Marketing
Tenth Edition

FOR THE INSTRUCTOR

- Want an easy way to test your students prior to an exam that *doesn't* create more work for you?

- Want to access your supplements *without* having to bring them all to class?

- Want to integrate current happenings into your lectures *without* all the searching and extra work?

- Want an *easy* way to get your course on-line?

- Want to *free up more time* in your day to get more done?

Of course you do!

Then check out your
Online Learning Centre!

- Downloadable Supplements
- PageOut
- Bonus CBC Segments

W9-BPN-388

Higher Learning. Forward Thinking.™

Marketing

Tenth Edition

Montrose Sommers

Ryerson University

James G. Barnes

Memorial University of Newfoundland

McGraw-Hill
Ryerson

Toronto   Montreal   Burr Ridge, IL   Dubuque, IA   Madison, WI   New York
San Francisco   St. Louis   Bangkok   Bogotá   Caracas   Kuala Lumpur
Lisbon   London   Madrid   Mexico City   Milan   New Delhi
Santiago   Seoul   Singapore   Sydney   Taipei

The McGraw·Hill Companies

McGraw-Hill Ryerson

MARKETING
Tenth Edition

Copyright © 2004, 2001, 1998, 1995, 1992, 1989, 1985, 1982 by McGraw-Hill Ryerson Limited, a Subsidiary of The McGraw-Hill Companies. All rights reserved. No part of this publication may be reproduced or transmitted in any form or by any means, or stored in a data base or retrieval system, without the prior written permission of McGraw-Hill Ryerson Limited, or in the case of photocopying or other reprographic copying, a license from The Canadian Copyright Licensing Agency (Access Copyright). For an Access Copyright licence, visit www.accesscopyright.ca or call toll free to 1-800-893-5777.

ISBN: 0-07-091438-9

3 4 5 6 7 8 9 10 TCP 0 9 8 7 6 5 4

Printed and bound in Canada

Care has been taken to trace ownership of copyright material contained in this text; however, the publisher will welcome any information that enables them to rectify any reference or credit for subsequent editions.

Vice President, Editorial and Media Technology: Patrick Ferrier
Sponsoring Editor: James Buchanan
Developmental Editors: Lesley Mann & Sandra de Ruiter
Marketing Manager: Kim Verhaeghe
Copy Editor: June Trusty
Production Coordinator: Madeleine Harrington
Photo and Permissions Research: Alison Derry & Christina Beamish
Cover Design: Dianna Little
Cover Image: Peter Griffith/Masterfile; Tattoo: Stu Jay, Lower East Side Tattoo
Interior Design: Dianna Little
Composition: Valerie Bateman/ArtPlus Design and Communications
Printer: Transcontinental Printing Group

National Library of Canada Cataloguing in Publication
Barnes, James G.
        Marketing / James G. Barnes, Montrose Sommers. — 10th ed.

Previous ed., 9th Canadian ed., written by Montrose S. Sommers and James G. Barnes under title: Fundamentals of marketing. Includes bibliographical references and index.

ISBN 0-07-091438-9

1. Marketing. I. Sommers, Montrose S., 1933- II. Title.

HF5415.S745 2003   658.8   C2003-900459-7

To Michael, Annie and the memory
of our dear old Jesse
M.S.S.

To Jennifer, Stephanie, and Karen
J.G.B.

About the Authors

Montrose Sommers is an author and special lecturer in marketing. He received his Bachelor of Commerce degree from the University of British Columbia, his MBA from Northwestern University, and his doctorate in marketing and sociology from the University of Colorado. Dr. Sommers has been a consultant to private and public sector organizations involved in petroleum marketing, financial services, telecommunications, various retailing specializations, marketing research, and advertising. His teaching background is extensive; he has worked with Bachelor, Master, and PhD students at the Universities of British Columbia, Texas, Hawaii, Toronto, Guelph, York, Nairobi in Kenya, Witwatersrand in South Africa, Huazhong and Tianjin in China, and the London School of Economics in Great Britain. Dr. Sommers has also served on the editorial boards of the *Journal of Marketing*, the *Journal of International Management and Organizations*, and the *Journal of the Service Industries*.

Jim Barnes is Professor of Marketing at Memorial University of Newfoundland. Dr. Barnes received his Bachelor of Commerce and BA degrees from Memorial, his MBA from the Harvard Business School, and his PhD from the University of Toronto. He has been a member of the faculty at Memorial University since 1968 and served as Dean from 1978 to 1988. He has been a visiting professor at Queen's University, the University of Bath (England), University College Dublin (Ireland), Université de Reims (France), and Macquarie University (Australia). He is co-founder and executive vice-president of Bristol Group, a full-service marketing communications and information firm with four offices in Canada. He serves as consultant to many national and international companies and regularly delivers seminars and lectures on marketing-related subjects in many countries. In 1997, Dr. Barnes received the national Leaders in Management Education award from the *Financial Post*, and was elected a Fellow of the Professional Marketing Research Society of Canada in 1999. He serves on the editorial boards of the *International Journal of Bank Marketing* and *The International Journal of Customer Relationship Management*. His book, *Secrets of Customer Relationship Management: It's All About How You Make Them Feel,* was published in 2001 by McGraw-Hill and is an international bestseller.

Contents In Brief

Available on the Sommers/Barnes Online Learning Centre at
www.mcgrawhill.ca/college/sommers:

COMPANY AND BRAND NAME INDEX

APPENDIX: *Planning Your Career in Marketing*

Contents

Part 4 Marketing Communications 281

Part 5   Distribution   375

Chapter 13 Retailing   376

Chapter 14 Supply Systems   410

Part 6   Pricing   451

Part 7   Tying Marketing Together   487

***Available on the Sommers/Barnes Online Learning Centre at* www.mcgrawhill.ca/college/sommers:**

COMPANY AND BRAND NAME INDEX

APPENDIX: *Planning Your Career in Marketing*

List of Cases

Marketing at Work Boxes

Preface

Ask yourself the question: "What does marketing have to do with me?" The answer is: "A lot more than you would think!" When you finish reading this book, we know you will agree.

Marketing is actually an integral part of your life, of all our lives. A surprising amount of your time is taken up by your efforts to market something — your ideas, your skills, your experiences, yourself — to others. And, of course, others spend a lot of time marketing to you. Whether you are a student, a small business owner, a lawyer, a professor, or an accountant doesn't make any difference — all are engaged in marketing. The challenge is to do it well, and that means you need an understanding of what today's marketing is all about and how you can perform it effectively. This requires a detailed understanding of customers and how they think and behave. It's only with this perspective that marketers can be successful in accomplishing the principal objective of marketing: the creation of customer satisfaction.

But there is much more to marketing than just learning what it is all about. A lot of the excitement of marketing is created by the context in which it occurs. The most obvious example today is the field of communications. How has greater access to faster computers, the Internet, and MP3 technology affected your life? Consider how the same changes have affected other areas of endeavour, such as manufacturing, transportation, entertainment, financial services, and agriculture. Add to this the continuing rapid globalization that the new communication technology enables. You, and the rest of us, are faced with new challenges, large and small, domestic and international, and they seem to come at us almost daily. But every change, every challenge, from whatever the source, creates new marketing opportunities.

What does this mean for marketers? In some respects, their jobs won't change. More than ever, they will need to create customer satisfaction to remain competitive. They will have to keep their customers at the centre of their thinking as they decide what products and services to offer, set prices they think customers will consider to provide good value for their money, distribute products so that customers can conveniently find them, and design promotional information to inform and persuade them. But the challenges they face and the tools they have available will change. In today's highly dynamic environment, managers of marketing and other functions will be faced with more new situations than ever before. They will have access to more information and information sources than did their predecessors — thanks mainly to the Internet. They will have to learn how to separate the essential from the interesting and how to use it effectively. They will have more strategic alternatives from which to select, but the cost of selecting the wrong one will be greater. They will be pursuing smaller market segments with products that have shorter lives. They will face a changing mix of competitors. In short, marketers will be operating in a faster-paced, higher-risk, and more technically complex environment. And the task of satisfying increasingly sophisticated customers will grow in complexity.

What does this mean for you? Your career is beginning during a time of unprecedented challenge and change. You could translate this into success. To make the most of this opportunity, you need an understanding of marketing and how it works in the dynamic world of today. The objective of this new edition is to help you gain that understanding.

Special Features of the Tenth Edition

Since the first edition, this book has been a leader — easy and enjoyable to read, practical and comprehensive in its content and orientation, full of current topical information and examples and illustrations of marketing as it is done "best" in Canada and around the world by leading Canadian and global firms, large and small. This edition not only continues this tradition, but also steps out to meet the challenges we face in our ever-changing environment.

We present marketing as a total system of business actions focused on customers and carried out by managers in individual organizations in the context of the larger economy and society. Regardless of whether managers are employed by a business or not-for-profit organization, are providers of goods or services, or are doing business domestically or globally, they need to understand the essential ideas — the big ideas — that are responsible for the marketing of today and the future.

We share those big ideas with you through the framework of the marketing management process. An organization first sets objectives, taking into consideration the environmental forces and competitors that influence its efforts. The managers then select target markets and build a marketing program to achieve the organization's objectives. The four elements integrated by managers in designing a marketing program — product, price, distribution, and promotion — are at the heart of marketing. But it is with people and their knowledge of their roles in the marketing process that the successful implementation of marketing programs begins and ends. Finally, an organization evaluates its performance and makes adjustments to its marketing strategy.

To help you understand and appreciate the big ideas of marketing and the marketing management process, we have not only provided clear, focused explanations but also many real-life, current examples. Each chapter opens with a real marketing story that illustrates the basic content of the material that follows. In addition to the text explanations, there are many current examples and illustrations of large and small Canadian firms in the form of Marketing At Work features. These features illustrate how firms actually work with the ideas you are reading about, both in the Canadian and the global marketplace. We have used photographs, reproductions of advertisements, and tables and figures to illustrate and highlight text materials for you. We also kept in mind that you have many demands on your time and designed this edition to help you learn rapidly and effectively in as short a time as possible.

Now, turn to Chapter 1 and start discovering that marketing is much more than you thought!

To the Instructor

The tenth edition of this text is newly entitled *Marketing*. In this edition, we have placed customers in a central role and then highlighted how the leading edge concepts of managerial marketing can be used to provide customer value, customer satisfaction, and — through relationship-building — customer acquisition and retention. This customer focus and managerial orientation is presented in the highly readable fashion that has been a hallmark of this book since its beginning. The new structure and new content of this tenth edition seamlessly integrates the new marketing ideas with new technologies and newly emerging concepts and practices — creating a very contemporary and effective learning tool for today's students and tomorrow's practitioners.

What's New and Improved

- An enhanced and integrated focus and emphasis throughout the book on the new view of marketing, featuring the importance of customer relationships, consumer expectations and satisfaction, service quality, and customer retention.
  - The highlighting of marketing strategies and tactics that enable the development of positive customer relationships, consumer value, and satisfaction in all marketing activities
  - A greater emphasis on really understanding the customer and his or her needs as the essence of marketing and the foundation for customer acquisition and retention.
  - A major realignment and integration of text material, resulting in a text that is more consistent with the amount of time you have to teach the course. The new edition consists of 16 chapters instead of the 21 of the previous edition. This significant change

has been made possible by the development of new content, as well as the major rede-velopment and revision of existing chapters.

- The enhanced use of exhibits, tables, advertisements, and photographs to more con-cisely communicate concepts and illustrations in a more compact and integrated fash-ion that facilitates student comprehension.

- International marketing, in keeping with globalization, is fully integrated throughout, with emphasis on consumer behaviour, business-to-business marketing, and channels of distribution.

- The basic pricing coverage has been greatly simplified and made more accessible to students, with less emphasis on the "economics" of pricing and more on today's business practices.

- Complete integration of the Internet, multimedia, and global issues through the use of chapter openers, Marketing at Work features, text illustrations, and examples of Internet and e-commerce marketing activity — much of it linked to Canadian and other companies with which students will be familiar and that are relevant to them.

- Numerous Web site references are placed throughout the text material and margins. These references direct students to companies and other sites that provide more infor-mation or allow the students to explore topics in greater detail.

- There are selected Web-based end-of-chapter problems and questions, as well as CBC video cases with supporting Internet resources at the end of each part of the book.

- Increased focus on student relevance and readability, with major emphasis on rapid stu-dent recognition and involvement in material with easy follow-through reading.

- Not only are illustrations, both text and graphic, well integrated for efficient commu-nication, but also these materials use situations, companies, and examples that are eas-ily recognized by your students and are easy for them to relate to. The colourful new design will aid students' comprehension and visually entice them at the same time.

● Shorter, easier-to-read chapter openings, text discussions and examples, and Marketing At Work features are written in familiar and comfortable language to further enhance our book's reputation as a "fun text to read."

● Completely new four-colour design, with careful page set-up for easy reading and changes of pace in presentation form, and convenient use in terms of locating materials, structure of presentations, and centrality of discussions.

- Revising a successful book is a delicate process. It is essential that new developments and material be incorporated into a revised edition and that the presentation be lively and engaging. At the same time, many of the features that have been eminently suc-cessful over time should be retained. We have worked hard to maintain this balance by updating and revising the book while preserving our basic strengths. This book has always been described by students as being enjoyable and "fun" to read, compared with others. We have made numerous changes so that this is an even more enjoyable edi-tion. Instructors have observed that it is well structured and comprehensive, contain-ing more Canadian perspectives, information, illustrations, and examples than other marketing textbooks. We have worked to increase these user benefits.

- The book is divided into seven parts to reflect the marketing management process.

● **_Part 1: Marketing and the Customer_** serves as an introduction and includes a new intro-ductory chapter, "What Marketing's All About," as well as chapters on the environment for strategic marketing planning and buyer behaviour.

● **_Part 2: Addressing Target Markets_** is devoted to segmentation analysis and selection of consumer and business target markets and positioning strategies. It also includes a discus-sion of the collection and use of market information.

- *Part 3: Products, Services, and Brands* contains separate chapters on product planning and development, services marketing, and branding and packaging.

- *Part 4: Marketing Communications* covers effective marketing communications and the management of advertising, as well as selling, sales promotion, and public relations, with a chapter devoted to each of these three topics

- *Part 5: Distribution* reviews the modern retailing scene and then looks behind retailing to examine the various elements of wholesaling and logistics that, taken together, form channels of distribution and thus the supply system.

- *Part 6: Pricing* introduces the real world of pricing mechanisms, pricing policies, and competitive pricing strategies and tactics.

- *Part 7: Tying Marketing Together* concludes the book with discussions on issues associated with successful marketing implementation and the performance of marketing, and presents our view of future developments.

Pedagogical Support

Chapter-Opening Vignettes — and Back to the Top

Each chapter begins with a contemporary case vignette that introduces some of the concepts, strategies, and techniques covered in the chapter. Subjects of the vignettes include Coke's Curious Vanilla advertising campaign and Amazon.ca's long-awaited appearance in Canada (highlighting services marketing and customer relationships); Air Canada, Tango, and seat sales (examining pricing issues); and the Birks Canada replacement of its blue box (focusing on retailing markets and institutions). And these vignettes are referenced throughout the chapter so students can relate what they're reading to the situation they encountered at the beginning of the chapter (look for the Back to the Top icon in the margin). At the end of each chapter, the Back to the Top heading introduces review questions related to the opening vignette.

Marketing at Work

Almost all of the Marketing at Work features, 48 of them, are new and illustrate new developments and successful implementations by recognizable companies and individuals. Some examples: "Always Talk to Strangers" (Lavalife); "The Osbournes Are a ★@#★@ Sellout!"; "And, In This Corner" (the Molson EXterminator). New in this edition, each feature highlights a key theme — Strategy, Relationships, Global, Technology, and Ethics. The colourful icon helps students to understand the focus and application of each Marketing at Work feature.

 **STRATEGY**

 RELATIONSHIPS

 GLOBAL

 **TECHNOLOGY**

 ETHICS

Backspace

We have added a new feature to this edition of *Marketing* called Backspace, because it allows students to pause as they study a chapter and reflect on what they have read. There are three Backspace sections in each chapter, introduced at appropriate points as major topics are completed. Backspace consists of three review questions that are intended to encourage students to think back over what they have just studied to make sure that they understand the material and concepts.

Cases

Each of the seven parts of the book ends with three cases. Almost all of these are new to this edition (a small number of successful cases from the previous edition have been retained and rewritten to reflect current situations). The format of the cases has been changed in response to feedback from instructors across the country. Each of the parts of the text ends with two short cases and one longer one. The short cases capture succinctly a concept or issue from the chapters just studied. They are valuable in that their length allows the instructor to assign them for in-class reading and discussion. The longer case that accompanies each part is approximately two pages in length and is more comprehensive in the concepts that it covers. It is appropriate for study and preparation before class, either as a written assignment or for in-depth discussion. The companies and topics presented in the line-up of cases are very student-friendly, dealing with companies with which students will be familiar, including Gap, Aveda, and Altoids. Finally, and this is a big plus, more than half of the cases in this edition are tied to CBC video clips that can be viewed in class to enhance the discussion. Students will be hooked by CBC videos on such intriguing topics as Krispy Kreme, Grocery Gateway, buzz marketing, mystery shoppers, and the Rethink advertising agency. Instructors can access two supplemental CBC video clips and their corresponding cases from the Online Learning Centre.

Summary/Key Terms and Concepts/Assignments

Every chapter concludes with a chapter summary, a list of key terms and concepts with chapter page references, and two types of assignments. The first is a set of 8 to 10 Questions and Problems designed to help students discover how to analyze issues and make applications based on the chapter discussion. The second type of assignment is called Hands-On Marketing. These assignments require the students to get out of the classroom and interact with customers or marketers as well as make use of the Internet. The Back to the Top feature wraps things up with a challenge to apply the lessons of the chapter to the situation outlined in the chapter-opening vignette.

Teaching and Learning Support

For the Instructor

Instructor's Resource CD-ROM: The new Instructor's Resource CD-ROM for *Marketing* contains the Instructor's Manual, Microsoft® PowerPoint® slides, and computerized test bank.

> ***Instructor's Manual*** by Montrose Sommers, James Barnes, and Peter Dunne: Peter worked closely with the authors throughout this revision. The *Instructor's Manual* uses a fresh approach that is based on the practical needs of instructors who want to help the students learn in the way that works best for the students. The goal is to help students learn more effectively by providing instructors with strategy suggestions (such as Internet activities, group work, and case studies) to encourage learning in the context of an introductory marketing course. Case solutions for the text cases are also provided. (ISBN 007-091439-7)

Microsoft® PowerPoint® presentation by James Barnes: This software includes a set of more than 300 slides. The slides include point-form summaries of key concepts discussed in the text. (ISBN 007-091441-9)

Test bank and computerized test bank: The test bank comprises multiple-choice and true/false questions, as well as caselettes — short, current case descriptions with accompanying multiple-choice questions. The 2,200 questions in the test bank are coded to identify the type — concept, definition, or application. (ISBN 007-091440-0)

Lecture Launchers: The lecture launchers, presented in Microsoft® PowerPoint® format, provide an overview of the key points in the chapters, as well as the graphic material from each chapter, including tables and figures.

CBC video cases and Video guide: This collection of video cases corresponds with selected companies or organizations profiled in the book's part-ending cases. They feature a variety of organizations and marketing topics. Suggestions for their use are provided in the Video Guide, which is included in the Instructor's Manual.

Transparency acetates: A comprehensive colour transparency program is available to enhance lectures and class discussions.

Online Learning Centre: Visit the Instructor Centre at **www.mcgrawhill.ca/ college/sommers** for downloadable supplements and other instructor information and updates.

*i***-Learning Sales Specialist:** Your *Integrated i-Learning Sales Specialist* is a McGraw-Hill Ryerson representative who has the experience, product knowledge, training, and support to help you assess and integrate any of the below-noted products, technology, and services into your course for optimum teaching and learning performance. Whether it's how to use our test bank software, helping your students improve their grades, or how to put your entire course on-line, your i-Learning Sales Specialist is there to help. Contact your local i-Learning Sales Specialist today to learn how to maximize all McGraw-Hill Ryerson resources!

For the Student

Study Guide by R. David Nowell: This useful study guide provides guidelines for analyzing marketing cases, chapter goals, chapter summaries, key terms and concepts, self-test questions (true/false, multiple choice, matching, and sentence completion), problems and applications questions, and interesting real-world cases and articles related to chapter concepts. The Study Guide contains almost all new, one-page cases and many new activities, with answers provided in the Instructor's Manual.

Online Learning Centre: Students and instructors can visit this Web site to gain access to a variety of aids and support, including student quiz questions and Internet Activities (prepared by Montrose Sommers), interactive Flash-based chapter concept illustrations with exercises, interactive glossary, learning objectives, downloadable interactive Marketing Math tutorial, Web links, cases, and video exercises. Visit **www.mcgrawhill.ca/college/sommers** today.

Marketing Magazine: McGraw-Hill Ryerson is pleased to offer special access to *Marketing Magazine's* online archive of marketing articles. It's an unbeatable research tool, invaluable for preparing assignments and exploring the hottest issues in Canadian marketing.

Acknowledgements

Through 10 editions of this book, many people have made important contributions. These include students, colleagues, clients, marketing managers in Canadian firms, and instructors at many universities and colleges. All have provided insights and commentary on the Canadian marketing scene and the teaching and learning of marketing. We sincerely thank them for their advice, thoughtfulness, and support.

We wish to acknowledge in particular those research and editorial assistants who contributed to the essential research and material-preparation process necessary for this revision. Peter Dunne, in St. John's, has provided his usual superb editorial and material-preparation assistance in a most exemplary fashion. We are thankful for his skill and diligence and pleased that he has also worked with us on the *Instructor's Manual*. Natalie Slawinski did a wonderful job of researching and developing cases and other material to support each chapter. We are also indebted to the business and other executives who allowed us to write cases on their companies or organizations and to include advertising and other material.

Another group that was instrumental in the preparation of this book was the group of reviewers used by our publisher. These include the following colleagues: Pat Browne, Kwantlen University College; Bill Clymer, Durham College; Dwight Dyson, Centennial College; Shannon Goodspeed, Mount Royal College; Mary Louise Huebner, Seneca College; Henry Klaise, Durham College; John MacGregor, Saskatchewan Institute of Applied Science and Technology (SIAST)/University of Regina; Marianne Marando, George Brown College; Jean-Paul Olivier, Red River College; Christopher Ross, Concordia University; Harvey Skolnick, Sheridan College; Jim Swaffield, University of Alberta; and Carla Gail Tibbo, Douglas College. They provided much useful insight and commentary and we would like to thank each of them. One colleague in particular requires special mention — David Nowell of Sheridan College. In addition to reviewing the manuscript, David made a significant contribution in the preparation of the supplementary materials for this edition of the book. As well, we would like to thank John McColl, Graham Davies, Harvey Skolnick, Bryce Hanna, and Steven Lee for taking time out of their busy schedules to meet with us during the initial stages of the project. Your suggestions have been very helpful in preparing this edition.

Finally, we would like to acknowledge with much appreciation the support and co-operation we received from the staff of McGraw-Hill Ryerson. We are grateful to James Buchanan, our Sponsoring Editor for this edition, for being there to get things moving. Lesley Mann, our Developmental Editor, really performed sterling development work. She kept both her team and us focused on the task. And in addition, she was fun to work with. Alison Derry and Christina Beamish, our Photo Researchers, extended themselves at doing just that. We owe special thanks to Kelly Dickson, Manager, Editorial Services, and June Trusty, Copy Editor, who provided important assistance and information and helped us ensure that this edition will meet the goals and objectives of all those involved. Thanks finally to Dianna Little, Art Director, for her inspired new design.

Montrose S. Sommers
James G. Barnes

PART 1

Marketing and the Customer

An overview of a new view of marketing, one that is truly focused on understanding customers so that we can better meet their needs and earn their loyalty

The successful practice of marketing requires an appreciation of the changing environment. It also demands a detailed understanding of customers and what's important to them in their dealings with businesses.

Marketing is dynamic, challenging, and rewarding, and it's never dull! Welcome to the part of the organization where everything comes together — where ideas, planning, and execution get the acid test of the marketplace.

Chapter 1 explains the new view of marketing, how marketing continues to change and to focus more on the building of customer relationships. Chapter 2 discusses the internal and external environmental forces that shape a marketing program. Then, Chapter 3 explores customers — the focal point of marketing — and helps us better understand what makes them tick. Unless we understand our customers, we can't begin to satisfy them.

CHAPTER 1

What Marketing's All About

"What is marketing?" Chapter 1 answers this question — and the answer may surprise you. Marketing today is widely considered to encompass many tasks within a company or organization. It's more than advertising and setting prices. It's more than retail stores and catchy jingles. In fact, it's just about anything that contributes to satisfying customers. After studying this chapter, you should have an understanding of:

- The focus of marketing on customer satisfaction.
- The relationship between exchange and marketing.
- Marketing's emphasis on creating customer loyalty and relationships.
- How marketing applies to business and non-business situations.
- The factors that drive customer satisfaction.
- The difference between selling and marketing.
- The evolution of marketing thinking.
- The creation of value and the value proposition.
- The modern marketing concept.
- Marketing's role in the economy and in an individual organization.

It's Not About the Shoes!

It's Saturday afternoon and you and your friend Bob decide to go shopping for a new pair of running shoes. You and Bob meet at Second Cup for a quick coffee and then walk down the street to your first stop, Sports Champs, where you notice a display of New Balance running shoes just inside the door, with a sign announcing "20% OFF!"

As you walk toward the shoe department, you notice that the store is quite untidy, with boxes in the aisles and clothing hanging off racks. Bob comments that the rock music blaring from the speakers in the ceiling is so loud that it's almost impossible to carry on a conversation. When you reach the display of shoes, you are pleased to see a good selection and that all New Balance shoes are indeed on sale at 20 percent off. You and Bob select two models and you look for someone to serve you.

But, there's no help in sight. Although there aren't many customers in the store and you can see three employees in the distance, dressed in the store's distinctive red-striped uniforms with their names on the back, no one shows any interest in serving you. In fact, they are gathered at the checkouts, apparently discussing something very important. Another employee walks by carrying an armload of jackets. When you ask if he's busy, he answers, "Yes!" and walks on. You approach the group at the checkouts and ask whether anyone is serving in the shoe department. One of the employees says, "That's Ted's department; he should be back soon." You and Bob wait, but Ted doesn't show. After 10 minutes, during which two other employees walk right by you, Bob says, "Let's get out of here."

Three blocks away, you walk into Blades & Boards. As you enter the store, you and Bob are approached by an employee who announces, "Hi! I'm Sandy. What can we do for you today?" You tell her that you are looking for running shoes and she leads you to the shoe department, where you notice that the selection is not as wide as it was at Sports Champs. They do carry New Balance shoes, but the prices are not reduced. Sandy asks what type of shoes you are looking for, and you explain that you have been running a lot lately and plan to run your first 10K road race next month. Sandy asks what size you wear and what price you are interested in paying; you tell her size 8 and approximately $125.

Sandy disappears into the storeroom and emerges with three boxes of shoes: two pairs of Nike and one of Saucony. After trying on the three pairs, you go back to the display wall and take a closer look at the New Balance shoes. There's one model priced at $119.95 that you looked at while waiting at Sports Champs, and you ask Sandy if she has your size in stock. She agrees that these shoes would be very suitable and again goes into the storeroom, emerging with the news that they have an $8\frac{1}{2}$, but no size 8.

Then, Sandy says "Rather than sell you a shoe that doesn't fit, let me call our other store in the Rosewood Mall to see if they have a size 8. If they have them, I'll get them sent over and you can come in and try them on; we're open tomorrow and I'll be here." She comes back in a couple of minutes to tell you that the size 8 New Balance shoes will be delivered that afternoon and that you can come back later tonight or tomorrow to try them on. Then she says, "By the way, there's a 10 percent discount for students at your school; couldn't help but notice your knapsack!"

At 2:30 Sunday afternoon, you walk out of Blades & Boards with your New Balance shoes, size 8.

What happened in this typical consumer experience that caused you to buy your new running shoes in one store rather than the other? And what does this have to do with marketing?

The answer is that this example is quite typical of situations that customers face every day. Some customer experiences are positive and others are negative; some are satisfying and others are not; some cause you to vow never to go back and others cause you to tell your friends about how well you were treated. This experience with two retail stores also illustrates how complex something as simple as buying a pair of running shoes can be. There are many factors involved and many things that contributed to your final decision to buy the shoes and how you felt afterward. This reflects the complexity of marketing and the importance of the customer's perspective in determining whether a company is successful.

Customer Satisfaction Is the Focus

marketing

A total system of business activities designed to plan, price, promote, and distribute need-satisfying products or services to target markets in order to achieve organizational objectives.

customer

An individual or organization that makes a purchase decision.

customer satisfaction

The degree to which a customer's experience with a product or organization meets or exceeds his or her expectations.

exchange

The voluntary act of providing a person or organization with something of value in order to acquire something else of value in return.

What is the focus of marketing today? What do we mean when we use the term **marketing**? To what aspects of a company's operations are we referring when we talk about marketing? Different people will have different views when they refer to marketing, and those views have changed over the years. We believe that *marketing* refers to just about anything that a company or other organization does that has an impact on the satisfaction of its **customers**. In other words, marketing is the most customer-focused part of a company and principally involves activities and programs that will contribute to high levels of **customer satisfaction**, through addressing customer needs and wants. In business, the objective of marketing is also to satisfy customer needs and wants at a profit.

Why are we interested in customer satisfaction as an objective of marketing and, indeed, of the company? It's really quite simple. Satisfied customers will buy more from us, they will come back again and again to do business with us, and they will often tell their friends and family members about us. A solid group of satisfied customers represents one of a company's most valuable assets — when one considers the potential lifetime value of loyal customers, it is obvious that these customers represent a stream of earnings that will last well into the future. Therefore, a marketing focus within a company today involves a long-term view. If we can satisfy a large percentage of customers, they will keep coming back again and again. They represent the future success of the business. Without them, we have to spend a great deal of time, energy, and money continually trying to attract new customers to replace those who are leaving.

How, then, can a company achieve long-term customer satisfaction? The most successful companies accomplish this by giving customers what they want, when they want it, for a price that the customers consider to be acceptable. The best companies make it easy for customers to deal with them and treat them pleasantly and politely. There is a process of **exchange** involved, but what is being exchanged is quite broad. The customer gives the company something and gets something of value in return. We need to consider precisely what this "something" is. It's not as simple as giving money to obtain a pair of jeans or a new tennis racquet. There's much more involved than that.

It's also very important to note that exchanges take place between many different groups and organizations and in different situations. So, marketing as we are discussing it does not apply only to businesses that are offering products and services to customers. There is an exchange involved when you buy a ticket to a concert, when you take a course at your school, when you donate to a charity, and when you visit a museum. In all cases, things are exchanged, some of them tangible, others intangible; sometimes involving the exchange of money, other times not. In all cases, the principles of marketing apply. Customers receive something of value in return for what they are giving. That perception of value is an individual thing and depends on the quality of the product and service, on how conveniently it is made available, on the time it takes to get it, on the price, and on many other factors. When customers perceive that they have received value, a feeling of satisfaction will be experienced, likely leading to a decision to buy, or donate, or visit that company or organization again.

THE CUSTOMER GIVES THE COMPANY GETS	THE COMPANY GIVES THE CUSTOMER GETS
Money	Product
Time	Price
Energy	Value
Commitment	Convenience
Referrals	Selection
Past experience	Service
Expectations	Warranty
Knowledge	Brand

Figure 1-1:

The Give and Get
of Marketing

"give and get"

An illustration of the
exchange process as both
customer and company giving
something and getting
something in return.

expectations

What customers expect to
encounter when dealing with
a company or buying a
product or service, based on
past experience and desired
outcomes.

value

The quantitative measure of
the worth of a product to
attract other products in
exchange.

It might be useful to consider the exchange that is involved in marketing as an exercise in "**give and get**" — the customer gives something and gets something in return (see Figure 1-1). What is given and received contributes to the level of satisfaction enjoyed by the customer. It's important to think very broadly about what is being exchanged, because this will help us understand that the scope of marketing itself is indeed very broad.

Think back to the example that opened this chapter. To buy your running shoes, you not only paid a certain price, you also invested time and effort. You had to make a certain commitment in order to obtain the shoes. You may have spent time planning the purchase by looking through magazines or talking with friends. Chances are you have had experience buying sports gear and were familiar with many of the brand names available. You may even have owned a pair of New Balance shoes.

And what did you get for this commitment of time, energy, and money and for the application of your past experience and knowledge? It's too simplistic to suggest that you got new shoes. You also got the time and attention of Sandy at Blades & Boards. You got the benefit of the selection that was available, the discount for students at your school, and the service involved in sending the running shoes over from the Rosewood Mall store. You received an implicit warranty that tells you that you can return the shoes if you have any problems with them. You also got a certain comfort level that goes with buying a recognized brand name like New Balance.

Now, where does customer satisfaction enter the picture? In simple terms, customers are satisfied as long as what they get is at least as great as what they have to give. Where *give* is perceived to be greater than *get*, the customer is generally dissatisfied. You were not satisfied with the service (or lack of service!) at Sports Champs, and you walked out. You were not prepared to give more of your time or make any further effort to get the shoes and the service that went along with them. On the other hand, you were satisfied at Blades & Boards because what Sandy was giving was greater than what you had to give. In fact, by acting as she did, Sandy reduced the time, commitment, and anxiety that you had to put into the exchange — not to mention the price of the shoes!

Two important concepts are evident in this early discussion about marketing. Sandy was successful in making the sale because she was able to exceed your **expectations** — you probably didn't expect her to be so friendly and helpful, you didn't expect her to call the Rosewood Mall store and to have the running shoes delivered, and you didn't expect the discount of 10 percent. Customer expectations are very important in determining whether satisfaction results.

Then, we must consider the concept of **value**. This is a central concept in marketing, since customers want to receive value when they buy products or services. In fact, it's value that leads to satisfaction. The greater the value that customers perceive they have received, the greater the satisfaction. You bought your shoes at Blades & Boards because you perceived that you were getting value. But, wait a minute! You could have saved 20 percent if you had bought them at Sports Champs — remember, all New Balance running shoes were on sale at a 20 percent discount *and* they had a wider range available.

What this tells us is an important lesson to be learned early: namely, that value is not only about price. Customers decide whether they are receiving value by taking into consideration (often subconsciously) all of the factors that are being exchanged: all of the "gives" and all of the "gets." Value for money is only one kind of value. One of the most important roles of marketers is to add value for their customers. Those that succeed in creating greater perceived value are generally more successful.

What's Involved in Marketing?

marketer
Any person or organization that desires to make exchanges.

This book focuses on the activities carried out by individuals, businesses, and other organizations to bring about exchanges that are beneficial to both sides and to develop long-lasting customer relationships. Virtually all organizations are involved in marketing activities, although some have only recently "discovered" marketing and some still practise it more with a sales focus than with an emphasis on creating customer satisfaction and long-term customer relationships. **Marketers** may be business firms in the conventional sense of the word, or they may be non-business, or not-for-profit, organizations, such as hospitals, universities, Big Brothers Big Sisters, churches, police departments, or museums. Both groups — business and non-business — face the same marketing issues and challenges and make use of the same marketing principles and concepts.

Our perspective on marketing — applicable in businesses, not-for-profit organizations, and personal situations — is as follows:

> Marketing is a total system of activities designed to plan, price, promote, and distribute need-satisfying products, services, and ideas to target markets in order to achieve the objectives of both the customer and the organization. It involves all aspects of how the organization interacts with the customer that have the potential to influence the customer's satisfaction with the organization and its value proposition.

This view of marketing has some significant implications when marketing is properly applied:

- It is a systems definition, which means that it should be understood and applied by everyone in an organization. Effective marketing demands an integrated view of the customer and of how value is created and customer satisfaction achieved.

- The entire system of activities must be customer-oriented and focus on the quality of the customer relationship — customers' needs and wants must be recognized and satisfied effectively. The ultimate objective of marketing is to achieve customer satisfaction.

- The marketing program starts with an idea for a product or service and does not end until the customer's needs and wants are satisfied, which may be some time after an exchange is made. This suggests that the process of customer satisfaction is an ongoing one and does not end with a sale.

marketing mix
A combination of the four elements — product, pricing structure, distribution system, and promotional activities — that comprise a company's marketing program. Many marketers now consider service and the "people" side of marketing to be a fifth component of the marketing mix, especially in the marketing of services.

- An organization's marketing program, generally termed the **marketing mix**, has traditionally been viewed in most organizations as consisting of four co-ordinated elements. These have been considered the essential components of what marketing is about. The four elements of the traditional marketing mix are:

1. A product or service assortment.
2. A pricing structure.
3. Distribution systems and channels.
4. Promotional activities.

Marketers have recently begun to express the view that although getting the components of the traditional marketing mix right is important or even necessary, this may not be sufficient to ensure high levels of customer satisfaction. In other words, as marketers have begun to pay more attention to the application of marketing to service organizations and to the development of long-term customer relationships, they have realized that other factors, such as how customers are treated and the physical facilities of the company, are important in influencing customer satisfaction. Consequently, in recent years, marketers have begun to consider an expanded marketing mix, one that incorporates customer service, processes, and technology with which the customer comes into contact, and even the employees of the company.

Much of what contributes to customer satisfaction lies outside the traditional responsibilities of the marketing department. The expanded view of the marketing mix has created a situation in some organizations in which there is confusion about the boundaries of what marketing is. Where does marketing begin and end in the modern company and not-for-profit organization?

Traditionally, the role and responsibilities of marketing executives and the marketing department extended principally to the four elements of the marketing mix — product development, pricing, communications, and distribution, so those marketers engaged in activities that dealt largely with these four areas. Such a view was popular until quite recently and many organizations still operate this way. This is a limited view of marketing that is inconsistent with our view that the scope of marketing extends to many other things that have the potential to affect customer satisfaction.

Today, progressive organizations have adopted a much broader view of marketing. They realize that there is a great deal more to marketing than is suggested by the traditional marketing mix. In fact, it is increasingly accepted that a company could get the four elements of the marketing mix right and still lose a customer. In fact, we saw this in the example with which we opened this chapter. Sports Champs had the shoes you wanted in stock (product and distribution) at a price that you considered attractive. There appears to have been nothing wrong with its advertising or other forms of marketing communications. Yet, you walked out and bought your shoes elsewhere, mainly because of things that went wrong that lie outside what is generally considered to be part of the marketing mix.

Increasingly, we find companies and other organizations allocating responsibility for customer satisfaction to a number of departments. In what are now often referred to as *marketing-oriented* or *customer-focused organizations,* it is acknowledged that satisfying the customer is a responsibility that must extend outside the traditional boundaries of the marketing department. As a result, we now see evidence that responsibility for achieving customer satisfaction has been extended to include, for example, customer-service departments and cross-functional groups responsible for implementing **customer-relationship management** programs.

customer-relationship management

A strategic orientation of a company toward the development of positive, long-term relationships with customers.

Long-term focus: Build genuine customer loyalty

Next time you need hockey equipment, or tennis balls, or running shoes, where are you going to go? Chances are you'll go first to Blades & Boards. The actions of Sandy and the policies and procedures of Blades & Boards suggest that this company has a long-term perspective on marketing. It realizes that it needs more than a good variety of products and attractive prices to satisfy customers and to keep them coming back. It probably realizes that making you happy that Saturday afternoon involved more than selling you a pair of running shoes.

Successful marketers look beyond the sale and look for ways to satisfy their customers to such an extent that a sense of loyalty develops. The most successful companies have a solid corps of loyal customers who account for the bulk of their business and who act as unpaid spokespersons for the firm. They not only come back again and again, but they also spread positive word of mouth that recommends the company to others.

Such **customer loyalty** is created when companies take a long-term, broad view of marketing. They pay attention to all things that have the potential to influence customer satisfaction. They realize that making a sale is not enough. They know that they must not only offer their customers great products at attractive prices, do good advertising, and have a wide selection to choose from, but that how customers are treated and ultimately made to feel also has a considerable effect on whether they will buy and, more importantly, on whether they will come back again.

customer loyalty

A state achieved when a customer not only deals regularly with a company, but also feels an emotional attachment to it and recommends it to others.

customer relationship

Close association between company and customers, characterized by strong feelings of loyalty, trust, and commitment; the ultimate connection, based not only on quality of products and service, but also on how the company makes its customers feel.

What these successful companies are doing is developing relationships with their customers that extend beyond the immediate transaction. Customer relationships have become the focus of many companies in recent years, as they have realized the costs and inefficiencies involved in high levels of customer turnover. If companies can succeed in having large numbers of customers come back willingly (or even enthusiastically!) again and again, they can be far more successful than companies that are constantly having to attract new customers to replace dissatisfied ones who leave to take their business elsewhere. The building of long-term **customer relationships** will be a central focus of this book.

What drives customer satisfaction?

Customer relationships begin with satisfied customers. If customers are satisfied when buying a certain brand of breakfast cereal or golf balls, chances are that they will buy that brand again. When satisfaction levels are high, there is little incentive to switch. But, the customer must be satisfied with all aspects of what is received from the company.

drivers of customer satisfaction

Factors that contribute to customer satisfaction.

The example at the beginning of this chapter illustrates the five factors that contribute to customer satisfaction, which could be called the **drivers of customer satisfaction**[1] (see Figure 1-2). To be genuinely or completely satisfied, a customer must be satisfied at all five levels. At the bottom of the "cone" is the core of the offer to customers. The *core* is the basic product or service provided by the organization — in the chapter opener, the running shoes. Generally, we tend to think of tangible products as the core because they are easy to visualize, but a service may be the core offering. For an Internet radio station, for example, the core product is the selection of channels (musical genres) from which visitors can choose. For a hair salon, the core product is the haircut.

The second level in the drivers of customer satisfaction model is that of support services and systems. It includes such things, in our shoe-buying example, as the hours when the stores are open, store location, the variety of models and sizes of shoes available, whether the store accepts major credit cards, the availability of staff, and the level of service they provide. Failing to provide satisfactory support services can cause customers to be dissatisfied and not return.

Moving farther up the "cone," the third level involves technical performance, which determines whether the service provider gets the core product and support services right. The emphasis is on meeting the expectations of the customer. Does the store provide the product the customer needs and make it available conveniently and without hassle? Customer dissatisfaction will result from a failure to meet customer expectations that things will go smoothly and as promised.

Figure 1-2:

Factors that Drive Customer Satisfaction

- Emotional elements of the interaction
- Interaction with the firm and its employees
- Technical performance
- Support services and systems
- Core

The fourth level of the drivers of satisfaction model concerns the customer's interaction with the company and its employees. This level can involve both face-to-face interaction and the connection that occurs over the telephone or through e-mail or the Internet. Satisfaction at this level is determined by whether the company makes it easy and pleasant for customers to do business with it. Are customers treated with respect? Is the staff efficient, pleasant, helpful, and courteous? Is the telephone system efficient and the Web site easy to navigate? Understanding this level indicates that a firm has thought beyond the provision of the core product and service and is focused on the delivery of service where it meets the customer.

Finally, marketers must think beyond the basic elements of the interaction with customers to consider the sometimes-subtle messages that firms send to customers. These messages may create either positive or negative feelings toward the company. Essentially, this final level at the top of the "cone" is concerned with emotional considerations — how the customer feels about dealing with the company. Often, a customer's satisfaction or dissatisfaction has nothing to do with the quality of the core product or service, its price, or how it is provided. Business may be lost because a customer is ignored by employees, an e-mail question is not answered, or some other "little thing" goes wrong and may not even be noticed by staff.

It's really interesting to remember that, in the chapter-opener example, you bought your running shoes at Blades & Boards, even though the store initially did not have your size in stock, you paid more than you would have at Sports Champs, and you had to make a second trip back to the store to get them. How can that be? Both stores had the shoes that you eventually bought. What caused you to buy them at Blades & Boards?

If we think about the drivers of customer satisfaction, it's obvious that the difference between the two stores lies mainly in the top two levels of the "cone" — your interaction with employees and how you were made to feel. Think about how you were treated by Sandy at Blades & Boards as compared with how the employees at Sports Champs handled the situation. How did you feel when you and Bob walked out of Sports Champs, as compared with how you felt on Sunday afternoon when you picked up your new shoes from Sandy?

BACKSPACE

1. What does marketing involve?
2. When we say that a company has a marketing focus, what do we mean?
3. What are the five drivers of customer satisfaction?

The Scope of Marketing

Our view of marketing, with its focus on the satisfaction of customer needs through a process of exchange, means that we will introduce certain concepts and terms that require some explanation and elaboration so we can be sure that our understanding of them is accurate from the beginning.

Marketers take the initiative in trying to stimulate and facilitate exchanges. They develop marketing plans and programs and implement them in order to create an exchange that can be satisfying to their customers. Marketers exist in all kinds of organizations and have the responsibility for creating customer satisfaction. Marketing, as we have observed, is not simply a business concept, but is used widely in virtually all organizations. Examples include Canadian Blood Services (**www.bloodservices.ca**) seeking the 245,000 donors it estimated would be needed for the peak summer months of 2002 with the help of billboard advertising and its "Roll up your sleeves, Canada" campaign. In addition to billboard advertising, television spots

Canadian Blood Services

This not-for-profit organization is obviously into marketing.

MARKETING AT WORK 1-1: STRATEGY

The Osbournes Are a *@#*@ Sellout!

How do you market Ozzy, an aging, absent-minded, heavy metal legend from the seventies? You give him a reality-based television show that follows his domestic life as, for example, he struggles to understand how to use the television remote control. Other highlights include the legendary substance abuser lecturing his teenaged children on the evils of drugs. The show, and its profanity-spewing cast of characters, represent the first real hit for any of the almost 50 digital cable channels introduced in Canada in 2002. The TV antics of the Osbourne clan have received incredible exposure in the media across North America, thereby creating a draw to watch the show and the advertising between segments. This has resulted in a must-have show for advertisers. Blue-chip brands such as Molson and L'Oréal have signed on for the entire run of the show.

What many viewers do not consider is the role of television shows as products — products not just to be sold to you, but to companies that want to sell their products to you. In fact, viewers are a very important (and, therefore, valuable) component of the product being sold. Television shows are vehicles to sell advertising time on television channels. The fact that viewers are entertained is simply a by-product of the formula. Like all products, television shows must be designed for particular market segments. The show and the characters are all designed with that purpose in mind — to reflect the audience and important events/activities in their lives. In turn, advertisers choose shows whose viewers reflect their target segments.

Many viewers of *The Osbournes* aren't old enough to remember Ozzy's bizarre onstage antics, while those who do remember tune in to see what happens when a rock star ages. The show appeals to today's viewing tastes for reality-based story lines and shock value.

A show like *Friends*, on the other hand, was carefully conceived to attract a broad market segment of younger consumers by assembling a diverse set of seven acquaintances who were in their twenties, or perhaps hitting their thirties (who actually knew?), and wrote about their varied life experiences with different types of relationships, careers, and life-altering decisions. In doing so, the network attracted a very valuable age demographic — 18- to 49-year-olds. The guarantee of those viewers represented a very attractive value proposition to companies who target this group.

SOURCE: Adapted from Chris Powell, "The Osbournes Are a @#$% Sellout," *Marketing Magazine,* May 13, 2002, p. 4.

MuchMusic

market
People or organizations with needs or wants to satisfy, money to spend, and the willingness to spend it.

featured action star Jackie Chan admitting to his lifelong fear of needles. When CHUM Television decided to spin off MuchMusic (**www.muchmusic.com**) into four separate music stations (MuchMusic, MuchMoreMusic, MuchVibe, MuchLoud), it was to better appeal to viewer (consumer) segments and hopefully attract more overall viewers. These are examples of marketers trying to communicate with potential customers.

On the other side of the exchange is the **market**, made up of people or organizations to whom marketing programs are directed and who will play a key role in the acceptance or rejection of a marketer's offer. Markets are made up of customers — any people with whom a business or organizational marketer wants to do business. While we tend to use the term *customers* to describe the individuals and entities to which a marketing initiative is directed, this is in fact a general term that is applied to the market for products and services. Markets also include employees, clients, passengers, patrons, donors, students, taxpayers, and patients. Markets may also be other organizations. For example, there are many companies that never sell to end-consumers, but rather market to other businesses and organizations; this is the so-called *business-to-business* (B2B) *market*, as distinct from the *business-to-consumer* (B2C) *market*. Markets for companies today also involve customers located in other countries or who are reached through the Internet.

This B2B company provides logistics services to other businesses.

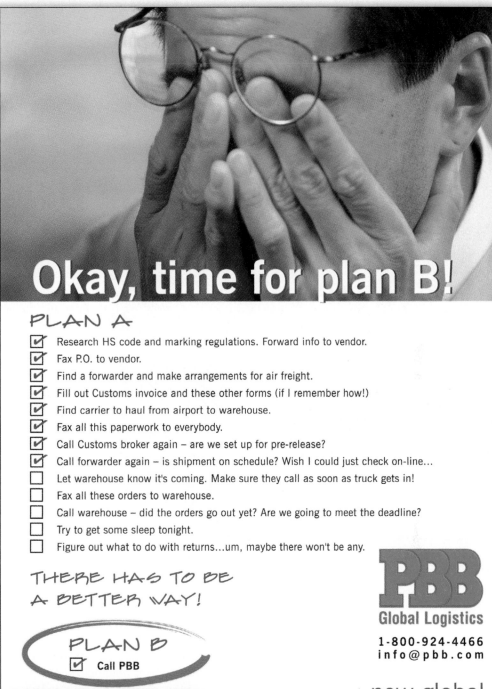

Okay, time for plan B!

PLAN A

☑ Research HS code and marking regulations. Forward info to vendor.
☑ Fax P.O. to vendor.
☑ Find a forwarder and make arrangements for air freight.
☑ Fill out Customs invoice and these other forms (if I remember how!)
☑ Find carrier to haul from airport to warehouse.
☑ Fax all this paperwork to everybody.
☑ Call Customs broker again – are we set up for pre-release?
☑ Call forwarder again – is shipment on schedule? Wish I could just check on-line...
☐ Let warehouse know it's coming. Make sure they call as soon as truck gets in!
☐ Fax all these orders to warehouse.
☐ Call warehouse – did the orders go out yet? Are we going to meet the deadline?
☐ Try to get some sleep tonight.
☐ Figure out what to do with returns...um, maybe there won't be any.

THERE HAS TO BE A BETTER WAY!

PLAN B
☑ Call PBB

www.pbb.com/planB

PBB
Global Logistics

1-800-924-4466
info@pbb.com

realizing **new global**
opportunities for your business

---

decision-maker
The individual in a household or organization who has the responsibility of deciding what to buy.

consumer
An individual or organizational unit that uses or consumes a product or service.

purchaser
The person in the household or organization who actually makes the purchase of a product or service.

influencers
The people in a buying centre who set the specifications and aspects of buying decisions because of their technical expertise, financial position, or political power in the organization.

The people who make up a market play a number of roles. First, there is the **decision-maker**, the individual or organizational unit that has the authority to make the decision to buy something. Then there is the **consumer**, the one who actually uses or consumes the product or service. The **purchaser** is the person who actually makes the purchase. Finally, there are **influencers**, who affect the decisions of others because of their expertise, position, or power. These definitions are not simply semantic distinctions. These roles are very important in determining how marketers carry out their marketing programs, what information they direct to whom, and what

When each year equals seven, nothing equals **Eukanuba® Senior.** An aging dog doesn't have to act like one. Or feel like one. That's why there's Eukanuba Senior with the **Vital Health System™**. Only Eukanuba Senior has advanced scientific ingredients that meet the unique nutritional needs of your aging dog, so his vital systems stay in optimum condition. Eukanuba Senior includes **ImmunoHealth™** antioxidants to promote a strong, healthy immune system, the **Joint Management System™** with Glucosamine and Chondroitin Sulfate to help maintain healthy joints, and **OmegaCoat Plus™** to help maintain a lustrous coat. All to make sure your dog's best years are ahead of him. To learn more, call 1-888-385-2682 or visit us today at www.eukanuba.com. **Eukanuba❖** Dog Foods *Results Oriented Nutrition™*

This consumer is neither decision-maker nor purchaser.

Science Diet
Eagle Pack
Purina

needs and wants
The focus of a customer-oriented company wanting to satisfy these in order to achieve customer satisfaction.

appeals are likely to work for different people in the process.

Let's illustrate the roles that various individuals (and others) play in the exchange process. As a society, we have become more open to acknowledging or recognizing family pets as important members of our families, and pet food marketers have capitalized on this through appeals to influence our purchase decisions and build brand relationships. The marketing problem for this industry was: How should we market effectively to pet owners? Increased focus has been placed on premium food products with all-natural ingredients. Science Diet (**www.sciencediet.com**) sales representatives have been known to consume the product straight from the tin to illustrate how superior the product is. Distribution of the company's Prescription Diet products is even restricted to veterinarians' offices (influencers). Brands such as Eagle Pack (**www.eaglepack.com**) appeal to owners wanting to take an holistic approach to their pets' health because the products contain certified organic chicken, dandelion, alfalfa, and apples, while the name of Purina's Beneful suggests that its wholesome, natural ingredients are healthful, beneficial, and flavourful. Purina (**www.purina.com**) has also utilized the Internet to forge relationships with pet owners (decision-makers and purchasers). Dedicated dog owners can use the site to set up home pages for the family pet, while the Cat Chow page offers a "mentoring program" to help provide support to the feline family member's nutritional, physical, and *emotional* needs. This example is unique in that the opinion of the actual *consumer* of this product is not targeted through marketing efforts. The cats and dogs that are the ultimate consumers get to voice their opinions only at the food dish.

In the case of the purchase of running shoes in the example that opened this chapter, you as an individual consumer played all three roles of decision-maker, consumer, and purchaser, as you were making the purchase of shoes for your own use. Your friend Bob played the role of influencer, and there may have been other influencers — friends with whom you discussed the purchase and others who may have recommended a particular brand of shoes.

Marketers, while keeping in mind the various roles played by people in the marketplace, must also remember that their principal task is to offer customers a product or service that will produce satisfaction. Marketing is a process of satisfying customer **needs and wants** through an exchange process. Technically, customer needs can be viewed in a strict physiological sense (related to food, clothing, and shelter) and everything else can be defined as a want. However, from a customer's perspective, the distinction is not clear. For example, many people consider a television set or a computer to be a necessity. When we speak of customer needs, we are actually extending our use of the term to include wants as well. Technically, it may be argued that most consumers really don't *need* a large percentage of the products and services that they buy, in the sense that they could continue to exist and get along very well without them. Therefore, we are often talking about wants, but we tend to refer to needs.

We also must remember that customer needs extend well beyond the actual product or service being offered. While we could debate whether you really *needed* those new running shoes or whether you and Bob really *needed* that cup of coffee at Second Cup, what we are saying is that you *want* to receive satisfaction when you engage in such exchanges. Here, we must return to a comment we made earlier: namely, that we should define what is being exchanged very broadly. So too, we must define customer needs very broadly. Customers shopping for running shoes (or any other product or service) not only need to find shoes that fit and that they like, but also need to find them conveniently located and reasonably priced. Customers also need to be treated politely and courteously by staff with whom they come into contact, and need to be made to feel good about their purchases. It is useful, in fact, to think about how customer needs exist at all five levels of the drivers of customer satisfaction model that we discussed earlier. If the needs that exist at each of these levels are addressed, chances are the customer will be satisfied and will be prepared to buy again and to tell others about the company.

Making the sale is only part of marketing success

As many organizations that are engaged in marketing emerge from the historic focus on sales to a broader view of achieving long-term customer satisfaction, there has been growing acceptance of the fact that making a sale is only part of marketing. In fact, it may be argued that in certain circumstances, it may be better for the company and the customer if no sale is made! How can this be? How can we talk about marketing unless we sell something?

Remember that our objective is to achieve high levels of long-term customer satisfaction. Are there not situations where it is better to have customers delay a purchase or even go to a competitor, rather than sell them something that doesn't fit, is inappropriate, or isn't needed, or something with which they will obviously be dissatisfied in the future? This raises an obvious ethical issue relating to an allegation that is occasionally made about marketing: namely, that it may cause customers to buy things that they may not really need or may not be able to afford. We will return to this and other ethics topics in Chapter 16.

Much marketing attention is focused on the point of purchase, on that interaction between a company and its customers that centres on making the sale. The importance of marketing begins long before this. Later in this book, we will discuss the process of communicating with prospective customers. At that time, we will identify one of the principal roles of advertising — creating high levels of awareness of a company and its brands. Communications in particular is used to create an interest in products and brands on the part of customers that will hopefully lead them to try a product for the first time. Then, we want to encourage repeat buying and, ultimately, a sense of loyalty.

Figure 1-3:

Stages of Customer Interaction

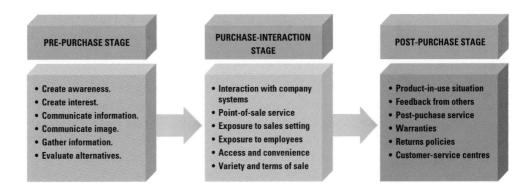

WEAR OUT WARRANTY

FULL WARRANTY ON ALL CHILDREN'S APPAREL AND
FOOTWEAR...FOR AS LONG AS THE CHILD FOR WHOM YOU
BOUGHT THIS ITEM WEARS THIS SIZE.
IF THE ITEM WEARS OUT, SEARS WILL, AT ITS OPTION,
REPAIR OR REPLACE IT WITH THE IDENTICAL
ITEM IN THE SAME SIZE, OR, IF UNAVAILABLE,
A SIMILAR ITEM OF EQUAL VALUE IN THE SAME SIZE.
EXCLUDES HOSIERY AND UNDERWEAR AND ITEMS SOLD IN OUR
OUTLET STORES AND ONLINE AT SEARS OUTLET SITE.
COVERS INFANTS TO SIZE 18 APPAREL AND
FOOTWEAR UP TO SENIOR KIDS' SIZE 6,
WITH PROOF OF PURCHASE.

NOTE: WARRANTY REPLACEMENTS/REPAIRS
MAY BE HANDLED THROUGH YOUR NEAREST
SEARS CATALOGUE LOCATION.

GARANTIE CONTRE L'USURE

GARANTIE COMPLÈTE SUR LES VÊTEMENTS ET CHAUSSURES
D'ENFANT...SI UN VÊTEMENT OU DES CHAUSSURES SONT USÉS
AVANT D'ÊTRE DEVENUS TROP PETITS POUR LE PREMIER ENFANT
QUI LES PORTE, SEARS, À SON CHOIX, RÉPARERA L'ARTICLE,
LE REMPLACERA PAR UN ARTICLE IDENTIQUE DE MÊME
TAILLE OU, SI CET ARTICLE N'EST PAS DISPONIBLE,
LE REMPLACERA PAR UN ARTICLE SEMBLABLE DE MÊME TAILLE
ET DE VALEUR ÉGALE. CETTE GARANTIE NE S'APPLIQUE PAS AUX
CHAUSSETTES ET COLLANTS, AUX SOUS-VÊTEMENTS OU AUX
ARTICLES DE NOS MAGASINS DE LIQUIDATION ET, EN LIGNE,
DU CENTRE D'AUBAINES SEARS. CETTE GARANTIE EST VALABLE
POUR LES VÊTEMENTS D'ENFANTS DE LA TAILLE NOUVEAU-NÉ
À LA TAILLE 18, ET POUR LES CHAUSSURES D'ENFANTS,
JUSQU'À LA POINTURE 6. PREUVE D'ACHAT REQUISE.

NOTE : POUR CETTE GARANTIE, LES DEMANDES
DE REMPLACEMENT/RÉPARATION SONT TRAITÉES
À VOTRE POINT DE VENTE DU CATALOGUE SEARS

Warranties such as this contribute to satisfying the customer after the sale.

product-in-use situation

The stage in the interaction when the customer has bought the product and is using it; evaluation of the success of the purchase takes place.

Much happens both before and after a sale to create satisfaction or dissatisfaction among customers and prospective customers. In fact, so much happens before a sale that a very large percentage of would-be customers never become customers. Think about situations when you really wanted to buy something. You had seen the advertising, found a certain product on the Internet, or you saw it while walking past a store in a shopping centre. You wanted the product, but you may have encountered a situation such as the one described in the chapter opener — you couldn't find someone to help you. Or you found the Web site so difficult to navigate that you gave up, or found after entering your order and other information, that the company does not ship its products to Canada. Or you got so frustrated after being kept on hold with a company's voice-mail system that you hung up.

Some companies make it very difficult for customers and would-be customers to deal with them, even though they have great products and services and through advertising have created an interest in their brands. Customers never buy something from such companies, because the companies have not paid sufficient attention to the second stage of the drivers of customer satisfaction model: support services and systems. They simply make it too difficult for customers to buy. What makes this particularly interesting is the fact that such customer dissatisfaction in many cases has nothing at all to do with the product or with the price being charged. In fact, customers are often prepared to pay *more* if they are simply treated well and the product is conveniently available.

Remember the purchase of your running shoes. Your final decision had very little to do with the shoes — you could have bought them in a number of different stores — or even with the price. Probably the most important factor that led you to buy them from Blades & Boards was Sandy and the way she treated you and handled the situation. Making things easy and pleasant for customers at the point of sale will often overcome other circumstances and result in a sale.

Much can go right or wrong at the point of sale, however. Regardless of whether the interaction with the customer takes place over the phone, via the Internet, or face to face, there are many opportunities to create customer satisfaction that will result in the sale being completed, or to dissatisfy customers so that they will abandon the attempt to buy. Much of the success of this interaction depends on how employees of the company interact with customers. An increasingly important aspect of that interaction is how the company has implemented customer-facing policies. While many customers appreciate the convenience of being able to deal with a bank, for example, through banking machines, the telephone, or the Internet, there are many others who want to deal with real people. They do not enjoy the impersonality of dealing with technology, and their long-term relationships with companies are weakened as a result. They are likely to leave in search of a company that will treat them like "a real person, rather than a number."

What happens after the customer buys something? This has as much potential to create satisfaction or dissatisfaction as anything that happens before or during the purchase process. This often relates to the so-called **product-in-use situation**, when a customer may enjoy or be dissatisfied with a tangible product after it has been has bought. The product may actually fail. Friends or family members may not like it. The customer may not know how to assemble it or even how to use it. And once it is ready to go, the opportunity to use the product may be limited, as, for example, when Web cameras were first introduced and few potential recipients had them attached to their computers. Much depends, of course, on the type of product purchased, but the point is that there is great potential for customer satisfaction or dissatisfaction after the sale.

As a result, we are seeing more and more companies paying greater attention to post-purchase service and the treatment of customers after the purchase. This includes increasing the flexibility of return and exchange policies. Increasingly, it is being recognized that it benefits the company to encourage the customer to return a product and/or complain if not completely satisfied. If you make it easy for your customers, they will return and purchase again, knowing the firm will stand behind its products. Wal-Mart allows customers to return merchandise to any of its stores, regardless of where it was purchased, and does not place a time limit on returns. Similarly, Sears makes it clear where it stands with its tag line "Satisfaction. Guaranteed." As well, both retailers will replace any children's clothing item if it wears out before the child outgrows it!

Firms are increasingly utilizing toll-free telephone numbers and Internet sites to provide post-sale support to answer questions, assist with assembly, and other customer requirements. Firms are offering guaranteed delivery times and faster service turnaround times, often involving on-site repairs or pick-up and delivery of the item. Such approaches are all about increasing the level of trust and reducing the feeling of risk involved in dealing with a particular company. Some companies are also using post-purchase opportunities to enhance relationships with their customers. General Motors dealers follow up with new car purchasers a couple of weeks after the purchase by sending a gift basket with a note of thanks and asking how everything is going with the new car.

Evolution of Marketing Thinking

The foundations of marketing were laid hundreds of years ago, when early settlers began trading among themselves and with various groups of Native peoples, thereby developing various exchange and barter relationships. However, it was not until the middle of the last century that marketing came to be recognized as a discipline within management and an important part of the organization of a company. We make specific reference to companies because the modern view of marketing grew out of businesses. The principles of marketing have in more recent years been applied to virtually every type of organization, including governments and cultural, charitable, and not-for-profit organizations.

Since then, marketing thinking has evolved through five successive stages of development or focus: a product focus, a sales focus, a new emphasis on the customer, a focus on service, and, most recently, on the development of customer relationships. These five stages reflect not only the development of the field over time, but also the state of mind of those who work in marketing. Although many firms have progressed to the third stage and beyond, the orientation of some firms and some individuals is still in the second or even the first stage, as shown in Figure 1-4.

Product-focus stage

product-focus stage

The stage at which a company is focused mainly on producing high-quality products and services.

Firms in the product-focus stage, typically manufacturers, place their emphasis on increasing output, while assuming that customers will seek out and buy reasonably priced and well-made products. Executives in production and engineering generally shape the firm's strategy. The function of the sales department is simply to sell the company's output at a price set by production and finance executives. The primary focus in business at this stage is to produce large

Figure 1-4:

Evolution of Marketing Thinking

PRODUCT FOCUS	SALES ORIENTATION	CUSTOMER INTEREST	CUSTOMER SERVICE	CUSTOMER RELATIONSHIP
1930s	1960s	1980s	1990s	2000s

quantities of goods and produce them efficiently. Finding customers is viewed as a relatively minor function. This focus on the production of physical goods was common during the first half of the twentieth century and into the 1950s, although some firms still think this way today: "If we make it, surely they will want to buy it." Many companies still do not understand why customers don't want to buy their perfectly good products. They don't yet realize that a lot more than great products is involved in producing customer satisfaction and marketing success.

Sales-orientation stage

As the economy grew through the 1950s and into the 1960s, it became clear that the main problem was no longer to produce enough products, but rather to sell the output. Just making a better product brought no assurance of success. Firms started to realize that the sale of products required substantial promotional effort. Thus began a period — the **sales-orientation stage** — when selling activities and sales executives gained new respect and responsibility. It was also during this period that selling acquired much of its bad reputation, as "hard-sell" approaches and shady sales tactics evolved. The emphasis on sales is still a feature of the operations of many companies, particularly in a business-to-business context. In such sales-focused companies, the emphasis is on selling more products, moving the inventory, getting the stuff out the door. Employees are rewarded mainly through commissions and bonuses, based on how much they sell.

Customer-interest stage

The pent-up demand for consumer goods that characterized the 1950s gave way to the need for companies to compete as they produced large quantities of goods, mainly as a result of new manufacturing technology and capacity. These early efforts to compete were characterized by the aggressive promotional and sales activities of the sales-orientation era. However, consumers became better educated and less willing to be persuaded, and they had greater variety from which to choose.

At roughly the same time, companies began to face increased competition, first from other local companies and then from national and, ultimately, international competitors. Competition became global and companies could no longer count on the patronage of their local clientele, who were now being exposed to marketing initiatives that originated in other countries. This combination of technology and global competition has, of course, been realized on the Internet, where companies now face competition from other organizations whose headquarters may be half a world away.

In this **customer-interest stage**, many businesses turn their attention beyond selling more products to addressing the customer's needs. The advent of this stage marked a profound change in marketing, as the orientation turned away from marketing as something companies do to people to an emphasis on finding out what customers want and then providing them with it. This was a much more sophisticated perspective on marketing, one that was for the first time truly customer-focused. The objective of a company at this stage is to satisfy customers, to meet their needs.

In this third stage, firms begin to do more of what is now considered marketing, rather than selling. Tasks that were once associated with other business functions become the responsibility of the top marketing executive, typically the marketing manager or vice-president. For instance, inventory control, warehousing, and some aspects of product planning are turned over to marketing as a way of serving customers better. And marketing research becomes an essential tool in the marketing manager's toolbox, providing important information on customer needs and behaviour.

sales-orientation stage
The stage in the evolution of marketing management in which the emphasis is on selling whatever the organization produces.

customer-interest stage
A company realizes that satisfying its customers is critical to its success; generally involves trying to know customers better.

Customer-service stage

Not until the 1980s did marketing managers really turn their attention to the marketing of services. Until then, marketing had been focused largely on tangible products turned out by well-known manufacturing companies such as General Electric, Kraft Foods, and Bombardier. But, as services began to account for more of the total value of the Canadian economy, firms began to pay greater attention to marketing in industries such as financial services, transportation, and hospitality. Some companies don't sell tangible products; what they offer their customers is entirely intangible. There was increasing acceptance of the fact that services are inherently different from tangible products and that customers approach their purchases differently. There was also a realization in the **customer-service stage** of the fact that all businesses, and indeed all organizations, are in the service business, in that some forms of service accompany the sale of all products. Thus, the era of services in marketing was born, as companies began to ensure that the intangible side of what they offered contributed to customer satisfaction.

Customer-relationship stage

Within the past 10 years, many companies have moved into yet another stage of the evolution of marketing thinking: the **customer-relationship stage**. The principal thrust of a company at this stage is to develop long-lasting relationships with customers, so that they will come back and buy from the company repeatedly and will recommend the company or brand to others. The objective is customer retention, based on the creation of long-term customer satisfaction. This seems to be such an obvious and sensible objective that you might well ask why companies took so long to get to this stage — in fact, it may be argued that many small, local businesses have been operating with this focus for years. They get to know their customers, treat them well, and are rewarded with repeat business. You can probably think of many small businesses that you and your family have been buying from for years, where you are well known to the owners and where you feel welcome or even "part of the family."

Many large national and multinational companies have for many years been motivated by short-term success, however. It was not until very recently that large companies have been able to track the business they get and the profits they make from individual customers, and have thereby gained an appreciation for the **lifetime value of customers**. With advances in information systems and customer databases, many companies were able only in the past decade or so to calculate the value of a customer and to realize what they are losing when customers leave and take their business elsewhere. Now these companies can focus on customer retention, on keeping as well as attracting customers. An even more recent extension of this thinking has been directed at creating the most solid relationships possible with customers through the building of an emotional connection with them. Through the 1990s and into the first decade of this century, we have witnessed more and more acceptance of a customer-relationship approach to marketing.

customer-service stage
A company at this stage places emphasis on providing excellent service to its customers, usually through improved systems and employee-customer interaction.

customer-relationship stage
A company actively tries to cultivate long-term relationships with its customers, based not only on great products, price, and service, but also on establishing an emotional connection.

lifetime value of customers
The value to a company of a customer over the lifetime of that customer's association with the firm; more than direct purchases.

BACKSPACE

1. What is the job of a marketer?
2. Beyond the actual product or service, what are some other customer needs?
3. What are the five successive stages through which marketing has evolved?

MARKETING AT WORK 1-2: RELATIONSHIPS

Pillsbury Hotcakes

The Pillsbury Doughboy® is as piping hot as ever — in fact, miniature beanbag toy versions of the famous character moved off grocery store shelves like hotcakes because consumers were eager to collect all three holiday versions of the little guy when these were introduced for a Christmas in-store promotion. Customers could purchase the beanbag doll for $2.99 with the purchase of two refrigerated dough products. In fact, the company's toll-free number received hundreds of calls wanting to know where the toy could be found. "We've had a fantastic response from customers and retailers," reported Chantal Butler, marketing manager for Pillsbury refrigerated baked goods at General Mills in Toronto. Citing proprietary research, Butler said, "The Doughboy® is the second-most-recognized icon in North America," after the Coca-Cola Polar Bears. "It was crazy not to leverage it."

How do you market cookie dough with beanbag dolls? Why would Pillsbury sell toys? The process sells the brand and it sells a relationship, that's why! Such activities can enhance the value of the brand, as well as relationships with customer segments — young and old. The influence can reach across decision-makers, buyers, and influencers of such purchases. "Logistically, it was not simple. We were getting into selling toys, which is not our core competency," said Butler.

But, it would seem worth the effort. The outstanding response caused Pillsbury to introduce other versions of the toy.

The promotion is a mainstream extension to the brand-building and relationship enhancement found on the company's Web sites (**www.pillsbury.com** and **www.dough boy.com**). There, aside from recipes and family activities, visitors can also find a veritable cyberboutique dedicated to the brand's icon, with about 100 items for sale bearing the Doughboy's® image — holiday decorations, plush figures, toy trucks, and kitchen curtains. Of course, there are also oven mitts for taking your piping-hot cookies out of the oven. It's part nostalgia, part toy store, and part shrine. Visitors can even sign up to receive messages from the Doughboy® himself! It's all about creating new memories for those who remember the little guy from their own youth and building memories for younger cookie eaters who will ask for them today and buy them for their own kids years from now.

SOURCE: Adapted from Lesley Young, "Pillsbury Promo Pops Off the Shelf," *Marketing Magazine*, January 14, 2002, p.2.

It All Begins with Value

We made the observation earlier that marketing involves the exchange of things of value between two parties who might simplistically be described as a customer and a marketer. We have commented that unless customers perceive that they have received good value from the exchange, satisfaction will not result. Only through the ongoing provision of value to its customers can a company achieve high levels of customer satisfaction, retention, and loyalty.

It is important to note that value, like many other concepts that we will examine in marketing, is intangible and exists largely in the mind of the customer. Value is perceived by the individual customer; where one may perceive value, another may see little or no value and may be unwilling to buy.

If a company or organization succeeds in creating value for its customers, generally high levels of customer satisfaction will be the result. If the company persists in satisfying its customers, a large percentage of these customers will continue to buy its products and services — customer retention will result. If customers are retained over time, they become better known to the company and its employees, a rapport begins to develop, and the customers feel more comfortable dealing with the company — the emotional characteristics of customer relationships begin to show. Once a company has succeeded in creating solid, long-lasting relationships with a large percentage of its customers, it will achieve a state of ongoing profitability and value for its owners. Thus, the creation of shareholder value, a goal of companies the world over, begins with the creation of value for the customer.

Figure 1-5:

Customer Value Drives
Shareholder Value

Value is, therefore, one of the most fundamental concepts in marketing. The essence of marketing is the creation of value for customers in order to produce high levels of satisfaction and to sustain that satisfaction over time. A central question in marketing deals with how to create value for customers.

value proposition
The sum total of what the company offers the customer; much more than product and price.

The answer lies in the development of what is termed the company's **value proposition**, encompassing literally everything that the company offers its customers and prospective customers. It is important again to define the value proposition quite broadly. Rather than focus on the core product or service, as we discussed earlier, a company must include in its value proposition everything that it does that has the potential to satisfy or dissatisfy customers. Thus, the value proposition must include not only what is being sold to the customer, but also how the product or service will be made available, what price is to be charged, the processes that will be used to provide the product, the level of post-purchase service to be provided, and many other aspects of the total offer.

It is important, finally, not to confine our discussion of value to aspects of the proposition relating to price. The simplest view of value is often expressed as value for money: How much does the customer have to pay for what is received from the company? But much more than monetary considerations influences a customer's decision on whether what is being offered or has been received represents good value. Value involves more than tangibles and more than money.

Think about a situation that would cause you to conclude that you will never go back to a particular clothing or sporting goods store. We have all had such negative experiences. In fact, one such experience may have been illustrated in the example that opened this chapter. Now, complete the following sentence: "I'll never go back there; it's just not worth the _____." Chances are that you completed the sentence with words like "time," "hassle," "trouble," "aggravation," or "frustration." It is surprising how infrequently customers will mention price in such a situation.

There is, of course, a very close connection between the stage of marketing thinking that a company has reached and how it defines its value proposition. Those companies that still have a product focus are most likely to define their value proposition quite narrowly, limiting its scope principally to having great products. As companies move into progressively more advanced stages of marketing thinking, they begin to include a broader range of things in their definition of the value proposition, until ultimately they are focused on the development of solid, long-term relationships with their customers. At this point, they tend to define the value proposition as broadly as possible to include literally everything the organization does that has the potential to influence long-term customer satisfaction.

Figure 1-6:

Marketing Thinking
Drives the Value
Proposition

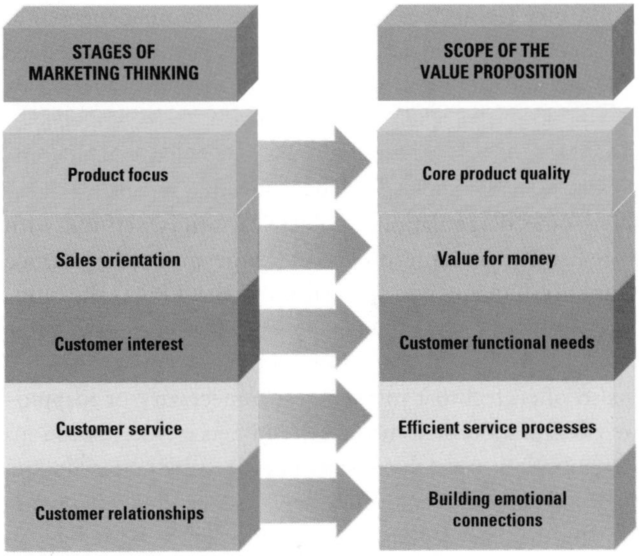

STAGES OF MARKETING THINKING	SCOPE OF THE VALUE PROPOSITION
Product focus	Core product quality
Sales orientation	Value for money
Customer interest	Customer functional needs
Customer service	Efficient service processes
Customer relationships	Building emotional connections

Customer-relationship thinking

The modern customer-relationship view of marketing is characterized by four concepts that are generally absent at the earlier stages in the evolution of marketing thinking, and especially at the early product- and sales-focused stages. First, an emphasis on building customer relationships is necessarily a *long-term strategy*. The payback may not be realized for two or three years and will last well into the future, unlike the sales-focused view where the objective is to make the sale today or this week. Second, companies that are focused on developing relationships with customers accept that they must understand the *customer's view* of the relationship, rather than the company's. It is the customer who decides whether quality and value are being offered and whether a solid relationship exists. Third, such companies also accept that they must *define very broadly what they offer the customer*, to include not only the core products or services, but also the service provided and the emotional connection with the customer. Finally, companies operating at this stage of the evolution of marketing *rely on new types of measures* to gauge their success. Rather than measuring success in conventional, short-term, financial terms such as sales, profits, and market share, they assess their performance against measures such as customer satisfaction, loyalty levels, and the strength of their relationships with customers.

Many business firms and other organizations are still operating in the early stages in the evolution of marketing thinking. Some believe they have the best products (and they may have), and can't understand why customers don't buy from them regularly, even though their service is terrible. Still others are focused almost entirely on selling, setting sales quotas, and paying their salespeople a commission on the amount they sell.

Admittedly, many of the firms that remain in the early stages of marketing thinking are long-established companies that manufacture tangible products. They continue to do business as they have done for years. Others have accepted the validity of the modern marketing orientation but have difficulty implementing it, for at least two reasons. First, implementation requires accepting the notion that the needs and wants of customers, not the needs of the company and its management, must direct the organization. Second, moving into the customer-focused advanced stages of marketing thinking requires that managers change their notion of what they offer the customer. Success in marketing today is about more than the products and services that we sell. Modern marketing thinking demands that companies realize that how they treat customers, the level of service provided, and ultimately how the customer feels about the company may in fact be more important in influencing long-term satisfaction and repeat business than the products that the company sells and the prices charged for them.

Placing customers first and taking a long-term view of dealing with customers affects the way a company describes what it does. Table 1-1 shows how some well-known organizations might define their businesses under a product or sales orientation and how differently the businesses would be defined using a more up-to-date service or relationship orientation.

In some situations, an organization may feel it does not need to be customer-focused to prosper. A monopoly service provider, such as a provincial power utility, is virtually guaranteed to have customers, since most people are not in a position to generate their own electricity. Nevertheless, customer satisfaction should remain the primary concern. In recent years in the telecommunications industry, former monopolies such as Bell Canada have faced competition from companies such as AT&T Canada, Sprint Canada, and cable television operators. Canada has also recently seen some deregulation of electrical utility service, with new providers beginning to provide service in some provinces. Large monopoly service providers are facing new direct competition in a newly deregulated arena. Unless they prepare to develop service and customer-focused environments, they are likely to suffer huge losses in the open market.

Free or not-for-profit services also often feel that marketing is unnecessary or inappropriate. Organizations such as Planned Parenthood or Canadian Blood Services have missions to fulfil and groups to serve. Such organizations can achieve greater success by understanding the needs of those with whom they deal. Issues of relevance in these cases can include understanding the critical role of empathy and patience when dealing with clients, as well as the

TABLE 1-1	What Business Are You In?	
Company	**Production-Oriented Answer**	**Marketing-Oriented Answer**
Bell Canada	We operate a telephone company.	We provide multiple forms of reliable, efficient, and inexpensive communications services.
Esso	We produce oil and gasoline products.	We provide various types of safe and cost-effective energy.
VISA Canada	We provide credit cards.	We facilitate the purchase of products and services and the transfer of funds.
Canadian National	We run a railway.	We offer a transportation and materials-handling system.
Levi Strauss	We make blue jeans.	We offer comfort, fashion, and durability in wearing apparel.
Kodak	We make cameras and film.	We help preserve beautiful memories.
Bombardier Inc.	We make airplanes.	We provide innovative ways of transporting people quickly and safely.
TELUS Mobility	We provide cellphones.	We enable people to communicate freely from practically anywhere in the world.
Pegasus Intelligence	We design cad/cam software.	We allow companies to reach a superior level in the optimization and business processes.
National Hockey League	We provide hockey games.	We create and promote events that are an excellent means of family entertainment.

importance of providers always conducting themselves with professionalism and providing assurance of confidentiality and privacy. Also, the timeliness, safety, and efficiency of service provision may be of concern to potential users.

1. The essence of marketing is the creation of _____ for customers.
2. What four concepts characterize the customer-relationship view of marketing?
3. What are the four elements of the traditional marketing mix?

Keeping As Well As Getting Customers

"four Rs" of marketing
Guideposts for the new way of thinking in marketing: customer retention, relationships, referrals, and recovery from negative experiences.

The recent focus of marketing on customer service and the creation of customer loyalty have brought about an important change in how marketers view their dealings with customers and prospective customers. In short, there has been a realization on the part of many marketing managers that the provision of the four elements of the conventional marketing mix — product, price, advertising and promotion, and distribution channels — is not sufficient to ensure customer satisfaction and repeat business. While we will devote a large portion of this book to coverage of these four components of the marketing mix, it is important to do so in the context of a new strategic view of marketing, one that focuses on all of the ways that companies create value for their customers, leading to customer satisfaction. We have labelled the components of our new strategic view the **"four Rs" of marketing** — retention, referrals, relationships, and recovery. These components focus our thinking on what the new approach to marketing is designed to accomplish. They also serve to put into context how the elements of the traditional marketing mix should be applied. Marketers today realize that getting the four elements of the marketing mix right is not enough; each of these must be applied in the context of what it does to support the building of long-term relationships with customers.

Retention

Most successful marketers today have accepted the principle of **customer retention** — that long-term customers are more profitable and that organizations should pay at least as much attention to keeping existing customers as they do to trying to attract new ones. Recent studies have demonstrated quite clearly that customers become more profitable the longer they continue to do business with a firm. This is the case because satisfied, long-term customers spend a larger portion of their total expenditures (often referred to as **share of wallet**) with a firm to which they are loyal. These customers also cost less to serve, because they are generally more satisfied and don't need to be convinced to buy. They make fewer complaints and are less likely to quibble over price, often being prepared to pay more for good service. And they tell others how satisfied they are.

Referrals

This last point leads to the second of our four Rs, **referrals**. One of the greatest benefits of satisfying customers is that they will refer their friends and associates to the firm that is providing them with superior value. This is one of the most important benefits to be gained from satisfying customers. Through positive **word of mouth**, satisfied customers can produce large volumes of new business. Conversely, a dissatisfied customer will either spread negative word of mouth or will simply never return. Companies that provide a high level of value to their customers always keep in mind the potential for existing customers to bring in new ones.

Again, consider your purchase of running shoes at the beginning of the chapter. If a friend sees your new purchase and mentions that she or he is in the market for a new pair of Vans or Skechers, what will you say? If you're really happy with your experience and your new footwear, you'll suggest that your friend should check out Blades & Boards and you'll explain why. That would be an example of positive word of mouth. Negative word of mouth would be if you advised your friends *not* to go to Sports Champs. Such informal communication between friends, family members, and co-workers can greatly affect the reputation of a firm.

customer retention
The behavioural connection between regular customers and a company; characterized by repeat buying behaviour, but not yet a relationship because it may be lacking an emotional component.

share of wallet
The share of a customer's total spending in a product or service category that is given to a particular company or brand.

referral
The process of recommending a company or brand to others; positive word of mouth.

word of mouth
The process of customers discussing companies and brands with which they have come in contact; may be either positive or negative.

He'll spread positive word of mouth about this video game.

VideoGameReview.com
GameZone Online

Some companies use word of mouth to introduce new products and generate interest. As a formal part of promoting a new video game, for example, the manufacturer will send copies to game critics who write for magazines, newspapers, or Web sites such as VideoGameReview.com (**www.videogamereview.com**) or GameZone Online (**www.gamezone.com**), where prospective users will read the reviews, discuss them in chat rooms, and hopefully go out and rent or buy the game as a result. Also, manufacturers often run local contests, giving away many of the new game consoles or cartridges as prizes to get the product in people's hands and start them talking about it to their friends — perhaps even submitting their own reviews to one of these many review sites.

Relationships

One of the most important developments in marketing in recent years has been the attention now being paid to the establishment of relationships between companies and their customers. This is an aspect of marketing that is gaining considerable attention and is linked very closely to the notion that long-term customer satisfaction is a direct result of the provision of superior customer value. The customers' definition of value very often extends to the establishment of a close relationship with a company — they come to value the relationship itself. However, the establishment of a long-term customer relationship is not a simple task and should be approached following much study of how the firm's customers define a relationship.

Many companies are now introducing relationship-marketing programs to try to get closer to their customers, so that they will feel more a part of the company. The most notable of these include examples like Saturn, the automaker, which holds picnics and barbeques for Saturn owners. The company also sponsors the construction of local community playgrounds, inviting Saturn owners to help in the day-long event. Other higher-end service providers deliver services that exceed customer expectations, providing memorable experiences that forge solid relationships.

NAC: Live Rush

All types of organizations are seeking to develop reliable, mutually beneficial relationships. The National Arts Centre (NAC) discovered great success in 2002 with its Live Rush program (**www.liverushnac.ca**). Like other arts organizations concerned with the "greying" of the Canadian population, the NAC wanted not only to attract a younger demographic, but also to create customers for life. And the very young were targeted to publicize the 125 annual music, dance, theatre, and variety productions — high school and post-secondary students, in fact. Those who registered for the program could take advantage of "the cheapest date in town." Unsold inventory to same-day performances was made available at what was sometimes one-tenth of the regular ticket cost. But it takes more than discount tickets to create relationships. Targeted direct and database marketing efforts went a long way in changing the perception of the "arts" as highbrow entertainment. Registration information assisted in the collection of much consumer information that could be used to build long-term relationships — hopefully, customers for life.[2]

service recovery
The process of correcting the situation when a customer is dissatisfied with service provided. A company may attempt to recover from a poor service experience by apologizing or by offering the customer a price reduction or other form of compensation.

Recovery

The final element in our four Rs of marketing relates to **service recovery** — what a company can do to recover customer satisfaction when something has gone wrong. Inevitably, customers will encounter problems and poor service when dealing with some companies. Even the most meticulous companies cannot completely avoid delivering poor service on occasion. The issue is: What can and should a company do when something goes wrong?

Certainly, the answer is not "Do nothing." Particularly in service companies in recent years, managers have been paying increasing attention to the development of procedures to deal with service problems as they arise, with a view to solving customers' problems before they decide to take their business elsewhere. Therefore, service recovery becomes an important component in a company's program to establish and maintain customer relationships. Taking the necessary steps to deal with customers' problems efficiently and effectively will lead to those customers being satisfied, even to the point that they will be more loyal than they would have been if the service problem had never occurred!

The Modern Marketing Concept

marketing concept

A philosophy of doing business that emphasizes customer orientation and co-ordination of marketing activities in order to achieve the organization's performance objectives.

The evolution of marketing thinking from an emphasis on the product to a focus on customer relationships has led to successive steps in the development of a particular philosophy of doing business. Often referred to as the **marketing concept**, this philosophy emphasizes customer orientation and the co-ordination of marketing activities to achieve the mutual long-term objectives of the customer *and* the organization. Although customer satisfaction is important, this focus will work only if it is accomplished at the same time that the organization's objectives are being met; in short, the company has to make a profit. Long-term customer satisfaction leads to the retention of customers and generates ongoing profits.[3] Developing satisfied customers is therefore an important way to meet the organization's performance objectives. By creating value for its customers, a company is creating long-term payback for its shareholders and securing the future of the company.

Nature and rationale

The marketing concept is based on four beliefs that are illustrated in Figure 1-7:

- All planning and operations should be focused on creating customer satisfaction. Every department and employee should contribute to the satisfaction of customers' needs. The attitude should be that "everyone is in marketing," because virtually everything that a company or organization does has the potential to affect the satisfaction of customers. Thus, the people who design and install the telephone system and the Web site are in marketing. The people who prepare and send out invoices are in marketing. So too are representatives of the human resources department, because they are responsible for putting the right employees in positions where they come into contact with customers.

Figure 1-7:

Components and Outcomes of the Marketing Concept

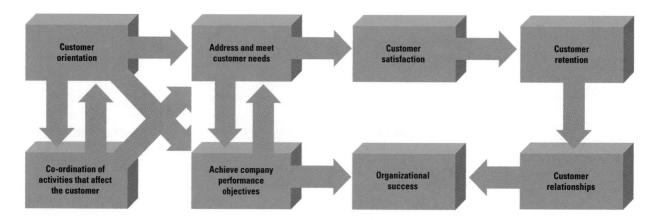

- All marketing activities in an organization should be co-ordinated. Marketing efforts (product and service planning, pricing, distribution, promotion, and customer service) should be designed and combined in a coherent, consistent way, and there should be one overall view of the importance of the customer. Responsibility for the marketing orientation of the company rests squarely on the shoulders of the chief executive officer (CEO) or president. This executive has the responsibility for creating the right culture within the company, one that ensures that customers are treated as the company's most important asset. Regardless of the department of the company in which employees work, they should be made aware of their roles in supporting a marketing orientation for the organization.

- Customer-oriented, co-ordinated marketing is essential to achieve the organization's performance objectives, while at the same time meeting the customer's needs. The primary objective for a business is typically to achieve profitability. In not-for-profit organizations, the objective might be to increase the number of people served or the variety of services offered. Since companies began to move into the service- and relationship-focused stages of marketing thinking, there has been a growing awareness that new and different measures of organizational performance are needed.

- Everything is focused on the long term and designed to create an emotional connection with the customer. Thus, an important component of the modern marketing concept relates to creating an environment and an experience for the customer that contributes to the building of a relationship. Concepts such as trust, communication, value, and quality are important parts of what building a relationship means. Thus, truly marketing-oriented organizations have a viewpoint that ensures that they act in an ethical and socially responsible manner, that they treat their employees and customers well, and that they generally behave as responsible members of the communities in which they operate.

Why Marketing Is Important

Marketing is important in a number of contexts: at the level of the national marketplace, at the level of the business or organization that practises marketing, and at the level of the customer.

Marketing in the marketplace

In the Canadian economy today, customers are probably better treated than at any time in the past. There is greater choice, a greater variety of products and services from which to choose, and higher levels of convenience and access to options than customers have ever had. This is a result of many factors, including competition from international competitors and through the Internet, and recent advances in technology that have enabled companies and other organizations to deliver higher-quality products and services more efficiently than in the past. But the current attractiveness of the marketplace is also a result of how businesses have responded to the challenges they have been facing. There is no doubt that companies are more marketing-oriented and customer-focused than at any time in the past, and customers are the beneficiaries of this. Canada is also one of the most marketing-friendly countries because, over the past 30 years or so, governments at all levels have put in place consumer protection legislation to ensure that companies act ethically and in the best interests of customers.

We can also get an idea of the importance of marketing in the Canadian economy by looking at how many people are employed in some way in marketing and at how much of what we spend covers the cost of marketing — upward of one-third of the Canadian labour force is engaged in marketing activities. This figure includes employees in retailing, wholesaling, transportation, warehousing, and communications industries, as well as people who work in marketing departments in manufacturing, agriculture, mining, and service industries.

Marketing in companies and organizations

Marketing considerations should be an integral part of all planning, because the success of any business comes from satisfying the needs and wants of its customers. Although many activities are essential to a company's growth, marketing is the only activity that directly produces revenue.

During the 1990s, many not-for-profit organizations realized that they needed effective marketing programs to counteract difficult economic times, shrinking government subsidies, and a decrease in charitable contributions. Charities with decreasing donations, service clubs with declining memberships, and symphony orchestras playing to empty seats all began to understand that marketing was essential to help them turn their situations around. Today, political organizations, museums, and even churches — all organizations that formerly rejected any thought of marketing — are embracing it as a means of growth and, for some, survival.

Marketing and you

Why is marketing important for you and for the millions of other consumers in this country? Why should you study marketing? There are a number of reasons.

Marketing pervades our daily activities. Consider how many marketers view you as part of their market. With people like you in mind, firms such as Nike, Loblaws, Air Canada, MuchMusic, and Tim Hortons have designed their products and services, set prices, created advertisements, and chosen the best methods of making their products and services available to you. They have devised customer-service strategies and developed programs to encourage you to come back and do business with them in the future. In response, you watch television commercials, buy various items from different retail stores or through the Internet, and sometimes complain about prices or the quality of service you receive. Marketing occupies a large part of your daily life. Studying marketing will make you a better-informed consumer. You'll understand more about what underlies a seller's pricing and how brand names are selected, as well as the roles of promotion and distribution.

Finally, marketing probably relates, directly or indirectly, to your career aspirations. If you are thinking about studying more marketing courses and considering employment in a marketing position, you can develop a feel for what marketers do. If you're planning a career in accounting, finance, or another business field, you can learn how marketing affects managerial decision-making in these areas. Finally, if you are thinking about a career in a non-business field, such as health care, government, music, theatre, or education, you will learn how to use marketing in these organizations. When you become serious about a job search, all of the marketing ideas and tools will be of great help to you in defining potential employer groups and their interests, and clarifying how you can present yourself to them.

An Integrated View of Marketing

This first chapter has presented a view of how marketing is addressed in modern businesses and organizations. A number of key points should be obvious from this early discussion of marketing. The first is that marketing has changed a lot over the past 50 years or so. This is because marketing is an extremely dynamic field — it is always changing, because customers are always changing. Marketing is all about satisfying customers, and these customers are influenced by many trends and changes in their lives. This is what makes marketing one of the most exciting fields of study.

Marketing applies to all forms of organizations. It is not something that is done by businesses only. Rather, it has been embraced as an essential activity by arts and cultural organizations that are trying to build their base of patrons, by charities that want their messages to reach more donors, and by universities and colleges such as your own that want to attract more students. Marketing is not simply a business department or function. It is a way of viewing an organization and how it operates.

The second key point that should be reinforced is that marketing is an all-pervasive approach to doing business that is represented by an attitude or focus that should pervade all parts of an organization. It could even be said that marketing today is too important to be left to the marketing department.

The final key point that we would reiterate to end the chapter suggests that marketing must be integrated throughout an organization. Many concepts have to be reflected in the marketing thinking of the modern organization. Management in the modern marketing-oriented company understands that virtually everything that the company and its employees do must be oriented toward the creation of value and the development of a solid corps of loyal customers.

◄ BACKSPACE

1. What are the four components of the new strategic view of marketing?
2. What is the marketing concept?
3. _____ are now much more important than goods as the object of a transaction.

Summary

The principal focus of marketing in most organizations today is the achievement of long-term customer satisfaction. This is accomplished through the provision by the company to its customers of something of value in exchange for something else of value. The end result, if marketing is practised well, is the creation of a base of loyal customers who not only continue to do business with the company, but also refer their friends and associates. Many will even develop an emotional attachment to the company, often referred to as a *customer relationship*.

All types of organizations engage in marketing. The things being marketed include tangible products, as well as services, ideas, people, and places. Marketing activities are targeted at groups of consumers that are termed *markets,* consisting of product purchasers and consumers, as well as the individuals and groups that influence the purchase decision.

In a business context, marketing is a total system of business activities designed to plan, price, promote, and distribute need-satisfying products to target markets in order to achieve consumer and organizational objectives. The main difference between marketing and selling is that, in selling, the emphasis is on the product; in marketing, the emphasis is on meeting customers' needs.

Marketing has evolved through five stages. It began with a production orientation, passed through a sales orientation, then through a stage focused on the customer, and then through one focused on service. The focus now is on customer relationships. In this fifth stage, a company's efforts are directed toward identifying and satisfying customers' needs in order to establish effective marketing relationships.

Many factors drive customer satisfaction. The most basic of these is the core product or service that is marketed by the firm, followed by various services and systems that the firm has in place and its ability to deliver these effectively and accurately. How the firm and its employees interact with customers also affects satisfaction. Ultimately, whether customers are satisfied depends on how they feel toward the company.

According to the modern marketing concept, a firm is best able to achieve its performance objectives by adopting a customer orientation and co-ordinating all of its marketing activities. A focus on the customer helps to build long-term relationships based on getting to know customers and understanding their needs in order to provide high levels of quality and service within a trusting and ethical framework.

Key Terms and Concepts

consumer 11
customer 4
customer-interest stage 16
customer loyalty 7
customer-relationship management 7
customer relationship 8
customer-relationship stage 17
customer retention 22
customer satisfaction 4
customer-service stage 17
decision-maker 11
drivers of customer satisfaction 8
exchange 4
expectations 5
"four Rs" of marketing 21
"give and get" 5
influencers 11

lifetime value of customers 17
market 10
marketer 6
marketing 4
marketing concept 24
marketing mix 6
needs and wants 12
product-focus stage 15
product-in-use situation 14
purchaser 11
referral 22
sales-orientation stage 16
service recovery 23
share of wallet 22
value 5
value proposition 19
word of mouth 22

Questions and Problems

1. Explain the concept of an exchange, including the conditions that must exist for an exchange to take place, and give an example of an exchange that does not involve money.

2. Name some retail stores that you frequently visit or some brands that you often buy. Are you loyal to these stores or brands? If so, why? If not, explain why you aren't.

3. Explain the five levels in the model of the drivers of customer satisfaction. Discuss how each level can influence the customer and generate satisfaction or dissatisfaction.

4. "The marketing concept does not imply that marketing executives will run the firm. The concept requires only that whoever is in top management be marketing-oriented." Give examples of how a production manager, a vice-president of finance, or a personnel manager can be marketing-oriented.

5. For each of the following organizations, describe what is being marketed.
   a. Toronto Maple Leafs.
   b. Human Resources Development Canada.
   c. www.monster.ca
   d. Canadian Blood Services

6. One way of explaining the value provided by marketing is to consider how we would live if there were no marketing facilities. Describe some of the ways in which your daily activities would be affected if there were no retail stores or advertising.

7. Name two service firms that, in your opinion, do a good marketing job. Then name some that do a poor marketing job. Explain your reasoning in each case.

8. Explain why it is sometimes better for a business not to make a sale. Describe a situation in which a customer would walk out of a store empty-handed but feeling satisfied or pleased.

9. Why is it that getting the traditional marketing mix right may not be enough to ensure high levels of satisfaction?

10. Why should a company want to develop a relationship with a customer?

Hands-On Marketing

1. Select a restaurant, hotel, dry cleaner, or other service company near your school and think about how it operates. If possible, observe the operation and interview a manager and some customers to identify: (a) what is being exchanged; and (b) whether the company is production-, sales-, or customer-oriented.

2. Go to **www.amazon.ca** and examine the Web site to determine how Amazon adds value for the customer. How does the company use technology to improve customer satisfaction and build relationships with customers?

Back to the Top

Think about the customer experience described in the chapter opener and what went on: why you bought your shoes at one store rather than the other. Think also about the many factors that contributed to your decision — what it was that made you satisfied with your experience at Blades & Boards and with your purchase. Why was Blades & Boards successful in selling you the shoes and Sports Champs was not? Now think about what this tells us about the scope of marketing. What can marketers learn from this everyday example?

Want to get better grades, tips on how to study more effectively, and up-to-date information on happenings in the world of marketing? Then, visit the Online Learning Centre for practice tests, Study Smart software, and much more! **www.mcgrawhill.ca/college/sommers**

Interested in finding out what marketing looks like in the real world? *Marketing Magazine* is just a click away on your Online Learning Centre!

CHAPTER 2

The Dynamic Marketing Environment

In this chapter, we'll examine how a company plans its total marketing program. After studying this chapter, you should have an understanding of:

- The concept of monitoring a firm's environment (environmental scanning) and how forces outside a company play a role in strategic marketing planning.
- The role of internal company factors (the internal environment) in guiding and supporting marketing strategies and their implementation.
- The nature and scope of planning and how it fits within the management process.
- Similarities and differences among mission, objectives, strategies, and tactics.
- The essential difference between strategic company planning and strategic marketing planning.
- The steps involved in strategic marketing planning.
- The purpose and contents of an annual marketing plan.
- How planning models can be useful aids in developing a marketing program.

ENOUGH ROOM FOR YOU AND YOUR STUDENT LOAN.

NAME
NOM 2002 Protegé5

MAZDA
GRADUATE
PROGRAM
GRADS GET $750 OFF
PURCHASE OR LEASE

$750 is above and beyond all other program offers.
See your local Mazda Dealer for details.

MAZDA
www.mazda.ca

Zoom–Zoom?

With the increasing realization of the importance of customer loyalty, retention, and lifetime value, it was only a matter of time before marketers came to the next logical conclusion — the earlier they develop such bonds, with their accompanying brand preference and loyalty, the greater the potential lifetime value they will have. Get 'em while they're young.

In an attempt to gain advantage in a mature product category such as the automobile market, many manufacturers have increased marketing efforts geared toward younger car buyers. With many consumers' tastes moving toward SUVs in recent years, new entries have been pouring into the marketplace, from compact to behemoth in size and moving more and more toward the high end of the price scale. But, many young consumers can't afford these vehicles.

Automobile marketers sat down to figure out how to get to young consumers and they seem to have decided to re-invent the station wagon. Who remembers the station wagon? Some time during the eighties, the "family wagon" became taboo — if you were under 40 years of age, you wouldn't be caught dead in one! The odd station wagon was available, but gone were the days when most North American cars were available in a wagon model. And it wasn't due to SUVs (they were just called "four-wheel-drives" in those days!), which didn't even become a part of the vernacular until well into the nineties.

In 2002, the Mazda Protegé 5 appeared, and for the 2003 model year, the Toyota Matrix and the Pontiac Vibe took to the road — aggressively designed, compact vehicles that look like they mean business. They exude an all-purpose, rough-and-tumble, go-anywhere, do-anything sort of look. They're new and they're radical, right? Well, sort of. Don't be fooled — these are station wagons, but marketers certainly aren't going to say that out loud. They're designed with boldly shaped body panels and flash aluminum wheels and equipped with boss-sounding audio systems to help you forget that. All with starting prices around $17,000 to $19,000. Much more affordable for young consumers than the average SUV price tag. Chrysler is already planning the next evolution, with the Pacifica managing to squeeze in third-row seating and a glass-panelled roof.[1]

Competing producers identified the importance of targeting and attracting younger consumers — those buying their first new car: post-secondary graduates, young couples, and young families. Also important are the many young consumers who are not yet old enough to get a driver's licence — reflecting trends of the growing influence of children in the household on the purchase of all sorts of big-ticket items, including the family car. Scanning the environment yielded a new strategic opportunity for some auto manufacturers. The opportunity was then translated into a goal for the organization — develop brand preference early — get 'em while they're young.

In Chapter 1, you were introduced to the ideas that make marketing contemporary and dynamic. You looked at such concepts as customer satisfaction, long-run customer loyalty, the stages of getting and keeping customers, customer value, and shareholder value. In this chapter, you will be looking at the framework that is used for taking these and other key marketing ideas and putting them to work, as illustrated by the actions of Mazda, Toyota, and Pontiac that you have just read about. While, from time to time, there are some great marketing successes that "just happen," the vast majority happen because they were carefully planned. To make marketing ideas work, you need to apply management concepts to them; you need to understand the management and planning framework that makes marketing work. Mazda, Toyota, and Pontiac did the work — their marketing programs should work.

In the first part of this chapter, we will describe the environment in which all businesses exist and with which they must deal, regardless of what they do or how big they are. If you know what's going on in the marketing environment, you can do a better job of dealing with it. Marketing people need to determine what makes up their firm's environment and then monitor it in a systematic fashion. Good monitoring of this environment provides the database and foundation ideas for developing successful strategies and plans for managing the business.

In the second part of this chapter, we examine three levels of management planning: strategic planning for the business or total organization, strategic planning for the marketing department or functions, and action planning for specific marketing activities. You will see where and how marketing environmental scanning plays a key role in the management process.

The Environment for Strategy and Planning

external macro-environmental forces
Market forces that are generally beyond the control of companies: demographics, economic conditions, competition, social and cultural trends, technological developments, and political and legal forces.

external micro-environmental forces
Forces affecting a particular firm that can readily be influenced by the company: the sets of marketing relationships a firm has with its customers, its suppliers, and the wholesalers and retailers through which the company sells its products and services.

internal non-marketing forces
The environment within a firm composed of working relationships between employees and departments.

The environment of all organizations, regardless of who they are and what they do, is composed of three sets of factors or forces:

- Those that affect all competing firms and that are generally, but not always, beyond the control of management: demographics, economic conditions, competition, social and cultural trends, technological developments, and political and legal forces. These forces are generally not controllable by the firms, and are often referred to as **external macro-environmental forces** — the market forces faced by our three auto manufacturers.

- Those that affect a particular firm and can more readily be influenced by management: the sets of marketing relationships a firm has with its customers, its suppliers, and the wholesalers and retailers through which the company sells its products and services. Relationships can often be developed with these groups as part of the firm's overall marketing strategy. These forces are often referred to as **external micro-environmental forces**. Mazda, Toyota, and Pontiac each had a different set of suppliers.

- Within the firm itself, an environment exists that is composed of working relationships between employees and departments. These, traditionally, have been referred to as **internal non-marketing forces**, but do influence the ultimate success of the organization. What are the internal efficiencies of our three auto manufactures and how smoothly are decisions made and implemented?

Sometimes a firm may be able to manage a part of its external environment that is generally not controllable. For example, through corporate and industry lobbying in Ottawa or provincial capitals, or in other cities and towns, a company may have some influence on how political and legal forces affect it. In addition, new-product research and development that is on the leading edge of technological innovation can influence a firm's competitive position. In fact, one company's technology may be the external environmental force of technology that is affecting other organizations.

The six interrelated macro-environmental forces that are generally beyond the control of management are presented in Figure 2-1: demography, economic conditions, competition,

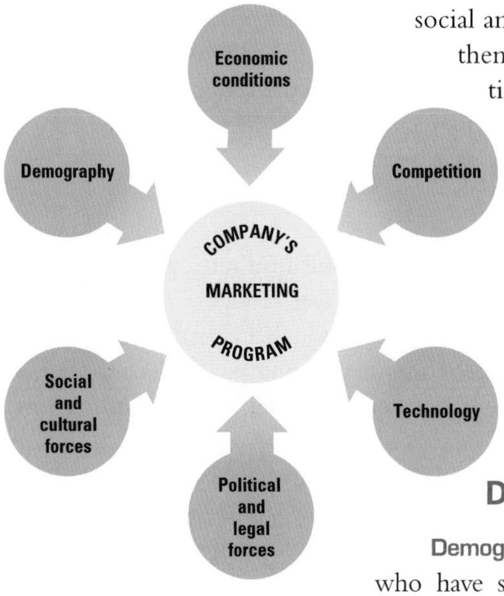

Figure 2-1:

Relationship-
Insensitive External
Environmental Forces
*Six largely
uncontrollable external
forces influence an
organization's
marketing activities.*

**relationship-
insensitive forces**

Forces that do not afford a firm
a particular advantage or the
opportunity to develop
particularly strong bonds or
connections with its customers.

demography

The statistical study of human
population and its distribution.

social and cultural forces, technology, and political and legal forces. Each force is then discussed in turn: the force is described and some examples of its potential implication are provided in terms of market opportunities or strategic approaches, or of marketing tactics that are commonly used as a result of each force's impact. Keep in mind that the forces and their magnitude keep changing. When they change, it can be at different rates — not all markets or consumers are affected by a given change in the same way, and sometimes, through industry and company pressure, some of these forces can be influenced. Such forces could be said to be relationship-insensitive, meaning that they do not afford a firm a particular advantage or the opportunity to develop particularly strong bonds or connections with its customers.

Demography

Demography is the statistical study of human population and its distribution. People who have similar demographic characteristics (such as age, geographic location, or income level) often share other relevant characteristics, creating a potential market for a particular product or service.

The Baby Boomers   Born between 1946 and 1966, Baby Boomers account for a larger percentage of the population of Canada than is the case in any other country (more than 33 percent in 2002). They are now passing through their middle years (late 30s to 50s),[2] bringing changes in "middle-aged" values, tastes, and concerns — indulging in well-earned vacations and luxury cars instead of family minivans. This demographic sector is likely to inherit more wealth from aging parents than any other group in the past. Baby Boomers represent growing and changing markets.

Seniors   For the first time in history, there are more people aged 65 and older than there are teenagers in Canada (almost 4 million in 2002). The cruise ship industry benefits greatly from this growing market, as do upscale retirement homes and communities, which are of interest to the mid-seniors. The oldest seniors have the lowest level of affluence and focus on affordable retirement services and products.

Singles   Almost 10 percent of Canadian households are made up of people who live alone. Increasingly, products such as single-serving prepared foods are being introduced for young and older singles alike, and homebuilders are designing homes, condominium units, and housing developments with older singles in mind.[3]

'Tweens   Youth between 9 and 13 years of age account for 10 percent of the population, and this number will continue to grow in size until 2006. Changes in demographics and culture mean that this group of savvy consumers influence about $1.5 billion of the spending in this country, as decisions about family purchases become more egalitarian within the family unit.

Economic conditions

People must have money to spend and be willing to spend it. A marketing system is affected especially by such considerations as the current stage of the business cycle, inflation, and interest rates.

Stages of the business cycle   We now think of a three-stage business cycle: prosperity, recession, and recovery. During prosperity, firms tend to expand their marketing programs, as they add new products and enter new markets. During a recession, on the other hand, with higher rates of unemployment and reduced consumer spending, firms typically retrench, as consumers become discouraged, scared, and angry. Recovery finds the economy moving from recession to prosperity, and as unemployment declines and disposable income increases, companies expand their marketing efforts to improve sales and profits.

Inflation   Inflation occurs when price levels rise at a faster rate than personal income, so that there is a decline in consumer buying power. Although inflation rates declined to just over 2 percent by 2002 from much higher levels previously,[4] a fear of higher rates continued to influence government policies, consumer psychology, and business marketing programs in the area of pricing and cost control. With inflation, consumer buying power declines but, at the same time, consumers may overspend today for fear that prices will be higher tomorrow.

Interest rates   When interest rates are high, consumers tend to hold back on long-term and large purchases such as housing and vehicles, since it is expensive to borrow money. Banks and other lenders, as well as retailers, sometimes offer below-market interest rates or no payments for a year as a promotional device to increase business.

Unemployment rates   Unemployment rates reflect the percentage of people who are employed and the percentage who are looking for work. These rates vary from market area to market area and affect greatly the amount of disposable income that consumers have to spend on products and services, as well as their willingness to spend. Regional variations in pricing and terms of sale may be necessary.

Competition

A company's competitive environment is a major influence in shaping its marketing system, so key aspects of competitors' marketing activities should be monitored. Expanded trade with other countries means that Canadian firms will have to pay greater attention to foreign competition and, with the movement toward global free trade, increasingly find opportunities for Canadian products and services in foreign markets. A firm generally faces competition from three sources.

Direct brand and store competition from marketers of similar and directly competing products and services   The Xbox, PlayStation 2, and GameCube compete with each other for many of the same gamers, while retailers such as Old Navy, Gap, and American Eagle compete with each other for many of the same clothing dollars at the local mall.

Indirect competition from substitute products that satisfy the same basic need   On any given evening, many people choose either to go to a movie or rent one at a video store. Courier companies and Canada Post have seen a portion of their business taken away by fax machines and e-mail. Traditional department stores and clothing retailers realize that their competition is coming not only from other stores down the street or elsewhere in the same town, but also from Internet retailers such as L.L. Bean, Lands' End, and J. Crew, headquartered in other countries.

Competition for the consumer's limited buying power   This is the final type of competition, where almost all companies are competing for the same consumer dollars. A marketer of tennis racquets faces competition from other companies that are marketing jeans or shoes or weekend ski holidays. Competition for discretionary spending is one of the greatest challenges for marketers.

Social and cultural forces

Social and cultural forces — lifestyles, social values, and beliefs — continue to change much more rapidly than in the past. The following are just some of these forces that have significant marketing implications.

Emphasis on quality of life Today, quality of life is a major focus for many people, including the demand for more quality goods and services. The theme is "Not more — but better value." People are more concerned about education and health, and less about keeping up with neighbours in terms of bigger and better purchases. A growing concern for the physical environment and discontent with pollution and resource waste also plays a key role.

Immigration and changing values Continued immigration results in the addition, often in subtle ways, of the unique values and preferences shaped by the cultures of many different home countries. The characteristics of some of these immigrant groups include a higher degree of control by family elders over purchasing power and buying decisions, a suspicion of government and government-sponsored programs, an aversion to the use of credit cards and the accumulation of debt, and a focus on household and family goals, including securing a job, home ownership, and education of the children.[5]

Roles of men and women The erosion of stereotypes of male and female roles in families, jobs, recreation, and product use continues, affecting all areas of marketing. These effects are particularly noticeable in product design, advertising, and promotion.

Attitudes toward physical fitness and food An increased interest in health and physical fitness is obvious across most demographic and economic segments of society. Stores supplying activity products and service organizations catering to this trend have multiplied.

MARKETING AT WORK 2-1: STRATEGY

The New Male Obsession

Traditionally considered an issue for females in our society, body image has now significantly become a male issue. If you don't believe that, look again! Today's newsstands are bulging with men's "lifestyle" magazines. And what exactly are those? Think about it — they're the mirror image of what we refer to for women as "beauty magazines." Keep thinking about it — they are about honing the ideal physique, diet, fashion, trends and gadgets, and, yes, sure-fire sex tips.

The number of young men having cosmetic surgery is rising and about 83,000 Canadians, mostly young men between the ages of 11 and 18, report using steroids at least once. It's not clear how many have done this knowing the link between use and testicular shrinking and kidney and liver failure. But with the possibility of shedding 11 kg in one month, some may be willing to gamble.

Male grooming is becoming more socially acceptable, and it's no longer about which razor blade gives the closet shave — it's face scrubs, moisturizers, and hair colour. Leading marketers are scrambling to develop new strategies for targeting the male demographic with new product lines. Many men still shy away from the cosmetic counter and women still account for a large proportion of actual purchasers. But, somewhere there is a guy who will end up with that product. Times are still a-changing and more and more men are going online to purchase items, while research shows that younger professional men, 19 to 34, are much more likely to buy skincare products for themselves and are far more comfortable talking to salespeople about them.

While more and more guys are detoxifying and exfoliating, perhaps the most obvious marketing efforts can be seen in the hair colour aisle at your local drugstore. Men's hair colour products are currently one of the largest growth areas in health and beauty products. It's an inexpensive image alteration that can have a big impact — and guys are going for it in a big way. Always-market-savvy L'Oréal is keenly aware of today's image-conscious male and is doing its bit by providing manly shades such as Camel, Brick, and Black Leather.

SOURCE: Adapted from Lucy Saddleton, "Marketers Refine Male Beauty Strategy," *Strategy*, May 20, 2002, pp. 36, 38, and Shannon McCarthy, "Body Image — The New Male Obsession," *Faze*, Spring 2002, pp. 1, 8.

Significant changes in the eating patterns of Canadians continue, as we become more sensitive to the relationship between what we eat and major diseases. Interest continues in weight-control eating, featuring foods low in fat, salt, food additives, and cholesterol, and foods high in vitamins, minerals, and fibre.

Emphasis on service and relationship quality   Consumers have become more confident of their rights and the power they wield in the marketplace — they are increasingly demanding to be treated better by businesses. Companies are now beginning to realize that the quality of appropriate customer interaction is important in service delivery, providing desired value, and maintaining and improving customer relationships.

Concern for the environment   Possibly one of the most important forces in the coming years will be a concern for the physical environment. There has already been a collective outpouring of support for programs and products that allow us to take action to protect the environment: Food manufacturers package products in less wasteful and more biodegradable materials; municipalities across the country have established recycling programs; and supermarkets stock many products labelled "environmentally friendly."

Desire for convenience   Since consumers now sometimes have more money and less time, the desire for convenience is continually increasing. Products must be ready to use or easy to prepare or assemble; purchasing systems must be convenient; products must be packaged in a variety of sizes, quantities, and forms; stores must be located nearby, easily accessible, and open at virtually all hours; and Web sites must be easily found, readily navigable, interesting, informative, and secure.

Impulse buying   Much retail purchasing involves impulse buying — purchasing that while done without much advance planning can be done on a very rational basis. Self-service and open displays allow planning to be postponed until buyers reach the retail outlet, so marketing emphasis continues to be placed on promotional programs designed to get people into a store so that they'll see displays that serve as silent salespersons. Marketers who sell their products through vending machines, catalogues, and home demonstration parties make their offerings as attractive as possible and offer free delivery, free catalogues, credit, and toll-free telephone numbers.

Technology

Failing to remain innovative and keep pace with technological advancements in its product category threatens a firm's ability to remain competitive. New materials, television, computers, lasers, miniaturization of components, robotics, compact discs, and closely targeted antibiotics have had a tremendous impact on our lifestyles. Major technological breakthroughs have three primary impacts on marketing:

Start entirely new industries   Many new businesses have been started for such products as computers, robots, lasers, fax machines, and microwave ovens. The Internet, CD-ROM and its heir-apparent DVD-ROM, and other digital technologies will account for more in the future.

Alter radically or virtually destroy existing industries   Television had a significant impact on movies and radio when it was first introduced; compact discs have eliminated vinyl records and threaten cassette tapes; fax machines and then e-mail cut into the conventional mail business of Canada Post, which now offers its own courier and electronic mail services; sensors imbedded in toll highways, such as on Highway 407 north of Toronto, record cars for

MARKETING AT WORK   2-2: TECHNOLOGY

Who Likes to Vacuum Anyway?

How would you like to have an appliance that wanders around the house on its own and can think for itself? Sound sort of creepy? It depends on what you're willing to do to get out of having to do the vacuuming! Just press "Go," select a speed, and the room gets vacuumed!

Currently being tested in home trials, the Dyson Dual Cyclone robotic vacuum cleaner (or DC06, for short) is just one example of how breakthroughs in technology are utilized or impact a firm's marketing strategy and planning and, by extension, the strategies and planning of all competitors in a product category.

The DC06 has more than 50 sensory devices that constantly feed data into the "brain" of the machine and three on-board computers assisting it in making 16 decisions per second to constantly make adjustments as it navigates its way around a room. The DC06 does not need to be programmed — it "thinks" for itself. Its "intelligence" stops it from falling down stairs and will pause the machine if the family pet or a child gets too close.

The DC06 can even tell you how it's feeling! Its mood light is blue when everything's A-OK, green when it's moving around an obstacle, and red when it "feels" it's in danger. The compact yellow-and-silver canister weighs about 9 kg and will retail initially in Canada for about $5000. The DC06 does not require bags and comes with an attachable hose for stairs and other hard-to-reach spots — those you will still have to do yourself. A high-tech electric motor has been specially designed and should last four times as long as a conventional motor. While the DC06 is not yet commercially available, the company has received inquiries from more than 1,100 people interested in buying the appliance.

Pertinent Web Sites
www.dyson.com
www.21century.co.uk/robotics/dyson

---

toll payment and eliminate toll collectors and toll booths, and have changed road design and building methods;[6] and downloading and ripping hardware and software are changing the music industry's marketing and distribution systems.

Stimulate other markets and industries not related to the new technology
New home appliances and entertainment products have altered the pattern of time use within the home and outside. Cable television, VCRs, CD players, video games, computer games, and microwave ovens have revolutionized the ways in which consumers use their time. These developments have also led to new industries, providing entertainment and food products used with these new devices that were not available a few years ago.

Political and legal forces

Every company's conduct is influenced by political and legal forces. Legislation at all levels exercises more influence on the marketing activity of a business than on any other part of its operations. These influences stem both from legislation and the policies established by a host of government agencies.

General monetary and fiscal policies   The level of government spending, the money supply, and tax legislation affect both consumers and companies.

Legislative framework and government agency codes and policies   Human rights codes, environmental legislation, and programs to reduce unemployment or increase national health all work to affect both firms and consumers in various ways. Direct-mail marketers, for example, are continually under pressure to reduce unsolicited mail and the waste involved by producing unwanted flyers.

Social legislation   Social legislation that is intended to protect society results in, for example, restraining people from smoking in various venues and tobacco firms from certain types of advertising and promotion.

MARKETING AT WORK 2-3: RELATIONSHIPS

Always Talk to Strangers

It was once something people did privately. And they certainly didn't tell their family and perhaps not even their closest friends about it. The shame of it was too much to bear — it was using a dating service! Whether you were matched up using computer-generated profiles or you waded through a stack of videotapes to select your next blind date — it was your dirty little secret.

But, somewhere along the way, all that tradition has been deserted, as have all those jokes about having to be so desperate. Nobody's snickering anymore! Since when have dating services become hip? Since they went online! And gone are the days when such services needed to advertise discretely. To many students today, such a service would probably seem a logical extension of the chat rooms and cyber-forums in which they so often participate. But, for everyone else, it's a big departure.

One such trailblazer in this renewed industry is Toronto-based Lavalife Inc. (www.lavalife.com), which heavily promotes its fun, friendly service on television and in print media. The company has had such success with its matchmaking that it found its way to the United States in 2002, and New Yorkers looking for love could find out about it on the subway. That's just one of the places where advertisements appeared during Lavalife's $2 million debut in the Manhattan marketplace. Print and television were also used. Four print executions, aimed at the 18- to 40-year-old urban single, consisted of funky illustrated characters on a bright red background, each with a witty tag line and an invitation to meet thousands of singles. The style was urban and sophisticated, yet fun. There's nothing embarrassing going on here!

SOURCE: Adapted from "Campaign Spotlight," *Strategy*, May 6, 2002, pp. 1, 6.

Government relationships with individual industries Governments provide subsidy programs for industries such as agriculture, passenger rail transportation, and many others. Governments have also affected the structure and operation of industries by selling publicly owned firms to the private sector, as well as by deregulating industries such as banking, telecommunications, airlines, and broadcasting. The movement toward deregulation and privatization appears to be continuing.

Legislation specifically related to marketing Marketing legislation is primarily administered by Industry Canada. Table 2-1 contains examples of this legislation that is relevant to marketers. Other pieces of legislation dealing with food products and advertising are administered by other government departments and will be discussed in later chapters. While marketing executives do not have to be lawyers, they do need to have an awareness of the major pieces of legislation and regulations and how these impinge on their strategies and tactics.

Provision of information and the purchase of products Illustrating the help provided by governments, Statistics Canada is a prime example of information provision by the government, and government procurement activities provide marketing opportunities for a host of businesses.

TABLE 2-1	Marketing-Related Legislation Administered by Industry Canada
• Bankruptcy and Insolvency Act	• National Research Council Act
• Boards of Trade Act	• Natural Sciences and Engineering Research Council Act
• Business Development Bank of Canada Act	• Patent Act
• Canada Business Corporations Act	• Precious Metals Marking Act
• Canada Co-operative Associations Act	• Public Servants Inventions Act
• Canada Corporations Act	• Radiocommunication Act
• Canadian Space Agency Act	• Small Business Investment Grants Act
• Companies' Creditors Arrangement Act	• Small Business Loans Act
• Competition Act	• Social Sciences and Humanities Research Council Act
• Competition Tribunal Act	• Standards Council of Canada Act
• Consumer Packaging and Labelling Act	• Statistics Act
• Copyright Act	• Telecommunications Act
• Department of Industry Act	• Textile Labelling Act
• Electricity and Gas Inspection Act	• Timber Marketing Act
• Industrial Design Act	• Trade-marks Act
• Integrated Circuit Topography Act	• Weights and Measures Act
• Investment Canada Act	• Winding-up Act
• Lobbyists Registration Act	

Controllable Environmental Forces

relationship-sensitive forces

Forces that can be managed to varying degrees and therefore are part of a firm's marketing system.

Three environmental forces that are external, but are still a part of a company's marketing system, are the company's market, its suppliers, and other businesses involved in getting the company's products to consumers. These forces are considered to comprise the firm's external micro-environment and can be influenced by the firm to varying degrees to help the firm in its efforts to establish ongoing working relationships. These forces can be referred to as being relationship-sensitive. In this sense, they are unlike the uncontrollable environmental forces; they are a part of a firm's marketing system since they can be managed to varying degrees, as opposed to the firm simply reacting to them. A marketing organization, for example, is able to influence its suppliers and other businesses involved in the distribution of its products concerning the services each will provide and the nature and type of information each will make available to the other to aid in strategy development. The better the relationship that exists between the parties, the better the strategy development and implementation. Through its advertising, promotion, and service provision activities, a company is able to influence its different markets in a variety of ways to increase perceived value and build long-term relationships. Relationship-sensitive external forces are illustrated in Figure 2-2.

Figure 2-2

Relationship-Sensitive External Environmental Forces

The Market Environment

The market really is what marketing is all about — how to reach it and serve it profitably and in a socially responsible manner. The market should be the focus of all marketing decisions in an organization. But just what is a market? A market may be defined as a place where buyers and sellers meet and where goods and services are offered for sale; as transfers of ownership occur, the foundations for future relationships are established, if they do not already exist. A market may also be defined as the demand made by a certain group of potential buyers for a good or service. For instance, there is an agricultural market for petroleum products and a college market for textbooks.

These definitions are not sufficiently precise to be useful to us here. For business purposes, we define a market as people or organizations with needs or wants to satisfy, money to spend, and the willingness to spend it. In short, the market is made up of customers and prospective customers, so in the market demand for any given product or service, there are three factors to consider:

1. People or organizations with needs or wants.

2. Their purchasing power.

3. Their expectations and buying behaviour.

When we say "needs," we mean what the dictionary says it means: something that is required, desired, or useful. As we pointed out in Chapter 1, we do not limit needs to the physiological requirements of food, clothing, and shelter essential for survival; the words "needs" and "wants" can be used synonymously and interchangeably. Also, we define the market very broadly to include the purchase of many different types of products and services, but also to include other forms of exchange, including the purchase of entertainment and the arts, and contributions to charitable and other public organizations.

Suppliers

To sell a product, you must first make it or buy it. That's why the people or firms who supply the goods or services that a company needs to produce goods are critical to marketing success. And that's why we consider a firm's suppliers as part of its marketing system and sensitive in relationship-building terms. Marketing executives often are not concerned enough with the supply side of the marketing system, but they do become very concerned when shortages or supply service problems occur. Then the need for co-operative relationships with suppliers is very apparent. A company or organization often has many suppliers on whom it relies for raw materials, operating supplies, electricity, cleaning services, and many other things. If one or more of these fail to deliver what's needed when it's needed and in the quantity and of the quality desired, the company may not be able to meet the needs of its own customers or may even have to cease operations.

Marketing intermediaries

marketing intermediaries
Firms that render services directly related to the purchase and/or sale of a product as it flows from producer to consumer.

distribution channel
The set of people and firms involved in the flow of ownership of a product as it moves from producer to ultimate consumer or business user.

Marketing intermediaries are independent business organizations that directly aid in the flow of goods and services between a marketing organization and its markets. There are two types of intermediaries: (1) the wholesalers and retailers and (2) various facilitating organizations that provide such services as the transportation, warehousing, and financing that are needed to complete exchanges and facilitate relationships between buyers and sellers. These intermediaries, since they operate between a company and its markets and between a company and its suppliers, are part of what are called **distribution channels**. In some cases, it may be more

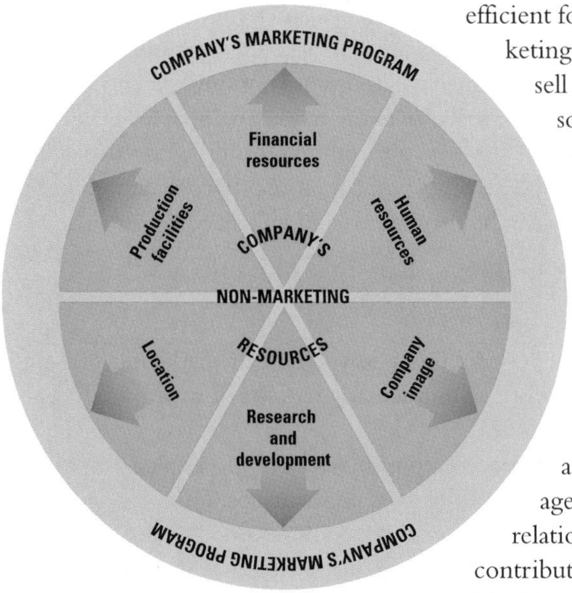

Figure 2-3:

Relationship-Sensitive Internal Environmental Forces

A company's internal non-marketing resources influence and support its marketing program.

efficient for a company to take a "do-it-yourself" approach and not use marketing intermediaries. A producer can deal directly with its suppliers or sell directly to its customers and do its own shipping, financing, and so on. But marketing intermediaries are specialists in their respective fields and often do a better job at a lower cost than the company can do by itself. Because the company relies on these other companies to get its products and services to market, many pay considerable attention to the cultivation of solid relationships with distribution channel members.

Internal non-marketing system forces

The internal resources of the firm also have a great influence on an organization's marketing system. These are controllable by management, relationship-sensitive, and require careful organizational relationship-building on the part of marketing personnel in order to contribute to the marketing system and its programs.[7] These forces are illustrated in Figure 2-3.

These internal resources and influences can affect marketing programs in a variety of ways:

- Production facilities and capabilities influence the availability of products and their quantities, quality, and costs; these factors also affect whether the marketing department has products available to sell.

- Financial resources play a part in determining marketing and promotion budgets, pricing strategies, terms of sale, and whether money is available to spend on marketing programs

- Human resource policies and capabilities affect the quality of personnel and their training, job satisfaction, and loyalty, as well as the quality of services and customer contacts provided.

- The company image projected to the public affects the acceptance of marketing programs to some extent, as inconsistencies threaten marketing's relationship-building activities and the overall trust and loyalty of customers, suppliers, and intermediaries.

- Research and development activities produce advances in product features, materials, production systems, product costs, packaging, quality enhancements, and overall competitive ability to be an industry leader.

- Location can determine access to markets, transportation costs, service frequency and quality, and even the number and quality of contacts with customers, suppliers, and intermediaries. Plant location often determines the geographic limits of a company's market, particularly if transportation costs are high or the company's products are perishable.

All of these factors (and more) that are part of a company's non-marketing system have the potential to influence the satisfaction of customers — the overall objective of marketing, as we discussed in Chapter 1. As a result, there is an obvious need for *all* parts of a business or organization to work together toward the goal of customer satisfaction and to realize that virtually everything that happens in all departments ultimately has the potential to increase or decrease customer satisfaction. So, while these factors have traditionally not been considered to be marketing variables, it can therefore be appreciated that they do actually contribute to the marketing mix (value proposition) offered by a firm.

One of the most important factors to consider, therefore, in a firm's internal environment is the need to co-ordinate its marketing and non-marketing activities. Customer, supplier, and intermediary contacts and communications must be carried out in a planned and consistent fashion in order to achieve the desired quality of relationships Sometimes this can be difficult because of conflicts in goals and executive personalities. Production people, for example, like to see long production runs of standardized items. However, marketing executives may want a variety of models, sizes, and colours to satisfy different groups of consumers. Financial executives typically want tighter credit and expense limits than the marketing people feel are necessary to be competitive. When customers or suppliers are communicating with various units in an organization, it is important that they be dealt with in an appropriate and consistent fashion, so that their goodwill and loyalty can be maintained and enhanced.

Marketing Planning

All of the environmental forces we have just discussed play a role in marketing planning. Figure 2-4 shows a company's complete set of environmental forces. We now turn to the planning process itself.

Marketing planning, as a management process, consists basically of (1) planning a marketing program, (2) implementing it, and (3) evaluating its performance. This process is illustrated in Figure 2-5.

The planning stage includes setting goals and designing strategies and tactics to reach these goals. The implementation stage involves staffing and orienting the marketing organization and directing its operations according to plan. The evaluation stage consists of analyzing the resulting performance in terms of the marketing goals originally established. This third stage demonstrates the continuous nature of the management process — the results of this stage of the management process are used in planning goals and strategies for future stages.

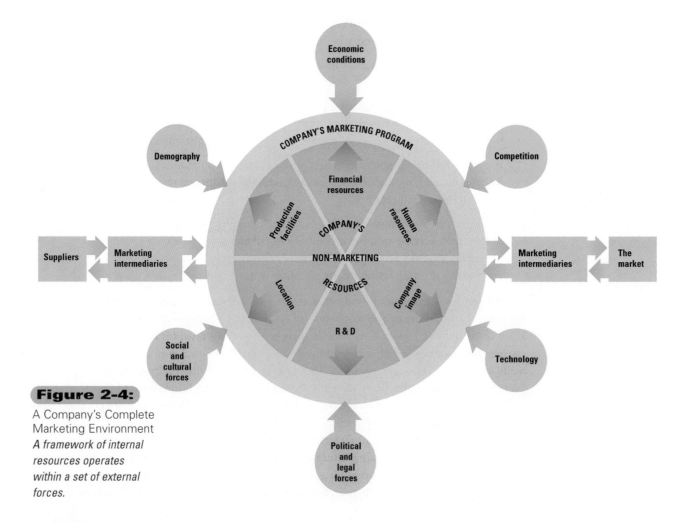

Figure 2-4:

A Company's Complete Marketing Environment
A framework of internal resources operates within a set of external forces.

Figure 2-5:

The Management
Process in Marketing

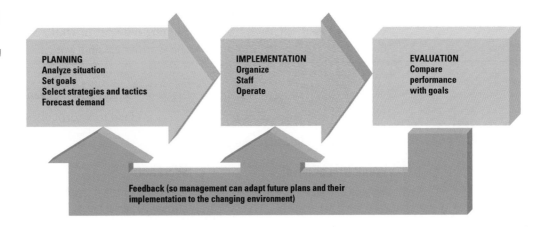

PLANNING
Analyze situation
Set goals
Select strategies and tactics
Forecast demand

IMPLEMENTATION
Organize
Staff
Operate

EVALUATION
Compare
performance
with goals

Feedback (so management can adapt future plans and their
implementation to the changing environment)

The nature of planning

"If you don't know where you're going, any road will get you there." The point of this axiom is that all organizations need both general and specific plans to be successful. Management first should decide what it intends to accomplish as a total organization and then develop a strategic plan to achieve these results. Given this overall plan, each department or business unit then determines its own plans. Of course, the role of marketing in each of these plans must be considered.

We begin our discussion of marketing planning by reviewing the basic terms used in the planning phase.

mission statement
Indicates the boundaries of an organization's activities.

Mission   An organization's **mission statement** details what customers it serves, what needs it satisfies, and what types of products and services it offers, indicating the boundaries of an organization's activities. It should be neither too broad and vague nor too narrow and specific. To say that a firm's mission is "to benefit Canadian consumers" is too vague; to state that its purpose is "to make tennis balls" is too narrow. Neither statement outlines meaningful benefits for customers or provides much guidance to management. Unless the firm's purpose is clear to the various levels of management, strategic planning will probably result in disagreement and confusion.

Some companies still state their mission in production-oriented terms, such as "We make furnaces" (or telephones or tennis racquets). Most express their mission in customer-oriented terms — satisfying needs and providing value. Instead of "We produce snowmobiles, ATVs, and small watercraft," Bombardier Inc.'s mission statement could be "We provide safe, comfortable travel for wherever our customer wants, or needs, to go." Recall that in Chapter 1, Table 1-1 illustrated different ways of stating a company's mission to provide more direction for management actions.

*Does this photo
represent a customer
or a production
orientation?*

objective

A desired outcome; same as *goal*.

Objectives and goals   We treat the terms *objectives* and *goals* as synonyms. An **objective** is simply a desired outcome. Effective planning must begin with a set of objectives that are to be achieved by carrying out plans. To be worthwhile and workable, objectives should be:

- Clear and specific.
- Stated in writing.
- Ambitious, but realistic.
- Consistent with one another.
- Quantitatively measurable whenever possible.
- Tied to a particular time period.

Consider the following examples.

Weak (too general)	Workable
Increase our market share.	Increase our market share to 25 percent next year from its present 20 percent level.
Strengthen relationships with our customers.	Increase customer satisfaction, customer retention, and customer loyalty scores by 20 percent.
Improve our company's public image.	Receive recognition awards next year from at least three consumer and/or environmental groups.

strategy

Broad, basic plan of action by which an organization intends to achieve its objectives.

Strategies and tactics   A **strategy** is a broad, basic plan of action by which an organization intends to reach its objectives. In marketing, the relationship between objectives and strategies may be illustrated as follows.

Objectives	Possible Strategies
Increase sales next year by 8 percent over this year's sales.	1. Intensify marketing efforts in domestic markets. 2. Expand into foreign markets. 3. Increase customer retention by reducing account closings by 10 percent.

Two organizations might have the same objective but use different strategies to reach it. For example, two firms might both aim to increase their market shares by 20 percent over the next three years. To do that, one firm might intensify its efforts in household markets, while the other might concentrate on expanding into institutional markets (e.g., food-service organizations). Conversely, two organizations might have different objectives but select the same strategies to reach them.

tactic

An operational means by which a strategy is implemented or activated.

A **tactic** is a means by which a strategy is implemented. A tactic is a more specific, detailed course of action than is a strategy. If the strategy is to increase customer retention, the tactics spell out how this is to be accomplished. Tactics can change rapidly and cover shorter time periods than strategies. Here is an illustration of tactics related to a strategy:

Strategy	Tactics
Direct our promotion to males aged 25 to 40.	1. Advertise in magazines read by this group. 2. Advertise on television programs watched by this group.
Increase revenue from existing customers.	1. Redesign the customer information system. 2. Create a loyalty program for light and medium users. 3. Retrain account analysts and service personnel.

◀ **BACKSPACE**

1. The environment of all organizations is composed of what three factors or forces?
2. Six interrelated macro-environmental forces are usually beyond the control of management. What are they?
3. What are the three relationship-sensitive external forces?

Scope of planning

The marketing strategies in a firm are planned at two different levels:

1. At the company level, senior management defines an organization's mission, sets long-range objectives, and formulates broad strategies to achieve these goals. These company-wide objectives and strategies then become the framework for planning the firm's strategies and tactics in such functional areas as production, finance, human resources, research and development, and marketing.

2. At the marketing unit or department level, the top marketing executives set objectives and strategies for the business's marketing efforts. Strategic marketing planning takes place within the framework of, and co-ordinated with, the company-wide planning level.

Within the marketing unit, a short-term plan of the firm's marketing activities is then developed, based on the marketing strategy. Such a plan covers a specific period, usually a year, and contains the tactics that will be used to implement the strategy for the specified time period.

Strategic Company Planning

strategic company planning
The level of planning that consists of defining the organization's mission, analyzing the situation the company is facing, setting organizational objectives, and selecting strategies to achieve the organization's objectives.

At the company level, strategic planning consists of four essential steps: (1) defining the organization's mission; (2) analyzing the situation the company is facing; (3) setting organizational objectives; and (4) selecting strategies to achieve these objectives. The **strategic company planning** process is shown in the top part of Figure 2-6.

Step 1 Define the organization's mission, which influences all subsequent planning. For some firms, this step requires only review of the existing mission statement to confirm that it is still suitable.

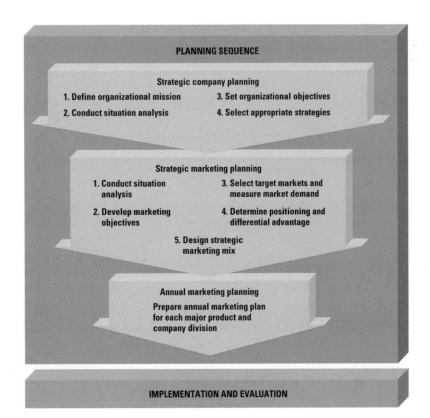

PLANNING SEQUENCE

Strategic company planning
1. Define organizational mission
2. Conduct situation analysis
3. Set organizational objectives
4. Select appropriate strategies

Strategic marketing planning
1. Conduct situation analysis
2. Develop marketing objectives
3. Select target markets and measure market demand
4. Determine positioning and differential advantage
5. Design strategic marketing mix

Annual marketing planning
Prepare annual marketing plan for each major product and company division

IMPLEMENTATION AND EVALUATION

Figure 2-6:
Three Levels of Organizational Planning

situation analysis
The stage in strategic company planning that involves gathering and studying information important to the strategies and tactics of an organization.

Step 2 Conduct a situation analysis. This is vital, because strategic planning is influenced by many forces both within and external to an organization. Situation analysis simply means gathering and studying information important to the strategies and tactics of an organization. We'll talk more about conducting a situation analysis in the following section.

Step 3 Management must decide on a set of objectives to guide the organization in fulfilling its mission. Objectives also provide standards for evaluating an organization's performance, such as gaining a 10 percent market share within five years.

Step 4 Select appropriate strategies that indicate how the firm is going to get to where it wants to go. Strategies are selected either for the entire company, if it is small and has only a single product, or for each division or business unit if the company is large or has multiple products.

According to one survey, almost 70 percent of companies have strategic marketing plans in place; among them, nearly 90 percent believe that their strategic plans have been effective.[8] Interestingly, a larger proportion of newer firms (1 to 10 years old) than older firms have formal strategic plans.

Strategic Marketing Planning

strategic marketing planning
The level of planning that consists of conducting a situation analysis, determining marketing objectives, identifying target markets and measuring the market, deciding on positioning and differential advantage, and designing a marketing mix.

After conducting strategic planning for the organization as a whole, management needs to lay plans for each major functional area, such as marketing and production. Of course, planning for each function should be guided by the organization-wide mission and objectives. Strategic marketing planning, as shown in the middle of Figure 2-6, is a five-step process: (1) conducting a situation analysis, (2) determining marketing objectives, (3) identifying target markets and measuring market demand, (4) deciding on positioning and differential advantage, and (5) designing a marketing mix.

Situation analysis

Conducting a situation analysis is the most critical step, since the results of this analysis establish the basic boundaries and conditions for further planning. The situation analysis usually has two parts: an environmental scan and a SWOT assessment.

environmental scanning
Gathering information regarding a company's internal and external environment, analyzing it, and forecasting the impact of the conditions and trends that the analysis suggests.

Environmental scanning normally starts with a review of those factors we discussed in the first part of this chapter: the external and internal environmental forces. The environmental forces considered in marketing planning are frequently the same or similar to those examined in developing the company or overall business plan: demographic shifts, economic conditions, competitive trends, social and cultural forces, technological changes, and political and legal forces.

SWOT assessment
Identifying and evaluating an organization's most significant strengths, weaknesses, opportunities, and threats.

A SWOT assessment is usually conducted after the environmental scan. In this second part of the situation analysis, a firm identifies and evaluates its most significant strengths, weaknesses, opportunities, and threats. For example, prior to the financial difficulties leading to Eaton's final closure in 1999, the company's strength was its large size, which gave it — among other things — clout in dealing with suppliers. Weaknesses included its frequent merchandising changes and its comparatively high operating expenses. High inventories and outstanding debts left the company in a vulnerable position. International retailer Wal-Mart (**www.wal-mart.com**), on the other hand, controls its suppliers so that a very efficient inventory supply system has been developed; almost no excess inventory is carried.

Wal-Mart

Opportunities and threats often originate from outside the organization. An opportunity identified by Wal-Mart when expanding into Canada was the large number of metropolitan

Zellers
Canadian Tire

areas in which it could open its highly efficient stores. An unknown threat was the competition that could come from such firms as Zellers (**www.zellers.com**) and Canadian Tire (**www.canadiantire.ca**) and their very successful loyalty programs — Generation Z and Canadian Tire money. These programs were potential threats to Wal-Mart, while being strengths for the Canadian retailers. Table 2-2 illustrates how selected environmental forces might be viewed in a SWOT analysis, using the entry of Mitsubishi Motors into the Canadian market in 2002.

TABLE 2-2 **Mitsubishi Motors: SWOT Implications for Selected Environmental Forces**

Mitsubishi Motor Sales of America has come to Canada. After a number of false starts, Mitsubishi autos, which we have always seen on U.S. TV channels, entered the Canadian market in September of 2002 — the date the automaker felt that both its organization and the market were ready. The firm had been experiencing record sales volume, market share, and profit for the previous three years and now offered a much wider range of cars and SUVs to buyers.[9] A SWOT assessment of selected environmental forces gives us some insight into market implications and the resulting company issues.

Environmental Trend	Market Dynamics	Company Issue
Traditional gender role	Females increasingly continue to independently purchase more vehicles than in the past and to participate in the family decision-making process.	**Opportunity:** Position the brand toward the female market with regard to products for individual and family use, using caution not to alienate male consumers.
State of the economy	Canada moving out of mild recession during this period, with most economic indicators pointing to good growth trends.	**Opportunity:** Car sales strong during early 2002. Publicized introduction of the brand well timed for this market. **Threat:** Although the brand would be familiar, a potential concern to be addressed is that it may still be seen by some as new and unproven.
Age demographics	The increasing average age of Boomers and seniors — referred to as the "greying" of Canada.	**Threat:** Current brand image is very youthful and may not widely appeal to Boomers and seniors.
Fertility rate/ household size	Fertility rates have been decreasing, meaning that the average household has fewer people.	**Threat:** Market size has limited the total potential in this competitive market category. **Threat:** Possible decreasing market for the brand's larger sedans and full-size SUVs.

SWOT conclusion: To enter the Canadian marketplace in September of 2002 (a high-volume sales month for vehicles) with a focus on the four-door, entry-level Lancer, along with both its compact and full-sized SUVs.

Marketing objectives

When environmental scanning and a SWOT analysis have been completed, the next step in strategic marketing planning is to determine marketing objectives, as illustrated in the Mitsubishi situation. These should be closely related to company-wide goals and strategies. In fact, a company strategy often translates into a marketing goal. For example, to reach an organizational objective of a 20 percent return on investment next year, one organizational strategy might be to reduce marketing costs by 15 percent. This strategy would become a marketing goal. In turn, converting all salespeople from salaried compensation to a commission basis might be one of the marketing strategies adopted to achieve this marketing goal.

segments
Parts of markets.

target market
A group of customers (people or organizations) to whom a seller aims its marketing efforts.

positioning
A company's strategies and actions related to favourably distinguishing itself and its products from those of competitors in the minds of selected groups of consumers.

differential advantage
Any feature of an organization or brand perceived by customers to be desirable and different from that of the competition.

Target markets and market demand

Selecting target markets and measuring market demand is the third step in marketing planning. A market consists of people or organizations with needs to satisfy, money to spend, and the willingness to spend it. For example, many people need transportation and are willing to pay for it. However, this large group is made up of a number of **segments** (that is, parts of markets) with various transportation needs. One segment may want low-cost, efficient transportation, while another may prefer luxury and privacy. Air Canada segments the air travel market by offering economy, business, and first-class travel, with each class offering a different service bundle that ranges from checking-in privileges to different seat widths at various prices. This is not very different from automakers offering products ranging from heavy-duty trucks to luxury cars to economical compact cars. Recently, in an attempt to reach more customer segments and stimulate demand in different markets across the country, Air Canada developed new brands such as Tango and Jazz to reach economy and commuter markets — new brands meant to evoke a young and fresh image with the intention of making price-conscious travel the trendy thing to do.[10]

Ordinarily, it is impractical for a firm to try to satisfy every market segment, since they all have different needs. Instead, a company targets its efforts at one or more of these segments. Thus, **target market** refers to a group of people or organizations to which a firm directs a marketing program. Few companies target a single segment — when they do, they are often said to be following a *niche strategy*. Designing the actual product is part of that marketing effort.

Target markets must be selected on the basis of opportunities. In a new company, management should analyze markets in detail to identify potential target markets. In an existing firm, management should routinely examine any changes in the characteristics of its target markets and alternative markets. A firm must forecast demand, that is, sales, in each market. The results of sales or demand forecasting will determine whether the firm's targets are worth pursuing or whether alternatives need to be identified.

Making a virtue out of an awful taste!

Positioning and differential advantage

The fourth step in strategic marketing planning actually involves two complementary decisions: how to position a product in the marketplace, and how to distinguish it from competitors' products. **Positioning** (discussed in detail in Chapter 4) refers to the image of a company or brand in relation to direct competitors' products, as well as to other products marketed by the same company. **Differential advantage** refers to any feature of a brand or organization that is perceived by customers to be desirable and different from the competition. For example, Buckley's cough syrup (**www.buckleys.com**), developed in a Toronto drugstore in 1919 and long famous for its horrible taste (what can you expect from pine needles!), has used taste to both position the product and to differentiate it: "It tastes awful. And it works." Buckley's competitors do not extol the awful taste of their products — in fact, some of their products even taste good! The Buckley approach has been memorable and successful not only in Canada but also in the United States and other international markets — a rare example of how a common strategy can work

Buckley's
Robitussin

across international markets. Robitussin, on the other hand, has positioned itself as "Mom's trusted partner in cough treatment — enabling her to have complete confidence that she's providing trusted care for her family." This is reinforced through repeated use of the tag line "Recommended by doctors, pharmacists, and 'Dr. Mom.'" Part of this strategy is to reassure the decision-maker that the product is alcohol-free and "goes down with a great cherry taste" (**www.robitussin.com**).

Marketing mix

Finally, management must design a marketing mix — the combination of a product or service, its price, and how it is distributed and promoted. Traditionally, the marketing mix has been considered in terms of four elements that together must satisfy the needs of the organization's target customers and, at the same time, achieve its marketing objectives, such as creating value for customers and achieving high levels of customer satisfaction. In recent years, as marketers have turned their thinking more toward the customer service and interaction elements that must accompany the sale and marketing of any product or service, some have expanded their view of the marketing mix to include the essential element of customer service. This refers to the way in which the customer is treated not only by marketing personnel, but also by all employees and by the company itself. Let's consider the elements of the expanded marketing mix and some of the concepts and strategies you'll learn about in later chapters:

Product Strategies are needed for managing existing products and services over time, adding new ones, and dropping unsuccessful ones. Strategic decisions must also be made regarding the types and levels of service required to accompany the core product or service, branding, packaging, and other product features, such as warranties.

Price Necessary strategies pertain to the prices that should be charged for the products and services that a company sells, taking into account such things as the location of customers, price flexibility, related items within a product line, discounts to be offered, and terms of sale. Also, pricing strategies for entering a market, especially with a new product, must be designed.

Distribution Here, strategies involve the management of the channel or channels by which products and services are transferred from producer to customer; in short, how things are made available to customers. In many cases, this involves the system by which tangible products are moved from the place where they are produced to the place where they are purchased by the final customer. It also involves creating access and convenience for customers. Strategies applicable to intermediaries, such as wholesalers and retailers, must be designed.

Marketing communications Strategies are needed to combine individual methods such as advertising, personal selling, and sales promotion into a co-ordinated campaign that communicates desired value. In addition, these strategies must be adjusted as a product moves from the early stages to the later stages of its life. Strategic decisions must also be made regarding each individual method of marketing communications.

Customer service This component of the marketing mix deals with how customers are to be handled or interacted with as they deal with the company or organization. Marketers must develop strategies concerning what types and levels of service are needed for different target market segments to allow the company to compete effectively and to create customer value and relationships.

The elements of the marketing mix are interrelated; decisions in one area often affect actions in another. To illustrate, the design of a marketing mix is certainly affected by whether a company chooses to compete on the basis of price or service, or on one or more of the other elements. When a company relies on pricing as its primary competitive tool, the other elements must be designed to support aggressive pricing. For example, the promotional campaign probably will be built around a theme of "low, low prices." In non-price competition, however, product, distribution, customer and service strategies, and/or promotion strategies come to the forefront. For instance, the product and supporting services must have features that can be perceived by target markets to offer superior value and so be worthy of a higher price. Marketing communications must help create a superior value image for the product if a premium price is to be sustained.

Each marketing-mix element contains countless variables. An organization may market one product and service or many, and these products may be related or unrelated to each other. The product may be distributed through wholesalers, to retailers without the benefit of wholesalers, or even directly to the consumer. Ultimately, from the multitude of variables, management must select a combination of elements that will satisfy target market needs for customer value and achieve organizational and marketing goals in terms of profitability and customer-relationship building.

Annual Marketing Plan

annual marketing plan

A written document that details the planned marketing activities for a business unit or product for a given year.

Besides strategic planning for several years into the future, more specific, shorter-term planning is also vital. For this reason, strategic marketing planning in an organization leads to the preparation of an annual marketing plan, as shown in the bottom part of Figure 2-6. An **annual marketing plan**, which is a written document, is the master blueprint for a year's marketing activity for a specified organizational division or major product.

A separate plan normally should be prepared for each major product and company division. Sometimes, depending on a company's circumstances, separate plans are developed for key brands and important target markets. As the name implies, an annual marketing plan usually covers one year, but there are exceptions. For instance, because of the seasonal nature of some products or markets, it is advisable to prepare plans for shorter time periods. In the clothing industry, for example, plans are made for each season, which lasts only several months.

Purposes and responsibilities

An annual marketing plan serves several purposes:

- It summarizes the marketing strategies and tactics that will be used to achieve specified objectives in the upcoming year — it is a "what-to-do" guide for executives and others involved in marketing.

- The plan also focuses on "how to do it," pointing to what needs to be done. The implementation details provide important basic information that gives direction to evaluation of the marketing program.

- It outlines who is responsible for which activities, when the activities are to be carried out, and how much time and money can be spent.

The executive responsible for the division or product covered by the plan typically prepares it. All or part of the task may be delegated to subordinates.

Preparation of an annual marketing plan may begin nine months or more before the start of the period covered by the plan. Early work includes necessary research and arranging for other information sources. The bulk of the work occurs one to three months prior to the plan's starting date. The last steps are to have the plan reviewed and approved by upper management. Some revision may be necessary before final approval is granted.

The final version of the plan, or relevant parts of it, should be shared with all employees who will be involved in implementing the agreed-on strategies and tactics. Failure to have a plan understood and accepted by those implementing it both within and outside the organization threatens both service quality and the quality of the market relationships ultimately established.

Recommended contents

The exact contents of an annual marketing plan should be determined by an organization's circumstances. For example, a firm in an intensely competitive industry might assess its competitors in a separate section, while a firm in another industry might present this assessment as part of the situation analysis. Similarly, some organizations include alternative (or contingency) plans; others don't. An example of a contingency plan is the set of steps the firm will take if a competitor introduces a new product, if this is being rumoured.

Annual marketing planning follows a sequence similar to strategic marketing planning. However, annual planning has a shorter time frame and is more specific, both in relation to the issues addressed and the plans laid out. Still, as shown in Table 2-3, the major sections of an annual marketing plan are similar to the steps in strategic marketing planning.

In an annual marketing plan, more attention is devoted to tactical details than is feasible at other levels of planning. As an example, a strategic marketing plan might stress an increased focus on personal selling within the marketing mix. The annual plan might recommend an increased focus on customer retention and provide for training in the tactics necessary for improving customer relations.

It's important to note that an annual marketing plan relates to all of the steps of the management process, not just to planning. That is, sections 5 through 7 in Table 2-3 deal with implementation, and section 8 is concerned with evaluation. We will return to implementation when we discuss the various components of the marketing mix in the chapters that follow.

TABLE 2-3 Contents of an Annual Marketing Plan

1. *Executive Summary.* In this one- or two-page section, the thrust of the plan is described and explained. It is intended for executives who desire an overview of the plan but need not be knowledgeable about the details.

2. *Situation Analysis.* Essentially, the marketing program for the strategic business unit (sbu) or product covered by the plan is examined within the context of pertinent past, present, and future conditions. It is vital that a reliable assessment of human resource needs and capabilities be part of the analysis. Much of this section might be derived from the results of strategic marketing planning. Additional information of particular relevance to a one-year planning period may be included in this section.

3. *Objectives.* The objectives in an annual plan are more specific than those produced by strategic marketing planning. However, annual objectives must help achieve organizational goals and strategic marketing goals.

4. *Strategies.* As in strategic marketing planning, the strategies in an annual plan should indicate which target markets are going to be satisfied through a combination of product, price, distribution, and promotion.

5. *Tactics.* Specific activities, sometimes called action plans, are devised for carrying out each major strategy included in the preceding section. For ease of understanding, strategies and tactics may be covered together. Tactics specifically answer the question of what is to be done, who will do it, and how the tasks will be accomplished. The who and the how tend to show that a plan is actually implementable, given the finances in section 6.

6. *Financial Schedules.* This section normally includes three kinds of financial information — projected sales, expenses, and profits in what's called a pro-forma financial statement, along with the amounts of resources dedicated to different activities in one or more budgets.

7. *Timetable.* This section, often including a diagram, answers the question of when various marketing activities will be carried out during the upcoming year.

8. *Evaluation Procedures.* This section addresses the questions of what, who, how, and when connected with measuring performance against goals, both during and at the end of the year. The results of evaluations during the year may lead to adjustments in the plan's strategies and/or tactics or even in the objectives to be achieved.

1. What are the four essential steps in strategic planning at the company level?

2. Describe the five steps involved in strategic marketing planning.

3. Explain the difference between positioning and differential advantage.

Selected Planning Models

A number of frameworks or tools — we'll call them *models* — have been designed to assist with strategic planning. Most of these models can be used with both strategic company planning and strategic marketing planning. In this section, we briefly discuss several planning models that have received much attention in recent years. First, however, you need to be more familiar with a form of organization called the *strategic business unit*.

Strategic business units

strategic business unit (SBU)
A separate division for a major product or market in a multi-product or multi-business organization.

Bombardier

Most large and medium-sized companies, and even some smaller firms, consist of multiple units and produce numerous products. In such diversified firms, company-wide planning cannot serve as an effective guide for executives who oversee the organization's various divisions. Consequently, for more effective planning and operation, a multi-business or multi-product organization should be divided according to its major markets, products, or services into **strategic business units** (SBUs). Each SBU may be a major market, product, or service division in an organization; a geographic organization, such as an international or country division; a group of related products; or even a single major product or brand that is marketed globally.

Bombardier Inc. (**www.bombardier.com**), a company probably best known to most Canadians as the manufacturer of Ski-Doo snowmobiles, provides a good example. The mission, objectives, and strategies of the divisions within the motorized consumer products group (which includes the Sea-Doo/Ski-Doo Division) are — and must be — quite different from those that guide marketing and other activities in its aerospace group (where the strategic business units include Canadair and De Havilland, manufacturers of airplanes) and its transportation equipment group (where the strategic business units are involved in the manufacture of subway and railway cars, shuttle-train cars for the tunnel under the English Channel, and people-moving transportation systems).

To be identified as an SBU, an entity should: (1) be a separately identifiable business; (2) have a distinct mission; (3) have its own competitors; and (4) have its own executive group with profit responsibility.

Let us now consider two of many different planning models: the Boston Consulting Group matrix and the product-market growth matrix.

The Boston Consulting Group matrix

Boston Consulting Group (BCG) matrix
A strategic planning model that classifies strategic business units or major products according to market shares and growth rates.

Boston Consulting Group

Developed by a management consulting firm, the **Boston Consulting Group (BCG) matrix** (**www.bcg.com**) dates back almost 30 years. Using this model, an organization classifies each of its SBUs (and sometimes its major products) according to two factors: its market share relative to competitors, and the growth rate of the industry in which the SBU operates. When the factors are divided simply into high and low categories, a 2-by-2 grid is created, as displayed in Figure 2-7. In turn, the four quadrants in the grid represent distinct categories of SBUs or major products: stars, cash cows, question marks, and dogs. The categories differ in relation not only to market share and industry growth rate, but also to cash needs and appropriate strategies.

Figure 2-7:

The Boston Consulting Group (BCG) matrix

COMPANY'S MARKET SHARE

stars

Strategic business units characterized by high market shares and high industry growth rates.

Xbox
Microsoft
Ford
Sony

- **Stars** are characterized by high market shares and high industry growth rates. However, an SBU that falls into this category poses a challenge for companies, because it requires lots of cash to remain competitive in growing markets. Aggressive marketing strategies are imperative for stars to maintain or even build market share. Adding new customers and retaining existing ones are both crucial at this stage. Examples of this category are Microsoft's Xbox (**www.xbox.com**) and Windows XP (**www.microsoft.com**) software packages, Ford Motor Company's Explorer SUV (**www.ford.ca**), and Sony's CLIÉ personal entertainment organizer (**www.sony.ca**).

cash cows

Strategic business units that are characterized by high market shares and do business in mature industries (those with low growth rates).

DaimlerChrysler

The CLIÉ personal entertainment organizer is an example of a market star. (CLIÉ is a registered trademark of Sony Corporation.)

- **Cash cows** are SBUs that have high market shares and do business in mature industries that have low growth rates. When an industry's growth diminishes, stars for which the strategies and tactics have resulted in the building of strong customer relationships move into this category. Because most of its customers have been with it for some time and remain loyal, a cash cow's marketing costs are not high and it generates more cash than can be reinvested profitably in its own operations. As a result, cash cows can be "milked" to support the firm's other SBUs that need more resources. Marketing strategies for cash cows seek to defend market share by maintaining or increasing perceived value, as well as by continuously improving customer relationships and reinforcing customer loyalty. When Chrysler (**www.daimlerchrysler.ca**) reorganized its Jeep-Eagle car division in the midnineties, it maintained the Jeep line of vehicles that continue to be popular

As a cash cow, the Jeep Liberty was designed to maintain market share at a low cost.

2002 LIBERTY.

Jeep

THERE'S ONLY ONE.

Sure, there are prettier angles. But none quite as impressive.

Look under a Liberty and you're looking at over sixty years of Jeep engineering. Tested on North America's most grueling off-road trails, the Liberty proved itself to be as tough as its legendary forefathers, and more impressively, earned the right to call itself a Jeep. To learn more about the Jeep Liberty's off-road capabilities visit jeep.ca.

AUTOMOBILE JOURNALISTS ASSOCIATION OF CANADA

2002 Canadian Truck of the Year

® Jeep is a registered trademark of DaimlerChrysler Corporation used under license by DaimlerChrysler Canada Inc., a wholly owned subsidiary of DaimlerChrysler Corporation.

today. The long heritage of the Jeep TJ has attained almost cult status, spawning the development of a four-door version called Liberty.

question marks
Strategic business units characterized by low market shares but high industry growth rates.

Question marks (sometimes called "problem children") are SBUs that are characterized by low market shares but high industry growth rates. A question mark has not achieved a strong foothold in an expanding but highly competitive market. The question surrounding this type of SBU is whether it can gain adequate market share and be profitable. If management answers "No," then the SBU should be divested or liquidated. If management instead answers "Yes," the firm must come up with the cash to build market share — more cash than the typical question mark generates from its own profits. Appropriate marketing strategies for question marks focus on creating an impact in the market by displaying a strong differential advantage that enhances perceived value, thereby, building customer support. Many examples can be found in Internet retailing, which represents an

dogs

Strategic business units that are characterized by low market shares and operate in industries with low growth rates.

product-market growth matrix

A planning model that consists of four alternative growth strategies, based on whether an organization will be selling its present products or new products to its present markets or new markets.

market penetration

A product-market growth strategy in which a company tries to sell more of its present products to its present markets.

market development

A product-market growth strategy in which a company continues to sell its present products, but to a new market.

area of rapid growth and development. Yet many e-tailers (Internet retailers) continue to lose money as they experiment in this new marketplace, trying to determine what marketing mix works best for them.

• **Dogs** are SBUs that have low market shares and operate in industries with low growth rates. A company normally would be unwise to invest substantial funds in SBUs in this category. Marketing strategies for dogs are intended to maximize any potential profits by minimizing expenditures or to promote a differential advantage to build market share. The company can instead say, "Enough's enough!" and divest or liquidate an SBU that's a dog. General Motor's Oldsmobile was once a crown jewel (that is, a star) of the company's automobile divisions. However, as the oldest brand in the U.S. automobile industry, it developed a grandfatherly image that no amount of product innovation or fresh marketing could seem to eliminate, despite repeated efforts throughout the nineties. As a result, the money-losing brand will be phased out by 2004.[11] This is only the second automobile brand to be discontinued in the last 30 years.

Ordinarily, one firm cannot affect the growth rate for an entire industry. An exception might be the leading firm in a fairly new industry. If growth rate cannot be influenced, companies must turn their attention to the other factor in the BCG matrix: market share. Marketing strategies based on the BCG matrix therefore tend to concentrate on building or maintaining market share, depending on which of the four SBU categories is involved. Various strategies require differing amounts of cash, which means that management must continually allocate the firm's limited resources (notably cash) to separate marketing endeavours.

In the financial arena, an investor needs a balanced portfolio in relation to risks and potential returns. Similarly, a company should seek a balanced portfolio of SBUs. Certainly, cash cows are indispensable. Stars and question marks are integral to a balanced portfolio, because products in growing markets determine a firm's long-term performance. While dogs are undesirable, it is rare that a company doesn't have at least one. As a result, the portfolios of most organizations with numerous SBUs or major products include a mix of stars, cash cows, question marks, and dogs.

Product-market growth matrix

Most organizations' mission statements and objectives focus on growth — that is, a desire to increase revenues and profits. In seeking growth, a company must consider both its markets and its products. Then, it has to decide whether to continue doing what it is now doing — only do it better — or establish new ventures. The **product-market growth matrix**, first proposed by Igor Ansoff,[12] depicts these options. Essentially, as shown in Figure 2-8, there are four product-market growth strategies:

• **Market penetration:** A company tries to sell more of its present products to its present markets. Supporting tactics might include improved customer handling, greater spending on targeted promotions, advertising, or telemarketing. A company can try to become a single source of supply by offering preferential treatment to customers who might then give that company all of their business. Examples of this include insurance companies that will provide increasingly higher discounts the more policies you carry with them. Banks will also negotiate reduced service charges or free services as clients broaden their relationship with the bank by increasing the number of bank products used or the value of their holdings.

• **Market development:** A firm continues to sell its present products, but to a new market. Frequently, firms turn to exporting to new foreign markets or to developing their own foreign organizations. Krispy Kreme (**www.krispykreme.com**) has been a

Krispy Kreme
Tim Hortons
Starbucks

Figure 2-8:

Product-Market Growth Matrix

	PRESENT PRODUCTS	NEW PRODUCTS
PRESENT MARKETS	Market penetration	Product development
NEW MARKETS	Market development	Diversification

product development

A product-market growth strategy that calls for a company to develop new products to sell to its existing markets.

Panasonic
Sharp
Sony

diversification

A product-market growth strategy in which a company develops new products to sell to new markets.

part of U.S. culture for more than 60 years and in that time has managed to pretty much tap-out its potential in its homeland. As a result, in 2002, we saw the much-promoted introduction of the brand in Canada. Tim Hortons (**www.timhortons.com**) has built an empire but Krispy Kreme's fellow American, Starbucks (**www.starbucks.com**), made a successful run for the border, so it only stood to reason that, with an average doughnut fat content twice that of Tim's offerings (meaning twice the tastiness), this marketplace should find Krispy Kreme a palatable alternative.

● **Product development:** This strategy calls for a company to develop new products to sell to its existing markets. To remain competitive, Panasonic (**www.panasonic.ca**), Sharp (**www.sharp.ca**), and Sony (**www.sony.ca**) have to continually develop and introduce new products and improved products in order to keep "Just Slightly Ahead of Our Time." While television is certainly not a new product, these companies are constantly introducing new high-definition and liquid crystal models. Sony previewed its new broadband personal television — the Airboard — in 2002. Equipped with a 10.4-inch colour LCD, the Airboard unclips from a base to resemble a tablet PC and allows users to access the Internet, send and receive e-mails, or watch TV from anywhere within about a 30-metre range of the base.

● **Diversification:** Diversification means that a company develops new products to sell to new markets. This strategy is risky because it doesn't rely on either the company's successful products or its position in established markets. Sometimes it works, but sometimes it doesn't. Roots is a brand familiar to most Canadians, but many don't realize what product the company began with or how far it has diversified. The company began in 1973 in Toronto when it introduced the negative-heel shoe — a leather shoe with a heel that was lower than the rest of the shoe's sole. The company has gone on to many other leather products, athletic clothing, a children's line, watches, and a home furnishings collection that features leather furniture, accent pieces, and towels. Then, there was the introduction of a river resort and, finally, an airline. All have been successful product diversifications except for the last one. While the image of the brand facilitated the success of most of these new products, it did not carry over into the airline industry, where the brand lasted much less than a year.

As market conditions change over time, a company may shift product-market growth strategies. For example, when its present market is fully saturated, a company may have no choice other than to pursue new markets within Canada, nearby U.S. states, or Asian countries.

Assessment of the Planning Models

Each of the planning models we've discussed has been praised and criticized. While each is somewhat distinctive, all share some common weaknesses and strengths.

The primary weakness is probably oversimplification. Each model bases its assessment of market opportunities and subsequent decisions on only two or three key factors. Another weakness is the possibility of placing an SBU on a grid or choosing a strategy without relevant, reliable information. For example, the extent to which market share is critical to a product's profitability is still debated. Whether a market share represents a high or low proportion of repeat purchasers does make a difference. A third possible weakness is that the results from one of the models might be used to contradict or substitute for the critical business judgements made by line managers (such as marketing vice-presidents).

The focus of all of these models is primarily the product portfolio of a company. While implicit attention is paid to the customer, one overriding assumption seems to be that value may be created and the customer satisfied largely through management of the product component of the marketing mix, either by selling more of the products, dropping some of them from the line, or developing new ones. In that sense, we suggest that these models may be characteristic of the thinking of companies that are at the product-oriented stage of their marketing evolution. While it is critical that a company have a well-developed product strategy, growth can in fact be achieved and customers satisfied through many other strategies as well, including enhanced levels of customer service, more effective distribution methods, improved communications, and the cultivation of solid relationships.

The models discussed do possess noteworthy strengths, however. Most notable is straightforward classification — each model permits an organization to examine its entire portfolio of SBUs or major products in relation to criteria that influence business performance. A second strength is that the models can pinpoint attractive business opportunities and suggest ventures to avoid. They encourage the careful, consistent assessment of opportunities, allocation of resources, and formulation of strategies. Without planning models, these activities might be haphazard — for example, using one set of criteria this month and, with no good reason, another set next month.

Overall, these and other planning models can help management in allocating resources and in developing sound business and marketing strategies. Of course, any planning model should supplement, rather than substitute for, managers' judgements and decisions. Also, no single model can accomplish all that managers need to accomplish in planning marketing programs for their firms. These planning models represent a starting point and should be used in combination with other planning tools to achieve as comprehensive a strategy as possible for the firm.

BACKSPACE

1. An annual marketing plan serves what purpose?
2. According to the BCG matrix, an organization classifies each of its strategic business units according to which factors?
3. What are the four product-market growth strategies?

Summary

Various environmental forces influence an organization's marketing activities. Some are external and uncontrollable, while some are external but subject to control and relationship-building. Other forces are internal, within the control of management and open to relationship-building.

Six broad variables constitute the external environment: demographic, economic, competitive, social and cultural, technological, and legal and political. Another set of factors — suppliers, market intermediaries, and the market itself — is also external to the firm but part of its marketing system and thus manageable to varying degrees. A set of internal non-marketing resources — production, personnel, financial, location, research and development, and company image — are both manageable and in constant need of co-ordination and relationship-building.

The management process, taking into consideration the environmental forces discussed above, consists of planning, implementation, and evaluation. Planning is deciding now what we are going to do later, including when and how we are going to do it. Planning provides direction to an organization. Strategic planning is intended to match an organization's resources with its market opportunities over the long run.

In any organization, there should be three levels of planning: strategic company planning, strategic marketing planning, and annual marketing planning. In strategic company planning, management defines the organization's mission, assesses its operating environment, sets long-range goals, and formulates broad strategies to achieve the goals. This level guides the planning in different functional areas, including marketing.

Strategic marketing planning entails five steps: conduct a situation analysis; develop objectives; select target markets and measure market demand; determine positioning and differential advantage; and design a marketing mix. Based on strategic marketing plans, an annual marketing plan lays out a year's marketing activities for each major product and division of an organization. An annual plan includes tactics as well as strategies and should be specific about the people involved — the who and how of implementation. It is typically prepared by the executive responsible for the division or product.

Management can rely on either or both of the models discussed for assistance with strategic planning: the Boston Consulting Group matrix and Ansoff's product-market growth matrix. A planning model helps management see how best to allocate its resources and to select effective marketing strategies.

Key Terms and Concepts

annual marketing plan 50
Boston Consulting Group (BCG) matrix 52
cash cows 53
demography 33
differential advantage (or disadvantage) 48
distribution channel 40
diversification 56
dogs 55
environmental scanning 46
external macro-environmental forces 32
external micro-environmental forces 32
internal non-marketing forces 32
market development 55
market penetration 55
marketing intermediaries 40
mission statement 43
objective (same as *goal*) 44

positioning 48
product development 56
product-market growth matrix 55
question marks 54
relationship-insensitive forces 33
relationship-sensitive forces 39
segments 48
situation analysis 46
stars 53
strategic business unit (SBU) 52
strategic company planning 45
strategic marketing planning 46
strategy 44
SWOT assessment 46
tactic 44
target market 48

Questions and Problems

1. A decline in university and college enrolments is predicted during the next several years. What marketing measures should your school take to respond to this forecast?

2. For each of the following products and services, give some examples of how its marketing program is likely to differ during periods of prosperity as contrasted with periods of recession.
   a. McDonald's.
   b. Mercedes-Benz.
   c. Rollerblades.
   d. Caribbean vacations.

3. What have been some of the marketing strategies used in recent years by fast-food restaurants in response to increasing public interest in health and physical fitness?

4. Using examples other than those given in this chapter, explain how a firm's marketing system can be influenced by the environmental force of technology, and particularly by the Internet.

5. Explain how each of the following resources within a company might influence that company's marketing program. How could each be a source or sources of differential advantage and/or disadvantage?
   a. Plant location.
   b. Company image.

c. Financial resources.
d. Personnel capability.

6. Should a small firm (either a manufacturer, a retailer, or an online enterprise) engage in formal strategic planning? Why or why not?

7. Considering the impact of changing technology on technology-based industries, should firms involved in these follow the same guidelines and time frames for strategic planning as traditional organizations? Explain.

8. Using a customer-oriented approach (benefits provided or needs satisfied), answer the question "What business are we in?" for each of the following companies:
   a. VIA Rail.
   b. Mountain Equipment Co-op.
   c. Subway Sandwiches and Salads.

9. In the situation-analysis step of strategic marketing planning, what specific external environmental forces should be analyzed by a manufacturer of equipment used for backpacking in the wilderness?

10. Using the BCG matrix, identify a major product or strategic business unit that would fit into each quadrant (stars, cash cows, questions marks, dogs).

Hands-On Marketing

1. Go to your school's library and obtain a copy of an annual report for a major corporation. Based on your examination of the year-end review, which of the following product-market growth strategies is being used by this company: market penetration, market development, product development, and/or diversification?

2. Talk with a marketing executive at a local firm. Based on the information you obtain, determine the differential advantage or disadvantage of the firm's primary product or service. Indicate how the advantage could be strengthened or the disadvantage alleviated.

3. Go to Gap's Web site (**www.gapinc.com**) and, by reviewing the content of the "About Gap Inc." section, determine Gap's objectives.

Back to the Top

So, what's the difference between an SUV and a station wagon? Did your parents have a station wagon to haul kids and their gear around when you were young? Think about the discussion in our chapter opener about the new models being introduced by Mazda and others to appeal to younger adults. Are you attracted? Are you in their target segment? What do you find attractive or unattractive about the concept and about the products themselves?

Want to get better grades, tips on how to study more effectively, and up-to-date information on happenings in the world of marketing? Then visit the Online Learning Centre for practice tests, Study Smart software, and much more! **www.mcgrawhill.ca/college/sommers**

Interested in finding out what marketing looks like in the real world? *Marketing Magazine* is just a click away on your Online Learning Centre!

CHAPTER 3

Understanding the Customer

Having looked at the basic ideas about marketing in Chapter 1 and how marketing planning is carried out in Chapter 2, we now examine the heart of all marketing ideas and planning efforts — the consumer. You will see how consumers, the key force in the controllable marketing environment, behave in the marketplace over time, and review the factors that influence this behaviour. After studying this chapter, you should have an understanding of:

- The process consumers go through in making buying decisions.

- The importance of commercial and social information sources in consumer decisions.

- The influence of cultures and subcultures on consumer behaviour.

- The direct impact of reference groups on consumer behaviour.

- Family and household buying behaviour.

- The roles of motivation, perception, learning, personality, and attitudes in shaping consumer behaviour.

- The importance of situational factors in buying.

I Need a New Computer, But Which One?

Now that you and your friends are enrolled in school and on your way, you've decided that you're going to take your studies seriously. So, to really get up to speed and prepare for the challenge, you've decided you need a new computer — up-to-date technology so you can efficiently access Web resources, download class notes, and participate in online class discussion forums.

You've had a Dell computer for the past few years and you like it, but it's time to trade up — and speed up! So, your plan is to call Dell's convenient toll-free number and order something newer, faster, and with a few more features. Two of your friends are taking somewhat different approaches to the same task. One of them believes there is very little difference between all of the PCs available and that as soon as you buy a new machine, it's practically out of date anyway. So, he has decided to quickly scan the local big-box and electronic discount stores for the fastest "no-name" machine at the cheapest price.

And your other friend? Well, she has taken pretty much the opposite strategy to choose her new computer. She really enjoys working, and entertaining herself, with her computer — to her, it's much more than a work tool. She has done a lot of surfing and looking in the local specialty stores to make sure she knows what's out there and that she gets everything she wants from her purchase. Of course, speed and word processing are important, but so is the entertainment component. So she has been attracted to the iMac, with its features such as iPod digital music player, digital photo capabilities, iMovie, and iDVD. And then there's its sleek look. The decision isn't easy — she would really like these features, some of which are optional, but it means spending a good deal more money than for a regular PC.

At the end of the day, what will each of you end up with? Who will have made the best decision? Why?

Why do you and your friends in this chapter opener approach the computer decision in different ways? Why do you all shop differently? What kind of decision process leads one to buy a Dell, another just a beige box at the best price, and another to spend a lot of time and energy putting together the right system? These are just some of the questions you can ask about the three different ways of buying a computer. And if you look around, watch yourself, your friends, your schoolmates, parents, and others, you will see similar kinds of consumer decision-making. You'll appreciate that, with growing experience, we have all become more sophisticated and demanding consumers.

Increased global competition and more knowledgeable consumers have combined to raise the bar for most companies as they strive to meet the increased expectations of their customers. And because the foundation for marketing success always depends on the ability to know what consumers are doing and to anticipate their future behaviour, in this chapter, we examine consumer behaviour from the perspective necessary to guide marketing planning. First, we examine the consumer decision-making process. Next, we consider the sources of information used by consumers and the factors that influence them — the Internet, various social and group forces in a consumer's environment, and the significant role that situational factors play in buying situations.

Figure 3-1 brings all of the dimensions of consumer behaviour together in a model that provides the structure for our discussion. At the core of the model is the six-stage buying-decision process, surrounded by four primary sets of forces.

The Buying-Decision Process

buying-decision process

The series of logical stages through which a prospective purchaser goes when faced with a buying problem. The stages differ for consumers and organizations.

Consumers deal with the marketing environment that surrounds them by engaging in a **buying-decision process**. This process, which divides nicely into six stages, can be thought of as a problem-solving approach. When faced with a buying problem ("I need a new computer before the start of term," "I need a new pair of shoes to wear to my cousin's wedding"), the consumer goes through a series of logical stages to arrive at a solution or a decision. Table 3-1 presents the stages in this process and some of the variations that commonly occur.

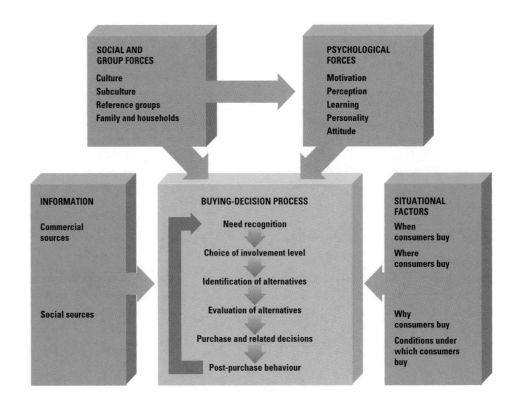

Figure 3-1:

The Consumer Decision-Making Process and Its Environment

TABLE 3-1 The Six-Staged Buying-Decision Process and Common Variations

Six Stages of Buying-Decision Process	Common Variations
1. **Need recognition**: The consumer is moved to action by an internally or externally generated need.	Not all stages are involved in all purchase situations, and the following variations are quite common.
2. **Choice of an involvement level**: The consumer decides how much time and effort to invest in satisfying the need and the energy to be devoted to the remaining stages of the problem-solving process.	• **Withdrawing from the decision process prior to actual purchase**: Need or desire may diminish, no satisfactory alternatives are available, or the search is not worth the effort.
3. **Identification of alternatives**: The consumer collects information about products, services, and brands that might address the need.	• **Skipping stages**: All six stages are likely to be followed when buying high-priced, infrequently purchased items; for frequently purchased, familiar products, purchasing is usually routine and is often satisfied by repurchasing a familiar brand, with the third and fourth stages of the process being bypassed.
4. **Evaluation of alternatives**: The consumer weighs the pros and cons of the alternatives identified.	
5. **Purchase and related decisions**: The consumer decides to buy or not to buy.	• **Different stages require different amounts of time and energy**: It may take only a moment to recognize the need for a new car, but picking out and evaluating the alternative models may go on for weeks. Sometimes stages can occur simultaneously — when, for example, a consumer identifies and evaluates alternatives at the same time, eliminating unsuitable options as the decision-making process proceeds.
6. **Consumption experience and behaviour**: The consumer seeks reassurance that the choice made was the correct one, experiences the product or service in use, assesses whether expectations have been met and satisfaction derived, becomes prepared to develop a relationship with the marketer, determines to engage in the decision process again as the need arises.	• **Not all stages may be performed consciously**: You don't consciously calculate the amount of time and effort you will put into reaching a decision about every purchase. But the fact that you spend more time on some purchases and less on others indicates that level of involvement is part of the process.

Let's now look at these stages in more detail. Keep in mind that once a buying decision has been made and a product purchased, consumers want their expectations met, value received, and satisfaction to be derived from product possession and use. As we observed in Chapter 1, many aspects of the interaction between buyers and sellers can affect expectations, perceptions of value, and the resulting satisfaction levels and relationships with marketers.

1. Need recognition

An unsatisfied need creates tension or discomfort for a consumer. This condition may arise *internally* and have a physiological basis; for example, a person feels hungry, or the need may be dormant until it is aroused *externally* by a stimulus such as a TV advertisement or the sight or smell of a favourite fast food being eaten by a passerby. Another possible source of tension that can create an impetus to act is dissatisfaction with a product currently being used. Perhaps you realize as you are getting into more advanced courses that you need a faster computer.

While hunger represents an actual physiological need that we all experience, the term *need*, as we have pointed out before, also refers to consumers' *wants* — like that new pair of sunglasses with the great shape that you really *need* to buy!

Once a need has been recognized, consumers often become aware of conflicting or competing uses for their scarce resources of time and money. Our desire to fulfil all of these needs must be balanced with a sense of practicality and the fact that we never have enough money (and probably never will!) to satisfy all of our wants as consumers. It is the existence of this conflict that forces consumers into some form of decision-making process.

Let's say that one of our computer-buying friends from the beginning of the chapter is torn between buying an iMac computer and a completely different purchase — a powerful, new audio system for her car. She would also like an in-dash CD/MP3 receiver/controller with dual cone speakers and a 12-inch subwoofer box. No, she's not a street racer, but she does like her music, and she likes it loud! Besides, she could probably make do with her old computer and this audio system would cost less than the iMac, considering that the iPod MP3 player would cost $600 more, on top of the price of the computer. This way, there would be money left over to buy new music and for her social life. On the other hand, she would then have to get someone else to download MP3 files from the Internet, because her old computer isn't up to it. And, of course downloading notes and information from the Web will be painfully slow! Our friend has to resolve these conflicts before proceeding — if she doesn't, the buying process stops. If she asks you what to do, what would you recommend? Which of her "needs" is the most important?

2. Level of involvement

high-involvement level

A purchase decision that involves all six stages of the buying-decision process.

low-involvement level

A purchase decision in which the consumer moves directly from need recognition to purchase, skipping the stages in between.

Very early in the process, a consumer can consciously (but most likely, subconsciously) decide how much effort to exert in satisfying a need; in other words, what level of involvement is required. Sometimes, when a need arises, a consumer is sensitive about a product, perceives some level of risk in the purchase, or is concerned with the quantity or quality of information available. Such situations are usually considered to be at the **high-involvement level** and result in extended problem solving, using all stages of the decision-making process. Your friend in the chapter opener who is carefully building a work and entertainment system is an example of this level. If the consumer is comfortable with the information on hand and satisfied that no more is needed (replace your Dell computer with anther Dell), or even if the consumer is indifferent about the situation, an unconscious or barely conscious **low-involvement level** results and the decision approach progresses in a routine problem-solving fashion. In this latter situation, the consumer will likely skip directly from need recognition and alternative selection to the purchase, ignoring the intervening evaluation stage. A moderate level of involvement, between the two extremes, leads to limited problem solving — shopping for the best-priced beige box. Some of the major differences in involvement and problem-solving approaches are presented in Table 3-2.

TABLE 3-2 Consumer Behaviour Differences in Involvement and Problem Solving			
Level of Involvement	**High**	**Moderate**	**Low**
Problem-Solving Approach	**Extended**	**Limited**	**Routine**
Resulting Behaviour:			
Time invested	Large amount	Moderate to little	Small amount
Information sources used	Many	Few	None
Response to information	Critically evaluate	Review	Ignore or accept without evaluation
Brands evaluated	Many	Small number	One
Brand attributes evaluated	Many	Moderate number	Few
Sources considered	Many	Moderate number	Few
Interaction with sales, service, and retail personnel	Committed, demanding	Focused, could be sensitive	Nominal

Generally, perceived risk is higher and involvement tends to be greater under any of the following conditions:

- The consumer lacks information about the purchase. It may be a new product on the market or the first time the consumer has bought this product or service.

- The product or its attributes and benefits are viewed as being important. Such a product may be heavily relied on to perform each day, or involve safety issues.

- The practical, psychological, or social consequence of making a bad decision is perceived as high. What if it is poor quality, has outdated technology, doesn't look right, or just isn't considered to be cool?

- The need for personal interaction about the purchase is important. Taking part in the interaction can yield important new information, clarify what is known, and generally be informative.

- The interaction process itself is satisfying or even enjoyable and builds confidence when the decision is complicated or difficult.

Most buying decisions for relatively low-priced products that have close substitutes would be low involvement and handled in a routine or limited problem-solving way. Typical examples are the majority of items sold in supermarkets, variety stores, and hardware stores. However, for a wealthy person, the purchase of a car could be low involvement and handled in a routine way, while for a person with a high need for social acceptance, purchasing toothpaste might be highly involving and handled with a moderate or even extended problem-solving approach. Such a consumer may look for new product features such as assurance of whiter teeth and fresher breath. It is important to remember that involvement must be viewed from the perspective of the consumer; it is not a characteristic of the product.

impulse buying
Low-involvement purchase made with little or no advance planning.

Impulse buying, or purchasing with little or no advance planning, is an important form of low-involvement decision-making. A shopper who goes to the supermarket with the intention of buying only vegetables and bread, but on noticing a display of peaches at an attractive price decides to buy some, engages in impulse buying.

The growing importance of the Internet as a product and purchase information source may result in consumers spending more time and involvement in what would otherwise be considered low-involvement decisions. Where once existed a clearer trade-off between time and effort expended in gathering more or better data for a more informed decision, now the time and involvement trade-off has changed. With the use of a good Internet search engine (or a battery of them operating simultaneously), you can collect a lot of very useful product and purchase information, using much less time and effort than in the past. But it is also true that the ease with which information (on anything and everything!) can be gathered — without stepping out of the house — can draw the consumer into extended problem solving with increased search time. This complicates the seemingly clear distinction presented in Table 3-2 regarding involvement levels and problem-solving approaches. In actuality, the distinction would lie more with consumer differences than with the type of purchase.

3. Identification of alternatives

Once a need has been recognized and the level of involvement determined, the consumer must next identify the alternatives capable of satisfying that need. First, alternative products and then alternative brands are identified. Product and brand identification usually starts with an internal search or memory scan, since previous personal consumer experiences are the most important. When a consumer is more than satisfied with a brand and really likes it — has an attachment to it or a degree of relationship with it — only one alternative is usually identified. For example, you are with your study group, it's coffee break time, and someone says, "Hey, there are three different places down the block where we could go." You say, "Yeah, but it's Tim Hortons for me — let's go!'" In this simple case, a nanosecond of internal or memory scanning yielded a brand alternative that had met a consumer's expectations and provided desired satisfaction and a developed brand-relationship experience.

But when sufficient or appropriate information is not available internally in a person's memory, a consumer can engage in an extensive external search of the physical or cyber-environment. For example, suppose a couple decides not to cook but to have an already-prepared item for their evening meal. Since neither can remember offhand what's in the refrigerator, identifying alternatives might mean first checking the freezer to see if any frozen dinners are on hand, then paging through the newspaper for supermarket specials or discount coupons, or looking in a local magazine or on the Internet to see if there are any reviews of nearby restaurants.

The search for alternatives is influenced by:

- How much internal information the consumer already has from past consumption experiences and information from other sources.

- The consumer's past experiences and other internal information.

- The consumer's confidence in information from external sources.

- The expected benefit or value of additional information or, put another way, what the additional information is worth in terms of the effort, time, or money required to obtain it.

4. Evaluation of alternatives

Once a set of reasonable alternatives has been identified, the consumer must evaluate them before making a decision. Consumer approaches to evaluation range from simple to complex, depending on the consumer's own experience as well as degree of product complexity technically and in use. A simple comparison can be determining which of five brands, all well known to the consumer, has the lowest purchase price. A more complex comparison, where the consumer has much less brand experience, could involve the evaluation of each of the seven important product and benefit characteristics of each of the five competing brands. Every evaluation involves establishing some criteria against which each alternative is compared. In the preceding meal example, the decision-maker may have a single criterion ("How quickly can we sit down to eat?") or several criteria (speed, taste, nutrition, price, decor, atmosphere). When multiple criteria are involved, they typically do not carry equal weight. For example, preparation time might be more important than nutrition.

Epinions

The criteria that consumers use in the evaluation result, first and foremost, from their past experience and feelings toward various brands, as well as the opinions of family members, friends, or even experts' comments in newspapers, magazines, or on the Internet. There is no shortage of people wanting to express their opinions on the Net, as evidenced by the Epinions Web site (**www.epinions.com**), where people can share their experiences and views on anything from brands of bowling balls to ski vacations and computer operating systems. Because experience is often limited or dated, and information from sources such as advertising or friends can be biased, evaluations may not be founded on facts. While a consumer may believe that the price of brand A is higher than that of brand B, the opposite may in fact be true. The degree to which consumer experience and information departs from reality is a problem that marketers must work to alleviate.

5. Purchasing and related decisions

After searching and evaluating, the consumer has decided what to buy; the next problem is whether to buy. If the decision is to go ahead and buy, a series of purchasing-related decisions must be made and perhaps the specific types of special features desired must be determined. The consumer must decide where and when to make the actual purchase, how to take delivery or possession, the method of payment, and other issues related to being able to begin making use of the purchase. So, the decision to make a purchase is really the beginning of an entirely new series of decisions that may be as time-consuming and difficult as the initial one. The outcome of these purchase-related decisions affects satisfaction in an important way. Consumers want their expectations met in terms of product value, the tenor and tone of the actual purchase transaction, and the ease and convenience with which they are able to gain satisfaction from their purchases.

patronage motives
The reasons why a consumer chooses to shop at a certain place.

Sources from which to make a purchase can range from Internet sites to manufacturers' outlets. The most common source is a retail store, and the reasons a consumer chooses to buy there as opposed to a cyberspace or electronic store are called patronage motives. Consumers have a variety of reasons for selecting a retail source for the brand they have decided to buy. Many want to feel comfortable when they shop. This may mean that they want the assurance of being around people like themselves and in an environment that reflects their values or that they can trust. Others may want the convenience, lack of pressure, and anonymity of an electronic store.

Patronage motives can range from something as simple as convenience when you want a bottle of water to something more complex, such as the atmosphere of a restaurant. While it is apparent that physical stores are quite different from Internet ones, patronage motives for e-shopping are as important as those for traditional shopping — but in a slightly modified form. The similarities and differences for patronage motives are illustrated in Table 3-3. Just as is the case for a building, the "look" of a Web site matters, as it gives an impression of the style and image of the brand. A good impression gives consumers confidence, as do clear evidence of security and privacy, and clearly displayed prices and delivery policies. Easy, convenient site navigation and helpful links ensure that consumers will stay the course and hit the button to submit an order. If shoppers are frustrated by the quality of the experience as they fill their cybercarts, they can simply "walk away," leaving their carts in the aisle. This is not as easy to do in a physical retail store environment.

6. The consumption experience

What a consumer learns from going through the decision-making process and making the actual purchase has an influence on how that consumer will behave the next time the same

TABLE 3-3	Common Patronage Motives Used By Consumers in Selecting Purchase Locations	
Buying Patronage Motive	**For "Bricks" (offline)**	**For "Clicks" (online)**
Convenient to find/access	Location, name	Memorable URL, easy navigation
Appearance	Physical appeal of premises	Attractiveness of Web site
Product assortment.	Reach, touch, feel, try	Clear, realistic, useful graphics and text
Service availability	Personal, flexible, range	Impersonal, limited range, fixed
Service quality	Variable comfort, speed, reliability	Standardized level
Reliability of product	Inspection, demonstration available	Product brand reputation
Confidence in supplier	Retailer brand, staff reputation	E-tailer brand reputation
Prices, credit, other terms	Fixed but sometimes negotiable	Fixed
Mix of other customers	Visible, known by reputation	Invisible, generally unknown
Reputation for after-sales delivery, service	Easy to find out and evaluate	Difficult to ascertain and evaluate

To which patronage motives does Amazon appeal?

post-purchase behaviour

Efforts by the consumer to reduce the anxiety often accompanying purchase decisions.

cognitive dissonance

Anxiety created by the fact that in most purchases the alternative selected has some negative features and the alternatives not selected have some positive features.

need arises. Having decided on what to purchase and where, if the consumer's expectations throughout the actual purchase or transaction have been met, transaction satisfaction results. You now have the brand of product you want on terms that are acceptable, and you believe you have received good value.

Your experience with the product over its useful life — useful as far as you're concerned — will dictate what other satisfactions you may derive. For example, if your experience over the life of a cellphone is negative for whatever reason (functional problems, lack of service when needed, rapid feature obsolescence), your dissatisfaction will feed back from this consumption-experience stage (**post-purchase behaviour**) to the next need-recognition stage — the feedback loop, as shown in Figure 3-1. This dissatisfaction will likely cause you to avoid the same brand the next time you buy a cellphone.

If, as is frequently the case, the product or service met your expectations and you are satisfied that it should be favoured in the next decision-making process, you'll be feeding back satisfaction information. Satisfaction itself can be derived from the performance or functional aspects of the product. In such a case, a functional relationship is being established. Favouring or preferring a brand does not always lead to it being the only one considered. You may be presented with new functional feature information, causing you to use a limited problem-solving approach and compare features rather than a routine approach that considers only one brand.

But when the brand purchased has more than met your expectations and you really enjoyed having it and using it, your feedback of information is based on more than your functional satisfaction. The satisfaction expressed here includes a degree of emotional attachment or liking — an emotional relationship is being established. The greater the degree of emotional information fed back to a need-recognition stage, the more likely the brand in question will be the only alternative considered. The buying-decision process itself will require limited involvement and be routine in nature. The brand name will say it all — a simple and highly satisfactory buying situation for the consumer and a more than happy event for the marketers involved. As long as the consumer's relationship with the brand is maintained or enhanced by marketers, both continue to enjoy the long-term benefits that flow from it. In the chapter opener, it may be concluded that you have developed an emotional relationship with the Dell brand; you really like their products and feel you can count on them. Consequently, you plan to call them again to buy your new computer, without even considering other brands.

Something else often occurs following a purchase. You went through a careful decision process for a major purchase (perhaps a stereo, video game system, or expensive item of clothing), selected what you thought was the best alternative, but then had doubts about your choice after the purchase. You asked yourself if maybe you should have bought the other one you were considering. What you were experiencing is post-purchase **cognitive dissonance** — a state of anxiety brought on by the difficulty of choosing from among several alternatives. Unfortunately for marketers, dissonance is quite common and can easily lead to dissatisfaction with the chosen brand and a weakening of any relationships that existed. You may be unhappy with the chosen product even if it performs adequately!

Post-purchase cognitive dissonance occurs when each of the alternatives seriously considered by the consumer has both attractive and unattractive features. For example, in purchasing a stereo system, the equipment selected may be the most expensive (unattractive), but provides superior sound (attractive). The brand of system not chosen may be popular among your friends (attractive), but has a very limited service warranty (unattractive). After the purchase is made, the unattractive features of the product purchased grow in importance in the consumer's mind, as do the attractive features offered by the rejected alternatives. As a result, we begin to doubt the wisdom of the choice and experience anxiety over the decision.

Dissonance typically increases (1) the higher the dollar value or perceived risk of the purchase, (2) the greater the similarity between the item selected and items rejected, and (3) the greater the importance of the purchase decision to the consumer. Buying a new colour laser printer creates more dissonance than buying the paper for it.

To avoid or reduce post-purchase anxiety, consumers ignore information (such as ads for the rejected products) that is likely to increase the dissonance. They seek out information that supports their decision, even to the extreme of reading ads for a product after it has been purchased. Also, prior to the purchase, putting more effort into evaluating alternatives can increase a consumer's confidence and reduce post-purchase dissonance.

Marketers can protect and nurture the relationship they have with consumers by providing dissonance-reducing information. For example, anything sellers can do in their advertising, personal selling, and other communications activity to reassure buyers — stressing the number of satisfied owners, for example — will reduce dissonance. Also, the quality of a seller's follow-up and post-purchase service programs can be significant factors in reducing dissonance and strengthening relationships, particularly emotional relationships. Online marketers have a good opportunity to reassure buyers and strengthen any emotional relationship, since they have easy access to all of the customer information they need and can communicate supportive information or direct customers to helpful Web sites and chat rooms, as well as to favourable product reviews.

With this background on the buying decision process, we can now examine specific influences on the buying decision and consumer experience. We'll begin with the sources and types of information used by consumers.

BACKSPACE

1. When a consumer is making a purchase decision, under which conditions is risk perceived to be higher and involvement greater?

2. What does *functional satisfaction* refer to?

3. _____ is a state of anxiety brought on by the difficulty of choosing from among several alternatives.

- -

Information and Purchase Decisions

Consumers need to know what products and services are available, which brands offer what features and benefits, what services are available to support the purchase, who sells them at what prices, where they can be purchased, and what kind of follow-up service is likely. Without this information, there wouldn't be any decision to make. Fortunately, more and more information is available, as the Internet makes possible the collection of vast amounts of information with relatively little effort.

As shown in Figure 3-1, two information sources — commercial and social — enable the buying decision process. The **commercial information environment** includes all of the marketing organizations and individuals that attempt to communicate with consumers — manufacturers, retailers, advertisers, e-commerce Web site sponsors, and sales and service people, whenever any of them are engaged in efforts to inform or persuade.

commercial information environment

All marketing organizations and individuals that directly or indirectly communicate with consumers.

social information environment

Family, friends, and acquaintances who directly or indirectly provide information about products.

The social information environment is made up of family, friends, and acquaintances who directly or indirectly provide information about products. Think how often your conversations with friends at the coffee shop or in a chat room deal with purchases you are considering or those you have made. You probably have more discussions about products, brands, and services in a day than the number of commercial messages to which you pay attention. Also, it is interesting to note that people report negative experiences with products and services to other people more often than they report positive experiences.

Advertising is the most common type of commercial information. Other commercial sources are direct sales efforts by store clerks, telemarketing, and direct mail and e-mail to consumers' homes and computers, as well as consumers' physical involvement with products (examining packages, trial product use, and sampling). More and more consumers are obtaining the important information they need about products and services through the Internet. Both in e-commerce and e-business (business-to-business marketing), one of the first sources of information on products, services, and prospective suppliers is a Web site.

The most important kind of social information is word-of-mouth communication, in which two or more people simply have a conversation about a product or service. The proliferation of product review sites and special-topic discussion groups and chat rooms on the Internet has enhanced this effect. Other social sources include the observations of others using products and exposure to products in the homes and offices of others.

When all of the different types of information are considered, it's clear that there is enormous competition for consumer attention. It's estimated that the typical adult is exposed to about 300 ad messages a day — almost 10,000 per month.[1] To understand how a consumer handles this information, we begin by examining the social and group forces that influence the individual's psychological make-up and also play a role in specific buying decisions.

Social and Group Forces

The way we think, believe, and act is determined to a great extent by social forces and groups. In addition, our individual buying decisions — including our needs, the alternatives we consider, and the way we evaluate them — are affected by the social forces that surround us. To reflect this dual impact, the arrows in Figure 3-1 extend from the social and group forces in two directions: to the psychological make-up of the individual and to the buying-decision process. Our discussion begins with culture, the force with the most indirect impact, and moves to the force with the most direct impact, the household.

Definition of culture and cultural influence

culture

A complex of symbols and artifacts created by a given society and handed down from generation to generation as determinants and regulators of human behaviour.

Culture is the complex of symbols and artifacts created by a given society and handed down from generation to generation as determinants and regulators of human behaviour. The symbols may be intangible (attitudes, beliefs, values, languages, religions) or tangible (tools, housing, products, works of art). Culture implies a totally learned and "handed-down" way of life. It does not include instinctive acts. However, standards for performing instinctive biological acts (eating, eliminating body wastes, and sexual relationships) can be culturally established. So, while everybody gets hungry, what people eat and how they act to satisfy the hunger will vary among cultures.

Our sociocultural institutions (family, schools, churches, and languages) provide behavioural guidelines for us. "Culture . . . regulates our lives at every turn. From the moment we are born until we die there is constant conscious and unconscious pressure upon us to follow certain types of behaviour that [others] have created for us."[2] People living in a culture share a whole set of similarities and beliefs — and these often differ from those originating in other cultures.

When a culture is relatively homogeneous, as in Japan, using cultural factors for marketing purposes can be very effective. As well, within a given culture such as Canada, for those goods and services where the cultural characteristics of consumers have no effect, it is suitable to use the notion of "homogeneity of the market." For example, if all Canadians, regardless of where they live and whatever their ethnicity, believe equally in the need for efficiency, then goods and services that are presented with efficiency claims would be equally acceptable. But if there is less homogeneity in terms of values and way of life or lifestyle, culture is not as effective a guide for the development of marketing programs as is subculture.

Canada: A culturally complex society

subculture
Groups that exhibit characteristic behaviour patterns sufficient to distinguish them from other groups within the same culture.

OMNI.2 Television

Cultural complexity varies from big-city sidewalks to small-town ones.

Compared with many other countries, Canada is a culturally complex society — it has many **subcultures**, as opposed to being homogeneous. Marketers need to understand the concept of subcultures and analyze them as potentially profitable market segments. They also need to be careful not to step on culturally sensitive toes — it can easily be done. Our subcultures are based on factors such as race, nationality, religion, geographic location, age, and urban-rural distribution. Ethnicity, for example, is a cultural factor that has significant marketing implications. According to Dr. Elizabeth Hirschman of New York University, "Ethnicity contributes to consumers' imaginal tendencies and sensory arousal-seeking, and that affects consumption motives and preferred leisure activities."[3] Concentrations of Middle or Eastern Europeans in the Prairies provide a market for some products that would go unnoticed in Italian or Chinese sections of Toronto, Montréal, or Vancouver.

The cultural diversity of the Canadian market has taken on an increasing importance for many companies. Not too long ago, most ignored ethnic and linguistically based segmentation. However, as groups grew in size due to immigration, French-English differences became emphasized, and marketplace competition escalated, segmentation became accepted as a viable marketing strategy. Besides the large French Canadian population, there are also large communities of Italian, Chinese, German, and Portuguese in this country. Although many of these

people have been here for 50 years or more, language loyalty continues to remain high, indicating the pervasive influence of original cultures within our cultural mosaic.[4] In 2002, it was estimated that visible minorities numbered 5.7 million and it is expected that this number will climb to 7.7 million by 2016.[5]

The most obvious marketing efforts to reach ethnic market segments are found in major markets such as Toronto, Vancouver, and Montréal. In Toronto, for example, Fairchild Radio reaches 24 percent of the Chinese population, while CHIN reaches 11 percent. The OMNI.2 television system in Ontario (**www.omnitv.ca/OMNI2**) boasts the number-one Cantonese language newscast in Ontario, with a 71 percent weekly reach. OMNI.1 and OMNI.2 also broadcast Armenian, Filipino, Greek, Iranian, Japanese, Korean, Macedonian, Maltese, Polish, Russian, South Asian, and Ukrainian productions. In the 10 largest Canadian cities, the proportion of visible minorities is more than 20 percent of the population.[6] The ethnic market is highly concentrated, with four-fifths of visible minorities living in Ontario (50 percent), British Columbia (17 percent), and Québec (15 percent).

Television and newspapers are available to the Chinese communities in Vancouver, Toronto, Montréal, and elsewhere. Toronto's Spanish-language *El Popular* is targeted at the area's 250,000 Spanish speakers and is distributed from Québec to British Columbia. Edmonton's Aboriginal Media Services sells airtime for its Native radio station as well as advertising space in its 70 Native newspapers. These and similar media represent attractive advertising outlets for companies who want to reach growing subcultural and linguistic market segments.

The sharpest cultural differences of concern to marketers are portrayed in the attitudinal and behavioural differences between English- and French-speaking communities on a countrywide basis, including Acadian markets.

The Québécois market

While French Canada is technically, and politically for some, a subculture, its sheer size, homogeneity, main geographic location, purchasing power, and social and political orientation makes it a cultural rather than a subcultural market. The smaller French-speaking communities in other parts of the country can be considered to be subcultural markets. No other ethnic or non-English-speaking linguistic group comes close to comprising 14 percent of the Canadian population (in total, approximately 31 percent of the population speaks French).[7]

While French-speaking people are found from coast to coast, the major French-speaking market in Canada is relatively highly concentrated in one geographic area — Québec — with a long-established and fully developed set of cultural, social, artistic, and legal institutions. Québec consumers consistently exhibit consumption patterns unlike those in the rest of Canada. A number of studies have found that when demographics are either matched or controlled for, consumption differences exist between Québecers and other Canadians and that these differences are attributable to cultural factors — values and lifestyle preferences. Common examples of such generalized consumption differences are:[8]

- Better acceptance in Québec of premium-priced products, such as premium-grade gasoline and liquors.

- Willingness to pay higher prices for convenience items.

- Greater popularity in Québec of coupons and premiums.

- Greater per-capita expenditure in Québec on clothing, personal-care items, tobacco, wine, and beer. But there is a lower consumption of "hard" liquor, although stronger brands of beer are preferred.

- Greater per-capita consumption of soft drinks (regular, not diet), maple sugar, molasses, candy, and pre-sweetened cereals in Québec than in the rest of Canada — and lottery tickets, as well.

- Much higher consumption rates for instant and decaffeinated coffee in Québec.

- More time spent with television and radio in Québec than in the rest of the country.

- Women in Québec show different patterns of cosmetics use, including more use of perfumes, colognes, and hair-colouring products.

- Québec consumers are wary of new products, often waiting for them to prove themselves before purchasing them.

- A difference in banking and financial practices results from the popularity of credit unions (caisses populaires). There is also a trend away from the use of credit and credit cards.

- Consumers exhibit strong relationships with brands, but are susceptible to special offers and sale prices. Perceived value is often linked to price.

In what language is the text of this ad? Does it matter?

The impact of cultural differences on marketing

The fact that French Canada as well as the various ethnic minority communities in Canada represent distinctively different markets requires marketers who wish to be successful in, for example, the Québec market, to develop unique marketing programs for the segment. There must be an appreciation of the fact that certain products will not be successful in French Canada simply because they are not appropriate to the French Canadian culture and lifestyle. In other cases, products that are successful in English Canada must be marketed differently in French Canada, because French Canadians have a different perception of these products, their importance, and the way in which they are used. It may be necessary for companies to develop new products or appropriate variations of existing products specifically for the Québec market. Similarly, the retail buying behaviour of residents of that province may necessitate the use of different channels of distribution.

A similar case can be made for other ethnic-minority and linguistically based markets in our country. Because most of these communities are so much smaller in both scale and purchasing power than Francophone Québec, the scope for and amount of marketing program adaptation that is feasible for firms to engage in is frequently limited to advertising in the appropriate language and using, where possible, culturally acceptable themes. While the large Asian population represents a most attractive ethnic market, there are intricacies that must be considered. Within this population group, there are differences in origin that amount to significant differences. Those from Hong Kong primarily speak Cantonese; those from Taiwan primarily speak Mandarin and Taiwanese; those from China primarily speak Mandarin or standard Chinese.[9] Within the Chinese community, the words used may differ according to place of origin, and of course differences in expressions and puns exist. Common understanding of illustrations, copy, and message must be ensured. There is also the possibility of insult through stereotyping. Burger King faced language concerns head-on with its "Now we're speaking the same language" campaign, in which they chose Cantonese as it is the most common dialect in the Canadian Chinese community.[10] Special attention was given, as Cantonese is quite complex when sung. It is very important to use the correct tones and colloquialisms. Even colours are important in such advertising. White flowers, for example, are a sign of death in this culture and may have been used in the background of advertisements — the point being you must know the target culture or risk making such errors.

MARKETING AT WORK 3-1: GLOBAL

Chevy Nova Awards?

In selecting the name, a slogan, or even choosing package colours and design, a firm has to be sensitive to the fact that even if the product is to be sold in a single geographic region, it is likely that consumers of many different cultures are likely to encounter the product and its advertising. This cultural sensitivity becomes even more critical if that firm has chosen to target certain groups based on their culture or heritage. Failing to take enough precautions in this regard can often have humorous results — but usually not for the firm marketing the product!

Popular belief is that the Chevy Nova Award is bestowed on marketing efforts that have failed to cross language and/or cultural barriers successfully. The idea behind the award can perhaps be best understood by explaining the name of the award. It is named in "honour" of General Motors' attempts, years ago, to market a car of this name in Central and South America. "Chevy Nova" in Spanish is "*No va*," which means "It doesn't go"! Hardly a good omen of how the car will perform! This classic gaffe thus gave birth to the title of the award.

The following are some recent examples of award nominees.

- The Dairy Association's great success with the "Got Milk?" campaign led to a decision to expand the promotion into Mexico. It wasn't good news when the association found out that the Spanish translation for the tag line is "Are you lactating?"

- Coors beer also decided to use an existing slogan in the Spanish marketplace. Somehow the slogan "Turn it loose" was interpreted as "Suffer from diarrhoea."

- Scandinavian vacuum cleaner manufacturer Electrolux used the following in an American campaign: "Nothing sucks like an Electrolux."

- Clairol introduced the "Mist Stick," a curling iron, in Germany, only to find out that "mist" is slang for "manure." Not too many people had use for a "Manure Stick."

- Pepsi's "Come alive with the Pepsi generation" translated into "Pepsi brings your ancestors back from the grave" in Chinese.

- When the Pope visited Miami, a T-shirt manufacturer, in an attempt to cater to the large Spanish population, printed T-shirts that promoted the visit. But, instead of "I saw the Pope" (*el papa*), the shirts displayed "I saw the potato" (*la papa*).

In fact, the Chevy Nova story is nothing more than urban legend — yes, "*no va*" is Spanish for "doesn't go," but this is pronounced differently from "*nova*" and it is unlikely that there would have been confusion between the terms. It still serves as the classic cautionary tale, though, about the pitfalls of doing business with consumers of other cultures. The Chevy Nova legend lives on in many marketing textbooks, and is repeated in numerous business seminars. Perhaps some day this tale will become what it should be — an illustration of how easily even "experts" can sometimes fall victim to the very same dangers that they warn others about.

Sadly, the other stories above about award nominees are true!

SOURCE: Adapted from www.snopes2.com/business/misxlate/nova and www.urbanlegends.about.com.

Reference Group Influences

reference group
A group of people who influence a person's attitudes, values, and behaviour

Consumers' perceptions and buying behaviour are also influenced by the reference groups to which they belong. These groups include small **reference groups** such as the family — the strongest social group influence on a person. For teens and young adults, peer group relationships can be more important and influential when it comes to food, clothing, entertainment, and a host of related consumption decisions. For many teens, shopping is still a top leisure activity that they share with their core group, experimenting with different styles.

Small group effects

Consumers' behaviour is influenced by the small groups to which they belong or with whom they aspire to associate. These groups may include family, sports clubs or teams, or a circle of close friends from school, work, or the neighbourhood. Each of these groups has its own standards of behaviour that serve as guides or frames of reference for actual or aspiring members. A person may agree with all of the ideas of the group or only with some of them. Also, a person does not have to belong to a group to be influenced by it. Actual and potential reference groups operate to influence a person's attitudes, values, and behaviour.

Studies have shown that personal advice in face-to-face reference groups is much more effective in influencing buying behaviour than is advertising in newspapers, television, and other mass media. That is, in selecting products or changing brands, you are more likely to be influenced by advice, comments, or word of mouth from satisfied (or dissatisfied) customers in your reference group. This is true especially when you consider the speaker to be knowledgeable about the particular product or service or about the problem a product or service is designed to address. There is now growing awareness of the importance and influence that Internet-based reference groups or special-interest communities have on those who spend a significant amount of time in online conversations with individuals as well as in chat rooms — either in giving opinions or monitoring them. Notoriously popular among today's 'tween generation (between child and teenager, 9 to 13 years old), online groups and chat rooms make 'tweens feel empowered. The experience allows their creativity to roam wild, and unleashes their imagination as they role-play while communicating with faceless individuals at the other end.[11]

Advertisers rely on reference group influence when they use celebrity spokespersons. Professional athletes, musicians, models, and actors can influence people who admire them or want to be like them in some small way. Recent examples include Wayne Gretzky for Tylenol products and McDonald's restaurants, Mark Messier for Lay's potato chips, MusiquePlus VeeJay Genevieve Borne for Procter & Gamble, and Shania Twain for Revlon. A variation on this is marketers who actually supply professional organizations with their products. Bauer Inc., for example, as part of its parent company Nike's sponsorship deal with the International Ice Hockey Federation, dressed the Canada hockey team in Bauer uniforms and equipment.[12]

The importance of reference group influence is evident when charities and not-for-profit organizations use endorsements by well-known figures to champion their causes in print and broadcast media advertising. Recent examples of Canadian-born stars who have spoken out to educate the public and promote research support for causes close to them include Michael J. Fox and Neve Campbell — Fox for Parkinson's Disease, from which he suffers, and Campbell for Tourette's Syndrome, which has afflicted her brother.

Reference group influence in marketing is not limited to well-known personalities. Any group whose qualities a person admires can act as a reference. The physically fit, the environmentally conscious, and the professionally successful have all served as reference groups in advertisements. Another useful reference group factor pertains to the flow of information between and within groups — it tends to flow horizontally from group to group on a similar social level, rather than trickle down from high-status to lower-status groups.[13]

The proven role of small groups as behaviour determinants, plus the concept of horizontal information flow, suggests that a marketer is faced with two key problems. The first is to identify the relevant reference group likely to influence a consumer in a given buying situation. The second is to identify and communicate with two key people in the group — the innovator (the early buyer — which one of your friends got "it" first) and the influential person — the person you would ask for advice (the opinion leader) about a specific topic. Every group has a leader — a taste-maker or opinion leader — who influences the decision-making of others in the group. The key is for marketers to convince that person of the value of their products or services. The opinion leader

innovator
The member of a reference group who is most likely to adopt something new (good, service) first.

opinion leader
The member of a reference group who is the information source and who influences the decision-making of others in the group.

Using a celebrity with credibility for a good cause

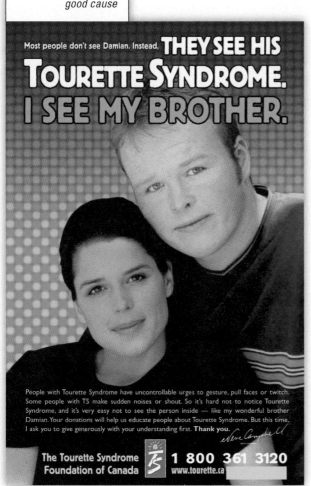

The Tourette Syndrome Foundation of Canada
1 800 361 3120
www.tourette.ca

in one group may be an opinion follower in another. A person who is influential in matters concerning food, because of a special interest or skill in that area, may follow the opinions of another when it comes to buying gardening equipment, software, or home office equipment.

Family and household influence

family

A group of two or more people related by blood, marriage, adoption, or common practice living together in a household.

household

A single person, a family, or any group of unrelated persons who occupy a housing unit.

A **family** is still commonly viewed as a group of two or more people related by blood, marriage, adoption, or common practice, living together in a household. During their lives, most people will belong to at least two families — the one into which they are born and the one they form at marriage. The birth family primarily determines core values and attitudes. The marriage family, in contrast, has a more direct influence on specific purchases. For example, family size is important in the purchase of a car.

A **household** is a broader concept than a family. It consists of a single person, a family, or any group of unrelated persons who occupy a housing unit. Thus, an unmarried homeowner, college students sharing an off-campus apartment, and people who are cohabiting are examples of households.

Since households are not necessarily composed of a couple with children, sensitivity to household structure is important in designing marketing strategy. It affects such dimensions as product type and form (semi-processed or prepared gourmet meals for singles or busy working couples), product size (how large a serving for older couples, how large a refrigerator or microwave oven), and the design of advertising (Who should be depicted in a TV ad: a traditional family or a couple? What kind of couple?).

In addition to the direct, immediate impact households have on the purchasing behaviour of members, it is also interesting to consider the buying behaviour of the household as a unit. Who does the buying for a household? Marketers should treat this question as five separate ones, because each may call for different strategies:

1. Who influences the buying decision?

2. Who makes the buying decision?

3. Who makes the actual purchase?

4. Who uses the product or service?

5. Who follows up on service and performance concerns?

The answers to these questions allow marketers to design marketing programs that take into consideration the nature of the interaction patterns within the household and thereby create effective marketing programs. Different household members may assume these various roles, or one individual may play several roles in a particular purchase. For many years in families of an earlier generation, the stay-at-home female household head did most of the day-to-day buying. However, these days, this behaviour has changed, since such a high proportion of married women are in the workforce and men have assumed more responsibility for household matters. Knowing this allows for more effective development of product features and the targeting of appeals.

Teenagers and young children are important decision-makers in family buying, as well as actual shoppers, than ever before. They could represent a $10 billion-plus market by the year 2005. According to a study by YTV, the more than 2.3 million Canadian 'tweens (who are between being kids and being teenagers) have $1.1 billion in disposable income to spend.[14] This certainly is enough to warrant the attention of many manufacturers. Even very young children influence buying decisions today, because they watch TV advertising and ask for products when they shop with their parents. Children are also making their way onto the

Internet and "window shopping" — there have yet to be reports of them making massive use of parents' credit cards on an unauthorized basis.

The power this market holds is evidenced by recent changes in retail offerings aimed at this group. Ch!ckaboom is a clothing store for girls 5 to 14 years of age. Girls can shop, fiddle with accessories, or hang out in a place all their own. The store's database tracks birthdays, so these customers can receive cards with gift certificates. There are also theme days and activities such as Valentine's Day and Halloween parties. Other retailers have also focused on this segment of young girls who are in control of Mom's credit cards. Le Château and La Senza also have developed product lines and marketing for this segment.[15]

When children aren't influencing the process, purchasing decisions are often made jointly by the male and female partners. Young couples are much more likely to make buying decisions on a joint basis than older couples are. Apparently, the longer a couple lives together, the more they feel they can trust each other's judgement.

Knowing which family member is likely to make the purchase decision will influence a firm's entire marketing mix. If children are the key decision-makers, as is often the case with breakfast cereals, then a manufacturer will produce something that tastes good to children, design the package with them in mind, and advertise on Saturday morning cartoon shows. Even sedate and wholesome products such as milk and yogurt can have added appeal with a packaging makeover. Canada's major dairies have in recent years launched loudly packaged, single-serving milkshakes and flavoured milks, whose cool design, advertising, and convenience aim for strong teen appeal. Yogurt products have had similar makeovers, making them more convenient to carry and even possible to drink from the package, eliminating the need to arm oneself with a spoon. Other strategies to broaden the appeal of yogurt include adding cream or cereal products to reduce the sharp taste and hopefully making it more appealing to younger consumers. Such strategies are employed regardless of who actually makes the purchase and who else (besides the children) in the household might eat cereal or yogurt.

BACKSPACE

1. Which social force has the most direct impact on our individual buying decisions?
2. Consumers from which province consistently exhibit consumption patterns unlike those in the rest of Canada?
3. For the marketer, what is the difference between a family and a household?

Psychological Factors

psychographics
A concept in consumer behaviour that describes consumers in terms of a combination of psychological and sociological influences.

In discussing the psychological component of consumer behaviour, we continue to use the model in Figure 3-1. One or more motives within a person activates goal-oriented behaviour. One such behaviour is perception — the collection and processing of information. Other important psychological activities are learning and attitude formation. We then consider the roles that personality and self-concept play in buying decisions. These psychological variables help to shape a person's lifestyle and values. The term **psychographics** is used in marketing as a synonym for those variables that include lifestyle and values.

Motivation — the starting point

motive
A need sufficiently stimulated that an individual is moved to seek satisfaction.

To understand why consumers behave as they do, we must first ask why a person acts at all. The answer is "Because the individual experiences a need." All behaviour starts with a recognized need. Security, social acceptance, and prestige are examples of needs. Thus, a **motive** is a need sufficiently stimulated to move an individual to seek satisfaction.

A buying decision is often the result of balancing or ordering multiple motives. Moreover, various motives may conflict with one another. In buying a jacket, a young man may want to (1) please himself, (2) please his girlfriend, (3) be considered fashion-savvy among his friends, and (4) strive for value. To accomplish all of these objectives in one purchase is truly a difficult assignment. Also, a person's buying behaviour changes because of changes in income, lifestyle, and other factors. Finally, identical behaviour by several people may result from quite different motives, and different behaviour by the same person at various times may result from the same motive. In our example in the chapter opener, you and your friends all decide that you need new computers, but for different reasons.

Classification of Motives   Psychologists generally agree that motives can be grouped in two broad categories:

- Needs aroused from physiological states of tension (such as the need for sleep).

- Needs aroused from psychological states of tension (such as the need for affection and self-respect).

A refinement of these two categories is Maslow's hierarchy of five levels of needs, arrayed in the order in which people appear to seek to gratify them.[16] Maslow's hierarchy of needs, shown in Figure 3-2, recognizes that a normal person is most likely to be working toward need satisfaction on several levels at the same time and that rarely are all needs on a given level fully satisfied. However, the hierarchy indicates that the majority of needs on a particular level must be reasonably well satisfied before a person is motivated at the next higher level.

In their attempts to market products or communicate with particular segments, marketers often must go beyond a general classification such as Maslow's to understand the specific motives underlying behaviour. For example, to observe that a consumer on a shopping trip may be satisfying physiological and social needs because the person purchases food and talks to friends in the store may be useful, but much more detail is required to identify marketing-specific motives and to measure their strengths.

One proposed model suggests that all behaviour is determined by 15 fundamental motives, and that individual differences are the result of varying priorities and intensities among these motives.[17] These fundamental motives are curiosity, food, honour, rejection, sex, physical exercise, order, independence, power, citizenship, pain avoidance, prestige, family, social contact, and vengeance. Appealing to a relevant motive in marketing efforts will gain the attention of some group of consumers. The curiosity motive is what appears to drive many to surf the Web, not just to see what is out there, but also to gather information on a myriad of topics of interest, as well as for shopping and product comparison information.

Perception

A motive is an aroused need. It, in turn, activates behaviour intended to satisfy the aroused need. One form that behaviour takes is collecting and processing information from the environment, a process known as perception. We constantly receive, organize, and assign meaning to stimuli detected by our five senses. In this way, we interpret or give meaning to the world around us. Perception plays a major role in the alternative-identification stage of the buying-decision process. Our perception of a company or brand generally will guide our behaviour toward it, whether or not we will consider buying it. Perceptions are slow to change and may or may not have a lot to do with reality. In fact, many

Maslow's hierarchy of needs
A needs structure consisting of five levels and organized according to the order in which people seek need gratification.

perception
Collecting and processing information from the environment in order to give meaning to the world around us.

Figure 3-2:

Maslow's Hierarchy of Needs

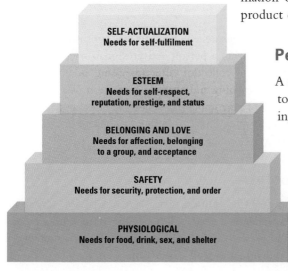

marketers agree that the customer's perception of a company or brand is *more* important than reality in terms of guiding a consumer's decision-making and purchase behaviour.

What we perceive — the meaning that we give something we sense — depends on the object and our experiences. In an instant, the mind is capable of receiving information, comparing it with a huge store of images in memory, and providing an interpretation.

Although important, visual stimuli are just one factor in perception. Consumers make use of all five senses. Scents, for example, are powerful behaviour triggers. Who can resist the aroma of popcorn in a theatre? A recent study of common odours that evoke pleasant childhood memories found that older consumers identified the natural smells of horses, flowers,

MARKETING AT WORK 3-2: RELATIONSHIPS

Classless, Yet Oozing with Class

Bigger is better? Newer is better? Right? So why all the anticipation and attention for the launch of a tiny car that looks just like it did when they stopped selling it in the sixties? Who buys an old new car like the Mini Cooper?

Well, we need to start with a little history, as that seems to be part of the appeal of the Mini. John Cooper began building cars in the 1940s in the United Kingdom and was instrumental in the early development of motor racing in post-war Great Britain. It wasn't until 1961 that the Mini found its way to races at Indianapolis, where it came to be known affectionately as the "funny car" because, according to Americans, the engine was in the "wrong place." Even to this day, the car is still famous, with something of a cult following and "fan" clubs made up of those who own restored models from the halcyon days of the 1960s.

Michael Caine used one to escape the authorities in *The Italian Job*. It was the original econo-car and the first front-mounted, four-cylinder engine mated to front-wheel drive. It also won three Monte Carlo rallies. It's the most ubiquitous of British motorcars. It's the Mini! And German-based BMW (now the owner of the nameplate) put it back on the streets in 2002. The Mini and Michael Caine are both in the movies again, with Michael as Austin Powers' father in *Austin Powers in Goldmember*.

Oh, it's a little bigger and a lot more streamlined, but it can't be mistaken for anything other than a Mini. Those cute little headlights peering out from each side of that familiar grille, that truncated rear roof line, and the wheels at the four corners of the body. Yep, that's it all right! Oh, there are some changes, of course. It comes with up to 163 HP available, leather, and CD, and oh, yeah, a price tag of about $30,000.

Colour selections allow a great deal of customization, as body and roof have different options and possible combinations. It comes with lots of chrome and a go-cart look, and thanks to the corner wheel locations, it certainly is loaded with retro appeal. But can you still call the appeal retro when the consumers buying the car aren't old enough to remember it from its first pass around? The aging population with disposable income is part of what is driving the renaissance of retro designs (including the Beetle, Thunderbird, and PT Cruiser), but

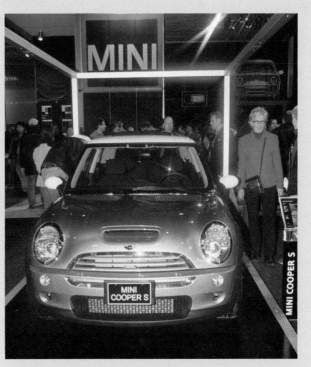

MINI COOPER S

increased attention to the growing force of women and young car buyers is contributing to the momentum. And there is momentum — the company had to increase production in its first year, as sales of the Mini were 15 to 20 percent higher than anticipated.

How do we know who the primary targets are for this retro product? Fashionable launch parties were held in Montréal, Toronto, and Vancouver, with food, dancing, and live DJ music. And, of course, lots of Minis were interspersed among the party-goers, who danced and cavorted late into the night. Guests were mostly twenty- and thirty-something urbanites and singles.

SOURCE: Adapted from www.edmunds.com; cairns.mistral.co.uk; "New-Look Mini Cruises Past Sales Target," *Financial Post*, Reuters, p. FP13, May 17, 2002; and Deidre McMurdy, "The Car Buyer's Clout," *Maclean's*, March 19, 2001, p. 37.

selective attention
The process that limits our perceptions so that, of all of the marketing stimuli to which our senses are exposed, only those able to capture and hold our attention have the potential of being perceived.

selective distortion
The process of mentally altering information that is inconsistent with one's beliefs or attitudes.

selective retention
The process of retaining in memory some portion of what is perceived.

and hay. However, younger ones associated pleasant recollections with the scent of Play-Doh and even jet fuel! Marketers are using this type of information to associate odours with products and shopping environments to create positive perceptions.

Every day, we come into contact with an enormous number of marketing stimuli. However, a process of selectivity limits our perceptions. As an illustration, consider that:

● We pay attention by exception. That is, of all of the marketing stimuli to which our senses are exposed, only those with the power to capture and hold our attention have the potential of being perceived. This phenomenon is called **selective attention**.

● We may alter information that is inconsistent with our beliefs and attitudes. Thus, someone may say, "Despite the evidence, I don't believe smoking will be hazardous to my health." This is **selective distortion**.

● We retain only part of what we have selectively perceived. We may read an ad but later forget it. This is known as **selective retention**.

There are many communications implications in this selectivity process. For example, if an ad is too familiar, it will be ignored. On the other hand, if it is too complex, the ad will be judged not worth the time and effort to understand it. A useful communications approach is to create a mildly ambiguous first impression that heightens the consumer's interest.

Selective distortion operates so that we cannot assume that a message, even if it is factually correct, will necessarily be accepted as fact by consumers. In designing a message, the distance between the audience's current belief and the position proposed by the message must be considered. If the distance is large, a moderate claim may be more believable than a dramatic claim and therefore more effective in moving consumers in the desired direction.

Even messages received undistorted are still subject to selective retention. Consequently, ads are repeated many times. The hope is that numerous exposures will etch the message into the recipient's memory. This partially explains why a firm with very familiar products, such as Wrigley's, spends more than $100 million a year in Canada and the United States to reinforce its brand name. In order to have something to say in its ads about its over 100-year-old Juicy Fruit gum, the company in 2002 redesigned the packaging and shape of the gum pieces to look more like newer brands, and informed consumers of the changes in television ads that poked fun at the brand's own theme song for which it had been so well known. Such practices are intended to create ease of recall and top-of-mind awareness. It is hoped that the particular brand will be the first brand remembered when buying gum occurs to the consumer. Today, Juicy Fruit remains the number-one selling gum in the United States.

learning
Changes in behaviour resulting from previous experiences.

stimulus-response theory
The theory that learning occurs as a person responds to some stimulus and is rewarded with need satisfaction for a correct response or penalized for an incorrect one

Learning

Learning can be defined as changes in behaviour resulting from previous experiences. It excludes behaviour that is attributable to instinct, such as breathing, and temporary states, such as hunger or fatigue. The ability to interpret and predict the consumer's learning process enhances our understanding of buying behaviour, since learning plays a role at every stage of the buying-decision process. The recognition of brand satisfaction and the subsequent development of functional and emotional relationships with the brand are the results of learning from consumer experience. Customers learn about companies and brands in part from prior experience: their own and that of others. In the chapter opener, your leaning toward buying another Dell computer is a good example of learning at work. No simple learning theory has emerged as universally workable and acceptable. However, the one with the most direct application to marketing strategy is the stimulus-response theory.[18]

According to **stimulus-response theory**, learning occurs as a person (1) responds to some stimulus and (2) is rewarded with need satisfaction for a correct response or penalized for an incorrect one. When the same correct response is repeated in reaction to the same stimulus, a behaviour pattern or learning is established. Learning is at the root of building positive customer relationships. As the customer learns to expect positive results and treatment from the company or brand, that person will go back and buy again and again.

Once an habitual behaviour pattern has been established, it replaces conscious, wilful behaviour to search for alternatives. This is the same as saying that a consumer, having been satisfied or more than satisfied, develops and continues a relationship with the brand or the seller or both over repeated purchases. The task for a competitor is to find a way to arouse need in a different way or, once need has been aroused, to break into the process and cause the consumer to pay attention to competing information. This would be most easily done when a relationship is weak or is functionally based. It would be more difficult when a strong emotional relationship exists.

Marketers have taught consumers to respond to certain cues:

- End-of-aisle displays and Day-Glo price stickers in supermarkets suggest that an item is on sale.
- Sale signs in store windows suggest that bargains can be found inside.
- Large type in newspaper grocery ads suggests that featured items are particularly good bargains.

But the sad fact for marketers is that what is learned can be unlearned, and effective competitors search the decision-making process and the detail of each stage to find ways of disrupting habitual learned behaviour. Of course, the consumer adds to a marketer's frustration by seeking variety, by being short of time or money and thus prepared to behave differently, or by facing an empty store shelf where a favourite brand should be.

Personality

personality

An individual's pattern of traits that influences behavioural responses.

The study of human **personality** has given rise to many, sometimes widely divergent, schools of psychological thought. As a result, attempts to inventory and classify personality traits have produced a variety of different structures. In this discussion, personality is defined broadly as an individual's pattern of traits that influence behavioural responses. We speak of people as being self-confident, aggressive, shy, domineering, dynamic, secure, introverted, flexible, or friendly, and as being influenced (but not controlled) by these personality traits in their responses to situations.

It is generally agreed that personality traits do influence consumers' perceptions and buying behaviour. However, there is considerable disagreement about the nature of this relationship, that is, about how personality influences behaviour. Although we know that people's personalities often are reflected in the clothes they wear, the cars they drive (or whether they use a bike or motorcycle instead of a car), and the restaurants they patronize, we have not been successful in predicting behaviour from particular personality traits. The reason is simple: Many factors besides personality enter into the consumer buying-decision process.

self-concept

A person's self-image.

Self-Concept   Your **self-concept**, or self-image, is the way you see yourself. At the same time, it is the picture you think others have of you. Social psychologists distinguish between (1) the actual self-concept (the way you really see yourself) and (2) the ideal self-concept (the way you want to be seen or would like to see yourself). To some extent, the self-concept theory is a reflection of other psychological and sociological dimensions already discussed. A person's self-concept is influenced, for instance, by innate and learned physiological and psychological needs. It is conditioned also by economic factors, demographic factors, and social group influences.

We know that people generally prefer brands and products that are compatible with their self-concept. Your friend in the chapter opener is seriously considering purchasing an iMac computer, which seems to fit with her self-image. The compatibility is what allows brand relationships to develop, and the greater it is, the more emotional the relationship. There are

actual self-concept

The way you really see yourself, as distinguished from *ideal self-concept*.

ideal self-concept

The way you want to be seen or would like to see yourself, as distinguished from *actual self-concept*.

mixed reports concerning the degree of influence of the actual as opposed to the ideal self-concept on brand and product preferences. Some researchers contend that consumption preferences correspond to a person's **actual self-concept**. Others hold that the **ideal self-concept** is dominant in consumers' choices.

Perhaps there is no consensus here, because in real life we often switch back and forth between our actual and our ideal self-concepts. A middle-aged man may buy some comfortable but not fashionable clothing to wear at home on a weekend, reflecting his actual self-concept. Then, later, he buys some expensive, high-fashion exercise clothing, envisioning himself (ideal self-concept) as a young, active, upwardly mobile guy. This same fellow may drive his old, beat-up minivan for his weekend errands (actual self-concept), but he'll drive his new, European sports sedan to work, where he wants to project a different (ideal) self-concept. Self-concept theory argues that individuals express themselves in the artifacts that they acquire, or would like to acquire, thus representing personality by the kinds of things they own and use. While this show-me-what-you-have-and-I'll tell-you-what-you-are notion is appealing and we can easily think of examples of people we know who would seem to fit this abstraction, this is but one force acting on consumers in their purchase decisions.[19]

The various self-concept frames of reference can be used to design marketing research projects as well as help to organize approaches to interviewing consumers and analyzing research results. The actual self-concept and/or ideal self-concept frames of reference can be used in advertisements as a before-and-after approach, as well as by sales and service personnel in determining customer problems, needs, and aspirations.

Attitudes

attitude

A learned predisposition to respond to an object or class of objects in a consistently favourable or unfavourable way.

Attitude is traditionally defined as a learned predisposition to respond to an object or class of objects in a consistently favourable or unfavourable way. In our model of the buying-decision process, attitudes play a major role in the evaluation of alternatives. Numerous studies have reported a relationship between consumers' attitudes and their buying behaviour regarding both types of products and services selected and brands chosen. Surely, then, it is in a marketer's best interest to understand how attitudes are formed, the functions they perform, and how they can be changed.

Attitudes are also critically important in the formation of customer relationships. Since relationships are based to a very great extent on how customers feel toward a company or brand, their attitudes represent an important component of those feelings. They represent the deeply held views and opinions that customers have toward the companies and brands that they encounter in the marketplace.

All attitudes have the following characteristics in common:

salon.com

- *Attitudes are learned.* The information individuals acquire through their direct experiences with a product or an idea, indirect experiences (such as reading about a product in *Wallpaper** magazine or at **www.salon.com** on the Internet), and interactions with individuals in their social groups all contribute to the formation of attitudes. For example, the opinions expressed by a good friend about diet foods, plus the consumer's favourable or unfavourable experience as a result of using diet foods, will contribute to an attitude toward diet foods in general.

- *Attitudes have an object.* By definition, we can hold attitudes only toward something. The object can be general (professional sports) or specific (Toronto Raptors); it can be abstract (college life) or concrete (the computer lab). In attempting to determine consumers' attitudes, it is very important to define carefully the object of the attitude, because a person might have a favourable attitude toward the general concept (exercise) but a negative attitude toward a specific dimension (running).

- *Attitudes have direction and intensity.* Our attitudes are either favourable or unfavourable toward an object. They cannot be neutral. In addition, they have strength. For example, you may mildly like this textbook or you may like it very much (we hope!). This factor is important for marketers, because strongly held positive attitudes are the foundation of strong emotional relationships and are difficult to change.

- *Attitudes are arranged in structures that tend to be stable and generalizable.* Once formed, attitudes usually endure, and the longer they are held, the more resistant to change they become. People also have a tendency to generalize attitudes. For instance, if a person is treated well by a salesperson in a particular store, there is a tendency to form a favourable attitude toward the entire store and develop a relationship with it.

A consumer's attitudes do not always predict purchase behaviour. A person may hold very favourable attitudes toward a brand but not buy it because of some inhibiting factor. Typical inhibitors are not having enough money or discovering that your preferred brand has been replaced by a new model or is out of stock when the purchase must be made. Under such circumstances, purchase behaviour may even contradict attitudes.

As the preceding discussion suggests, it is extremely difficult to change strongly held attitudes. Moderately held or weakly held attitudes are much more amenable to change. Marketers need to know what consumer attitudes are to many aspects of their products, services, personnel, and advertisements, as well as the strength of such attitudes. Only then can they determine the bases for either satisfaction or dissatisfaction and where their relationships with consumers are vulnerable. When a company is faced with strongly held negative or unfavourable attitudes, it has two options. The first is to try to change the attitude to be compatible with the product. The second is to change the product, or more likely its image, to match attitudes. Ordinarily, it is much easier to change the product image than to change consumers' strongly held attitudes.

Nevertheless, in many situations, attitudes have been changed. Consider how negative attitudes have changed in favour of trucks and sports utility vehicles, how positive attitudes have changed about tobacco products, and how yellow tennis balls and off-season vacations have been accepted.

Values and lifestyles

lifestyle
A person's activities, interests, and opinions.

One of the most valuable ways of looking at a market and its potential involves consideration of consumer values and lifestyles. Marketers develop programs based not only on how old their customers are or where they live, but also on how they spend their leisure time, what type of movies they like to watch, and what things they consider to be important in their lives — what they hold near and dear. This is an integral part of the concept of market segmentation, which will be discussed in Chapter 4. Essentially, the Canadian market is made up of many types of people. Once we can identify how these various groups think and live, we can do a better job of developing products, services, advertising, and other marketing techniques to appeal to them.

The field of psychographic research was developed through the study of thousands of consumers by measuring their opinions, interests, attitudes, values, beliefs, and activities in a variety of different areas. Today, psychographic research is considered by many in marketing to have transcended the demographic categories of age, gender, religion, social class, and ethnicity. Michael Adams, president of Environics Research Ltd., has produced the social-value "tribes" of Canada (see the box on the next two pages), which presents the three major generational divisions that exist in Canada: the Elders, the Boomers, and the GenXers. Everyone in the country fits into one of these three on the basis of age alone.

Each of these generational groups is further subdivided pyschographically, resulting in thumbnail sketches for defined social-value tribes of Canada. Each sketch provides a quick review of the group size, age distribution, geographic location, common motivation factors, social values, catchphrases, and, finally, heroes or icons. Locate yourself, your parents, friends,

The Social Value "Tribes" of Canada

In the book *Sex in the Snow*, author and pollster Michael Adams proposes that Canadians can be segmented into a number of social-value tribes. Initially, Adams divides the Canadian population into three sections: Elders, Boomers, and GenXers. Each of these three categories can be further divided by distinguishing the fundamental motivators, key values, words of advice, and icons of each of the defined groups. Take a look at the categories below to determine where you fall in Michael Adams' social tribes.

The Elders (aged 50+)

Rational Traditionalists
(54 percent of Elders)
Financial independence, stability, and security are the fundamental motivators of this population group. Some of their key values include primacy of reason, deferred gratification, duty, and guilt. A rational traditionalist could be heard saying, "Better safe than sorry," "A woman's place is in the home," or "A bird in the hand is worth two in the bush." These Canadians would idolize individuals such as Sir Winston Churchill, fifties TV character Ward Cleaver, and Franklin D. Roosevelt.

Extroverted Traditionalists
(26 percent of Elders)
This category includes a higher–than-average proportion of women and individuals from the Maritimes and Québec. Their fundamental motivators include social status, institutions, and traditional communities. Religion, family, fear, and respect for tradition and institutions are highly valued, and words of wisdom would include epitaphs such as "Duty above all else" "A woman's work is never done," and "A penny saved is a penny earned." Icons of the Extroverted Traditionalists would include Mother Teresa and Jesus Christ.

Cosmopolitan Modernists
(20 percent of Elders)
The category of Cosmopolitan Modernists includes a higher-than-average proportion of individuals who are from British Columbia, are over 50, and have post-secondary education. Traditional institutions and experience-seeking are the fundamental motivators of this group, and they place high value on things such as education, innovation, and a global perspective. Cosmopolitan Modernists believe that people should "take time to smell the roses" and that "the world is their oyster." Icons of this group include author Pierre Berton and former Prime Minister Pierre Trudeau.

The Boomers (aged 30–49)

Autonomous Rebels
(25 percent of Boomers)
This category of Boomers has fundamental motivators that include personal autonomy and self-fulfilment. They place a high value on freedom and individuality and are sceptical about traditional institutions. Words of advice from an individual in the Autonomous Rebel category could be "To each his own," "Knowledge is power," or "I did it my way." Icons include Bill and Hillary Clinton, John Lennon, and Scully and Mulder from *The X-Files*.

Anxious Communicators
(20 percent of Boomers)
Traditional communities, institutions, and social status are considered to be the fundamental motivators of this social tribe. They value family, community, respect, and fear. The Anxious Communicators believe that "wisdom comes with age" and "children are our future." The icons of this category would include individuals such as Oprah Winfrey and Ann Landers.

Disengaged Darwinists
(41 percent of Boomers)
This is the largest group within the Boomers category. It includes a higher proportion of men and blue-collar workers who are motivated by financial independence, stability, and security. Key values of the Disengaged Darwinists are fear and nostalgia for the past. Advice from this group would include "Look out for number one" and "Every man for himself." Icons include Chuck Norris and David Frum.

GenXers (aged 15–29)

Aimless Dependants
(27 percent of GenXers)
These GenXers crave the financial independence, security, and stability that their parents, members of the Boomers, possessed. Their key values include a desire for independence and fear. Words of wisdom from this group would include "What's the point," "I couldn't care less," and "What's the system going to do for me?" The icons for this group include Eric Lindros, Courtney Love, and the Smashing Pumpkins.

Thrill-Seeking Materialists
(25 percent of GenXers)
The fundamental motivators of Thrill-Seeking Materialists include traditional communities, social status, and experience-seeking. Their key values include the desire for

The Social Value "Tribes" of Canada continued

money, material possessions, respect, and admiration. Words of advice from this group would be "Live dangerously" and "Money is power." Icons of the Thrill-Seeking Materialists are Pamela Anderson and Calvin Klein.

New Aquarians
(13 percent of GenXers)
This group is characterized by its desire for new experiences and new communities. They believe in hedonism, ecologism, and egalitarianism. Advice from the New Aquarians could include "There is no being, only becoming" and "Unity is diversity." Their icons include Tori Amos, Sarah McLachlan, and William Gibson.

Autonomous Post-Materialists
(20 percent of GenXers)
The fundamental motivators of this group of GenXers are personal autonomy and self-fulfilment, and their key values

include freedom and respect for human rights. In the mind of an Autonomous Post-Materialist, words to live by would include "It's my life," "Image is nothing," and "There is more to life than money." Icons of this group include Dennis Rodman, Bart Simpson, and Ashley MacIsaac.

Social Hedonists
(15 percent of GenXers)
This group of GenXers seeks new experiences and new communications. They value immediate gratification, sexual permissiveness, and hedonism. They advise people "Party hard," "If you look good you feel good," and "Don't worry, be happy." The icons of this group include Janet Jackson and Chris Shepard.

Source: Adapted from Michael Adams, "The Demise of Demography," *The Globe and Mail*, January 18, 1997, p. D5, and based on *Sex in the Snow: Canadian Social Values at the End of the Millennium* (Toronto: Penguin Canada, 1997).

employers, or potential employers in these groups. The social-value tribes classification provides marketers with a quick, comprehensive, and integrated multivariate view of the basic segmentation of the country. This kind of information signals who is interested in what kinds of products and services, their location, their preferred information themes, their orientations to product claims, and the kinds of events they would likely attend.

Situational Influences

You know that you and your friends act differently in a classroom from the way you act in your favourite coffee shop. The same holds true of buying behaviour. You might get a haircut because of an upcoming job interview when you would not get one otherwise. On vacation, you might buy a souvenir that seems very strange when you get home. For a close friend's wedding gift, you might buy a more prestigious brand of small appliance than you would buy for yourself. These are all examples of how temporary forces associated with the immediate purchase environment affect behaviour. Situational influence tends to be less significant when the consumer has a strong relationship with a brand and when the consumer is highly involved in the purchase. However, it often plays a major role in buying decisions. The five categories of situational influences and their effects are explained next.

situational influences

Temporary forces, associated with the immediate purchase environment, that affect behaviour.

Time effects — when consumers buy

Marketers should be able to answer at least two time-related questions about consumer buying: Is it influenced by the season, week, day, or hour? What impact do past and present events have on the purchase decision?

The time dimension of buying has implications for promotion scheduling. Promotional messages must reach consumers when they are in a decision-making frame of mind. Marketers also adjust prices in an attempt to even out demand. For instance, supermarkets may offer double coupons on Wednesdays, usually a slow business day. If seasonal buying patterns exist, marketers can sometimes extend the buying season. There is obviously (or so

Less time at home means more time in family restaurants.

you'd think) little opportunity to extend the buying season for Easter bunnies or Christmas ornaments, although some "Christmas" stores operate year round. Even the traditional season for vacations has been shifted to such an extent that winter and other "off-season" or "shoulder-season" vacations are now quite popular.

The second question concerns the impact of past or future events. For example, the length of time since you last went out to dinner at a nice restaurant may influence a decision on where to go tonight. Or the significance of an upcoming event, such as a vacation trip to a resort area, could result in a greater than normal level of clothing purchases. Marketers need to know enough about the targeted consumers to anticipate the effects of these past and future events.

Dual-income Baby Boomers are finding it difficult to make time in their busy schedules to prepare meals at home, yet they can afford to take the family out to eat at a restaurant that offers something more in terms of quality than do the mainstream fast-food outlets such as McDonald's, Burger King, and Harvey's. Rather than standing in long lines for burgers and fries, these families head for restaurants that offer a wider menu selection, table service, and a family atmosphere. There has been considerable growth in the sector of the restaurant business labelled "family restaurants," which include Swiss Chalet, White Spot, and Golden Griddle, and in the slightly more pricey casual-dining sector, where we find East Side Mario's, Jack Astor's, and such regional chains as Milestone's.[20]

The growth and popularity of fast-food restaurants, quick-oil-change outlets, highly specialized Web sites, and catalogue retailers are marketers' responses to consumers' time pressures. Dual-income households, job activity (including business trips and travel to and from work), and mandatory leisure-time activities (such as carpooling children to social and sports events) leave little time for relaxed shopping. The results are measurable. In 1988, the average consumer spent 90 minutes on a mall shopping trip. Today, this figure has fallen below 65 minutes. Some photo-processing operations return developed prints by mail or e-mail, or send them to their customer's Web site to save time and effort. Internet-based marketers are open for business 24 hours a day. Whether purchases are of the pure "click" or "click and brick" variety, time of buying can and is being changed.

Where consumers buy — the physical and social surroundings

Physical surroundings are the features of a situation that are apparent to the senses, such as lighting, smells, weather, and sounds. Music can be an important element in a store's strategy. Colours, smells, and sounds can all be engineered to control consumers' retail experience and attempt to influence their behaviour.

The social surroundings are the number, mix, and actions of other people at the purchase site. You probably would not go into a strange restaurant that has an empty parking lot. And in a crowded store with other customers waiting, you probably ask the clerk fewer questions and spend less time comparing products.

Surroundings also impact experiences on the Internet. The ease with which product information can be obtained and orders can be placed in the virtual surroundings will decide if a site will be considered for future purchases. The Internet also places greater control in consumers' hands. Wherever the purchase is made, consumers can now arm themselves with huge quantities of technical and pricing information that allows greater leverage when making unfamiliar and/or large purchases. This knowledge combined with information regarding actual and virtual locations to buy a product helps to prevent a consumer from being taken advantage of, or simply making uninformed purchasing decisions.

How consumers buy — the terms and conditions of the purchase

How consumers buy refers to the terms and conditions of sale as well as the transaction-related activities that buyers are willing to perform. Many more retailers sell on credit today than just a few years ago. Not only do consumers use credit for instalment purchases (to buy things today with future income), but many now use credit for convenience. The ability to use VISA or MasterCard or debit cards to make a wide variety of purchases while not carrying cash is an attractive option to many consumers. The growth of catalogue distribution, telephone and mail order, and e-commerce has enabled consumers to buy everything from food to a new house without setting foot outside the door.

Finally, with the increasing pressures on our time, the trend toward one-stop shopping has encouraged traditional retailers to add unrelated items to their basic mix of products. Consider, for example, the wide variety of goods found in what we call a drugstore. Many Shoppers Drug Mart locations, for example, carry household cleaning supplies and grocery items and have postal outlets. Gas bars have added convenience foods and sundries. E-tailers attempt to design and develop Web sites that carry more and more items. Amazon.com continues to experiment with adding new product lines to what was originally a "books only" Internet site.

Conditions under which consumers buy — states and moods

Sometimes consumers are in a temporary state that influences their buying decisions. When you are ill or rushed, you may be unwilling to wait in line or to take the time or care that a particular purchase deserves. Your expectations and decision-making are different when you want to grab a quick lunch with a business associate than they are when you go out for dinner with family or friends to celebrate a special occasion. Moods can also influence purchases. Feelings such as anger or excitement can result in purchases that otherwise would not have been made. In the exciting atmosphere of a rock concert, for example, you might pay more for a commemorative T-shirt than you would under normal circumstances. Salespeople must be trained to recognize consumers' moods and adjust their presentations accordingly.

Marketers must also monitor long-term situational influences. The optimistic consumers of the 1980s were free-spending and apparently carefree. Household debt grew 50 percent faster than disposable income during the decade, as the Baby Boom generation acquired cars, homes, and household possessions. However, the recession that rocked the economy at the end of the 1980s produced many changes. It created more conservative buyers who save more, avoid debt, and purchase more carefully. As we moved into the twenty-first century, consumers of all ages were more sophisticated and demanding than in any previous times. More education and access to information are largely responsible for these changes, along with lessons from the past. Although it is difficult to predict if changes such as these in consumer psychology are temporary or permanent, they have important implications for virtually all marketers.

What about the impact of catastrophic events such as 9/11? Suddenly all of the United States felt like a target. Airlines, hotels, and other travel- and tourist-related services immediately felt a tremendous impact. People were afraid to travel: Would they ever feel safe again? Would people refrain from using public transportation unless absolutely required? People became afraid to spend on large purchases because of the uncertainty of what would happen next. The impact was felt far beyond New York — it swept around the world for a period of time. If it wasn't for the confidence-building programs spearheaded by the United States and other governments, there could have been a devastating recession.

When a particular situational influence becomes widely accepted and strongly embedded (such as shopping on particular days of the week), overcoming it can be difficult. The marketer may have to carry out an extensive campaign with no guarantee of success.

BACKSPACE

1. What is selective distortion?
2. What are the four common characteristics of attitudes?
3. What three major generational divisions exist in Canada?

MARKETING AT WORK 3:3: STRATEGY

Cocooning Boosts Retail

One outcome of the 9/11 terrorist attacks and the events associated with them that has affected the retail world is what is referred to as "cocooning." The response to the attacks and the prevailing concerns across North America that these would not be isolated incidents seems to have resulted in many consumers seeking comfort and security at home. What does this have to do with retail sales? Marketing? Consumer behaviour? A great deal!

No longer can we afford the smug self-assuredness that life in peaceful, prosperous North America seemed to have engendered. The unspoken promise of a safe, comfortable world has been shattered.

The idea of consumers cocooning actually began prior to these events, with trends such as the increase in the number of people working from home. Such changes in lifestyle affect how we behave as consumers — what we do, think, and buy. The events of 9/11 seemed to reinforce this trend, as people became more likely to spend more time in their own homes — and therefore to pay increased attention to them.

On the retail level, this led to a significant boost in the sales of home goods. Coupled with the lowering of interest rates to help restimulate the economy, this also helped the sales of high-ticket items. This effect was still felt strongly a year later as, in the summer of 2002, the Hudson's Bay Company announced plans to open 17 new stores under its Home Outfitters banner. Winners also made plans to open four or five more of its HomeSense stores in Canada.

The impact spread beyond the decision to spend more time at home — it also influenced many holiday decisions, as more and more North Americans became "rubber-tire travellers" opting to spend more time on the road with the family and enjoying more local holidays. For example, Albertans have traditionally had something of a love-hate relationship with their national parks — these had become more of a destination for overseas tourists, as that was who usually dominated the areas at peak times. Following the events of 9/11, the Banff Springs Hotel alone received 2,700 cancellations. The response was an aggressive local marketing campaign, which was eagerly received by Albertans with the same concerns about travelling, considering the prevailing mood. Many Albertans decided to stay home during 2002 and avail themselves of their local hospitality.

SOURCE: Adapted from Norma Ramage, "Lassoing the Locals," *Marketing Magazine*, April 29, 2002, p. 8.; Jason MacDonald, "The End of Irony," *Marketing Magazine*, September 24, 2001, p 8.

Summary

The buying behaviour of ultimate consumers can be examined by using a five-part model: the buying-decision process, information, social and group forces, psychological forces, and situational factors.

The buying-decision process is composed of six stages through which consumers go in making purchases. The stages are need recognition, choice of an involvement level, identification of alternatives, evaluation of alternatives, purchase and related decisions, and post-purchase consumer experience behaviour.

Information fuels the buying-decision process. Without it, there would be no decisions. There are two categories of information sources: commercial and social. Commercial sources include advertising, personal selling, selling by telephone or the Internet, and personal involvement with a product. Word of mouth, observation, and experience with a product owned by someone else are social sources.

Social and group forces consist of cultures, subcultures, reference groups, families, and households. Culture has the broadest and most general influence on buying behaviour, while a person's household has the most immediate impact. Social and group forces have a direct impact on individual purchase decisions, as well as a person's psychological make-up.

Psychological forces that affect buying decisions are motivation, perception, learning, personality, and attitudes. All behaviour is motivated by some aroused need. Perception is the way we interpret the world around us and is subject to three types of selectivity: attention, distortion, and retention. Learning is a change in behaviour as a result of experience. Continued reinforcement leads to habitual buying and brand loyalty.

Personality is the sum of an individual's traits that influence behavioural responses. Personality patterns predispose consumers to certain types of information, product features, and interactions. The self-concept is related to personality. Because purchasing and consumption are very expressive actions, they communicate to the world our actual and ideal self-concepts.

Attitudes are learned predispositions to respond to an object or class of objects in a consistent fashion. Besides being learned, all attitudes are directed toward an object, have direction and intensity, and tend to be stable and generalizable. Strongly held attitudes are difficult to change.

Situational influences deal with when, where, how, and why consumers buy, and with the consumer's personal condition at the time of purchase. Situational influences are often so powerful that they can override all of the other forces in the buying-decision process.

Key Terms and Concepts

actual self-concept 82
attitude 82
buying-decision process 62
cognitive dissonance 68
commercial information environment 69
culture 70
family 76
high-involvement level 64
household 76
ideal self-concept 82
impulse buying 65
innovator 75
learning 80
lifestyle 83
low-involvement level 64
Maslow's hierarchy of needs 78

motive 77
opinion leader 75
patronage motives 67
perception 78
personality 81
post-purchase behaviour 68
psychographics 77
reference group 74
selective attention 80
selective distortion 80
selective retention 80
self-concept 81
situational influences 85
social information environment 70
stimulus-response theory 80
subculture 71

Questions and Problems

1. When might the purchase of a laptop computer be a low-involvement decision?

2. When a consumer's experience with a product equals the consumer's expectations for the product, the person is satisfied. Is there any disadvantage for a marketer whose product causes the consumer's experience to greatly exceed expectations?

3. From a consumer-behaviour perspective, why is it incorrect to view the European Union or the countries of Asia as single markets?

4. Explain how your family or household might influence your choice of a product or brand for the following items:
   a. Toothpaste.
   b. Auto tune-up.
   c. Haircut.
   d. Breakfast cereal.

5. How would a soft drink company market its product to the Québécois market? How would the company's marketing activities differ in Québec, compared with the rest of Canada?

6. Explain how self-concept might come into play in the purchase of the following products:
   a. Eyeglasses.
   b. New suit.
   c. Perfume or cologne.
   d. College or university education.

7. List three products or services for which usage would not be greatly affected by cultural or ethnic differences. List three that would be affected by such differences. Explain how.

8. How could you assess your product for its appeal to different cultures or subcultures in or outside of your own country? In other words, how do you find a market for your product?

Hands-On Marketing

1. Interview the manager of a store that sells big-ticket items (furniture, appliances, electronic equipment) about what methods, if any, the store uses to reinforce purchase decisions and reduce the cognitive dissonance of its customers. What additional methods can you suggest?

2. Have a friend describe a high-involvement purchase that he or she recently made. Show how each of the six stages described in this chapter are reflected in the description. Identify the primary social influences that played a part in the decision.

Back to the Top

Think about the decisions that you and your friends are about to make in selecting new computers and apply some of the concepts covered in this chapter, so that you can better explain what is going on. What are your motives in buying new computers? What evidence is there that motives are at work? Is there any evidence of reference group influence? What information sources are being used? Where is there evidence of learning having occurred? What are the implications of all of this for marketers in the computer business?

Want to get better grades, tips on how to study more effectively, and up-to-date information on happenings in the world of marketing? Then, visit the Online Learning Centre for practice tests, Study Smart software, and much more! **www.mcgrawhill.ca/college/sommers**

Interested in finding out what marketing looks like in the real world? *Marketing Magazine* is just a click away on your Online Learning Centre!

Case 1-1

Modrobes
Resisting the Mainstream

Steve "Sal" Debus, the creative mind behind Modrobes Saldebus Lounge Clothing Inc., is faced with a dilemma that's not uncommon for successful entrepreneurs. Modrobes is growing fast, but Debus is not sure what direction the company should take. Of greater concern is how to stay cool with its target market as the brand becomes more popular. The problem is that if Modrobes becomes too mainstream, the company will lose touch with its target customers, 14- to 25-year-olds who look for street wear and rave clothing that is out of the ordinary. But, the more popular Modrobes becomes, the more clothes it will sell and the more money it will make. If the company's goal, however, is to stay connected to its main clientele, it will have to consider its marketing goals very carefully.

Modrobes has always understood its target market. In fact, owner Debus shares characteristics with his customers. He is young, charismatic, and like other members of his generation, he believes comfort is as important as design in clothing. He was still in university when he came up with the Modrobes idea. Basically, he was tired of getting a sore butt when he had to sit through exams for hours, so he came up with the exam pant — a lightweight, extremely comfortable utility pant. Since then, Modrobes has continued to put out tops and bottoms that are both functional and comfortable.

Debus began marketing his pants in 1996 by setting up tables at universities and using the pitch "If these aren't the most comfortable pair of pants you've had in your life, return them and I'll give you your money back." Debus has resisted the pressure to use traditional advertising and, instead, relies mostly on word of mouth. He wants to speak directly to the customer by, for example, distributing stickers that young customers can put on their skateboards or snowboards. Despite its success, Modrobes has stuck to its roots. The company still does university tours and continues to show up at events such as Edgefest, where its target market can be found in droves.

Today, the company continues to grow and spread its message. Visitors to its Web site enter the world of "post-modern functional sportswear clothing," aka Modrobes. White letters glide onto the black screen, transmitting to viewers what the company and its clothing are all about. "I want you in my pants" is followed by "Saving the world one crotch at a time," and, finally, "Technology for your ass." Modrobes sells clothing, hats, and accessories online in addition to having stores in Toronto, Vancouver, Cookstown, Windsor, and London, Ontario. The company has also hooked up with an online distributor of cool, non-mainstream, rave clothing, Radical Planet.

So far, Moderobes has managed to resist becoming ordinary. But as its clothing becomes more widespread, will Modrobes be pushed into the mainstream?

Pertinent Web Sites
www.modrobes.com
www.radicalplanet.com

Questions
1. What has Modrobes done to appeal to its target market?
2. Can the company continue to grow and still remain cool with its current customers?

Case 1-2

Aveda
A Way of Life

Jessica loves everything about Aveda products — the way they smell, the fact that they are all-natural, even the philosophy behind the brand. She couldn't imagine using anything else on her skin or hair. Products that aren't natural make her feel dirty. Aveda, on the other hand, always makes her feel healthy and clean.

Every morning, Jessica starts her usual morning routine. She works out with an exercise video, takes a shower, and eats her breakfast of fresh fruit and low-fat yogurt. Once she's dressed, she moisturizes her face with her favourite Aveda hydrating lotion and applies her Aveda foundation, eyeshadow, and lipstick, as she has done for the past six years.

Jessica was first introduced to Aveda beauty products when she was in her first year of university. Her roommate Elaine led a very healthy lifestyle, exercising regularly, eating only natural foods, and meditating. Elaine wouldn't use anything but Aveda products. That was the first time Jessica had ever heard of Aveda's all-natural line. Later, Jessica switched hair salons and her new stylist used Aveda products on her hair. When Jessica learned that the hairstylist had completed a course on Aveda's products and philosophy, she was impressed. She had finally found a product that fit nicely with her own approach to health and wellness.

Jessica, now in the first year of a Master of Science degree, is studying nutrition, which she has always found fascinating. This is not surprising, given her passion for healthy living. That's why Aveda appeals so much to her. To Jessica, Aveda is more than a line of beauty and hair products — it's a way of life. She often refers to her book on Aveda, entitled *Aveda Rituals: A Practical and Inspiring Guide to Holistic Beauty and Well-Being By the Visionary Founder of Aveda*. The book talks about the Aveda philosophy — that a healthy lifestyle is key to healing, preventing illness, and overall well-being. The book also discusses healthy eating, exercise, and stress management. Jessica has followed these principles as closely as she can, and it makes her feel good about herself. In fact, she can't imagine her life without Aveda. And while she knows that many of her friends find the prices exorbitant — a 28-ml vial of Aveda pure jasmine oil costs $60 — Jessica feels that the products are worth every cent.

Jessica doesn't know a lot of people who use Aveda, so she feels that it is *her* product. In fact, once when she was out shopping with her friends, she visited her hairstylist to purchase some Aveda products. One of her friends suggested she try another brand. Jessica just looked at her and said, "No way. I don't use anything but Aveda. I'm addicted." Jessica just can't imagine life without Aveda. She has come to rely on the brand to make her feel great.

Pertinent Web Site

www.aveda.com

Questions

1. What does Jessica perceive to be the value of Aveda products?
2. Would you say that Jessica has a relationship with Aveda? Why or why not?

Source: This case is based on a study conducted by Gillian Kennedy, Memorial University of Newfoundland.

Case 1-3

CBC
Krispy Kreme
Leah Tries Them All

Leah became a coffee drinker in her first year of university. As a University of Toronto engineering major, there were many late nights when the only thing that kept her awake was a strong cup of coffee. At the time, she drank instant coffee because it was fast and cheap. On weekends, when she visited her parents in Mississauga, she would go to the neighbourhood Country Style to grab a coffee and a doughnut with her high school friends. Then, during the week, it was back to drinking instant coffee.

One day, when Leah was in her second year at the university, her friend Jack introduced her to Second Cup. On a warm Saturday in October, the two friends were walking down Yonge Street when Jack suggested they stop into Second Cup for a cappuccino. Leah thought it was a cool spot but a little on the pricey side. After ordering a cappuccino, Leah sat down in a comfy armchair, listened to the jazz music, and glanced around at the decor. She felt completely relaxed and in her element. After a couple of hours of sipping coffee, chatting, and people-watching, Leah and

Jack headed back to campus. They had a long day of studying ahead of them. Leah knew she would soon return to Second Cup. As far as she was concerned, the atmosphere more than made up for the steep prices. Saturday mornings at Second Cup with Jack became a weekly ritual. Now, whenever she visited her parents in Mississauga, she would go to Second Cup. She liked the atmosphere there much more than at Country Style. It was a cool place to hang out and she was always sure to run into old friends.

When she was in her final year of engineering, Leah was more of a coffee drinker than she had ever been. In fact, she had become very picky about what constituted good-quality coffee and what was cheap stuff. She no longer bought instant coffee. Instead, she had purchased a coffee maker and a coffee grinder so she could enjoy fresh, aromatic coffee whenever she wanted. The only coffee beans she bought were either Second Cup or Van Houtte from her local supermarket. She refused to drink cheap coffee.

One morning as she walked from her apartment to campus, Leah noticed a brand-new Starbucks. She had heard a lot of hype about the U.S. chain moving into Canada. Some of her friends had told her that Starbucks coffee was better than the Second Cup's. Leah stood there for a moment examining the green Starbucks sign and finally decided to go in. The decor was quite different from Second Cup's. The place had a very hip, retro feel to it. Leah decided to try a dark roast coffee. As she drank the coffee, she decided that while it had a slightly stronger taste than Second Cup's dark roast, it was not all that different. The real difference, she thought, was in the atmosphere of the two coffee shops. Lately, Leah had grown tired of Second Cup and was ready to try somewhere new, so she began frequenting Starbucks. It was a nice place to sit down with a coffee and read the paper. She also hung out there with friends regularly.

When Leah graduated with her engineering degree, she found a job with an aerospace engineering firm in north Mississauga. She decided to buy a house that was located about 10 minutes by car from where she worked. Just around the corner from her office, Leah discovered a Tim Hortons. Every morning, on her way to work, Leah would pick up a medium "double-double" and a Fruit Explosion muffin. She found the drive-through to be quick and convenient, and the coffee was always hot and fresh. It was exactly what she needed to start her day. She also liked the lunch menu when she was in a hurry and needed to grab a quick lunch.

While Tim Hortons was convenient, Leah still preferred the local Starbucks on weekends. She would go there to read the Saturday paper or she would meet her friends to catch up on the events of the week. Leah now knew by name everyone who worked at Starbucks. She often stopped at the counter to have a chat with one of the employees. For Leah, coffee drinking had become both a social ritual and a necessity on weekdays when she worked long hours. Where she grabbed a coffee depended very much on her mood and on how much time she had.

One Saturday morning, as she sat at Starbucks sipping a coffee and reading the *The Globe and Mail*, Leah noticed an article on Krispy Kreme, the popular U.S. doughnut chain. She had heard about it before, but had never tried the famous doughnuts. All she knew was that Americans were so crazy about Krispy Kreme doughnuts that the chain had practically achieved cult status in the United States. Even celebrities like Nicole Kidman and Rosie O'Donnell sang the praises of Krispy Kreme. Now, Krispy Kreme was planning to move into Canada. The company would build its first outlet in Mississauga. Leah continued reading.

The chain was planning to build 32 stores in Ontario, Québec, and the Maritimes over six years. Leah thought for a moment. That didn't seem like a lot of doughnut shops, when she figured that there were probably more than 32 Starbucks in Toronto alone! She wondered if Krispy Kreme doughnuts would catch on the way they had in the United States. The author of the article suggested that Krispy Kreme would be competing with Tim Hortons in an already saturated coffee and doughnut market, but Leah disagreed. Canadians were too loyal to Tim Hortons and besides, she thought, Krispy Kreme seemed to focus on doughnuts, while Tim Hortons was more about coffee than anything else. By the time Leah had finished reading the article, she was curious about the hype surrounding Krispy Kreme doughnuts. As she glanced at her watch, she realized that she had been sitting in Starbucks for three hours. It was time for her to leave. She put the newspaper down, waved goodbye to Jeannette behind the counter, and left.

Several months later, as Leah was driving to the dry-cleaner, she noticed some steam rising from behind a building. When she rounded the corner, she spotted a Krispy Kreme billboard featuring a box of doughnuts from which the steam was rising. Clever advertising, thought Leah. It was just a couple of weeks ago that she had seen the opening of the first Canadian Krispy Kreme outlet on the news. People were so excited about the grand opening that they had actually lined up all night waiting for the doors to open the next morning. Leah couldn't believe the buzz surrounding a doughnut! What was more surprising was that on its first day, sales at the Mississauga outlet had surpassed opening day records at all U.S. Krispy Kreme stores. Leah was now more curious than ever. She decided she would stop into Krispy Kreme on her way back from the dry-cleaner.

On entering the store, Leah enjoyed the smell of fresh, hot doughnuts. A doughnut-making operation was visible through a glass panel, and Leah watched as the steaming doughnuts made their way down the assembly line. The store had a totally different feel to it than any doughnut shop she had ever visited. The only word that came to Leah's mind was "fun." It was therefore not surprising to find a bunch of kids running around the store.

As Leah approached the counter, the first thing she noticed was that Krispy Kreme didn't have a lunch menu. Strange, she thought. It didn't really matter, though, since she had come just to try their doughnuts. She ordered an original glazed and watched as the girl behind the counter grabbed a hot doughnut and slipped it into a bag. "Will that be everything?" asked the girl. "Uh, could I also get a coffee?" As she paid, Leah realized that the doughnut was more expensive than those at Tim Hortons. It had better be good, she thought. When Leah bit into the soft, warm doughnut, it almost melted in her mouth. Delicious, thought Leah, as she quickly swallowed the last piece. She was tempted to get another one, but had been watching her weight lately. With her busy career, she didn't have a lot of time to work out, so she tried as much as possible to avoid fatty foods. But she had to admit that Krispy Kreme's original glazed was amazing. The coffee, on the other hand, was not that great.

Now, every time she drove past Krispy Kreme and smelled the doughnuts, Leah was tempted to stop in, but she allowed herself to drop by only a couple of times a week to indulge in an original glazed. Sometimes, she would pick up a dozen to take to her friends at work. Leah had never really been keen on doughnuts before Krispy Kreme, but now she loved them. She hoped it was just a phase she was going through, because she was sure their doughnuts were loaded with fat. The fat content in the doughnuts certainly didn't seem to bother other patrons, though. So far, the doughnut shop had remained popular. Every time she dropped in, Leah had to stand in line. She wondered whether Krispy Kreme was gaining in popularity. Or maybe it was still just hype.

Pertinent Web Sites

www.countrystyle.com   www.timhortons.com

www.secondcup.com   www.krispykreme.com/can.html

www.starbucks.com

Questions

1. How have the different coffee and doughnut shops mentioned in the case positioned themselves?

2. What is Krispy Kreme's target market? How has the chain differentiated itself? Who is its major competitor?

3. Does Leah have a relationship with any of the coffee shops mentioned?

4. How has Leah's taste in coffee changed over the years? Has that affected her choice of coffee shops?

5. What exactly does Leah find appealing about Krispy Kreme?

Source: Unknown, "Recommended Readings: Krispy Kreme's siren song," *Marketing Online*, August 14, 2000; Sarah Smith, "Krispy Kreme heats up doughnuts," *Marketing Online*, January 29, 2001; Scott Gardiner, "In praise of St. Timmy: Behind the folksy façade, Tim Hortons is arguably Canada's best-oiled marketing machine," *Marketing Online*, August 21, 2000; Andrea Kryhul, "The Krispy Cult: PR is at the heart of a mission to convert doughnut-mad Canadians to the passion for Krispy Kreme that fires up so many of their American neighbours," *Marketing Online*, January 28, 2002; Lisa D'Innocenzo, "Doughnut wars: Can anyone catch Tim?" *Strategy Magazine*, April 22, 2002.

Video source: CBC *Marketplace*, "Krispy Kreme," March 20, 2002.

PART 2

Addressing Target Markets

An exploration of the strategies behind effective marketing, the nature of business-to-business marketing, and the information needed to guide marketing decisions

In Part 2, we delve into strategies to guide successful marketing programs, including segmentation, differentiation, and positioning. We apply those strategies to the business market and examine what information marketing managers need to make effective decisions.

Chapter 4 examines the very important concepts of market segmentation as it relates to the selection of target markets and positioning as a means to ensure that a company's offerings appeal to its target segments. In Chapter 5, we examine the business-to-business market, a massive market that many end-consumers rarely see — the one that involves marketing to businesses and organizations. Finally, Chapter 6 discusses marketing research and information systems, the ways in which marketers learn about their markets and consumers.

CHAPTER 4

Market Segmentation and Other Strategies

After studying this chapter, you should have an understanding of:

- The fundamental principles behind market segment identification and selection.

- The concept of market segmentation — its meaning, benefits, limitations, and applications.

- The difference between end-consumer markets (B2C) and business markets (B2B).

- The principal bases for segmenting consumer markets.

- Segmentation of the market based on income and other demographic factors.

- Segmentation of markets from a lifestyle- or product-related perspective.

- The importance of positioning a brand or company to appeal to target market segments.

- Niche marketing and other positioning strategies to appeal to different consumers or segments.

So You Think You Need a Holiday

It's almost the end of the winter semester and you and your friends have been talking about getting away for a week of sun and sand before starting that summer job. You've been checking out the Internet and have found a package deal that will get you to Cuba on an all-inclusive deal for $499. Saving $20 a week from your part-time job since September gives you just enough to finance this getaway. How do you go about planning this trip with the three friends who are as eager to go as you are?

Contrast this pre-summer break with an end-of-summer trip cycling along the Cabot Trail through Cape Breton Island. You have just finished your summer job and want to spend the week leading up to Labour Day on that

cycling trip. You'll fly on a Tango flight to Halifax. Then what? Where to stay? Motels? Campsites?

Now, contrast this also with your parents planning a European vacation to celebrate their twenty-fifth wedding anniversary. They want to go back to Italy and France to revisit some of the places they went that summer when they first met while backpacking through Europe almost 30 years ago. How do they plan that trip? Probably they will use a travel agent, maybe even fly business class to Paris, book into nice hotels, and eat at good restaurants.

Contrast this finally with your mother or father planning a business trip that has just come up that requires arrival in Boston for a meeting next Tuesday afternoon. How will that trip be booked? What airline? What hotel?

Today, travellers are faced with many more options than were available even a few years ago. Depending on who is taking the trip, the purpose of the trip, and who is actually paying for it, the decision-making process will differ, as will each consumer's perception of the value involved. As consumers, our shopping habits have been altered in recent years, largely as a result of technology and the increasing competition occurring in many industries. As consumers, we are more sophisticated, knowledgeable, and demanding. Technology has mainly created these changes through advances in service quality and widespread access to the Internet — no longer do we require travel agents or have to call different hotels, airlines, and car rental companies to determine the best price or availability. Competition among providers has also made us more aware that there is almost always another way to get a lower rate or fare. The scenarios in the chapter opener represent consumers with differing needs who represent various market segments with a variety of requirements in scheduling, quality and type of accommodation, and financial resources.

In some cases, a trip will come up at the last minute and there will be no flexibility in schedule or destination, while at other times the departure and arrival times and dates, as well as the actual destination, are more flexible. Some consumers will be willing to search for the best rates through online services such as Expedia.com or Travelocity.ca, even allowing the service to make the decisions, based on a budget, while others will use agents to ensure that all details match their preferences, right down to the airline taken and the type of car rented.

This glimpse into travel planning from the customer's perspective reflects a number of different market segments of the travel industry. Clearly, there are business and vacation segments. Within the vacation segment, our examples illustrate that there are many sub-segments, based on such factors as the occasion, ability to pay, and desired outcomes. How the customer behaves in planning and buying the travel products and services depends on many factors. How marketers in the travel agency, airline, hotel, cruise line, and car rental businesses market their products and services depends on which segments are being targeted and on what occasions.

What segments of the market are companies in the travel industry trying to reach? Who is making the travel decisions? What is the reason for travel? What series of decisions have to be made (there are always several)? What factors are considered in making these decisions? Why does a travel customer choose one travel agency, airline, hotel, or rental car company over another?

Once we address such questions, it should be obvious what the primary target markets are for a marketer's products. This travel example serves to introduce a number of very important topics in marketing: the selection of a target market segment; the fact that the target segment should be characterized on the basis of a number of factors, only some of which may be demographic; and the need to position a product so that it appeals to the target segment.

Selecting a Target Market Segment

target market segment

A group of customers (people or firms) to whom a company specifically aims its marketing efforts.

In Chapter 1, we defined a *market* as people or organizations with (1) needs to satisfy, (2) money to spend, and (3) the willingness to spend it. The market is not homogeneous; it is divided into segments that exhibit different characteristics and behaviours. A **target market segment** is a group of customers (people or firms) at whom a company specifically aims its marketing efforts. The careful selection and accurate definition and identification of market segments are essential for the development of an effective marketing program. One of the fundamental principles underlying the practice of market segmentation is that most companies and brands cannot aspire to be "all things to all people." If they try to do so, a company or brand will actually mean very little to those looking for specific, and different, characteristics in the products and services that they buy.

This is particularly true because of the changes taking place in the competitive environment. Companies in most industries today are faced with competition from many sources. Not only is the global nature of business creating new competitors from other countries, but customers are now able to buy products from companies with which they would never have dealt a few years ago. With access to the Internet, Canadians can access products from companies all over the world. The e-commerce environment fragments a market by exposing customers to companies with which they were once totally unfamiliar. With this fragmentation of the marketplace and the increased level of competition from local, domestic, and international competitors, most marketers practise a strategy of carving out of the mass market a manageable number of target segments on which they will concentrate. They can't serve them all, so they focus on those for whom they can do the best job.

Firms select target segments that they believe are most likely to be interested in and purchase their products or services. Often, products are specifically designed for a particular group. MuchMusic focuses on a core target of viewers 18 to 24 years of age, while actually attracting an audience ranging in age from 12 to 34. In the last few years, Much has increased the number of channels it offers by developing new stations based on musical taste to better search out specific groups within this larger demographic. So Nice Soyganic beverage's advertising has a target audience of women aged 25 to 49, while Sun-Rype Fruit & Veggie bars are gunning for busy, active adults aged 30 to 49 and living in major urban centres. Molson Canadian targets male beer drinkers aged 19 to 24, while Molson Black Label goes for the slightly older beer drinker: 25- to 35-year-olds. Lavalife.com aims its Cupid's arrow primarily at 18- to 40-year-old urban singles.[1]

Guidelines in segment selection

Four general guidelines govern the selection of target market segments. The first is that the segments selected should be compatible with the organization's goals and image. A firm marketing high-priced personal computers should not sell through discount chain stores in an effort to reach a mass market.

A second guideline is to match the market opportunity with the company's resources. Essentially, this means serving those segments where the company believes it can do well. Not all video game consoles are marketed toward the same spending dollars. Nintendo's new GameCube is geared toward 14- to 16-year-olds, while Sony and Microsoft's offerings are aiming for the 17- to 24-year-old (and older) gamers. The latter have the ability to offer more technologically powerful equipment, multimedia capabilities, and a greater number of more sophisticated game titles.[2]

Over the long run, a business must generate a profit if it is to survive. This translates into what is perhaps an obvious segment selection guideline: An organization should consciously seek markets that will generate sufficient sales volume at a low enough cost to result in a profit. Surprisingly, companies often have overlooked the profit factor in their quest for high-volume markets. Their goal was sales volume alone, not profitable sales volume.

Finally, a company ordinarily should target segments where the number of competitors and their size are such that the firm is able to compete effectively. An organization should not enter a market that is already saturated with competition unless it has some obvious competitive advantage that will enable it to take customers from existing firms.

Market opportunity analysis

Theoretically, a market opportunity exists at any time and at any place where there is a person or an organization with an unfilled need or want. Such opportunities present themselves, for example, when the population's demographics change, as discussed throughout this textbook. As the population ages, more age-relevant products and services will be needed, providing increased opportunities for entrepreneurial firms to create and develop new products and services for an older customer group.

Realistically, of course, a company's market opportunity does have restrictions. Thus, selecting target segments requires an appraisal of market opportunities available to the organization. A market opportunity analysis begins with a study of the environmental forces that affect a firm's marketing program. Then, the organization must analyze the three components

MARKETING AT WORK 4-1: STRATEGY

How Campbell's Warmed Up Hockey Fans (and Moms)

After a long winter filled with negative press about youth hockey, the Campbell Soup Company, a long-time supporter of hockey in Canada, decided it was time for a little good news. It was the year when we all heard and read about bans on street hockey, eight-year-olds competing in cash-prize tournaments, and angry hockey dads in court.

Hockey has been one of the Campbell Chunky brand's most successful marketing vehicles and a strong complement to its "hearty" positioning. After a brainstorming session at the Hockey Hall of Fame, marketers came up with the "Campbell's Chunky Soup Most Valuable Hockey Moms" program. The first year of the program featured a contest encouraging hockey players between the ages of 6 and 16 to describe why their moms deserved to be the Most Valuable Hockey Mom. Finalists got to meet Mario Lemieux and received Team Canada prize packs. One grand-prize winner was flown to Montréal to meet Lemieux and attend a Penguins-Canadiens game.

What wasn't expected (but hoped for) was that hockey parents, especially hockey moms, would energize so quickly and rally around the program. It seems that the grass-roots hockey community decided that hockey moms, after their countless hours of driving, feeding hungry players, waiting at cold rinks, and working overtime to pay for equipment, were due a little recognition, so local hockey communities took it on themselves to spread word of the program. One Nova Scotia entrant saw program information posted at a local Wal-Mart, a Saskatchewan entrant heard about the program from his teacher, and the local Zamboni driver handed one Manitoba entrant a brochure. Many hockey associations also carried information about the program on their Web sites, and stories were seen in community newspapers and hockey newsletters. Campbell's built the wings, but community credibility and word of mouth is what made the program fly.

The program complemented well the "Hockey Mom" television ads featuring players such as Lemieux, Wendel Clark, Trevor Linden, and Mats Sundin with their mothers, communicating the brand's attributes: It's the soup that eats like a meal, and is the choice of both caring mothers and hungry athletes.

SOURCE: Adapted from Dan Howe, "The Power of Grassroots Marketing," *Marketing Magazine*, July 1, 2002, p. 16.

of a market — people or organizations, their buying power, and their willingness to spend. Analysis of the "people" component involves a study of the characteristics of the population. The second component is analyzed through the distribution of consumer income and expenditure patterns. Finally, to determine consumers' "willingness to spend," management must study consumer buying behaviour.

Target market strategy: Aggregation or segmentation

In defining its target markets or segments, an organization has its choice of two approaches. In one, the total market is viewed as a single unit, as one mass, aggregate market. This approach leads to the strategy of market aggregation. In the other approach, the total market is seen as many smaller, more homogeneous segments. This approach leads to the strategy of market segmentation, in which one or more segments are selected as the top target market(s). Deciding which target market strategy to adopt is a key in selecting target markets.

Measuring selected markets

When selecting target segments, a company should make quantitative estimates of the sales potential for its product or service. This process requires estimating (1) the total industry potential for the company's product in the target segment and (2) the share of this total market that can be achieved. It is essential for management to also prepare a realistic sales forecast, usually for a one-year period. The existence of a group large enough to target is not a guarantee of equivalent sales. Consumers must become aware of your product or service, be able to obtain it, and then must choose it over your competitors' offerings and other alternative purchases. Knowing that customers buy a certain volume of such products and services is not enough. The firm must give them a reason to buy its product or service.

Nature of Market Segmentation

The total market for most types of products is too varied — too heterogeneous — to be considered a single, uniform entity. To speak of the market for vitamin pills or electric razors or education is to ignore the fact that the total market for each product or service consists of sub-markets that differ significantly from one another. This lack of uniformity may be traced to differences in customer buying habits, in ways in which the product or service is used, in motives for buying, or in other factors.

Not all consumers want to wear the same type of clothing, use the same brand of shampoo, or take the same holiday. Nor do all business firms want to buy the same type of computers or delivery vans. Similarly, not all want to have the same kind of relationship with a retail store or bank, or to be treated in the same way. At the same time, a marketer usually cannot afford to provide a different product or service for every single customer (although there are companies today that are doing just that by delivering custom-made products on order to individual customers). Consequently, market segmentation is the strategy that most marketers adopt as a compromise between the extremes of one product or service for all and a different one for each customer.

market segmentation

The process of dividing the total market for a product into several parts, each of which tends to be homogeneous in all significant aspects.

Market segmentation divides the total heterogeneous market for a product or service into several segments, each of which tends to be homogeneous in many significant aspects. Management selects one or more of these market segments as the organization's target market. A separate marketing program and approach is developed for each segment or group of segments in this target market. A major element in a company's success is its ability to select the most effective location on this segmentation spectrum between the two extremes. In other words, this means to find the blend of product or service customization and mass appeal that will produce the greatest sales potential for the firm.

Benefits of market segmentation

Market segmentation is a customer-oriented approach, so it is consistent with the marketing concept. We first identify the needs of customers within a sub-market (segment) and then develop an approach to marketing that will satisfy those needs.

By tailoring marketing programs to individual market segments, management can do a better marketing job and make more efficient use of marketing resources. A small firm with limited resources might compete very effectively in one or two market segments, but the same firm would be buried if it aimed for the total market. By employing the strategy of market segmentation, a company can design products and services that really match market demands. Advertising media can be used more effectively because promotional messages can be aimed specifically toward each segment of the market. Some of the most successful marketers are small or medium-sized firms that have decided to concentrate on a small number of market segments and to gain a strong market position and greater market share in these segments — an application of the principle of niche marketing, in which goods and services are tailored to meet the needs of small market segments.

Even very large companies with the resources to engage in mass marketing supported by expensive national advertising campaigns have in recent years abandoned mass-marketing strategies. Instead, these companies have accepted market segmentation as a more effective strategy to reach the many fragments that once were thought to constitute a mass, homogeneous market. Procter & Gamble's (**www.pg.com**) marketing program nicely illustrates these changing conditions. Once the epitome of a mass marketer with innovative but utilitarian products, P&G advertised heavily on network television. But, today, it's a different ball game. Fewer people are at home during the day to watch television. Those who spend time in front of the TV may be watching programs, viewing videos or a movie or program that was recorded a day or two earlier, or playing video games.

Procter & Gamble

Faced with fragmentation of the television audience, Procter & Gamble developed a variety of marketing campaigns, each designed to appeal to a different target market segment. The company now offers several varieties of its market-leading Tide detergent, each targeted to consumers with different needs and reasons for buying laundry detergent. In its line of hand and bath soaps, P&G offers Ivory, Zest, Coast, Safeguard, Camay, and Olay. Many of these brands come in different sizes, various colours to match bathroom decor, and different forms — bar soaps, body wash, and liquid soap in pump dispensers. Procter & Gamble, by offering such a wide range of options to the consumer, is competing in a soap market that is segmented by skin type (oily versus dry, normal versus sensitive), fragrance, aesthetics, the desire for convenience, economy, and the primary benefit sought — clean skin. It is clear that all consumers buy soap for cleansing, but they also expect other benefits from the soap they use. Hence, many segments exist.

Advances in technology have made market segmentation easier for companies in many industries, as they have created efficiencies by permitting the targeting of specific segments. For example, many companies regularly collect data on their customers and their purchasing patterns. Data can be collected that offer specific information on individuals or groups of individuals. Telephone companies, for example, can identify the types of services used by individuals or groups of people, and can assess that information in relation to demographics or other individual characteristics. Firms that utilize the Internet can easily gather consumer information from visitors, track customer purchasing, and develop electronic mailing lists.

Although a market segmentation strategy will involve a firm developing and delivering different products and services for different market segments, it is not necessarily a more costly strategy. Any additional costs actually represent an investment in a much more efficient and effective approach to marketing. Not to engage in a segmentation approach, but rather, using a broad-brush, mass-market approach, results in much lost effort. Many customers are reached through such marketing efforts who are not at all interested in the product or service or who do not want any kind of association with the firm. A segmentation strategy increases the likelihood that the marketing effort reaches those who are most likely to be interested in buying.

Conditions for effective segmentation

Ideally, management's goal should be to segment markets in such a way that each segment finds its company's offer attractive and responds positively to its marketing program. Three **conditions for effective segmentation** will help management move toward this goal.

1. The basis for segmenting — that is, the characteristics used to allocate customers to segments — must be measurable, and the information on those customers must be accessible. The "desire for low levels of cholesterol" may be a characteristic that is useful in segmenting the market for a given food product, but data on this characteristic among customers may not be readily accessible or easily quantified.

Maclean's
Chatelaine

2. The market segment itself should be accessible through existing marketing institutions — distribution channels, advertising media, company sales force — with a minimum of cost and waste. To aid marketers in this, some national magazines, such as *Maclean's* (**www.macleans.ca**) and *Chatelaine* (**www.chatelaine.com**), publish separate regional editions. This allows an advertiser to run an ad aimed at, for example, a western segment of the market, without having to pay for exposure in other, non-target areas.

3. Each segment should be large enough to be profitable. In theory, management could treat each single customer as a separate segment. But in segmenting a consumer market, a firm must not develop too broad an array of styles, colours, sizes, and prices. Usually the diseconomies of scale in production and inventory will put reasonable limits on this type of over-segmentation.

From a customer-oriented perspective, the ideal method for segmenting a market is on the basis of customers' needs and desired benefits. Certainly, using benefits to segment a market is consistent with the idea that a company should be marketing benefits and not simply the physical characteristics of a product. After all, a carpenter wants a smooth surface (benefit), not sandpaper (the product); a young family needs a home, not a mortgage. However, in many cases the benefits desired by customers do not meet the first condition described above — they are not easily measured, because customers are unwilling or unable to reveal the necessary characteristics. For example, what benefits do people derive from clothing that has the designer's label on the outside? Conversely, why do others refuse to wear such clothing?

Bases for Market Segmentation — End-Consumers and Business Users

A company can segment its market in many different ways, and the bases for segmentation vary from one product category to another. At the top of the list, however, is the division of the entire potential market into two broad categories: end-consumers and business users.

end-consumers
People who buy products for their personal, non-business use.

The sole criterion for placement of customers in one of these categories is the customer's reason for buying. **End-consumers** buy goods or services for their own personal or household use. They are satisfying strictly non-business wants, and they constitute the "consumer market." This large segment is today often described as the business-to-consumer or B2C market.

business user
An organization that buys goods or services to resell, use in its own business, or make other products.

Business users are business, industrial, or institutional organizations that buy products or services to use in their own businesses or to make other products. A manufacturer that buys chemicals with which to make fertilizer is a business user of these chemicals. Farmers who buy fertilizer for use in commercial farming are business users of the fertilizer. (If homeowners buy fertilizer to use on their yards, they are end-consumers, because they buy it for personal, non-business use.) Businesses selling to other businesses and organizations are targeting the business-to-business or B2B market.

The segmentation of all markets into two groups — B2C and B2B — is extremely significant from a marketing point of view because the two markets buy differently. Consequently, the composition of a firm's marketing mix — products and services, distribution, pricing, and promotion — will depend on whether it is directed toward the B2C market or the B2B market.

◀ BACKSPACE

1. What is a target market segment?
2. What are four general guidelines for selecting target market segments?
3. An organization chooses a strategy of _____ when the total market is viewed as a single unit.

Bases for Consumer Market Segmentation

Dividing the total market into consumer and business segments is a worthwhile start toward useful segmentation, but it still leaves too broad and heterogeneous a grouping for most companies. We need to identify some of the bases commonly used to segment these two markets further. As shown in Table 4–1, the following characteristics may provide bases for segmenting the B2C market:

- Geographic.
- Demographic.
- Psychographic.
- Behaviour toward product or service (product/service-related bases).

TABLE 4-1	Segmentation Bases for Consumer Markets
Segmentation Basis	**Examples of Typical Market Segments**
Geographic	
Region	Atlantic provinces; Québec; Ontario; Prairie provinces; British Columbia: census regions.
City or CMA size	Under 25,000; 25,000 to 100,000; 100,000 to 250,000; 250,000 to 500,000; 500,000 to 1,000,000; over 1,000,000.
Urban–rural	Urban; rural; suburban; farm.
Climate and topography	Mountainous; seacoast; rainy; cold and snowy; etc.
Demographic	
Age	Under 6, 6–12, 13–19, 20–34, 35–49, 50–64, 65 and over.
Gender	Male, female.
Family life cycle	Young single; young married; no children; etc.
Family size	Single, couple, 3–5, 6 or more.
Education	Elementary school only, high school graduate, college graduate.
Occupation	Professional, manager, clerical worker, skilled worker, salesperson, student, homemaker, unemployed.
Religion	Protestant, Catholic, Jewish, other.
Ethnic background	White; Black; Asian. British; French; Chinese; German; Ukrainian, Italian; Indian; etc.
Income	Under $10,000; $10,000–$25,000; $25,000–$35,000; $35,000–$50,000; over $50,000.
Psychographic	
Social class	Upper class, upper middle, lower middle, upper lower, etc.
Personality	Ambitious, self-confident, aggressive, introverted, extroverted, sociable, etc.
Lifestyle	Conservative, liberal, health- and fitness-oriented, adventuresome.
Value perception	Kinds of value the customer finds most attractive.
Relationships	Close, more close, less close, trusting, personal, distant.
Behaviour Toward Product or Service (or Product/Service-Related Bases)	
Benefits desired	Examples vary widely, depending on product or service:
	appliance: cost, quality, life, repairs.
	aerobics class: fitness, appearance, health, fellowship.
	toothpaste: no cavities, plaque control, bright teeth.
	hairdressing: image, style, price, self-confidence.
Usage rate	Non-user, light user, heavy user.
Loyalty/brand recognition	More or less loyal to particular companies and brands.

Marketing managers should be particularly aware of trends taking place in the demographic, psychographic, and behavioural characteristics of the markets in which they are operating. For example, if the population of Victoria is increasing because of a large number of people moving there to retire, this has obvious implications for businesses that operate in and around Victoria. According to census results released in 2002, 17.8 percent of its population was over 65 — the highest percentage of seniors in the country. Contrast this with our newest territory, Nunavut, where the median age is a mere 22 years of age and the birth rate is three times higher than in the rest of Canada.[3]

Similarly, a company should be interested in knowing if the customers it has been serving are gradually reducing their usage of its product and using more of a competing product. This is precisely what has been happening in the beer market in Canada in recent years, as per-capita consumption of the product has been declining gradually and as consumers have switched to more wine and non-alcoholic drinks. Most industry representatives will agree that this change in consumption patterns is largely a result of the fact that the percentage of the Canadian population in the heavier beer-drinking age group has been declining in recent years, as the Baby Boomers moved into their thirties and forties and began drinking a lot more wine and less beer. The key word that marketers should keep in mind when examining such trends or changes in consumption and other segmentation variables is *implications*. Marketers should always look into the implications of such change and seek information to guide an appropriate response to the changing market.

In using the bases outlined in Table 4–1 to segment markets, we should bear in mind two points. First, buying behaviour is rarely a result of only one of these segmentation factors. Including variables from several bases develops useful segmentation. To illustrate, the market for a product rarely consists of all people living in Québec or all people over 65. Instead, the segment is more likely to be described through a combination of these variables, so a market segment for notebook computers might be travelling businesspeople who earn above-average incomes, are well educated, and are older than 30. As another example, one clothing manufacturer's target market might be affluent young women (income, age, gender).

The other point to observe is the interrelationships among these factors, especially among the demographic factors. For instance, the age and life-cycle stages typically are related. Income depends to some degree on age, life-cycle stage, education, and occupation.

Geographic segmentation

geographic segmentation

The process of segmenting a market into geographic regions and developing a different marketing strategy for each region.

Subdivisions in the geographical distribution and demographic composition of the population are widely used bases for segmenting consumer markets. The reason for this is simply that consumer wants and product usage often are related to one or more of these subcategories. Geographic and demographic groupings also meet the conditions for effective segmentation — they are measurable, accessible, and large enough. Let's consider how the geographic distribution of population can be used for **geographic segmentation**.

Total population

A logical place to start is with an analysis of total population. The rapid growth in population that was experienced during the Baby Boom years from 1945 to the early 1960s has slowed to the point that Canada now has a declining population growth rate. According to census data released in 2002, the Canadian population reached 31.1 million in 2001. The current low birth rate is expected to continue, so projections for total population indicate slow population growth for the next two decades, reaching 34 million by 2016 and just over 36 million by 2026. It is unclear at this point if the population will continue to grow or if we will see some decline in the numbers as we experience what could be referred to as a "grandchild bust." The Boomer generation typically had two, maybe three children — one or two fewer than their parents. Boomer children, it would seem, are typically having one or two children — and quite a few are just getting a dog instead![4]

Other factors, such as the flow of inhabitants into and out of a country also influence total population size. In recent years in Canada, concerns have been expressed about an outward movement of educated, high-income-potential professionals from Canada to the United States (the so-called "brain drain"), and controversy has surrounded certain immigration policies. Another trend of interest includes Canada's increasingly aging population.

The total market is so large and diverse that it *must* be analyzed in segments. Significant shifts are occurring in regional and urban-rural population distribution patterns. Market differences traceable to differences in age, gender, household arrangements, lifestyles, and ethnic backgrounds pose real challenges for marketing executives.

Regional distribution

The **regional distribution** of population (see Figure 4-1) is important to marketers because people within a particular geographic region often tend to share the same values, attitudes, and style preferences. However, significant differences do exist across regions, because of differences in climate, social customs, and other factors. Ontario is a more urbanized province and represents the greatest concentration of people in Canada, especially in the corridor between Oshawa and Niagara Falls. This market is attractive to many marketers because of its sheer size and the diversity of consumers living there. On the other hand, the Atlantic region and the Prairie provinces are characterized by a much more relaxed and rural lifestyle, which suggests a demand for different types of products and services. People in the West appear to be more relaxed and less formal than eastern Canadians, and they spend more time outdoors. As this western Canadian market grows, there will be a growth in demand for products associated with an outdoor lifestyle, from clothing to leisure activities.

Urban, rural, and suburban distribution

For many years in Canada, there has been a decline in the farm population; this decline in the rural market is expected to continue. The declining farm population has led some people to underestimate the importance of rural markets. However, both as an industrial market for farm machinery and other resource industry equipment and supplies, and as a consumer market with increased buying power and more urban sophistication, the rural market is still a major one. Sociological patterns (such as average family size and local customs) among rural people differ from those of city dwellers. These patterns, affected by the **urban-suburban-rural distribution**

Figure 4-1

Provincial Distribution of Canadian Population, 2000, and Projected Growth to 2006

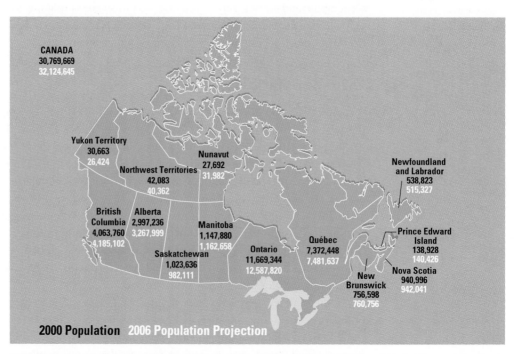

CANADA
30,769,669
32,124,645

Yukon Territory
30,663
26,424

Nunavut
27,692
31,982

Northwest Territories
42,083
40,362

Newfoundland and Labrador
538,823
515,327

British Columbia
4,063,760
4,185,102

Alberta
2,997,236
3,267,999

Manitoba
1,147,880
1,162,658

Saskatchewan
1,023,636
982,111

Ontario
11,669,344
12,587,820

Québec
7,372,448
7,481,637

Prince Edward Island
138,928
140,426

Nova Scotia
940,996
942,041

New Brunswick
756,598
760,756

2000 Population 2006 Population Projection

SOURCE: Statistics Canada, *Annual Demographic Statistics, 2001,* catalogue no. 91-213, and *Market Research Handbook, 2001,* catalogue no. 63-224.

of populations, have considerable influence on buying behaviour. Per-capita consumption of cosmetics and other beauty aids, for example, is much lower in farm and rural markets than in city markets. At the same time, consumption of these types of products is higher in certain regions, such as in areas of Québec. Marketers need to think about how consumption of various products and services differs across regions, as this will influence the marketing programs that should be prepared and implemented.

Census Metropolitan Areas

Census Metropolitan Area (CMA)
One of the major population centres of Canada, as defined by Statistics Canada; generally contains population centres of 100,000 or more.

As the rural population has shrunk, the urban and suburban population has expanded. Statistics Canada has established the concept of a **Census Metropolitan Area** (CMA) as a geographic market-data measurement unit. A CMA is defined by Statistics Canada as the main labour market of a continuous built-up area having a population of 100,000 or more. Table 4-2 indicates the growth in Canadian CMA populations from 1997 to 2001. By 2001, these 25 areas accounted for about 60 percent of the total population of Canada. A discernable trend is the continued growth of larger CMAs over the time illustrated. Immigration is partially responsible for this, as most immigrants settle in urban areas. Obviously, these Census Metropolitan Areas represent attractive, geographically concentrated market targets with considerable sales potential.

Suburban growth

As the metropolitan areas have been growing, something else has been going on in them: The central parts of many larger cities are being revitalized as attractive areas in which to live. At the same time, growth is occurring in the fringe areas of cities and in the suburbs outside these cities. For the past 50 years, one of the most significant social and economic trends in Canada has been the shift of population to the suburbs. As middle-income families have moved to the suburbs, the economic, racial, and ethnic composition of many central cities (especially their core areas) has changed considerably, thus altering the nature of the markets in these areas. Now those central cities are being repopulated, often with young, dual-career, higher-income professionals with considerable buying power.

The growth of the suburban population has some striking marketing implications. Since a large percentage of suburban people live in single-family residences, a vastly expanded market exists for lawn mowers, lawn furniture, home furnishings, and home repair supplies and equipment. Suburbanites are more likely to want two cars than are city dwellers and they are inclined to spend more leisure time at home, so there is a larger market for home entertainment and recreation items.

Demographic segmentation

The most common basis for the **demographic segmentation** of consumer markets is some characteristic of the population such as age, gender, family life-cycle stage, income distribution, education, occupation, or ethnic origin.

Age groups

Analyzing the consumer market by age groups is a useful exercise in the marketing of many products and services. Age is one of the most fundamental bases for demographically segmenting markets, as we can see from the large number of products and services directed at seniors, children, teens, young adults, and so on. But marketers must be aware of the changing nature of the age mix of the Canadian population. Looking ahead, we see a rapidly

TABLE 4-2 Census Metropolitan Area Population as of July 1, 1997–2001 (thousands)

	1997	1998	1999	2000	2001
Toronto (ON)	4,499.0	4,586.7	4,669.3	4,763.2	4,881.4
Montréal (PQ)	3,408.9	3,423.9	3,447.6	3,474.9	3,511.8
Vancouver (BC)	1,967.6	1,998.4	2,028.4	2,058.7	2,078.8
Ottawa-Hull (ON-PQ)	1,045.5	1,055.6	1,068.6	1,086.1	1,107.0
Calgary (AB)	873.2	903.0	926.1	947.3	971.5
Edmonton (AB)	897.3	914.3	928.1	941.8	956.8
Québec (PQ)	685.4	686.6	688.4	690.5	693.1
Winnipeg (MB)	677.8	677.8	679.7	682.1	684.8
Hamilton (ON)	650.4	657.8	664.7	672.2	680.6
London (ON)	413.1	415.9	418.5	422.1	426.3
Kitchener (ON)	402.1	408.5	415.5	423.2	431.7
St. Catharines-Niagara (ON)	385.5	387.5	388.8	390.9	393.1
Halifax (NS)	345.3	348.9	352.8	355.9	359.2
Victoria (BC)	317.6	316.8	317.0	317.1	318.8
Windsor (ON)	291.6	295.9	300.6	306.8	313.8
Oshawa (ON)	282.0	287.5	292.4	298.9	305.3
Saskatoon (SK)	227.6	229.5	230.7	231.0	230.5
Regina (SK)	199.1	199.2	199.8	199.3	198.1
St. John's (NF and Labrador)	176.5	175.2	175.3	175.8	176.2
Chicoutimi-Jonquière (PQ)	162.7	162.6	161.9	160.5	158.7
Sudbury (ON)	163.9	162.0	159.4	158.1	156.7
Sherbrooke (PQ)	151.3	152.3	152.6	153.6	154.9
Trois-Rivières (PQ)	142.2	141.9	141.9	141.6	141.5
Thunder Bay (ON)	128.5	127.5	126.9	125.8	124.6
Saint John (NB)	127.9	127.5	127.6	127.7	128.1

SOURCE: Statistics Canada, CANSIM II, Table 051-0014, catalogue no. 91-213-XIB.

aging population. In 1993, for example, there were almost 3.9 million people in Canada aged between 10 and 19. By 2001, this age group was at 4.2 million, but by 2016, this will drop to 3.6 million and is forecasted to stay at that level through to 2026. On the other hand, in 1986, there were only 2.7 million Canadians aged 65 and older. By 2001, this age bracket contained almost 4 million, and by 2021, this group will increase in number to 6.67 million and to 7.75 million by 2026.[5]

The youth market (aged roughly 5 to 13) carries a three-way market impact. First, these children can influence parental purchases. Second, millions of dollars are spent on this group by their parents. Third, these children make purchases of goods and services for their own use and satisfaction, and the volume of these purchases increases as the children get older. Promotional programs are often geared to this market segment. Manufacturers of breakfast cereals, snack foods,

Jeep TJ. The ultimate thrill ride. What are you waiting for?

Jeep

THERE'S ONLY ONE
jeep.ca

Clearly targeting a specific segment

and toys often advertise on television programs that are directed at children — except on the CBC television network, which prohibits advertising on children's programs.

Recently, Kellogg Canada joined with children's broadcaster YTV in a promotion called *YTV Gigabytes*. Kellogg launched a limited-time cereal named for the children's show, complete with Y-, T-, and V-shaped marshmallows. In the cereal, kids could find a pass code that allowed them to check in at the *Gigabytes* Web site. There, users could trap computer bugs when they joined one of three "virus-hunting missions," and also enter to win computers or IBM shopping sprees. The promotion was launched shortly before the 2001 holiday season, partly because Kellogg and YTV were counting on kids being online more often at that time of year.[6]

The teenage market is also recognized as an important one, yet many companies find it difficult to reach. The mistake they make might be in attempting to lump all teenagers together. Certainly, the 13 to 16 age group is very different from the 17 to 20 age group. Yet marketers must understand the teenage market because of the size of the segment and because its members have a great deal of money to spend. "The advantage of marketing to the 15–24 age group is that these people have a disposable income. They are the consumers of today and they'll be the consumers of tomorrow," according to the president of Youth Culture Inc., a research firm. This is becoming increasingly recognized, as even auto manufacturers such as DaimlerChrysler, among others, focus more of their advertising toward the college market. Advertising for entry-level vehicles such as the Neon and PT Cruiser have been designed with this in mind. The new Dodge Ram 2002 is also being launched with a TV spot geared to appeal to this segment.[7]

The second-largest teen population in Canadian history will peak this decade at 4.2 million strong. More than 60 percent of them say that advertising helps them decide what to buy. Teens have more influence than ever over household purchases and have about $19.1 billion dollars in disposable income. Nike, Ecko, Silver (a made-in-Canada brand), Phat Farm, Tommy, FUBU, and Brody are the top seven brands of clothing among Canadian teens who are known as "early style adopters," according to Youth Culture Inc. research. Video game manufacturer Activision grossed $425 million ($US) over the last three years on sales of Tony Hawk's Pro Skater, a game based on an icon of the sport. In Canada, the Tony Hawk game franchise was one of the top three game choices of males aged 14 to 17. Vancouver-based animation studio Mainframe Entertainment Inc. plans to build further on the now-retired pro boarder's following, with Tony Hawk's Feasters, a 3-D animated action sports series planned for the 2003 fall broadcast season.[8]

For marketers who set their sights on the much-sought-after 18- to 24-year-old crowd, the university or college campus is the ideal frontier: Where else can they find a captive audience so closely matching the desired traits? Marketing activities vary from campus to campus and can range from washroom advertising to sampling and event sponsorship. And while marketing is currently on the rise, this doesn't mean it's entirely acceptable to the target. Part of the issue is that students are cynical about corporations, which they believe take advantage of these usually cash-strapped institutions by using deep pockets to declare "open season" on academic institutions, according to Stephen Wicary, a student at Ryerson who also attended Ontario's University of

Guelph for four years. "The amount of revenue gained is minuscule compared to the costs associated with the sacrifice in scholastic integrity." Administrators need to look into the matter more seriously because, according to Wicary, "It's still an issue to politically minded students and to those who still believe an academic environment should be kept as pristine and free of commercial messages as possible."[9]

Because the size of the young-adult segment will decline in coming years, Canada's universities and colleges are aggressively competing for students by taking new strategic approaches to recruiting and introducing advertising and marketing campaigns, new scholarships, integrated student services, and enrolment management systems.[10]

The aging Baby Boom generation makes an attractive market segment as they move into middle age. They are in their high-earning years and are contemplating retirement; some have already retired, taking advantage of early-retirement packages offered as companies and other organizations have downsized in recent years. Typically, the values and lifestyles of this group are different from those of people in the same age category in previous generations. Already, companies are adjusting to these changing demographics. While toothpaste manufacturers like Procter & Gamble and Colgate-Palmolive capitalized on concern about cavity prevention in children's teeth in the 1950s and 1960s, 35 or more years later, they are producing toothpaste to fight tartar — an adult dental problem. This generation, with more dual-income families and fewer children, have more money to spend on themselves. As a result, they are a prime market for products that promise convenience and for home and garden services.

Many are seeing their children graduate from college and university and have probably paid off the mortgage on the family home. Suddenly, they have a lot more disposable income to spend on themselves and on indulging their grandchildren. Many have a lot of leisure time on their hands. Consequently, this age group makes an attractive target for vacation travel, entertainment, recreation, smaller homes and condominiums, and long-term investments intended to finance a long retirement. This group may be aging, but this should not be confused with being old. Those born at the peak of the Baby Boom will not reach 65 until 2026. Many of these consumers want to shop at their neighbourhood bakeries, butcher shops, and clothing boutiques, where staff members know their names and their likes and dislikes — the specialty retailer is on the comeback trail. Clearly, their needs are different, as we can see in our chapter opener. Your parents planning an anniversary celebration represent quite a different segment than you and your friends planning a vacation trip to Cuba.

A very important older age group is made up of people over 65 — a segment that is growing both absolutely and as a percentage of the total population. Companies are beginning to recognize that people in this age group are logical prospects for small, low-cost housing units, cruises and foreign tours, health-related products and services, and cosmetics developed especially for older people. Many firms are also developing promotional programs to appeal to this group because their purchasing power is surprisingly high. On a per-capita basis, seniors are increasing their spending faster than average in areas such as health care, entertainment, recreation, gifts, and charitable contributions. In this latter category, seniors give more dollars than the average Canadian, making them an attractive market segment for charities and religious groups.

This is a rapidly growing market segment that is spanning new products and presenting opportunities for marketers. The Canadian Home Income Plan (CHIP) wants elderly Canadians to get off their assets — namely, their already-paid-for houses. It wants them to consider a "reverse-mortgage," which gives them a lump-sum payment or a monthly income in return for a stake in their homes. The idea is to use the money for whatever they want — holidays, a sailboat, gifts to the kids. It's not an easy proposition, as many in this target group remember hard times and were raised to avoid debt — they are also a little suspicious of smooth-talkers possibly trying to scam them out of their savings![11]

The Internet is becoming an increasingly attractive way to reach seniors. Now that Gramps is retired, he's got lots of time on his hands, and money is no object anymore. He's still hungry

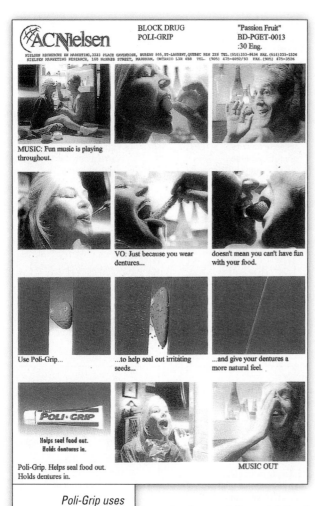

MUSIC: Fun music is playing throughout.

VO: Just because you wear dentures...

doesn't mean you can't have fun with your food.

Use Poli-Grip...

...to help seal out irritating seeds...

...and give your dentures a more natural feel.

Helps seal food out.
Holds dentures in.

Poli-Grip. Helps seal food out.
Holds dentures in.

MUSIC OUT

Poli-Grip uses creative approaches to appeal to seniors.

for knowledge and to fill his time. With a click of the mouse, he has joined the meteoric growth of the online senior market. The mature market is becoming increasingly comfortable with the Internet — and as more of the 50-plus set spend more and more time online, they are becoming increasingly attractive targets for online marketers. Of the approximately nine million Canadians aged 50-plus, about 25 to 30 percent are regular Internet users. Although still lagging in transactional activity, seniors account for about one in five online buyers, and their selective use of Web activities makes them easy to spot.[12]

Gender

Gender is an obvious basis for consumer market analysis. Many products are made for use by men or women, not both. In many product categories (automobiles, for example), women and men typically look for different product benefits. Market segmentation by gender is also useful because either men only or women only have traditionally purchased many products.

Some of these traditional buying patterns are breaking down, however, and marketers certainly should be alert to changes involving their products and services. According to Statistics Canada, women comprise more than 46 percent of the Canadian workforce. The entry of women into the workforce has occurred in great numbers since the 1970s. Participation rates have levelled off in recent years and almost 60 percent of Canadian women 15 to 24 years of age are in the workforce, while almost 79 percent of Canadian women 25 to 44 are in the workforce. These facts are significant for marketers.[13]

Family life cycle

family life cycle
The series of life stages that a family goes through, starting with young, single people and progressing through married stages with young and then older children, then ending with older married and single people.

Frequently, an important factor accounting for differences in consumption patterns relates to consumers being in different life-cycle stages. The concept of the **family life cycle** implies that there are several distinct stages in the life of an ordinary family. The traditional six-stage family cycle is shown in Figure 4-2, along with three alternative stages that reflect significant changes from traditional patterns. In addition to the family configurations represented in Figure 4-2, numerous other examples exist, from same-sex marriages to families with shared child custody to cohabitation arrangements between mixed-sex groups. Lifestyles that do not reflect the traditional norm are often more the rule than the exception. We can think of life-cycle position, in any of its various patterns, as a major determinant of buyer behaviour, so it can be a useful basis for segmenting consumer markets.[14]

A young couple with two children (the full-nest stage) has quite different needs from those of a couple in their mid-50s whose children no longer live at home (the empty-nest stage). A single-parent family (divorced, widowed, or never married) with dependent children probably faces social and economic problems quite different from those of a two-parent family. Young married couples with no children typically devote a large share of their income to clothing, vehicles, and recreation. When children start arriving, expenditure patterns shift, as many young families buy and furnish a home. Families with teenagers find larger portions of the budget going for food, clothing, and educational needs.

Figure 4-2:

The Family Life Cycle

1. Bachelor stage: young, single people

2. Young married couples with no children

3. Full nest I: young married couples with children

ALTERNATIVE STAGES

A. Young or middle-aged person with dependent children — the single parent

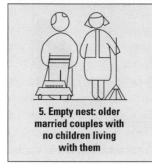

B. Divorced person without dependent children

C. Middle-aged married couples without children

4. Full nest II: middle-aged married couples still with dependent children

5. Empty nest: older married couples with no children living with them

6. Older single people, still working or retired

Consumer Income and Its Distribution

People alone do not make a market; they must have money to spend. Consequently, **consumer income**, its distribution, and how it is spent are essential factors in any quantitative market analysis.

What is income? When we talk of consumers and their income, we tend to be most interested in **personal disposable income**, that is after-tax income available for personal consumption expenditure and savings. We also are interested in a household's **discretionary purchasing power**, the amount of disposable income that is available after fixed commitments (mortgage and loan payments, rent, insurance) and essential household expenditures for food, clothing, household utilities, and transportation have been covered. Compared with personal disposable income, discretionary purchasing power is a better (more sensitive) indicator of consumers' ability to spend for non-essentials.

personal disposable income

Personal income remaining after all personal taxes are paid.

Income distribution

To obtain full value from an analysis of income, we should study the variations and trends in the distribution of income across regions and population segments. Regional income data are especially helpful in pinpointing the particular market to which a firm may wish to appeal. Income data on cities and even on areas within cities may indicate the best locations for shopping centres and branches of retail stores, and for targeting direct-marketing programs.

discretionary purchasing power

The amount of disposable income remaining after fixed expenses and essential household needs are covered.

A genuine **income distribution** revolution has occurred in Canada over the past 30 years or so — there has been a tremendous growth in the middle- and upper-income segments, and a corresponding decrease in the percentage of low-income groups. The purchasing power of the average Canadian household is expected to continue to increase in the future. We will see the effects of higher personal incomes and higher participation rates in the labour force. It is very likely that more than half of all Canadian families will have a total annual income in excess of $60,000 by the year 2016. This anticipated increase in the number of affluent households is the result of several factors, including (1) the large growth in the number of people in the prime earning years of 35 to 50, (2) the increase in dual-income families, and (3) the wider distribution of inherited wealth. We will still have low-income families; however, there will be fewer below the poverty line, even though that level (by government definition) is moving up, in recognition of a society that is generally better able to provide its members with reasonable incomes.

Marketing significance of income data

The declining percentage of families in very low income brackets, coupled with sharp increases in the upper-income groups, points to growth in discretionary purchasing power. As discretionary income increases, so too does the demand for items that once were considered to be luxuries.

The middle-income market is large and growing, and it has forced many changes in marketing strategy. Some stores that once appealed to low-income groups have traded up to the huge middle-income market. These stores are upgrading the quality of the products they carry and are offering additional services.

In spite of the considerable increase in disposable income in the past 30 years, many households are still in the low-income bracket or find their higher incomes inadequate to meet all of their needs. Furthermore, many customers are willing to forgo services in order to get lower prices. One consequence of this market shift has been the development of self-service retail outlets, discount houses, and superstores, where the emphasis is on convenience and low prices.

Consumer Expenditure Patterns

How consumer income is spent is a major market determinant for most products and services. Consequently, marketers need to study **consumer spending patterns**, as well as the distribution of consumer income. Marketers also should be aware of the shifts in spending patterns that have occurred over the past three decades. Families have increased the percentage of their total expenditures on housing, health, and utilities. Spending (as a percentage of total) has decreased for food, beverages, clothing, and home expenses (except utilities). But, expenditure patterns are not the same for all families. These patterns vary considerably, depending on family income, life-cycle stage, and other factors.

Relation to stage of family life cycle

Consumer expenditure patterns are influenced by the consumer's stage in the life cycle. There are striking contrasts in spending patterns between, for example, people in the full-nest stage with very young children and people in the empty-nest stage. Table 4–3 summarizes the behavioural influences and the spending patterns for families in each stage of the cycle. (This table expands the number of stages shown earlier in Figure 4–2.) Young married couples with no children typically devote large shares of their income to clothing, automobiles, and recreation. When children start arriving, expenditure patterns shift as many young families buy and furnish a home. Families with teenagers find larger portions of the budget going for food, clothing, and educational needs. Families in the empty-nest stage, especially when the head of the family is still in the labour force, are attractive to marketers; typically, these families have more discretionary buying power.

TABLE 4-3 Behaviour Influences and Buying Patterns, by Family Life-Cycle Stage

Bachelor stage: young single people not living at home

Few financial burdens.

Fashion opinion leader.

Recreation-oriented.

Buy: basic kitchen equipment, basic furniture, cars, equipment for the mating game, vacations.

Newly married couples; young, no children

Better off financially than they will be in near future.

Highest purchase rate and highest average purchase of durables.

Buy: cars, refrigerators, stoves, sensible and durable furniture, vacations.

Full nest I; youngest child under 6

Home purchasing at peak.

Liquid assets low.

In some cases, both spouses work outside the home.

Dissatisfied with financial position and amount of money saved.

Interested in new products.

Like advertised products.

Buy: washers, dryers, TV sets, baby food, chest rubs and cough medicine, vitamins, dolls, wagons, sleds, skates.

Full nest II; youngest child 6 or over

Financial position better.

In many cases, both spouses work outside the home.

Less influenced by advertising.

Buy larger-sized packages, multiple-unit deals.

Buy: many foods, cleaning materials, bicycles, music lessons, pianos.

Full nest III; older married couples with dependent children

Financial position still better.

In many cases, both spouses work outside the home.

Some children get jobs.

Hard to influence with advertising.

High average purchase of durables.

Buy: new, more tasteful furniture, auto travel, non-necessary appliances, boats, dental services, magazines.

Empty nest I; older married couples, no children living with them, head in labour force

Home ownership at peak.

Most satisfied with financial position and money saved.

Interested in travel, recreation, self-education.

Make gifts and contributions.

Not interested in new products.

Buy: vacations, luxuries, home improvements.

Empty nest II; older married couples, no children living at home, head retired

Drastic cut in income

Keep home.

Buy: medical appliances, medical care, products that aid health, sleep, and digestion.

Solitary survivor, in labour force

Income still good but likely to sell home.

Solitary survivor, retired

Same medical and product needs as other retired group; drastic cut in income.

Special need for attention, affection, and security.

SOURCE: William D. Wells and George Gubar, "Life Cycle Concept in Marketing Research," *Journal of Marketing Research*, November 1966, p. 362. Reprinted with permission from the American Marketing Association.

Relation to income distribution

The pattern of consumer expenditures is influenced significantly by the income level of the household. For example, as we can see in Table 4-4, families with annual incomes of less than $20,520 spend an average of 17.8 percent of their expenditures on food. This percentage drops to 12.5 percent for those with annual incomes between $20,520 and $36,015, and to only 8.7 percent for those with incomes over $79,654 per annum. These and other findings from an analysis of Statistics Canada data suggest the type of information that marketers might obtain from analyzing spending patterns by income groups.

TABLE 4-4 Detailed Family Expenditure by Selected Family Income Categories, All Families and Unattached Individuals			
Expenditure	Family Income Up to $20,520	Income Between $20,520 - 36,015	Income Over $79,654
Food	17.8%	12.5%	8.7%
Shelter	31.9	20.7	15.3
Household operation	6.6	4.7	3.8
Household furnishings and equipment	2.6	2.8	2.8
Clothing	4.0	4.2	4.4
Transportation	11.0	13.9	12.2
Health care	3.5	2.8	1.7
Personal care	1.7	1.4	1.1
Recreation	4.6	5.7	5.6
Reading materials and other printed matter	0.7	0.6	0.4
Education	1.5	1.3	1.7
Tobacco products and alcoholic beverages	3.3	2.6	1.6
Miscellaneous	1.7	1.5	1.7
Gifts and contributions to persons outside household	4.0	2.5	2.6
Personal taxes	3.0	16.6	30.1

SOURCE: Statistics Canada, *Market Research Handbook*, cat. no. 63-224, 2001, page 67.

Psychographic and Relationship Segmentation

Demographic data are used to segment markets because these data are related to easily measured characteristics and to consumer behaviour. However, demographics are not themselves the causes of behaviour. People don't buy in-line skates because they are young — they buy them because they enjoy an active, outdoor lifestyle, and it so happens that such people are also typically younger. Thus, demographics often correlate with behaviour, but they do not explain it.

Marketers have gone beyond demographic attributes in an effort to better understand why consumers behave as they do. They now engage in a deeper kind of segmentation, which involves examining attributes such as personality and lifestyles. When demographics and psychological attributes are combined, richer descriptions of segments are produced.

Psychographics The term *psychographics* was coined to describe a wide variety of psychological and behavioural descriptions of a market. The development of psychographics evolved

MARKETING AT WORK

4-2: GLOBAL

Si, Si, Espanol!

At first glance, Hispanic Canadians might seem too small in number to be considered a market worth specifically targeting, but those catering to this community say its impressive growth merits greater attention and that marketers who target this group will see strong returns in the years to come.

Certainly, interest in this community in the United States has grown, thanks to the huge influx of immigrants and due to celebrities such as Jennifer Lopez and Enrique Eglesias. Wal-Mart, McDonald's, Ford, and Wendy's are just a few of the big players introducing Spanish-language advertising south of the border.

In Canada, Hispanic immigration has been a little slower. Statistics Canada ranks home-language Spanish sixth behind English, French, Chinese, Italian, and Punjabi. The Spanish population numbered about 204,000 (based on ethnic origin) in the last census, with the vast majority located in Ontario, Québec, and British Columbia. Current immigration estimates peg this number to be increasing by about 10,000 per year.

That's part of the reason why CFMT, owned by Rogers Broadcasting, applied for its newest station, CFM2, set to hit the airwaves in the fall of 2002. "It's one of the groups we focused on in our application as having a tremendous upside potential because of the growth in the population," said Malcolm Dunlop, general manager. Hispanic Publications is equally optimistic, having launched its thrice-weekly newspaper *Correo Canadiense* in the Greater Toronto Area in 2001 to provide international Spanish and Latin American news.

According to specialty TV broadcasting company Telelatino, of those Spanish speakers immigrating to Canada, 42 percent are making their way to the Greater Toronto Area and 38 percent are moving to metropolitan Montréal. An advantage of this Spanish-speaking population is that it skews younger — 58 percent are under 35 years of age, making it a young and vibrant populace. And while these initial waves of immigrants will age, the sense of history and origin will remain strong and they will still like to be able to follow the culture-based programming with which they are familiar.

SOURCE: Adapted from Sarah Smith, "Si, Si, Espanol!" *Marketing*, June 3, 2002, p. 14.

activities, interests, and opinions
The bases of an individual's lifestyle; these characterize how people leads their lives.

from attempts by marketers to find measures more directly related to purchase and consumption than to demographics. Lifestyles are often considered to be part of the broad topic of psychographics, although we are treating this subject separately here.

Early work on consumer psychographics tended to focus on variables such as the consumer's **activities, interests, and opinions**. It was widely felt that a much richer and deeper view of a person is possible once a marketer better understands that person's interests and opinions on certain topics. Research on psychographics includes variables relating to activities such as leisure time and media usage. Where people go for their vacations, what books they read, and what television programs they watch can tell a marketer a great deal about their likelihood to buy.

values (as distinct from *value*)
The principles that individuals hold to be important and by which they lead their lives.

Values are another important psychographic descriptor. According to psychologists, values are what we hold to be important, so they are a reflection of our needs, adjusted for the realities of the world in which we live. Researchers at the Survey Research Center at the University of Michigan have identified nine basic values that relate to purchase behaviour, which they call the List of Values (LOV):

1. Self-respect.

6. Sense of accomplishment

2. Self-fulfilment.

7. Fun and enjoyment in life.

3. Security.

8. Being well respected.

4. Sense of belonging.

9. Having warm relationships.

5. Excitement.

While most people would view all of these values as desirable, their relative importance differs among people, and their importance changes over a person's life. For example, people who value fun and enjoyment especially like skiing, dancing, bicycling, and backpacking, and people who value warm relationships give gifts for no particular reason. Thus, the relative strength of these values could be the basis for segmenting a market.

Lifestyles The term *lifestyle* is a broad concept that sometimes overlaps personality characteristics. Being cautious, sceptical, ambitious, a workaholic, a copycat — are these personality or lifestyle traits? Lifestyles relate to activities and interests. They reflect how you spend your time, what books you read, which television programs, specialty channels, or DVDs you watch, where you surf on the Internet, and where you spend your leisure time and your money.

There is no commonly accepted terminology of lifestyle categories for segmenting markets. Nevertheless, people's lifestyles undoubtedly affect their choice of products and their brand preferences. Marketers are well aware of this and often attempt to segment their markets on a lifestyle basis.

Nike
NIKEgoddess

As consumer tastes and lifestyles have changed in recent years, most companies have had to make adjustments in their products and services to ensure that these remained attractive to their target customers. One company that has taken an aggressive approach in the retail industry is Nike (**www.nike.com**). Nike continues to capture lifestyle images with NikeTowns — single-brand stores — set up to reflect and represent the brand's desire to appear action-oriented and "with it." These stores are decorated in cyber-age video glyphs with screens showing athletes continuously in motion, giving visitors the complete brand experience. This "experiential" chain of shops is directly targeted at the young, athletic consumer who responds positively to the electronic age.[15] Taking this one step further the company introduced NIKEgoddess (**www.nike.com/nikegoddess.com**) stores in 2002. These are designed to deliver the "best selection of Nike athletic gear for women who like to look good and kick ass." Stores are staffed with expert salespeople to help customers find "fitness and lifestyle solutions that work from the gym to the street." Initial stores were opened in California, with clean, crisp styling and contemporary furnishings. They don't look or feel like "sporting goods" stores. The stores are the evolution of Nike's megalogue Goddess and a Web site that features female athletes and everyday women and offers information on various sports. The focus is not just toward female youth or specifically toward athletes, but rather on how fitness can give a person confidence. The stores would seem to be a natural development after preliminary efforts resulted in a 46 percent increase in the sale of women's items in NikeTown stores in 2001.[16]

Although it is a valuable marketing tool, lifestyle segmentation has some serious limitations. It is very difficult to measure accurately the size of lifestyle segments in order to determine their viability. Another problem that may affect the marketer's ability to deal with specific lifestyle segments relates to their accessibility. Although certain of the mass media (particularly magazines and television) offer options that appeal to particular lifestyle groups, such options for advertising may be out of the cost range of many smaller companies, making it difficult for them to reach their lifestyle targets in a cost-effective manner.

Relationships   With the increased attention being paid to customer relationships in marketing, many companies are focusing on segmenting their customer base in terms of the kind of relationship their customers currently have with a company or the kind of relationship they would like to have. In recent years, many progressive companies have come to realize that the long-term future of their operations is very much linked to the extent to which they are able to develop appropriate relationships with customers. Those customers who feel that a relationship exists are more likely to remain customers, spend more money with the company, and refer other customers.

But not all customers want the same kind of relationship. While some want to feel very close to a company and to develop something approaching a friendship with a company and its employees, others will be content with a more distant and businesslike relationship. Similarly, some customers want to hear from a company frequently with information about new products and services or simply to be asked if there is anything they need. Others don't want to hear from a company very often. Their view is that the company simply has to be there when needed; they don't want what they would consider "in-your-face" service.

relationship segmentation

The process of segmenting a market on the basis of the types of relationships that customers want to have with a company or brand.

It is extremely important, if a company intends to practise relationship segmentation, that the company develops appropriate relationships with customers so that their satisfaction is increased and they remain loyal customers. To do so requires a detailed understanding of the type of relationship that customers will find satisfying and a strategy to develop different types of relationships with different segments of customers.

Personality Characteristics   An individual's personality characteristics are usually described in terms of traits that influence behaviour. Theoretically, they would seem to be a good basis for segmenting markets. Experience tells us that compulsive people buy differently than cautious consumers do, and quiet introverts do not buy the same things nor in the same way as gregarious, outgoing people. However, personality characteristics pose problems that limit their usefulness in practical market segmentation. First, the presence and strength of these characteristics in the population are virtually impossible to measure. For example, how many people in Canada could be classified as outgoing? Another problem is associated with accessibility — no advertising medium provides unique access to a particular personality type; that is, television reaches introverts as well as extroverts, aggressive people as well as timid people. So one of the major goals of segmentation — to avoid wasted marketing effort — is not likely to be accomplished using personality as a basis for market segmentation.

Nevertheless, many firms tailor their advertising messages to appeal to certain personality traits. Even though the importance of the personality dimension in a particular decision may not be measurable, the seller believes that it does play an influential role. Thus, we see products and services advertised to consumers who are "on the way up," or are "people with taste," or who "want to break away from the crowd."

Behavioural Segmentation

behavioural segmentation

Market segmentation based on consumers' product-related behaviour; typically, the benefits consumers desire from a product and the rate at which they use the product.

Some marketers regularly attempt to segment their markets on the basis of product-related behaviour, utilizing **behavioural segmentation**. This section briefly considers three of these bases for segmentation: the benefits desired from a product, the rate at which the consumer uses the product, and occasions when it is used.

Benefits Desired   Let's consider a hypothetical division of the toothpaste market based on the benefits desired. The segment names and the benefits sought by each segment might look like this:

- **Sensories:** Flavour and appearance
- **Sociables:** Brightness of teeth
- **Worriers:** Decay prevention and plaque control
- **Independents:** Low price

There was a time when a particular brand of toothpaste such as Crest or Colgate was "positioned" to appeal to one of these **benefit segments**. Today, with the concept of brand extension very much in evidence, each of the major brands will have at least one version to appeal to each segment.

Two things determine the effectiveness of benefit segmentation. First, the specific benefits consumers are seeking must be identified. This typically involves several research steps, beginning with the identification of benefits related to a particular product or behaviour through brainstorming, observing consumers, focus groups, and later, surveys to determine how important the benefits are and how many consumers seek each one. An airline or a travel agency would target different marketing programs to reach your parents, who are taking a business trip, than to reach you and your friends, who are booking a charter to Cuba, as described in the chapter opener.

To illustrate, the ExxonMobil Corporation (**www2.exxonmobil.com**) conducted a market segmentation study of gasoline buyers. The study identified five primary segments. Contrary to conventional wisdom, only one, accounting for about 20 percent of the buyers, consisted of price shoppers. To attract the four more profitable non-price segments, Mobil has begun offering things that appeal to those segments, such as quick service, with features such as Speedpass, which enables customers to be identified and billed by waving a special keychain across the pump. This personal ID device is linked to a credit card for payment.[17] The company is also attempting to appeal to these segments by positioning itself as a leading convenience store retailer. In Canada, under its Esso brand, the company has recently penned a deal to see up to 300 of its "On the Run" convenience stores house full-menu Tim Hortons outlets instead of the small kiosks that are currently in some stations. It is an exclusive deal in which the doughnut maker commits not to enter into any new business dealings with convenience stores or other petroleum companies.[18]

ExxonMobil Corporation

usage rate

The rate at which people use or consume a product.

A second task, once the marketer has identified the various benefits that are to be used to segment the overall market, is to develop detailed **profiles** of each of the market segments that have been identified. The purpose of the profiling exercise is to develop as detailed an overview as possible of the consumers who make up each of the segments of interest, in terms of their demographic, psychographic, and lifestyle characteristics. The main premise behind this profiling is "The better we know the customers in each of the segments we plan to target, the more likely it is that we can put together an integrated marketing program that they will find attractive."

Procter & Gamble targets several different segments with the Crest brand.

Usage Rate   Another product-related basis for market segmentation is **usage rate** — the rate at which people use or consume a product. Thus, we can have categories for non-users, light users, medium users, and heavy users. Normally, a company is most interested in the heavy users of its product. In most categories, 50 percent or less of users typically account for 80 to 90 percent of the total purchases of a given product or service.

That is not to say that this percentage applies precisely in all product or service categories; rather, it is the principle that is important. Typically, a company can identify a number of different segments among its target customers. Among these segments, there are usually one or two that contain disproportionately heavier consumers of the product or service. For example, one segment may contain only 15 percent of customers, but these customers may account for 25 percent of all purchases of the company's product. Another segment may have a comparatively smaller number of consumers, accounting possibly for only 8 percent of customers, but their consumption patterns may be such that they account for 20 percent of all sales of the product or service. These segments, because they include such heavy consumers, represent important target segments. In such circumstances, most companies would prefer to be the market leader among the heavy users, rather than targeting their marketing efforts at customers who use relatively little of the product.

For example, Heinz's share of the ketchup market has declined, as lower-priced and private-label brands have captured more of this market. To win back customers, Heinz is going after the heavy half of ketchup users — children and teenagers — with a variety of new product variations. The goal is to build an extreme brand personality through extreme products! Introducing Heinz Ketchup in green and purple has greatly revived interest in the brand and product sales. Not to stop there, in the summer of 2002, Heinz introduced the EZ Squirt Mystery Color — with one of the nation's largest grocery retailers selling out in only two weeks. Not until the first squirt would consumers know what colour they had — Passion Pink, Awesome Orange, or Totally Teal. All of this plus a special nozzle for accurate squirting and an ergonomically smart shape that allowed smaller hands to hold on tight, allowing for some mealtime masterpiece creations from little artists. Limited-time "talking labels" were also introduced, with messages such as "Makes hot dogs chase their tails," "Comes out quicker for curly fries," or "Are your French fries lonely?" For the 2003 sequel, consumers can enter their own "Ketchuppy" quips to be featured, with their names, next time around.

Not banking everything on the fickle tastes of the young, Heinz also has introduced something for mature tastes and considerations. There is Heinz Organic Ketchup, made with 100 percent certified organic ingredients. For something a little zestier, there are Heinz Ketchup Kickers — the old regular enhanced in three varieties: Zesty Garlic, Hot & Spicy (with Tabasco pepper sauce), and Smokey Mesquite.[19]

Sometimes the target market is the non-user or light user, and the objective is to woo this customer into a higher-use category. Or light users may constitute an attractive niche for a marketer, simply because they are being ignored by other firms that are targeting heavy users. Once the characteristics of these light users have been identified, a marketer might try to increase usage rates by promoting (1) new uses for a product (baking soda as a deodorant), (2) new times for usage (off-season vacations), or (3) multiple packaging (a 12-pack of soft drinks).

Occasions Another popular approach to benefit segmentation is segmenting the market based on the occasions that customers would associate with the use of a product or service. Certain brands tend to be associated with certain occasions. For example, you may buy one brand of beer if you are taking a six-pack to a party, and another if you are at a special restaurant with a friend. Many restaurants and hotels cater to special occasions such as weddings by offering entertainment and all-inclusive rates. Some companies have grown up around meeting special-occasion needs.

◀ BACKSPACE

1. Name three bases for demographic segmentation.

2. What is psychographic segmentation?

3. How do people's lifestyles affect their choice of products?

Target Market Strategies

Let's assume that a company has segmented the total market for its product. Now management is in a position to select one or more segments to which it will target its marketing efforts. The company can follow one of three **target market strategies**: market aggregation, single-segment concentration, or multiple-segment targeting, as illustrated in Figure 4-3. To evaluate the strategies, management must determine the market potential of each segment that it has identified. But, before a strategy is chosen, the potential of the identified segments must be determined. This calls for establishing some guidelines for target market selection.

Selecting target segments

Holt Renfrew

Four guidelines govern how to determine which segments a company should target. The first is that target markets should be compatible with the organization's goals and image. One business that is keenly aware of this is Toronto-based Holt Renfrew (**www.holtrenfrew.com**), which recently changed its emphasis to focus more on national and international brands. This focus is in line with Holt Renfrew's positioning as an upscale store catering to the needs of an elite clientele.

Figure 4-3:

The Three Target Market Strategies

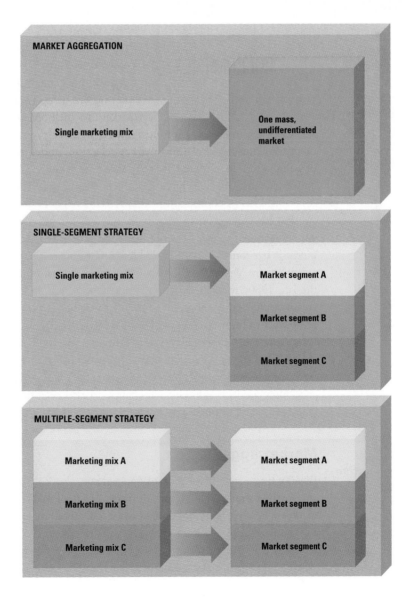

BURBERRY CANALI DOLCE & GABBANA ERMENEGILDO ZEGNA ESKANDAR GIORGIO ARMANI,
GUCCI HUGO BOSS JIL SANDER MICHAEL KORS PIAZZA SEMPIONE PRADA RALPH LAUREN ST JOHN

COMPLIMENTARY PERSONAL SHOPPING

HOLT RENFREW

QUEBEC MONTREAL OTTAWA TORONTO CALGARY EDMONTON VANCOUVER WWW.HOLTRENFREW.COM

There's no doubt about what segments Holt Renfrew is targeting.

To quote Andrew Jennings, the company's president, "It's all about advancing our goal of being one of the world's leading fashion and lifestyle experiences." This is a clear statement of Holt Renfrew's goals and image. Its recent store renovations and its pull-back from an earlier strategy to have up to 40 percent private-label merchandise, suggest a renewed emphasis on its wealthy clientele. It kicked off this re-emphasis on the country's elite with a month-long promotion of Italian fashion, food, design and lifestyle, called *Viva Italia*. Its glossy magazine named simply *holt's* features such items as Russian sable jackets and Gucci shirts. While Holt Renfrew targets a wealthier segment, Jennings' view is that "It's not about expense, it's about perceived value." Holt Renfrew's clientele clearly appreciates the difference.[20]

A second guideline — consistent with our definition of strategic planning — is to match the market opportunity represented in the target markets with the company's resources. For example, in examining new product opportunities, 3M considered many options but chose the do-it-yourself home improvement market because of the marketing economies that could be achieved. The firm's name was already well known to consumers, and the products could be sold through many of the retail outlets already selling 3M products, so entering this market was much less expensive than entering a market in which 3M was inexperienced.

Over the long run, a business must generate a profit to survive. This rather obvious statement translates into our third market-selection guideline. Some companies make the mistake of going after sales volume, not *profitable* sales volume. Companies that target the higher-yield customer must offer products or services that are perceived by the customer to have value. In some instances, a combination of approaches may be beneficial.

Fourth, a company ordinarily should seek a market where there are the fewest and smallest competitors. A company should not enter a market that is already saturated with competition unless it has some overriding differential advantage that will enable it to take customers from existing firms. When the Häagen-Dazs brand of premium ice cream entered Europe and Asia in the late 1980s, it had little competition at the high end of the market. Because per-capita ice cream consumption on these continents is well below that of North America, many viewed the prospects of a high-priced brand in a low-usage market as not very attractive. However, Häagen-Dazs, now with sales well over $500 million, proved the doubters wrong. It wasn't that consumers disliked ice cream; rather, many simply had not been exposed to a high-quality version. By getting to the market first, Häagen-Dazs now has a significant advantage over later entrants.[21]

These are only guidelines for target market selection. A marketer still has to decide how many segments to pursue as its target market, as we will see next.

Market aggregation

market aggregation
A strategy whereby an organization treats its total market as a unit — as one mass market in which the parts are considered to be alike in all major respects.

By adopting a strategy of **market aggregation**, also known as a mass-market or an undifferentiated-market strategy, an organization treats its total market as a single unit. This unit is one mass market whose parts are considered to be alike in all major respects. Management then develops a single marketing program to reach as many customers as possible in this aggregate market.

When is an organization likely to adopt the strategy of market aggregation? Generally, when a large group of customers in the total market tends to have the same perception of the product's need-satisfying benefits. Firms that are marketing a non-differentiated, staple product such as gasoline, salt, or sugar often adopt this strategy. In the eyes of many people, sugar is sugar, regardless of the brand. All brands of table salt are pretty much alike, and one unleaded gasoline is about the same as another.

Basically, market aggregation is a production-oriented strategy. It enables a company to maximize its economies of scale in production, physical distribution, and promotion. Producing and marketing one product for one market means longer production runs at lower unit costs. Inventory costs are minimized when there is no (or a very limited) variety of colours and sizes of products. Warehousing and transportation efforts are most efficient when one product is going to one market.

Market aggregation will work only as long as the seller's single marketing mix continues to satisfy enough customers to meet the company's sales and profit expectations. The strategy of market aggregation typically is accompanied by the strategy of **product or service differentiation** in a company's marketing program. Differentiation is the strategy by which one firm attempts to distinguish its product from competitive brands offered to the same aggregate market. By differentiating its product or service, an organization hopes to create the impression that what it offers is better than the competitors' brands. The seller also hopes to engage in non-price competition and thus avoid or minimize the threat of price competition.

A seller implements this strategy either (1) by changing some feature of the product (for example, packaging colour or label design), (2) by using a promotional appeal that features a differentiating benefit, or (3) by using advertising and other promotional strategies to create a differentiating image for the brand, product, or service. Gatorade has used a combination of these to maintain its image and market share in an increasingly competitive marketplace for energy beverages. It has introduced its own line of water, Propel, which is lightly flavoured and "vitamin-packed." It has also altered its existing product mix with Ice and Fierce lines, which are clearer, lightly flavoured beverages. In Canada, Montréal Canadiens' Jose Theodore promotes Ice in TV spots. Gatorade has also introduced a line called Xtremo, which was "specially created for our Latino consumers" in citrico, tropical, and mango flavours.[22]

Differentiation is an important strategy in any situation where there is little difference across the offerings of various companies, or where the consumer is unable to understand or appreciate the differences that do exist. Increasingly, companies are turning to service and how they treat customers to differentiate their companies. With so many products now being perceived by consumers to be quite similar, companies that can offer the best service to their customers are getting the business.

Single-segment concentration strategy

A **single-segment concentration strategy** involves selecting as the target market one homogeneous segment from within the total market. One marketing mix is then developed to reach this single segment. A small company may want to concentrate on a single market segment rather than to take on many competitors in a broad market.

Modrobes (pronounced "mode robes") clothing provides an example of targeting a very specific target group (see also Case 1-1, following Chapter 3). Modrobes targets the student population that prefers a casual, baggy, and sort of retro look. It started with a product that Steve "Sal" Debus created for an entrepreneurship project at Brock University in St. Catharines. He thought students needed "exam pants" — something in which you could eat and sleep, and then get up the next day and go to class in. They were stain-resistant, dried in 10 minutes, and needed no ironing. Modrobes started in the student market because it allowed the company to concentrate on a core audience.

Although, today, Modrobes clothing is available in outlets across Canada, the company still concentrates its marketing on small segments of the market and through company-owned stores

---

product or service differentiation

The strategy of setting a company or brand apart from its competition in the minds of its customers or prospective customers.

---

single-segment concentration strategy

The selection of one homogeneous segment from within a total market to be the target market.

---

in Toronto and Vancouver. With edgy slogans like "I want you in my pants," Modrobes promotes at concerts, raves, sports events, and campuses, and advertises in youth niche magazines such as *Vice* and *Tribe*. The founder/designer Steve Debus still keeps a close handle on how Modrobes is advertised and wants to remain close to its "original market" for product development and trends.

This focused strategy enables a company to concentrate in depth on one segment and to acquire a reputation as a specialist or an expert in this limited market. Young consumers who appreciate Modrobes clothing feel that the company "gets them." A company can enter such a market with limited resources and, as long as the single segment remains a small market, large competitors are likely to leave the single-segment specialist alone. However, if the small market shows signs of becoming a large market, bigger companies may well jump in. This is exactly what happened in the market for herbal and specialty teas.

The big risk and limitation to a single-segment strategy is that the marketing firm has all of its eggs in one basket. If that single segment declines in market potential, the seller can suffer considerably. Also, a seller with a strong name and reputation in one segment may find it difficult to expand into another segment.

Multiple-segment strategy

multiple-segment strategy

A strategy that involves the selection of two or more groups of potential customers as target markets.

Under a **multiple-segment strategy**, two or more different groups of prospective customers are identified as target segments. A separate marketing mix is developed to reach each segment. A marketer of personal computers, for example, may identify three distinct market segments — university and college students, small businesses, and a home market — and then design a different marketing mix to reach each segment. Dell, for example, has classified its target markets into three categories: consumer, business, and public. Each is then broken down further in order to determine the appropriate hardware, software, pricing strategies, etc. Public, for example, is broken down into federal government, provincial government, K–12 education, higher education, and health care. Each has different product and support requirements, as well as procurement policies. Dell manages this online distribution network of more than 55,000 third-party software and computer-related products in 27 languages and 40 currencies.[23]

In a multiple-segment strategy, a seller frequently develops a different version of the basic product for each segment. However, market segmentation can also be accomplished with no change in the product, but rather with separate distribution channels or promotional appeals, each tailored to a given market segment. Air Wair, the company that markets and distributes Doc Martens footwear, now develops products for a wider range of target segments. The company's original products (such as the 1460 boot) have always been associated with subcultures such as psychobilly, skins, goth, or grunge. Now older, many from these ranks have joined the adult world and have responsibilities, such as their own children. The company still features its classic lines, but also has developed products for casual business dressing for men, women, and children. For 2002, adult product lines included classic, street, urban, and leisure. Still true to their original image, the company participates in the music industry and features an online magazine — *Iconic* — intended to represent the voice of youth culture.[24]

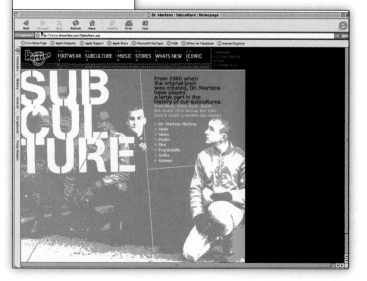

Doc Martens has extended its appeal to several new segments.

Positioning

The concept of market positioning is closely related to segmentation: A marketer must determine how the company's brands or stores or image are perceived by the public in general and, more particularly, by the market segment that has been selected as the principal target. As part of a company's marketing strategy, decisions must be made concerning how the company and its brands are to be portrayed to convey the correct image to the target segment. **Positioning**, therefore, relates to the use of various marketing techniques and marketing-mix variables to create the desired image and consumer perception of the company and its products or services.

A company may develop a positioning strategy for a particular brand or group of brands, for a retail store or chain, or for the company itself. The process involves answering questions such as: Who are the target market segments for this brand or store or company? On what basis do we want to appeal to this segment? What do we want people to think of when they hear our name? What do we want to be known for? What should our brand stand for and what should we mean to people? How do we want to be seen to be different from our competitors or from other brands or companies in the market? In dealing with questions such as these, the company is really asking: What position do we wish to occupy in this market or, more correctly, in the minds of target customers?

A food company that has successfully positioned itself is the youth-oriented, fast-food chain New York Fries. Sold as a premium product, some people even refer to it as "designer fries." This company is marketing quality fries described as "with the potato skins on to ensure protein is retained." Although the fries are higher priced, they are purchased because the product is perceived to be distinctive. The brand has developed a "personality" or "image" through its tongue-in-cheek marketing efforts, such as its campaign to support the ethical treatment of potatoes. Positioning has also been bolstered by its presence in many of the newly themed movie megaplexes across the country. The extra value created by this positioning seems to work, as avid buyers of New York Fries are prepared to pay more. This positioning is enhanced with promotional deals such as the "strategic alliance" they have with Alliance Atlantis to be a part of promoting particular movies such as Adam Sandler's *Little Nicky* and *Jackie Chan's Rush Hour 2*.[25]

Positioning, therefore, is a strategy for locating a brand or store in the consumer's mind in relation to its rating on certain dimensions or attributes that the consumer considers to be important. It involves staking out a place in the collective perception of consumers in which the brand or store or company can establish an image that will be appropriate for certain segments of the market. This image is created through the effective use of marketing-mix variables, including advertising, product design, pricing, packaging, store decor, and level of service.

The creation of the appropriate image may be approached in a combination of ways. In the first place, a firm may wish to occupy a position in a market in relation to that occupied by competitors. It may choose a position that is distinct from the one occupied by a competitor or may choose to challenge a competitor directly, thereby trying to occupy roughly the same position. On the other hand, the positioning strategy may be developed to position the brand or firm through the creation of an image tailored to the characteristics, preferences, attitudes, and feelings of a particular segment of the market. This approach is dependent on the company having selected certain target segments. The image of the product, brand, or store is then tailored to appeal to those segments.

Finally, a brand or company may be positioned on the basis of its inherent characteristics. In other words, the marketing staff of the company would have to decide what the brand or retailer is to be known for and set about creating the appropriate image. Such an approach deals implicitly with positioning against competition and meeting the needs of particular segments, but is often undertaken in response to the identification of a market gap, where no company has established a dominant position. There has been a dramatic increase in the number of overweight people in Canada over the past 20 years, particularly among young people. While the health implication of this should not be glossed over, the point here is that this trend is creating a new market of apparel

MARKETING AT WORK   4-3: TECHNOLOGY

A Segment of One — The End of Mass Marketing?

When Tom Cruise walked down the street in Steven Spielberg's movie *Minority Report*, he was bombarded with messages from talking billboards that addressed him by name. And while this 2002 film was set nearly 50 years into the future, its vision of a world in which people are pursued by personalized advertising messages is firmly rooted in today's marketing technologies and trends — this isn't science fiction according to John Pliniussen, associate professor of e-marketing at the Queen's University School of Business.

It's a practice that Pliniussen calls "shadow marketing." He says the technology is already available through cellphones and wireless messaging to track people's whereabouts and send them messages geared to their personal interests and present circumstances. As radio- and satellite-tracking technologies are incorporated into cars, electronic cash cards, and portable and wearable computers, consumers will find themselves in a world where they "are always connected, always being tracked," he says.

Personalized advertising that takes advantage of the interactivity and location-tracking capabilities of wireless messaging and other new media is still in its infancy, but it represents the beginning of a major trend — personalized, or one-to-one, advertising.

"There is no question, the industry is driving to build relationships on a more individual basis," says Michael Wood of Toronto-based advertising agency Leo Burnett Co. Ltd. "It's far more efficient than mass communications," he says. "With increased targeting, you are able to track whether or not the ads lead to purchase."

We soon may be able to wake up to clock radios that will blend personalized messages with traffic reports tailored to our daily commutes. Instead of tuning into regular broadcast commercial television, we may find ourselves with interactive programming with advertising tailored to our personal interests.

Pliniussen says that privacy legislation will ensure that this shadow marketing is carried out with the permission of the consumer, who will of course always have the capability to turn it off. But, it is believed that a growing number of people will choose to remain connected, as we all become more dependent on services such as links to home-security systems and day-care Web cams.

SOURCE: Adapted from Kevin Marron, "Personalized Advertising a Virtual Reality," *The Globe and Mail,* July 26, 2002, p. B9.

retailers. Toronto-based Toni+ has also been expanding — its stores, that is. Serving the plus-size market has done well by the company, particularly now that it also caters to the plus-size youth demographic. The company has a database of about 120,000 members to whom it sends brochures about the season's hottest looks for women of various ages, including teens.[26]

Niche marketing

niche marketing
A strategy in which goods and services are tailored to meet the needs of small market segments.

Some marketers may stake out "niche" positions for their brands; they create an image that is quite distinct and intended to appeal to a fairly narrow segment of the market. This is called niche marketing. Within the Canadian beer market, for example, brands such as Schooner and Celtique, imported beers such as Stella Artois, Sol, Guinness, and Corona, and the "handmade" brands are considered to be niche brands, while mainstream brands such as Molson Canadian and Labatt's Blue are positioned to appeal to much larger segments. Niche brands generally are not positioned to meet major competitors head-on, but rather to be leaders in a very narrow area of the market. Smaller companies often successfully carve out a niche for themselves. To continue with our beer examples, successful microbrewers such as Upper Canada Brewing, Les Brasseurs du Nord, Steam Whistle, Unibroue, and Granville Island Brewery are really niche marketers; they are satisfied with occupying a relatively small position in a very large market by catering to the tastes and preferences of consumers who want something different. Brands aren't just about function anymore, they're about entertainment. Currently, microbrews and imports hold only 4 percent and 6 percent, respectively, of the market. Continued growth is expected in "premium" products, because consumers seem increasingly willing to pay a premium for perceived value or a "hand-crafted" touch.[27]

Sleeman's Red Rock marketing strategy has enjoyed considerable success with its "chatty" commercials featuring John Sleeman talking informally about his company. The company has conveyed an image of a homespun cottage-industry operation. Brasserie McAuslan of Montréal has brewed an image of good corporate citizenship through community involvement and sponsorship. This has included tie-in promotions with bookstores, the Montréal International Film Festival, and on-screen ads in art-house theatres and other venues in sync with their micro-niche market of sophisticated, better-educated-than-average consumers. New Brunswick-based Alpine's slogan "Alpine. You gotta live here to get it" conjures up the notion of exclusivity, with humour supplied by Spot the dog. In TV spots, our hero Spot recruits attractive females for his owner by posing as lost and having a bad limp. On being returned home by a helpful brunette who joins the party going on inside, his owner whispers, "We're a little short of blondes." Spot once again hits the streets, looking for his next unwitting, but this time fair-haired, victim.[28]

Niche marketing is generally a successful strategy for smaller companies that do not have the financial and other resources generally available to large companies. In the travel business, for example, many travel agencies are seeking ways to set themselves apart from their competitors by specializing in narrow parts of the market. As travel has become more complex and travellers more demanding, some travel agencies have found it impossible to serve all segments equally well. Consequently, some become niche players, specializing in cruises, business travel, the ethnic market, or adventure travel. Weary of commercial travel but can't afford your own jet? Here's a new option — Lufthansa has begun operating "all-business-class" flights from Newark International Airport to Dusseldorf, Germany, using planes and crew from the elite Swiss charter company Privatair. Passengers are escorted through security by an airline agent and board from a special gate next to Lufthansa's club lounge. The aircraft are outfitted with 48 large seats (each with its own Sony Watchman), on-board plainclothes security, and an attendant for every 12 passengers. Fares rival those of regular business-class prices.[29]

To be successful in positioning itself as a niche player in the market, a company or the managers of a niche brand must have identified a segment of the market that is not now being served adequately by the brands and companies that are in the market. That segment must have sufficient potential buying power to warrant the development of a marketing program, it must be sufficiently small that larger companies are unlikely to retaliate if the niche brand is successful, and the niche marketer must have detailed knowledge of the characteristics of the members of the segment and their needs and preferences. One author has suggested that a company should follow four steps in implementing a successful niche marketing strategy.[30]

1. *Identify an appropriate niche* through marketing research that will indicate segments of the market that are not being well served by existing brands or where competition is not intense.

2. *Exploit the niche* by determining the likelihood of competitive retaliation and the length of time the company will enjoy a competitive advantage.

3. *Expand the niche* by meeting changing needs of the market segment, expanding the customer base, and making more effective use of marketing variables.

4. *Defend the niche* by continuing to meet the needs of segment members through improving the product and offering better service or lower prices.

Positioning strategies

Once a company has determined its market segmentation objectives and has identified the segments toward which its brands are to be targeted, it may adopt a number of **positioning strategies** to accomplish its objectives.

1. *Take on the competition head-on:* By deciding to challenge the market leader or to target large segments of the market with a broad appeal, a marketer is saying, "Our brand is as

good as or better than the leader." Such a strategy is exemplified in the so-called "cola wars," in which Pepsi-Cola and Coca-Cola have been fighting for market leadership by attempting to create the widest appeal to attract as many consumers as possible.

2. ***Occupy a gap in the market:*** A number of companies have moved to fill a gap in a market by positioning a brand to appeal to a certain segment of consumers or to take advantage of the disappearance of a competitor. For example, Volvo differentiates its cars from competitors by emphasizing safety.

3. ***Set a brand apart from the competition:*** Often a company will decide to employ a strategy that says, "Our brand is not like all of the others; this is why you should buy ours." This involves positioning a brand or store to avoid head-to-head competition with market leaders or with brands that have an established image or reputation and a secure market share. Jumbo Video distinguishes itself with its "guaranteed in-stock" policy for featured new releases. Office Depot offers a 150-percent price guarantee, assuring customers that if they find a product cheaper anywhere else, they will be reimbursed 150 percent of the purchase price (some restrictions apply).

4. ***Occupy position of leadership:*** Some companies that are clearly market leaders are not particularly interested in positioning themselves against the competition, but rather are likely to stake out a position as clear market leader, known to be ahead of the pack and leader in such areas as product quality, service to customers, profitability, innovations, or technology. Companies such as Loblaws and the Royal Bank of Canada tend to be regarded by many consumers as market leaders whose market franchises are so large and well established that competitors often try to emulate them and to position themselves against them. This approach can also work in cyberspace, as with Google.ca — the Google search engine positions itself to be almost overwhelmingly comprehensive, stating that it searches more than two billion Web pages at each request.

5. ***Position to appeal to lifestyle segments:*** Often a company will position itself to appeal to certain segments of the market that are defined not only by demographic characteristics but also by lifestyles. For example, there are two equally large segments of Porsche buyers with quite different lifestyles and reasons for buying the car. One group is driven by power and control. Called "top guns" at Porsche, they buy the car to be noticed. Another group, the "proud patrons," views a Porsche as a reward for hard work. To them, owning the car is an end in itself. They don't need the acknowledgment of others to derive satisfaction from a Porsche. Clearly, an ad that would appeal to the top guns could easily alienate the proud patrons.[31]

Repositioning

repositioning
The process of moving a company, store, or brand to a new position in the minds of target customers, usually by changing its image.

Repositioning is a variation of a positioning strategy that involves changing the market position of a brand or store in response to changes taking place in the broader market environment. The need to reposition a brand or retail store may result from one of three market conditions. First, management may identify a gap in the market that may be filled by altering the image of the store or brand — that is, changing the position it occupies in the minds of consumers. For example, a retailer in a local market may realize that the average age of its customer base is increasing and decide to reposition the store to have greater appeal to an older market segment.

Second, repositioning may be required by an increase in competitive activity. For example, Canada's retail industry has suffered considerable upheaval with the entry of new U.S. competitors. PharmaPlus, a Toronto-based drugstore, is positioning itself as a store that focuses on the core product categories of pharmacy, over-the-counter drugs, health and beauty aids, and baby care. This firm is finding it difficult to compete in non-pharmacy areas because of the increased number of low-priced chains such as Wal-Mart (**www.walmart.com**), who can undercut conventional

Wal-Mart
Zellers

drugstores in these product categories.[32] Zellers (**www.hbc.com/zellers**) has responded to Wal-Mart by renewing focus on its loyalty program and by introducing "best-value" format stores that offer convenience through smaller store sizes located in densely populated areas, offering less stock variety than regular outlets but "awesome deals" not possible from large chain stores.[33]

With the acquisition of Mark's Work Warehouse, an ambitious expansion strategy, and a new "Let's Get Started" positioning, Canadian Tire isn't sitting on its advertising laurels. It can't, with Home Depot, Wal-Mart, and home-grown Loblaws breathing down its neck. It's a very familiar brand — partly because of what is often jokingly referred to as our second official currency (Canadian Tire money) — but it's not a new one. In fact, it's more than 80 years old and that has been an integral part of its positioning: invoking memories of your first bike, hockey stick, or baseball glove. This sense of being a part of growing up in Canada has often been spun into the fabric of the store's advertising. The store's new positioning is intended to evolve and refresh this, while keeping the equity that has developed with many consumers. The new campaign that debuted during the 2002 Academy Awards shows people enjoying life with products purchased from Canadian Tire. It's less about reflecting on past memories and more about creating energy and inspiration — creating new memories. The message is that it's still the ideal place to start something: a new sport, new season, whatever.[34]

Third, it may be necessary to reposition a brand or store in response to a change in the demographic characteristics, attitudes, or values of the target consumer market. Packaged-food producers have addressed these trends in recent years as a result of significant changes in eating habits. High-fat foods are no longer appealing to mass markets. This is becoming particularly evident now that labels must carry information about package contents. Heinz, Nabisco, Kraft, and other major packaged-food suppliers are creating new products such as flavoured cream cheeses and ultra-low-fat salad dressings, Linda McCartney vegetarian cuisine (introduced by Paul McCartney's late wife), and Ore Ida Funky Fries in flavours such as cocoa, cinnamon, and sour cream, and colours such as electric blue.

Another change has been in the demand for "convenience" foods or "meal solutions." This has led manufacturers and supermarkets to alter their product offerings. Manufacturers have increased the number of meal "kits" they offer, including prepared frozen main courses that require only cooking or the addition of a certain amount of the consumer's meat of choice. The delicatessen sections of supermarkets have expanded to offer consumers greater selections of home meal replacements: any frozen or fresh meal prepared in-store for immediate consumption at home. This includes items as varied as salad-in-a-bag, to prepared entrées bought by the kilogram, to individual meal packages that have main and side dishes pre-selected.

← BACKSPACE

1. What are the three target market strategies that a firm can follow?
2. A firm that develops a different version of the basic product for each segment would use a _____ target market strategy.
3. How is positioning related to segmentation?

Summary

An effective marketing program begins with the identification and analysis of target markets for the products and services that the organization wants to sell. It is not usually wise for organizations to try to sell to all available consumers. Markets consist of people and organizations with needs or wants, resources to spend, and the willingness to spend them. There are some general guidelines to follow when trying to determine appropriate target markets for a firm.

In the interest of targeting the consumers who would be most interested in its product or service, the organization will utilize some form of market segmentation. This is a customer-oriented process in which the total heterogeneous market is divided into several homogeneous segments. A separate marketing program is then developed for the segments to be pursued. These programs attempt to portray, or position, the organization (or a product or service) in the most appealing way to each group. Many effective positioning strategies are available to the firm. At times, a product will appeal to only a small niche segment of the marketplace, but this can still be profitable.

The requirements for effective segmentation include that (1) the bases for segmentation be measurable with accessible data, (2) the segments themselves be accessible, and (3) the segments be large enough to be potentially profitable. Segmentation allows the company to make the most efficient use of its marketing resources and makes it possible for even small firms to compete effectively in those segments where they are most suited.

The total market can be divided into two broad categories: end-consumers and business users. The four major bases that are used to further segment the consumer market are (1) geographic, (2) demographic, (3) psychographic, and (4) product/service-related.

In the consumer market, the distribution and composition of the population has a major effect on target market selection. Other useful divisions can be made on a regional basis or by urban, suburban, or rural segments. In this context, the bulk of the population is concentrated in metropolitan areas — these areas continue to expand and even join together in some parts of the country.

Age groups are another significant basis for market analysis. The stage of the family life cycle influences the market for many products and services. Other demographic bases include education, occupation, religion, and ethnic origin. Consumer income, particularly disposable and discretionary income, is a meaningful measure of buying power and market potential. Income distribution has shifted considerably in recent years, with more families in the over-$90,000 bracket and a much smaller percentage that earns under $30,000. Income level and life-cycle stage are both significant determinants of spending patterns. The increasing use of psychographic and relationship segmentation approaches is permitting the marketing department to better understand how to establish bonds with consumers, enabling higher levels of customer satisfaction and loyalty.

Key Terms and Concepts

activities, interests, and opinions 117
behavioural segmentation 119
benefit segments 119
business users 103
Census Metropolitan Area (CMA) 107
conditions for effective segmentation 102
consumer income 112
consumer spending patterns 113
demographic segmentation 107
discretionary purchasing power 112
end-consumers 103
family life cycle 111
geographic segmentation 105
income distribution 113
market aggregation 122
market segmentation 101
multiple-segment strategy 124

niche marketing 126
personal disposable income 112
personality characteristics 118
positioning 125
positioning strategies 127
product or service differentiation 123
profiles 119
regional distribution 106
relationship segmentation 118
repositioning 128
single-segment concentration strategy 123
target market segment 98
target market strategies 121
urban-suburban-rural distribution 106
usage rate 119
values 117

Questions and Problems

1. What benefits can a company expect to gain from segmenting its market?

2. Take a look at the range of channels currently offered by the MuchMusic network. Why would the network embark on such a strategy and what segments is each channel targeting?

3. In which stage of the life cycle are families likely to be the best prospects for each of the following products or services?

a. Braces on teeth.
b. Suntan lotion.
c. Second car in the family.
d. Vitamin pills.
e. Refrigerators.
f. Life insurance.
g. Aerobics classes.
h. Two-week Caribbean cruise.

4. Using the demographic and income segmentation bases discussed in this chapter, describe the segment likely to be the best market for:
   a. Skis.
   b. Good French wines.
   c. Power hand tools.
   d. Birthday cards.
   e. Gas barbecues.

5. Describe what you believe to be the demographic characteristics of heavy users of:
   a. Dog food.
   b. Ready-to-eat cereal.
   c. CD players.
   d. The Internet.

6. Suppose you are marketing automobiles. How is your marketing mix likely to differ when marketing to each of the following market segments?
   a. High school students.
   b. Retired teachers.
   c. Blue-collar workers.
   d. Mothers.
   e. Young single adults.

7. Explain the similarities and differences between a single-segment and a multiple-segment target market strategy.

8. Assume that a company has developed a new type of portable headphone-type cassette player in the general product category of a Sony Walkman. Which of the three target market strategies should this company adopt?

9. Identify a number of brands, retailers, or restaurants with which you are familiar that have chosen to occupy a niche in the market. How would you describe the niche that each occupies? Why do you feel each has chosen this niche?

10. Why would a company decide that one of its brands needs to be repositioned? What market conditions are likely to lead to a decision to reposition a brand or company? Can you think of any brands or stores with which you are familiar that have recently been repositioned? What were their original positions? How would you describe the new position that each occupies in the market? How was the repositioning accomplished in each case?

Hands-On Marketing

1. Interview three friends or acquaintances who all own running shoes, but who are from different demographic groups (for example, different education, age, or gender). Using demographic characteristics only, describe in as much detail as possible the market segment each of your friends represents. Is yours a very complete segment picture? Why or why not?

2. Consider three retailers or three restaurants in your home town or the town or city in which your university or college is located and describe in as much detail as possible the target market segment that each of the stores or restaurants is serving.

Back to the Top

Knowing what you now know about market segmentation and positioning, think back to the chapter opener on the travel industry and outline how various players in that industry address different market segments. Select two different airlines, hotel chains, and car rental companies, and discuss the target segments of each and how each is positioned to appeal to these segments

Want to get better grades, tips on how to study more effectively, and up-to-date information on happenings in the world of marketing? Then, visit the Online Learning Centre for practice tests, Study Smart software, and much more! **www.mcgrawhill.ca/college/sommers**

Interested in finding out what marketing looks like in the real world? *Marketing Magazine* is just a click away on your Online Learning Centre!

CHAPTER 5

B2B Marketing

In this chapter, we turn our attention specifically to the situation in which a company is marketing to other businesses and organizations, which today is commonly referred to as B2B (business-to-business) marketing. In many ways, business markets are similar to the consumer markets we examined in the early chapters of this book, but there are also important differences. After studying this chapter, in addition to being able to describe how business markets differ from consumer markets, you should have an understanding of:

- The nature and scope of the B2B market.
- The components that make up the B2B market.
- The characteristics of business market demand.
- The determinants of business market demand.
- The buying motives, buying processes, and buying patterns in business markets.

About Us   Company   News   Online Demo   Grocery Stores   Contact Us

The MyWebGrocer
Internet Shopping
Solution connects the
traditional Supermarket
to its customers by
providing a state of the
art online shopping
experience. For
consumers, it is as easy
as pointing and clicking
through the aisles of
their neighborhood
grocery store!

MyWebGrocer.com

Connecting the consumer
to their local grocer

| Home | About Us | Company | News | Online Demo | Grocery Stores | Employment | Contact Us |

©2002 by MyWebGrocer.com
All Rights Reserved

Intel Inside the Grocery Van — Bagging Customers in a Difficult Sector

Internet grocers are re-emerging and beginning to find success online after several years of trying to find the right mix of bricks and clicks. But, what does it take to get from a grocery list in your hands to the bag of groceries delivered to your door by your local grocer? In some cases, it has meant the outsourcing of certain functions and working with solutions providers in the business-to-business marketplace. In this case, it takes the services of providers called MyWebGrocer.com and Intel.

Online grocery stores have had a difficult time, with giants such as WebVan and Kozmo disappearing from the market after spending billions. But MyWebGrocer.com has taken a different approach from its deceased competitors, and instead of establishing its own entire infrastructure, has utilized outsourcing and other business services.

MyWebGrocer.com is an Internet-based "shopping solution" designed specifically for the retail grocery industry. It isn't a grocery store, but it helps grocery stores offer their services via the Internet. Consumers can shop the aisles from their computers, with orders routed directly to the store. Orders are completed by either delivery or customer pick-up, depending on store policy. The easy-to-use customer interface accurately reflects each store's inventory and pricing, including specials and frequent-shopper program discounts. MyWebGrocer.com has been designed to work for multiple stores in various geographic areas, offering different inventory at varying prices. Inventory tracking and price changing are obviously easier than in traditional bricks-and-mortar stores. How is all of this possible? That's where Intel enters the story.

Intel provided the architecture that gave MyWebGrocer.com rapid deployment, flexibility, and a wide range of software choices, helping the company to grow tenfold, while others have tanked. This service was facilitated by equipment from other familiar names as well, including various Compaq servers equipped with Intel Xeon and Pentium III processors, as well as Microsoft Internet Information Servers and software.

Intel does more than just push out the well-recognized processors used in our home PCs. It also provides a wide range of scalable products to help business-solution providers meet the needs of their clients, clients such as MyWebGrocer.com, which boasted a clientele of more than 160 stores in 2002 — up from just 12 in 2000. Growth has been impressive, with more than 120,000 specific product items (called stock-keeping units or SKUs) and stores experiencing 12 to 15 percent monthly growth in online order volumes. While competition exists, only MyWebGrocer.com is positioned to extend and enhance the existing brands of thousands of established supermarkets.

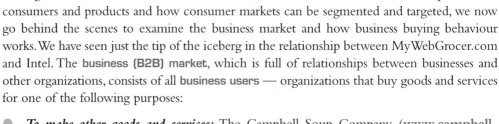

The Nature and Scope of the B2B Market

Having discussed consumer behaviour and introduced the role of the relationships between consumers and products and how consumer markets can be segmented and targeted, we now go behind the scenes to examine the business market and how business buying behaviour works. We have seen just the tip of the iceberg in the relationship between MyWebGrocer.com and Intel. The **business (B2B) market**, which is full of relationships between businesses and other organizations, consists of all **business users** — organizations that buy goods and services for one of the following purposes:

business (B2B) market
The market consisting of business users.

- *To make other goods and services:* The Campbell Soup Company (**www.campbell-soup.com**) buys fresh vegetables for its Leamington, Ontario, plant; Bombardier (**www.bombardier.com**) in Montréal and its other Canadian and worldwide locations buys a great variety of different materials to make products as varied as its Ski-Doo snowmobiles, Sea-Doo personal watercraft, and regional jets.

Campbell Soup Company
Bombardier

- *To resell to other business users or to consumers:* Loblaws buys canned tuna fish from South America and Asia to sell across Canada; Western Pipe buys lawn sprinkler equipment and supplies from Canadian, U.S., and offshore manufacturers and resells them to sprinkler contractors.

- *To conduct the organization's operations:* The school that you attend buys office supplies and electronic office equipment (many fitted with Intel chips) for use in the registrar's office; Canadian Tire buys software to co-ordinate and manage its inventory system across the country.

B2B marketing
The marketing of goods and services to business users, rather than to end-consumers.

The business market deals with both consumer products and business products. **B2B marketing**, then, is the marketing of goods and services to business users, rather than to end-consumers.

Because the business market is largely invisible to the average consumer, its significance is underrated — it is actually huge in total sales volume and the number of firms involved. Approximately 50 percent of all manufactured products are sold to the business market. In addition, about 80 percent of all farm products and virtually all forest, sea, and mineral products are business goods. All of these products are sold to firms for further processing.

The magnitude and complexity of the B2B market are also evident from the web of relationships and the many transactions required to produce and market a product. You have an idea of the nature of such relationships from the MyWebGrocer.com-Intel chapter opener but, closer to home, think about what goes into getting those thick-soled, leather boots to you and other end-users. First, cattle are sold through one or two intermediaries before reaching a meat packer. Then the hides are sold to a tanner, who in turn sells the leather to a specialized footwear manufacturer. The footwear manufacturer may sell the finished boots to a wholesaler, who markets them to select retail stores. Finally, they are then available to you, the end-consumer. At least five transactions are involved here, and each sale but the last one is a business-to-business market transaction relying on myriad relationships. Each of the B2B transactions can be made in a market that operates for that type of transaction.

Our footwear manufacturer also buys metal eyelets, laces, thread, glue, heels and soles, and zippers, as well as polishes and dyes. Consider something as simple as the bootlaces. Other industrial firms must first buy the raw cotton and then spin, weave, dye, and cut it so that it becomes shoestring material. All of the manufacturers involved have factories and offices with furniture, machinery, furnaces, lights, computer hardware and software, and maintenance equipment and supplies, which also are business goods that have to be produced and marketed. Imagine, then, the number of relationships that have developed and the transactions that have occurred from the cattle and cotton fields to the footwear you are now wearing. In short, hundreds of business products and business marketing activities may come into play before almost any consumer or business product reaches its final destination.

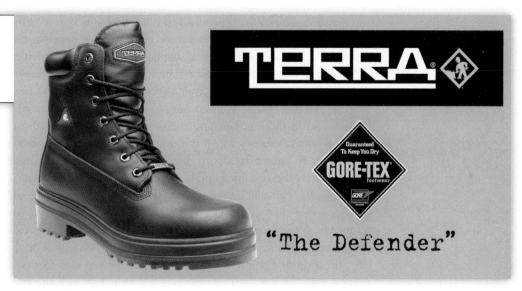

How many B2B markets are involved in getting these boots onto your feet?

The magnitude and complexity of the B2B market looms even larger when we consider all of the business services involved throughout our "simple" footwear example. Each firm engaged in any stage of the production process probably uses outside accountants, computer systems designers, and law firms. Several of the producers may use advertising agencies. All of these companies will use the services of various financial institutions.

Every retail store and wholesaling establishment is a business user. Every bus company, airline, and railroad is part of this market, as is every hotel, restaurant, bank, insurance company, software provider, hospital, theatre, and school. In all, there are close to half a million business users in Canada. While this falls far short of the more than 30 million Canadian consumers, the total sales volume in the business market far surpasses total sales to consumers. And it is mostly behind the scenes.

Components of the B2B Market

Traditionally, business markets were referred to as "industrial markets." This caused many people to think that the term referred only to the 105,000 or so manufacturing firms operating in Canada, varying in size from 2 or 3 to more than 500 employees. These firms alone have an estimated shipment value of approximately $450 billion.[1] But, as you can see from our discussion so far, the business market is a lot more than that. Certainly, manufacturers constitute a major portion of the business market, but there are also five other components: resellers, government agencies, service companies, agriculture, and not-for-profit organizations. Although they are often underrated or overlooked because of the heavy attention devoted to manufacturing, each is a significant part of the business market. And it must be kept in mind that some of Canada's most important and fastest-growing business markets are outside Canada, in the United States and many other countries.

The reseller market

reseller market
Wholesaling and retailing intermediaries that buy products for resale to other business users or to consumers; a segment of the business market.

Intermediaries in the Canadian marketing system — the few hundred thousand wholesalers, retailers, and other organizations — constitute the **reseller market**. The basic activity of resellers, unlike that of any other business market segment, is buying products from supplier organizations and reselling these items in essentially the same form to the resellers' customers. In economic terms, resellers create time, place, and possession utilities, rather than form utility.

Resellers also buy many goods and services for use in operating their businesses, such as office supplies, information and communication equipment, materials-handling equipment, legal services, electrical services, and janitorial supplies. In these buying activities, resellers are essentially no different from manufacturers, financial institutions, or any other segment of the business market.

It is their role as *buyers for resale* that distinguishes resellers from their suppliers. To resell an item, you must please your customer. Resellers must decide what products will be popular or useful to those comprising their markets. It is more difficult to determine what will please an outside customer than to find out what will satisfy someone in your own organization. When an airline decides to design new foul-weather jackets for its flight crews, it can carefully study the conditions under which the jackets will be worn and ask for the opinions of the people who will be wearing the jackets. As a result, it should be able to select an all-weather jacket that will be lightweight and safe to wear when working, easy to clean, and acceptable to the employees. Contrast that with retailers trying each year to anticipate what outerwear to purchase and place on their shelves. What will be the next trend — short or long, function or fashion — and what about colours and fabrics? In both cases, clothing is being purchased, but the opportunity for interaction with the users and the variety of uses and purposes differ greatly between the groups. This makes buying for resale for the "anonymous" consumer market more difficult and much more risky.

Buying for resale, especially in a large reseller's organization, can be a complex procedure. For a supermarket chain such as Sobeys, Loblaws, or Safeway, a buying committee made up of experts on market demand, trends, supply, and prices frequently does the buying. This is necessary, as hundreds of products may be proposed to these stores each week for consideration — up to 10,000 each year.[2] Department stores may retain resident buyers — independent buying agencies — located in Toronto, London, Hong Kong, or other major market centres to be in constant touch with the latest fashion developments.

The services market

services market
The market for service activities, including all transportation carriers and public utilities; communications firms, financial, insurance, legal, and real estate firms; and organizations that produce and sell services such as rental housing, recreation and entertainment, repairs, health care, personal care, and business services.

Firms that produce services greatly outnumber firms that produce goods: Service firms outnumber the total of all manufacturers, mining companies, construction firms, and enterprises engaged in farming, forestry, and fishing. The **services market** includes all transportation carriers and public utilities, communications firms, and the many financial, insurance, legal, and real estate firms that make purchases to enable their provision of services. This market also includes organizations that produce and sell such diverse services as rental housing, recreation and entertainment, repairs, health care, personal care, and business services.

Service firms constitute a huge market that buys goods and other services. Four Seasons Hotels, for example, buys blankets and sheets from textile manufacturers. Hospitals in Canada and abroad buy supplies from Baxter Healthcare. As in the chapter opener, MyWebGrocer.com buys software and hardware from Intel and Microsoft. These and other service firms buy legal, advertising, accounting, information technology equipment and systems, and consulting advice from other service marketers. The importance to Canadian marketers of the services market is dealt with in greater detail in Chapter 8.

The government market

government market
The segment of the business market that includes federal, provincial, and local government units buying for government institutions such as schools, offices, hospitals, and research facilities.

The large **government market** includes federal, provincial, territorial, Native, and municipal governments, as well as various Crown agencies and corporations that spend millions of dollars each year buying for institutions such as schools, offices, hospitals, and military bases. At the federal level, Public Works and Government Services Canada purchases in excess of $191 billion worth of goods and services annually for its own use and for other government units.[3] The largest "consumers" among these are Public Works and Government Services Canada itself and the

competitive bidding
The characteristic form of government procurement, in which a government agency advertises both offline and online for bids, using a format that states the specifications of the intended purchase. The agency must accept the lowest bid that meets these specifications.

Contracts Canada

Canada Business Service Centre

MERX

Department of National Defence. Collectively, however, the other levels of governments listed are even more important markets than is the federal government.

Government procurement processes are different from those in the private sector of the business market. A unique feature of government buying is the **competitive bidding** system. Much government procurement is done on a bid basis and a growing amount of it is now taking place online. The government agency advertises both offline and online for bids, using a format that states the specifications of the intended purchase. Any size of firm can usually bid, as individual contracts vary greatly in size across departments. The agency must accept the lowest bid that meets these specifications. Contracts Canada (**www.contractscanada.gc.ca**) is the interdepartmental program assigned to simplify access and improve awareness of federal government purchasing. Also, the Canada Business Service Centre provides information regarding provincial and federal programs, as well as opportunities for bidding on government contracts (**www.cbsc.org**). The electronic tendering service utilized by the federal government is MERX (**www.merx.cebra.com**), operated by Cebra Inc., a member of the Bank of Montreal group of companies.

The potential of the government business market is sufficiently attractive that some firms concentrate almost exclusively on government markets. Despite the opportunities, however, many companies make no effort to sell to the government, because they are intimidated by the red tape. Dealing with the government to any significant extent usually requires specialized marketing techniques and information. Some firms, such as Spar Aerospace and Bombardier, have established special departments to deal with government markets. For firms wanting to sell to the government, information and guidelines are available from Public Works and Government Services Canada on the proper procedures for doing business.

The agriculture market

Both the proportion of farmers of the total population of Canada and the number of farms have been decreasing and probably will continue to decline. Counterbalancing this has been an increase in large corporate or "business" types of farms. Even the remaining "family" farms are expanding in order to survive. Farming continues to be more automated and mechanized, which means, of course, that capital investment in farming is increasing. **Agribusiness** — farming, food processing, and other large-scale, farming-related businesses — is big business in every sense of the word.

agribusiness
The business side of farming; usually involves large, highly mechanized farming operations.

Like other business executives, farmers are looking for better ways to increase their productivity, cut their expenses, and manage their cash flows. For example, one large business farmer has developed a sensor and remote steering system that guides a tractor between the rows in a field to avoid destroying any crops. Caterpillar Equipment, in order to service large equipment in remote locations, has a satellite that can monitor on-board systems, detect equipment wear, and perform diagnostic tests, automatically shipping replacement parts within hours so that they will arrive before they are required.

As farms become fewer and larger, marketing to them effectively requires carefully designed strategies. Some large fertilizer producers have salespeople who visit individual farms and, working with the farmer, analyze the soil and crops to determine exactly what fertilizer mix is best. Based on the analysis, the manufacturer prepares the appropriate blend of ingredients as a special order.

non-business market
Includes such diverse institutions as churches, colleges and universities, museums, hospitals and other health institutions, political parties, labour unions, and charitable organizations.

The "non-business" business market

The **non-business market** includes such diverse institutions as churches, colleges and universities, museums, hospitals and other health institutions, political parties, labour unions, and charitable organizations. Each of these non-business organizations is actually a business organization. However, our society (and the institutions themselves) in the past did not perceive a museum or a hospital as being a business, and many of those involved still feel uncomfortable thinking of their church, school, or political party as a business organization. Nevertheless, these organizations do virtually all of the things that any business does — offer and consume products or services, collect money, make investments, hire employees — and therefore require professional management.

Not-for-profit organizations also conduct marketing campaigns — although under a different name — in an effort to attract millions of dollars in contributions. In turn, they spend millions of dollars buying goods and services to run their operations.

The international dimension

Since Canada exports more than $180 billion (nearly 30 percent) of its gross domestic product, and since a major portion of this export trade is conducted on a business-to-business basis, the international market, comprising the same components as those that exist within Canada, is a vibrant collection of foreign-based business markets. The value of international B2B commerce can be expected to rise as the Internet continues to be a favoured tool for these buyers. While the total value of goods and services exchanged online by U.S. businesses was more than $230 billion ($US) in 2000, this is estimated to reach almost $600 billion ($US) by 2004.[4] Further, it is estimated that worldwide B2B e-commerce will be worth $2.7 trillion ($US) by 2004.[5] It is not possible, however, to predict accurately how quickly vendors,

MARKETING AT WORK   5-1: GLOBAL

B2B Relationships in the Global Marketplace

As more and more organizations do business across international boundaries, executives are becoming increasingly aware of the non-business factors that influence the ultimate success or failure of their ventures. Consider these tips on what marketers going abroad can expect:

- In Germany, executives are thorough, systematic, well prepared, and quite systematic. They tend to be assertive — even intimidating — and not very willing to compromise. They are especially punctual and prize efficiency and directness.

- In Egypt, the pace is slow and a "hard-sell" approach will neither be appreciated nor successful. Your counterparts must get to know you and decide they like you for negotiations to go anywhere. Egyptians love language, so they expect a lot of rhetoric, exaggeration, poetics, emotion, and flowery language.

- In France, managers may insist on doing business in French, and because they feel that speaking is an art form, the French don't like being interrupted. Lengthy lunches with lots of wine usually accompany negotiations. Appropriate clothing is suggested, and never use first names without an invitation to do so.

- In Brazil, initial meetings will be formal, but relaxed once rapport is established. Small talk is very important. Businesspeople are very keen to exchange business cards, which should be printed in English and Portuguese. Book appointments far ahead of time, as it is unacceptable to show up unannounced.

- In England, the style is friendly and easy-going. Executives are more likely to be underprepared than overprepared.

They are generally flexible and open to initiatives. However, this can be misleading and they can become stubborn if they sense a lack of respect.

- In Mexico, personal relationships are very important, as is face-to-face contact. The idea is to socialize first and work later. To rush business matters when being offered hospitality may be seen as insulting. Businesspeople can be flexible when it comes to trade-offs, but it is often best to negotiate privately in one-on-one conversations.

- In China, small courtesies and follow-up gifts are important in establishing friendships. Meticulous preparation and consistency are important, because the Chinese are very thorough. Again, social engagements will often precede business discussions. Most negotiations will involve government, as there are many joint ventures and state enterprises.

- In Japan, first impressions are critical. Introductions and the exchange of business cards are very ceremonial events, as the order of presentation and business cards is tightly linked to rank. Meetings tend to be large, with many levels involved in decision-making. Non-verbal communication, smiling, laughing, and eye contact are all important communication cues.

SOURCE: Adapted from Sergay Frank, "Global Negotiating: Vive Les Differences!" *Sales & Marketing Management*, May 1992, pp. 65–69; Brian Banks, "English Too," *Canadian Business*, January 1995, pp. 20–35; *Business Culture* (www.businessculture.com), March 2000; *Executive Planet* (www.executiveplanet.com), June 2002.

buyers, and product classes will adapt to the medium, since traditionally the development of personal relationships has always played an important part in B2B international marketing.

The Internet, however, is invaluable for making international contacts, even if a site does no more than list products or services and contact information. Even sites providing only traditional contact by snail mail or telephone will still turn up in Web search results.[6] However, many B2B buying decisions continue to require face-to-face contact. Marketing to businesses based abroad, whether in the United States, Japan, the United Kingdom, or the Gulf states, requires more work on developing relationships than you would expect. This is the case because, whether the marketer is dealing with a foreign subsidiary of a Canadian firm or with foreign firms, the cross-cultural dynamics of negotiation and relationship-building cannot be taken for granted. Canadian marketers doing business abroad must become familiar with the values, customs, symbols, and standard practices and expectations of their foreign-based buyers, including the individuals with whom the marketer must negotiate and the firms that they represent. Marketing at Work 5-1, "B2B Relationships in the Global Marketplace," provides a sample of what marketers doing business abroad can expect.

◀ BACKSPACE

1. The business market consists of _____ .
2. What are the six components of the business market?
3. There are more _____ firms than firms that produce goods.

Characteristics of B2B Market Demand

Four demand characteristics differentiate the business market from the consumer market: Demand is derived, tends to be inelastic, and is widely fluctuating, and the market is well informed.

Demand is derived

The demand for a business product or service is based on (derived from) the demand for the consumer products in which that business product is used. The demand for steel or plastics depends partially on consumer demand for automobiles and refrigerators, but it also depends on the demand for computer graphics boards, butter, and hockey pads and equipment. This is because the tools, machines, and other equipment needed to manufacture these items are made of steel and plastic. When the demand for hockey equipment increases, The Hockey Company may need more sewing machines and computers — each requiring plastic and steel.

There are two significant marketing implications of the fact that business market demand is derived. First, to estimate the demand for a product, a business marketer must be very familiar with how it is used. This is fairly easy for a company such as Pratt & Whitney, a manufacturer of jet engines. But what about the manufacturer of rubber O-rings (doughnut-shaped rings of all sizes that are used to seal connections, often referred to as "washers")? Considerable research may be necessary to identify uses, users, and potential new opportunities.

Second, the producer of a business product sometimes engages in consumer marketing efforts to encourage the sale of its buyers' products. Intel consistently advertises to consumers, urging them when buying computers to ask specifically for products with an Intel processor. Further, name-brand computers will often also be labelled, "Intel Inside." The NutraSweet Company (www.nutrasweet.com) ran a consumer advertising campaign designed to build consumer loyalty for goods sweetened with its product. The idea, of course, is that increases in consumer demand will in turn trigger increases in **derived demand** for these business products.

NutraSweet Company

derived demand
A situation in which the demand for one product is dependent on the demand for another product.

Demand is inelastic

inelastic demand
A price-volume relationship in which a change of one unit on the price scale results in a change of less than one unit on the volume scale.

Mountain Equipment
Co-op

Another characteristic of the business market is that the demand for business products does not change easily because of price fluctuations. In economic terms, this **inelastic demand** refers to an item's price elasticity — how responsive demand is to a change in the price of a product.

The demand for many business products responds very little to changes in price, as long as the cost of a business product is a small proportion of the product's total cost. In these situations, the demand for the product is relatively inelastic. If the price of a business product such as Velcro fastening materials suddenly rises or falls considerably, how much effect would it have on retail prices at a store such as Mountain Equipment Co-op (MEC)? MEC (**www.mec.ca**) uses these materials in its jackets, pants, vests, and knapsacks. In fact, Velcro is used to some degree in most MEC apparel, so a price increase could mean a significant increase in the company's purchasing cost for this item. Because the fasteners are such a small part of a jacket, pant, or knapsack, however, the price increase would not likely change the retail price noticeably. As a result, Canadians would still flock to MEC and demand for these products would not change. This would also be the case for all other Velcro buyers — a price change in either direction would not alter demand for the business product. But not all business products form a small part of the total consumer product. In such situations, *the greater the cost of a business product as a percentage of the total price of the finished good, the greater the elasticity of demand for this business product.*

Demand is widely fluctuating

Although the demand for business goods does not change much in response to price changes, it does respond to other factors. In fact, market demand for most classes of business goods fluctuates considerably more than the demand for consumer products. The demand for installations — major plant equipment, factories, and so on — is particularly subject to change. Substantial fluctuations also exist in the market for accessory equipment — office furniture and machinery, delivery trucks, and similar products. These tend to accentuate the swings in the demand for business raw materials and fabricating parts. We can see this very clearly when declines in demand in the construction and auto industries affect suppliers of lumber, steel, plastics, and other materials and parts.

Fluctuations in the demand for business products can influence all aspects of a marketing program. In product planning, fluctuations in demand may stimulate a firm to diversify into other products to ease production and marketing problems. Changes within the industry, competition, and technology may also cause concerns. For example, in the last few years, IBM has retreated in a major way from mainframe computer manufacturing and, using mass-market television and magazine advertising, placed much emphasis on its digitally based consulting services. Microsoft decided in 2001 to diversify into more consumer markets by moving into the lucrative video game console market that, with the Xbox, is estimated to be valued at $700 million in Canada alone. This was not only an entry into an established market, but represented an opportunity to establish itself with this product in the burgeoning interactive multimedia market.

Buyers are well informed

Typically, business buyers are better informed about what they are buying than are consumers. They know more about the relative merits of alternative sources of supply and competitive products for three reasons. First, there are relatively few alternatives for a business buyer to consider, while consumers typically have many more brands and sellers from which to choose. Consider, for example, how many options you would have in purchasing a TV set. In most business situations, however, a buyer will find only a few firms that offer the particular combination of product features and service desired. Second, the responsibility of a buyer in an organization is ordinarily limited to a few products. Unlike a consumer who buys many different things, a purchasing agent's job is to be very knowledgeable about a narrowly defined set of products. Third, for most consumer purchases, an error is only a minor inconvenience. However, in business buying, the cost of a mistake can easily be tens of thousands of dollars or even the decision-maker's job!

Manufacturers and marketers of business products place a much greater emphasis on product information and personal contact to communicate than do firms that market consumer products. This makes business buyers more reliant on both Internet contact and personal relationships with their suppliers. Business salespeople and service representatives must be carefully selected, properly trained, and adequately compensated. They must give informative and effective presentations, furnish satisfactory service, form relationships with their client firms, and work to build and maintain relationship strength. This is increasingly important, because the Internet makes searching for other suppliers, up-to-date information, and new products easier than ever before.

Determinants of B2B Market Demand

To analyze a consumer market, a marketer would study the distribution of population and various demographics, such as income, and then try to determine the consumers' buying motives and habits. A firm selling to the business market can use essentially the same type of analysis. The factors affecting the market for business products are the number of potential business users and their purchasing power, buying motives, and buying habits. In the following discussion, we'll identify several basic differences between consumer markets and business markets.

Number and types of business users

The business market contains relatively few buying units compared with the consumer market. There are approximately 500,000 business users, with about 40,000 of these being manufacturing establishments. In contrast, there are more than 30 million consumers divided among more than nine million households. The business market will seem even more limited to most companies because they sell to only a segment of the total market. A firm selling to meat-processing plants, for example, would have about 45 potential customer plants. If you were interested in providing services to battery manufacturers, you would find about 25 companies as basic prospects. Consequently, marketing executives must try to pinpoint their markets carefully by type of industry and geographic location. A firm marketing hard-rock mining equipment is not interested in the total business market nor even in all firms engaged in mining and quarrying.

North American Industry Classification System (NAICS)

System that allows business marketers to locate codes for present customers and obtain coded lists of similar firms, and provides a rapid, low-cost approach to identifying changes in the growth of various industry sectors.

One very useful source of business market and segmentation information is the **North American Industry Classification System (NAICS)**. This system provides common industry definitions for Canada, the United States, and Mexico, and is consistent with United Nations industry classifications used for measuring global economic activity. NAICS, which replaced the Standard Industrial Classification System that was in use for more than 50 years, comprises 20 industry sectors, with 96 subsectors and many industry groups. Table 5-1 shows the breakdown for one industry — pagers, a segment of the wireless telecommunications industry in the information sector.

The NAICS allows business marketers to locate codes for present customers and obtain coded lists of similar firms, and provides a rapid, low-cost approach to identifying changes in the growth of various industry sectors.

Size of Business Users Although the business market may be limited in the total number of buyers, it is large in purchasing power. Business users range in size from very small companies

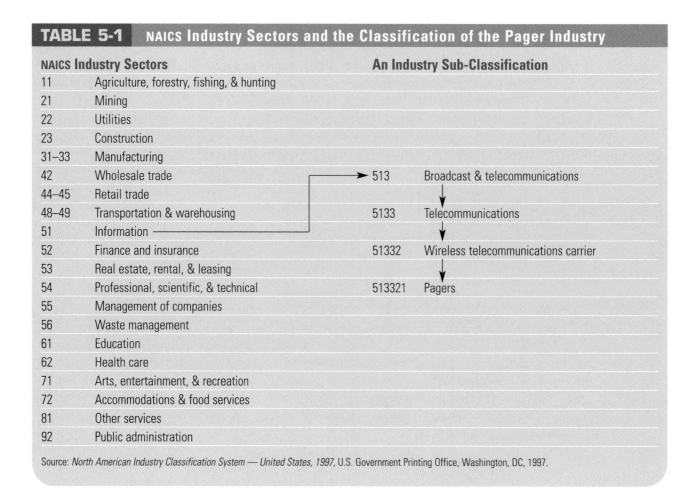

TABLE 5-1 NAICS Industry Sectors and the Classification of the Pager Industry

NAICS Industry Sectors		An Industry Sub-Classification	
11	Agriculture, forestry, fishing, & hunting		
21	Mining		
22	Utilities		
23	Construction		
31–33	Manufacturing		
42	Wholesale trade	513	Broadcast & telecommunications
44–45	Retail trade		
48–49	Transportation & warehousing	5133	Telecommunications
51	Information		
52	Finance and insurance	51332	Wireless telecommunications carrier
53	Real estate, rental, & leasing		
54	Professional, scientific, & technical	513321	Pagers
55	Management of companies		
56	Waste management		
61	Education		
62	Health care		
71	Arts, entertainment, & recreation		
72	Accommodations & food services		
81	Other services		
92	Public administration		

Source: *North American Industry Classification System — United States, 1997*, U.S. Government Printing Office, Washington, DC, 1997.

with fewer than five employees to firms with staff numbering more than a thousand. A relatively small percentage of firms account for the greatest share of the value-added production by a given industry. For example, Statistics Canada data on the manufacturing sector in Canada indicate that slightly more than 1 percent of manufacturing firms — those with 500 or more employees — account for approximately 40 percent of the total value added by manufacturing and for more than 30 percent of the total employment in manufacturing. The firms with fewer than 50 employees, while accounting for more than 80 percent of all manufacturing establishments, produce less than 15 percent of the value added by manufacturing.

The marketing significance in these facts is that buying power in the B2B market is highly concentrated in relatively few firms. This market concentration has considerable influence on a seller's approach to target marketing, as well as on policies regarding its channels of distribution and customer contact. Intermediaries in concentrated business markets are not as essential as in the consumer market and the opportunity (in fact, the competitive need) to build strong relationships is very apparent.

Regional concentration of business users   There is substantial regional concentration in many of the major industries and among business users as a whole. A firm selling products usable in oil fields will find the bulk of its market in Alberta, the Northwest Territories, offshore Newfoundland, the United States, and abroad. Rubber-products manufacturers are located mostly in Ontario, shoes are produced chiefly in Québec, and most of the nation's garment manufacturers are located in southern Ontario and Québec. There is a similar regional concentration in the farm market.

Although a large part of a firm's market may be concentrated in limited geographic areas, a good portion may lie outside these areas. Consequently, a distribution policy must be developed that will enable a firm to deal directly with the concentrated market and also to employ intermediaries (or a company sales force, at great expense) to reach the outlying markets.

vertical business market

A situation in which a given product is usable by virtually all of the firms in only one or two industries.

Vertical and horizontal business markets   For effective marketing planning, a company should know whether the market for its products is vertical or horizontal. If a firm's product is usable by virtually all firms in only one or two industries, it has a **vertical business market**. For example, some precision instruments are intended only for the marine market, but every builder of boats or ships is a potential customer. If the product is usable by many industries, then it is said to have a broad or **horizontal business market**. Business supplies, such as Esso lubricating oils and greases and Canadian General Electric small motors, may be sold to a wide variety of industries.

horizontal business market

A situation in which a given product is usable in a wide variety of industries.

A company's marketing program ordinarily is influenced by whether its markets are vertical or horizontal. In a vertical market, a product can be tailor-made to meet the specific needs of one industry and personal relationship-building can easily be pursued. However, the industry must buy enough to support this specialization and form of buyer contact. In addition, advertising and servicing can be directed more effectively in vertical markets. In a horizontal market, a product is developed as an all-purpose item, to reach a larger market. In such markets, a strategy of building strong personal relationships may not be as easily accomplished but is still necessary because, given the larger potential market, the product is likely to face more competition.

Buying power of business users

Another determinant of business market demand is the purchasing power of business users. This can be measured either by the expenditures of business users or by their sales volume. Many times, however, such information is not available or is very difficult to estimate. In such cases, it is more feasible to use an **activity indicator of buying power** — that is, some market factor that is related to income generation and expenditures. Sometimes, an activity indicator is a combined indicator of purchasing power and the number of business users. Following are examples of activity indicators that might be used to estimate the purchasing power of business users.

activity indicator of buying power

A market factor that is related to income generation and expenditures; sometimes, a combined indicator of purchasing power and the number of business users.

Measures of manufacturing activity   These market indicators include the number of employees, the number of plants, and the dollar value added by manufacturing. One firm selling work gloves used the number of employees in manufacturing establishments to determine the relative value of various geographic markets. Another company, with a product that controls stream pollution, used two indicators: (1) the number of firms processing wood products (such as paper mills and plywood mills) and (2) the manufacturing value added by these firms.

Measures of mining activity   The number of mines operating, the volume of their output, and the dollar value of the product as it leaves the mine may all indicate the purchasing power of mines. This information can be used by any firm marketing industrial products to mine operators.

Measures of agricultural activity   Indicators of the buying power of the farm market include cash farm income, acreage planted, and crop yields. A chemical producer that sells to a fertilizer manufacturer might study the same indices, because the demand for chemicals in this case is derived from the demand for fertilizer.

Measures of construction activity   Construction activity indicators include the number and value of building permits issued and the number of construction starts by type of housing (single-family residence, apartment, or commercial). If a firm is marketing building materials (such as lumber, brick, gypsum products, or builders' hardware), its market is dependent on construction activity.

BACKSPACE

1. What are the four demand characteristics of the business market that differentiate it from the consumer market?
2. What are the factors affecting the demand for business products?
3. What is the difference between vertical and horizontal business markets?

Business Buying Behaviour

Business buying behaviour, like consumer buying behaviour, is initiated when an aroused need (a motive) is recognized. This leads to goal-oriented activity designed to satisfy the need. Once again, business marketers must try to determine what motivates the buyer, and then understand the buying process and buying patterns of business organizations in their markets.

The importance of business buying

Business buying or purchasing is an activity of great interest to top management. Once viewed as an isolated activity that focused primarily on searching out low prices, purchasing has become an important part of overall strategy for at least three reasons:

1. **Companies are making less and buying more**. For example, 93 percent of the cost of an Apple computer is purchased content and, for all manufacturers, purchased content is more than 50 percent of their final products. Managing all of these supply relationships is time-consuming and therefore also consumes additional financial resources. While low price is important, savings can also be found through reducing the number of suppliers and maintaining those who provide dependable, quality service and products. Honda at one time had different suppliers producing mirrors for the inside and outside of its cars. Very happy with the relationship and working style of the Donnelly Corporation in its agreement to supply interior mirrors, the car company asked that this supplier develop exterior mirrors for its cars, thereby reducing Honda's supplier list by one. This trend can be found across this industry, as there may be up to 2000 supply relationships to manage in automobile manufacturing.

2. **Firms are under intense quality and time pressures.** To reduce costs and improve efficiency, firms no longer buy and hold inventories of parts and supplies. Instead, they demand that raw materials and components that meet specifications be delivered "just in time" (JIT) to go into the production process. To take advantage of this, Canadian automaker Magna establishes its facilities near its main clients — the Big Three auto producers. This ensures that the automakers' inventories can be kept at a minimum, yet fluctuations in demand will be met with guaranteed on-time delivery. This is achieved through computerized data interchange systems that link suppliers to their JIT clients.[7] To ensure quality, companies such as Xerox require suppliers to be ISO 9000 certified. Certification means that a supplier has undergone an audit that ensures quality-management and quality-assurance systems are operating within the firm and meet the international standards of this certification.[8]

3. **To get what they need, firms are concentrating their purchases with fewer suppliers and developing long-term "partnering" relationships.** This level of involvement extends beyond a purchase to include such things as working together to develop new products and providing financial support.[9] For example, at the Chrysler Design Institute in Michigan, as many as 30 offices are available at any time for the full-time use of personnel who, instead of being Chrysler employees, actually work for various suppliers.

A low-involvement consumer purchase can require a related high-involvement B2B purchase.

Buying-decision process in business

The buying-decision process in B2B markets is a sequence of six stages similar to the ones followed by consumers, as discussed in Chapter 3. Not every purchase involves all stages. First, we'll illustrate the process by providing an example and then we'll examine some of the details of each stage, as we did in the review of consumer decision-making. Assume that Montréal-based Culinar, Inc., makers of Vachon, Jos. Louis, and MayWest snack cakes, is considering the use of a fat substitute in a special line of baked goods.

Simple replacement purchases (termed "straight rebuy" and discussed later) are usually low-involvement situations for a buyer, so purchasers typically skip some stages. But the first-time purchase of an expensive product or service is likely to be a high-involvement, total-stage buying decision.

1. **Need recognition** Culinar's marketing executives are sensitive to the concern of consumers about fat in their diets. They see the strategic opportunity of producing a line of high-quality, good-tasting baked goods without fat as very attractive for segments of the consumer market. Finding the right substitute for fat ingredients is a challenge for those concerned with purchasing.

2. **Choice of involvement level** The marketing executive who will be responsible for the product development project discusses with production and purchasing personnel the feasibility of finding the right substitute, and the decision is made to carefully research what is available and on what terms, since the firm has no experience with these types of ingredients.

3. **Identification of alternatives** The marketing staff draws up a list of product-performance specifications for fat-free baked goods — attractive appearance, special features, good taste, and reasonable cost. The product specifications are similar to the expectations that consumers develop. The purchasing department also develops a set of supplier specifications or, in consumer marketing terms, patronage motive criteria. An external search then identifies the potential suppliers and the alternative brands of fat substitutes that generally meet functional specifications.

4. **Evaluation of alternatives** The production, research, and purchasing people jointly evaluate both the alternative products and sources of supply against the product and supplier specifications. They discover that some brands cannot withstand high temperatures, there are differences in how well they simulate the taste and texture of fat, and some have not received final approval from federal health authorities. The complete evaluation considers such factors as product performance, appearance, and price, as well as the suppliers' abilities to meet delivery schedules and provide consistent quality.

5. **Purchase decision** Based on the evaluation, the buyer decides on a specific brand and supplier. Next, the purchasing department negotiates the contract, having achieved negotiation satisfaction with the selected supplier. Since large sums are involved, the contract will likely include many details. For example, if Culinar feels confident about the supplier, the contract relationship might go beyond price and delivery schedules. This could include the low-fat substitute producer gaining access, through electronic data interchange to production, quality-control, shelf-life, and product-movement data in order to be able to provide a higher degree of accuracy in product delivery and better-

targeted service. A more effective schedule can help ensure a consistently fresher product, perhaps leading to higher product sales. In such a situation, a long-term relationship appears to be in the baking — um, we mean making.

6. **Consumption experience**   Culinar, Inc. continues to evaluate the performances of the fat substitute and the selected supplier to ensure that both meet expectations. Continued dealings will depend on this performance evaluation and on how well the supplier handles the total interaction process. Formal evaluations of the purchase will be made and satisfaction recorded for future reference. A functional relationship is developing. Consumer market success with this product line would increase the likelihood of future projects involving the two firms. Buyer-supplier success in their information interchange, mutual problem solving, and personal communications aid in developing an emotional relationship.

In the following sections, we explore several differences between consumer buying behaviour and the business buying behaviour reflected in the Culinar scenario.

Buying motives of business users

buying motive

The reason why a person buys a specific product.

One view of buying motives is that business purchases are methodical and structured. Business buying motives, for the most part, are presumed to be practical and unemotional. Business buyers are assumed to be motivated to achieve the optimal combination of price, quality, and service in the products they buy and any relationships that are developed are considered to be functional. An alternative view is that business buyers are human and thus their business decisions are influenced by their attitudes, perceptions, and values and therefore any relationships developed will be emotional in nature. In fact, many salespeople would maintain that business buyers seem to be motivated more toward personal goals than organizational goals, and the two are often in conflict.

As is usual in such cases, the truth is actually somewhere in between. Most B2B relationships are a combination of the functional and emotional. Business buyers have two goals — to further their company's position (in profits, in acceptance by customers) and to protect or improve their position in their firms (self-interest). Sometimes these goals are mutually consistent. For example, the firm's highest priority may be to reduce costs, and the buyer knows that there will be a reward for negotiating a low price. Obviously, the more consistent the goals are, the better for both the organization and the individual, and the easier it is to make buying decisions and develop good relationships.

However, there are often significant areas where the buyer's goals do not coincide with those of the firm, as when the firm insists on dealing with the lowest-price supplier, but the buyer has developed a good personal relationship with another supplier and doesn't want to change. In these cases, a seller must appeal to the buyer both on a rational "what's good for the firm" basis and on a self-interest "what's in it for me" basis. Promotional appeals directed to the buyer's self-interest are particularly useful when two or more competing sellers are offering essentially the same products, prices, and post-purchase services.[10]

Types of buying situations

buy classes

Three typical buying situations in the business market: new-task buy, straight rebuy, and modified rebuy.

In Chapter 3, we observed that consumer purchase decisions can range from routine to complex. Similarly, the buying situations in business organizations vary widely in their complexity and, most importantly, in the number of people involved in the decision and the time required to make it. Three buy classes or types of business buying situations characterize the field: new-task buy, straight rebuy, and modified rebuy.

new-task buy

In the business market, a purchasing situation in which a company considers buying a given item for the first time.

● **New-task buy**   This is the most difficult and complex buying situation because it is a first-time purchase of a major product. New-task buys are not, however, that common.

Typically, more people are involved in new-task buying than in the other two situations, because the risk is great. Information needs are high and the evaluation of alternatives is difficult because the decision-makers have little experience with the product. Sellers have the challenge of finding out the buyer's needs and communicating their product's ability to provide satisfaction. A hospital's first-time purchase of laser surgical equipment or a company buying robots for a factory (or buying the factory itself) are new-task buying conditions. In these situations, firms with established relationships could work with buyers to help them define the buying task and suggest solutions because these firms are known and trusted. Unknown potential suppliers must provide information and aid in the buying task in a form that engenders trust and allows them to begin the task of establishing a relationship.

straight rebuy

In the business market, a routine purchase with minimal information needs.

● **Straight rebuy**   This is a routine, low-involvement purchase with minimal information needs and little or no consideration of alternatives. **Straight rebuys** are very common. The buyer's extensive experience with the seller has been satisfactory or more than satisfactory, so at least a functional and possibly an emotional relationship has been developed. In such a case, there is no incentive to search. An example is the repeat purchase of steering wheels by Freightliner, a truck manufacturer. These buying decisions are made in the purchasing department, usually from a predetermined list of acceptable suppliers. Suppliers who are not on this list may have difficulty getting in to make a sales presentation to the buyer. But as more buyers gain experience in making use of the Internet to both gather product and service information and actually buy online, the predetermined list is easily expanded by asking for bids from a broader base of suppliers.

modified rebuy

In the business market, a purchasing situation between a new-task rebuy and a straight rebuy in terms of time required, information needed, and alternatives considered.

● **Modified rebuy**   This buying situation is somewhere between the other two in time and people involved, information needed, and alternatives considered. **Modified rebuys** are also quite common. Where straight rebuys have existed and a degree of dissatisfaction has developed, signalling a possible breakdown of functional performance or personal relationships, a modified rebuy would result. The availability of important new products or product performance information could also cause a modified rebuy. In either case, a new list of acceptable suppliers would be developed. Commonly, two or more suppliers are in constant competition. In selecting diesel engines for the trucks it manufactures, Freightliner considers Cummins and Caterpillar products, among others. However, because these engine makers frequently introduce new design and performance features, Freightliner evaluates each on a regular basis. Close relationships are common in situations where modified rebuys are frequent and, of course, should work to benefit both buyer and seller.

multiple buying influences

A situation in which a purchasing decision is influenced by more than one person in the buyer's organization.

Multiple buying influences — the buying centre

One of the biggest challenges in B2B marketing is to determine which individuals in the organization play the various buying roles. That is, who influences the buying decision, who determines product specifications, and who makes the buying decision? In the business market, these activities typically involve several people. In other words, there are **multiple buying influences**, particularly in medium-sized and large firms. Even in small companies where the owners or managers make all major decisions, knowledgeable employees are usually consulted before certain purchases are made.

buying centre

All of the people in an organization who participate in the buying-decision process.

Understanding the concept of a **buying centre** is helpful in identifying the multiple buying influences and understanding the buying process in business organizations. A buying centre may be defined as all of the individuals or groups involved in making a decision to purchase. Thus, a buying centre includes the people who play any of the following roles:

users

The people in a buying centre who actually use a particular product.

● **Users:** The people who actually use the business product — perhaps a secretary, an executive, a production-line employee, or a truck driver.

influencers
The people in a buying centre who set the specifications and aspects of buying decisions because of their technical expertise, financial position, or political power in the organization.

deciders
The people in a buying centre who make the actual buying decision regarding a product and/or supplier.

gatekeepers
The people in a buying centre who control the flow of purchasing information within the organization and between the buying firm and potential vendors.

- **Influencers:** The people who set the specifications and aspects of buying decisions because of their technical expertise, their organizational position, or even their political power in the firm.

- **Deciders:** The people who make the actual buying decision regarding the business product and the supplier. A purchasing agent may be the decider in a straight-rebuy situation. But someone in top management may make the decision regarding whether to buy an expensive computer.

- **Gatekeepers:** The people who control the flow of purchasing information within the organization as well as between the firm and potential suppliers. These people may be purchasing agents, secretaries, receptionists, or technical personnel.

- **Buyers:** The people who interact with the suppliers, arrange the terms of sale, and process the actual purchase orders. Typically, this is the purchasing department's role but, again, if the purchase is an expensive, complex new buy, the buyer's role may be occupied by someone in top management.

Several people in an organization may play the same role — there may be several users of the product. Or the same person may occupy more than one role — a secretary may be a user, an influencer, and a gatekeeper in the purchase of office equipment.

The size and composition of a buying centre will vary among business organizations. In one study, the average size of buying centres ranged from 2.7 to 5.1 persons.[11] Within a given organization, the size and make-up of the buying centre will vary, depending on the product's cost, the complexity of the decision, and the stage of the buying process. The buying centre for a straight rebuy of office supplies will be quite different from the centre handling the purchase of a building or a fleet of trucks.

> *Well-trained purchasing professionals will always be, at the very least, gatekeepers.*

Hitting high notes with your bottom line

Today, more than ever, purchasing and supply management play a strategic role in bottom line performance and profitability. As 'big picture' thinkers working in harmony with suppliers and partners, purchasing professionals help enhance organizational effectiveness, customer satisfaction, and shareholder value. PMAC is the recognized leader in the development and advancement of world class supply management. We offer an accredited program leading to the highly-acclaimed Certified Professional Purchaser (C.P.P.) designation. For more information, please call PMAC at (416) 977-7111, e-mail info@pmac.ca or visit www.pmac.ca

PMAC
Purchasing Management Association of Canada™

Strategic Perspective. Competitive Advantage.

www.pmac.ca

The variety of people involved in any business buying situation, plus the differences among companies, present real challenges to salespeople. As they try to determine "who's on first" — that is, determine who does what in a buying situation and influences which aspect of the decision-making process — sales reps often call on the wrong executives. Even knowing who the decision-makers are at a certain time is not enough, because these people may be very difficult to reach and people move into and out of the buying centre as the purchase proceeds through the decision process. This, in part, explains why a salesperson typically has only a few major accounts.

Certainly the challenges presented in the business buying-decision process should suggest the importance of co-ordinating the selling activities of the business marketer with the buying needs of the purchasing organization.

Buying patterns of business users

Buying behaviour in the B2B market differs significantly from consumer buying behaviour in several ways. These differences stem from the products, markets, and buyer-seller relationships in business markets.

Direct purchase In the consumer market, consumers rarely buy directly from the producer, except in the case of services. In the business market, however,

buyers
The people in a buying centre who select the suppliers, arrange the terms of sale, and process the actual purchase orders.

direct purchase by the business user from the producer is quite common, even for goods. This is true especially when the order is large and the buyer needs much technical assistance. Computer-chip makers deal directly with personal computer manufacturers because the chip technology is changing so rapidly. From a seller's point of view, direct sale in the business market is reasonable, especially when there are relatively few potential buyers, when they are big, or when they are geographically concentrated. With telephone, fax, and the Internet readily available, smaller sellers can both concentrate their efforts and work to expand their reach into markets that in the past were too expensive to serve at an appropriate level.

Internet purchase   Online buying between businesses is much greater, both in absolute terms and proportionately than in the consumer market. Business buying accounts for more than 80 percent of the total value of all online transactions.

value chain
The relationships by which the roles of suppliers, producers, distributors, and end-users contribute to the final product.

Nature of the relationship   Many business marketers take a broad view of exchanges. Rather than focus only on the immediate customer, they approach marketing as a **value chain**. That is, they consider the roles of suppliers, producers, distributors, and end-users to see how each contributes value to the final product. This perspective leads to recognition of the importance of all of the parties involved in successfully bringing a product to market and an emphasis on building and maintaining relationships along the chain. For example, Apple Computer, which once relied exclusively on dealers, recognized that many of

MARKETING AT WORK   5-2: TECHNOLOGY

B2B Builds New Markets in Great Web Bazaar

B2B transactions are usually worth at least 10 times as much as consumer sales. This shouldn't come as any surprise, as these are usually bulk purchases, while consumers buy most things one at a time. Therefore, the most successful e-commerce businesses tend to be B2B ones. It's only logical that organizations in the B2B marketplace would adopt this channel through which to conduct business, as most routine business transactions take place at a distance — fax, telephone, mail, private electronic links. Moving to the Internet reduces transaction costs, speeds up transactions, and makes them easier and more efficient to conduct.

The total value of electronic commerce sales rose by 73 percent in 2000 to $7.2 billion from $4.2 billion a year earlier. In 2001, this number rose another 43 percent to $10.4 billion. Despite this, e-commerce remains a small portion of Canadian economic activity, accounting for about half a percent of total operating revenue as of 2001. In that year, it was estimated that 7 percent of businesses in Canada were selling goods and services online. The e-commerce market remained volatile, as four firms stopped selling over the Internet for every five that started in 2001. This should not be taken as a sign that the Internet will not continue to be a viable sales channel — instead, it should be seen as a normal pattern as industries and companies determine the suitability of this new means of conducting business.

Only about one-fifth of online sales are to consumers and households — about 78 percent of Internet sales are B2B transactions. Wholesalers and manufacturers alone account for almost 50 percent of the value of all Internet transactions in Canada. More than 35 percent of sales are export sales to clients outside Canada.

Although only a small percentage of Canadian firms currently appear to offer goods and services on the Internet, this is expected to grow. A great number of enterprises do use the Internet to *buy* the goods and services they need. And what industries are utilizing this channel the most? According to Statistics Canada, they include information and cultural industries (publishing, broadcasting, telecommunications, information services, and data processing), finance and insurance, utilities, manufacturing, wholesalers, and professional, scientific, and technical services.

In some cases, entire industries are moving their supply and procurement arrangements to the electronic marketplace. The Big Three automakers each established their own online parts exchanges, forcing their suppliers to move online to bid and conduct transactions if they wanted to continue doing business. Suppliers are also able to use these sites to make their purchases and sell excess inventories. In 2001, the Big Three combined their procurement exchanges, creating a market hosting tens of thousands of suppliers and more than $500 million in annual spending.

SOURCE: Adapted from *The Economist*, online edition, "Survey of Commerce," April 1, 2000; Julie Landry, Red Herring.com, "Big Three Automakers Face Big B2B Challenges," February 29, 2000; "Statcan.ca," *The Daily*, April 2, 2002.

its larger customers needed specialized service. To satisfy this segment of the market and maintain strong ties to these key customers, the firm now has its own sales force calling directly on large accounts. However, many of the orders taken by the sales force are contracted out to dealers to ensure that they are protected.[12]

supply partnership
A partnership that occurs when a buyer and seller with mutual trust and interests adopt certain policies, procedures, and co-ordinated relationships to lower production and supply costs and increase consumer product value.

Among those businesses where good relationships exist, a **supply partnership** can be created. This occurs when a buyer and seller have developed sufficient trust and mutuality of interest so that, through the mutual adoption of certain policies and procedures, the use of electronic data interchange, and co-ordinated personal and professional relationships, production and supply costs are lowered for both parties and consumer product value is increased.

Wal-Mart, for example, is connected electronically with almost all of its major suppliers, such as Proctor-Silex and Rubbermaid, through an inventory control system that increases efficiency and reduces inventory held at each store. As items are scanned at the checkout, the information about each item is transferred back to manufacturers, so they always have current information about inventories at all locations and are able to better schedule shipments of products to each store. Wal-Mart seldom runs short of a product, ensuring that customers are not disappointed. And by maintaining lower inventories, operating costs are reduced. For suppliers, making the investment in this technology and co-operating with this retailer provides access to an international retail distribution network.

reciprocity
The policy of "I'll buy from you if you'll buy from me."

A highly controversial business buying practice is **reciprocity**, the policy of "I'll buy from you if you'll buy from me." Reciprocity was once common among firms marketing homogeneous basic business products (oil, steel, rubber, paper products, and chemicals). There has been a significant decline in, but not an elimination of, reciprocity. This decline has occurred for two reasons, one legal and the other economic. The Competition Act applies to reciprocity when the practice is similar to price discrimination. A firm can buy from a customer, but it must be able to prove that the customer is not given any special privileges regarding price, quality, or service that are not made available to competing buyers.

From an economic point of view, reciprocity may not make sense, because the price, quality, or service offered by the seller may not be competitive. In addition, when a firm fails to pursue objectives that maximize profits, the morale of both the sales force and the purchasing department may suffer.

Reciprocity is an area in which firms run into problems in doing business overseas. In many parts of the world, it is taken for granted that if I buy your product, you'll buy mine.

Frequency of purchase   In the business market, firms buy certain products very infrequently. Large installations are purchased only once in many years. Small parts and materials to be used in the manufacture of a product may be ordered on long-term contracts, so that a selling opportunity exists as seldom as once a year. Even standard operating supplies, such as office supplies or cleaning products, may be bought only once a month.

Because of this buying pattern, a great burden is placed on the personal-selling programs of business sellers. The sales force must call on potential customers often enough to provide the first-hand information that other media, such as a Web site, e-mail, or fax cannot effectively provide, and to know when a customer is considering a purchase.

Size of order   The average business order is considerably larger than its counterpart in the consumer market. This fact, coupled with the infrequency of purchase, highlights the importance of each sale in the business market. A salesperson losing the sale of a pair of shoes to a consumer is not nearly as devastating as Canadair losing the sale of 10 airplanes.

Period length of negotiation   The period of negotiation in a business sale is usually much longer than in a consumer transaction. General Electric, for example, negotiated over a five-year period before completing the purchase of a $9.5 million Cray supercomputer to aid in managing operations and research activities in Canada and the United States. Some reasons for extended negotiations are:

- Several executives participate in the buying decision.
- The sale involves a large amount of money.
- The business product is made to order and considerable discussion is required to establish the specifications.

Demand for service The user's desire for excellent service is a strong business buying motive that may determine buying patterns. Frequently, a firm's only differentiating feature is its service, because the product itself is so standardized that it can be purchased from any number of companies. Consider the choice of suppliers to provide elevators for a major office building or hotel. The installation of the elevators is no more important than keeping them operating safely and efficiently. Consequently, in its marketing efforts, a firm such as Otis emphasizes its maintenance service as much as its products.

Sellers must be ready to furnish a continuous service program, not just before or just after a sale. For example, suppliers such as Kraft Foods conduct a careful analysis of a supermarket's customers and sales performance and then suggest a product assortment and layout for the store's dairy department. In the case of office copiers, manufacturers train the buyer's office staff in the use of the equipment and, after the machines have been installed, offer other services such as repairs by specially trained technicians.

Dependability of supply Another business buying pattern is the user's insistence on an adequate quantity of uniform-quality products. Variations in the quality of materials going into finished products can cause considerable trouble for manufacturers. They may be faced with costly disruptions in their production processes if the imperfections exceed quality-control limits. Also, the right quantities at the right time are as important as the right quality. A work stoppage caused by an insufficient supply of materials is just as costly as one caused by the inferior quality of materials. In one study of problems faced by purchasing agents for smaller manufacturers, the problem most often reported was the failure of sellers to deliver on schedule.

MARKETING AT WORK 5-3: STRATEGY

Good to the Last Drop!

Everyone knows the Kraft brand. Kraft Foods supplies us with 61 brands of various products. Many of the foods, beverages, and condiments we have grown up with in Canada come from this company, including Kraft Dinner, Tang, Grape-Nuts cereal, Maxwell House coffee, Ritz crackers, and Oreo cookies.

But it is not only in the supermarket that we come across many of the Kraft products we enjoy. We have all been in a cafeteria, on an airplane, or even at some sort of banquet or function where we have used those small packages of coffee, crackers, jam, or even peanut butter or cream cheese. And most often we recognize the brand on the package — Sanka coffee, Philadelphia cream cheese, Kraft salad dressing. While the contents of these packages are the same as we can get at our local grocery store, these small packages actually are products that are not available for sale in the consumer marketplace. Kraft offers them only in the B2B marketplace — sold to other businesses for resale — products

that enable other companies and organizations to offer their own products and services.

This is an example of a firm that sells to both B2B and B2C markets. And while you may think that strawberry jam is strawberry jam — whether it is in a jar or a single-serving package — you would be wrong! These are actually two different products. Why? Because they each require their own marketing mix. Yes, it is the same strawberry jam, but "'product" also refers to size and packaging, which is a very important detail for creating utility in these two different marketplaces. Also, unit pricing will be different because of the packaging and because the small packages will be sold in bulk as a "component" product. Promotion and distribution will differ as well: Sales representatives will attempt to address the very different concerns of different clients — hotel chains and airlines, instead of supermarkets.

SOURCE: Kraft Foods Internet site (www.kraft.com).

The emphasis on total quality management has increased the significance of dependability. Now that it has been established that firms can operate with virtually zero defects, buyers expect a very high standard of performance.

Leasing instead of buying   A growing tendency among firms in the B2B market is leasing business goods instead of buying them. In the past, this practice was limited to large equipment, such as large computers, packaging equipment, and heavy construction equipment. Industrial firms are now expanding leasing arrangements to include delivery trucks, vehicles used by salespeople, machine tools, and items such as software site licences that are generally less expensive than major installations.

Leasing has several merits for the lessor, the firm providing the equipment:

- Total net income — the income after charging off repairs and maintenance expenses — is often higher than it would be if the equipment was sold.

- The lessor's market may be expanded to include users who could not afford to buy the product, especially for large equipment.

- Leasing is an effective method of getting users to try a new product. They may be more willing to rent a product than to buy it. If they are not satisfied, their expenditure is limited to a few monthly payments.

From the lessee's, or customer's, point of view, the benefits of leasing are:

- Leasing allows users to retain their investment capital for other purposes.

- Firms can enter a new business with less capital outlay than would be necessary if they had to buy equipment.

- Leased products are usually repaired and maintained by lessors, eliminating one headache associated with ownership.

- Leasing is particularly attractive to firms that need equipment seasonally or sporadically, such as food canning or construction.

Bases for Business Market Segmentation

Several of the bases used to segment the consumer market can also be used to segment the broad business market. For example, we can segment business markets on a geographical basis. Several industries are geographically concentrated, so any firm selling to these industries could easily use this segmentation basis. Sellers also can segment on product-related bases, such as usage rate or benefits desired.[13]

Let's look at three of the bases that are used solely for segmenting business markets — type of customer, size of customer, and type of buying situation.

Type of customer

Any firm that sells to customers in a variety of business markets may want to segment this market on the basis of customer types. We discussed the NAICS codes as a very useful tool for identifying business and institutional target markets. A firm selling display cases or store fixtures to the retail market could use the codes, as could a firm selling janitorial supplies or small electric motors that has a broad potential market among many different industries. Management in this firm could segment its market by type of customer and then perhaps decide to sell to firms in only a limited number of these segments.

Size of customer

In this situation, size can be measured by such factors as sales volume, number of production facilities, or number of sales offices. Many business-to-business marketers divide their potential market into large and small accounts, using separate distribution channels to reach each segment. The large-volume accounts, for example, may be sold to directly by the company's sales force. To reach the smaller accounts, however, the seller may use a telemarketing or Internet approach, a manufacturers' agent, or some other form of intermediary.

Type of buying situation

Earlier in this chapter, we discussed the three types of buy classes — new-task buy, straight rebuy, and modified rebuy. We also recognized in that discussion that a new-task buy is significantly different from a straight rebuy in several important respects. Consequently, a business seller might well segment its market into these three buy-class categories. Or the seller could at least set up two segments by combining new-task buy and modified rebuy into one segment. Then different marketing programs would be developed to reach each of these two or three segments.[14]

BACKSPACE

1. Business buyers have two goals. What are they?
2. What are the three types of buying situations?
3. In business marketing, to what does *reciprocity* refer?

Summary

The B2B market consists of organizations that buy goods and services to produce other goods and services, to resell to other business users or consumers, or to conduct the organization's operations. It is an extremely large and complex market, spanning a wide variety of business users that buy many different types of business goods and services. Besides manufacturing, the business market includes the agriculture, reseller, government, services, not-for-profit, and international markets.

Business market demand generally is derived, inelastic, and widely fluctuating. Business buyers usually are well informed about what they are buying. Business market demand is analyzed by evaluating the number and kinds of business users and their buying power.

Business buying, or purchasing, has taken on greater strategic importance because organizations are buying more and making less, under intense time and quality pressures, and developing long-term partnering relationships with suppliers.

Business buying motives are focused on achieving a firm's objectives, but the business buyer's self-interests must also be considered.

The buying-decision process in business markets may involve as many as six stages: need recognition, choice of involvement level, identification of alternatives, evaluation of alternatives, purchase decision, and consumption experience. The actual number of stages in a given purchase decision depends largely on the buying situation, whether new-task buy, straight rebuy, or modified rebuy.

The concept of a buying centre reflects the multiple buying influences in business purchasing decisions. In a typical buying centre, people play the roles of users, influencers, deciders, gatekeepers, and buyers.

Buying patterns (habits) of business users often are quite different from patterns in the consumer market. In the B2B market, direct purchases (without intermediaries) are more common, purchases are made less frequently, and orders are larger. The negotiation period usually is longer, and reciprocity arrangements can exist. The demand for service is greater, and the dependability of supply is more critical. Finally, leasing (rather than product ownership) is quite common in business marketing.

Three segmentation bases that are used solely for segmenting the B2B market are customer type, customer size, and type of buying situation.

Key Terms and Concepts

activity indicator of buying power 143
agribusiness 137
B2B marketing 134
business (B2B) market 134
business users 134
buy classes 146
buyers 149
buying centre 147
buying motive 146
competitive bidding 137
deciders 148
derived demand 139
gatekeepers 148
government market 136
horizontal business market 143

inelastic demand 140
influencers 148
modified rebuy 147
multiple buying influences 147
new-task buy 146
non-business market 137
North American Industry Classification System (NAICS) 141
reciprocity 150
reseller market 135
services market 136
straight rebuy 147
supply partnership 150
users 147
value chain 149
vertical business market 143

Questions and Problems

1. What are some marketing implications for business goods whose demand:
   a. Fluctuates widely?
   b. Is inelastic?
   c. Is derived?

2. What are the marketing implications for a seller of the fact that business customers are geographically concentrated and limited in number?

3. What differences would you expect to find between the marketing strategies of a company that sells to horizontal business markets and those of a company that sells to vertical business markets?

4. A manufacturer has been selling specialized software to a large oil company in Norway. In which of the three buy classes would you place this buyer-seller relationship? Is there any aspect of the relationship that is likely to fall into the straight-rebuy category?

5. Explain how the six stages of the buying-decision process might be applied in the following buying situations:
   a. New-task buying of a conveyor belt for a soft-drink bottling plant.
   b. Straight rebuy of maintenance services for that conveyor belt.
   c. Modified rebuy of advertising agency services for a hotel chain.

6. How would you go about determining who influences the buying decisions of business users?

7. Steelcase, IBM, Xerox, and other manufacturers of office equipment make a substantial proportion of their sales directly to business users. At the same time, wholesalers of office equipment are thriving. Are these two market situations inconsistent? Explain.

Hands-On Marketing

1. Find an ad for a business product or service that is directed toward the B2B market and another ad for the same product that is directed toward the B2C market (such as an ad for leasing fleets of Chevrolets and an ad for Chevrolet aimed at consumers). Discuss the buying motives appealed to in the ads.

2. Interview a purchasing agent about buying a product that would qualify as a modified rebuy. Draw a diagram that shows the purchasing agent's perceptions of: (a) the stages of the decision process; (b) who was in the buying centre at each stage of the decision process; and (c) what role or roles each person played at each stage of the process. Comment on how this diagram might be useful to a salesperson representing the product in question.

Back to the Top

Think about the fact described in the chapter opener that Intel is a major supplier to MyWebGrocer.com. Most of us are familiar with Intel as the maker of computer chips that seem to be inside most PCs. What do you suppose is most important to Intel in marketing to companies like MyWebGrocer.com, as compared to marketing its Pentium chips to Toshiba, for example?

Want to get better grades, tips on how to study more effectively, and up-to-date information on happenings in the world of marketing? Then, visit the Online Learning Centre for practice tests, Study Smart software, and much more! **www.mcgrawhill.ca/college/sommers**

Interested in finding out what marketing looks like in the real world? *Marketing Magazine* is just a click away on your Online Learning Centre!

CHAPTER 6

Getting the Marketing Information We Need

The management of any business or organization, whether a major automobile manufacturer, a radio station, or an art gallery, requires one fundamental input in order to achieve success in a competitive marketplace — accurate and timely information. To be effective, marketing managers need up-to-date information about the markets they are trying to reach, the environment in which their particular industry operates, and the internal and external factors that affect their specific markets. We're about to see where and how this information can be obtained and how to use it. After studying this chapter, you should have an understanding of:

- Why organizations need marketing information, and the decisions it influences.

- The types of information sought by firms — in other words, the questions the firm needs to have answered.

- The different approaches and procedures available to obtain market information.

- How to plan and execute a research project.

- Organizations that conduct marketing research.

- The status of marketing research in Canadian organizations.

Hummus and Tofu to Go

Rhonda is a local entrepreneur who has been thinking for a long time about opening a vegetarian restaurant near your campus. She even has a name in mind: "Hummus a Few Bars!" Rhonda has been a vegetarian for many years and has always been bothered by the fact that few restaurants in the area provide vegetarian items on their menus. She has asked several of her friends, and they agree that such a restaurant is needed. She has also decided that students will represent the most important target market segment for her restaurant, because she knows quite a few students who are vegetarians.

Rhonda also realizes, however, that investing the money needed to open the restaurant would not be a good idea unless she can be satisfied that she can generate sufficient sales volume and margins to be profitable. Plus, she will have to borrow some money to get started, and she knows her bank won't lend her the money without a business plan that includes projected sales and profitability.

Research is necessary to accomplish a number of Rhonda's objectives. She needs to know what the likely size of the market is in the area — how many people are vegetarians or eat vegetarian food on occasion. She also needs to know where they eat now when they eat out and whether they share her view that the area needs a new vegetarian restaurant. Then, she needs to know what they would like to see on the menu, how often they would go to the restaurant, what price levels they would expect, and so on. She has never designed a survey, because such projects were never required in her English literature program. She also knows that if she is to get accurate information, this project will have to be done properly.

So, last Monday, she called your school and made an appointment with Professor Stewart, who teaches marketing research, to see if she could get a survey done this semester as a class project. She knows students always need practical projects to work on, and she is optimistic that she'll get the information she needs without spending a lot of money.

Need for Marketing Information

All organizations, even small start-ups like Rhonda's vegetarian restaurant, need information — lots of it — about potential markets, consumer tastes and preferences, and environmental forces in order to develop successful marketing plans and to respond to changes in the marketplace. More than ever before, a large volume of data is available both from external sources and from within a firm. The challenge is how to transform raw data into information and how to use it effectively. To see how to do this, we will begin by briefly discussing why organizations need information and why they need to do research. Then, we will focus our attention on how organizations actually conduct research.

Today, many forces dictate that every organization must have access to timely information. Consider some of these factors and their relationship to the management of information:

- *Focus on the customer:* New ways of viewing customers and of marketing to them demands that companies know their customers as completely as possible. Those companies that know their customers best have a distinct advantage when it comes to marketing to them.

- *Emphasis on retention and relationships:* As companies have become focused more on building customer relationships and less on making immediate sales, their need for information has changed as well. Companies now have more interest in information on complex concepts such as service quality, perceptions of value, loyalty, and the strength of relationships.

- *Competitive pressure:* To be competitive, companies must develop and market new products and services more quickly and effectively than ever before. Pressures continue to build as the Internet eliminates geographic borders, drawing new competitors from around the globe.

- *Expanding markets:* Marketing activity is becoming increasingly complex and broader in scope as more firms operate in both domestic and foreign markets, blurring distinctions between the two. Today, it doesn't matter where a company is located — if it is doing business on the Internet, it is competing globally.

- *Cost of a mistake:* Introducing and marketing a new product or service is enormously expensive. A failure can cause severe — even fatal — damage to a firm. Even making modifications to existing products is a risky business. Knowing what to change and when to ensure that a firm remains competitive are decisions that should not be made without input from customers.

- *Growing customer expectations:* The lack of timely, adequate information about a problem that consumers are having with some aspect of an organization's marketing program can result in lost business. Greater competition has allowed consumers to become more demanding and selective. To prosper, a firm must know what the customer expects and meet those expectations.

- *Increased market complexity:* The marketplace that most companies and organizations are facing today is far more complex than it was in the past. As a result, managers must be as well informed as possible, armed with information in which they can have complete confidence.

Managers in a wide variety of organizations make important marketing decisions on many different subjects. It is probably a self-evident fact that the best decisions are based on the best available information. Before embarking on marketing decisions related to new-product introduction, changes in the customer service program, the launch of an advertising campaign, or a program to target new customer segments, the marketing manager needs information. In most organizations, the necessary information is not generally available and must be obtained from some external sources. This is where marketing research comes in. The information obtained through research guides strategic decision-making. However, in order for the marketing manager to have complete confidence in the information, the research must be conducted professionally and in accordance with certain standards that will ensure minimization of bias and that the results accurately reflect the situation the manager is facing. Marketing research is viewed by many managers as insurance that will help them succeed.

What is marketing research?

marketing research
The process of specifying, assembling, and analyzing information used to identify and define marketing opportunities and problems; generate, refine, and evaluate marketing actions; monitor marketing performance; and improve the understanding of marketing as a process.

Marketing research includes all of the activities that enable an organization to obtain the information it needs to make decisions about its marketing mix and its present or prospective customers and consumers. More specifically, marketing research involves the development, interpretation, and communication of decision-oriented information to be used in the strategic marketing process. Businesses and other organizations spend millions of dollars each year obtaining information to improve the quality of decision-making. Obviously, research is an important part of marketing.

Marketing research is an important function within a business because it is responsible for providing accurate, timely information that can be relied on by management in making decisions related to marketing. Most firms don't conduct marketing research all of the time, however, and the vast majority are not large enough to employ research staff on a full-time basis. Only very large firms have a formal marketing research department; most rely on outside specialty firms to conduct research projects for them.

Therefore, most managers need to know when they require research information, and they need to know how to get research projects done. They rely on marketing research to help them reach accurate conclusions and make the best possible decisions in understanding their customers, in planning their marketing programs, in implementing those programs, and in determining how successful the programs have been. Marketing research is more than designing a questionnaire and collecting data. It must be very well planned to obtain the information that's really needed by marketers.

Scope of Marketing Research Activities

Marketing managers need a great deal of accurate information to better understand the marketplace in which they are operating, the customers who represent the target segments for their products and services, and what is or is not working. The challenge is to put in place a marketing research strategy and program that will result in management receiving the required information in a timely and accurate way. Let's start by outlining the types of information that are generally needed by the marketing managers of most organizations. This is not meant to be a complete or detailed list, but it will provide you with an overview of the kinds of information that are usually obtained.

The information that is generally collected extends from information about the marketplace and what marketers need to know about planning an entry into that market, to customers and how they buy, to how to plan the marketing mix, to evaluating how well the firm has performed and how satisfied its customers are.

What's happening out there? Companies must have a solid understanding about what is happening in the marketplace in general and the characteristics of the markets they plan to enter. Such information generally deals with the size of the market, the level of competition, changes that are occurring at the macro level that will affect customer buying power, and other factors that we discussed in Chapter 2. Keeping up to date on trends and changes is critical if a company is to respond appropriately.

What's going on in our market? The marketer must have somewhat more detailed information about the specific markets in which the firm operates — information about direct competitors, new products or brands entering the market, price and distribution changes, and new consumer interests. They also need to know how well they are doing against their competitors, what their market share is, sales trends, and much more. The marketplace is constantly changing. If marketers are not up to date on what's going on, they can be left behind very quickly, as other marketers will have caught the attention of customers.

Will this stuff sell?   Before launching a new product or service, or even before changing an existing product, marketers need to know how consumers will react. A very large percentage of new products that are introduced into the Canadian market each year fail, mainly because the companies that introduce them have not done sufficient research to know whether the customer is even interested. Rhonda, in the chapter opener, realizes that she needs to know a great deal about the market before opening her restaurant.

What are the customers like?   The more a firm knows about its customers and prospective customers for its products and services, the better the job it can do in marketing to them. There is a great deal to know. Profiling customers is a major role of marketing research, telling the marketing staff about its customers, including their characteristics, families, attitudes, lifestyles, and likes and dislikes. Understanding the various segments that exist is also of critical importance.

What's important to them?   To satisfy customers — the ultimate objective of marketing — a company must understand what customers consider to be important when buying its products and services. Some customers think obtaining a low price is very important, while others may be prepared to pay higher prices if they can access the product quickly and conveniently.

What do they buy and where?   A firm needs to know a great deal about customer buying patterns: what they currently buy, what brands, how often, what quantities and sizes. Do they buy from the same stores all of the time, or is location not particularly important? Customer buying patterns, if they are well established, may be difficult to break if a company is trying to unseat an existing brand.

What do they like about our products?   A company needs to know how customers respond to the various elements of its marketing program, in particular, to its products or services. Unless customers find these attractive, the company has little chance of success. Therefore, much marketing research is devoted to assessing customer reaction to existing and planned products, identifying strengths and weaknesses so that modifications can be made to make the product as attractive as possible.

What do they like about our advertising?   Advertising and other forms of promotion are also tested through research. A firm needs to know whether its planned advertising and promotions will be attractive to customers before the company spends possibly millions of dollars producing these promotions and placing them in the media. After advertising has run in the market for a time, it is tested again to determine customer reaction and the advertising's effectiveness.

Do they think our prices are acceptable?   Much pricing research is devoted to finding out what prices customers are prepared to pay for the products and services being offered. As we will discuss in Chapter 15, the real objective of such research should be to find out what customers value, what they will or will not pay for, and what will represent value for them. Companies need such information to be able to set reasonable and acceptable prices.

Do we make it easy for them?   A fundamental issue for most customers is how easy it is to deal with a company. Most want their interaction with a company to be hassle-free, convenient,

MARKETING AT WORK 6-1: STRATEGY

The Heart of Saturn

Every good ad campaign starts with a challenge. For Saturn Canada, that challenge was to develop a new way of expressing the Saturn difference after more than a decade in the marketplace. The company and its advertising agency, Cossette Communications-Marketing in Toronto, came up with a successful national TV campaign that got to the core emotion of the Saturn ownership and buying experience. Marketing research was the key to this project.

Research began with a series of workshops with Saturn stakeholders, followed by a thorough review of primary and secondary research. The objective: to continue to build brand awareness and its relevance in today's market. However, questions about the real (emotional) nature of the Saturn ownership experience and how Saturn could communicate this remained unanswered.

These grey areas were explored through focus groups with Saturn owners, prospective owners of small and mid-sized cars, and owners of competitive products. The results indicated that consumers had positive perceptions of the brand. As well, it became clear that most consumers had high recall of previous Saturn advertising, indicating strong brand awareness that could be built on.

Brand attributes expressed as rational or emotional statements were tested via the "Brand Explosion" technique, which has participants rank benefit statements until the most relevant are determined. This allowed researchers to learn more about customers' relationships with their cars and Saturn retailers, and then to incorporate those ideas into marketing messages.

What resulted were two real-life stories aired across English Canada. The common theme: Demonstrate the personal nature of the Saturn buying and ownership experience, while reinforcing its commitment to "do things differently." Featuring a woman named Susan Kelly, the ads highlight Saturn's flexible returns policy and shows how you can buy a Saturn online from anywhere. Susan loses her job and sadly returns her Saturn to the dealership, as allowed by the returns policy. Then, she gets a new job and orders another Saturn online. The ad ends with Susan's smiling face when she is met at the airport by the dealer with the keys to her new car. The spots emotionally touched viewers, and Saturn received an unprecedented number of positive comments about the ads.

SOURCE: Adapted from Eric LeBlanc and Kate Tutlys, "The Heart of the Matter," *Marketing Magazine*, July 16, 2001, page 10.

---

and quick. This means that a company needs to know how customers want its products distributed or made available for them to buy. Research on various aspects of the firm's distribution system is critical to make sure that customers not only find it convenient, but also that they agree it represents a good fit for the image of the company.

Do they like dealing with us? Much marketing research is devoted to determining customers' perception of the quality of products and services offered by a company, and the customers' overall satisfaction with those products and with the service provided by the firm. Customer satisfaction research is important in that it provides the company with feedback on how well it is doing in serving its customers. Based on that feedback, adjustments can be made in service levels and in other aspects of the marketing program.

What do they think of us? A company needs to know about its image and reputation among customers and the general public at large. Many companies conduct public opinion research that is not aimed at specific products and services or at aspects of the marketing program, but rather at how the company is regarded as a member of the community or as a place to work. Much of this type or research today is aimed at determining the image of brands.

How solid are our relationships? Finally, a firm needs to know how well it is doing in developing a base of loyal customers and in building solid relationships with them. As the attention of marketing shifts more toward customer retention and loyalty-building, companies are increasingly interested in measuring the health of their relationships with customers.

Examples of typical marketing research projects are described briefly in Table 6-1.

TABLE 6-1	Typical Marketing Research Projects
Project	**Objective**
Concept test	To determine if a new product idea is attractive to potential customers, or to determine how targeted customers will respond to advertising concepts.
Copy test	To determine if the intended message in an advertisement is being communicated effectively.
Price responsiveness	To gauge the effect a price change would have on sales of a brand.
Market-share analysis	To determine a firm's proportion of the total sales of a product or service and whether that share is increasing or declining.
Segmentation studies	To identify distinct groups within the total market for a particular product or service, so that these groups may be targeted with specific marketing programs.
Customer satisfaction studies	To monitor how customers feel about an organization and its products or services, and with how they are treated by the company.

Approaches To Marketing Research

There are many ways to carry out marketing research — there is no single right or wrong way to obtain the information that a company needs. The answer to what research approach should be used depends on the objectives of the research, the information needed, and many practical considerations, such as how much time and money the company has available to devote to the project.

Essentially, there are four approaches to carrying out marketing research: qualitative, quantitative, observational, and experimental. The approach chosen by a marketer to collect the required information depends on the nature of the problem or question being examined. A major point is that they are not competing approaches. In other words, a marketer or researcher rarely would have to decide whether to use qualitative research or an experimental approach. The approach selected will be dictated by the nature of the problem.

Qualitative research

qualitative research
A form of marketing research usually employed for exploratory purposes that examines consumers' deeply held views, opinions, and feelings; includes focus group interviews and one-on-one depth interviews.

When research is intended to probe more deeply into opinions and attitudes, qualitative techniques are usually required. **Qualitative research** involves interviewing relatively small numbers of people in considerable depth and for as long as 90 minutes or two hours. The two most widely used qualitative research techniques are the individual depth interview and the focus group interview.

An **individual depth interview** is used when the researcher wants to probe the consumer's thoughts concerning purchase and use of a certain product or service. It is conducted with an individual rather than with a group, because sometimes the topics to be discussed are sensitive ones or because the people are difficult to reach and would be unlikely to attend a focus group session. For example, an individual depth interview is often used to interview business executives and professionals. Such interviews will generally take an hour or more to complete and range over a number of topics. The interviewer usually conducts the interview using a prepared interview guide.

In the case of a **focus group interview**, approximately 8 to 10 people are "recruited" to participate. They are usually selected to meet certain criteria relating to demographic characteristics, the use of a particular brand, frequent visits to certain vacation destinations, or similar criteria of interest to the researcher and client. The focus group interviewer or moderator orchestrates the discussion using a loosely structured interview guide, rather than the more

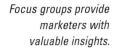

Focus groups provide marketers with valuable insights.

structured questionnaire of the typical face-to-face interview or telephone survey. Many interesting and enlightening findings are revealed through focus group interviews; this has become one of the most widely used techniques in marketing research.

These are qualitative marketing research techniques, so their results are completely non-quantifiable; typically, no statistics are generated and research reports contain few if any numbers. They do however produce valuable insights into how consumers feel about certain concepts and why they make decisions as they do. The principal use of the focus group interview, for example, is to allow the marketer to really understand why customers are buying one brand over another, why this bar of soap and not that one, why this locally owned fitness centre and not a national chain. The research explores what customers like and dislike about each, and what would have to happen for them to switch to the alternative. The loosely structured focus group is intended to provide marketers with insights that they simply cannot obtain through the more structured answers provided by survey research.

Online focus groups have also been utilized in recent years, as certain groups of consumers have become accessible through the Internet. Here, a focus group would be like a focused chat room with a moderator. Unfortunately, no systematic research has been conducted to gauge the effectiveness of this focus group format. While this format may be effective at targeting particular groups, these groups currently are not representative of the overall population, as only a minority of Canadians regularly surf the Internet. This will probably change over time as usage among all age groups increases. Also, there is the question of how people represent themselves online. While there are those who argue that people are more honest and expressive in this forum because of the anonymity afforded, studies have found that people often misrepresent themselves — perhaps as part of the entertainment value of the Internet. As for being expressive, these focus groups lack the richness of the traditional format, because moderators are unable to observe the facial expressions and body language of participants.

So, while the majority of Canada's population is online (about 60 percent), many marketing researchers are still uncomfortable about leaving out that other 40 percent. About 3 percent of all marketing research in Canada is conducted online, and only a small part of that is through online focus groups, as many marketers are still sceptical of this method. Despite its convenience and promise, the Internet paradigm shift in the research industry is still very new and currently is more hype than action.[1]

MARKETING AT WORK

6-2: ETHICS

The Recruiter

A few years ago, the Toronto marketing research community started noticing a familiar face in focus groups. Sometimes uninvited, this shady figure would show up in different disguises that even crossed genders. It soon became clear they were dealing with a focus group junkie, whose presence could easily taint research results.

Enter Dawn Smith. It took a while, but Smith and her colleagues were able to identify the person and that he was in effect making a living attending focus groups, which usually pay $50 per two-hour session. They nipped his burgeoning "career" in the bud!

Smith doesn't mince words when she says she considers it her personal mission to protect the reputation of all marketing research recruiters, because "Recruiters are at the bottom of the food chain," as Smith puts it — they often get caught in the crossfire when things don't work out as they should. Every now and then, a loose screw falls between the cracks — like that often-bearded focus group junkie, who was eventually flagged with 30 names and 15 different telephone numbers — but that doesn't happen too often.

Being a recruiter takes patience and good telephone skills. Recruiters rely on and build their databases most successfully by referral. Good respondents are later asked for potential contacts among friends and family. Of every 10 telephone calls made to referrals, about six people are interested, whereas cold calls average a 1-in-10 success rate.

Focus groups are an easy target for criticism because of the monetary incentive involved. However, while some do it for the money, others do it for the social aspect and yet others like the sense of having participated in the decision process. When recruiting over the telephone, Smith tries to determine how articulate, expressive, and creative the recruit is, but that's not easy. While a screening questionnaire is utilized, that doesn't prevent something from going awry. As Smith says, "It's impossible to tell what people look like, their level of personal hygiene — not to mention whether they'll show up drunk, which can and does happen."

SOURCE: Adapted from Lesley Young, "The Recruiter," *Marketing Magazine,* July 16, 2001, pp. 8, 9.

Quantitative research

quantitative research

A form of marketing research that is intended to obtain statistical information about a sample of consumers or members of the public; usually relies on surveys to collect the data.

benchmark

The process of comparing a company with its competitors and others in related industries.

survey

A method of gathering data by interviewing a limited number of people (a sample) in person or by telephone or mail.

Quantitative research is so named because it involves the measurement of concepts using standard numeric measures such as time, frequency, or monetary units, or specific measures that have been developed to assess customer- or marketing-related concepts, as when we are asked to express our satisfaction with shopping at Loblaws on a 10-point scale. Unlike qualitative research, which is intended to capture the deeply held views of customers, quantitative research has the advantage of using numbers that allow for statistical calculations and comparisons. For example, if a company measures customer satisfaction every six months, it can calculate average satisfaction scores for various groups of customers, compare its performance on customer satisfaction over time, and can then **benchmark** itself against other companies that also measure customer satisfaction.

Most forms of quantitative research involve carrying out a **survey** of customers or prospective customers. A survey consists of gathering data by interviewing people or by having them complete a questionnaire of some type. What distinguishes a survey from qualitative research is that, in a survey, the information is usually collected from a fairly large sample of customers, generally several hundred or more, and the results are entered into computer files for analysis. The results of survey research are quantitative in nature because they involve statistical analysis. The advantage of a survey is that information is first-hand. In fact, it may be the only way to determine the opinions or buying intentions of a group of customers or prospective customers.

Certain limitations are inherent in conducting surveys. There are opportunities for error in the construction of the survey questionnaire and in the data collection process. Moreover, surveys can be very expensive, and they take some time to complete. Other possible weaknesses are that potential respondents sometimes refuse to participate, and the ones who do respond often cannot or will not give accurate answers. We will discuss surveys in greater detail later in this chapter.

Observational method

observational method

Gathering data by observing personally or mechanically the actions of a person.

In the **observational method**, data are collected by observing some action of the respondent. No interviews are involved, although an interview may be used as a follow-up to obtain additional information. For example, if customers are observed buying beer in cans instead of bottles, they may be asked why they prefer that form of packaging to the other. We should not adopt a too-restricted view of what constitutes observational research. We can include any form of research that involves the automatic capture of information, where the customer or consumer is being observed by a machine or by technology rather than by another person. In each case, the information is often being collected without the customer's knowledge, which may raise ethical issues.

In using this approach, researchers may collect information by personal or mechanical observation. In one form of **personal observation**, the researcher may pose as a customer in a store. This technique is often referred to as "mystery shopping" and is useful in getting information about the calibre of the salespeople or in determining what brands they promote. One example of **mechanical observation** is the use of an electric cord laid across a highway to count the number of cars that pass during a certain time period. Technology has advanced so rapidly that data are now captured by technology in many different settings. Builders of highways now imbed sensors in the surface of roads to not only count but also to identify the vehicles that pass over them. Whenever we use banking machines, we enable the bank to capture a lot of information. The scanners that speed up the process of checking through our groceries at supermarkets also are automatically collecting information about what was purchased. If your supermarket has a frequent-shopper club, the system uses the list of items purchased to update your personal data file. The resulting databases that most large retail firms and others now maintain on their customers are a direct result of data captured through such technology-based observation.

Retailers also find that watching the customer is a valuable way to gauge reactions and attitudes toward store displays and merchandise. In fact, there has been a resurgence of observational research over the past five years, often involving watching customers doing tasks in their own homes. In doing research to develop its Dryel home dry-cleaning product, for example, Procter & Gamble watched people sort laundry in their own homes. Sico watched people paint rooms, and one food producer had researchers go into homes where the principal grocery shopper invited four or five friends over for coffee to chat about food around the kitchen table. Sometimes it's a little sneaky, such as video-recording consumer reactions without the consumers' knowledge; this has also provided valuable input. Urban Outfitters (**www.urbanoutfitters.com**), the specialty clothing and home accessory store, likes to use observation as a marketing research tool. By videotaping and photographing customers in its stores, Urban Outfitters doesn't plan to find out what customers are saying, but rather what they are doing. Managers are then able to determine what customers are wearing and their reactions to displays, etc. This helps them make future merchandise decisions.[2]

Urban Outfitters

Marketers have even found a way to keep an eye on us when we are surfing the Internet. Through the use of "cookies," inactive data files are placed on a visitor's computer hard drive when the person visits a particular Web site. The cookie records the visitor's activity while connected to the site — which pages were visited, how long was spent in which areas, the links used, and the previous site the person visited. The cookie allows the visitor to be identified and welcomed back, making the log-in process quicker; it can keep track of shopping-cart items, or provide customized news, weather, or sports information. Sometimes, based on past purchases, suggestions may be made about other products or services of possible interest. In theory, a cookie transmits information back only to the original Web site that put it there and cannot be accessed by other parties. It is only when companies link this information with individual e-mail addresses and make this available to third parties that your personally identifiable information is accessible to other marketers. A common complaint that arises out of this practice concerns consumers' privacy, but there is another issue that should make marketers question its effectiveness.

The cookie tracks the activity of the machine, not the actual person using it, so pop-ups and e-mails may be blindly sent to those not in the target group. Another scenario: You search the Web to find a gift for a niece or nephew and suddenly you're receiving banner ads for everything from toys to diapers. The problem: You don't actually have any children.[3]

The observational method has several advantages. It can be highly accurate. Often, it removes all doubt about what the consumer does in a given situation. Consumers are usually unaware that they are being observed, so presumably they act in their usual fashion. The observation technique also reduces interviewer bias. However, the technique is limited in its application: Observation tells what happened, but it cannot tell why. It cannot delve into motives, attitudes, or opinions.

To overcome the biases inherent in the survey method, some firms are using sophisticated observational techniques that involve a combination of cable TV, electronic scanners in supermarkets, and computers. For example, some marketing research companies in Canada and the United States have established "scanner panels." Selected households are invited to participate in a program that involves recording electronically every TV commercial watched in participants' homes. Also, every purchase the participants make in supermarkets equipped with checkout scanners is electronically recorded. With this observational method, researchers can measure which products members of the households are buying and determine which TV commercials they have seen. It provides an improved link between advertising and purchase that allows for more accurate measurement of the types of advertising that work and that don't work.

Experimental method

experimental method

A method of gathering primary data in which the researcher is able to observe the results of changing one variable in a situation while holding all others constant.

The **experimental method** involves the gathering of primary data in which the researcher is able to observe the result of changing one variable in a situation while keeping all others constant. Experiments are conducted in simulated or laboratory settings and in the field. In marketing research, the word *laboratory* is used to describe an environment over which the researcher has complete control during an experiment.

Consider the following example. A Vancouver film producer wanted to determine whether Canadian films would be rented more frequently from video stores if they were identified as being Canadian. To assess this, he set up an experiment with 10 Vancouver-area video stores, supplying them with a stock of Canadian videos to put on their shelves. In three stores, the tapes were mixed in with other videos. In another three stores, the Canadian films were displayed separately on their own rack and identified as being Canadian. The remaining four stores, known as the promotional group, put the Canadian tapes in their own section, stuck little bar signs on each cassette, and promoted them with stickers and posters. Rentals were tracked over six months, and the results indicated that people rented more Canadian videos when they were identified as such, and 45 percent more when they were promoted. These results, incidentally, conflict with the conventional view that Canadians are not interested in films made in this country — information that is of great interest to the Canadian film industry.[4]

test marketing

A marketing research technique in which, before committing to a major marketing effort, a firm markets its product in a limited geographic area, measures the sales, and then, from this sample, projects (a) the company's sales over a larger area and/or (b) consumer response to a strategy.

Laboratory experiments can be used to test virtually any component of marketing strategy. However, it is important to recognize that the setting is unnatural and that consumers' responses may be biased by the situation.

An experiment carried out in the field (that is, under actual market conditions), is called **test marketing**. It is similar to a laboratory experiment but is conducted under more realistic conditions. The researcher therefore has less control. In test marketing, the researcher duplicates real market conditions in a small geographic area to measure consumer response to a strategy before the company commits itself to a major marketing effort. Test marketing may be undertaken to forecast sales or to evaluate different marketing mixes. Test marketing methodology is also used to evaluate pricing strategies, to obtain feedback on aspects of an advertisement, or to establish the effectiveness of an advertising campaign in influencing buying behaviour. Advertising testing is sometimes done by running two versions of the same advertisement and assessing changes in purchasing behaviour relative to each area.

The advantage of field experiments over laboratory experiments is their realism; however, there are several disadvantages. Test marketing is expensive (spending $500,000 or more to complete a test is not uncommon), time-consuming (9 to 12 months is normal), and impossible to keep secret from competitors (who may intentionally disrupt the test by temporarily changing their marketing programs). Another problem is the researcher's inability to control the situation. For example, a company that is test marketing a new product may encounter a certain amount of publicity while the product is in the test market, simply because of the innovativeness of the product. Although such publicity would normally be considered a good thing, when faced with it in a test market situation, the marketer is not sure about the extent to which the publicity has distorted the sales results. In other words, what volume of sales resulted from the product and the regular marketing efforts of the company (what was actually being tested), and what resulted from the publicity that was generated?

Because of its inherent limitations, the use of traditional test marketing declined as faster, less expensive alternatives were developed. One of these alternatives is the **simulated test market**, in which a sample of consumers is shown ads for the product being tested as well as for other products. The subjects are then allowed to "shop" in a test facility that resembles a small grocery store. Follow-up interviews may be conducted immediately and also after the products have been used to better understand the consumers' behaviour. The entire set of data goes into a statistical model, and sales for the product are forecast.

simulated test market

A variation of test marketing in which consumers are shown advertising for a product and then are allowed to "shop" in a test facility in order to measure their reactions to the advertising, the product, or both.

← BACKSPACE

1. Firms must conduct _____ in order to obtain accurate, timely information used in marketing decision-making.

2. Name the four approaches that a firm can use when it conducts marketing research.

3. What is a focus group interview and why is it used by researchers?

Conducting Marketing Research Projects

The carrying out of occasional marketing research projects is a major part of marketing research. Some of these projects are non-recurring, in the sense that they are conducted only once to address a particular issue, such as a decision on a new package design. Others are repeated periodically, as they are intended to update management's knowledge about a particular subject; for example, a company may have a policy of measuring aspects of customer satisfaction and loyalty every 12 months. Examples of marketing research projects were described briefly in Table 6-1. Most marketing research projects follow the procedure outlined in Figure 6-1. Let's examine what goes into conducting a marketing research project.

1. Define research objectives

research objectives

The purpose of conducting the research; questions the marketer and researcher want to have addressed and areas that they want to have explored.

Marketers need a clear idea of what they are trying to learn — the **research objectives** of the project, why research is needed. Usually the objective is to solve a problem, but this is not always the case. Often the objective is to obtain information that will allow the firm to define the problem. Sometimes it's simply to determine if there is a problem. To illustrate, a manufacturer of commercial air-conditioning equipment had been enjoying a steady increase in sales volume over a period of years. Management decided to conduct a sales analysis. This research project uncovered the fact that, although the company's volume had been increasing,

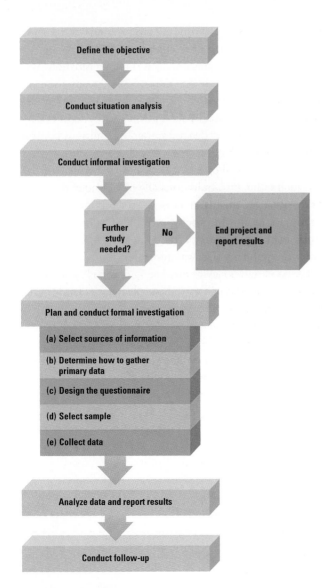

Figure 6-1:

Marketing Research Procedure

secondary data

Information already gathered by somebody else for some other purpose.

research hypothesis

A tentative supposition that, if proven, would suggest a possible solution to a problem.

its share of the market had declined because the industry was growing even faster. In this instance, marketing research uncovered a problem that management didn't know existed. It is critically important that the marketer clearly identifies the research objectives. Failure to do so often means that the most important information is not obtained. After specifying the research objectives, the marketer is ready for the next step — situation analysis.

2. Conduct a situation analysis

Next, the marketer and the researcher who is actually conducting the project will try to get a "feel" for the situation surrounding the problem. They analyze the company, its market, its competition, and the industry in general. Situation analysis is a background investigation that helps in refining the research problem and objectives. It involves obtaining information about the company and its business environment by library research and interviewing company officials. This process generally relies on the use of secondary data, meaning that the data already exist in some other form, often available from outside organizations such as Statistics Canada or trade associations.

In situation analysis, researchers also try to refine the problem definition and develop hypotheses for testing. A research hypothesis is a tentative supposition that, if proven, would suggest a possible solution to a problem. Some examples of testable hypotheses are:

- Sales of grocery items are significantly greater when the items are placed in end-of-aisle displays than when they are located only in their normal aisle positions.

- Sales of Nintendo Game Boy Advance units will experience a sharp increase following each introduction of a new Breath of Fire game cartridge.

- Bank customers who use ATMs and telephone banking services will accept and adopt PC-based banking systems once they have become aware of their availability.

- Demand for MP3 players will increase proportionally to the increasing availability of downloadable sampling via the Internet.

- Consumers in rural areas of Canada are more inclined to buy locally produced products and services than are those living in larger centres.

The project then turns to generating data that can be used to test the correctness of the hypotheses.

3. Conduct an informal investigation

Now having a feel for the problem, the researchers are ready to collect some preliminary data from the marketplace. This informal investigation consists of gathering readily available information from people inside and outside the company — distribution channel members, competitors, advertising agencies, and consumers, for example.

Marketers need research to understand why consumers buy products like Game Boy.

informal investigation

The stage in a marketing research study at which information is gathered from people outside the company, such as distribution channel members, competitors, advertising agencies, and consumers.

The informal investigation is a critical step in a research project, because it will determine whether further study is necessary. Decisions can frequently be made with information gathered in the informal investigation. For example, a company considering opening sales offices for its computer software support service in western Canada might first talk with representatives of trade associations representing the personal computer industry and with officials of companies that supply computers and software. Before contacting any prospective clients for its new service, the company would be interested in getting a feel for the market and for the extent to which demand for software support is being satisfied. The conclusion at this stage may be that the market is large enough to warrant further investigation. The company's representatives might then meet with office managers or information systems managers of prospective clients in cities such as Edmonton, Calgary, and Vancouver to discuss informally their needs for software support, where they are currently buying such a service, and what they would look for in a new entrant into the market.

Much valuable information is obtained through an informal market investigation. The company not only will learn a great deal about the market it proposes to enter, it will also determine whether further study is needed. A decision on the main problem can often be made with information gathered at the informal investigation stage.

4. Plan and conduct a formal investigation

If the project warrants continued investigation, the marketer and researcher must determine what additional information is needed and how to gather it. This usually involves the part of a marketing research project that we normally think of when we think of research — the actual design and carrying out of the project. At this stage, a series of decisions are made concerning the nature of the project to be conducted: Should it be qualitative or quantitative? From whom will information be obtained? How many people should we talk to? What questions should we ask? And so on. The first step is to decide where the necessary information can be obtained.

primary data
Original data gathered specifically for the project at hand.

syndicated data
Research information that is purchased from a research supplier on a shared-cost basis by a number of clients.

4(a) Select sources of information Primary data, secondary data, or both can be used in an investigation. **Primary data** are original data gathered specifically for the project at hand. Secondary data have already been gathered for some other purpose. For example, when researchers conduct personal interviews, perhaps to have individuals complete questionnaires over the telephone, they are collecting primary data. When they obtain information from Statistics Canada or from the local chamber of commerce, they are using a secondary source.

One mistake often made in marketing research is to collect primary data before exhausting the information available in secondary sources. Ordinarily, secondary information can be gathered much faster and at far less expense than can primary data.

Syndicated data represent a third source of information and are a hybrid between primary and secondary data. Syndicated data are collected by a research supplier and may be purchased from that supplier by a number of clients, some of whom may be in direct competition with one another. The most common form of syndicated data involves the collection of data on a regular basis from an established sample or panel of consumers or retail stores. Clients subscribe to the reports that are produced by the research company and essentially share the cost of collecting the data from the large sample. Although syndicated research does not provide privileged information to a single company, it does allow companies to obtain information on a shared-cost basis.

Several excellent sources of secondary information and syndicated data are available to marketers and marketing researchers in Canada. A detailed review of the main sources of secondary and syndicated data in this country can be found in a number of Canadian marketing research textbooks. See Table 6-2 for an overview of key secondary data resources for conducting marketing research in Canada.

4(b) Gathering primary data After exhausting all of the available secondary sources considered pertinent, researchers may still lack sufficient data. If so, they must turn to primary sources and gather or purchase the information. In a company's research project, for instance, a researcher may interview the firm's salespeople, wholesalers or retailers, or customers to obtain the market information needed. Important decisions have to be made regarding from whom the information is to be obtained.

There are four widely used methods of gathering primary data, as we discussed earlier in this chapter: qualitative research, quantitative research, the observational method, and the experimental method. Normally, all four are not used on the same project, although more than one may be. Because each method has strengths and weaknesses, the choice of which to use depends on the nature of the problem, but it will also be influenced by how much time and money are available for the project. Because it is the most frequently used approach to obtain marketing research information and is usually more complex than other approaches, we will use survey research to illustrate how a research project may be conducted.

Survey data collection is usually conducted either in person, by telephone, by mail, or through the Internet. **Personal interviews** are more flexible than the other types because interviewers can probe more deeply if an answer is incomplete. Ordinarily, it is possible to obtain more information by personal interview than by telephone or mail. Also the interviewer, by observation, can obtain data regarding the respondents' socio-economic status — their homes, neighbourhoods, and apparent standard of living.

Rising costs and other problems associated with door-to-door interviewing have prompted many marketing researchers to survey people in central locations, typically regional shopping centres. This technique is called the **mall intercept** method of interviewing. By interviewing people as they pass through a shopping mall, the interviewer is better able to encounter large numbers of people, as the urban mall has essentially become the "main street" of North America. Although data collection is made somewhat easier by this method, the

personal interview
A face-to-face method of gathering data in a survey.

mall intercept
A method of gathering data by conducting personal interviews in central locations, typically regional shopping centres

TABLE 6-2   Key Sources of Secondary Data

Internal Sources

Internal sources include annual reports, profit and loss statements, sales figures, balance sheets, and prior research conducted by the organization. Research should begin within the company's own files and records, as well as that of the parent company if one exists.

Directories, Guides, and Indexes

Business Periodical Index

Canadian Business Index

Canadian Periodical Index

Canadian Statistics Index

Canadian Trade Index

Directory of Association in Canada

Fraser's Canadian Trade Directory

Predicasts Index

Scott's Directories

Standards Periodical Directory

Ulrich's International Periodicals Directory

Selected Periodicals, Newspapers, etc.

Advertising Age

Adweek

Business Horizons

Canadian Business

Canadian Consumer

Canadian Markets

Financial Post Magazine

Forbes

Fortune

Harvard Business Review

Journal of Advertising

Journal of Consumer Research

Journal of the Academy of Marketing Science

Journal of Marketing

Journal of Marketing Research

Journal of Retailing

Marketing Magazine

Marketing News

National Post

Sales and Marketing Management

Strategy: The Canadian Marketing Report

The Globe and Mail

The Globe and Mail Report on Business Magazine

The Wall Street Journal

Selected Statistics Canada Publications

Annual Retail Trade

Canadian Economic Observer

Family Expenditure Guide

Market Research Handbook

Statistics Canada is also on the internet at www.statcan.ca. Industry Canada also provides statistical information regarding various industries at www.stategis.ic.gc.ca. Additional information may also be available from specific government departments that can be accessed through www.canada.gc.ca. Provincial government Web sites may also contain required information.

For Canadian companies researching international business opportunities: www.dfait-maeci.gc.ca, Department of Foreign Affairs and International Trade. Also, www.bdc.ca, the Business Development Bank of Canada.

Selected Trade Resources

A.C. Nielsen

Compusearch

Conference Board of Canada

Dun & Bradstreet

Equifax Canada

Find/SVP

Gale Research

Maclean-Hunter Research Bureau

MMRI (Simmons Market Research Bureau)

Predicasts International

PMB (Print Measurement Bureau)

R.L. Polk

Selected Databases

ABI/Inform (Proquest)

CANSIM (Statistics Canada)

CBCA (Canadian Business & Current Affairs)

Dialog

Dow Jones

Infoglobe

Infomart

Lexis-Nexis

PsycINFO

The Source

Wilson's Business Abstracts

Online Search Options

Canadian Corporate Newsnet at www.cdn-news.com/ Canada Newswire at www.newswire.ca/

General-purpose Internet search engines such as Google, Lycos, Excite, or Yahoo! also provide marketers with additional information on special topics. The most recent publication of *The Canadian Internet Directory* can also facilitate the search for reputable Canadian Web sites.

"On a scale from 1 to 10, how interested are you in eating at a vegetarian restaurant?" could be this interviewer's question.

telephone survey

A method of gathering data in a survey by interviewing people over the telephone.

researcher is less confident that a representative sample of the population of interest is being obtained. In such a situation, the ability to access large numbers of people at relatively low cost outweighs concerns about the representativeness of the sample. This might, for example, be the best approach for Rhonda, in our chapter opener, to collect information from students about whether they would be likely to patronize her planned vegetarian restaurant. Or Professor Stewart might suggest that some of his students station themselves at various points on campus and select passersby to be interviewed.

In a **telephone survey**, the respondent is contacted by telephone, and the interview is completed at that time. Participants in telephone surveys are usually selected at random from telephone directories or by random dialling of telephone numbers. If a company wants to obtain information from its own customers, it could provide the researchers with a list from which those to be called may be selected at random. Telephone surveys usually can be conducted more rapidly and at less cost than either face-to-face interviews or mail surveys. Since a number of interviewers can make many calls from a few central points, this method is quite easy to administer. Computer-assisted techniques have broadened the scope of telephone interviewing. These techniques involve automated random-number dialling and a facility for the interviewer to record the respondent's answers directly into the computer as they are received. This technology speeds up the entry and processing of data and the production of reports.

A telephone survey can be timely. For instance, people may be asked whether they are watching television at the moment and, if so, the name of the program and the advertiser. One limitation of the telephone survey is that interviews cannot be too long, although telephone interviews that take up to 30 minutes to complete are not uncommon. In fact, one of the myths of telephone interviewing is that the questionnaire must be very short, because participants will not be willing to stay on the line for more than a minute or so. This is simply not true, as many Canadians are quite co-operative in participating in telephone surveys that take 5 to 10 minutes to complete.

One difficulty with telephone research is that fewer people are at home today, and those who are at home are becoming more difficult to reach. Although there appears to be no dramatic increase in the frequency of unlisted numbers, more and more people are installing telephone answering machines or subscribing to services such as voice mail and call display. Many people who have such devices or services are using them to screen incoming calls, forcing callers to leave messages, or are choosing not to answer the call if they do not recognize the number or name displayed. The result is that telephone interviewers are unable to reach an increasing percentage of the population, thereby making telephone interviewing more costly and resulting in more biased samples. Low response rates generally translate into an under-representation of younger people, males, and professionals or senior executives.[5]

Telephone surveys have been used successfully to reach professionals and executives at work. When preceded by a letter introducing the study and a short call to make an appointment for the actual interview, these surveys can elicit a very high co-operation rate.

Collecting marketing research information through **mail surveys** involves mailing a questionnaire to prospective respondents and having them return the completed form by mail. Since no interviewers are used, this type of survey is not hampered by interviewer bias or problems connected with the management of interviewers. Mailed questionnaires are more economical than personal interviews and are particularly useful in national surveys. If the respondents remain anonymous, they are more likely to give true answers because they are not biased by the presence of an interviewer.

mail survey
Gathering data by means of a questionnaire mailed to respondents and, when completed, returned by mail.

A major problem with mail surveys is the compilation of a good mailing list, especially for a broad-scale survey. If the sample can be drawn from a limited list, however, such as taxpayers in a certain province, region, or municipality, or subscribers to a certain magazine, the list presents no problem. Another significant limitation concerns the reliability of the questionnaires returned. The researchers have no control over who actually completes the questionnaire or how it is done. For example, a survey may be addressed to an adult male member of the household but because that person is unavailable or not interested, a teenaged daughter "helps out" by completing it. In addition, because there is no personal contact with the respondents, it is impossible to judge how much care and thought went into providing the answers.

Still another limitation is that there is usually a low response rate to a mail survey. It is not uncommon to receive completed replies from only 10 to 15 percent of those contacted. The positive news is that average response rates for one-time random studies have increased slightly since 1997 from 15.5 percent to over 17 percent.[6] Response rates are important because if the respondents have characteristics that differentiate them from non-respondents on certain dimensions of the survey, the results will be biased. Techniques for improving mail response rates have been the subject of hundreds of experiments. Some of these include making the subject matter of the survey as interesting as possible, offering incentives to the participant to encourage involvement, and guaranteeing anonymity. In the case of mailed questionnaires, a higher response rate can be obtained by paying for return postage and by sending a reminder note or card, or even a second questionnaire, within a week or so of mailing the original.

Because of the lack of control over the process, increased postal rates, low response rates, and the time needed to mail out questionnaires and to receive the completed ones, most marketing researchers are using far fewer mail surveys than was the case several years ago.

Increasingly, the Internet is being used to collect survey data. Questionnaires can be posted on a firm's Web site or e-mailed to a sample of individuals. Speed and cost are the two most obvious advantages of this approach — transmission is electronic, providing speed and significant personnel and material savings. Perseus Development Corporation, a company that specializes in electronic research services and survey development software, says a five-minute survey to one hundred people would cost $550 conducted by telephone (including telephone costs, interviewers, and data entry), $500 by mail (including printing, postage, and data entry), and a mere $55 by Internet (including creation, delivery, and conversion of data).[7]

The disadvantages of **Internet research** are similar to those of traditional mail methods. Clearly, the risk of bias is great: The general population is not represented, as all consumers cannot be reached through the Internet. Use of the Internet continues to expand at a rapid pace, with about 60 percent of Canadians online. Canada is second only to Sweden in Internet usage and just ahead of the United States.[8] It is also often not possible to verify the identity of the respondent, quality lists of potential participants are hard to find, and it is difficult to provide effective incentives. This new medium also brings with it a new manifestation of bias. Reliability of data is a concern, because people have the tendency to "reinvent" themselves online. As many as 50 percent of high school kids lie about their identity online, as do 33 percent of university students. Adults aren't much better, misrepresenting themselves 25 percent of the time. While validity scales are built into almost all surveys to ensure consistency of responses, this is still a major concern with the use of this medium for research. To promote honest responses, online marketers sweeten the pot with offers of electronic coupons, instant online shopping coupons, contests, and sweepstakes. To participate in these, respondents are required to submit personal information such as e-mail and mailing addresses. As the Internet becomes a more universally used medium, there is no doubt that the use of online surveys will increase.

4(c) Designing the questionnaire   Whether interviewing or observing subjects, or having respondents complete questionnaires on their own, as in the case of a mail or Internet survey, researchers use a **questionnaire** or form on which there are instructions and spaces to record responses. It is not easy to design a data gathering form that elicits precisely the information needed. When conducting surveys, researchers use questionnaires that are fairly structured and generally provide a number of responses, asking respondents or interviewers to check the most appropriate response or to write in an answer. When conducting focus group interviews or depth interviews, researchers use **interview guides** that are much less structured and ensure that the interviewer raises all of the topics that must be covered during the interview.

Depending on whether questionnaires or interview guides are being used, different considerations apply. If the researcher is to obtain qualitative information through focus groups or depth interviews, no statistical analysis can be performed. The interpretation of these results is quite subjective and will consist of conclusions drawn from the comments made by participants during the interviews. On the other hand, if the researcher chooses to obtain quantitative data, usually through survey research, such information will lend itself quite readily to

questionnaire
A data-gathering form used to collect information in a personal, telephone, or mail survey.

interview guide
The equivalent of a questionnaire used in qualitative research; a list of questions or areas of enquiry designed to guide the depth interview or focus group.

MARKETING AT WORK   6-3: TECHNOLOGY

Surveying the Internet

While marketing research conducted on the Internet is still in its infancy and arguments abound over the pros and cons of this method, some research firms are making significant investment in trying to control the nature of the sample and know who their respondents are.

One firm, Ipsos-NPD of Toronto, currently does about 17 percent of its surveys online. With public disaffection for telephone interruptions at mealtime, such an approach is less intrusive and allows people to respond at their own convenience. The firm uses four main approaches in conducting these surveys.

The first, and least-favoured, is e-mail surveying via purchased database lists. In many cases, the original source of the list and its recency are unknown. There can also be software compatibility problems if e-mails with elaborate formatting are used.

The remaining are Web-based. According to Ipsos-NPD, this is where better surveys are executed. Site-based surveys feature pop-up banners at appropriate sites that invite visitors to participate in a survey — respondents can click yes or no.

Next is the subscriber or customer study. A company such as an online bank or cyberbookstore supplies a list of customers to the researcher to survey customer satisfaction levels or to rate different aspects of the service provided.

The last, and most favoured for many applications, is panels. It is also the most expensive — infrastructure, software engines, and expert recruitment and management are required. But, once a panel is in place, it can be used for a number of studies. Respondents have expressed an interest in participating, so response rates can be as high as 50 to 60 percent, where other research often results in single-digit response rates. Ipsos-NPD has the largest representative panel in Canada, with 55,000 members.

Omnitel Research has reported little difference between online and telephone survey respondents, but the differences are revealing. Participants seemed more comfortable about sharing their beliefs online and the online participants skew somewhat younger. Such demographic differences can be overcome, however, by weighting samples, requiring that data be collected until certain pre-set targets are reached.

SOURCE: Adapted from Sharon Younger, "Online Surveys More Hype Than Action," *Strategy*, January 28, 2002, page 25.

---

statistical analysis. Therefore, the appropriate instrument, whether a questionnaire or a less formal interview guide, must be designed in such a way as to ensure that the relevant information is obtained and that it is collected in a form that will allow for analysis.

The following represent some factors that must be considered when designing forms for the collection of research data:

- **Question wording:** If a question is misunderstood, the data it produces are worthless. Questions should be written with the potential respondent in mind. Vocabulary, reading level, and familiarity with jargon all must be considered. A common wording error is to inadvertently include two questions in one. For example, the question "How would you evaluate the speed and efficiency of our service?" followed by a rating scale that ranges from "poor" to "excellent" is likely to cause problems. Some respondents may see the service as fast, which is good, but with too many mistakes, which is bad.

- **Response format:** Questions asked in survey research are generally designed either for check-mark responses (such as yes or no, multiple choice, agree or disagree scales) or open-ended replies. Open-ended questions are more often associated with depth interviews, are easier to prepare, and frequently produce richer answers, but they require more effort from the respondent and therefore lower the level of co-operation. In addition, in a mail survey, it is often difficult to read and interpret open-ended responses. Open-ended questions are used most often in personal or telephone interviews, when the interviewer can probe for explanations and additional details.

- **Questionnaire layout:** The normal procedure when constructing a questionnaire for use in a survey is to begin with easy, general questions and move to more difficult, complicated, and specific questions. To understand behaviour, researchers must sometimes ask questions about possibly sensitive topics (for example, personal hygiene) or private matters (age, income). These questions are normally placed close to the end of a questionnaire.

- **Pre-testing:** All questionnaires should be pre-tested on a small group of respondents who are similar to the intended sample. **Pre-testing** is designed to identify problems in the design of the questionnaire and to allow for corrections and refinements to be made prior to the actual study.

Many books have been written on questionnaire design. Extreme care and skill are needed to produce a questionnaire that maximizes the likelihood of obtaining a response while minimizing bias, misunderstanding, and respondent irritation.

pre-testing
The process of testing a questionnaire before it is used in a survey, to identify problems and areas of confusion.

4(d) Sampling   It is, of course, not necessary to interview or observe every person who could shed light on a research problem. It is sufficient to collect data from a sample if its reactions are expected to be representative of an entire group. We all use sampling in our everyday activities. Often we base our opinion of a person on only one or two conversations. We test-drive a car and check a CD before buying it, and we taste a little bit of an unfamiliar food before taking a larger quantity. The key in these personal examples and in marketing research is whether the sample provides accurate information.

The fundamental idea underlying sampling is that a small number of items — a **sample** — if properly selected from a larger number of items — a **population** — will have the same characteristics in about the same proportion as the larger number. Obtaining reliable data with this method requires the right technique in selecting the sample. The two main issues to be addressed in selecting a sample are, first, to ensure that the sample is representative of the population of interest and, second, to have a large enough sample to have confidence that the results can be generalized for a larger population.

Improper sampling is a source of error in many studies. One firm, for example, selected a sample of calls from all of the calls made to its toll-free number and used the information to make generalizations about its customers. Would you be comfortable saying that these callers are a representative sample of all of the firm's customers or even all of the dissatisfied ones? Many airlines, hotels, and restaurants use comment cards to obtain feedback from customers. The danger in generalizing from this information relates to the issue of who completes comment cards. The sample is self-selected and as such has built-in biases. Although numerous sampling techniques are used, only **representative samples** of the population of interest are appropriate for making generalizations from a sample to the population. A random sample is selected in such a way that every member of the population has a known probability of being included. In fact, unless the researcher has a list of all members of the population, it is virtually impossible to select a **random sample**. As a result, marketing researchers generally attempt to select a sample that is as representative of the population as possible.

Most of the samples used in surveys would be considered **convenience samples**. For example, interviews are often conducted in shopping centres, where large numbers of people are conveniently available. These are quite common in marketing research for two reasons. First, random samples are very difficult to obtain. Even though the researcher may select the subjects in a random fashion, there is no guarantee that all of those who are selected will participate. Some will be unavailable and others will refuse to co-operate. As a result, researchers often resort to carefully designed convenience samples that reflect the characteristics of the population as closely as possible. Second, not all research is done with the objective of generalizing to a population. Sometimes the company is interested in interviewing customers who visit a certain store or who telephone for service. In these cases, a convenience sample may be considered representative of the overall population. For example, if we want to assess whether regular users of a shopping centre are favourably disposed to the idea of installing lockers, a convenience sample may be appropriate for this situation.

How large should a sample be? With random sampling methods, a sample must be large enough to be truly representative of the population; thus, the size will depend on the diversity of characteristics of the population. All basic statistics books contain general formulas for calculating sample size. It is not, however, a simple matter to determine the appropriate size of a sample. The choice of sample size is normally made after consideration of a wide variety of factors. The researcher must determine whether there are natural groupings in the population, if the research objectives will require an investigation of whether one factor is associated with another, and the budget available to conduct the research.

Many researchers have rules of thumb that they use in deciding on sample size. Some, for example, would not consider using a sample of fewer than 400, as this sample size provides an acceptable level of confidence in the results. Generally, a sample of 1,000 or more would be considered acceptable by any standards, as it will provide a high degree of confidence. A problem arises, however, if the marketer wants to examine a subgroup of, for example, Volvo drivers out of a sample of 1,000 owners of luxury cars. If there are only 47 Volvo owners in the sample, the research is constrained in drawing conclusions about Volvo owners because it is based on such a small sample.

4(e) Data collection Earlier in this chapter, we outlined the various approaches that can be used to collect research information. Collection of primary data by interviewing, observation, or distributing questionnaires through the mail is often the weakest link in the research process. Ordinarily, in all other steps, it's possible to ensure accuracy. However, these efforts may be lost if interviewers are inadequately trained or supervised. Data collectors need to understand the importance of maintaining the integrity of the data collection methods. In other words, if it has been decided that they need to interview every third person entering a store and this is how the sample is being selected, they cannot decide to interview the first 20 people because it is more convenient. Such interference with methodology can significantly bias the results. In their training, data collectors need to be given a basic understanding

---

random sample
A sample that is selected in such a way that every unit in the defined universe has a known probability of being selected.

convenience sample
A sample that is selected in a non-random way, so that every member of the universe does not have an equal chance of being included.

of research methodologies so that they can relate to the importance of the procedures used and understand why these must not be changed in any way.

Motivating data collectors is often difficult, because they frequently are part-time workers doing what is often a monotonous task. As a result, many problems may crop up at this point. For instance, poorly trained interviewers may fail to establish rapport with respondents or may change the wording of questions. In extreme cases, there have even been instances where interviewers have attempted to fake the responses!

5. Data analysis and reporting

data analysis
The process of extracting relevant information from data collected through research; usually associated with the application of statistical tools.

The value of research is determined by its results. Since data cannot speak for themselves, analysis and interpretation are key components of any project. **Data analysis** software packages have made it possible for researchers to tabulate and process masses of quantitative data quickly and inexpensively. This tool can be abused, however. Managers have little use for large volumes of computer output. Researchers must be able to identify pivotal relationships, spot trends, and find patterns — that's what transforms data into useful information. Proper coding of information assists in this process. Coding enables the researcher to determine how the data are to be presented to ensure efficiency of interpretation. Qualitative data, such as the results of focus groups and depth interviews, are more time-consuming and more difficult to analyze than quantitative data. It is very important to have clearly articulated the research objectives at the beginning of the project. Understanding what questions the research is designed to address makes it much easier to determine what the results are saying. Sometimes trends or patterns will develop that are not anticipated in the planning stages. Good researchers must be able to interpret these findings relative to the research objectives.

The end-product of the investigation is the researcher's conclusions and recommendations. Most projects require a written report, often accompanied by a presentation to management. Here, communication skill becomes a factor. Not only must researchers be able to write and speak effectively, they also must adopt the perspective of the manager in presenting research results.

6. Following up

Researchers should follow up their studies to determine whether their results and recommendations are being used. Management may choose not to use a study's findings for several reasons. The problem that generated the research may have been wrongly defined, become less urgent, or even have disappeared. Or the research may have been completed too late to be useful. Without a follow-up, the researcher has no way of knowing if the project was on target and met management's needs or if it fell short, and an important source of information for improving research in the future would be ignored.

By this time, you have probably realized that doing good research is not easy. It takes a well-designed set of objectives with a research methodology suitable to address these objectives. Unfortunately, research is not always done well. When interpreting research information, you should assess the methods used and be careful not to make generalizations that are not substantiated.

◀━━━ **BACKSPACE**

1. What is a research hypothesis?

2. What is the difference between primary data and secondary data?

3. What are some of the disadvantages of conducting Internet research?

- -

Automatically Collected Data

database

A set of related data that is organized, stored, and updated on a computer.

A great deal of information is available in most companies today for the use of marketers; much of this information is automatically collected by various systems. These data are organized, stored, and updated in computer **databases**. Often, a database will contain separate data modules on such topics as customers, competitors, industry trends, and environmental changes.

Internally, data are provided by the sales force and the marketing, manufacturing, and accounting departments. One of the most lucrative sources of customer data, for example, already exists in customer account and billing files in many companies. Some organizations, such as banks and telephone companies, maintain such detailed accounts that they know precisely what a customer has purchased, when it was bought or used, and what price was paid. Some users of databases use this kind of data for predictive modelling, which seeks to determine which customers would be interested in a particular type of product or service. For example, by scanning its database of credit card customers for individuals who have used their cards to purchase a computer in the past year, a bank could develop an excellent list of customers who would probably be interested in online banking and investment services.

data warehouse

A collection of data from a variety of internal and external sources, compiled by a firm for use in conducting transactions.

Some organizations move beyond databases to create large and complex data repositories. These are called **data warehouses** and comprise enormous collections of data from a variety of internal and external sources compiled by a firm that is conducting transactions with millions of customers. For example, large companies such as banks, major retailers, telephone companies, and credit card companies maintain massive data warehouses that contain data files on each customer, including detailed records of each and every transaction, right down to each use of the credit card, each ATM transaction, and each telephone call.

data mining

Method used to identify patterns and meaningful relationships in masses of data that might be unrecognizable to researchers.

The data in data warehouses can be analyzed in the same way as databases, searching for predetermined patterns in the data. But, because of their size, this would be a slow and cumbersome process. Therefore, more advanced statistical and artificial intelligence techniques are utilized for such processes. Referred to as **data mining**, these techniques have the capability to identify patterns and meaningful relationships in masses of data that otherwise might be overlooked or unrecognizable to researchers.

The way in which a company analyzes and combines the data from databases determines their usefulness in planning and implementing marketing strategy. An impressive example of data mining is Zellers. When it scrapped its infamous Club Z loyalty program, combining it with sister retailer the Bay and Hbc Rewards, Zellers created the most comprehensive and potentially far-reaching customer database in Canada. And size is everything — about 85 percent of Canadians go through its doors every year and the product selection covers something like 80 percent of the things Canadians buy. When someone buys children's clothes at either store, the retailer has the ability to identify details that effectively identify the gender and age of the customer's children. With data-mining techniques, the company can link and understand cross-shopping behaviour in a way that it may not have been able to understand before. "It's a 3-D picture," according to Senior Vice-President of Marketing David Strickland. "We've got a Bay credit file, a Zellers' credit file, and a basket of goods and services purchased at Zellers." The bar that rides through all of this, according to Strickland, "is what we call our customer information file." Why is the company doing this? To better understand the people it is dealing with and to find out how to deliver the products and services customers want. Also to figure out answers to things such as: Where's the optimal future use coming from? From what segments can we get more spending?

Marketers then take it to the next level. Knowing who uses services such as a pharmacy and who doesn't, they have the capability to develop a program to convince more moms to use the pharmacy, in addition to buying clothing for their kids. It also takes research to another level, allowing the retailer to use samples of 500,000, according to Strickland, who

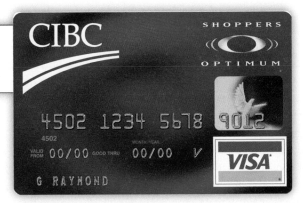

You provide data every time you swipe this card.

Eddie Bauer

retail scanner
The electronic device at retail checkouts that reads the bar code on each item.

single-source data
Data that allow marketers to trace to individual households any connection between exposure to television advertising and product purchases.

says that he'd ultimately like to combine the credit and loyalty cards — perhaps some day even restricting markdowns to holders of that card. And for offering up all of this information, consumers get points they can redeem for flights or merchandise.[9]

Research has allowed marketers to move from undifferentiated, mass marketing to focusing on well-defined market segments. It is now suggested that, through the management of databases, marketers will be able to reach the ultimate level of segmentation — the individual. For example, many online retailers, such as Eddie Bauer (**www.eddiebauer.com**), greet returning visitors by name, make recommendations and special offers based on previous purchases, and can hold items in your "shopping basket" between visits, while you are deciding whether or not to buy. Online retailers have the ability to monitor and log which site pages were visited and for how long, as well as what site you came from when you came to their sites. These data can be used to prepare special offers to a market of one — especially if you join their mailing list.

The data used by researchers and managers in databases and data warehouses are gathered from many sources. Internally, data can come from various departments and data files. Externally, computer systems are able to gather information from retail checkout systems and other technology-based customer interfaces.

Perhaps the most important data source for databases is the retail scanner, the electronic device at retail checkouts that reads bar codes located on each product that is purchased. Originally, these were meant simply to speed up the checkout process and reduce errors in supermarkets. With unique bar codes on each item indicating price information, prices did not need to be memorized or checked, and no keying errors could be made entering the price. However, it was soon discovered that the scanner could also be used to improve decisions regarding inventory control and the allotment of shelf space for products.

Many retailers quickly discovered how to extend the use of this technology as a marketing tool and developed what are known as frequent-shopper or loyalty programs. Some benefit or convenience is offered to a consumer for carrying a store's program card and allowing this card to be "swiped" at the time of purchase. To receive the card, the customer provides some personal information that the store retains in a data file. This system enables the store to combine data stored on the card about household demographics and lifestyle with the shopper's scanned purchases. The store is then able to relate product choices to household characteristics and plan product assortment and store layouts to maximize sales potential.

Knowing what customers buy is even more important if a firm knows what advertising the customers have been exposed to. In many countries, research companies such as ACNielsen have developed consumer household panels to create databases of information on advertising exposure and retail purchases. A representative sample of households agrees to have its television viewing monitored by an electronic device known as a "people meter" and to have its purchases recorded when sample members buy at scanner-equipped retail stores. Demographic information is obtained from each household when its members agree to be part of the scanner panel. The result is that household demographics can be correlated to television advertising exposure and product purchases. The result is called single-source data, because any connection between exposure to television advertising and product purchases can be traced to individual households, providing a single source for both types of data.[10]

Marketing Information Systems

marketing information system (MkIS)
An ongoing organized set of procedures and methods designed to generate, analyze, disseminate, store, and retrieve information for use in making marketing decisions.

In addition to special research projects, some companies have implemented another source of the important marketing information needed by managers. This is a **marketing information system (MkIS)**, which provides a scheduled flow of standardized marketing reports to managers. In some cases, the information system allows managers to interact directly with data online to answer specific questions.

In recent years, firms have come to rely on the increasing power and sophistication of computerized information systems to assist in the compilation and analysis of a sea of potentially useful marketing information. Out of this capability developed the MkIS — software that can collect massive volumes of data to generate, analyze, disseminate, store, and retrieve information for use in making marketing decisions. The MkIS has become even more important in recent years, as many companies have access to data that are captured automatically every time a customer buys something or interacts with the company in some other way.

The ideal MkIS:

- Analyzes data using statistical analysis and mathematical models that represent the real world.

- Generates regular reports and recurring studies as needed.

- Integrates old and new data to provide information updates and identify trends.

Designing an MkIS

To build an MkIS, marketing managers must identify what information is needed to make better decisions. Is it available within the organization (for example, in the daily reports made by salespeople, cost data from the accounting department, or customer records) or must the information be obtained from outside sources? For example, the product manager responsible for jeans for Gap needs to know the retail sales of all adult jeans by province or state, geographic region, and climate on a monthly basis for Canada and the United States. With 18 adult styles and six wash finishes, Gap offers up to 50 different options at some locations. This information is also required for the dozen children's styles. The same manager may want quarterly reports on the selection and prices that competitors are charging in each of these areas and how much advertising they are doing. Less frequently, possibly once a year, this manager needs to know about developments in the marketplace, such as demographic changes that might affect long-term planning.

A well-designed MkIS can provide a continuous flow of this type of information to support management decision-making. With this capability, managers can continually monitor the performance of products, markets, salespeople, and other marketing units.

How well an MkIS functions depends on three factors:

1. The nature and quality of the data available.

2. The ways in which the data are processed to provide usable information.

3. The ability of the operators of the MkIS and the managers who use the output to work together.

MkIS limitations

When an MkIS doesn't do what management expects it to do, there are several possible explanations:

- It is not always obvious what information is needed on a regular basis to make better decisions, resulting in either wrong or irrelevant information being collected and/or too much information being collected, confounding the decision-making process. It may produce exactly what was requested, yet be of no benefit.

● Gathering, organizing, and storing data and disseminating reports customized to the needs of many managers can be extremely expensive, in addition to the cost of operating and updating the system.

● Possibly most important, an MkIS is not well suited to the solution of unanticipated problems. The biggest challenges managers face are situations in which a decision must be made quickly, without all of the details clearly defined nor the implications of the options known. Under these conditions, standard reports produced according to prede-termined schedules are unlikely to be of much value.

Highly trained programmers working on large computers to produce the MkIS informa-tion requested by managers are no longer required, as a great deal of the information now avail-able in MkIS files is automatically "captured" when a customer interacts with the business.

New customer-relationship technologies allow the integration of sales, marketing, and customer-service applications operating from a common database, and offer easier-to-use Web interfaces, more robust functionality, and simpler integration with back-office systems. Such solutions are becoming less expensive, more effective, and quicker to deploy. Automation has also enabled companies to shorten sales cycles, increase customer face-to-face time, guide the sales process, and promote team selling. Less computer expertise is required, but more mar-keting expertise may be necessary to make effective use of such applications.

The ease of access and the proliferation of data have led to another concern. It has become quite easy to generate reports, but generating meaningful reports that have validity and that the firm can act on is not always what results. It has become easy to weigh manage-ment down with a lot of interesting but meaningless data.

Who Does Marketing Research?

Marketing research can be done by a firm's own personnel or by outside researchers. Sometimes a job is divided, with company personnel doing parts of a project and using an outside research specialist for such tasks as collecting data or developing approaches for the analysis of data.

Within the company

Separate marketing research departments exist primarily in larger companies and are usually quite small. The department might consist of only a single manager or could have as many as four or five professionals in large consumer-products companies. In most of these situations, the marketing research department rarely conducts research utilizing its own staff, but rather contracts the work out to suppliers. The primary role of the marketing research department, therefore, is to organize, monitor, and co-ordinate marketing research, which may be done by a number of different suppliers across the country. The manager of the marketing research department reports either to the chief marketing executive or directly to top management. The researchers who staff this department must be well versed in company procedures and know what information is already available within the company. They must also be familiar with the relative strengths and weaknesses of potential marketing research suppliers.

Outside the company

A sign of the growth in the use of marketing research is the fact that there are a great many companies across the country from which a marketing manager may seek help for marketing research problems. In Canada today, several hundred companies operate in the field of marketing research. When a marketing manager requires information on Canadian marketing research suppliers, a number of sources exist that can be consulted to obtain a list of potential suppliers. One listing of such suppliers is the *Directory of Canadian Marketing Research Organizations* (**www.pmrs-aprm.com**), produced by the Professional Marketing Research Society. This directory provides detailed information on companies that operate in Canada in marketing research and related fields.

Professional Marketing
Research Society
Creative Research
International
NFO CF
Market Facts of Canada
Bristol Group

Well over 30 full-service marketing research companies are operating in Canada, including Creative Research International (**www.crii.com**), NFO CF (**www.cfgroup.ca**), Market Facts of Canada (**www.marketfacts.ca**), and Bristol Group (**www.bristolgroup.ca**). These firms provide a full range of marketing research services, from the design of a research study to the submission of a final report. In addition to full-service marketing research companies, dozens of smaller Canadian firms operate in various specialized areas of marketing research, conducting research by geographic region, by industry, or by service performed, for example. Some concentrate on either consumer or industrial research or carry out studies that involve the application of specialized techniques. Other companies provide specialized marketing research services, such as the analysis of survey data. Some marketing research is also conducted in Canada by advertising agencies and management consulting firms.

Privacy and Other Issues

The field of marketing research has always had to address issues of privacy and research ethics. These are receiving even more attention, as consumers are expressing increasing concern about what happens to their personal information, particularly today when data are automatically captured every time we use a credit card or a banking machine or make a long-distance call. Many consumers want assurance that this information remains confidential and is not used to target them for marketing campaigns.

The Personal Information Protection and Electronics Documents Act went into effect in Canada in January 2001, a move intended to make consumers feel more comfortable about how their personal information is being used. The legislation applies to all federally regulated industries, including transportation, financial services, and telecommunications, and to any interprovincial transfer of personal information for even the simplest information exchange, such as the use of an address for a mailing label. The provinces have until 2004 to develop their own privacy laws, at which point the Act will also apply to businesses in provinces that fail to enact similar legislation. The exception is Québec, which enacted sweeping legislation in 1994.

As of January 1, 2001, companies require the consent of an individual to collect information, to use information, and to transfer information, as well as for use of the information for other than the original purpose for which it was collected. Marketers are no longer able to go on "fishing expeditions" for personal information without specifying exactly why the data are being collected. Companies also have to clearly identify the individual in the organization responsible for managing privacy issues, ensure access to that individual, and create an official system for handling privacy-related complaints and requests. Companies need to assess information flaws and implement privacy-sensitive policies. Many organizations do that on an ad hoc basis but not systematically throughout the firm. Those who don't may find themselves under investigation by the Office of the Privacy Commissioner of Canada, as Air Canada did in 2001 when it distributed a brochure to Aeroplan members explaining the different circumstances in which their personal information may be disclosed. The onus was placed on members to "opt out" of these circumstances, which violates the legislation requiring individual permission (positive consent) to be sought in order to allow such disclosure. These rules apply to marketers requesting information for contests or promotions, membership drives for loyalty programs, and direct-to-consumer e-mail campaigns.

Three levels of consent are recognized by the new law: implied (for example, where personal information may be used to contact consumers regarding renewal of service), negative option (people are given a box to check, indicating whether or not their information may be passed on to other organizations), and express (individuals must give specific consent for use of personal data in cases where the data may be considered sensitive).[11]

Status of Marketing Research

Marketing research is a major growth area, partially as the result of advances in technology. These advances include computer accessibility, point-of-sale data collection equipment (such as supermarket scanners), the Internet and its proliferation, and improved data analysis software, all of which have enabled more efficient collection, analysis, and processing of data. The cost of computer technology has plummeted in the last decade to the point where even small businesses can collect and store data in their customer databases. Most large companies now collect considerable amounts of data at each purchase. Frequent-shopper cards, such as those used by Zellers, A&P, and Shoppers Drug Mart, allow businesses to determine purchasing behaviour and patterns.

The challenge for marketers in the future will be to decide what information is needed and how it is to be integrated into decision-making. Database development and design are critical in ensuring that information is collected efficiently and meets management's needs. The role of managing databases is, therefore, a crucial one, and more emphasis is being placed on proper management. One example of this is the integration of customer files throughout business departments; previously, separate data were often maintained in each. Hotels, for instance, now compile data on their guests that can be accessed at check-in. The individual's file tells the front-desk clerk that the guest may require a smoke-free room, a 6 a.m. wake-up call, and business services, such as access to fax or e-mail, throughout the day. In addition to providing immediate information to management, the integration of this information in research design on lifestyles or travel patterns can identify for marketers the areas to be explored and the types of information to be collected.

As we observed earlier, the marketing environment is changing. For example, increased competition through globalization means new competitors to understand, thereby making it more difficult for some businesses to operate. Lifestyles and value systems are changing. Since marketing research is all about obtaining information to support marketing decision-making, the changing environment is increasing its importance. The more competently marketers can zero in on what is wanted and needed, the more effective they will be in marketing their products and services and in developing high levels of customer satisfaction and loyalty.

It is still true, however, that many companies are spending very large amounts on product-development research and on opening new channels of distribution, without spending enough on determining whether customers find their new offerings attractive or on determining what it will take to ensure high levels of customer satisfaction in the long run. We still find companies that launch new marketing initiatives without having talked with customers in advance. Several factors may explain this less-than-universal acceptance of marketing research:

● *Predicting behaviour is inexact:* Because of the many interrelated variables involved, marketing research often cannot predict future market behaviour precisely. When dealing with consumer behaviour, it is difficult to determine present attitudes or motives, let alone predict what they may be next year. As a result, it is difficult to make predictions regarding sales increases for the following period. Unless it is able to convince management of the concrete value of such research, the marketing research department will often not receive enough resources to do a good job.

- **Conflicting objectives between researchers and managers:** Poor communication between researchers and managers continues to be a problem. Researchers tend to be product-focused, while managers are usually market-focused. Managers are often forced to make quick decisions in the face of uncertainty, while researchers have been trained to approach problems in a more cautious, scientific manner. It can be appreciated how this leads to disagreements regarding what research to conduct, how long it should take, the way it should be presented, and even what the goals of the research should be.

- **A project orientation to research:** Management is often reluctant to treat marketing research as a continuing process and, further, to relate it and decision-making in a more systematic fashion. Too often, marketing research is viewed in a fragmented, one-project-at-a time manner and utilized only when management feels it has a "marketing problem." The expansion of marketing information systems into firms of various sizes will likely improve this situation.

Marketing Research, a magazine dedicated to management and applications issues within marketing, performed its own survey of research professionals, asking what they believed would be the key influences in shaping marketing research in the years ahead. The top responses were as follows: the Internet, globalization of business and research, one-to-one marketing, Internet/online research, privacy issues, computer technology, and e-commerce. As can be seen, the very technology issues that have come up repeatedly throughout this chapter dominate these responses. It is safe to conclude, however, that the future for marketing research is bright, as more and more companies realize the risk associated with making major decisions in the marketing area without good information to back them up. We'll see more and more companies spending larger amounts on marketing research in the future.

◄■ BACKSPACE

1. What is data mining?

2. A _____ (MkIS) provides a scheduled flow of standardized marketing reports for managers.

3. What is the primary role of the marketing research department?

Summary

Competitive pressure, expanding markets, the cost of making a mistake, growing customer expectations, and increased emphasis on customer retention and relationships all reinforce the need for marketing research. For a company to operate successfully today, management must have methods for gathering and storing relevant data and converting it into usable information. Tools used in research include research projects and marketing information systems.

A marketing research project is undertaken to help resolve a specific marketing problem. The problem must first be clearly defined. Then, a researcher conducts a situation analysis and an informal investigation. If a formal investigation is needed, the researcher decides which secondary and primary sources of information to use. To gather primary data, a survey, an observation, or an experiment may be used. The project is completed when the data are analyzed and the results reported. Follow-up provides information for improving future research.

A marketing information system (MkIS) is an ongoing set of procedures designed to generate, analyze, disseminate, store, and retrieve information for use in making marketing decisions. An MkIS provides a marketing manager with a regularly scheduled flow of information and reports.

Researchers have recently developed a stronger interest in finding out what competitors are currently doing and forecasting what they are likely to do in the future. Research can be conducted internally by marketing research staff members and/or purchased externally from firms that specialize in doing research. New technologies have helped marketers to keep track of competitors, but it has also raised ethical issues related to consumers' privacy. While these technologies are still evolving, so is legislation to monitor information use and protect consumers.

Marketing research has not yet achieved its potential, because the value of research often cannot be directly measured, research does not always accurately predict the future, and researchers are often too production-oriented. Further, researchers do not always communicate effectively with management, and research frequently is used in an ad hoc manner.

Key Terms and Concepts

benchmark 164
convenience sample 176
data analysis 177
data mining 178
data warehouse 178
database 178
experimental method 166
focus group interview 162
individual depth interview 162
informal investigation 169
Internet research 173
interview guide 174
mail survey 173
mall intercept 170
marketing information system (MkIS) 180
marketing research 159
mechanical observation 165
observational method 165
personal interview 170
personal observation 165

population 175
pre-testing 175
primary data 170
qualitative research 162
quantitative research 164
questionnaire 174
random sample 176
representative sample 176
research hypothesis 168
research objectives 167
retail scanner 179
sample 175
secondary data 168
simulated test market 167
single-source data 179
situation analysis 168
survey 164
syndicated data 170
telephone survey 172
test marketing 166

Questions and Problems

1. Explain how a marketing information system differs from marketing research.

2. How involved should marketing researchers be in setting strategy for their organizations?

3. A group of wealthy business executives regularly spends some time each winter at a popular ski resort at Whistler, British Columbia; Banff, Alberta; or Grey Rocks, Québec. The executives were intrigued with the possibility of forming a corporation to develop and operate a large ski resort in the BC Rockies, near the Alberta border. This would be a totally new venture and would be on federal parkland. It would be a complete resort, with facilities appealing to middle- and upper-income markets. What types of information might the group want to have before deciding whether

to go ahead with the venture? What sources of information would be used?

4. Evaluate surveys, observation, and experimentation as methods of gathering primary data in the following projects:
   a. A sporting goods retailer wants to determine college students' brand preferences for skis, in-line skates, and golf clubs.
   b. A supermarket chain wants to determine shoppers' preferences for the physical layout of store fixtures and traffic patterns, particularly around checkout stands.
   c. A manufacturer of equipment used in making ice cream wants to know who makes buying decisions for its product among present and prospective users.

5. Using the steps in the research process as presented in this chapter, describe how you would go about investigating the feasibility of opening a used-book store on your campus.

6. What kind of sample would you use in research projects designed to answer the following questions?
   a. What brand of running shoes is most popular among the students on your campus?
   b. Should retail stores in or near your home town be open all day on Sundays?
   c. What percentage of the business firms in the city closest to your campus have automatic sprinkler systems?

7. Would it be appropriate to interview 200 students as they left your college hockey arena about their feelings regarding funding for athletics, and then generalize the results to the student body? Why or why not?

8. If you were asked to conduct a research project for a venture capital company, what suggestions would you have if your client proposed that you conduct a consumer study to determine the feasibility of introducing a National Basketball Association franchise in Calgary or Montréal?

Hands-On Marketing

1. Assume that you work for a manufacturer of a liquid glass cleaner that competes with Windex and Glass Wax. Your manager wants to determine the amount of the product that can be sold throughout the country. To help her in this project, prepare a report that shows the following information for your home province and, if possible, your home municipality or region. Carefully identify the sources that you use for this information.
   a. Number of households or families.
   b. Income or buying power per family or per household.
   c. Total retail sales in the most recent year for which you can find reliable data.
   d. Total annual sales of food stores, hardware stores, and drugstores.
   e. Total number of food stores.

2. Interview the manager of your campus bookstore about the marketing information system used in the store (keep in mind that it may be a very informal system).
   a. What are the data sources?
   b. How are the data collected?
   c. What reports are received, and on what schedule?
   d. What problems arise with the marketing information system?
   e. How could the system be improved?

Back to the Top

Go back to the chapter opener and place yourself in the shoes of Professor Stewart. Now that you have studied how to conduct a marketing research project, what advice would you give Rhonda on doing some research before she opens her vegetarian restaurant?

Want to get better grades, tips on how to study more effectively, and up-to-date information on happenings in the world of marketing? Then, visit the Online Learning Centre for practice tests, Study Smart software, and much more! **www.mcgrawhill.ca/college/sommers**

Interested in finding out what marketing looks like in the real world? *Marketing Magazine* is just a click away on your Online Learning Centre!

Case 2-1

SC Johnson
Bug Off!

SC Johnson (SCJ) has been around for a long time. The 116-year-old company is known for its core brands, which include Windex, Fantastik, Glade, and Off! It has positioned itself as a trustworthy family company with a long-standing reputation for quality products. SCJ may be a conservative company, but its new ad campaign for its well-known mosquito repellent Off! is far from traditional. Instead of explicitly demonstrating the effectiveness of the product in its ads as it once did — showing, for example, an arm covered with the company's repellent entering a box full of mosquitoes and remaining unbitten — the company has shaken up its advertising and is now taking creative risks. Its ad agency, FCB Toronto, has moved away from conservative advertising and has developed quirky, funny ads. One of its print ads for Off! reads: "Something's in the air and it's not love." Still another ad, this time on grocery carts, has a picture of a giant mosquito, along with a warning: "Don't leave your children unattended."

So, why has such a conservative company taken risks with its advertising? Because SC Johnson wants to portray a modern image that is more in tune with the times. The company is livening up its brands to get people's attention. It must somehow differentiate Off!, a fairly standard product, from other mosquito repellents, and witty advertising is one way to do it. SCJ has gone to new lengths to be different. Its magazine and newspaper ads show mosquitoes in a bug-collector's box with the sign "Got Blood?" And if that's not enough, in some stores, you can find "bug avengers," people dressed up in Superman-style costumes, handing out bug control information and displaying live bugs in containers.

There's even a Web site that looks like a public service announcement, which includes regional bug forecasts by expert entomologists. There's also an insect encyclopedia, featuring pictures and descriptions of common insects, including tips on how to avoid and treat the bites of various bugs. Possibly most intriguing of all are the giant billboards on Highway 400, the route from Toronto to cottage country. They look suspiciously like city-limits signs, blue with white lettering, but as you get closer, they read: "Welcome to Cottage Country. Mosquito Population: 87,500,000." Billboards like this certainly catch travellers' eyes. More importantly, they send a message that SC Johnson may be an old company, but it certainly hasn't lost touch. It shows that the company not only has a sense of humour, but also that it takes bugs very seriously!

Pertinent Web Sites
www.scjohnson.com
www.bugfreeliving.com

Questions

1. Can SC Johnson retain its reputation as a family company when its advertising campaign is decidedly quirky and edgy? Does the ad campaign affect the image of the company?

2. Who is SC Johnson's target market? How does the company hope to reach out to its target customers?

3. Discuss SCJ's strategy for differentiating Off!

Source: Andrea Zoe Aster, "Ads With Bite," *Marketing Magazine*, July 29, 2002.

Case 2-2

CBC

Spin Master Toys

High Flyers

In the industry, they call it "magic" — the ability to make kids say "Cool," or "Neat," or perhaps more importantly, "I gotta have one!" And the Air Hogs Sky Shark air-pressure plane has it in spades, or more accurately in aces: high-flying aces!

The story of Spin Master Toys is one of almost religious belief in the power of public relations and how it can turn a good idea into magic. It's what happens when innovation meets marketing savvy. It's actually the story of a little purple-and-yellow foam plane that became one of the biggest hits of the 1998 holiday season, receiving stellar reviews and flying out of stores faster than new stock could be delivered. At $49.99, the preassembled plane came with the needed pump, an instructional video, and a toll-free number to speak to Captain Air Hog for advice and flying tips. After more than two years and the half-million dollars required to develop the concept, the Air Hogs Sky Shark had taken to the skies successfully.

The first air-powered toy of its kind, it launched the small company into big markets and big distribution deals, and the partners' style of marketing and promotion opened many doors for the company. Initially, small and independent retailers formed most of the distribution network for Spin Master Toys, but increasing media attention about the product began to attract the attention of major specialty toy stores across North America and from even farther away. Founders Ben Varadi, Anton Rabie, and Ronnen Harary were able to build business-to-business relationships with some of the top department stores, including Wal-Mart and Toys 'Я' Us.

In addition to developing close relationships with distribution network members, the company also focused on developing ties with the media. Soon, there was a buzz in the toy market. A small company with a product as simple as a toy airplane was now competing with the major toy manufacturers, Mattel, Hasbro, Fisher-Price. The guys behind Spin Master had clearly succeeded in spinning their product to major distributors. They had a new toy concept: The Air Hogs was the first-ever, air-powered model airplane. But of equal importance were Rabie, Varadi, and Harary's marketing skills and their ability to convincingly pitch their product to major stores. By early 1999, the trio had turned an entrepreneurial partnership into a global company, with an entire line of air-pressure toys.

For a while, it seemed that the company's string of successes would never end. But, in May 2002, the company's luck seemed to run out — Spin Master Toys had to recall about 140,000 Firestormer and Skyblazer toy planes. The company received seven reports of their planes bursting and, in four cases, the bursts caused injuries to children. Spin Master Toys now had to find a way to rebuild confidence in their products.

Pertinent Web Site

www.spinmaster.com

Questions

1. What can Spin Master Toys do to continue its relationship with its major distributors?

2. What responsibility does the company have to its consumers?

3. How does a company like Spin Master protect its brand name against such events, particularly since its products are targeted to children?

Video source: CBC *Venture*, "High Flyers," February 15, 2000.

Case 2-3

The Science of Shopping

It's All About the Customer

Peter Taylor was nearing the end of his MBA program at the University of Ottawa and looking forward to moving to Toronto after graduation. There, he was sure he would find a job related to sports marketing, something he found very interesting. Peter had always been athletic and through the years had played many sports. During the often-gruelling, two-year MBA program, however, Peter had found the workload too demanding to spend much time on sports. He did find some time to swim in the university pool and he also played squash a couple of times a week. Peter fully intended to continue his active lifestyle when he moved to Toronto and had been thinking for some time about which sport would be suitable once he began working. Having done quite well in middle-distance track-and-field competitions during high school, Peter decided to take running more seriously. While working on his degree, he had done a little jogging from time to time along the Rideau Canal and had enjoyed it. He also appreciated that running was one physical activity he could do on his own schedule.

Although Peter considered himself quite knowledgeable about most sports, he felt there was probably more to running than just putting on a pair of sneakers and going out for a jog. Walking through the Rideau Centre one day after an exam, he stopped at a bookstore to buy a magazine about running. If he was going to take running seriously, Peter would have to do some research before buying the right pair of running shoes. As he flipped through *Running Times*, Peter realized that he knew very little about the engineering and technology of running shoes. Although he had bought other athletic footwear during the past few years, he had not appreciated the diversity of styles, models, and colours available, as well as the range of prices.

Peter wanted to make sure that he bought the right brand of running shoe. As he mulled over his decision, he identified what criteria were most important to him. He was willing to spend more than $100 for a pair of quality running shoes, but his tight budget would not allow him to go much higher. Comfort and protection against injury were critical, but colour was not at all important. Peter preferred lightweight shoes, because they seemed better for running long distances.

Having decided more or less what he was looking for, Peter headed to Sports Experts the next day, after his last exam. As he scanned the huge wall display of running, court, squash, tennis, aerobic, basketball, cross-training, and volleyball shoes, a sales clerk approached him and offered her assistance. Peter was looking closely at several Nike and Brooks styles, as he had worn both brands in the past and had been very satisfied with them. He asked Donna, the sales clerk, which of the brands was considered to be the best. Donna explained that neither was necessarily the best brand. His decision should be based on comfort and fit, ensuring that the width was neither too narrow nor so wide that his feet shifted from side to side. She felt that price was generally a good measure of the quality of a shoe, but not necessarily of a brand. She recommended that Peter try one style of each of the major brands so that he could determine which one fit him best. Donna also suggested that sturdiness could be tested by bending the shoes from right to left and by ensuring that the heel components of the shoe felt firm.

Peter proceeded to try one Nike, one Brooks, one Saucony, and one Asics running shoe, all within the same price range. He decided that he felt most comfortable with the Air Max Nike shoes, because the air cushioning and light weight seemed to offer more spring. The only problem was that they felt a little too wide on his narrow feet. Donna suggested another shoe, the Nike Air Stab, and it fit perfectly on Peter. He had finally found what he was looking for, but asked Donna to hold the shoes for him until closing. He wanted to make sure that other stores were not offering the shoes at a lower price than $129.99.

Peter headed for Elgin Sports on Bank Street, an established Ottawa sporting goods store. There, he found the same shoes for exactly the same price, so he quickly left in search of a lower price. Peter then went to Sports-4, a newer store that specialized more in running shoes. Peter was pleasantly surprised to find that the Air Stabs were on a special promotion for $99.99. He asked Geoff Wallace, the sales clerk, whether he had a size 9. The sales clerk disappeared to the back and returned with an apologetic look and a size $9\frac{1}{2}$ instead. He explained that $9\frac{1}{2}$ was the smallest size the store had in stock. Peter decided to try them on just in case. Maybe the extra half-size wouldn't matter much, and he really wanted to save $30. The extra space in the toe was quite noticeable, however, even with the thick socks that Geoff supplied. Peter shook his head and declined when the clerk offered a different style of shoe to try on; he had his heart set on the Nike Air Stabs.

It was closer to walk back to Elgin Sports, but Peter realized that Donna at Sports Experts had been a great help, so he walked back to the Rideau Centre. As he walked, Peter wondered if he might be able to strike a deal at Sports Experts, considering that he probably should buy a rain suit, too. When he returned to Sports Experts, Donna recognized Peter right away and welcomed him with a smile. Peter requested the running shoes that he had asked her to hold for him, but mentioned the better deal offered by Sports-4. Peter asked if he might speak to the manager about the possibility of matching the Sports-4 price.

While Donna disappeared to get the manager, Peter spotted a Nike rain suit that appealed to him and had been marked down in price. As he took the rain suit off the display rack, he was greeted by the manager. Peter explained his dilemma and asked if Sports Experts would match Sports-4's sale price on the Nike Air Stabs, provided that he purchase the rain suit he had selected. The manager was eager for business and goodwill, especially since he considered Sports-4 to be Sports Experts' main competitor for running and triathlon equipment in the city. So the manager agreed to the deal and offered to ring in the sale for Peter, all the while making conversation about running in Ottawa. Peter appreciated the concession that Sports Experts had made and thanked the manager and Donna, telling them he would be sure to shop at Sports Experts stores in Toronto on a regular basis.

Paco Underhill, a retail anthropologist, would be fascinated by this scenario. Underhill studies people's shopping patterns and behaviours for a living, and could have been watching Peter Taylor's shopping experience either directly from inside the store or on a video monitor. Through his studies of consumer behaviour, Underhill has turned shopping into a science. He observes people as they wander through malls and shops, monitors their purchasing habits, and compiles the results of his observations. Using these results, Underhill draws conclusions that can help retailers better understand their customers and determine what mistakes, if any, they are making.

In the case of Peter Taylor, Underhill would have picked up on everything from the store layout to the mannerisms of the sales clerks. He might have pointed out that the clerk in Sports-4 should have offered to contact another store to check if they had Peter Taylor's correct size, rather than make him try on a larger size with thick socks. The point Underhill is making is that the twenty-first century belongs to the consumer, not the marketer. As Underhill says, "If the twentieth century was about marketers being leaders, the twenty-first century is about marketers being followers." He means that consumers have a right to demand more respect and to have their specific needs met. In the above case, Donna at Sports Experts recognized that Peter wanted to be taken seriously as a runner and she offered advice that was more technical to meet Peter's needs. This particular shopping experience was more about the consumer, Peter, and that's the way it will have to be in the future, as consumers become increasingly sophisticated and better informed. Peter Taylor understood his power as a consumer and acted on it. He knew about the lower price at Sports-4 and asked that the price be matched at Sports Experts in exchange for his buying a rain suit. The manager quickly agreed, understanding that there was more at stake then simply one pair of shoes.

Questions

1. What objectives do you feel Peter was trying to accomplish in the selection of running shoes? What motivated his final selection?

2. Why did he buy his shoes at Sports Experts? What could Geoff Wallace have done to persuade Peter to buy a different shoe at Sports-4?

3. What does Paco Underhill mean when he says, "If the twentieth century was about marketers being leaders, the twenty-first century is about marketers being followers"? Explain, with specific reference to the Peter Taylor case.

Source: Malcolm Gladwell, "The Science of Shopping," *The New Yorker*, November 4, 1996.
Video source: CBC *Marketplace*, Paco Underhill: "The Science of Shopping," November 7, 2000.

PART 3

Products, Services, and Brands

The planning, development, and management of the products and services that represent the essence of an organization's core offer to its customers

The next step in the marketing process is to develop a marketing mix that will achieve the company's goals in its target markets. The marketing mix is a strategic combination of components, all broadly defined — the organization's products or services, its communications and promotional programs, its distribution system, the prices it charges, and the value it creates for its customers. Each of these is closely interrelated with the other variables in the mix.

Part 3 is devoted to the product component of the marketing mix. In Chapter 7, we define the term *product* very broadly to incorporate services as well, and discuss the importance of product planning and the new-product development process. Chapter 8 deals mainly with organizations whose core product is actually an intangible service and the importance of service in cultivating customer relationships. Chapter 9 addresses the very important concept of branding and other product features, including packaging and labelling.

CHAPTER 7

Product Planning and Strategies

After studying this chapter, you should have an understanding of:

- The meaning of the word *product* in its fullest sense.
- The classification of consumer and business products.
- The major product-mix strategies.
- The importance of product innovation.
- The steps in the product-development process.
- Organizational structures for product planning and development.
- Adoption and diffusion processes for new products.
- Managing products throughout the product life cycle.

Developing Intimate Products — Trading Cards, Anyone?

What do you see in the future for condoms? How would you improve the product? What else can manufacturers do to encourage the use of the product and distinguish their brands from those of the competition? Well, now you have the opportunity to weigh in with your two cents' worth on the topic!

How does a company develop new products or refine a product strategy for young adult consumers such as today's college students? A firm such as, for example, Québec-based LifeStyles? Well, it helps to go to where these consumers gather — the Internet. That's one place where Toronto-based Hotspex (**www.hotspex.com**) gathers information for its clients. This innovative marketing think tank has the task of figuring out what LifeStyles and other clients will introduce next.

These futurists offer Hotspex "innovators" the opportunity to have their say in product development for its clients. And how do you become an "innovator"? By signing up at the Hotspex Web site. And why would you do this? For X-points, of course. And what do you do with them? You spend points in your account for chances to win prizes such as a Sony MD, Uproar MP3 player, or Rollerblades. Innovators can choose brands or products to comment on and sometimes receive e-mail invitations to comment on products that might be of particular interest to them. Basic points are awarded for responding to the core questions and there are opportunities along the way to rack up bonus points.

To test a "top-secret concept" intended to make the typical LifeStyles customer a "sex expert," the firm has participants follow a five-step process: So what do you look for in a condom? What size? Where do you usually buy them, how many at a time, and how important are brand and price?

What's the latest totally new idea from LifeStyles? Intimate sexual secrets made public on collector's cards! Possibly three cards would be in every box of condoms. Collect them all! Trade with your friends! What do you think? What name would you suggest for these cards? Do you have any ideas that you'd like to see turned into one of these cards? Answers to these types of questions get you the really big bonus points. At the end of the questionnaire, the company asks for input on how many cards should be in each package and what you'd expect to pay for the product.

At last count, 65 percent of the more than 1,500 participants at the Hotspex site were clamouring for the new product, and suggestions for the trading cards ranged from pointers for clumsy men to finding out-of-the-ordinary places to "get it on." Although a novel idea, it still might be a little too risqué for LifeStyles, according to the sales and product manager: "We are concerned about the image of the brand…we're still not sure if the cards will give us a bad name." What do you think?[1]

Remember the stars, cash cows, question marks, and dogs of the Boston Consulting Group matrix? Or the product-market growth matrix? Both are marketing planning models presented and discussed in Chapter 2. Product strategy played a key role in each of the models. In this chapter, we review the major product strategies as well as their consumer behaviour foundations. Both LifeStyles and Hotspex use the Internet to research consumer behaviour in order to provide new ideas for new products. But before we discuss strategy and approaches to new-product idea generation, we need to look at some basics — the meaning of the word *product* and the main product classification systems.

The Meaning of *Product*

Each PDA version provides a different benefit set.

What is a product? The word is potentially confusing, in that most of us would probably use it to refer to physical, tangible items. In a narrow sense, a product is a set of attributes assembled in an identifiable form. Each product is identified by a commonly understood descriptive or generic name, such as "steel," "insurance," "tennis racquets," or "entertainment." But in the reality of the marketplace, we need a broader definition of product; essentially, it is the essence of what a company or organization is offering its customers. We need to indicate that consumers are not really buying a set of attributes, but rather the valuable benefits that those attributes provide. Consumers don't want sandpaper — they want a smooth surface. They don't want a wireless hand-held personal digital assistant (PDA) — they want quick and convenient communication. And a product that provides the desired benefits, whether tangible or intangible, provides satisfaction. A bank's product is a host of services that provide, among other things, the benefits of convenient and secure transactions, as well as asset growth and management for personal financial security.

Marketers usually offer the consumer multiple versions of their products — sandpaper, PDAs, or bank services. Each offering is made up of a set of tangible and intangible attributes that combine to provide the benefits in which a target market segment is interested, benefits that will give the satisfaction consumers in that segment want. Figure 7-1 illustrates the range of attributes that comprise the benefits offered by a product. Competing marketers may offer a range of designs, colours, brands, quality levels, warranties, packaging, services, prices, and sellers' reputations. Each combination is designed to provide a somewhat different set of benefits.

What, then, is a **product**? It is a set of tangible and intangible attributes, including packaging, colour, price, quality, and brand, plus the seller's services and reputation, that provides a set of perceived consumer benefits. A product may be a tangible product, service, place, person, or idea. But consumers are buying much more than a set of physical

product

A product might be a tangible product, service, place, person, or idea; it has a set of tangible attributes, including packaging, colour, price, quality, and brand, plus the services and reputation of the seller.

Figure 7-1:

Product Attributes

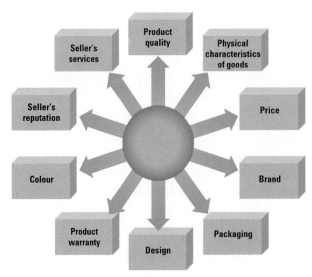

attributes when they buy a product. They are buying want satisfaction in the form of the benefits they expect to receive from the product.

You should consider how different marketers develop the product they are promoting. In other words, what is the nature of the product for which they are responsible? As a manufacturer, you might be responsible for developing a product strategy for a new multimedia cellphone. What features should it have? Colours? Price? On the other hand, as a retailer you might be responsible for developing a product strategy for a chain of hardware stores. What new products should you introduce? Should you carry housewares? Electronics? High-end merchandise?

Product Classification Systems

To design effective marketing programs, firms must organize their approaches. We begin this organization process by dividing all products into two categories — consumer products and business products — that parallel our initial description of the market. Then, we will subdivide each category still further.

Consumer and business products

consumer product
A product that is intended for purchase and use by household consumers for non-business purposes.

business product
A product that is intended for purchase and use in producing other products or in rendering services in a business.

Consumer products are intended for use by household consumers for non-business purposes. **Business products** are intended for resale, for use in producing other products, or for providing services in an organization. The two types of products are distinguished on the basis of who will use them and how they will be used.

Kellogg's Corn Flakes are categorized as consumer products, even if they are in the manufacturer's warehouse, in a freighter's trucks, or on retailers' shelves, if ultimately household consumers will use them in their existing form. However, Kellogg's Corn Flakes sold to restaurants and other institutions are categorized as business products, no matter where they are in the distribution system. Similarly, the Ericsson P800 cellphone can be purchased by your employer and provided to you to conduct business from any location, or you may purchase the product yourself to use when you go camping on the weekend.

Often it is not possible to place a product in only one class or the other. Seats on an Air Canada flight from Toronto to Vancouver may be considered as a consumer product if purchased by students going on vacation or a business product if bought by a sales representative on a business trip. Air Canada, or any other company in a similar situation, recognizes that its product falls into both categories and therefore develops separate marketing programs for each market.

These distinctions may seem like "splitting hairs," but they are necessary for the strategic planning of marketing programs. Each major category of products ultimately serves a distinctive type of market and requires different marketing methods.[2]

Classification of consumer goods

convenience goods
A class of consumer products of which the consumer has prior knowledge and purchases with minimum time and effort.

One method of classifying consumer goods is based not on the nature of the goods themselves, but on the nature of the buying process most commonly used in their acquisition. Table 7–1 shows three of the four categories of goods — convenience, shopping, and specialty — and the marketing considerations associated with each one. The fourth category, unsought goods, is explained below.

Convenience goods are products that consumers know enough about before going out to buy them that the products can be bought with minimum effort. The consumer usually takes a routine problem-solving approach to decision-making or, sometimes, a very limited problem-solving approach. Convenience goods include many food items, inexpensive candy, drugstore sundries such as shampoo and toothpaste, and staple hardware items such as light bulbs and batteries. Convenience services include such things as banking transactions, pay telephones calls, and photocopying.

TABLE 7-1 Categories of Consumer Goods: Characteristics and Marketing Considerations

	Type of Product*		
	Convenience	**Shopping**	**Specialty**
EXAMPLES	Canned fruit	Furniture	Expensive suits
Characteristics			
Time and effort devoted by consumer to shopping	Very little	Considerable	Cannot generalize; consumer may go to nearby store and buy with minimum effort or may have to go to distant store and spend much time and effort
Time spent planning the purchase	Very little	Considerable	Considerable
How soon want is satisfied after it arises	Immediately	Relatively long time	Relatively long time
Are price and quality compared?	No	Yes	No
Price	Usually low	High	High
Purchase frequency	Usually frequent	Infrequent	Infrequent
Marketing Considerations			
Length of channel	Long	Short	Short to very short
Retailer	Relatively unimportant	Important	Very important
Number of outlets	As many as possible	Few	Few; often only one in a market
Stock turnover	High	Lower	Lower
Gross margin	Low	High	High
Responsibility for advertising	Producer's	Retailer's	Joint responsibility
Point-of-purchase display	Very important	Less important	Less important
Brand or store name important	Brand name	Store name	Both
Packaging	Very important	Less important	Less important

*Unsought products are not included. See text explanation.

shopping goods
A class of consumer products purchased after the buyer has spent some time and effort comparing price, quality, colour, and/or other attributes of alternative products.

specialty goods
A class of consumer products with perceived unique characteristics; consumers are willing to expend special effort to buy them.

unsought goods
A type of consumer product that consists of new products of which the consumer is not yet aware or products that the consumer does not yet want.

Shopping goods are those for which consumers want to compare quality, price, and perhaps style in several stores or on several Web sites before purchasing — and the decision-making can be limited or extended problem solving. For most consumers, shopping goods are clothing, furniture, major appliances, computer components, and automobiles. The process of searching and comparing continues as long as the customer believes that the potential benefits from a better purchase more than offset the additional time and effort spent shopping.

Specialty goods are those for which consumers have a strong brand preference and are willing to expend substantial time and effort in locating the desired brand. The consumer is willing to forgo more accessible substitutes to search for and purchase the desired brand — a strong brand relationship exists. This can even result in a buyer searching the Internet and purchasing a preferred brand as an imported item from another country, subject to duties and taxes. Examples include ultra-expensive clothing brands, sound equipment, health foods, photographic equipment, and, for many people, automobiles and certain home appliances. Various brands, such as Prada, Jaguar, and Nikon, have achieved specialty-good status in the minds of consumers around the globe.

Unsought goods are different. They are so unlike the other three categories that we have not included this category in Table 7-1. One form of unsought good is a newly developed product. Consumers are often not aware it exists or may not understand its function or purpose. Alternatively, unsought goods can be products that the consumer is aware of but does not want right now. Newly created products and innovations begin as unsought goods, because it is difficult to look for a product if you don't know it exists. For that matter, some goods you may not really want to buy at all! Many new high-tech products and services may very well be unsought goods simply because, while they are technologically feasible, they do not offer consumer benefits that are easily recognized as having value. Traditional unsought goods include such things such as burial services, gravestones, and life insurance.

Classification of business goods

Business goods are separated into five categories in Table 7-2. This classification is based on the product's broad uses, not the manner in which buyers shop for the goods. For example, a business good may be used in producing other products, in operating an organization, and in other ways that we will discuss.

TABLE 7-2 Categories of Business Goods: Characteristics and Marketing Considerations

	Type of Product				
	Raw Materials	Fabricating Parts and Materials	Installations	Accessory Equipment	Operating Supplies
EXAMPLES	Iron ore	Engine blocks	Blast furnaces	Storage racks	Paper clips
Characteristics					
Unit price	Very low	Low	Very high	Medium	Low
Length of life	Very short	Depends on final product	Very long	Long	Short
Quantities purchased	Large	Large	Very small	Small	Small
Frequency of purchase	Frequent delivery; long-term purchase contract	Infrequent purchase, but frequent delivery	Very infrequent	Medium frequency	Frequent
Standardization of competitive products	Very much; grading is important	Very much	Very little; custom made	Little	Much
Quantity of supply	Limited; supply can be increased slowly or not at all	Usually no problem	No problem	Usually no problem	Usually no problem
Marketing Considerations					
Nature of channel	Short; no intermediaries	Short; intermediaries only for small buyers	Short; no intermediaries	Intermediaries used	Intermediaries used
Negotiation period	Hard to generalize	Medium	Long	Medium	Short
Price competition	Important	Important	Varies in importance	Not main factor	Important
Pre-sale/post-sale service	Not important	Important	Very important	Important	Very little
Promotional activity	Very little	Moderate	Salespeople very important	Important	Not too important
Brand preference	None	Generally low	High	High	Low
Advance buying contract	Important; long-term contracts	Important; long-term contracts	Not usual	Not usual	Not usual

raw materials
Business goods that have not been processed in any way and that will become part of another product.

Raw materials are business goods that become part of another tangible product before being processed in any way (except as necessary to assist in handling the product). Included are goods found in their natural state (minerals, land, and products of the forests and the seas), and agricultural products. For raw materials in their natural state, competition is built around price and the assurance that a producer can deliver the product as specified. This makes these products very amenable to Internet marketing approaches. Since transportation and warehousing costs are likely to be high relative to the product's unit value, close attention must be given to logistical matters such as transportation and warehousing.

manufactured parts and materials
Materials that become part of other finished products; distinguished from raw materials in that they have already been processed and bought by manufacturers for assembly into their final products. Some undergo further processing and may be referred to as *fabricating materials*.

Manufactured parts and materials become part of other finished products. Some of these undergo further processing and may be referred to as fabricating materials. Examples include yarn that is woven into cloth and flour used in making bread. What distinguishes them from raw materials is that they have already been processed and are bought by manufacturers for assembly into their final products. Examples are the small motors that are bought by manufacturers of furnaces and lawnmowers and the zippers used by clothing manufacturers. While branding manufactured materials and parts is generally unimportant, some firms have successfully pulled their business goods out of obscurity by branding them: Gore-Tex fabrics (**www.goretex.com**), YKK zippers, and Intel Pentium processors (**www.intel.com**) are examples.

Installations are manufactured products that are an organization's major, expensive, and long-lived equipment, such as a factory building, diesel engines for a railroad, and servers for an Internet service provider. The characteristic of installations that differentiates them from other categories of business goods is that they directly affect the scale of operations in an organization producing goods or services. Adding 12 new Steelcase desks will not affect the scale of operations at Jetsgo or Tango, but adding 12 jet aircraft certainly will.

The marketing of installations presents a real challenge, because each unit sold represents a large dollar amount. Often each unit is made to the buyer's detailed specifications and much pre-sale and post-sale servicing is essential, making buyer trust and confidence in the supplier essential. A large printing press requires installation, maintenance, and — inevitably — repair services; good relationships are vital. Because installations are technical in nature, a high-calibre, well-trained sales force is needed to provide careful, detailed explanations, quality service, and personal selling

Gore-Tex
Intel

installations
In the business market, long-lived, expensive, major industrial capital goods that directly affect the scale of operation of an industrial firm.

accessory equipment
In the business market, capital goods used in the operation of a firm.

Accessory equipment has substantial value and is used in an organization's operations. This category of goods neither becomes an actual part of a finished product nor has a significant impact on the organization's scale of operations. The life of accessory equipment is shorter than that of installations but longer than that of operating supplies. Some examples are point-of-sale terminals (computerized register systems and scanners) in a retail store, small power tools, hand-held wireless scanners, forklift trucks, and office desks.

operating supplies
The "convenience goods" of the business market: short-lived, low-priced items purchased with a minimum of time and effort.

Operating supplies aid in an organization's operations without becoming part of the finished product. They are usually of a low dollar value and have a short life; examples are lubricating oils, ink cartridges for printers, copy paper, and other stationery. Purchasers want to buy operating supplies with fairly little effort, so they are the convenience goods of the business sector.

Because they are low in unit value and are bought by many different organizations, operating supplies (like consumer convenience goods) are distributed widely, so the producing firm uses wholesaling intermediaries extensively. Also, because competing products are quite standardized and there is little brand insistence, price competition is normally stiff.

◀ BACKSPACE

1. To the marketer, what is a product?
2. _____ products are intended for use by household consumers while _____ products are intended for use by organizations.
3. What are the four types of consumer goods?

Product Strategies

product mix

All products offered for sale by a company.

breadth of product mix

The number of product lines offered for sale by a firm.

depth of product line

The assortment within a product line.

product line

A broad group of products intended for essentially similar uses and possessing reasonably similar physical characteristics.

At any given time, firms specializing in business or consumer products will be marketing some new products and some old ones, while other products are being planned and developed. In this section of the chapter, we'll cover the main strategic decisions pertaining to an organization's assortment of products and services

Product-mix and product-line strategies

Very few firms rely on a single product or service; instead, most sell many products. What each firm does about products and services is dictated by the product strategy it chooses to devise and implement (see the product–market growth matrix discussion in Chapter 2). The set of all products offered for sale by a company is called a **product mix** or product portfolio. The structure of a product mix has both **breadth** and **depth**. The number of product lines carried is a measure of the breadth of the product mix. The depth is measured by the variety of sizes, colours, and models offered within each product line. A product-mix strategy is illustrated in Figure 7-2.

A broad group of products, intended for essentially similar uses and having similar physical characteristics, constitutes a **product line**. Panasonic's product lines (**www.panasonic.ca**) include televisions, videocassette recorders, DVD players, telephones, small home appliances, and several lines of audio components. To examine the depth of one particular product line, DVD players, for example, we would count the various models that are connected to external screens, the number of portable models offered, and then include the in-dash model for cars.

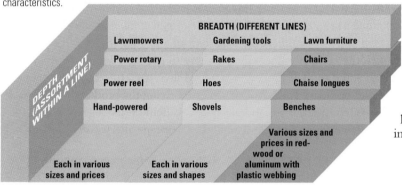

Figure 7-2:

Product Mix — Breadth and Depth *Part of the product mix in a lawn and garden store*

Panasonic

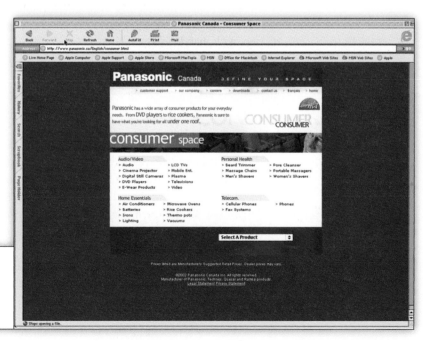

Panasonic lets you explore product mix, breadth, depth, and a line at your leisure.

Planned Product-Mix Strategies

Many firms offer a large number of products to consumers — Johnson & Johnson and Sony are prime examples. In service industries, firms such as Bell Canada (telephone, Internet, etc.) and Loblaws (groceries, dry-cleaning, photo services, financial services) offer customers many services and many ways to access them. These diverse assortments of goods and services did not develop by accident: They reflect a planned strategy by the company.

Product positioning

Management's ability to position a product appropriately in the market is a major determinant of company profitability. Equally important is the ability of management to reposition a product over the long run. In addition to the **positioning strategies** based on market segmentation discussed in Chapter 4, a variety of other positioning strategies are available.

Positioning in relation to a competitor   For some products (Coca-Cola and Pepsi-Cola, for example), the best position is directly against the competition. This is a particularly effective approach if a product has better features or some other differential advantage over the competition. Québec-based Lassonde Industries Inc., makers of Oasis orange juice and Fruité beverages, recently marketed the first refrigerated vegetable juice. Eighty-five percent of consumers surveyed said that this product was fresher tasting, of better quality, and more practical than shelf products currently available.[3] When Kool-Aid drink mix decided to "age-up" its consumer base with the addition of iced-tea flavour in order to get a piece of the exploding 'tween market, the company knew the best way to get these young consumers to try it was to get moms to add it to their grocery lists. So, while it tried to create demand from kids with ads featuring the legendary Kool-Aid character receiving the product intravenously after wiping out on his skateboard, the ads also alleviated "caffeine fears" of moms by highlighting the fact it was caffeine-free — unlike many other beverage alternatives.[4]

Positioning in relation to a product class or attribute   Sometimes a company's positioning strategy entails associating its product with (or dissociating it from) a product class or attribute. Some firms promote their wares as being in a desirable class, such as "Made in Canada," or having an attractive attribute, such as "low energy consumption," "all-natural," or "environmentally friendly." A survey of consumers' opinions of manufactured goods made in various countries revealed that Canadians rate their own manufactured goods more favourably than products produced in Japan, Germany, and other countries.[5] This is good news for Canadian firms that want to position their products on a "Made in Canada" basis, particularly since it seems that this positioning is also effective outside of Canada. Canada, as seen from abroad, is credited with expertise in everything to do with ice — from hockey to beverages — as evidenced by the success of Canadian beer, ice wine, ice vodka, and bottled water made from iceberg or glacial water.[6]

Mighty Ducks

Positioning works for services as well as for tangible products.   The Mighty Ducks of Anaheim (**www.mightyducks.com**) have been positioned as the "fun" team of the National Hockey League. The team's logo and colour scheme were selected with merchandising in mind, to appeal not only to hockey's traditional audience — men — but also to women and children.[7] The Disney-owned club chose teal and purple as the team colours and the Ducks' colourful merchandise is sold in retail stores throughout North America, including Disney stores.

Positioning in relation to a target market   Regardless of which positioning strategy is used, the needs of the target market always must be considered. This positioning strategy doesn't suggest that the other strategies ignore target markets. Rather, with this strategy, the target market — rather than another factor, such as competition — is the focal point in positioning the product.

Daytimers
Sony

Day-Timers, Inc. (**www.daytimer.com**), widely known for its daily planners and organizers targeted at businesspeople, has also developed a product for the home. This was the result of a realization by the company that there was a general untapped market of consumers looking for products to use for time management. The majority of this market was anticipated to be female. When researching the target market to design the product, the manufacturer learned that the proposed users wanted the planner to be basic; made of softer, leather-like material; with a closure such as a zipper or clasp. The product was introduced in a variety of colours, designs, and sizes, and sold at very low prices in comparison with the business products. To appeal to younger groups, the styles now offered include brighter colour schemes and more generic filler sheets that can be used for a variety of purposes. Sony (**www.sonystyle.com**) has decided that PDAs should do more and has created the CLIÉ line of hand-helds that serve as complete personal entertainment organizers, offering gaming, MP3, and remote-control capabilities, making this product of interest to younger markets.[8]

Halls cough drops were pretty much targeted to anyone suffering from a cold or flu until recently. In 2001, the company began promoting the product to those who experience "throat irritation due to overuse." In other words, they might be a good thing to keep in your desk or briefcase if you talk or yell a lot for a living — teaching, public presentations, even yelling in outdoor venues such as construction sites or over noisy equipment. Effective television ads demonstrated how useful they could be for day-to-day activities.[9]

Positioning by price and quality Some retail stores are known for their high-quality merchandise and high prices (Harry Rosen, Birks, Holt Renfrew). Positioned at the other end of the price and quality scale are discount stores such as Wal-Mart and Zellers. This doesn't mean that such retailers position themselves as lacking quality, but rather that value and low price are stressed.

Four Seasons Hotels
Choice Hotels
International

In the hotel industry, positioning by price and quality is common. The Four Seasons Hotels chain (**www.fourseasons.com**) in Canada and elsewhere is well known for its high standards in rooms and services. Luxurious furnishings and guest courtesies clearly differentiate this chain from others that target a lower-paying clientele. Choice Hotels International (Comfort Inn, Quality, Econo Lodge, Sleep Inn), on the other hand, has positioned itself as offering clean, comfortable rooms and economical prices (**www.choicehotels.com**).

Product-mix expansion

product-mix expansion
Increasing the depth within a particular product line and/or the number of lines a firm offers to consumers.

Product-mix expansion is accomplished by increasing the depth within a particular line and/or the number of lines a firm offers to consumers. Let's look at these options.

Line extension is the term used when a company adds a similar item to an existing product line with the same brand name. For examples, look at the coupons in your local newspaper or the ones that appear in your mailbox. You will probably see lots of examples of new products that are actually line extensions. After decades of success, Kraft Foods introduced Easy Mac for the microwave and the Reese Candy Company gave us a crunchy version of its famous peanut butter cups and then Reese's Pieces in the eighties, Reese's Peanut Butter Sticks in the nineties, Reese's Bites in 2000, and Reese's FastBreak nougat bar in 2002. Also in 2002, Code Red Mountain Dew and Vanilla Coke were introduced.

line extension
One form of product-mix expansion in which a company adds a similar item to an existing product line with the same brand name.

While the Mach3 was still enjoying the number-one position in wet shaving, Gillette introduced Mach3 Turbo, showing men that there was no longer a difference between up and down when shaving. Lever Brothers Company offers Dove skincare products in addition to Dove bar soap. Procter & Gamble, manufacturer of Pringles potato chips, has introduced fat-reduced and pizza-licious flavour products as extensions to its existing chip line.

The line-extension strategy is also used by service organizations. Universities and colleges are offering more and more programs to appeal to older and working students, such as distance courses and part-time programs. Some group medical practices and some hospitals have added nutrition counselling clinics and forms of exercise counselling to their services, acknowledging that an important part of their role is to keep people well. Canadian banks continually offer expanded services, such as telephone and Internet banking, trust services, and insurance.

The main reason for a line extension is that the firm wants to appeal to more market segments by offering a wider range of choices for a particular product. Another reason is that companies want to take advantage of the considerable functional and emotional relationship value that resides in their established brands. There is often a much lower risk involved in introducing a new product as an extension to an existing line under a recognized brand than there would be in launching a completely separate line with a new brand name. Marketers have found that a line extension has a greater chance of success than a totally new brand.

mix extension

A way of expanding the product mix by adding a new product line to the company's current assortment.

Another way to expand the product mix, referred to as **mix extension**, is to add a new product line to the company's current assortment. Sometimes this is an innovative new product never seen before, but more often it is simply something that the company has never offered previously. When Procter & Gamble introduced the Swiffer, it was doing both of these things. As a totally new and innovative product (to be discussed in the next section), it created a new category of product that other companies quickly tried to copy and add to their mixes. When P&G created SwifferWet, Mitt, Max, and WetJet, these were line extensions.

Under a mix-extension strategy, the new line may be related or unrelated to current products. Furthermore, it may carry one of the company's existing brand names or may be given an entirely new name. The following are examples of these four alternatives:

● *Related product, same brand:* Tim Hortons added canned ground coffee and then introduced a line of Tim Hortons home coffee makers. In 2002, McDonald's introduced its Lighter Choices Menu to entice health-conscious Baby Boomers with veggie burgers, new salads, and a fruit and yogurt parfait. The company hoped to encourage a McHealthier and McLeaner brand image.

● *Unrelated product, same brand:* Swiss Army Brands, the maker of the original Swiss Army knife, extended its mix by adding Swiss Army watches and sunglasses. Other examples include the extension into home furnishing by clothing manufacturer Roots and into cosmetics and housewares by Club Monaco.

● *Unrelated product, different brand:* This diversification strategy, adopted when a company adds a new division in a different field, was very popular in the early 1990s. Many companies today are more likely to eliminate unrelated product lines. For example, Pepsi-Cola amassed a number of diversified companies such as Pizza Hut and KFC and now is spinning-off these fast-food outlets.[10] On the other hand, Swatch (**www.swatch.com**), the Swiss watch company, diversified by adding a clothing line and then announced an even more unlikely mix extension — small cars (**www.smart.com**)!

Swatch
Smart Car

● *Related product, different brand:* Procter & Gamble introduced Luvs to store shelves right beside its Pampers disposable diapers. Black & Decker produced a line of professional/industrial tools under the DeWalt brand; Panasonic produced some of its audio equipment under the Technics brand.

Most often, a new line is related to the existing product mix, since the company wants to capitalize on its expertise and experience. IKEA, which has been known for offering reasonably priced, medium-quality Scandinavian home furnishings, has expanded into a line of office furniture.[11] Thomson Minwax Ltd., an Ontario firm, is expanding beyond its line of wood stains and producing a new line of decorative paints. In both cases, the new lines benefit from consumers' familiarity and relationships with the brand.

Trading up and trading down

The product strategies of trading up and trading down involve a change in product positioning and an expansion of product line. Trading up means adding a higher-priced product to a line to attract a broader market. The seller also intends that the new product's prestige will help the sale of its existing lower-priced products.

trading up
A product-line strategy in which a company adds a higher-priced, prestige product to its line in order to increase sales of the existing lower-priced products in that line and attract a higher-income market.

Consider some examples of trading up. Facing stiff competition in the middle-price market, Holiday Inns introduced the higher-price Crowne Plaza Hotels, with nicer surroundings and more amenities. To its line of inexpensive casual watches, Swatch added the higher-priced Chrono stopwatch, James Bond Collection, and other upgraded watches, as well as the SwatchTalk, the first watch with an integrated cellphone. Hyundai has tried to de-emphasize its position as an economy car manufacturer by continuing to offer more expensive and diversified products. These have recently included the Tiburon coupe and the Sante Fe SUV. The new models have helped attract a wider range of auto buyers and help shift the image of the company toward being a producer of more rugged and performance-oriented products.

trading down
A product-line strategy in which a company adds a lower-priced item to its line of prestige goods in order to reach a market that cannot afford the higher-priced items.

A company is said to be trading down when it adds a lower-priced item to its line of prestige products. The company expects that people who cannot afford the original product will want to buy the new one because it carries some of the status of the higher-priced product. Major manufacturers of 35-mm, single-lens reflex cameras, such as Pentax, Canon, and Minolta, have introduced smaller, simplified cameras for photography buffs who want to be seen to be using the major brands but who do not want to be bothered with the intricacies of 35-mm photography. Mont Blanc, the West German manufacturer of the "world's most famous fountain pen," introduced a lower-priced ballpoint pen, thereby allowing its purchasers to own a Mont Blanc without having to pay more than $300 for the top-of-the-line fountain pen. The 2002 C230 Kompressor coupe was introduced at around $33,000 — the lowest price Mercedes-Benz has offered. It was intended to attract younger, and more female, buyers to the brand.

Trading up and trading down are risky strategies, because the new products may confuse buyers, resulting in negligible net gain. It is equally undesirable if sales of the new item or line are generated at the expense of established products. When trading down, the new offering may permanently hurt the firm's reputation and that of its established high-quality product. To reduce this possibility, new lower-priced products may be given different brand names to distinguish them from the established brands. Gap (**www.gap.com**) chose Old Navy Clothing Co. (**www.oldnavy.com**) as the name for its lower-price outlets.[12]

Gap
Old Navy

In trading up, on the other hand, the problem depends on whether the new product or line carries the established brand name or is given a new name. If the same brand name is used, the firm must change its image enough that new customers will accept the higher-priced product. At the same time, the seller does not want to lose its present customers. The new offering may present a cloudy image, not attracting new customers but driving away existing customers. If a different brand name is used, the company must create awareness for it and then stimulate consumers to buy the new product. The latter strategy means that the company will not be able to trade on the reputation of its existing brand.

Modifying existing products

product modification
Improvement of an established product as a less risky and more profitable alternative to developing a completely new product.

As an alternative to developing a completely new product, management should take a fresh look at the organization's existing products. Often, improving an established product — product modification — can be more profitable and less risky than developing a completely new one. The substitution of NutraSweet (**www.nutrasweet.com**) for saccharin in diet soft drinks increased sales of those drinks by improving flavour and reducing health-related concerns about saccharin. Similarly, the use of all-natural or organically grown products is popular with certain market segments. Product modification, however, is not without risks.

NutraSweet

For some products, redesigning is the key to relaunching or repositioning. Many companies frequently redesign or reformulate their products to give them fresh appeal. In recent years, disposable diapers have been redesigned to be less bulky and are now available in separate styles for girls and boys. To revitalize its brand, Polaroid developed less-expensive and funkier accessory-type cameras such as the I-Zone pocket camera and the JoyCam, with features such as sticky-back film and different-size photo options, for $25 to 35 each. Clairol has tried to move away from the belief that hair colour is for hiding the grey and instead position it as a fun product for the 15 to 29 age group.[13] Sometimes the redesign might simply involve the addition of a new flavour, in which case the product becomes more of a line extension, as when General Mills launched Apple Cinnamon Cheerios.

Another example involves changing the shape or basic look of a product. Canada's own Polar Ice Vodka decided it needed a new look for 2002 to distinguish its quadruple-distilled beverage with the exceptionally clean taste — the new look would also help justify charging $30 per bottle in a very competitive category. The dreary, nondescript bottle was redesigned with a crisp blue colour and broad, proud shoulders at the end of the bottleneck, compared with the existing sloping bottleneck style. A pressure-sensitive vinyl label bearing the brand logo was the finishing touch. The redefinition of Polar Ice provided the brand with "a perspective of depth and a window into the soul of the purity of the product."[14]

As a variation of this strategy, developing new uses for the existing product can be part of the relaunch and repositioning. Eagle Brand, for example, redesigned the labelling of its sweetened condensed milk and promoted its use in mocha and other specialty coffees, five-minute fondues, no-bake bars, and as an after-school beverage.[15]

Alternatively, especially for consumer products, only the packaging is altered. Kraft Canada relaunched its Honey Toasted Shredded Wheat cereal with new packaging and a multimedia ad campaign. The line extension to Shredded Wheat debuted a year earlier, but sales quickly tailed off as it became lost in a sea of other cereals with yellow packaging.[16] Made to look like a bee, the packaging communicated the flavour and created a striking image when stacked together on the store shelf. Tylenol introduced its products in red-capped bottles with ridges for ease of opening; Evian redesigned its bottle with ridges to improve its ability to be crushed for recycling. Packaging can be altered to enhance appearance or to improve a product's usefulness. According to a Point-Of-Purchase Advertising Institute survey, consumers make 70 percent of their buying decisions while in a store and the package is often the ultimate salesperson.[17]

Product-mix contraction

product-mix contraction

The elimination of an entire line or simplification of the assortment within a line to weed out low-profit and unprofitable products.

Another product strategy, **product-mix contraction**, is carried out either by eliminating an entire line or by simplifying the assortment within a line. Thinner and/or shorter product lines or mixes can weed out low-profit and unprofitable products. The intended result of product-mix contraction is higher profits from fewer products. General Mills decided to concentrate on its food business and, consequently, sold its interest in Izod (the "alligator" apparel maker) and its lines of children's toys and games. In service fields, some travel agencies have shifted from selling all modes of travel to concentrating only on cruises or tours focused on certain destinations or tailored to certain age groups.

◀━▶ **BACKSPACE**

1. The set of all products offered for sale by a company is called a _____.
2. A company can expand its product mix in two ways. What are they?
3. What is the difference between trading up and trading down?

- -

Developing New Products

Most of the strategies just discussed call for the development of **new products**. It is obvious that without a flow of new products, a company will have great difficulty surviving over the long run. For many, a substantial portion of this year's sales volume and net profit will come from products that did not exist five to ten years ago, and in the high-technology world, from products that did not exist two years ago or less. Sales of a product grow and then almost inevitably decline; eventually, most products are replaced.

● Every company's current products eventually become obsolete, as their sales volume and market share are reduced by changing consumer desires and/or superior competing products.

● As a product ages, its profits generally decline. Introducing a new product at the right time can help maintain a company's profits.

Risks of new-product development

Typically, some 25,000 new consumer products are introduced each year in North America alone. And, just as typically, as many as 95 percent of them crash and burn, often within months (or even weeks) of their launch.[18] Why do new products fail? The single most important reason is that most new products are not perceived by consumers to be different from existing ones — regardless of what marketers think, say, or do. Some new products simply do not deliver what they imply or promise. Others do not have a large enough market, a fact missed because of faulty or insufficient market research (see Marketing at Work 7-2 later in this chapter, "All Charged Up!"). Other factors contributing to product failure include poor positioning and lack of marketing support. Large numbers of dot-com companies failed because of their inability to provide useful benefits or to attract Internet consumer attention. Another reason a new product can fail is that it is perceived as offering poor value in relation to its price.

Fortunately, many of these marketing mistakes seem to exist to bring humour to the lives of marketing students. In the late 1980s, R.J. Reynolds "spent a fortune" to bring us the smokeless cigarette. In one sense, the company succeeded — Premier cigarettes were pretty much smokeless. But there was a rub — the idea appealed only to non-smokers, and they don't buy too many cigarettes! There seems to have been another problem, too — according to the then-president of R.J. Reynolds, they "tasted like crap."[19]

What then is a "new" product?

Just what is a "new" product? Are the auto manufacturers' annual models new products? Was Toyota's 2003 Vibe "cross-utility" vehicle new? Or, in other product categories, is a new version of Microsoft's Windows XP software for word processing, communications, and spreadsheet work new? Nintendo's GameCube? Nike's spring-loaded Shox shoe? Or must a product be revolutionary, never before thought of, before we can classify it as new?

How new a product is will affect how it should be marketed. There are numerous connotations of "new product," but we will focus our attention on three distinct categories:

● ***Products that are really innovative*** — truly unique. A recent example is a security device that electronically compares the shape of a person's hand with the image of a hand encoded on an identification card.[20] A new model of a car is not a new product, but what if it's a hybrid gas-electric car that recharges itself and gets about 110 kpg on the highway, like the Honda Insight coupe?[21]

Is the Insight an innovation or an extension?

Johnson & Johnson
Panasonic

Products in this category satisfy a real need. Electric or hybrid vehicles are new since they provide new solutions to fossil fuel and pollution problems. Other models have quickly followed from Toyota and Honda. Still-to-be-developed products in this category would be a cancer cure and easily and inexpensively repaired automobiles.

● *Replacement products that are significantly different* from existing products in form, function, and — most important — benefits provided. Johnson & Johnson's Acuvue2 extended-wear, disposable contact lenses (**www.jnjvision.com**) and Panasonic's (**www.panasonic.com**) very thin Plasmatv (110-cm screen, 9 cm thick, and only 32 kg) are both replacing traditional models. At times, even new fashions in clothing are different enough to fit into this category.

● *Imitative products that are new to a company but not new to the market:* Usually, annual models of autos and new versions of cereals are appropriately placed in this category. In another situation, a firm may simply want to capture part of an existing market with a "me-too" product. To maximize company-wide sales, makers of cold and cough remedies routinely introduce imitative products, some of which compete with a nearly identical product from the same company. Computer manufacturers and assemblers do this all the time.

Ultimately, of course, whether a product is new or not depends on how the intended market perceives it. If buyers consider it to be significantly different from competitive products in some relevant characteristic (such as appearance or performance), then it is indeed a new product. As in other situations, perception is reality!

Criteria for new products

When should a company add a new product to its current assortment of products? The following are guidelines that some producers use in answering this question:

Shoppers Drug Mart

There must be adequate market demand. Too often management begins with the wrong questions: Can we use our present sales force? Will the new item fit into our production system? Can we just put it up on our Web site, since we get a lot of traffic? The necessary first question is: Do enough people really want this product?

Shoppers Drug Mart (SDM) (**www.shoppersdrugmart.com**) made sure it knew what it was doing before it introduced a new private-label make-up line, Quo. Research indicated that the average Canadian woman visited SDM every eight days, and yet bought most cos-

MARKETING AT WORK 7-1: STRATEGY

When All Else Fails — Turn Two Products into One New Idea!

It's hard to define what a "new" product is, but we all pretty much know one when we see it. Sometimes it's not so much what makes up the product itself that is really new — it can be kind of familiar looking — but rather, what it allows us to do is new or it makes it possible to do it in a new way or even in a new place.

This is where Freebord and Crosskates enter the story. Their creation has given us street snowboarding and off-road skiing. You see, they already sound familiar — even if you don't know exactly what they are yet.

First, we have the Freebord (www.freebord.com). This puppy carves and slides just like a snowboard. You can hug a tight turn or drift a long, gentle slide; flip the board into a fakie or float a 360. Only thing is, you're doing it on pavement on something resembling a skateboard with really low-profile wheels. How? Outer wheels and spring-biased inner wheels! Four outer wheels simulate the board's edges, while tucked away underneath are two casters that can swivel 360 degrees. By keeping weight over the board's edges, you can carve turns. As you apply more weight to the base, your board will start to slide. To execute 180s and the like, unweight your edges. That's all there is to it!

Next, the sensation of carving your own trail down a fresh alpine slope. Exhilarating — but there's no ski lift! Actually, there's no snow, either. That's because you're cross-skating on your 616 Backcountry skates (www.crosskate.com). Basically, what you have is a traditional ski boot mounted on a frame attached to two 10- by 2-inch knobby pneumatic tires, providing quite a bit of ground clearance, and disc brakes engineered into the rear wheels. Designed for every type of skier, there is the PowerCurve pivoting front-wheel set-up that helps you steer the skates in your turning direction as you sail downhill. For those who prefer the bunny slope, the spring system that controls the front-wheel pivot is adjustable. It allows you to replace the normally stiff springs with softer ones that give more speed to scrub off in turns. For cross-country enthusiasts, there is the special lifting-heel system worked into the boot binding, allowing classic strides across flats and up hills. And for ascent, the 616s have a locking system on the front wheels to prevent you from rolling back.

Two products that when described component by component seem quite familiar to many of us. Yet, when the elements described are combined, the result is innovative new products and challenging activities.

INTERNET SOURCES: www.freebord.com; www.crosskate.com.

metics at department store brand-name cosmetic counters. No department store, however, can boast such a customer frequency. SDM's new private-label line was positioned between pricey high-end department store brands and inexpensive mass-market offerings, filling a very real gap in the marketplace. With no visible tie-in to SDM on the packaging and with a timeless quality design featuring clean, sleek lines and displayed in a special showcase in the cosmetics department, the product had the high-end brands in its sights.

The product must satisfy key financial criteria. At least three questions should be asked: Is adequate financing available? Will the new item reduce seasonal and cyclical fluctuations in the company's sales? And, most critical: Can we make sufficient profit with the product? Adequate financing means more than that required to produce the product; it must ensure that enough market research is carried out and that sufficient marketing support is provided to bring the product to the awareness of the targeted segments.

The product must be compatible with environmental standards. Key questions include: Do the production processes avoid polluting the air or water? Will the finished product, including its packaging, be friendly to the environment? And: After being used, does the product have recycling potential?

The product must fit into the company's present marketing structure. Sherwin-Williams Paint Company would probably find it quite difficult to add margarine to its line of paints. Specific questions related to whether a new product will fit the company's marketing expertise and experience include: Can the existing sales force be used? Can the present channels of distribution be used? To reduce risk, many firms rely on brand extensions. For example, Sunlight successfully moved out of the laundry room and into the kitchen with Sunlight dishwashing products. It seems that the idea of removing stubborn dirt and stains carried over well from clothing to greasy dishes. The name was less successful, however, when it came to hand soap, and its furniture polish never made it past the test market phase.[22]

Bayer

Besides these four issues, a proposed product must satisfy other criteria. For instance, it must be in keeping with the company's objectives and image. Bayer (**www.bayer.com**), to promote a new garden bug spray, used an aggressive marketing push that included television ads with animated insects choking and wheezing before their final demise. The question is: What image might come to parents' minds the next time that they give their children that little pink Bayer Aspirin?

The new-product strategy statement

It's clear that every new-product project or venture should have an explicit strategy statement identifying the role the new product is expected to play in achieving company and marketing goals. A new product might be designed to protect market share or maintain the company's reputation as an innovator. Or a new product's role might be to meet a specific return-on-investment goal or establish a position in a new market. With computer technology, the imperative is often to be the first to market.

As shown in the box below, given a stated company goal, specific product strategies — such as those discussed in the previous section — can be implemented to aid in achieving that goal. Thus, a line extension, product modification, or completely new product-development approach may be what is needed.

Goal	Strategy	Example
Defend market share	Introduce addition to existing line	Mike's Hard Lemonade introduction of new flavours — orange, raspberry iced tea, etc.
Strengthen reputation as an innovator	Introduce significantly new product	Sony's introduction of the CLIÉ line of hand-held personal entertainment organizers that combine PDA capabilities with multimedia and remote-control capabilities for other home electronics
Increase customer satisfaction	Develop mass customization to improve service	Johnson & Johnson's development of a contact lens system that can be fitted within 10 minutes and can be used for one-week extended wear

With the availability of new communication and information technology, firms are now beginning to orient their **new-product strategies** toward mass customization in order to provide increased product value. Individual consumer preferences can be built into new products either by requiring that a modular strategy be used for product design or by positioning the final step of individual product differentiation at the last minute in the product creation process, the delivery or consumer "try-on" stage. Auto manufacturers continue to refine their Internet presence in the hope of increasing online ordering. By allowing consumers to custom-order their new cars, manufacturers hope to reduce the inventories held at dealerships by producing more on demand.

Stages in the development process

Guided by a company's new-product strategy, a new product is best developed through a series of six stages, as shown in Figure 7-3. Compared with unstructured development, the formal development of new products provides benefits such as higher success rates, increased customer satisfaction, and greater achievement of time, quality, and cost objectives.[23]

At each stage, management decides whether to proceed to the next stage, abandon the product, or seek additional information.[24] A brief description of what should happen at each stage of the **new-product development process** follows:

1. ***Generating new-product ideas:*** New-product development starts with an idea or a concept. A system must be designed for stimulating new ideas within an organization and then acknowledging and reviewing them promptly. Customers should also be encouraged to propose innovations. In a research study, 80 percent of companies pointed to customers as their best source for new-product ideas.[25] Take another look at how Hotspex and LifeStyles approach this.

2. ***Screening:*** At this stage, new-product ideas are evaluated to determine which ones warrant further study.[26] Typically, a management team with representatives of various functions screens the pool of ideas.

3. ***Business analysis:*** A surviving idea is expanded into a concrete business proposal. In the business analysis, management (a) identifies product features, (b) estimates market demand, competition, and the product's profitability, (c) establishes a program to develop the product, and (d) assigns responsibility for further study of the product's feasibility.

4. ***Prototype development:*** If the results of the business analysis are favourable, then a prototype or trial model of the product is developed. In the case of tangible products, a small quantity of the trial model is manufactured to designated specifications. Laboratory tests and other technical evaluations are carried out to determine whether it is practical to produce the product. A firm may be able to construct a prototype of a new type of cellular telephone but be unable to manufacture the new product in large quantities or at a cost low enough to stimulate sales and still yield a profit. In the case of services, the facilities and procedures necessary to produce and deliver the new product are designed and tested. That certainly is a necessary step in the development of a new roller-coaster ride at an amusement park!

new-product strategy
A plan that defines the role new products are to play in helping the company achieve its corporate and marketing goals.

business analysis
The stage of new-product development in which a surviving idea is expanded into a business proposal and management identifies product features; estimates market demand, competition, and profitability; establishes a development program; and assigns responsibility for further study.

Figure 7-3:

Major Stages in the New-Product Development Process

market tests

The stage of new-product development that involves tests with actual consumers.

5. *Market tests:* Unlike the internal tests conducted during prototype development, **market tests** involve actual consumers. A new tangible product may be given to a sample of people for use in their households (in the case of a consumer good) or their organizations (a business good). Beta versions of all types of software are made available free to those who will download and make use of it. Following this trial, consumers are asked to evaluate the product. Consumer-use tests are less practical for pure services, due to their intangible nature. If a service can be simulated on a computer, however, some form of trial can be achieved.

This stage in new-product development often entails test marketing, in which the product is placed on sale in a limited geographic area. Results, including sales and repeat purchases, are monitored by the company that developed the product and perhaps also by competitors. In this stage, the product's design and production plans may have to be adjusted as a result of test findings. Following market tests, management must make a final "go" or "no-go" decision about introducing the product.

6. *Commercialization:* Finally, full-scale production and marketing programs are planned and implemented. Up to this point in development, management has virtually complete control over the product. Once the product is "born" and enters the introductory stage of its life cycle, however, the external competitive environment becomes a major determinant of its destiny.

In the six-stage process, the first three stages are particularly critical, because they deal with ideas and are therefore the least expensive. More importantly, many products fail because the idea or the timing is wrong — and the first three stages are intended to identify such situations. Each subsequent stage becomes more costly in terms of the budget and human resources necessary to carry out the required tasks.

Some companies, trying to bring new products to market faster than their competitors, skip stages in the development process. The most common omission is the fifth stage: market tests. Without this stage, however, the company lacks consumer reactions to the proposed product.

Historically, the marketing of goods has received more attention than the marketing of services, so it is not surprising that the new-product development process is not as advanced in services fields as it is in goods industries. However, on the positive side, this means that services firms have more flexibility to devise a new-product development process that suits their distinctive circumstances.

Organizing for Product Innovation

If new-product programs are to be successful, they must be supported by a strong, long-term commitment from top management. This commitment must be maintained even when some new products fail. To implement this commitment to innovation effectively, new-product programs must be soundly organized.

Types of organization

There is no "best" organizational structure for product planning and development. Many companies use more than one structure to manage these activities. Some widely used organizational structures for planning and developing new products are:

- **Product-planning committee:** Members include executives from major departments — marketing, production, finance, engineering, and research — and, especially in small firms, the president and/or another top-level executive.

MARKETING AT WORK   7-2: ETHICS

All Charged Up!

It's not easy being green, and being green can mean different things in different countries. Terry Spyropolous, brand manager of Ford of Canada's TH!NK Group, believes in green — or he did. TH!NK, created in 1999, was a business unit of Ford dedicated to developing and marketing environmentally responsible vehicles. Consisting of two units, TH!NK Mobility focused on the development of battery electric vehicles, while TH!NK Technologies focused on developing fuel cell vehicles.

The TH!NK Group thinks very differently. For example, "vehicle" doesn't always mean "car" in the traditional sense. The culture of the firm was to develop "personal mobility solutions" — certainly an interesting venture for a company better known for its tough trucks, gas-guzzling SUVs, and the Mustang muscle car. Perhaps that's why a separate unit, mindset, and working environment were required, a new working culture where the products and practices of the past didn't influence (or limit) the thinking of the future.

Ford believed that there was a growing interest in and demand for earth-friendly vehicles, and it hopes to work toward zero-emission mobility products in the near future. The company has already launched several products in Europe (www.thinkmobility.com).

And what of the actual market size for environmentally friendly vehicles? The company just didn't know, because it felt the vehicles were "so different from what we are used to seeing." Sales of hybrid vehicles were slow to take off. Unlike previous offerings that certainly resembled traditional cars, TH!NK products have been quite different. TH!NK City is a micro two-seater, while the TH!NK Traveler and TH!NK Fun are electric bicycles. These are products intended for commuting within the city. The City was to be launched in Canada by 2003 (a similar product is already offered in Europe) and was designed as a battery-powered vehicle with a driving range of 85 km and a top speed of 90 km/h, with a charging time of eight hours. The Traveler and Fun are already available in the United States and run about $1,000 ($US) each.

But the market and tough competitive conditions in the auto industry seem to have derailed this product innovation for the time being. Ford had hoped to sell 5,000 City cars per year, but sold only 1,000 in three years. In mid-2002, Ford gave up on TH!NK and announced it would invest in other forms of alternative fuel technology. Is this a new-product failure? Was Ford too far ahead of the consumer?

SOURCE: Adapted from Jason MacDonald, "All Charged Up," *Marketing Magazine*, August 27, 2001, pp. 9, 10; Catherine Greenman, "Bike Power: Tired Legs Get A Leg Up," *The New York Times*, April 19, 2001, pp. D1, D8; and Michelle Maynard, "Ford Abandons Venture in Making Electric Cars," *The New York Times*, August 31, pp. 13, 14.

- **New-product department:** These units are small, consisting of five or fewer people. The department head reports to the president (which, in a large firm, may be the president of a division).

- **Venture team:** A small group responsible for the development of new products, with representatives from engineering, production, finance, and marketing research, that operates like a separate small business. Typically, the team reports directly to top management and has a great deal of flexibility.

- **Product manager:** This individual is responsible for planning new products as well as managing established products. Although still effective in some firms, we'll discuss in the next section why this structure is being displaced in many firms by one of the other structures discussed above.

Which organizational structure is chosen is not the key point here — each has strengths and weaknesses. What's critical is to make sure that some person or group has the specific responsibility for new-product development and is backed by top management. Product innovation is too important an activity to handle in an unorganized, nonchalant fashion, which presumes that somehow the job will get done. To maximize the chances for successful new-product development, it is vital that employees responsible for product planning have the right skills, particularly the ability to work well with other people and operate in a supportive environment.

As the new product is completed, responsibility for marketing it usually is shifted either to an existing department or a new department established just for this new product. In some cases, the team that developed the product may continue as the management nucleus of the new unit.

Integrating new products into departments that are already marketing established products does carry at least two risks, however. First, executives who are involved with ongoing products may have a short-term outlook as they deal with day-to-day problems of existing products. Consequently, they may not recognize the long-term importance of new products and, as a result, neglect them. Second, managers of successful existing products often are reluctant to assume the risks inherent in marketing new products.

Product and brand management

product-adoption process

The stages that an individual goes through in deciding whether to accept a new product or innovation.

Companies with many brands, such as Procter & Gamble and Kraft Foods, assign the responsibility for planning new products as well as co-ordinating the marketing efforts of existing ones to a product manager. Essentially, a product manager, sometimes called a *brand manager*, plans the complete marketing program for a brand or group of products. Specific tasks include setting marketing goals, preparing budgets, and developing plans for advertising and personal selling and service activities. Developing new products along with improving established products is usually part of the job description.

product diffusion

The process by which a new product or innovation is spread through a market or social system over time.

The likelihood of achieving success with a new product — especially a really innovative one — as well as an established one, is increased if management understands two natural processes: (1) product adoption and diffusion and (2) product evolution or product life cycle. First, we will discuss the process of the diffusion of new products and then follow up that discussion with a review of product life-cycle concepts. We will illustrate how both sets of concepts can aid product and marketing managers to determine when and in what sequence the strategies we have already discussed in this chapter can be most usefully implemented.

New-Product Adoption and Diffusion

The **product-adoption process** describes the set of successive decisions an individual makes before accepting a new product or innovation. **Product diffusion** is the process by which a new product or innovation spreads throughout a market or social system over time.[27] By understanding these processes, marketing and product managers gain insight into how a product is or is not accepted by consumers and which groups of consumers are likely to buy a product soon after it is introduced, later on, or never.

stages in the product-adoption process

The six stages a prospective user goes through in deciding whether to purchase something new, including awareness, interest, evaluation, trial, adoption, and confirmation.

Stages in the product-adoption process

A prospective user goes through six **stages in the product-adoption process** — deciding whether to purchase something new. These stages are summarized in the box below.

Stage	Activity in That Stage
Awareness	Individual is exposed to the innovation; becomes a prospect.
Interest	Prospect is interested enough to seek information.
Evaluation	Prospect judges the advantages and disadvantages of a product.
Trial	Prospect adopts the innovation on a limited basis. A consumer buys a sample, if the product can be sampled.
Adoption	Prospect decides whether to use the innovation on a full-scale basis.
Confirmation	After adopting the innovation, prospect becomes a user who immediately seeks assurances that the decision to purchase the product was correct.

Adopter categories

innovation-adopter categories
Five categories, based on the point in time when individuals adopt a given innovation, comprising innovators, early adopters, early majority, late majority, and laggards.

innovators
The first group of people — a venturesome group — to adopt a new product or service.

early adopters
The second group (following innovators) to adopt something new. This group includes opinion leaders, is respected, and has much influence on its peers.

early majority
A more deliberate group of innovation adopters that adopts just before the "average" adopter.

Some people will adopt an innovation soon after it is introduced. Others delay before accepting a new product, and still others may never adopt. Research has identified five **innovation-adopter categories**, based on the point in time when individuals adopt a given innovation. Non-adopters are excluded. The characteristics of early and late adopters are summarized in Table 7-3.

Innovators, representing about 3 percent of the market for a specific product, comprise the small group of venturesome consumers who are the first to adopt an innovation. In relation to later adopters, they tend to be younger, have higher social status, and are in better financial shape. They also tend to have broad social relationships involving various groups of people in more than one community. They are likely to rely more on non-personal sources of information, such as advertising and the Internet, rather than on salespeople or other personal sources.

Early adopters make up about 13 percent of the market and purchase a new product after innovators but sooner than other consumers. Unlike innovators, who have broad involvement outside a local community, early adopters tend to be involved socially within a local community. Notably, they are greatly respected in their social circles and communities, and other people are interested in and influenced by their opinions. The early-adopter category includes more **opinion leaders** than any other adopter group. Salespeople are probably used more as information sources by early adopters than by any other category.

The **early majority** group is large, representing about 34 percent of the market. It consists of those more deliberate consumers who accept an innovation just before the "average" adopter in a market segment or social system. This group is a bit above average in social and economic terms. Consumers in the early majority group rely quite a bit on ads, salespeople, and contact with and observation of early adopters.

TABLE 7-3	Characteristics of Early and Late Adopters of Innovations	
	Early Adopters	**Late Adopters**
Key Characteristics		
Venturesome	Innovators (3% of total adopters)	
Respected	Early adopters (13%)	
Deliberate	Early majority (34%)	
Sceptical		Late majority (34% of total adopters)
Tradition-bound		Laggards (16%)
Other Characteristics		
Age	Younger	Older
Education	Well educated	Less educated
Income	Higher	Lower
Social relationships: within or outside community	Innovators: outside Others: within	Totally local
Social status	Higher	Lower
Information sources	Wide variety; many media	Limited media exposure; limited reliance on outside media; reliance on local peer groups

late majority

The sceptical group of innovation adopters who adopt a new idea late in the game.

laggards

Tradition-bound people who are the last to adopt an innovation.

non-adopters

Consumers who never adopt an innovation.

The late majority, another 34 percent of the market, is a sceptical group of consumers who usually adopt an innovation to save money or in response to social pressure from their peers. They rely on their peers — late or early majority — as sources of information. Advertising and personal selling are less effective with this group than is word-of-mouth communication.

Laggards are consumers who are bound by tradition and therefore are last to adopt an innovation. They make up about 16 percent of the market. Laggards are suspicious of innovations and innovators; they wonder why anyone would pay a lot more for a new kind of light bulb, for example. By the time laggards adopt something new, it may already have been discarded by the innovators in favour of a newer concept. Laggards are older and usually are at the low end of the social and economic scales.

Keep in mind that we are discussing only adopters of an innovation. For most innovations, there are many people who are not included in our percentages. They are non-adopters, who never adopt the innovation.

How new-product characteristics affect adoption

Five innovation characteristics affect the rate at which new products are adopted, as discussed below. Firms would like their new product to be able to satisfy all five, but this can happen only if the characteristics and their affects are attended to in the product-development process. While some firms are careful about the characteristics that aid the adoption of an innovation, others are not.

3M

1. *Relative Advantage:* The degree to which the new item is superior to existing ones. The new product may cost less, be safer, and be easier to use. Safest Stripper, a paint and varnish remover introduced by 3M (**www.3m.com**), scored much higher than existing ones on safety, since it contains no harmful chemicals, is odourless, and allows users to refinish furniture indoors rather than having to work outdoors.

2. *Compatibility:* The degree to which the innovation is seen as coinciding with the values and predispositions of potential users. Since most North American consumers want to save time and satisfy their desires now rather than later, microwave popcorn eminently meets this value and predisposition. Supermarkets cater to values by offering ethnic foods in large urban areas and many foods are now microwave-friendly, if not developed specifically for microwave use, consistent with how important time is to consumers.

3. *Complexity:* The degree of difficulty in understanding or using an innovation. The more complex a new item is, the more a consumer must learn to be able to use it and the less rapidly it will be adopted — if it is adopted at all. Combined shampoo-conditioners posed no challenge to consumers, but many forms of insurance and some consumer electronics products are hard to understand and use. In such cases, marketers often use toll-free telephone numbers and special Web sites to provide assistance and reduce adoption-resistance due to product complexity.

4. *Trialability:* The degree to which an innovation may be sampled on some limited basis. The greater the trialability, the faster the adoption rate. New modular home air-conditioning systems are likely to have a slower adoption rate than an easily sampled new seed or fertilizer. Costly products will be adopted more slowly than less expensive ones; many services (such as insurance) are difficult to use on a trial basis, so they tend to be adopted rather slowly.

5. *Observability:* The degree to which an innovation actually can be seen to be effective. In general, the greater the observability, the more rapid the adoption rate. A new weed killer

that works on existing weeds will be accepted sooner than a product that prevents weeds from sprouting. The latter product, even if highly effective, produces no dead weeds to show to prospective buyers.

Kodak

Kodak's camcorder videotape is a good example to use to assess these characteristics. Kodak (**www.kodak.ca**) sells this product as "backcoated," which it claims enables the videotape to perform better in a VCR, especially if it's an old VCR. The backcoating reduces the likelihood of losing images. This product comes pre-packed in a cassette and is easy to use (reducing complexity), is a well-known brand name (alleviating concerns about trialability and tangibility), and offers a feature that other film does not have — the backcoating that prevents damage to the film (representing relative advantage). The customer can observe the backcoating by checking the back of the film: A flat surface as opposed to a shiny one indicates that the product is backcoated. The product is widely distributed, which enhances compatibility with consumers' desire for convenient purchase.[28]

BACKSPACE

1. What percentage of new consumer products introduced each year in North America fail?
2. What are the three categories of new products?
3. In marketing, what is a laggard?

MARKETING AT WORK   7-3: STRATEGY

What Were They Thinking?

In the quiet town of Ithaca, NY, sits the New Products Showcase and Learning Center. It's a dreary little building, with all the appeal of a nuclear fallout shelter — suitable, considering it's home to about 80,000 items representing some of the biggest consumer product bombs ever unleashed on the public.

Cucumber antiperspirant spray? Aerosol ketchup? Chocolate-covered Ritz crackers? Nestea's Tea Whiz (which was, well, urine-coloured)? Meat jerky made with (gulp!) bunnies? Oh yes, they're all tucked away in there somewhere. Robert McMath, proprietor of the establishment, could write a book on fiascos and flops. Wait a minute — he did and it's called *What Were They Thinking?* He's trying to make sure these blunders aren't forgotten for fear they'll be repeated, which actually happens from time to time.

McMath has distilled these failures down to a few basic truisms:

No one wanted it in the first place   Pepsi A.M. was an attempt to steal some thunder from the coffee market. It featured less carbonation and a whole lot more caffeine. Thing is, few people want a cold soft drink at the crack of dawn, regardless of carbonation and caffeine levels.

Failure to deliver   Johnson's Hot Scoop Microwave Sundae, as you have guessed, was for the microwave. But only the sauce should have melted, not the ice cream. Not all freezers or microwaves are created equal, so what often resulted was liquefied ice cream with lava-molten syrup steaming through it.

Me-too madness   McMath believes "me-too" marketing is the number-one killer of new products. Simply too many similar products are often introduced. Coca-Cola has long been a target, with products such as Yum Yum Cola, French Wine of Cola, Toca Cola, Afri-Cola, and even Coco-Cola.

Corporate Alzheimer's   "Those who ignore history are doomed to repeat it." Sound familiar? As employees come and go in a company, so do the same bad ideas occasionally. Listerine-flavoured toothpaste? Not likely! The mouthwash known for its awful flavour was not once but twice offered in the form of toothpaste. While consumers will accept vile-tasting mouthwash, marketing researchers have long known they will not accept the same in toothpaste.

Marketing to marketers   For some reason, marketers sometimes think that we all think like they do, so we'll "get it." Not always the case, as with Kellogg's Ensemble, a line of 17 breakfast products launched in the mid-nineties to help people cut their cholesterol. Great idea, but wrong name, wrong packaging, and way too confusing for average consumers to follow how it was all supposed to work for them.

SOURCE: Adapted from David Menzies, "The Museum of Mortal Marketing Mistakes," *Marketing Magazine*, April 23, 2001, pp. 9–11.

Product Life-Cycle Management

product life cycle

The stages a product goes through from its introduction, to its growth and maturity, to its eventual decline and death (withdrawal from the market or deletion from the company's offerings).

Kraft
Gillette
Intel

All consumer and business products, whatever their classifications, come to an end through obsolescence of one form or another. The life cycle of a product consists of four stages: introduction, growth, maturity, and decline. The concept of product life applies to a generic category of product (microwave ovens, for example). The category can consist of a number of product lines: high-powered and fully featured, medium-powered with standard features, or low-powered with basic features. The category thus consists of all brands of all lines being offered by competitors, not specific brands such as Sony or Braun. A **product life cycle** consists of the aggregate sales over an extended period of time for all brands making up a generic product category.

Stop at this point and think about the distinction being made between product category and brands of a product. Intuitively, this sounds simple, but a little more thought may be required to ensure that you understand what this cycle refers to. Many students assume they understand, but when asked for an example on an exam, often provide a brand of a product to illustrate a stage of the cycle.

A product life cycle is graphed by plotting aggregate sales volume for a generic product category over time, usually years. It is also worthwhile to accompany the sales-volume curve with the corresponding profit curve for the product category, as shown in Figure 7-4. After all, we are interested ultimately in profitability, not just sales.

The shapes of these two curves vary from one product category to another. Still, for most categories, the basic shapes and the relationship between the sales and the profit curves are as illustrated. In this typical life cycle, the profit curve for most new products is negative (signifying a loss) through much of the introductory stage.

In the latter part of the growth stage, the profit curve starts to decline, while sales volume is still rising. Profits decline because the companies in an industry usually must increase their advertising and selling efforts or cut their prices (or both) to sustain sales growth in the face of intensifying competition during the maturity stage. The length of time it takes a product to reach maturity varies considerably, depending on the nature of the product. Some products remain in the maturity stage much longer than others. Electronic equipment, such as computers, has a very short maturity stage. Continuous new developments in technology cause the life cycle of these products to be quite short.

Introducing a new product at the proper time will help maintain a company's desired level of profit. Building on its original product lines, Kraft (**www.kraftcanada.com**) is constantly extending product life cycles with innovations. Kraft Dinner a good example of a product that has been sustained in this way. Over the past 15 years, the company has introduced Alfredo, Rugrats, and Easy Mac versions. These products have all sold at premium prices. The Gillette Company (**www.gillette.com**) has had to constantly evolve to compete against the disposable variety of razors in the wet-shave market. The Sensor featured independently suspended blades and consumers were willing to pay a little more for the superior shave it provided. Trading up, Gillette produced the triple-blade Mach3, which is more expensive. Trading up again, the Mach3 Turbo was introduced, which allows the shaver to be pulled in any direction on the face without irritation, thanks to anti-friction blades and twice as many microfins.[29] Will consumers continue to be convinced to spend more and more for such disposable products?

Intel Corp. (**www.intel.com**) sought a measure of control over the product life cycle of microprocessors and their prices by introducing new generations only two or three years apart. They did this even though demand was still growing for the

Figure 7-4:

Typical Life Cycle of a Product Category
During the introduction stage of a life cycle, a product category — and virtually all brands within it — are unprofitable. Profits are healthy during the growth stage, but then start to decline while a product's sales volume is still increasing.

| INTRODUCTION | GROWTH | MATURITY | DECLINE |

Sales Volume

Profit

Dollars

0

Loss

Time in years

current versions. In recent years, however, Intel has had to rely more on price cuts of existing lines than on new-product introductions in order to maintain its share of the market for micro-processors used in personal computers.[30]

The product life-cycle concept is both straightforward and powerful, but it is too general to be useful in specific cases and therefore must be adapted to fit different circumstances. A company's marketing success can be affected considerably by its ability to determine and adapt to the life cycles of each of its product categories.

Characteristics of each stage

Management must be able to recognize in which part of the life cycle its product is at any given time. The competitive environment and marketing strategies that should be used ordinarily depend on the particular life-cycle stage. Table 7-4 contains a synopsis of all four stages, and then each stage is discussed.

introduction stage
The first part of a product life cycle, during which a generic product category is launched into the market in a full-scale marketing program.

Introduction   During the introduction stage, a product is launched into the market in a full-scale marketing program. It has gone through product development, including idea screening, prototype, and market tests. The entire product may be new, such as a substitute for fat in prepared foods. Or it may be well known but have significant new features that, in effect, create a new product category — PDAs and multimedia cellphones are examples. A total program would be designed to achieve awareness, arouse interest, elicit evaluation, promote adoption, and confirm that adoption. Prime target consumers would be those who are considered innovators for the type of product being launched, followed by those who would be considered to be early adopters.

This introductory stage (sometimes called *pioneering*) is the most risky and expensive, because substantial amounts of money must be spent in seeking consumer adoption of the product. However, many products are not accepted by a sufficient number of consumers and therefore fail at this stage. For really new products, there is very little direct competition. Promotional programs designed to stimulate demand affect the entire product category, not just the seller's brand. Advertising and promotion should emphasize product features that aid in speeding up the rate of adoption.

TABLE 7-4   Characteristics and Implications of Different Product Life-Cycle Stages

Each stage of a product's life cycle has different characteristics; as a result, marketing must be modified over the course of the cycle.

	Stage			
	Introduction	**Growth**	**Maturity**	**Decline**
Characteristics				
Customers	Innovators	Mass market	Mass market	Loyal customers
Competition	Little, if any	Increasing	Intense	Decreasing
Sales	Low levels, then rising	Rapid growth	Slow/no annual growth	Declining
Profits	None	Strong, then at a peak	Declining annually	Low/none
Marketing Implications				
Overall strategy	Market development	Market penetration	Defensive positioning	Efficiency or exit
Costs	High per unit	Declining	Stable or increasing	Low
Product strategy	Undifferentiated	Improved items	Differentiated	Pruned line
Pricing strategy	Most likely high	Lower over time	Lowest	Increasing
Distribution strategy	Scattered	Intensive	Intensive	Selective
Promotion strategy	Category awareness	Brand preference	Brand loyalty	Reinforcement

SOURCE: Adapted from material provided by Professor David Appel, University of Notre Dame, Notre Dame, IN.

growth stage

The second part of a product life cycle, during which the sales and profits of a generic product category rise and competitors enter the market; profits start to decline near the end of this part of the cycle.

maturity stage

The third part of a product life cycle, during which sales of a generic product category continue to increase (but at a decreasing rate), profits decline largely due to price competition, and some firms leave the market.

decline stage

The fourth, and final, part of a product life cycle, during which the sales of a generic product category drop and most competitors abandon the market.

Growth   In the **growth stage**, sales and profits rise at a rapid rate as early majority, a portion of the late majority, and some of the laggard group of potential customers purchase the product. Competitors enter the market, often in large numbers if the profit outlook is particularly attractive. Mostly as a result of competition, profits start to decline near the end of the growth stage.

Maturity   During the first part of the **maturity stage**, sales continue to increase, but at a decreasing rate, as late majority and laggard groups become product users. When sales level off, profits of both producers and intermediaries decline. The primary reasons: intense price competition, as well as much demand being replacement sales rather than coming from new customers. Seeking to differentiate themselves, some firms extend their product lines with new models. During the latter part of this stage, marginal producers, those with high costs or without a differential advantage, are forced to drop out of the market. They do so because they lack sufficient customers and/or profits.

Decline   For most products, a **decline stage**, as gauged by sales volume for the total category, is inevitable for one or more of the following reasons:

● Very few or no new consumers are available in the market and almost all sales are replacement sales.

● The need for the product disappears, as when frozen orange juice generally eliminated the market for juice squeezers.

● A better or less expensive product is developed to fill the same need. CDs have replaced tapes and vinyl records because the sound, durability, and storage capability of the new product is far superior to that of the old product. CDs require CD players, which have, for the most part, replaced tape machines and turntables.

● People simply grow tired of a product (a clothing style, for instance), so it disappears from the market, goes out of favour or fashion.

Seeing little opportunity for revitalized sales or profits, most competitors abandon the market during the decline stage. However, a few firms may be able to develop a small market niche and remain moderately successful in this stage. Some manufacturers of wood-burning stoves have been able to do this. Whether a product at this stage has to be abandoned or can be continued on a profitable basis often depends on the skills and creativity of the marketing manager responsible for the product.

Length of product life cycle

The total length of the product life cycle — from the start of the introduction stage to the end of the decline stage — varies across product categories. It ranges from weeks or a short season (for a clothing fashion) to many decades (for cars or telephones). This varies because of differences in the length of individual stages from one product category to the next. Furthermore, although Figure 7-4 suggests that all four life cycle stages cover nearly equal periods of time, the stages in any given product's life cycle usually last for different periods.

Three variations on the typical life cycle are shown in Figure 7-5:

● In one variation, the product gains widespread consumer acceptance only after an extended introductory period (see Part A). The hand-held computer is an example of a current product that, for this category, has experienced a long introductory period with a relatively slow adoption rate after innovators and early adopters entered the market.

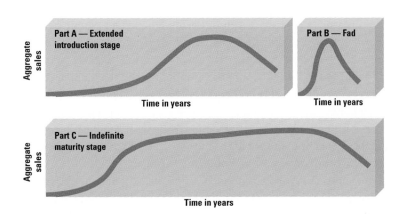

Figure 7-5:

Product Life Cycle
Variations

In another variation, the entire life cycle begins and ends in a relatively short period of time (Part B). This variation depicts the life cycle for a fad, a product or style that becomes immensely popular nearly overnight and then falls out of favour with consumers almost as quickly. Beta format VCRs and videodisc players are examples of entertainment technology that did not survive very long in the consumer marketplace.

• In a third variation, the product's mature stage lasts almost indefinitely (Part C). This life cycle is illustrated by canned, carbonated soft drinks and also by the automobile with a gasoline-powered, internal-combustion engine.

Product life cycles are becoming shorter. If competitors can quickly introduce a "me-too" version of a popular product, it may move swiftly into the maturity stage — or rapid changes in technology can make a product obsolete virtually overnight. Some said that would occur in the audio field, with digital audiotapes replacing CDs, but that didn't happen. The latest forecast is that even newer formats, notably Super Audio CDs and DVD-Audio, will turn the CD into a dinosaur.[31] What possible impact will MP3 technology have on CDs in the long term?

Life cycle is related to a market

Ortho Pharmaceuticals

When we say that a product is in a specific stage of its life cycle, implicitly we are referring to a specific market. A product may be well accepted (growth stage) in some markets (consisting of innovators and early adopters) but still be striving for acceptance in other markets consisting of early majority or even late adopters. At the time that Ortho Pharmaceuticals (**www.orthomc neil.com**) introduced Retin-A as a treatment for acne, existing products already served this purpose, so the acne-treatment category probably was in the maturity stage. However, it was then discovered that Retin-A might be effective in reducing facial wrinkles. In effect, this created a new product category, so Retin-A fit into both the acne-treatment category that was in the maturity stage among teenagers and into the wrinkle-remover category that was in the introductory or perhaps early-growth stage among the middle-aged. Rapid growth is now occurring in this category as many cosmetic firms rush to get products into the marketplace, greatly increasing the level of competition as Baby Boomers start to sag around the edges — or at least around the eyes! But not just those who are already starting to sag are being targeted: L'Oréal, for example, is targeting women in the 25 to 45 age range, with a skew toward the 30 to 35 category.[32]

Life-cycle management

To a surprising extent, the shape of the sales and profit curves for a product category can be controlled. The collective actions of firms offering competing products in the same category shape the curves, but even single companies can have an impact. A giant firm may be able to shorten the introductory stage by broadening the distribution or increasing the promotional effort supporting the new product.

Most firms, however, cannot substantially affect the sales and profit curves for a product category. Their task, therefore, is to determine how best to achieve success with their own brands within the life cycle for an entire product category. For an individual firm, successful life-cycle management depends on (1) predicting the shape of the proposed product's cycle even before it is introduced and (2) successfully adapting marketing strategies at each stage of the life cycle.

Entry strategies   A firm entering a new market must decide whether to plunge in during the introductory stage. Or it can wait and make its entry during the early part of the growth stage, after innovating companies have proven that there is a viable market.

Perrier

The strategy of entering during the introductory stage is prompted by the desire to build a dominant market position right away and thus lessen the interest of potential competitors and the effectiveness of actual competitors. This strategy worked for Sony with the Walkman, Perrier (**www.perrier.com**) with bottled sparkling water, and Nike with running shoes. The hurdles may be insurmountable when you enter with a "me-too" product or service and try to play catch-up — to grow market share against an entrenched competitor.

Sometimes, delaying entry until the market is proven can pay off. Pioneering requires a large investment and the risks are great — as demonstrated by the high failure rate among new products. Large companies with the marketing resources to overwhelm smaller innovating firms are most likely to be successful with a delayed-entry strategy. In one such case, Coca-Cola introduced Tab and Diet Coke, and Pepsi-Cola introduced Diet Pepsi — and the two giants surpassed Diet Rite Cola, an early pioneer. It's not clear-cut which is the better entry strategy. Each has its advantages and disadvantages, its successes and failures. As with nearly all marketing decisions, sound managerial judgement is critical.[33]

Managing on the rise   When sales are growing strongly and profits are robust in a product category, you might think that a marketing manager has little to do except tally up an anticipated bonus. During the growth stage of the life cycle, a company has to devise the right strategies for its brand(s) and Web sites in that product category. Promotion that will cause consumers to desire the company's brand of product must be considered. Distribution must be expanded and made more efficient and rapid, and product improvements must be considered. Decisions made during the growth stage influence (a) how many competitors enter the market and (b) how well the company's brand does within a product category both in the near and distant future.

Home video games were introduced in the 1970s, but the more captivating (and perhaps addictive) Nintendo brand, in effect, created a new product category in the 1980s. As the 1990s began, this product appeared to be in the growth stage of its life cycle. However, in the mid-1990s, video games stagnated. To stimulate sales, Nintendo and its competitors Sega and Sony have been engaged in a game of "technological leapfrog." As revenue potential grew to about $700 million in Canada alone, Microsoft even entered the category with its first contender, the Xbox, in 2002. These firms are in a constant struggle to gain some sort of differential advantage, even if it's only temporary, by increasing the video, audio, or graphics capabilities of their systems. At the same time, they are trying to control prices.[34]

Managing during maturity   Various strategies may be effective in maintaining or boosting sales of a product during the maturity stage of its life cycle. Of course, what works magnificently for one product may perform dismally for another. Common strategies during maturity include modifying the product, designing new promotions, and devising new uses for the product. The Campbell Soup Company recently celebrated its hundredth birthday and used this event as an opportunity to redesign its labels, giving a more mature look to the product.[35] Such steps may lead to added purchases by present customers and/or attract new customers. As sales in the North American cruise industry flattened out, some cruise lines modified their services by adding fitness programs and offering special theme cruises (sometimes in conjunction with a professional sports team or celebrity entertainers). Playskool, a division of Hasbro Canada Inc., has modified its mature product line of children's toys, equipment, and furniture. To make the products more competitive, the company has added an anti-bacterial agent to the plastic in the manufacturing stage.[36]

Surviving the decline stage   Perhaps it is in the decline stage that a company finds its greatest challenges in life-cycle management. For instance, the advent of video camcorders and filmless cameras may hint at the decline of photographic film as a product category. Kodak Canada is trying to prevent the decline of this product while keeping pace with competitors in examining bold new products. With one such product, which Kodak calls Photo CD, consumers take pictures as they normally have; the big difference comes at the time of film processing, when the prints can be stored on a compact disc. Then they can be shown on a TV, if you have a videodisc player. Kodak is also extending the life of the traditional film product by maintaining an aggressive research and development process to improve the overall performance of each roll. Film recently released offers improved colour accuracy, saturation, detail, and sharpness. A new product designed especially for "zoom" cameras improves light sensitivity and eliminates photographic problems with light reduction.

When sales are declining, management has the following alternatives:

- Ensure that marketing and production programs are as efficient as possible.

- Prune unprofitable sizes and models. Frequently, this tactic will decrease sales but increase profits.

- "Run out" the product; that is, cut all costs to the bare minimum to maximize profitability over the limited remaining life of the product.

- Best (and toughest) of all, improve the product in a functional sense, or revitalize it in some manner. Some publishers of printed dictionaries have attempted to do this. Other reference materials, including dictionaries available on personal computers and online encyclopedias, seemed to have pushed such traditional reference materials into — or at least toward — decline. However, some publishers are working hard to maintain the appeal of the dictionary. St. Martin's Press has introduced a dictionary that includes workplace slang, 5,000 biographical references, geographical and cultural notes, and more than 4,000 illustrations. A collaboration with Microsoft, the *Encarta World English Dictionary* (**www.worldenglishdictionary.com**) is available on CD-ROM and in the traditional printed format.[37]

Encarta World English Dictionary

If one of these alternatives doesn't work, management will have to consider product abandonment. The expense of carrying profitless products goes beyond what shows up on financial statements. For example, there is a very real cost for the managerial time and effort that is diverted to terminally ill products. Management often is reluctant to discard a product, however, partly because it is easy to become attached to the product over the years. John Fluke Manufacturing began in 1928 as a provider of traditional testing and measurement devices for manufacturers. As manufacturing became more and more technologically advanced, these products became less useful and effective. In fact, they eventually became obsolete. The company is still in the same business, but the products sold for decades had to be completely discarded in favour of the development of electronic testing and measurement devices.[38]

In the final analysis, the most compelling — but often painful — alternative may be product abandonment. Knowing when and how to abandon products successfully may be as important as knowing when and how to introduce new ones. Certainly, management should develop systematic procedures for phasing out weak products.

← BACKSPACE

1. What are the four stages of the product life cycle?

2. During the _____ stage, sales and profits rise at a rapid rate.

3. The _____ stage is the most risky and expensive.

Summary

The first commandment in marketing is "Know thy customer" and the second is "Know thy product." The relative number and success of a company's new products are a prime determinant of its sales, growth rate, and profits. A firm can best serve its customers by producing and marketing need- and want-satisfying goods or services.

To manage its products effectively, a firm's marketers must understand the full meaning of *product*, which stresses that consumers are buying need and want satisfaction. Products can be classified into two basic categories — consumer products and business products. Each category is then subdivided, because a different marketing program is required for each distinct group of products.

Many strategic decisions must be made to manage a company's assortment of products effectively. To start, a firm must select strategies regarding its product mix. One decision is how to position the product relative to competing products and other products sold by the firm. Another strategic decision is whether or how to expand the product mix by adding items to a line and/or introducing new lines. Alternatively, management may elect to trade up or trade down relative to existing products. Altering the design, packaging, or other features of existing products is still another option among the strategies of selecting the best mix. The product mix also can be changed by eliminating an entire line or by simplifying the assortment within a line.

Potential new-product users go through six stages in deciding whether to adopt a new product. Adopters of an innovation can be divided into five categories, depending on how quickly they accept an innovation such as a new product. These categories are innovators, early adopters, early majority, late majority, and laggards. In addition, there usually is a group of non-adopters.

Five characteristics of an innovation seem to influence the adoption rate: relative advantage, compatibility, complexity, trialability, and observability.

Executives need to understand the concept of a product life cycle, which reflects the total sales volume for a generic product category. Each of the cycle's four stages — introduction, growth, maturity, and decline — has distinctive characteristics that have implications for marketing. Managing a product as it moves through its life cycle presents challenges and opportunities. Eventually, a product category may lack adequate acceptance from consumers; at that point, all or most companies will abandon their versions of this product.

Key Terms and Concepts

accessory equipment 198
breadth of product mix 199
business analysis 209
business product 195
consumer product 195
convenience goods 195
decline stage 218
depth of product line 199
early adopters 213
early majority 213
fabricating materials 198
growth stage 218
innovation-adopter categories 213
innovators 213
installations 198
introduction stage 217
laggards 214
late majority 214
line extension 201
manufactured parts and materials 198
market tests 210
maturity stage 218
mix extension 202
new products 205
new-product department 211

new-product development process 209
new-product strategy 209
non-adopters 214
operating supplies 198
opinion leaders 213
positioning strategies 200
product 194
product-adoption process 212
product diffusion 212
product life cycle 216
product line 199
product manager 211
product mix 199
product-mix contraction 204
product-mix expansion 201
product modification 203
product-planning committee 210
raw materials 198
shopping goods 196
specialty goods 196
stages in the product-adoption process 212
trading down 203
trading up 203
unsought goods 196
venture team 211

Questions and Problems

1. In what respects are the products different in each of the following cases?
   a. A Whirlpool dishwasher sold at an appliance store and a similar dishwasher sold by Sears under its Kenmore brand name. Assume that Whirlpool makes both dishwashers.
   b. A Sunbeam Mixmaster sold by a leading department store and the same model sold by a discount house.
   c. An airline ticket purchased through a travel agent and an identical ticket purchased directly from the airline.

2. Compare the elements of a producer's marketing mix for a convenience good with those of the mix for a specialty good.

3. In developing new products, how can a firm make sure that it is being socially responsible with regard to scarce resources and the environment?

4. Assume that the following organizations are considering additions to their product lines. In each case, does the proposed product meet the criteria for adding a new product? Explain your decisions.
   a. McDonald's: salad bar.
   b. Safeway: automobile tires.
   c. Esso: personal computers.
   d. Banks: life insurance.
   e. General Motors Canada: outboard motors for boats.

5. Describe the kinds of people who are most likely to be found in (a) the innovator category of adopters and (b) the late-majority category.

6. "Trading up and trading down are product strategies closely related to the business cycle. Firms trade up during periods of prosperity and trade down during recessions." Do you agree? Why or why not?

7. Name one category of tangible products and one category of services that you believe are in the introductory stage of their life cycles. For each product, identify the market that would consider your examples to be truly new.

8. What are two products that are in the decline stage of the life cycle? In each case, point out whether you think the decline is permanent. What recommendations do you have for rejuvenating the demand for either of these products?

9. How might a company's advertising strategies differ, depending on whether its brand of a product is in the introduction stage or the maturity stage of its life cycle?

10. Planned obsolescence is criticized as a social and economic waste because we are urged to buy things we do not like and do not need. What is your opinion? If you object to planned obsolescence, what are your recommendations for correcting the situation?

Hands-On Marketing

1. Arrange a meeting with the manager of a large retail outlet in your community. Discuss two topics with the manager:
   a. What recently introduced product has been a failure or seems destined to fail?
   b. Did this product, in retrospect, satisfy the criteria for adding a new product? (Remember to consider not just the intermediary's criteria but also applicable producer's criteria.)

2. Go to **www.honda.com** and discuss the depth and breadth of the company's product mix.

Back to the Top

Think about the example of new-product development described in the chapter opener. What do you think of the idea of offering consumers incentives to provide their opinions on new-product ideas online? Will this work for some product categories and not for others? Where will it work best? Consider the pros and cons of including trading cards in packages of condoms.

Want to get better grades, tips on how to study more effectively, and up-to-date information on happenings in the world of marketing? Then, visit the Online Learning Centre for practice tests, Study Smart software, and much more! **www.mcgrawhill.ca/college/sommers**

Interested in finding out what marketing looks like in the real world? *Marketing Magazine* is just a click away on your Online Learning Centre!

CHAPTER 8

Services Marketing and Customer Relationships

This chapter focuses on the marketing of services and the role of services in supporting marketing in all of its forms. It discusses the implications for marketing resulting from the growth in services industries and from an increased emphasis on service provision and quality across all industries. The concept of service quality and the connection between quality and profit, the linkage between human resources practices and marketing, and the development and implications of a customer-relationship focus in marketing are key issues addressed in this chapter. After studying this chapter, you should have an understanding of:

- The nature of marketing in services companies.
- The importance of services in our economy.
- The characteristics of services and the marketing implications of these characteristics.
- The value proposition in services companies.
- Issues related to planning the marketing mix for services.
- The importance of supplementary services in all firms.
- The role of customer service in driving customer satisfaction.
- The importance of service in building customer relationships.
- The prospect for improved productivity in services.
- The impact of technology in the provision of services.

Tim Hortons: Coffee Shop or Friend?

Sandra is a junior computer analyst at EMD, a Calgary-based software company specializing in software solutions for the health-care sector. She graduated from Red Deer College three years ago and moved to Calgary last year to join EMD. She and her boyfriend Jack live about five kilometres from the EMD office.

Each morning, just before 7:30, Sandra leaves for work and stops for coffee at Tim Hortons on MacLeod Trail South, just a couple of blocks from EMD's offices. She always parks her car and goes into the restaurant, never using the drive-through. She once observed to Jack, "I like to see the people who are serving me. They're always so friendly there." She also thinks that the drive-through is actually slower.

Sandra has noticed in the past few weeks that the employees seem to recognize her. Just last week, one of them (Francine, according to her name tag) smiled as Sandra approached the counter and said, "Medium, double milk, no sugar; right?" The staff members also engage in quick conversations while the coffee is being poured or the bagel toasted — conversations about the weather, how the Flames won a big game last night, or a customer's new car. Sandra has noticed that this seems to please the customers.

Sandra has also noticed that many of the tables are occupied when she drops in each morning, and that she sees many of the same faces there most days. These "regulars" are often chatting with each other or with the employees as they clean the tables. She has even seen some of these customers helping out with the clean-up when the restaurant was really busy.

Yesterday, Sandra made her usual stop at Tim Hortons on her way to work and, leaving the store in the rain, placed her coffee on the roof of her car as she unlocked the door. The coffee slid off the wet roof and fell to the ground, spilling across the parking lot. Frustrated, Sandra went back into the store, stood in line, and on reaching the counter, was greeted by Francine, who said, "You're back awfully quickly." Sandra explained what had happened and Francine went off to get her a replacement coffee. When she came back to the counter, Sandra handed her $2, but Francine refused, saying, "No, no, anyone can have an accident like that. There's no charge."

The food-services industry (of which Tim Hortons is a part) is a prime example of how tangible and intangible elements combine to create service industries. While industries such as food services, airlines, hotels, financial services, and others often provide tangible products, their main role is the provision of intangibles. In other words, their "core products" are actually services. They provide customers with an array of products and services from which to choose, and they deliver these conveniently.

Potentially, some confusion can arise in a discussion on services in marketing. So, let's clear up that confusion now. In this chapter, we will talk about services in three contexts. First, there are the services industries that we've just mentioned, whose core offering to their customers is intangible. They don't manufacture things. Second, we often refer to services that *all* companies and organizations offer to their customers. We will refer to these in this chapter as *supplementary services*. In this sense, all businesses are services businesses, because all of them potentially have to offer their customers credit terms, delivery, post-purchase service, and so on. Finally, we will discuss "service" principally in the context of how the word is used by customers. We often hear customers comment on a business where service is excellent, or of another that they'll never go back to because of terrible service. The delivery of service in this sense is an integral part of marketing, dealing mainly with how customers interact with the business and how they are treated.

Nature and Importance of Services

Over the past 30 years or so, a major change in the role of services in the Canadian economy has changed the thinking of marketers. Now, more than three-quarters of working Canadians are employed in the services sector. The services sector is widely seen as holding the key to improved economic growth and job creation in the future, as services industries currently account for more than two-thirds of Canada's gross domestic product. Virtually all growth in employment experienced in the past decade was due to growth in the services sector.

Some of the reasons for the rapid growth of this sector, which is undoubtedly the fastest-growing part of the Canadian economy, stem from major marketing environmental changes we discussed in Chapter 2. You will recall that these included such things as a more technologically oriented world and massive communication changes, as well as changing workforce demographics. Demands for and the ability to provide services have increased. For example, an entire industry has grown up around servicing the Internet. Other examples include increased requirements for eating out, since both partners in many households are in the workforce; more interest in time-saving and convenience, through home cleaning services and Internet banking, for example; and the rapid growth in television networks and home entertainment products such as DVD rentals and direct-to-home television. All of these marketing environmental changes have placed greater emphasis on services and increasing demands on the quality of service provision. Marketers have gradually changed their focus from marketing tangible goods to identifying customer needs and wants in services, either to accompany those goods or on their own.

This discussion of the growth in the services sector tends to focus on the expansion of areas that traditionally have been classified as service industries. When we consider that this service sector includes transportation, entertainment, education, health care, government services, and financial services, it is no wonder that such a large portion of the Canadian economy is included. Advances in technology that have dramatically improved productivity in goods-producing industries have contributed to a decline in the percentage of jobs in manufacturing. While this is all very important, we should not lose sight of the extremely important fact that service is an integral component of the marketing of any product, whether tangible or intangible.

Traditionally, services marketing has been thought to be different from the marketing of tangible products. In fact, however, they are essentially the same. In each case, the marketer must select and analyze target markets. Then, a marketing program must be developed. There are characteristics of services that differentiate them from tangible products, and these must be considered in developing the marketing program. All tangible goods have a service element, and as consumers place more value on the services that accompany the purchase of tangible goods, the distinctions between services marketing and tangible-goods marketing become less significant.

Definition and scope of services

We are talking about services in marketing, but do we have a clear understanding of what we mean by *services*? The term is potentially confusing because, in addition to being the core product in many organizations (such as in banking or education, where the core is intangible), services are also an important part of the marketing of tangible products. Services require supporting products (you need an airplane to provide air transportation services) and products require supporting services (delivery, credit, and repair services accompany the sale of a refrigerator). Furthermore, a company may sell a combination of goods and services. Thus, along with repair service for your car, you might buy spark plugs or an oil filter. It may be helpful to think of every offer or value proposition of a company as a mix of tangible products and intangible services located on a continuum ranging from pure products to pure services, as shown in Figure 8-1.

core services
Services that are the main purpose or object of a transaction.

To move closer to a useful understanding of services, two classes of services can be identified. In the first group are services that are the main purpose or object of a transaction. These are known as **core services**. As an example, suppose you want to rent a car from Avis. The rental car company needs a car (tangible product) to provide the rental service. But you are buying the use of the car, not the car itself. The second group consists of **supplementary services** that support or facilitate the sale of a tangible good or another service. Thus, when you buy a compact disc player, you may want technical information from a salesperson and the opportunity to pay with a credit card. Virtually every transaction involves both tangible and intangible elements. It is useful to distinguish between situations where the core of what is being exchanged is intangible — this is the situation that we refer to as the marketing of services — and the supplementary services and general level of customer service that accompanies the sale of practically everything that we buy.

supplementary services
Services that support or facilitate the sale of a tangible good or another service.

services
Identifiable, intangible activities that are sometimes the main object of a transaction and at other times support the sale of tangible products or other services.

Consequently, our definition of services in this chapter is as follows: **Services** are identifiable, intangible activities that are sometimes the main object of a transaction and at other times support the sale of tangible products or other services. In the first part of the chapter, we will focus primarily on the marketing of services that are the principal objective of a transaction, as in financial, entertainment, hotel, and car rental services. Then, we will turn our attention to the very important services associated with the marketing of every product, whether tangible or intangible. These include delivery, after-sale service, credit, and so on. Finally, marketers are realizing more and more that one of the most effective ways to compete and to differentiate one's company from the competition is to offer excellent service. This topic is approached principally from the view of the customer and addresses mainly the interaction between the company and its customers, how quickly they are served, whether

Figure 8-1:
A Goods-Services Continuum

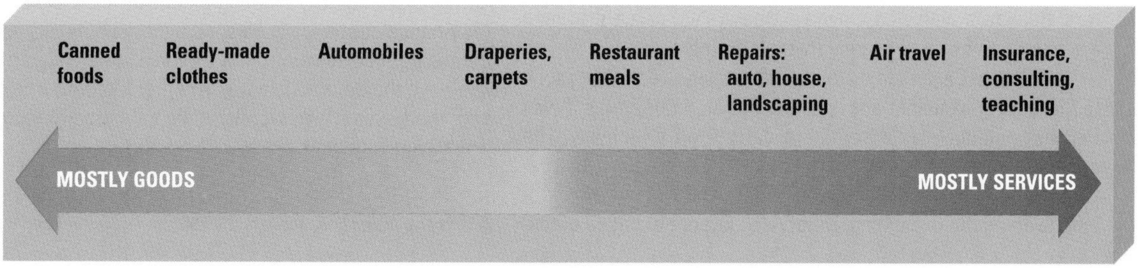

| Canned foods | Ready-made clothes | Automobiles | Draperies, carpets | Restaurant meals | Repairs: auto, house, landscaping | Air travel | Insurance, consulting, teaching |

MOSTLY GOODS ←————————————————————————————————→ MOSTLY SERVICES employees are helpful, whether calls are returned, and generally how customers are treated in their dealings with the firm.

We are concerned initially, then, with the services marketed by business or professional firms with profit-making motives — **commercial services**. Other important services are provided by not-for-profit organizations, such as churches, universities and colleges, arts and cultural organizations, and the government. A useful classification of commercial services by industry is as follows:

commercial services

The services marketed by business or professional firms with profit-making motives, as compared with the services offered by public and not-for-profit organizations.

- *Accommodations* (includes rental of hotel and motel rooms, apartments, houses, and cottages).

- *Household operations* (includes utilities, home repairs, painting and decorating, repairs of equipment in the home, landscaping, and household cleaning).

- *Recreation and entertainment* (includes rental and repair of equipment used to participate in recreation and entertainment activities; admission to all entertainment, recreation, and amusement events).

- *Food services* (includes restaurants, fast-food outlets, and catering services).

- *Personal care* (includes laundry, dry-cleaning, and beauty care).

- *Medical and other health care* (includes all medical services, dental, nursing, hospitalization, optometry, and other health care).

- *Education* (includes courses taken at a community college, university, or private college).

- *Business and other professional services* (includes legal, accounting, marketing research, management consulting, and computer services).

- *Insurance, banking, and other financial services* (includes personal and business insurance, credit and loan services, investment counselling, and tax services).

MARKETING AT WORK 8-1: STRATEGY

Do It for His Health's Sake

With the slogan "His health in your hands," British women are being encouraged to examine their partners for signs of male cancer. In a campaign launched by the NetDoctor health information Web site (www.netdoctor.co.uk) and the Institute of Cancer Research Everyman health charity, posters bearing the slogan and featuring a pair of walnuts can be seen in women's washrooms throughout the United Kingdom. The posters also provide advice about obtaining more information.

The appeal to women to carry out the sensitive examination recognizes that not only do few men examine themselves, but they are also not too happy about being examined by their doctors. Research indicates, however, that only 3 percent of men are averse to being examined by their partners.

While this is a personal and sensitive topic and the approach to increasing examinations is a little out of the ordinary, it was felt that humour was essential to carry it off effectively. The goal is to carry the message and encourage regular testicular examination to detect lumps or abnormalities, regardless of who is doing the examining. Ninety-six percent of cases of tes-

ticular cancer, which affects mainly men 20 to 35, can be cured if detected early enough.

The added benefit of this approach is the free publicity and word of mouth it generates, and while there were some embarrassed and nervous giggles from journalists at the campaign's launch, people realize it is educational and important in saving lives. The campaign recognizes that British women are more influential in making health decisions in the family and are more likely to consult doctors.

Other attempts in the United Kingdom to raise awareness of male cancers include renowned photographer Lord Lichfield, a cousin of the Queen, shooting photos of top soccer players with their hands strategically clasped over their "family jewels," as if defending themselves from a free kick. The billboard read: "Do You Have the Balls to Join In?" Another featured a pair of breasts with the tag line: "No wonder male cancers are ignored. These are all you ever think about."

SOURCE: Adapted from Lee Lester, "Male Cancer Gets Female Touch," *Marketing Magazine*, January 29, 2001, p. 6.

- *Transportation* (includes freight and passenger services on airplanes, trains, and ferries; automobile repairs and rentals).

- *Communications* (includes telephone, facsimile, Internet, e-mail, and specialized business communications services).

Importance of services

North America has become a true service economy. According to 2001 Canadian statistics, 11,214,200 people (74.4 percent of our labour force) were employed in the services-producing sector, compared to 3,862,500 (25.6 percent) in the goods-producing sector.[1] In addition, well over 70 percent of the country's gross domestic product is accounted for by services. Notably, service jobs typically hold up better during a recession than do jobs in industries that produce tangible products.

The highest-paying jobs in the services sector include a mixture of transportation, the public sector, and financial services. The absolute top dogs of the services sector work in brokerage houses and stock exchanges.[2] The rapid growth of technology industries has created a corresponding explosion in the number of technology jobs. For example, the Internet and other advances in computer systems have created a need for systems analysts, program co-ordinators, network support specialists, systems support specialists, technical writers, and instructional technologists, among others.

The growth in the market for **personal services** is at least partially explained by the relative prosperity and increasing standard of living that Canadians have enjoyed. It could be argued that many of the tangible products that we buy tend to be necessity purchases. People buy food, housing, clothing, and automobiles to meet essential needs. On the other hand, many services tend to be purchased, by end-consumers at least, from discretionary spending. The consumer usually purchases such things as travel, entertainment, restaurant meals, and home cleaning services after the essentials have been paid for. This spending has increased as the standard of living has increased.

The Canadian population today is more sophisticated than the previous generation and more active in leisure and entertainment activities. Increased global transportation systems have resulted in a high-growth travel industry, and advanced communications systems have stimulated increased awareness of travel destinations. Affluence and lifestyle changes have contributed significantly to this rapid growth in personal services.

The growth of **business services** may be attributed to the fact that business has become increasingly complex, specialized, and competitive. As a consequence, management has been forced to call in experts to provide services in marketing research, taxation, advertising, labour relations, and many other areas. Technology has also played a major role in the expansion of demand for business services. Even with relatively high rates of unemployment in parts of Canada, jobs in high-technology fields may still go unfilled because of a shortage of trained individuals to fill these vacancies.

Characteristics of services

The special nature of services stems from a number of characteristics that distinguish services from tangible products. These features create special marketing challenges and opportunities for those companies whose core product is intangible. As a result, services firms often require marketing programs that are different from those found in the marketing of tangible goods.

Intangibility   Because services are intangible, it is impossible for customers to sample — taste, feel, see, hear, or smell — a service before they buy it. As a result, there is often some degree of uncertainty or risk associated with a decision to eat at a restaurant or stay in a hotel

intangibility

A characteristic of a service indicating that it has no physical attributes and, as a result, is impossible for customers to taste, feel, see, hear, or smell before buying.

inseparability

A characteristic of a service indicating that it cannot be separated from the creator/seller of the service.

for the first time. Unlike a physical product such as a bicycle or DVD player, we can't examine or test-drive a service. As a result of the intangibility of services, a company's promotional program should portray the benefits to be derived from the service, rather than emphasizing the service itself, so prospective customers can have some idea of the service before deciding to buy. Four promotional strategies that may be used to suggest the benefits associated with services are as follows.[3]

● *Visualization:* For example, banks that offer Internet banking services depict the convenience and freedom of 24-hour banking by showing clients at home late at night in their comfy clothes doing their banking or on holiday, sitting on the beach with their laptops.

● *Association:* Connect the service with a tangible object, person, or place. The Australian airline, Qantas, uses a cuddly koala in its advertising to project a warm, friendly image of Australia. Prudential Insurance suggests stability and security with its logo depicting the Rock of Gibraltar, a landmark often referred to as a symbol of stability and strength.

● *Physical representation:* GM Goodwrench uses the image of its service representatives. Ads show clean-cut employees in their familiar, freshly pressed black-and-red uniforms beaming a warm smile to communicate trustworthiness, dependability, and cleanliness.

● *Documentation:* Midas muffler shops have used the company's warranty in print advertisements. This represents the company's commitment to the customer and supports the claim of performance, dependability, and customer satisfaction.

What exactly do MetLife customers associate with Snoopy?

WE CAN POINT YOU IN THE RIGHT DIRECTION.

When it comes to planning your future, we believe a little guidance goes a long way. So with the help of nationally recognized authorities, MetLife's Consumer Education Center has created the Life Advice℠ series. It's an information resource that can help you plan for more than sixty important events in your life, events that can have a major impact on your health, property and financial well-being.

Each Life Advice brochure includes practical information on the issues involved, to help

you make sense of it all. Our Directory lists Life Advice pamphlets on a wide range of topics such as saving for college, getting married, becoming a parent, buying a car or home, starting a business and planning for your retirement.

They're all significant events where MetLife's Life Advice can point you in the right direction.

For your free Life Advice Directory, just visit the MetLife Web site at www.metlife.com or call 1-800-MetLife today.

INSURANCE · MUTUAL FUNDS · ANNUITIES · EMPLOYEE BENEFITS · PENSIONS · INVESTMENT MANAGEMENT

GET MET. IT PAYS.®
1-800-MetLife®

Inseparability Services typically cannot be separated from the creator or seller of the service. Moreover, many services are created, delivered, and consumed simultaneously, so we can't separate production from consumption. For example, dentists and hairstylists create and dispense their services at the same time, and they require the presence of the consumer for the services to be performed. Because of this inseparability feature, consumers are usually directly involved in production and marketing in services firms, and customers receive and consume services at the production site. Consequently, customers' opinions regarding a service frequently are formed through their contact in face-to-face or telephone meetings with service personnel and their impressions of the physical surroundings of the company's premises.

From a marketing standpoint, inseparability frequently means that direct sale is the only possible channel of distribution. Also, a seller's services cannot be sold in very many markets, because one person can repair only so many cars in a day or treat only so many patients. This characteristic limits the scale of operations in a firm.

The inseparability of a service from the people providing it has important implications for companies that are operating in services businesses. This includes not only those companies in true "service" industries, such as financial services, entertainment, hotels, and restaurants, but also those that must pay particular attention to the services that support the marketing of their tangible products. For example, although Eastern Bakeries is technically a manufacturer of bakery products such as breads and cakes, it is also in the business of making sure that its products are delivered on time and in the quantity and condition the customer ordered.

Heterogeneity   It is impossible for a services company to standardize output. Each "unit" of the service is somewhat different from other "units" of the same service. This is principally so because of the individualized approach that service providers take to the production of a service. Because most services are delivered by people, service delivery is prone to the differences that exist across human beings. Because we are all different and our interaction with other people is affected by personality, mood, and a number of other factors, service delivery and quality are bound to vary considerably. For example, an airline does not give the same quality of service on each flight. All repair jobs done by an auto mechanic are not of equal quality.

An added complication is the fact that it is often difficult to judge the quality of a service. It is particularly difficult to forecast quality in advance of buying a service. A person pays to see a ball game without knowing whether it will be exciting or dull. Some companies are able to address this by allowing customers to sample a service before buying — for example, cable television companies will give new subscribers a free trial month's service on new channels. However, it is difficult for most services companies to provide samples. How can you sample dental services, for example?

Both dentist and patient have to be present for this service to be delivered.

heterogeneity
A characteristic of a service indicating that each unit is somewhat different from other units of the same service.

The **heterogeneity** of services is of concern to service providers, but the ability to deliver customer satisfaction is further complicated by the fact that customer expectations are not at all consistent. Although a student on a short lunch break may spend only 15 minutes grabbing a quick meal at a restaurant near campus, the same student may take more than an hour to enjoy a pizza with a friend after a Saturday night movie. In the first case, the customer wants to be served as quickly as possible; in the second, the customer is prepared to wait a little longer for service. Because service expectations differ across customers and even over time for the same customers, it is very difficult for service businesses to standardize their level of service.

In recent years, some services companies have turned to technology in an attempt to standardize the type and quality of service provided. Unfortunately, this is at the expense of losing personal contact and the ability to respond to customers' questions or concerns. Nevertheless, some technology-delivered services, such as those provided by ATMs, telephone banking, and self-service gas stations, can become standardized and are accepted by a large number of customers. Canada's telephone companies have automated directory-assistance services and have introduced a voice-response system for handling third-party collect calls.

While such technology-based services achieve standardization of service, in part by delegating much of the service provision or delivery to the customers themselves, some risks are inherent in their use. Some customers may resent having to do all of the work, especially when they are paying for the service. Also, some customers simply prefer to deal with real people and become confused or irritated when they encounter technology. Finally, in some industries, management is faced with the dilemma of not being able to keep in touch with customers or to establish relationships with them, since the customers are dealing primarily with machines or computers.

Perishability and fluctuating demand   Services are highly perishable and they cannot be stored. Unused telephone time, empty seats in a stadium, and idle mechanics in a garage all represent business that is lost forever. Furthermore, the market for services fluctuates considerably by season, by day of the week, and by hour of the day. Most ski lifts are idle all summer and golf courses go unused in the winter. The use of city buses fluctuates greatly during the day.

perishability

A characteristic of a service indicating that it is highly perishable and cannot be stored.

There are notable exceptions to this generalization regarding the **perishability** and storage of services. In health and life insurance, for example, the service is purchased by a person or a company. Then it is held by the insurance company (the seller) until needed by the buyer or the beneficiary. This holding constitutes a type of storage. Similarly, many services generally considered to be "public utilities" are able to store services until they are needed. For example, telephone and electricity services are available on demand. We can access them whenever we need them. Because of this, there is a very real probability that consumers will take such services for granted, simply because they are always there. This causes potential problems for companies that are marketing such services, because it makes it difficult for them to interest their customers in buying more or in adopting new services. It certainly creates a challenge for the establishment of close customer relationships.

The combination of perishability and **fluctuating demand** offers planning, pricing, and promotion challenges to services marketing managers. Some organizations have developed new uses for idle plant capacity during off-seasons; for example, during the summer, several ski resorts operate their ski lifts for hikers and sightseers who want access to higher elevations. Advertising and creative pricing are also used to stimulate demand during slack periods. Hotels offer lower prices and family packages on weekends, for example, and telephone companies offer lower rates at nights and on weekends.

◀ BACKSPACE

1. What is the difference between core services and supplementary services?
2. Define *services*.
3. Education and insurance are both examples of _____ services.

- -

The Value Proposition for Services

For companies that operate in the services sector, the development of a value proposition that customers will find attractive is a challenge, made all the more so by the characteristics of services that we have just discussed. We think it is important at this stage to clarify the three levels of the value proposition that pertain in services organizations. It is also important to note that this discussion is not only important in companies that have services as their core offer to customers, that is, those that operate in what are generally referred to as services industries. The concept of the **services value proposition** is also critically important for non-businesses, particularly organizations that operate in the not-for-profit sector, such as symphony orchestras, theatre companies, and colleges and universities, as these too provide services to their target segments.

services value proposition

The value proposition of a services company, which must include elements of the service provided to customers and the emotional value created.

The three levels of the value proposition that pertain especially in companies and organizations that operate in the services and not-for-profit sectors are presented in Figure 8-2. We

Figure 8-2:

The Services Value
Proposition

Figure 8-2:

The Services Value
Proposition

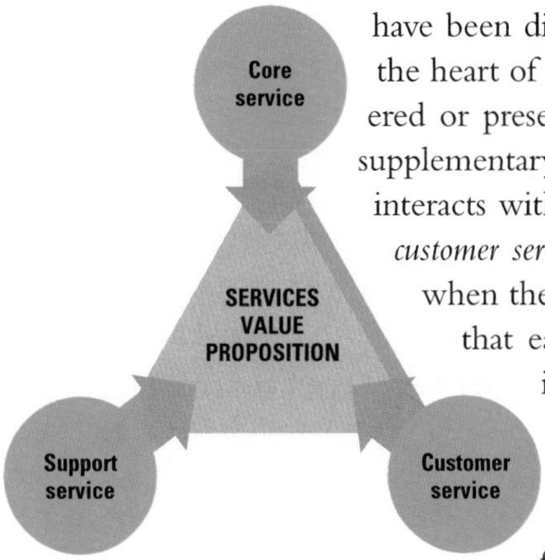

have been discussing characteristics of the core service that lies at the heart of the value proposition. This core service must be delivered or presented to the customer using a number of support or supplementary services. Finally, the way in which the company interacts with, treats, or serves its customers is often referred to as *customer service* and is what customers generally are referring to when they talk about "service." What is important, of course, is that each of these components of the value proposition is important in creating value for the customer and in contributing to customer satisfaction.

It is also important to remind ourselves that what principally distinguishes services companies from those that operate in a product-based environment is the intangibility of the core offering. While companies such as Burger King, Best Western, and Amazon.ca are considered services companies, companies that make things, such as Kraft Foods, Honda, and Burton Snowboards, are not. The businesses in this latter group are considered to be manufacturers, whose core products are tangible. But it is critical to appreciate that *all* companies must be aware of the implications of being successful at the second and third levels of our services value proposition. *All* companies and organizations must have effective supplementary services to surround and support their core offerings, and all must deliver effective customer service in order to achieve customer satisfaction.

The remainder of this chapter will be devoted to examining in greater detail each of these three levels of the services value proposition.

Strategic Aspects of the Services Core

Because of the characteristics of services (notably, intangibility), the development of a marketing program in an organization that has services as its core offering is often challenging. Nevertheless, as we have observed before, the fundamental principles of marketing are the same, regardless of what is being marketed. Ultimately, we are interested in achieving long-term customer satisfaction. Let's consider some of the strategic implications of putting a marketing program together in the services sector.

Understanding the customers of services

Marketers of services should understand the customers who buy their services. What are their buying motives? Sellers must determine buying patterns for their services: When, where, and how do customers buy, who does the buying, and who makes the buying decisions? The psychological determinants of buying behaviour — attitudes, perceptions, and personality — become even more important when marketing services rather than tangible goods, because typically we cannot touch, smell, or taste a service offering. This has implications for how consumers buy and for the need to gain a complete understanding.

For consumers, the purchase of services may be more problematic and potentially risky than is the case for tangible products, which can be examined and even tested before purchase. As a result, customers of services tend to rely more on conversations with and referrals from other customers than they do when they are buying tangible products, where more marketing information is generally available.

Planning core services

Launching new services is just as important to a service company as the launch of new products is to a goods-marketing firm. Similarly, the improvement of existing services and elimination of

PetCare Insurance

unwanted, unprofitable services are also key goals. Product planning and development has its counterpart in the marketing program of a services organization. Management must select appropriate strategies based on answers to these questions:

● What services products will be offered?

● What will be the breadth and depth of the services mix?

● How will the services be positioned? What attributes will they have?

Services offering Many firms have become successful by identifying a previously unsatisfied consumer need and then developing a service to address that need. Examples of this are everywhere. How about pet insurance covering 3,500 illnesses and all types of accidents? PetCare Insurance Brokers (**www.petcareinsurance.com**) will cover the family's cat or dog from head to tail for about $10 per month. In a society that is placing increased importance, and resources, on the family pet, many see this insurance as being well worth the money.

When it comes to youth, the wireless industry is banking on the prediction that they will want to! Canadian carriers are investing in many new services to capture the discretionary income of this target market: intercarrier capability, Web content-related programs, and text messaging. Rogers AT&T has even launched a Web site that lists definitions for short text.[4] When companies are developing such services, attention must be paid (as with tangible product development) to addressing customer needs and to knowing what will appeal to the customer.

Service-mix strategies Several of the product-mix strategies discussed in Chapter 7 can be employed effectively by services marketers. Consider the strategy of expanding or enhancing the line of services offered. This is often referred to as a process of adding value for the customer. In fact, one of the most effective ways of adding value to existing products and services is by adding new support services. Many hotel chains and even some "bed and breakfasts" have added desks, fax machines, and computer data ports to their rooms and provide photocopier and printer services on request for business guests. Rental car companies offer no-smoking cars and GPS, and rent cellular telephones. Most now have computerized the process of returning rental cars at airports to speed travellers on their way.

Managing the life cycle of a service is another strategy that is being practised more and more by services marketers. Recognizing that the competitive credit card industry is in its maturity stage, Canadian banks have explored new ways of gaining consumer popularity. The result in many cases is that consumers now carry several credit cards when they had only one previously. One of the many variations on the VISA card is the CIBC Shoppers Optimum VISA (CIBC Pharmaprix Optimum VISA in Québec), a co-branded, loyalty-based card from CIBC and Shoppers Drug Mart that allows holders of the VISA card to earn five Shoppers Optimum Points for every dollar spent using the card. When used at Shoppers Drug Mart stores in conjunction with the Shoppers Optimum card (which offers 10 Shoppers Optimum points for every dollar spent), the

Tiger Woods has teamed up with American Express — he's featured on a special credit card that offers benefits to golfers. How does using Tiger's image enhance the appeal of American Express to a younger generation?

cardholder receives 15 points for every dollar spent. These points can then be redeemed for free products at Shoppers Drug Mart stores. American Express has teed up with Tiger Woods to offer a card featuring the superstar golfer. Features of the new AMEX card include a free round of golf each year and discounts on golf equipment and apparel, as well as the usual membership reward program.[5] The Bank of Montreal introduced the Star Trek MasterCard — the only credit card approved by the United Federation of Planets. These varied programs have all served to extend the life of the credit card by developing new uses and increased usage.

Possibly one of the most difficult decisions relating to the services mix deals with deleting services from the line. Often, it is difficult to know what it costs to deliver particular services. As a result, management often is unable to determine which services are profitable and which are not. Deciding which to keep and which to drop therefore may be more difficult than it is for a firm that manufactures tangible products.

Service features In some respects, product planning is easier for services than for tangible goods. Packaging and labelling really are non-existent in services marketing. However, other features, such as branding and quality management, for example, present greater challenges for services industries.

Branding of services is a problem because maintaining consistent quality (a responsibility of brand ownership) is difficult. Also, a brand cannot be physically attached to a label or to the service itself. A services marketer's goal should be to create an effective brand image. In most successful services companies, the company or organization name is the brand name. Thus, customers become loyal to Tim Hortons or to Air Canada or to Hilton. Although there are some exceptions, most services companies have not been successful in creating strong brands for their individual service products.

The strategy to achieve a strong services brand image is to develop a total theme that includes more than just a good brand name. To implement this strategy, the following tactics may be used:

- ***Include a tangible component as part of the brand image*** — like the elephant of Jumbo Video or the torn movie ticket for Blockbuster Video, the Greyhound dog suggesting the speed of the Greyhound Bus Line, or the koala of Qantas Airlines.

- ***Tie in a slogan with the brand*** — for instance, Jumbo Video's "Home of the Guarantee" or the American Express slogan "Membership has its privileges."

- ***Use a distinctive colour scheme*** — such as the red-and-yellow signage for McDonald's or the blue and gold of the Royal Bank.

Pricing of services

In the marketing of services, nowhere is there a greater need for managerial creativity and skill than in the area of pricing. Since services are intangible, perishable, usually cannot be stored, and often have a fluctuating demand, there are significant pricing implications. To further complicate the situation, customers may perform some services themselves (auto and household repairs, for example).

Because of the heterogeneity and difficulty of standardizing quality, most services are highly differentiated. Also, it is virtually impossible to have complete market information; customers often have considerable difficulty assessing the quality of the service and, therefore, the perceived value that they have received. As an example, consider the issue of auto repairs. Many customers of auto dealers and repair shops do not understand how cars work, particularly with the on-board computer systems that are in most cars today. As a result, they are unable to assess whether they have received good value from a repair job. It's little wonder that auto repair businesses bear the brunt of large numbers of consumer complaints.

Distribution of services

franchising
A type of contractual vertical marketing system that involves a continuing relationship in which a franchiser (the parent company) provides the right to use a trademark plus management assistance in opening and operating a business in return for financial considerations from a franchisee (the owner of the individual business unit).

Geeks on Call
Mad Science

Traditionally, most services have been sold directly from producer to consumer or business user. No intermediaries are used when the service cannot be separated from the seller or when the service is created and marketed simultaneously. For example, medical care, auto repair, and other personal services are typically sold without intermediaries, simply because the service could not exist without the people who are providing it. Not using intermediaries does limit the geographic markets that service providers can reach, because they have to be there in person to provide the service. But it also enables sellers to personalize their services and get quick, detailed customer feedback.

The only other frequently used distribution channel for services involves one agent intermediary. Some type of agent or broker is often used in the marketing of securities, travel arrangements, entertainment, and housing rentals. Sometimes dealers are trained in production of the service and then are **franchised** to sell it. This is the case with Geeks on Call (**www.callthegeeks.com**), which supplies on-site computer services such as repairs, networking, and one-on-one training, or Mad Science (**www.madscience.com**), which offers over 1,000 hours of customized experiments for schools, parties, camps, and community events.

In recent years, some firms have realized that the characteristic of inseparability is not an insurmountable limitation to a seller's distribution system. With a little imagination, a services marketer can broaden distribution considerably. Let's look at some examples.

The use of intermediaries is another way to expand distribution of services. Banks have arranged for companies to deposit employees' paycheques directly into their bank accounts. The employer thus becomes an intermediary in distributing the bank's service. Insurance firms have broadened distribution by setting up vending machines in airports. Canada Post now operates post offices in drugstores across Canada. Canada's lottery corporations sell their tickets through kiosks in shopping malls and through thousands of retail agents in convenience stores and gasoline stations across the country. Courier services such as Purolator and Federal Express have made it convenient for their customers by installing drop boxes on street corners in the downtown business districts of major cities.

McDonald's uses franchising to reach consumers around the world.

The characteristic of intangibility essentially eliminates physical-distribution problems for most service producers. For example, other than office and other supplies, accountants and consultants have no physical inventory to store or handle. However, not all service producers are free from physical-distribution headaches. Those who are unable to deliver their services without the support of tangible products still have to address issues relating to physical storage and logistics. Retailing, for example, is considered to be a service industry, but retailers certainly have to deal with inventory issues and questions relating to location.

Many companies have succeeded in separating some services from the people who provide them by delegating the delivery of their services to technology. While we normally associate the concept of a vending machine with the ones that supply candy bars and soft drinks, much of the equipment and technology that deliver services are essentially service vending machines. When we make a telephone call from a payphone, we are using a vending machine of sorts. Similarly, ATMs supply financial services in much the same way that "Coke machines" supply soft drinks. When you use a coin-operated photocopying machine in your college library, you are buying a service.

Promotion of services

Several forms of promotion are used extensively in services marketing, but because services are often inseparable from the people who provide them, personal selling and word of mouth play a dominant role. For example, any employee of a service firm who comes in contact with a customer is, in effect, part of that firm's sales force. In addition to a regular sales force, customer-contact personnel might include airline flight attendants, receptionists, couriers, bank tellers, and ushers at theatres. We use the term **service encounter** to describe a customer's interaction with any service employee or with any tangible element such as a service's physical surroundings (bank, ballpark, law office). Customers often form opinions of a company and its service on the basis of service encounters, and they talk with their friends and associates about those encounters. Consequently, it is essential that management recognize the strategic importance of service encounters and prepare contact personnel and physical surroundings accordingly. A key step in preparing to sell a service is to provide sales training and service information for contact personnel, impressing on them the importance of their role.

For years, of course, advertising has been used extensively in many service fields — hotels, transportation, and insurance, for example. What is newer is the use of advertising by professional-services firms, including legal, accounting, physiotherapy, and chiropractic. Previously, professional associations in such fields prohibited advertising on the grounds that it was unethical. While some associations still control the type of advertising that may be done, the promotion of professional services is much more open and accepted than ever before.

service encounter
In services marketing, a customer's interaction with any service employee or with any tangible element, such as a service's physical surroundings.

Supplementary Services

All organizations, regardless of the nature of their core product or service, must offer a range of supplementary services. These are additional to the core and have a very important role to play in enhancing the customer's perception of the core and in contributing to customer satisfaction. They are support services that relate to the provision of information, the physical delivery and care of the core product, the processing of transactions, and generally to making it easy and less frustrating for the customer.

Such supplementary services are essential in enabling the company to add value to its core product or service. There is little point in having a superbly crafted and excellent-quality product if the company is unable to deliver it to customers in a timely and convenient way. Essentially, the supplementary services that we are discussing in this section apply to all types of organizations, and they are essential to the successful management of interaction with customers. In many

The hours that a retailer's store is open comprise part of the supplementary services that it offers customers.

cases, these supplementary services are critical to achieving customer satisfaction, even more important than the core product itself. This is particularly true when the core product is in danger of becoming a commodity. For example, in financial services, virtually all banks offer approximately the same services. There is very little different in a mortgage or a savings account at the Royal Bank of Canada as compared with CIBC or Scotiabank. The supplementary services made available are what is important in differentiating one from the other and in attracting customers.

We can divide the range of supplementary services offered into a number of categories. The first of these relates to the provision and management of information. Today, many companies provide information to customers through their Web sites, including where to buy their products and how to order them or to make reservations. Organizations have to make it easy for customers and others to communicate and interact with them. Services relating to the company's Web site, telephone system, and e-mail are all critical in contributing to that ease of interaction. Accurate and timely billing systems, provision of credit, and customer feedback processes are also part of the communications-information component of supplementary services.

Other supplementary services relate to access and convenience; thus, the hours that a retailer's store is open and WestJet's flight schedule are part of the services that surround the core. So, too, is FedEx's pick-up and delivery schedule, the location of its drop boxes, and the planning of routes. Auto dealers offer courtesy wagons to deliver customers to their homes and offices after they have dropped off their cars for service. Airport hotels have shuttle buses that meet guests at the airport to bring them to the hotel.

Figure 8-3:

Types of Supplementary Services

Provision and management of information

Access and convenience

Services that pertain to physical products

Provision of choice

Reduction of risk and anxiety

Physical surroundings in which service is delivered

Manufacturers in particular offer a range of supplementary services that pertain to the physical objects they provide. General Electric, for example, must have a distribution system that allows for the delivery and installation of its major appliances. The company must also put into place post-purchase services, including repair and the provision of information to customers when things go wrong. Many companies now use the Internet to allow customers to troubleshoot problems themselves before calling the manufacturer's toll-free number for assistance. The call centre itself is, of course, a supplementary service.

Choice is a large part of supplementary services. Retailers and others must offer customers a wide enough range of options from which to choose or they will go to the competition. Honda must manage its inventory of new cars and parts to make sure that they are in the right place at the right time to meet customer demand. Menu planning is part of the supplementary service offered by restaurants.

Supplementary services also contribute to the reduction of risk and anxiety. Many manufacturers and some services companies offer their customers guarantees and warranties. Air Canada allows you to check its Web site to see if the flight you are planning to meet is on time. On its Web site (**www.fedex.com**), Federal Express allows you to track a package that you have sent to Australia as it makes its way across Canada, to Los Angeles, then to Hawaii, and on to Sydney, and actually see the signature of the person who signs for it in Melbourne.

There are often physical aspects to the provision of supplementary services. Doctor's offices, airport lounges, and bank branches must be designed and operated to make waiting tolerable or even enjoyable. Comfortable seating, current magazines, water coolers, and acceptable music are all part of the services, as are washroom facilities and parking. Movie theatres have expanded the range of services that surround the core (the movies) in recent years to include parking and food courts.

Supplementary services should be viewed, therefore, as an essential component of the value proposition of a firm. Not only do they support and enhance the core, but also they often become the factors that lead to a customer deciding on one company versus another. We often deal with the company that offers the best choice, that is more conveniently located, or that is open when we want to deal with them.

BACKSPACE

1. What is meant by *services value proposition*?
2. Why is pricing difficult in services marketing?
3. What does the term *service encounter* mean?

Customer Service

When customers speak of "service," they are usually referring to how they are treated in their interaction with a business or to the processes to which they are exposed in dealing with a firm. So, while standing in a slow-moving queue on a busy day at the auto parts counter in the local Canadian Tire, one aspiring home mechanic might turn to the person waiting next to her in line and observe, "The service here is terrible!" Or, having looked without success for someone to offer advice on the various models of lawnmowers available at Sears, an impatient gardener might complain, "What do you have to do to get some service around here?" Conversely, when you encounter a retail salesperson who offers to check with another of the company's stores to see if she can locate that dress in your size and then arranges to have it delivered for you, your comment probably relates to the fact that you *feel* that you were treated well and received great service.

customer service

That part of the company's value proposition that addresses how the company interacts with its customers, as compared with the core service or services that it offers.

We are dealing here with **customer service**, or more correctly with service as defined by the customer, with how that customer interacts with a company and its employees, and the processes, systems, and procedures that are encountered along the way — service encounters. Some people also refer to them as "moments of truth," as they represent opportunities for a company to impress or disappoint the customer. These encounters represent the situation where the "rubber hits the road," in that the company's reputation is on the line and it either performs or it doesn't.

Service encounters do not have to involve in-person meetings with employees, as companies are increasingly interacting with their customers through technology such as the Internet, banking machines, self-service gas pumps, and telephone-based interactive ordering systems for concert tickets. All of these are service encounters, as they involve the customer-service experience at the hands of the company.

service quality

The value that consumers perceive they are receiving from their purchase of services; generally very difficult to measure.

Service quality   Quality, whether of tangible products or intangible services, is difficult to define, measure, control, and communicate. Yet, the quality of the service provided to customers is critical to a firm's success. Two airlines each fly a Boeing 747 on the Toronto–Paris route for approximately the same fare, two auto repair shops each use Ford or Chrysler parts and charge the same price, and two banks each offer the same investment accounts at identical interest rates. Assuming similar times and locations, **service quality** is the only factor that differentiates the offerings in each of these situations.

However difficult it may be to define the concept of service quality, management must understand one thing: Quality is defined by the consumer and not by the company that provides the service. Your hairstylist may be delighted with the job she did on your hair, but if you think your hair looks terrible, then the service quality was poor. What counts is what *consumers* think about a service. Service quality that does not meet customer expectations can result in lost sales from present customers and a failure to attract new ones. Consequently, it is imperative that management strives to maintain consistent service quality at or above the level of consumer expectations. Yet, it is sometimes virtually impossible to standardize service quality, that is, to maintain consistency in service output. No two service encounters are identical.

As part of managing service quality, many companies have implemented an ongoing quality-improvement program that monitors the level and consistency of service quality. They also measure the quality of the service they provide as perceived by their customers. Many businesses have existed for years under the assumption that management knew what customers wanted and how they wanted to be treated. The most successful companies have now abandoned that way of thinking and have subscribed to the idea that "Good service is whatever the customer says it is." A program to measure the perceived quality of a business's service therefore must start by defining the aspects of the contact with the company that the customer considers to be most important.

Let's illustrate the components of service by considering customers of Bell Canada and other telephone companies that are interested, first of all, in ensuring that their telephone systems work properly, that calls go through, and that reception is clear (the "core product" aspects of the service). In fact, as technology has improved in the telecommunications industry, customers do not expect their telephone systems ever to fail — the core service in this industry is largely taken for granted by customers; they almost never think about it.

The next component of service relates to the processes and support services that the telephone company has in place to deliver and support the core service — telephone bills, installation of new lines, telephone directories, directory-assistance services, and optional vertical services such as voice mail and call forwarding.

Finally, we must also appreciate that the quality of service as perceived by customers is related to the way in which employees of the company interact with their customers — whether operators are courteous and polite, whether salespeople know the technology, and how complaints are resolved. This not only relates to such aspects of personal service as courtesy, politeness, and product knowledge, but also to the ultimate effect of service — how the customer is made to feel while dealing with the service provider.

It may be suggested that as the nature of service moves farther away from the actual product or service and more toward the "people" aspects of service, the less control management has over the delivery and, therefore, the quality of the service offered. For example, WestJet can control the actual flight from Calgary to Vancouver (the core service, getting passengers from one city to another). Barring unforeseen circumstances, management can also control, to a greater or lesser extent, the services that support that core product: frequency of flights, departure and arrival times, the number of ticket agents at the counter, baggage-handling systems, and meal or beverage service.

Management loses much more control over the details of the service provided at the interface between customer and employee — how the passenger agent greets the customer at the

MARKETING AT WORK — 8-2: STRATEGY

When a Cocktail Onion Becomes a Service Experience

It all started with a simple request — instead of the usual olives in his dry martini, our friend decided to try something different and ordered cocktail onions. The waitress smiled and sped away, only to quickly return with a panicked look on her previously cheery face — the bartender had run out of these sweet little garnishes. Oh, no!

After some teasing that the International Tribunal of Bartending Arts and the Canadian Cocktail Board would have to be notified of this catastrophe, it was agreed that the usual would suffice — olives would have to do.

A few minutes later, she reappeared, this time accompanied by a young man carrying a tray with a shimmering martini and something under a white linen napkin. He apologized for the confusion, saying that he wanted to personally deliver the drink as he managed to find a couple of the missing cocktail condiments previously requested. With an elaborate gesture, he unveiled two onions the size of softballs, decorated with a dozen little paper umbrellas and various other garnishes.

Everyone at the table, as well as at the next table, exploded in laughter and then applause in appreciation for the imagination and effort shown by the restaurant employees. It was a wonderful joke, done in the right place at the right time in the right way.

But what was it really? It was a positive brand experience that differentiated this restaurant from hundreds of others in the city. All due to the response of a couple of employees who wanted to try to make right something that was beyond their control — a small service faux pas turned into a memorable experience for several from one customer's minor disappointment.

Such responses by committed, well-selected, and prepared staff help to reduce the impact of service failures, ensure service recovery attempts, and possibly can be responsible for enhancing brand equity, as the experience can create brand apostles who spread positive word of mouth (or word of mouse in the e-market) about the service provider, enhancing that provider's reputation.

SOURCE: Adapted from Alan Quarry, "When a Cocktail Onion Is a Brand Experience," *Strategy*, March 25, 2002, p. 25.

---

check-in counter, whether the baggage handler puts the suitcase on the right plane, whether the flight attendants are pleasant and helpful. In fact, it is in this latter component of service that many companies feel their greatest potential lies to differentiate themselves from the competition.

The realization that employees have the greatest potential to influence service quality and ultimately customer satisfaction has led many companies to introduce **internal marketing** programs. These programs are intended to ensure that employees "buy in" to the concept of customer service and appreciate that every satisfied customer means a returning customer. Again, the more progressive companies, and those that are most committed to exceptional levels of customer service, have developed elaborate training and motivation programs that emphasize excellence in treating the customer and reward those employees who treat customers well. It is at this level that marketing and human resources divisions of a company must co-operate, as both are ultimately responsible for the quality of service delivered by their employees.

Service failure and recovery No matter how diligent a company's employees and how well designed its service processes, **service failure** is inevitable. It may or may not be the fault of the company, but eventually something will go wrong. An important issue relating to customer satisfaction is how a company responds when service fails. The process of dealing with service failure to make amends with the customer is called **service recovery**, as discussed in Chapter 1.

Service recovery may be necessary when the core service fails. When the electricity fails because of a powerful thunderstorm or because ice build-up causes the toppling of hydro towers, the electrical utility works around the clock to restore power. An error on a bill will prompt immediate correction and an apology from a manager. Failure of a flight to depart and arrive on time may prompt an airline to offer its best customers a bonus of 500 frequent-flyer points as compensation.

The issue relating to service recovery is: What can and should the company do when something goes wrong? Certainly, the answer is not "Do nothing." In many companies in recent years, managers have been paying increasing attention to the development of procedures to deal

internal marketing
The process of directing programs to staff members with the intention of encouraging them to deliver superior service to customers and generally to adopt a customer focus in all that they do.

service failure
The failure of a service to meet customer expectations or standards, resulting in disappointment, frustration, or similar emotions.

with service problems as they arise, with a view to solving the customers' problems before they decide to take their business elsewhere. Therefore, service recovery becomes an important component in a company's program to establish and maintain customer relationships. Research has shown that a company taking the necessary steps to deal with customers' service problems efficiently and effectively will lead to those customers being satisfied, even to the point that they will be more loyal than they would have been if the service problem had never occurred!

Companies have to ask themselves to what lengths they should go to recover from service failures. The answer is that it depends on many factors. The seriousness of the problem is undoubtedly one factor to be considered. Mixing up a family's dinner reservations when they are celebrating their grandparents' fiftieth wedding anniversary is a more serious service failure than losing a lunch reservation for two businesspeople when there are lots of empty tables available. In addition, the importance of the customer to the company is another factor to be considered. This is not an easy one to deal with, as defining the importance or value of a customer is not a simple task.

Finally, some companies are so committed to recovering from service failure that they even take remedial steps in situations that are not their fault. We saw this in the chapter opener, when Francine at Tim Hortons gave Sandra a replacement coffee free, even though the company was not responsible for the fact that Sandra's first cup of coffee fell off the roof of her car.

Some companies are so intent on dealing with customer service problems that they actually encourage their customers to complain if they have a problem. If the dissatisfied customer who encounters a service failure simply leaves, vowing never to return, the company has missed a chance to deal with the problem, management may never know that the problem exists, other customers may experience the same problem, and the exiting customer has the opportunity to spread the bad news. Complaints provide an opportunity to restore customer satisfaction and even to impress the customer.

Service in driving customer satisfaction

It should be obvious that the quality and level of service provided by a company is an important determinant of the satisfaction level of its customers. In fact, business is often lost because of poor service, even though the quality of the core product is excellent. We saw this in the Chapter 1 opener, where the running shoes were bought at the store that offered the best customer service, even though they could have been purchased at a lower price at another store.

There are a couple of important lessons here. First, excellent customer service is an important differentiator. It sets a company apart from its competitors and gives it an advantage. Second, providing excellent service often allows a company to command a price premium. That is, customers are often prepared to pay higher prices in order to receive superior service. They'll say, "I know I'm paying more, but it's worth it." They clearly place a value on receiving great service and being treated well.

Many things contribute to customer satisfaction. We observed in Chapter 1 that customers are more satisfied when they perceive value in what they are offered by a firm. Value is created through product quality, attractive pricing, the provision of supplementary services, and how the customer is treated. Thus, a company can create high levels of perceived value among its customers by employing well-trained, helpful, and courteous employees, by having an efficient Web site and telephone system, and generally by making it easy for customers to deal with the company.

We also observed in Chapter 1 that satisfied customers will generally return to buy from a company again, while dissatisfied ones will not. Producing high levels of customer satisfaction is essential, therefore, if companies want to retain customers, to have them come back again and again. Think about the companies that you deal with, some of which you have probably being going back to for a number of years. What makes them different? Chances are, you could probably get just as good a product or service somewhere else. You go back because of how you are treated and, ultimately, how you are made to feel.

Another aspect of service delivery that is receiving a lot of attention in businesses today relates to the idea of exceeding **customer expectations**. As customers, we are most impressed when we encounter service that is better than we were expecting. Some companies offer such good service or recover from service problems so well that the only possible response from customers is "Wow!" Whenever a company succeeds in generating a "Wow!" response from customers, high levels of satisfaction have been achieved and the customers are likely to tell others about their favourable experiences.

Let's close this discussion of service delivery by returning to the question of what level of service is necessary and appropriate. Just as we asked what level of service recovery is necessary, so too it is important to ask what level of service in general a company should provide. The answer will depend to some extent on the company's positioning. Does it want to be known as a superior service provider, or is it content to deliver acceptable but not superb service and to compete on some other basis?

The level of service provided to specific customers will depend to some extent on the value the firm places on each customer. Some are more valuable than others. Many services companies have begun to develop information systems to allow them to measure or estimate the value of a customer to their firms. The question of **customer value** is important when companies are trying to decide on the level of service to provide and which customers they should retain. The principle here is one that many firms and organizations often find difficult to accept — they may not want all of their customers! Typically, companies earn as much as 80 percent of their profits from as few as 20 percent of their customers. The issue is to decide which are the most valuable ones so that a company can deliver superior service and protect its relationships with these. Some larger companies collect information on customers and their purchases and utilize this database information to assess the value of each customer. By categorizing customers, for example, into A, B, C, and D categories based on their value to the firm, a company can ensure that its best customers receive the highest levels of service and that attempts are made to address their problems immediately.

The role of service in building customer relationships

There is no doubt that the provision of excellent service leads to customer loyalty and causes customers to return to do business again. If this happens often enough, there is a possibility of a customer relationship developing. As we have observed throughout this book, achieving high levels of customer satisfaction, leading to the establishment of customer relationships, is the principal objective of marketing.

A company achieves the status of a relationship with a customer when it has succeeded in creating an emotional bond or attachment. There is a special feeling toward the firm on the part of the customer, who enjoys dealing with the company and its employees. A high level of trust exists and the customer may even feel a sense of ownership toward the company or service provider. This is reflected when the customer refers to the firm as "my bank," "my supermarket," or "my hairdresser." When the status of customer relationship is achieved, there is a high degree of loyalty toward the firm; these customers refer others to the company and give it a large share of their business. So, how is such a status achieved?

Essentially, relationships are interpersonal and emotional concepts. When we speak of our relationships, they are usually with people, and we reserve the word for those people toward whom we feel particularly close. We feel closest to people we trust, those we feel we can rely on, those with whom we feel comfortable, and those with whom we share things — common backgrounds, shared interests, and values. Companies have begun to realize the importance of creating such an emotional bond with customers.

customer expectations

What customers expect to occur when they enter a service encounter, or what they would like to happen, based in part their personal experiences.

customer value

The categorization of customers based on their value to the firm.

MARKETING AT WORK 8-3: RELATIONSHIPS

The Rewards of "Loyalty"

Are Canadians the loyal subjects they used to be? No, this isn't about how fond we are of the Royal Family, or how interested we are in the latest gossip out of Windsor Castle. This is about frequent-buyer programs — often referred to as "loyalty programs." You know, those little cards in your wallet that make you feel warm and fuzzy about being a member of the "Club" and collecting points every time you buy CDs, clothes, toilet paper, or lawn furniture.

Almost two-thirds of Canadians have at least one of these "loyalty" cards in their wallets or purses, but it seems that only slightly less than one-quarter of them actually like the cards!

A recent study by Montréal-based Léger Marketing found that 62 percent of Canadians belong to loyalty programs (21 percent to one program, 27 percent to two or three, 7 percent to four or five, and 7 percent to more than five). A paltry 27 percent of those card-holders said that they liked loyalty and reward programs to the point that these influence their buying behaviour. But, let's face it — would you admit to being influenced by one of those little cards? Another 41 percent of these card-holders said they don't much like loyalty programs, but use them on occasion. Some consumers may not be admitting, or even be aware of, the impact of these programs on their behaviour.

The reasons given for liking such programs include cash discounts, free gifts, and extra privileges. The naysayers think that such programs are often too complicated. The president of the company conducting the study believes that "If you can't explain your loyalty program in less than 10 words, you've got a problem."

So, who likes to hoard frequent-shopper points? Most likely to belong to a loyalty program are women (67 percent of participants), people aged 25 to 34 (67 percent), Anglophones (65 percent), Prairie residents (72 percent), those with household incomes of $60,000 or more (74 percent), and people with university educations.

SOURCE: Adapted from Danny Kucharsky, "Consumers Drawn to Loyalty Rewards," *Marketing Magazine*, May 6, 2002, p. 3.

---

functional value
The value that a company creates for its customers that is based on the quality of its products and the efficiency of its services.

emotional value
The value that an organization is able to create for its customers that addresses the feelings that the customer has toward the company or its brands.

Many companies now realize that customer satisfaction depends on the creation of two different types of value for customers — functional value and emotional value. **Functional value** is related to the provision of quality products, delivering them in a timely and convenient manner, and making sure that they work well. These are things that customers expect of well-run companies, but they may not be enough to lead to the establishment of customer relationships.

Emotional value, on the other hand, is created largely through the interpersonal interaction between the company and its customers, by how the company treats them, and ultimately how they are made to feel as a result. There is, therefore, a direct connection between the delivery of what the customer perceives to be excellent service and the emotional value that the customer experiences as a result. When customers are treated well, when they enjoy dealing with companies, and when they are recognized when they call, positive emotions are created and negative ones removed. Customers say that they feel comfortable dealing with their preferred service providers; they are made to feel valued and important, they trust these companies and feel that they can rely on them. Frustration, anxiety, and other negative emotions are removed.

We referred earlier to relationships as an emotional, largely interpersonal concept. Thus, relationships are best developed when customers are able to interact easily and comfortably with employees of the firm and when those employees have been selected, trained, and motivated to provide superior service.

Increasing Service Productivity

The boom in the services economy in recent years has been accompanied by a significant increase in competition in many service industries. This competition has been stimulated by several factors. One is the reduction in government regulation in many industries, such as airlines, telecommunications, and banking. Relaxed regulations of professional organizations now permit advertising by the medical, legal, and other professions. New techniques have opened new service fields, in solar and wind energy and information technology, for instance. Technological advances have also brought automation and other "industrial" features to service industries in which employees generally performed many manual tasks. Service chains and franchise systems are replacing the small-scale independent in many fields, including take-out food, auto repair, beauty, and real estate operations.

Companies and other organizations in virtually every industry still continue to face the challenges of becoming more efficient and productive. The pressure on businesses is to deliver greater returns to shareholders, while in public sector organizations, governments at all levels have been looking for new ways to produce better value for taxpayers. Because service industries are very labour-intensive compared with manufacturing, the pressure to become more efficient has led in some organizations to a phenomenon that has become known as "downsizing": reducing costs by reducing the number of employees. Services firms are employing other strategies to improve productivity. One is to invest in employee education and training programs, not just to teach basic skills, but also to improve efficiency. Another strategy is to bring in new technology and adopt methods used in manufacturing. Machines have enhanced or even replaced labour in a wide range of service industries. As technology has become more efficient, industries such as financial services are able to operate with far fewer customer-contact employees than ever before.

Elimination of many routine tasks may also occur as simple transactions are passed down to the consumer. Many banking transactions can be conducted at ATMs or through the Internet. Consumers pump their own gas and pay for it without ever meeting an employee. We obtain our own information on the Internet and complete our own course registration through our university or college computerized registration system. We interact with automated telephone systems that allow us to reach individuals or to leave messages without ever talking to a receptionist or operator. While this use of technology and the downloading of service tasks to the customer make for greater efficiency and lower per-transaction costs for the company that uses these systems, they are not without their disadvantages.

Moving forward

The basic premise of the manufacturing model is that machines and technology are the primary keys to increased productivity and successful operations. The people who deliver the services are less important — so goes the premise. But this premise simply no longer works in the competitive services environment of today. Instead, we need a model that puts customer-contact employees first and then designs the business operations around these people. Four key elements in this new model are:[6]

- Companies value investments in people at least as much as investments in machines.

- Firms use technology to support the work of customer-contact people, rather than using it to monitor or replace these workers.

- Companies make recruiting and training as important for salespeople and other customer-contact employees as for executives.

- Management ties compensation to performance for employees at every level, from bottom to top.

Impact of technology

One of the most important issues facing services companies relates to how technology affects the way services are delivered to customers and how it influences the quality of service provided to them. Certainly, we are unable to avoid technology today. Probably no other force has had the impact on services industries that technology has had in recent years and will continue to have in the future. Everywhere we turn, there is evidence of technology-delivered service, from the myriad ways we can access financial services at our banks to the 1,000-channel universe that crept up on us in 2002, when more than 50 new digital television channels hit Canadian airwaves,[7] to the Internet and all that it delivers.

Many advances in technology certainly make the life of the customer easier, even though the consumer may not even realize the role that technology is playing. Companies that operate call centres to receive incoming calls from customers use sophisticated number-recognition software to direct a customer's call to the person to whom the customer last spoke, thereby helping to build a more personal relationship between an employee and the customer. Manufacturers like Caterpillar use on-board computers to measure the wear on parts and to send a signal to a satellite, which informs the nearest Caterpillar dealer to contact the customer to replace the part before the customer's equipment fails.

Such use of technology to deliver improved levels of customer service is impressive. But, in service industries, technology has the potential to be a two-edged sword, particularly when you consider the quality of service delivered. The reason for this is simply that all consumers are not similarly comfortable and familiar with technology. Not everyone wants to use an ATM or bank through the Internet. To people who are not technologically literate or who simply long for the "good old days," technology often gets in the way of good service. Some customers resent efforts by their banks to encourage them to use ATMs, because they are used to dealing with their favourite bank employee. They are uncomfortable with the interactive voice-response system they encounter when they want to place a collect call. They don't enjoy dealing with voice mail. Encountering technology may discourage these customers from doing business with a company. This is an issue that some companies have begun to address, but many also seem to want to rush headlong into implementation of more technology, without giving much thought to its impact on customers and on their view of the firm.

Growth in the services sector

Services will continue to take an increasing share of the consumer dollar, just as they have over the past 50 years. This forecast seems reasonable even for periods of economic decline. History shows that the demand for services is less sensitive to economic fluctuations than is the demand for goods. The demand for business services should also continue to expand as business becomes more complex and as management further recognizes its need for business-service specialists. In professional services especially, the use of marketing programs is expected to increase considerably during the coming decade. This expansion will occur as more health-care organizations, lawyers, engineers, and other professionals come to understand the economic benefits they can derive from an effective marketing program.

Unfortunately, many service firms today still do not provide a satisfactory level of service quality. Most consumers undoubtedly would agree with this assessment by Leonard L. Berry, one of the leading researchers and authors in services marketing. Any prediction of profitable growth in services firms is based on senior management's raising their aspirations, learning from past mistakes, and providing effective leadership. More specifically, future profitability depends on a company's ability to correct the following basic mistakes related to service quality:[8]

- ● *Spending money on the wrong priorities:* A major hotel planned to install colour TV sets in some guest bathrooms when 66 percent of customer calls to the housekeeping department were requests for irons and ironing boards. The hotel later reversed these priorities.

● ***Reducing quality by flaws in service design:*** Computer-generated billing statements that are impossible for customers to understand; clothing store dressing rooms with fewer than two hooks — one for street clothes and one for try-on clothes.

● ***Seeking easy solutions to quality problems:*** Short-term, superficial, pep-talk solutions when the real need is an investment in managerial time, energy, and ego to change employee and management habits and attitudes regarding service quality.

● ***Short-changing fairness to customers:*** Hotels and airlines that do not honour confirmed reservations; insurance companies that inadequately disclose important information.

● ***Under-investing in leadership development:*** At all managerial levels, companies need leadership for employees faced with large numbers of demanding, sometimes rude customers and other conditions that breed stress, fatigue, and discouragement.

Even manufacturers are taking an increasing interest in services as a basis for growth. Most tangible goods can quickly and easily be imitated. Consequently, manufacturers see their accompanying services as a key factor in giving a company a competitive advantage. The idea is to bundle services with goods to respond to a full range of customers' wants and to deliver the highest quality of service possible.

◀ BACKSPACE

1. What is service quality and why is it difficult to measure?
2. What is service recovery?
3. What is the difference between functional value and emotional value?

Summary

Most product offerings are a mix of tangible goods and intangible services, located on a spectrum ranging from pure goods to pure services. Services are separately identifiable, intangible activities that are the main objective of a transaction designed to provide need and want satisfaction for customers. The scope of services marketing is enormous. Not only are services of considerable significance in our economy today, but significant continued growth is expected. Conceptually, tangible-goods marketing and services marketing are essentially the same. In reality, however, the characteristics that differentiate services from goods usually call for quite different marketing programs.

Services generally are intangible, inseparable from the seller, heterogeneous, and highly perishable, and they have a widely fluctuating demand. Each of these distinctive characteristics has several marketing implications that must be considered in new-service planning and the development of services marketing programs. Management must first identify its target market and then design a marketing mix to provide need and want satisfaction for that market. In the product-planning stage, the element of service quality is critical to a company's success. The communication of value is challenging, but critical in services marketing. In distribution, inter-mediaries are used less often, and location of the services marketer in relation to the market is important, particularly when the service is delivered in person. Personal selling is the dominant promotional method used in services marketing.

Service failure will occur. A firm's response (or that of its employees) is critical. Firms must have programs or processes in place to deal with these situations when they occur. Firms must understand customers' expectations and definition of quality in order to understand customer satisfaction and to foster long-term customer relationships. It is those retained customers who bring the greatest value to the firm over time.

As we move further into the twenty-first century, the service environment will continue to change. One of the biggest challenges for service industries today is to develop ways to improve efficiency and productivity without impairing the quality of the service provided. Productivity becomes more important as services account for a growing share of consumer expenditures and as organizations look for ways to provide better returns for their stakeholders. Service quality is often at risk in such situations, but it should remain a priority of service companies and not-for-profit organizations, as consumers pay increasing attention to the quality of service that they receive.

Key Terms and Concepts

branding of services 235
business services 229
commercial services 228
core services 227
customer expectations 243
customer service 239
customer value 243
emotional value 244
fluctuating demand 232
franchising 236
functional value 244
heterogeneity 231

inseparability 230
intangibility 230
internal marketing 241
perishability 232
personal services 229
service encounter 237
service failure 241
service quality 240
service recovery 241
services 227
services value proposition 232
supplementary services 227

Questions and Problems

1. How do you explain the substantial increase in expenditures for services relative to expenditures for tangible products in the past 40 years?

2. What are some marketing implications of the fact that services possess the characteristic of intangibility?

3. Why are intermediaries rarely used in the marketing programs of service firms?

4. Services are highly perishable and are often subject to fluctuations in demand. In marketing its services, how can a company offset these factors?

5. Discuss how loyalty programs such as Air Miles and Delta Privilege add value for customers.

6. Present a brief analysis of the market for each of the following service firms. Make use of the components of a market discussed in Chapters 3 through 5.
   a. Destina.ca.
   b. Toronto Airport Hotel.
   c. Indoor tennis club.
   d. Credit union.

7. What are some of the ways in which the following service firms might differentiate themselves? (**Hint:** How can they provide better service than their competitors?)
   a. Blockbuster Video.
   b. Hairstyling salon.
   c. Internet service provider.

8. Discuss why it is impossible for a services company to standardize its services.

9. Present in brief form a marketing program for each of the following services. Your presentation should start with a description of the target market you have selected for the service. Then, explain how you would plan, price, promote, and distribute the service.
   a. A disc jockey for private parties.
   b. A small vegetarian restaurant near your campus.
   c. A mobile phone company.

Hands-On Marketing

1. Identify a clothing store in your community and examine the supplementary services this company must also supply to support the sale of its tangible products (clothing).

2. Review a service encounter in which you have recently participated and in which you were not pleased with the outcome. Consider what went wrong. Was the problem with the core product or service or with the supplementary service? Or was there something wrong with the service in general? What could the service provider do to improve your experience next time?

Back to the Top

Think about the example in the chapter opener. Why do you suppose Sandra makes a trip to Tim Hortons almost every day? What evidence is there that she has developed a relationship with the Tim Hortons brand and with the staff at this particular store? What is her perspective on customer service? What is important to her? What evidence is there that the service she receives has contributed to the relationship she has developed?

 Want to get better grades, tips on how to study more effectively, and up-to-date information on happenings in the world of marketing? Then, visit the Online Learning Centre for practice tests, Study Smart software, and much more! **www.mcgrawhill.ca/college/sommers**

 Interested in finding out what marketing looks like in the real world? *Marketing Magazine* is just a click away on your Online Learning Centre!

CHAPTER 9

Branding, Packaging, and Other Product Features

As the Birks example that opens this chapter illustrates, the success of a company depends to a very great extent on the image communicated by its brand. Otherwise, how do you account for some people paying more for Bayer Aspirin, while others prefer to buy a significantly lower-priced private-label or generic brand of ASA tablets, when both products are commonly known to contain the same medicinal ingredients? Consumer choice is influenced not only by the brand but also, in the case of tangible products, by the package, warranty, design, and other features of the product or service. Because these features of products and services are important elements in a marketing program, we devote this chapter to them. After studying this chapter, you should have an understanding of:

- The meaning and relevance of brands in our lives.
- Developing brand equity, loyalty, and relationships.
- Characteristics of a good brand name.
- Branding strategies of producers and intermediaries.
- Strategies for branding services.
- The nature and importance of packaging and labelling.
- The marketing implications of other image-building features — design, quality, warranty, and post-purchase service — and how these can increase value for the customer.

This Package Communicates Brand Value

Many Canadians have grown up with some recollection of having received a special gift in a Birks blue box. Since 1944, the high-end jewellery retailer has packaged jewellery and gift items in distinctive blue boxes with an embossed silver lion. For generations of Canadians, this has meant something special, that the gift-giver has gone to a lot of trouble and probably spent a lot of money. The only way to get a Birks box was to buy something from the store.

Now Birks has decided to phase out the blue box in favour of a new line of packaging in an earthy shade of brown. A source close to the retailer was quoted as saying, "Birks is repositioning. Surveys show that many younger customers no longer identify with the blue box. It is perceived as old-fashioned, a little intimidating, a symbol of the old Birks." A spokesperson for Birks' public relations agency observed that the new colour "is not really brown. [It's] a shade of taupe that is warm and alluring."

Some people were surprised at the announcement that Birks was changing its famous package. Robert Soroka, a marketing professor at McGill, even admitted to recycling a Birks box when he was a student, to make a better impression. He said, "If the gift came in a Birks blue box, it had more value." Soroka went on to say, "One of the most difficult things to do is to cultivate a brand tradition and an image. Birks did it magnificently. The blue box has given them brand equity and brand position. But that is only one of its identifiers. A brand is more than just a name."

Reaction among customers was mixed. For some, the Birks box has become something of a collector's item. One commented, "No. No. Blue means Birks. They can't change that. The blue box means that someone went to the extra trouble of going to Birks, and that means something." Another concluded, "When you think of Birks, you think of blue boxes. The brown boxes don't really jump out at you."[1]

The approach that Birks has taken over the years in differentiating itself from the competition has been embodied in part by its distinctive packaging. The chapter opener illustrates two of the chapter's most important topics: the importance of branding and the role of packaging in supporting a company's branding initiatives.

Brands and Branding

When we think of brands, most of us tend to think of products that we use often and that we have been using, or at least have been familiar with, for many years. Certainly, many well-established brands have been part of our lives and the lives of our families and friends for 50 years or more — Tetley tea, Campbell's soup, Kodak film, Gillette shaving products, and Wrigley chewing gum, to name just a few. But brands are just as important in the marketing of services. A retail store name, such as Aldo and Cotton Ginny, is really a brand, as are such names as Air Canada, Delta Hotels, and Canada's Wonderland, although these are not applied to tangible products. As we will see in this chapter, some retailers' names have become so trusted and accepted by Canadians that they constitute widely regarded brands in their own right.

The word **brand** is a comprehensive term that has come to mean a great deal in marketing in recent years. In fact, many organizations today are very conscious of the importance and value of their brands and have made **branding** an important part of their management strategy. They pay a lot of attention to what their brands represent and what they mean to customers and prospective customers. The concept of branding refers to the management of the company's brand in such a way as to protect it and to increase its perceived value in the minds of customers.

As consumers and customers of various companies, we recognize certain companies, products, and services as legitimate brands and others as mere names. Few would deny that Heinz is a major brand, but very few would consider Bob's Ketchup to be a recognizable brand. So, if Bob was to establish a ketchup company, it would take some time to reach the status of Heinz — a status where we would refer to Bob's Ketchup as a recognized brand. What is it, then, that distinguishes brands from mere names? What has to happen for a new company to achieve the status of a brand?

As with many such concepts in marketing, brand is an intangible, perceptual concept that resides in the mind of the consumer. On hearing the name Heinz (or Nike, or Loblaws, or Gap), most of us would be able to conjure up images of what the name stands for. The company or brand may mean different things to different people, but there would be some agreement that there is a certain meaning behind the brand, that it stands for something. It is this consistency of brand meaning that companies strive for and that is the objective of their branding strategies. A brand, then, is a name that has over time acquired certain meaning and comes to stand for something in the minds of target customers.

Not all brands have the same meaning for all consumers. In fact, few brands are universal. While the Harley-Davidson brand may mean a great deal to an avid middle-aged biker who enjoys weekend rallies, it may mean nothing at all to someone who has no interest in such pursuits.

The meaning associated with a particular brand is acquired over time as a result of how the brand performs and is very closely related to concepts such as **reputation** and **image**, both of which also are perceived by consumers. A company such as FedEx is a recognized and respected brand in the minds of many people because of how it performs. It is a brand that has a reputation for service and an image as a company that is trustworthy and reliable.

We see this view of a brand when we consider some of the comments made in our chapter opener. Clearly, Birks is a recognized Canadian brand. It is a company that has been in business for generations, and one that is seen by many consumers as always providing great products and

brand

A name, term, symbol, special design, or some combination of these elements that is intended to identify the products of one seller or a group of sellers.

branding

The process of a company or product name acquiring a certain meaning over time; it comes to stand for something in the minds of customers.

service. When a customer is moved to comment, "*The blue box means that someone went to the extra trouble of going to Birks, and that means something*," there is clear evidence of meaning in a brand. To receive a gift in a Birks blue box has held special meaning for millions of Canadians.

A brand is, therefore, a name, term, symbol, or special design, or some combination of these elements, that is intended to identify the goods or services of one seller or a group of sellers. But it is much more than that. As Professor Soroka of McGill observed in our chapter opener, "A brand is more than just a name." A brand differentiates one seller's products or services from those of competitors. It sets a company apart as one that can be trusted to provide quality and service that will contribute to customer satisfaction.

In addition to the perceptual side of brands, there are a number of more practical aspects of branding. A brand is indeed a name, consisting of words, letters, and/or numbers that can be vocalized. But it is more, as we discussed above. A **brand mark** is the part of the brand that appears in the form of a symbol, design, or distinctive colouring or lettering. It is recognized by sight but may not be expressed when a person pronounces the **brand name**. Xerox, Bell Canada, Sony, and Maple Leaf are brand names. Brand marks are illustrated by the distinctive lettering and styling of the name: the Nike "swoosh," the picture of the little girl with pigtails on the Wendy's sign, and the Pillsbury Doughboy. These marks, logos, or designs are usually registered and may be used only by the company that owns the mark. In many cases, the company name is the brand, particularly for services companies such as Loblaws, Four Seasons, and Speedy Muffler.

A **trademark** is defined as a brand that is given legal protection because, under the law, it has been used for some time by one company or organization. A trademark is essentially a legal term, therefore. Trademark protection gives the legal owner of the brand the exclusive right to use that brand. All trademarks are brands and thus include words, letters, or numbers that can be pronounced. They may also include a pictorial design (brand mark).

One major method of classifying brands is on the basis of who owns them — producers or retailers. Major brands such as Sony, Zenith, Lexus, Sunlight, Levi, and Ivory are **producers' brands**, while Motomaster, President's Choice, Kenmore, Body Shop, and Life are all brands that are owned by retailers.

The term *national brand* has been used for many years to describe producer-brand ownership, while brands owned by retailers are generally referred to as *private brands* or **private labels**. However, more acceptable terminology for many marketers would be the terms *producers'* and *retailers' brands*. To say that a brand of a small manufacturer of poultry feed in British Columbia that markets in only two or three western provinces is a national brand, while those of Canadian Tire, Shoppers Drug Mart, Loblaws, and Sears are private brands seems to be misusing these terms to some extent. Nevertheless, the brands of retailers generally continue to be referred to as private labels.

How We View Brands

Companies and other organizations can consider brands and branding in a number of different ways. As is generally the case when we discuss such concepts, some will view the concept very simplistically, while others will have a greater appreciation for the potential for the concept to add value to their organizations. Such is the case with brands. While some managers think of their brand as the name of the company or product, others will realize that the brand is much more than this and that it has the potential to bond the customer to the company. This is very much related to the role of brands in building customer loyalty and relationships. How marketers manage their brands will determine whether the brand reaches its potential.

The most basic thinking views the brand as the name of the company or product and has as its objective "getting the name out there." In other words, at this stage a company is interested in

---

brand mark
The part of a brand that appears in the form of a symbol, picture, design, or distinctive colour or type of lettering.

brand name
The part of a brand that can be vocalized: words, letters, and/or numbers.

trademark
A brand that is legally protected.

producer's brand
A brand that is owned by a manufacturer or other producer; same as *national brand*.

brand awareness

The first stage in building an association between customers and a brand; they become aware of it.

brand recognition

The stage in a brand's association with customers where it is recognized and many customers are familiar with it.

brand characteristics

The stage of the development of a brand relationship in which customers are able to associate certain characteristics with the brand.

brand personality

The acquisition by a brand of certain characteristics normally associated with people; reflects the people who are most likely to buy the brand.

brand relationship

The ultimate stage of association between customers and a brand: They have an emotional attachment to it.

publicizing its brand, gaining exposure, leading to high levels of **brand awareness** and **brand recognition**. Companies at this stage of their view of the brand make little distinction between a brand and a name. This is mostly the view of the brand that is held by companies that are launching new products. Their objective is to create brand awareness and gain exposure, often through the expenditure of large amounts on advertising. The thinking is that people are not likely to buy the product if they have never heard of it.

A more sophisticated view of the brand requires that marketers think about what **brand characteristics** they want their product or company to possess. This is part of the brand positioning decision and addresses the question of what the company wants people to think of the brand. The positioning is then achieved through appropriate advertising, packaging, and other forms of communications that are intended to send consumers a message about the kind of product or company this is. At this level of sophistication, marketers would be deciding whether their brand gives the image or impression of being old or young, modern or old-fashioned, simple or complex, local or foreign, fun or boring, high priced or low priced, exclusive or ordinary, and so on.

As it becomes more advanced in its view of branding, a company may begin to think of its product or company as having a certain **brand personality**. At this stage, a company will address the age-old question often asked by marketing researchers: "If this brand was a person, what sort of person would it be?" Again, largely through its communications efforts, a company at this level of thinking would have a strategy to give its brand an appropriate personality. Should the brand be portrayed as friendly or distant, outgoing or reserved, confident or reticent, moody or bubbly? It this sense, the brand begins to take on the characteristics of a person, and marketers can ask themselves whether this is a person with whom a consumer would want to spend time.

This leads nicely into the final and most up-to-date thinking surrounding brands: the creation of **brand relationships**. Consumers develop relationships with brands in precisely the same way that they develop relationships with other people and with companies, as we discussed in Chapter 1. Most of us as consumers have products and companies that we have been dealing with for many years that are important to our lives. We use a certain shampoo, drive across town to buy a particular brand of clothing, and read certain magazines regularly, for example. Consumers often view brands as old friends; they can rely on them. Certain brands contribute to their definition of self and become central to their lives. They develop high levels of brand loyalty, a concept that we will address in the following section. A very important issue that marketers face is how to create a situation in which consumers have a genuine relationship with their brands.

Cultivating Brand Equity and Relationships

brand equity

The value a brand adds to a product.

brand loyalty

The situation in which a customer buys a certain brand on a regular basis because of its performance and appeal.

Companies as diverse as Coca-Cola, Microsoft, Hallmark, Sony, and McCain recognize that the brands they own may be more valuable than physical assets such as buildings and equipment. What we are talking about here is **brand equity**, one of the hottest topics in marketing in recent years. Brand equity relates to the value of a brand as reflected in the loyalty that consumers feel toward it. Thus, Heinz Ketchup has much greater brand equity than Bob's Ketchup. Companies take some time to achieve high levels of brand equity, because it usually takes a long time to develop high levels of **brand loyalty** and relationships. These result from the ongoing provision of value by the firm to its customers.

Where does the equity in a brand originate? If, over time, large numbers of people enjoy using a particular product or shopping at a certain store, to the point where they buy that product or visit that store on a regular basis and are likely to recommend it to others, we can conclude that they have developed a loyalty to that brand. This loyalty represents a stream of earnings for the company in that the loyal customers keep coming back, buying more, and bringing in their friends or family members. It is the sum total of all such relationships that constitutes the equity in the brand.

A company will often realize the equity in its brands only when it decides to sell the company or one of its product lines to a competitor or a new investor. When Eatons department store went under the first time, it was because it was unable to restructure its debt. So, what could it have that was of any value? What was it that Sears was so eager to buy? Prime retail locations, of course, but more importantly, brand names! The name of the store as well as ownership of the more than 40 private labels belonging to the venerable retailer. Although Eatons had literally lost its shirt, the brand had been a part of many people's lives growing up around the country and many were sad to think that the store would close forever. And the private labels? These were store brands that represented quality and value to many consumers — whether or not they recognized them as belonging to Eatons or some other company. Unless some such exchange occurs, the equity in a company's brands will usually never appear in its financial statements. It is what is often referred to as an **intangible asset**.

Brand equity is also the value a brand adds to a product from the perspective of the customer. In the minds of many consumers, just having a brand name such as Sony, Kenmore, or New Balance on a product adds value to it. Beyond a product's value in its potential to do what it's supposed to do, a brand adds value to that product through its name awareness and its connotations of favourable attributes (such as quality or economy).

If you're not convinced that a brand name by itself can have much value, consider the results of two studies. In one, the proportion of subjects choosing Corn Flakes cereal jumped from 47 percent when the brand was not known to 59 percent when the brand was identified as Kellogg's. In another study, when a sample of computer buyers were asked how much more or less they would pay for particular brands than they would pay for the average computer brand, there was a range of $364. Consumers said they would pay $295 and $232 more for the IBM and Compaq brands, respectively. Other brands commanding a premium include Apple, Digital, and Dell.[2] It's evident that Kellogg's, IBM, Compaq, and many other brands have substantial equity.

Today, creating brand equity is about more than positioning, packaging, and imagery. It involves developing a relationship with customers. Customers want brands that they can trust and be happy to tell others about. Developing a brand is a process of creating loyal followers who provide word-of-mouth support and ultimately add value to the product.[3] Substantial brand equity provides many benefits to the firm that owns the brand:

● The brand itself can become a differential advantage, influencing consumers to buy a particular product. Examples include Volvo, Tetley, Häagen-Dazs, and Michelin.

● Because it is expensive and time-consuming to build brand equity, a barrier is created against competing companies that want to enter the market with a similar product.

● The widespread recognition and favourable attitudes surrounding a brand with substantial brand equity can facilitate international expansion. For example, brands such as Pizza Hut, McDonald's, and Baskin-Robbins are now found literally all over the world. It also explains why new branches of companies such as Tim Hortons are often instant successes as soon as they open.

● Brand equity can help a product survive changes in the operating environment, such as a business crisis or a shift in consumer tastes. Although the Gap brand is undergoing some pressure to remain relevant as its target market matures, it probably has enough brand equity to allow it to transition to its next positioning.[4]

MARKETING AT WORK

9-1: ETHICS

A Brand Called Martha

She's a New Jersey girl who done good, building from nothing Martha Stewart Living Omnimedia, a $295-million concern that controls magazines and books, a syndicated television show, thousands of products, a radio program, a newspaper column, and a direct marketing business. But, what does the brand mean to consumers? Rumours of insider trading and investigation by federal authorities in 2002 caused her company's stock prices to falter, but many remained loyal to the brand and, in some cases, the woman behind it.

Stewart came from humble beginnings, did a little modelling, and even worked on Wall Street before turning her hand to creating domestic perfection for a living. Over time, she developed a reputation as a perfectionist who could be more than a little difficult to work with, even anal-retentive at times. In some respects, that has created her image as a survivor — she's got pluck!

One consumer, a 35-year-old attorney who has Martha Stewart curtains hanging in her bedroom, says the only reason she goes to Kmart is for Martha's merchandise. She is aware of Martha's reputation and current problems, but says that doesn't influence how she sees the products. "She never pretended to be the girl next door, like Kathy Lee Gifford did. She's a smart, sophisticated woman. Anyway, I'm not inviting her for dinner."

Stewart seems to summon more admiration than resentment. A resident from Martha's home town says, "It's hot or cold, you either love her or hate her. I like her. She made it okay to be a homemaker." Another New Jersey resident says she watches Martha's show religiously. "I'd love to be that calm and detailed-oriented. I just get a kick out of her. Nothing but the

best for Martha." She understands it's all airbrushed domestic fantasy — watching Martha make her own soap, tint sugar cubes pastel colours, cure her own salmon, and even make gilded quail-egg Christmas tree ornaments.

"You know what?" she says. "I feel really bad she's all tied up in this. If she's smart enough to get out fast, good for her," she says referring to the stock sale. She doesn't appear to be concerned about whether Stewart might be guilty.

SOURCE: Adapted from Anne Kingston, "Loyal Shoppers Stand," *National Post*, August 17, 2002, p. A10.

---

brand extensions

New products or services that are launched by a company under an existing brand name.

Ocean Spray
SC Johnson

Brand equity is often valuable in allowing a company to expand a product line, especially to extend a brand into new varieties or even new products. A company will use a strategy of **brand extensions** when it has a very strong brand with lots of equity, bringing out new related products under the existing brand. The view is that the relationship consumers have with the original brand is so strong that it will allow the firm to transfer that confidence and trust to new products under the same name. In fact, it may be argued that brand extensions are not possible unless the brand has established considerable equity. Examples include a wide variety of Ocean Spray (**www.oceanspray.com**) products, including juices that extend far beyond the cranberry flavour the company is known for and Craisins, dried cranberries in assorted flavours usually found in the produce department. SC Johnson (**www.scjbrands.com**) is well known for a variety of household care products such as Pledge furniture polish. The recognition and equity of both of these names allowed the company to successfully extend the Pledge brand into a new product category, using the name Pledge Grab-it for its line of sweepers and cloths. The rationale for using an existing, strong brand name on a new item or line is that the brand's equity will convey a favourable impression of the product and increase the likelihood that consumers will at least try it.

The fact that a brand has abundant equity does not necessarily mean that it should be applied to a wide range of other products, however. When Campbell was developing a spaghetti sauce, the company determined that its popular brand name would not convey an

Its strong brand has allowed Heinz to launch several brand extensions under the same trusted name.

Italian image, so it selected Prego as the name for its new sauce. Also, strong equity does not guarantee success for new items. Examples include Harley-Davidson cigarettes, Levi's tailored men's clothing, Dunkin' Donuts cereal, and Swatch clothing, to name a few. When Swatch and Mercedes-Benz collaborated to develop a new, very small car for the urban European market, they chose a new name (Smart) rather than risk extending their original brands too far.

Some retailer brands have succeeded in acquiring considerable brand equity, often in competition with long-established manufacturers' brands. Examples include President's Choice (Loblaws), Motomaster (Canadian Tire), and Life (Shoppers Drug Mart). In these cases, what started out as private-label brands have now, because of the trust that consumers place in them, evolved into full national brand status, because they have the strength of major retailers behind them. Some online retailers have succeeded in achieving a similar status, to the point where companies such as Lands' End, L.L. Bean, and Eddie Bauer stock only their own brands.

BACKSPACE

1. What is a brand? How is it different from a name?
2. Define *brand equity*.
3. When a company has a very strong brand, it will often bring out new, related products under the existing brand. This strategy is called _____.

What's in a Name?

The history of brand marketing shows that once a brand establishes a position of leadership in a product category, this position is often maintained over a very long period of time. Many of the leading brands that we buy today were purchased regularly by our parents and even our grandparents. Brands that continue to dominate their consumer product categories include Kodak, General Electric, Kellogg, Levi, Kraft, Nabisco, Heinz, Tide, Crest, and Campbell.

The development and protection of brand names has become a very important element of marketing management and one that demands increased attention all of the time. Companies such as Colgate-Palmolive have made conscious decisions to manage their brand names in such a way that they dominate a product category. For example, this company has made a commitment to position Colgate as an all-purpose supplier of oral health products. The importance of the Colgate name is summed up in a comment by Patrick Knight, former vice-president of marketing for Colgate-Palmolive: "We now consider the most valuable assets we have to be our trademarks."[5]

When Canadian Pacific (CP) Hotels and Fairmont Hotels and Resorts joined to create a new hotel management company, instead of renaming and marketing these destinations under either luxury moniker, the company opted to leave the names of the hotels as they were, but to advertise the locations under both names. Each brand has an established image and clientele, so why not let each brand name benefit from the equity of the other? The brands are now associated with quality accommodations at resort destinations and central-city locations. CP Hotels has strong brand recognition in Canada for providing superior accommodations. Each brand strengthened its name in both Canada and the United States with this association. Fairmont Hotels have "grand hotel" locations in major U.S. cities, including such landmark properties as The Plaza in New York. It was not until mid-2001 that the company decided it would finally drop the historic CP name — it felt that the two brands were finally merged in the minds of consumers in North America and that the Fairmont name (**www.fairmont.com**) was the better choice to retain as it was more "global expansion-friendly."[6]

Fairmont Hotels

Some companies have succeeded in keeping their brands successful with the purchasing public for many years. Nabisco, maker of such cookies and crackers as Oreo, Ritz, Arrowroot, Chips Ahoy!, and Triscuit, has been making cookies in Canada since 1861. Triscuit Crackers date from 1895, Honey Maid Graham Wafers from 1900, and Ritz from 1935. Today, the success of the Nabisco brands is obvious, and many have spawned brand extensions.

By stretching the original successful brand name to cover a number of brand extensions, the marketer is trading on the success of the original brand, but is also running some risk. Clearly, there may be some new products to which the original brand should not be applied. This raises the question of how far the successful brand can be extended before the marketer is stretching the credibility of the link between the brand and the product. Club Monaco, which successfully marketed casual wear aimed at young adults in Canada moved into lifestyle marketing, producing a wide range of home goods to sell in its stores. Roots, the Canadian company once famous for its revolutionary leather footwear, has long sold leisure wear but has tried to extend the brand to include home furnishings and a remote forest getaway resort.[7] Colgate can with confidence launch a line of toothbrushes, dental floss, and mouthwash, but would consumers buy Colgate sunglasses or suntan lotion?

Brands make it easy for consumers to identify goods and services. Brands also help to assure purchasers that they are getting comparable quality when they reorder. For sellers, brands can be advertised and recognized when displayed on shelves in a store. Branding also helps sellers control their markets, because buyers will not confuse one branded product with another. Branding reduces price comparisons because it is hard to compare prices on two items with different brands. Finally, for sellers, branding can add a measure of prestige to otherwise ordinary commodities (Sunkist oranges, Sifto salt, Lantic sugar, Highliner fish, Chiquita bananas).[8]

> CP Hotels in Canada are now branded "Fairmont."

Reasons for not branding

The two major responsibilities inherent in brand ownership are (1) to promote the brand and (2) to maintain a consistent quality of output. Many firms do not brand their products because they are unable or unwilling to assume those responsibilities.

Some items are not branded because of the difficulty of differentiating the products of one firm from those of another. Clothespins, nails, and industrial raw materials (coal, cotton, wheat) are examples of goods for which product differentiation (including branding) is generally unknown. The physical nature of some items, such as fresh fruits and vegetables, may discourage branding. However, now that these products are often packaged in typically purchased quantities, brands are being applied to the packages.

Producers frequently do not brand the part of their output that is below their usual quality. Products graded as seconds, or imperfects, are sold at discount prices and are often distributed through different channels and under different brand names than those used for usual-quality goods.

Selecting a good brand

Some brands are so good that they contribute to the sales success of the product or service; others are so poor or inappropriate that they appear to contribute little if anything to sales success and may even seem to be a factor in market failures. Some products appear to have been successful despite having names that may seem to add little to their appeal. Some brand names attain considerable value over time and remain consumer favourites for many years. It takes some time for the name of a product, service, or company to achieve the status where it becomes a "brand." The word itself implies that customers recognize the name and attach some meaning to it.

The challenge   Today, selecting a good name for a product or service is more challenging than ever. The reason is that we are running out of possibilities — many of the good names have already been used. Many thousands of new products are launched annually in North America, yet the standard desk-size dictionary contains only about 50,000 words. When you consider that a new brand can't be labelled Panasonic, Oreo, Esso, or Timex because these brands have been used successfully for many years, and that there are many other words you would not want to have associated with your product or service, it is no surprise that companies often resort to words that aren't really words, or that they bring out the new product as an extension of an already successful brand.

Many company and brand names have now achieved a certain status, but at one time they probably meant very little to consumers. Only over time have these names become recognizable and respected brands. Consider, for example, the names of companies such as Ford and Kraft. At one time, these were family names only — the name of the person who started the company. What if Henry Ford had been born into the Murphy family? Would many families all over the world now have Murphys parked in their driveways? It will be interesting to see how long it takes to achieve brand status for some of the new companies that are being established to do business on the Internet.

Meaningless words also are becoming more and more popular as names for companies and products. Names such as Invensys and Avaya — both technology companies — may well become widely known brands in the future. Drug companies have also created some unique names — Novartis and Astrazeneca, for example. Even good old Hewlett-Packard is becoming a little creative. The company, named after its two founders, hired a top-flight management team that went through a five-stage process to select a brand name for its instrumentation division. Consultants said they came up with a name that was "broad-shouldered and luscious, tempered with oaky notes of maturity, courage and character." What was the result? They made up a word, of course —Agilent![9]

The need for names and brands that are likely to contribute to a product's success has led to the establishment of companies that specialize in coming up with attractive and appealing brand names. These firms use database searches and rely on unusual sources to identify likely names. Some even employ qualified linguists on staff, often coming up with names that aren't part of any language: Pentium (Intel's microprocessor chip), Zoloft (a new pharmaceutical product), Lexus, Acura, and Compaq. Branding on the Internet through Web addresses has been approached in a similar manner, with sites such as fundu.com or imandi.com. The creation of a new brand name often involves research to determine whether consumers will react positively to the brand being proposed. It's an expensive process, as some firms will charge $25,000 or more for a new brand name.[10]

On the Internet, restrictions apply to the selection of names. Although e-addresses often ignore rules of grammar, such as the removal of spaces between words, there are limits: While two or more companies can have the same word, that word can be the basis for only one domain name in cyberspace. The most widely recognized top-level domain (TLD) is the dot-com extension — more than 28 million were registered in 2002. As a result, the dot-com options available to companies have begun to dwindle. Today in Canada, consumers and businesses seem to be favouring the dot-ca TLD over the once universally sought dot-com. The number of dot-ca domains has risen from about 60,000 in 2000 to about 300,000 in 2002.[11]

Concern over limited choices led the Internet Corporation for Assigned Names and Numbers (ICANN) to approve seven new TLDs: dot-biz, dot-info, dot-name, dot-pro, dot-aero, dot-coop, dot-museum. The name extension is proposed as an individual's digital identity and will work on a two-dot system (e.g., jane.doe.name). ICANN is the international body in charge of running the mechanisms by which new names are dispensed and resolving issues over name disputes. It is made up of representatives of industry, government, and Internet users. The dot-ca domain is overseen by the Canadian Internet Registration Authority.[12]

Once a company chooses and registers its name for doing business on the Internet — bearing in mind that it is really only borrowing the domain — registration has to be regularly renewed: Cybervultures are waiting to snap up addresses that expire, and little can be done to stop them from grabbing long-established domain names. Often, as many organizations have discovered, these occurrences can be quite embarrassing, as this address-grabbing is most often done by providers of adult content, such as gambling and pornography. At one point, the Tourism Toronto Web site was showing "Cheerleader Luv," while the New Brunswick Information Technology Alliance site featured similar content from Japan — all because someone forgot to renew the domain registration! Cybervultures are particularly fond of educational, governmental, and civic organization addresses.[13]

Desirable characteristics Five characteristics determine the desirability of a brand name for a product or service.[14] While it is difficult to think of a brand that has all five, a brand should possess as many of these characteristics as possible:

- *Suggest something about the product's characteristics (its benefits, use, or action):* Some names that suggest desirable benefits include Beautyrest, Motomaster, and — perhaps best of all — DieHard. Product use and action are suggested by Hi-Liter, La-Z-Boy, Mr. Clean, and Easy-Off. Or Web site addresses such as GardenCrazy.com, or click-abid.com.

- *Be easy to pronounce, spell, and remember:* Simple, short, one-syllable names such as Tide, Ban, Aim, and Raid are helpful. Top-Cuts, Weedman, and Speedy are other examples of brand names that are easy to remember. However, even some short names, such as NYNEX and Aetna, aren't easily pronounced by some customers.

- *Be distinctive:* Brands with names like National, Star, Ideal, or Standard fail on this point. Many services firms begin their brand names with adjectives connoting strength and then add a description of the business, creating brands such as Allied Van Lines and United Parcel Service. Some brand names play on patriotism as, for example, Maple Leaf food products, Air Canada, and Molson Canadian.

- *Be adaptable to new products that may be added to the product line:* An innocuous name such as Kellogg or Lipton may serve the purpose better than a highly distinctive name suggestive of product benefits. Frigidaire is an excellent name for a refrigerator and other cold-image products. But when the producer expanded its line of home appliances and added Frigidaire kitchen ranges, the name lost some of its sales appeal. Amazon.com suggests a huge selection and/or inventory of any product, but has come to be associated so far with a huge choice of books and music.

● ***Be capable of being registered and legally protected under the Trade-marks Act and other statutory or common laws:*** Names that are generic and in common usage in the English language would not meet this criteria. For example, the word "water" used as a name could not by itself be registered and legally protected. Names must also not already be registered or in use by other firms.

Protecting a brand name

Over a period of years, some brands have become so well accepted that the brand name is substituted for the **generic name** of the particular product. Examples of brand names that legally have become generic are linoleum, celluloid, cellophane, kerosene, shredded wheat, and nylon. Originally, these were trademarks limited to use by the owner.

A brand name can become generic in several ways. Sometimes the patent on a product expires. There is no simple generic name available, so the public continues to use the brand name as a generic name. This happened with shredded wheat, nylon, and cellophane. Sometimes a firm just does too good an advertising and selling job with an outstanding brand name. While not yet legally generic, names such as Xerox, Aspirin, Band-Aid, Scotch Tape, Ski-Doo, and Kleenex are on the borderline in Canada. Some of these brands have already lost their trademark protection in other countries. For example, in the United States and Great Britain, one can buy many brands of aspirin.

It is the responsibility of the trademark owner to assert the company's rights in order to prevent the loss of the distinctive character of the trademark. A number of strategies are employed to prevent the brand name from falling into generic usage. The most common strategy is to ensure that the word "trademark" or "TM®" appears adjacent to the brand name wherever it is used. A second strategy is to use two names — the brand name together with either the company's name or the generic name of the product. Examples of this include Polaroid Land camera and Dacron polyester. A third strategy for protecting a trademark involves the incorporation into the trademark of a distinctive signature or logo.

This protection is as important as ever because, according to the latest estimates, imitation products cost U.S. companies as much as $200 billion annually. Nintendo alone estimates that the piracy of its video games cost the company more than $700 million in 1998. In the United States, a top FBI official has called product counterfeiting "the crime of the twenty-first century."[15]

Branding Strategies

Both producers and intermediaries face strategic decisions regarding the branding of their goods or services. Whether a firm is branding a product or a service, some fundamental things need to be kept in mind. Branding is a means of creating and maintaining a perception of customer value. There is an expectation on the part of the customer that the brand name stands for quality. Branding also provides the means of differentiating products and services from those of the competition. When consumers see the offerings as all being alike, there is a tendency to shop on the basis of price. Branding provides consumers with another reason to choose a product. When brands provide better quality in products and services, they tend to be remembered by the consumer.[16] This is brand differentiation.

Product-branding strategies are often viewed differently than are services-branding strategies. Services branding is generally synonymous with the name of the company. The best example of services branding is franchising, in which companies such as Second Cup,

Wendy's, and Tim Hortons sell the rights to their name and products. The brand or name has come to stand for a service encompassing recognizable features. For example, McDonald's represents fast service, a children's focus, and consistent products. Other examples of services branding include hotel chains like Fairmont or Hilton, and professional-service companies, including consulting firms such as KPMG and Ernst & Young. Sometimes, service products are licensed for sale by intermediaries. An example of this is a training facility that delivers Microsoft training programs. The following strategies generally are used to brand tangible products. The strategic branding of services is dealt with later in the chapter.

Producers' strategies

Producers must decide whether to brand their products and whether to sell any or all of their output under intermediaries' brands.

Marketing entire output under producers' own brands   Companies that market their entire output under their own brands usually are very large, well financed, and well managed. Procter & Gamble, Maytag, and IBM are examples. They have broad product lines, well-established distribution systems, and large shares of the market. They generally have enough demand for products branded with their own names that they have no need to make products for other companies.

Some reasons for adopting this policy have already been covered in the section on the importance of branding to the seller. In addition, intermediaries often prefer to handle producers' brands, especially when the brands have high consumer acceptance.

Branding of fabricating parts and materials   Some producers of fabricating materials and parts (products used in the further manufacturing of other goods) brand their products.[17] This strategy is used in the marketing of Fiberglas insulation, Pella windows, Dolby

MARKETING AT WORK 9-2: TECHNOLOGY

Going Online to Keep the Brand Young!

"BMW has built an internationally recognized brand for its automobiles and motorcycles by building and delivering on a promise" — something the company is dedicated to continue online, according to Randy March, business manager of BMW Group Canada. The Internet is becoming an increasingly important tool in communicating brand messages to these younger market segments.

"Consistency across all marketing media — both nationally and internationally — is absolutely essential to maintaining and building the brand. Whatever we do," says March, "it must reflect what BMW stands for: It must be dynamic, innovative, inspirational, engaging, and reliable, with the ability to capture the imagination."

The strength of marketing online is that it allows BMW to be all of this and more. It allows a product to touch customers in new, informative, meaningful, and useful ways. The Internet can allow a company like BMW to bring the brand to life as no traditional medium can. The company does not sell cars over the Web. Rather, BMW uses the Web to provide people with the tools and information they need to assist in their purchasing decisions.

One idea that worked well was "The Hire," a BMW digital film series (www.bmwfilms.com) showcasing the industry's best talent, such as Ang Lee and Guy Ritchie. These were provocative films with interesting, interactive, and secret features. The initial series of five films brought the power and quality of feature-length movies to a format designed for the Internet. The BMW film player ensured that everyone had the opportunity to view the films. This was a huge hit for BMW, attracting a younger demographic to the brand.

The film series allowed the company to start a conversation with a whole new generation of potential BMW drivers and reaffirmed BMW's brand position as creative, innovative, and performance-driven. Often, online campaigns lack the emotional appeal necessary to capture people's attention, but this series generated excitement for the brand and enhanced the passion that customers feel for "The Ultimate Driving Experience."

SOURCE: Adapted from "Big Brands Make Their Mark Online," *Marketing Magazine*, April 22, 2002, pp. 10–12.

noise reduction, Intel processors, and many automotive parts — spark plugs, batteries, oil filters. DuPont has consistently and successfully used this strategy, notably with its Lycra spandex fibre and Stainmaster stain repellent for carpets.

Underlying this strategy is the seller's desire to develop a market preference for its branded part or material. For instance, G.D. Searle Ltd. wants to build a market situation in which customers will insist on food products sweetened with NutraSweet, so that food manufacturers will be convinced that their sales will be increased if their products contain NutraSweet. Similarly, a parts manufacturer wants to persuade a producer of a finished item that using its branded materials will help to sell the end-product.

Certain product characteristics lend themselves to the effective use of this strategy. First, it helps if the product is also a consumer good that is bought for replacement purposes. This factor encourages the branding of Champion spark plugs, Atlas batteries, and Fram oil filters, for example. Second, the seller's situation is improved if the item is a major part of the finished product — a microprocessor in a personal computer, for instance. Intel Corp. developed the slogan "Intel Inside" to strengthen its product's position.[18]

Marketing under intermediaries' brands   A widespread strategy is for producers to brand part or all of their output with the brands of their intermediary's customers. For example, a manufacturer of salad dressing makes products for Loblaws, and they are sold under the President's Choice label. For the manufacturer, this intermediary's brand business generates additional sales volume and profit. Orders typically are large, payment is prompt, and a producer's working-capital position is improved. Also, manufacturers may use their production resources more effectively, including their plant capacities. Furthermore, refusing to sell under a retailer's or wholesaler's brand will not eliminate competition from this source. Many intermediaries want to market under their own brands, so if one manufacturer refuses their business, they will simply go to another.

Intermediaries' strategies

The question of whether or not to brand the products they carry must also be answered by intermediaries. There are two usual strategies, as follows:

Carry only producers' brands   Most retailers and wholesalers follow this policy because they are not able to take on the dual burdens of promoting a brand and maintaining its quality. This is especially the case with smaller retailers, such as local shoe stores, whose volume of business is not sufficient to allow them to contract with a manufacturer for products labelled with the store's own brand.

Carry intermediaries' brands alone or with producers' brands   Many large retailers and some large wholesalers have their own brands. In fact, some of the most successful brands in recent years have been retailers' own brands, including President's Choice, Sobeys' Our Compliments, and Life from Shoppers Drug Mart. Intermediaries may find it advantageous to market their own brands for several reasons. First, this strategy increases their control over their market. If customers prefer a given retailer's brand, they can get it only from that retailer's store. Furthermore, intermediaries can usually sell their brands at prices below those of producers' brands and still earn higher gross margins. This is possible because intermediaries can buy at lower prices. The costs may be lower because (1) manufacturers' advertising and selling costs are not included in their prices or (2) producers are anxious to get the extra business to keep their plants running in slack seasons.

In addition to the two strategies mentioned above, some companies carry brands of other producers in association with their own. For example, Air Canada has entered into an agreement to provide Second Cup coffee on all of its flights.[19] McDonald's has an agreement with Wal-Mart to set up outlets inside its stores, and Starbucks has a similar arrangement with Chapters.

Loblaws, the grocery retailer, has private-labelled financial services.

Intermediaries have more freedom in pricing products sold under their own labels. Products carrying a retailer's brand become differentiated products, and this hinders price comparisons that might be unfavourable to that retailer. Also, prices on manufacturers' brands can be cut drastically by competing retail stores. This last point is what has been happening in recent years in the marketing of clothing with designer labels such as Calvin Klein, DKNY, Ralph Lauren, Fendi, and Hugo Boss. Some of the large retailers' upper-priced clothing departments have increased their stocks of apparel carrying the store's own brand. These stores have cut back on products with designer brands such as Calvin Klein and others. The reason for this brand-switching is that some designer-labelled products are now available at much lower prices in stores such as Wal-Mart, Zellers, and other "off-price" retailers.

The strategy of marketing as many products as possible under the retailer's own label has met with considerable success for such Canadian retailers as Loblaws and Canadian Tire. In fact, Loblaws is among the leading companies in the world in the private-label business, creating a situation where more than 30 percent of all Loblaws sales are accounted for by private-label products such as President's Choice Decadent cookies, Too Good To Be True cereals, and PC Cola. In fact, Loblaws has been so successful at developing the market for private-label products that the company has licensed the President's Choice brand to chains around the world. It has even extended the PC brand into financial services. Loblaws is an excellent example of how private-label products can replace national brands in the consumer's mind when the retailer develops products and value in which the consumer can be confident.[20]

Strategies common to producers and intermediaries

Producers and intermediaries alike must adopt some strategy in relation to branding their product mix and branding for market saturation

Branding a line of products/services   At least four different strategies are widely used by firms that sell more than one product or service:

● The same "family" or "blanket" brand may be placed on all products. This policy is followed by Heinz, Catelli, Campbell, McCain, and others in the food field. Other examples include the YM–YWCA and Pizza Hut.

● A separate name may be used for each product. This strategy is employed by Procter & Gamble and Lever Brothers. Pampers are produced by Procter & Gamble; Dove soap is a Lever product.

● A separate family brand may be applied to each grade of product or to each group of similar products or services. Sears groups its major home appliances under the Kenmore name, its paints and home furnishings under Harmony House, and its insurance under Allstate.

● The company trade name may be combined with an individual name for the product or service: Johnson's Pledge, Microsoft's Excel, Kellogg's Rice Krispies, Molson Export, the Bank of Montreal's MasterCard, and Ford Mustang.

family-brand strategy
A branding strategy in which a group of products is given a single brand.

When used wisely, a **family-brand strategy** has considerable merit. This strategy makes it much simpler and less expensive to introduce new related products to a line. Also, the general prestige of a brand can be spread more easily if it appears on several products rather than on only one. A family brand is best suited for a marketing situation when the products are related in quality, use, or some other manner. When Black & Decker, a manufacturer of power tools, purchased General Electric's line of small appliances, the Black & Decker brand was put on those appliances — but not immediately. Because of the perceived differences between kitchen products and workshop products, Black & Decker realized it was a risky proposition to switch brands. Consequently, the company mounted a year-long brand-transition campaign before making the change. Also during those years, Black & Decker introduced several other houseware products, and this helped in the General Electric–Black & Decker brand transition.

The success of major brands and families of brands certainly makes it easier for companies, whether manufacturers or intermediaries, to introduce new products under an established family brand or as brand extensions to well-established brands. This is obvious when one considers the number of varieties of Oreo cookies and Ritz crackers now produced by Nabisco and the wide array of products marketed under the Motomaster label by Canadian Tire. But the use of family brands and established brands to launch new products places a burden on the brand owner to maintain consistently high quality across all products marketed under that brand. One bad item can reflect unfavourably on other products that carry the brand and may even lead to the creation of a negative image for the overall brand.

Branding for market saturation   Frequently, to increase its degree of market saturation, a firm will employ a **multiple-brand strategy**. Suppose, for example, that a company has built one type of sales appeal around a given brand. To reach other segments of the market, the company can use other appeals with other brands. For example, Procter & Gamble markets a line of detergents that includes Tide, Bold, Cheer, and Ivory Snow. There may be some consumers who feel that Tide, even with its many varieties (phosphate-free, with bleach, unscented, liquid, regular, and most recently, high-efficiency HE Tide), is not suitable for washing lingerie and other delicate clothing. For these people, Procter & Gamble offers Ivory Snow, a detergent whose image is gentler than that of Tide and trades on its association with the purity and gentleness of Ivory soap. With this brand line-up, Procter & Gamble is assured of having a brand or a brand variation to appeal to every segment of the detergent market.

multiple-brand strategy
A strategy in which a firm has more than one brand of essentially the same product, aimed either at the same target market or at distinct target markets.

BACKSPACE

1. To be successful, a brand name should have many or all of five characteristics. What are they?
2. What is the difference between a brand name and a generic name?
3. When would a firm use a multiple-brand strategy?

Strategic Branding of Services

Throughout this chapter, we have discussed the competitive edge that a well-selected brand can give to a product. These advantages are equally applicable to tangible goods and intangible services. Furthermore, the marketers of services have to make many of the same strategic branding decisions as do the marketers of tangible products. Perhaps the first of these decisions is to select a good brand name for the service.[21] In services marketing, more so than in the marketing of tangible goods, the company name typically serves as the brand name. For example, H&R Block has become synonymous with tax-return preparation.

The characteristics of an effective service brand are much the same as for tangible goods. Thus, a service brand should be:

● ***Relevant to the service or its benefits:*** The name "Ticketron," the sales agency that sells tickets to sporting events, concerts, and other major attractions, conveys the nature of the service and the electronic speed with which it is delivered. "VISA" suggests an international activity and is relevant for a global financial service. "Instant Teller" is a good name for the automatic banking machines of the CIBC. "Budget" implies the best price for people who rent cars from that company. "Four Seasons" suggests a hotel chain that has something to offer year-round.

● ***Distinctive:*** This characteristic is difficult to communicate. The point is that companies should avoid branding their services with names that others could use. Names like National, Canadian, and Royal should probably therefore be avoided because, standing alone, they tell us nothing about the service or its benefits. When names such as these are used, the company will usually add words that indicate what service is being offered, such as Canada Trust, Royal Trust, and National Life Insurance.

Some services marketers differentiate themselves from the competition by using a symbol (usually referred to as a *logo*) or a distinctive colour. We are all familiar with the golden arches of McDonald's, the lion of the Royal Bank of Canada, and Air Canada's maple leaf. For colour, we see the green of the Toronto Dominion Bank, the red of Scotiabank, the claret of CIBC, and the blue of the Bank of Montreal. The use of a person's name, such as Harvey's or Tilden, or a coined word, such as Avis, RE/MAX, and AMEX, also offers distinctiveness, but it tells us little about the service being offered. This is the case until the name has been firmly established and it comes to mean something to the consumer. Certainly, many such names have become very well established in the marketplace.

● ***Easy to pronounce and remember:*** Simple, short names, such as Delta and A&W, usually meet this criterion. Others, such as Aetna, Clarica, and Overwaitea, pose pronunciation problems for some people. Sometimes, unusual spelling aids in having the consumer remember the name — the reversed R in Toys "Я" Us, for example.

● ***Adaptable to additional services or regions:*** Companies that change their mix of services and their geographical locations over time should be flexible enough to adapt to these extensions of their operations. Alberta Government Telephone (AGT) became a publicly held company and changed its name to TELUS, and the four telecommunications companies of Atlantic Canada merged to form Aliant, as traditional telephone service became a smaller part of their business with the move into Internet services, information technology, and a range of other technology-based services. The Canadian Imperial Bank of Commerce shortened its name to CIBC in anticipation of expanding its range of financial services beyond banking. When companies have names with geographical connotations, they are often abbreviated when expansion takes place, so Canadian Pacific became CP.

Packaging

packaging
For products, the activities in product planning that involve designing and producing the container or wrapper for a product; for services, bundling and promotion activities are involved.

Packaging is usually defined as all of the activities of designing and producing the container or wrapper for a physical product. Generally, we think of packaging in the context of physical products, and consumer products in particular — breakfast cereal, toothpaste, soft drinks — but services can also be packaged, even though they are not wrapped in brightly coloured boxes or displayed in containers.

There are two aspects of what is often referred to as the packaging of services. The first of these is **bundling**, which involves the marketer putting together an attractive "bundle" of services that can be bought as one unit but can include many elements. Financial services

bundling

The process of grouping together a number of services that are sold as a single unit.

companies bundle many services with a credit card, so that the customer receives several of the services, including travel insurance and access to travel information, for example, for a single monthly fee. Tour operators do the same thing when they bundle air travel, car rental, and an all-inclusive stay at a resort for one total fee. Telecommunications companies are now able to bundle local and long-distance telephone service, cellular telephone service, Internet access, and cable TV for a single monthly fee.

The second aspect of services packaging relates to how the services are promoted. With services, the container is not the tangible package we associate with products, but it does represent a package of value for the consumer. Because of the intangibility of services, it is often difficult to communicate effectively about the quality of the service being provided. Services companies must "tangibilize" their offer through the production of point-of-sale displays, brochures, and other promotional materials that play the same promotional role as attractive product packages. These will be discussed in greater detail in Chapter 15.

Packaging involves making the appearance of the collection of goods or services more attractive to the consumer. There are three reasons for packaging:

● Packaging of tangible products often serves several safety and utilitarian purposes. It protects a product on its route from the producer to the final customer, and in some cases, even while it is being used by the customer. Effective packaging can help prevent product tampering. Some protection is provided by child-proof caps on containers of pharmaceutical products and others that are potentially harmful to children. Also, compared with bulk items, packaged goods generally are more convenient, cleaner, and less susceptible to losses from evaporation, spilling, and spoilage.

● Packaging may play an important promotional role in a company's marketing program. Packaging helps identify a product and so may prevent substitution of competitive products. At the point of purchase, the package can serve as a silent salesperson. Furthermore, the advertising messages on the package will last as long as the product is used in its packaged form. A package may be the only significant way in which a firm can differentiate its product. In the case of convenience goods or business operating supplies, for example, many buyers may feel that one well-known brand is about as good as another. The package may be designed in such a way as to set a largely undifferentiated core product apart from its competition. Altoids, "the curiously strong mints," are packaged in a metal tin — not because they have to be, but because it sets them apart from "ordinary" mints. The NikeTown retail stores could be considered as one big "package" for Nike products.

Certainly, we saw in our chapter opener how important a package can be in communicating the reputation and image of a retailer. It can be a true differentiation tool. To Canadians, the Birks blue box has come to truly mean something, almost regardless of what's actually in the box!

Some feature of the package may add sales appeal — a reusable jar or a self-applicator (a bottle of shoe polish or glue with an applicator top, for example). Heinz Ketchup introduced squeezable no-drip bottles (contoured for little hands) that mothers love, which eliminate spills and that messy crust that used to form around the neck of the bottle. Colgate introduced 2-in-1 toothpaste and mouthwash in slim, easy-to-carry, flip-top bottles. Other marketers have been quick to duplicate these strategies. Concentrated formulations of cleaning solutions can be marketed as adding convenience by virtue of being smaller, lighter, and more environmentally friendly. Refill pouches for several household cleaning products serve this purpose.

● A firm can package its product in a way that increases profit and sales volume. A physical package that is easy to handle or minimizes damage losses will cut marketing costs, thus boosting profit. The previously discussed changes to several cleaning products helped to reduce transportation and storage costs, as well as attracting environmentally sensitive consumers. On the sales side, packaged goods typically are more attractive and therefore can be perceived as being better than items sold in bulk. Many companies have increased the sales volume of an article simply by redesigning its package. Diet Pepsi redesigned the look of its can in 2002 to revitalize its image in light of increasing competition from energy and health beverages. Sometimes, consumers just need a little nudge to remember that a product is still there. That same year, Gatorade came to the realization that its packaging was not too child-friendly — it was hard for little hands to hold and there was too much product in the bottle. The result? The company offered identical but smaller plastic bottles, as well as freezer-friendly tetra packages.[22]

Importance of packaging in marketing

Historically, packaging was a production-oriented activity in most companies, performed mainly to obtain the benefits of protection and convenience. Today, however, the marketing significance of packaging is fully recognized, and packaging is truly a major competitive force in the marketer's attempt to attract consumers. The widespread use of self-service selling and automatic vending means that the package must do the selling job at the point of purchase. Shelf space is often at a premium, and it is no simple task for manufacturers even to get their products displayed in a retail outlet. Most retailers are more inclined to stock the products of producers that have used effective packaging.

In addition, the increased use of branding and the public's rising standards in health and sanitation have contributed to a greater awareness of packaging. Safety in packaging has become a prominent marketing and social issue in recent years. Extensive consumer use of microwave ovens also has had a significant impact on packaging. Many food products are now packaged so that they can go straight from the shelf or freezer into a microwave oven. Environmental concerns, as mentioned, are also influencing package design.

New developments in packaging, occurring rapidly and in a seemingly endless flow, require management's constant attention. We see new packaging materials replacing traditional ones, new shapes, new closures, and other new features (measured portions, metered flow). These all increase convenience for consumers and selling points for marketers.

Packaging is an important marketing tool for companies that operate in international markets. Most countries have regulations governing the packaging of products and the wording that must appear on labels. A company that wants to export its product to another country must, therefore, be aware of the packaging laws of that country. For example, companies in other countries that export to Canada and the Canadian importers that represent them have to be aware of Canadian packaging regulations pertaining to metric package sizes, bilingual labelling, and the standard sizes of packages used in some industries. In addition to regulations, exporters must understand that packages that work in one country may not be accepted in another, because of design, illustration, or colour. Cultural differences as well as traditions and attitudes affect how consumers respond to brand colours and image, as well as situations and usage portrayed in advertisements.

Packaging strategies

Changing the package　In general, management has three reasons for considering a package change: to combat a decrease in sales, to extend the brand's life cycle, and to expand a market by attracting new groups of customers. More specifically, a firm may want to correct a poor feature in the existing container or it may want to take advantage of new materials. Some companies change their containers to aid in promotional programs. A new package may be used as a major appeal in advertising copy or because the old container may not show up well in advertisements. A package change may be an important element in a brand repositioning strategy. It is also a way of breathing new life into a tired brand, thereby rekindling interest and extending the product's active life.

This family package can be recognized instantly.

Packaging the product line A company must decide whether to develop a family resemblance in the packaging of its several products. Family packaging involves the use of identical packages for all products or the use of packaging with some common feature. Campbell, for example, has used virtually identical packaging for its condensed soup products for many years. Management's philosophy concerning **family packaging** generally parallels its feelings about family branding. When new products are added to a line, promotional values associated with old products extend to the new ones. On the other hand, family packaging should be used only when the products are related in use and are of similar quality.

Reuse packaging Another strategy to be considered is **reuse packaging**. Should the company design and promote a package that can serve other purposes after the original contents have been consumed? Decorative cookie tins can be used for any number of household functions, such as button boxes, containers for school supplies, or children's small-toy storage. Baby-food jars make great containers for small parts such as nuts, bolts, and screws. Reuse packaging also should stimulate repeat purchases, as the consumer attempts to acquire a matching set of containers.

family packaging
A strategy of using either highly similar packages for all products or packages with a common and clearly noticeable feature.

Multiple packaging For many years, there has been a trend toward **multiple packaging**, the practice of placing several units in one container. Dehydrated soups, motor oil, beer, golf balls, building hardware, candy bars, yogurt, and countless other products are packaged in multiple units. Test after test has proved that multiple packaging increases total sales of a product.

multiple packaging
The practice of placing several units of the same product in one container.

Criticisms of packaging

Packaging is one aspect of marketing that is criticized today because of its relationship to environmental pollution issues. Perhaps the biggest challenges facing packagers is how to dispose of used containers, which are a major contributor to the solid-waste disposal problem. Consumers' desire for convenience (in the form of throwaway containers) conflicts with their desire for a clean environment. Consequently, many manufacturers of consumer products in particular, and the package manufacturers who supply them, are actively engaged as partners in recycling projects across the country.

In many ways, the debate over the environmental impact of packaging often appears impossible to resolve, as the issue of the disposability of packaging is weighed against that of the use of energy and other effects associated with manufacturing it. Over the last decade, the use of environmentally friendly containers has become common. LMG Reliance, a Winnipeg company, manufactures the Enviro-Chem agricultural chemical container, part of a closed-loop recycling system that involves the collection of used containers from landfill sites for recycling. Refills of Fantastik all-purpose cleaners are available in a stand-up pouch, as are refills of other cleaners and detergents. The issue is, however, not a simple one. Environmentalists argue that companies should abandon disposable products, but the alternatives are often fraught with problems, as considerable energy may be required for their production and in recycling them for reuse.

Some question whether companies have an ethical obligation to the communities in which they operate, indeed to society itself, to take responsibility for the packaging they produce and distribute with their products. Some provincial governments, such as in Québec and Ontario, have begun drafting legislation that will require companies to pay 50 percent or more of the cost of municipal recycling programs. The ultimate cost of such legislation to companies is unknown right now, but clearly these costs will be passed down through the supply chain and, concerns are, ultimately to the consumer. Some estimates of this extended producer responsibility (EPR) have been pegged in excess of $25 million. EPR is a political concept in Europe, where industry and its customers have been made responsible for subsidizing the entire cost of collecting and recycling post-consumer packaging waste. These pending regulations could pose a major barrier to the healthy growth enjoyed by Canada's $14-billion packaging industry over the last 10 years.[23]

Companies that for years have been supplying the restaurant industry and providing Canadians with convenient disposable products have been greatly affected by the environmental movement and have had to adopt strategies aimed at developing products that are less harmful to the environment. In keeping with current environmental trends and to reduce packaging costs, many beer companies have increased their efforts to recycle the cans and bottles in which their products are sold. In the United States, Anheuser-Busch has created the Anheuser-Busch Recycling Corporation that, as the world's largest recycler of aluminum beverage holders, now recycles *more* than 100 percent of the beer cans it ships domestically.[24]

Other criticisms of packaging are:

- *Packaging depletes our natural resources:* This criticism is offset to some extent by the use of recycled materials in packaging and the fact that packaging reduces spoilage.

- *Packaging is excessively expensive:* In producing beer, for example, as much as half of the production cost goes for the container. On the other hand, effective packaging reduces transportation costs and losses from product spoilage.

- *Health hazards occur from some forms of plastic packaging and some aerosol cans:* Government regulations have banned the use of several of these suspect packaging materials.

- *Packaging is deceptive:* Excessive packaging may convey the impression of containing more than the actual contents. Government regulation plus improvements in business practices regarding packaging have reduced the intensity of this criticism, although it is still heard on occasion.

- *Package disposal:* Throwaway containers contribute significantly to the volume of solid waste in landfills, as well as contributing to litter problems.

Labelling

label
The part of a product that carries written information about the product or the seller.

Labelling is another product feature, primarily of tangible consumer products, that requires managerial attention. The label is the part of a product that carries information about the product or the seller. A label may be part of a package or it may be a tag attached directly to the product. Obviously, there is a close relationship among labelling, packaging, and branding.

Types of labels

brand label
The application of the brand name alone to a product or package.

Typically, labels are classified as brand, grade, or descriptive. A brand label is simply the brand name alone applied to the product or to the package. Some oranges are brand-labelled (stamped) Sunkist or Jaffa, for example, and some clothes carry the brand label Sanforized. A grade label identifies the product quality with a letter, number, or word. Canadian beef is grade-labelled A, B, or C, and each grade is subdivided by a number from 1 to 4, indicating an increasing fat content.

grade label
Identification of the quality (grade) of a product by means of a letter, number, or word.

Descriptive labels give objective information about the use, construction, care, performance, or other features of the product. On a descriptive label for a can of corn, there will be statements concerning the type of corn (golden sweet), the style (creamed or in kernels), and the can size, number of servings, other ingredients, and nutritional content. There is also growing interest in eco-labelling, such as the Canadian government's Environmental Choice Program, which encourages environmentally safe products by awarding seals of approval.[25] Many companies are now redesigning their products to qualify for environmental labels offered through such programs, which are now in operation in many countries worldwide.[26]

eco-labelling
Seals of approval awarded by a government to encourage environmentally safe products.

Statutory labelling requirements

statutory labelling requirements

Federal and provincial laws regulating packaging and labelling.

The importance of packaging and labelling in its potential for influencing a consumer's purchasing decision is reflected in the large number of federal and provincial laws that contain statutory labelling requirements to regulate this marketing activity. At the federal level, the Competition Act[27] regulates the area of misleading advertising, and a number of companies have been convicted of misleading advertising for the false or deceptive statements that have appeared on their packages. In this case, the information that appears on a package or label has been considered to constitute an advertisement.

The Hazardous Products Act[28] gives the Government of Canada the power to regulate the sale, distribution, advertising, and labelling of certain consumer products that are considered dangerous. As such, cleaning substances, chemicals, and aerosol products must carry on their labels a series of symbols that indicate the danger associated with the product and the precautions that should be taken with its use.

Similarly, the federal Food and Drugs Act regulates the sale of food, drugs, cosmetics, and medical devices. Certain misleading and deceptive packaging and labelling practices are specifically prohibited. Without question, the strictest regulations applied to packaging in Canada pertain to the cigarette industry. Canadian regulations required as of January 2001 that packaging used to sell these products in this country display health warnings that constitute 50 percent of the primary display surface of the package. Further, these warnings contain graphic depictions of the potential damage that can result from use of these products. This represents the largest and most graphic of such warnings required anywhere in the world.[29]

MARKETING AT WORK 9-3: RELATIONSHIPS

Water, Water, Everywhere — But Nothing to Put It In!

From coast to coast, there was a Nalgene crisis — people couldn't find them anywhere. What would they use to carry their water? What is a Nalgene? Could it be that you haven't heard of them by now? It's a water bottle, of course!

The brand of super-durable plastic bottles is beloved by campers, canoers, hikers, and birdwatchers. Most recently, they have become hip accessories, spotted at raves and skateboard parks. But, if you needed a new one for the summer of 2002, you were out of luck — the supply had dried up!

The news about the bottles, which started out as a laboratory product, spread by word of mouth. They don't absorb taste or smell, can be frozen or boiled, and have been known to hold water even after being gnawed by bears. It reached the point where Nalge Nunc International couldn't keep up with demand. Mountain Equipment Co-op posted signs on empty racks asking customers to "Please stay calm, we're doing all we can." Since his supplier had 10,000 bottles available, one retailer waited two days before reordering. When he called back — they were all gone!

Fledgling camper Stephanie Chambers was left high and dry when she went to purchase one: "I was a Nalgene novice, this was going to be my first bottle and I was crestfallen." Eventually, she did find one — the wide-mouth, one-litre bottle in cheery orange, for which she paid $12.99. On realizing the severity of the shortage, the resourceful Chambers mused, "Maybe I'll sell it on e-Bay."

Invented in 1946 by a U.S. chemist who started a company that supplied laboratory products, the bottles are made of a polycarbonate called Lexan, sold by General Electric. Although still primarily manufactured for industrial use, the company heard rumours in the mid-70s of adventurous scientists smuggling bottles out of the lab to use on weekend trips. But, only in the past five years has the outdoor and urban-hipster market taken off — the factory now operates 24 hours a day.

SOURCE: Adapted from Stephanie Nolan, "Polycarbonate's Properties Make Bottles Hip — and Scarce," *The Globe and Mail*, August 6, 2002, p. A5.

The Textile Labelling Act requires that manufacturers label their products according to the fibre content of the product, with the percentage of each fibre in excess of 5 percent listed.

The Consumer Packaging and Labelling Act regulates all aspects of the packaging and labelling of consumer products in this country. The regulations that have been passed under this Act require that most products sold in Canada bear bilingual labels. The net quantity of the product must appear on the label in both metric and imperial units. This Act also makes provision for the standardization of container sizes.

The provinces have also moved into the field of regulating packaging and labelling. A number of provinces have passed legislation regarding misleading advertising, and any information that appears on a package or label is considered to be an advertisement. Many of the provincial and municipal governments across the country have established recycling programs and regulations about what packaging materials may be disposed of in public landfill sites.

We can expect to see further changes in the labels required on food and grocery items in the future, as consumers demand more information about the products they are consuming and using. The most likely changes relate to the listing of nutritional information on food products, brought about by the increasing interest of consumers in health and nutrition.

Other Image-Building Features

A very important part of a company's marketing initiative is the support of the brand and the cultivation of a reputation and image. The packaging and labelling that is used mainly by tangible-product companies are a major part of that image-building initiative. A well-rounded program for product and service planning and development includes a company policy on several other attributes intended to build a solid image for the brand: product design, colour, quality, warranty, and after-purchase service.

Product design and colour

One way to satisfy customers and gain a competitive advantage is through skilful **product design**. In fact, a distinctive design may be the only feature that significantly differentiates a product. Many firms feel that there is considerable glamour and general promotional appeal in product design and in the designer's name. In the field of business products, engineering design has long been recognized as being extremely important. Today, there is a realization of the marketing value of appearance design as well. Office machines and office furniture are examples of business products that reflect recent conscious attention to product design, often with good sales results. The marketing significance of design has been recognized for years in the field of consumer products, from major items such as automobiles and refrigerators to small products such as fountain pens and clothing.

Good design can improve the marketability of a product by making it easier to operate, upgrading its quality, improving its appearance, and/or reducing manufacturing costs. Ford reintroduced its Thunderbird in 2002 — with unmistakable sixties styling in response to the popularity of retro designs. Apple Computers has been put back on the map with its eye-catching iMac line of computers.

Not even cosmetics can escape "reinvention" from time to time. The trend toward more natural-looking cosmetics has led trendy MAC Cosmetics to introduce a line of lipstick made with butter and soybeans. At the opposite end of the spectrum is Wet Diamonds lip colour from Montréal-based L'Oréal that has "silver-toned diamond-cluster pearls" and a "shine-boosting polymer" to give the appearance of diamond-coated lips! Recognizing the strategic importance of design, many companies have elevated the design function in the corporate hierarchy. In fact, it has been pointed out that design changes have assisted the iMac in saving Apple and that the new Volkswagen Beetle has provided needed revitalization of the image of Volkswagen.[30]

Product colour often is the determining factor in a customer's acceptance or rejection of a product, whether that product is a dress, a table, or an automobile. Colour by itself, however, has no selling advantage, because many competing firms offer colour. The marketing advantage comes in knowing the right colour and in knowing when to change colours. Sometimes just the presence of colour can be enough. When Apple introduced the Apple iMac PC in vibrant colours such as grape and tangerine — expected to be popular for home use — the products sold out within months and were a hit in both homes and offices. If a garment manufacturer or a retail store's fashion co-ordinator guesses wrongly about what will be the fashionable colour in the coming season's clothing, disaster may ensue.

Product quality

The quality of a product is extremely significant, but it is probably the most difficult of all of the image-building features to define. Users frequently disagree on what constitutes quality in a product, whether it is a cut of meat or a work of art or music. Personal tastes are very much involved. One guideline in managing **product quality** is that the quality level should be compatible with the intended use of a product; the level need not be any higher. In fact, *good* and *poor* sometimes are misleading terms for quality. *Correct* and *incorrect* or *right* and *wrong* may be more appropriate. If a person is making a peach dessert, Grade B or C peaches are the correct quality. They are not necessarily the best quality, but they are right for the intended use. It is not necessary to pay Grade A prices for large, well-formed peaches when these features are destroyed in making the dessert. Another key to the successful management of quality is to maintain consistency of product output at the desired quality level.

Quality of output also is a primary consideration in the production and marketing of services. The quality of its service can determine whether a firm will be successful. Yet it is virtually impossible for a firm to standardize performance quality among its units of service output. We frequently experience differences in performance quality from the same organization in appliance repairs, haircuts, medical examinations, football games, or marketing courses. You might want to return to our discussion of service quality in Chapter 8.

To aid in determining and maintaining the desired level of quality in their products and services, many companies have established quality-improvement programs. Such a program should be an ongoing group effort of the design, production, marketing, and customer-service departments. A firm may then justifiably claim in its advertising that its product quality has improved or is better than the competition's. Of course, companies must live up to their claims of superior quality in products or services, or consumers simply won't believe these claims.

Warranties and guarantees

Warranties represent a promise from the manufacturer of a product that, if something goes wrong or if the customer is not satisfied with the performance of the product, it may be returned or repairs will be carried out at no cost to the consumer. Sometimes warranties are referred to by consumers as *guarantees*. The purpose of a **warranty** is to assure buyers they will be compensated in case the product does not perform up to reasonable expectations. In years past, courts seemed to recognize only **express warranties** — those that were stated in written or spoken words. Usually these were quite limited in their coverage and seemed mainly to protect the seller from buyers' claims. Some companies were reluctant to honour a warranty unless it had been formally provided in writing.

But times change! Consumer activism in the last half of the twentieth century led to a campaign to protect the consumer in many areas, including product warranties. Courts and government agencies have broadened the scope of warranty coverage by recognizing **implied warranties**. This means that a customer can now assume that a warranty was intended, although not actually stated by the seller. In other words, a consumer today can assume that a warranty is in place even if the seller has not provided one in writing. Therefore, a consumer can assume a certain level of quality to be present and, if it is not, that the manufacturer or

warranty
An assurance given to buyers that they will be compensated in case the product does not perform up to reasonable expectations.

express warranty
A statement in written or spoken words regarding restitution from seller to customer if the seller's product does not perform up to reasonable expectations.

implied warranty
An intended but unstated assurance regarding restitution from seller to customer if the seller's product does not perform up to reasonable expectations.

retailer will replace or repair the product. Furthermore, manufacturers are being held responsible even when the sales contract is between the retailer and the consumer.

In recent years, manufacturers have responded to legislation and consumer complaints by broadening and simplifying their warranties. Many sellers are using their warranties as promotional devices to stimulate purchase by reducing consumers' risks. Advertising may be designed around claims regarding the quality of the warranty. This has been popular with high-ticket items such as automobiles, claiming coverage for a certain number of years or kilometres. The effective handling of consumers' complaints related to warranties can be a significant factor in strengthening a company's marketing program.

service guarantees
Guarantees that companies offer to their customers that attest to the quality of their service.

Some companies have even extended the concept of warranties to the offering of **service guarantees**. They have essentially guaranteed the quality of service that the consumer will receive, often offering money-back guarantees if the customer is not satisfied. This has become a fairly common practice in very competitive industries such as hotels and airlines. But, it is also a practice that may be difficult to implement because of some of the characteristics of services discussed in Chapter 8. It is, of course, more difficult to control the quality of service than that of a manufactured product, so service quality is highly variable. Also, as we discussed in Chapter 8, quality of service is based to a very great extent on the perception of the customer. The customer decides whether service is of an acceptable quality, influenced by past experience, expectations, and other factors. As a result, companies that offer service guarantees must be extremely diligent in their training of employees and in other aspects of service delivery to ensure that the best possible quality is being provided to customers.[31]

Post-purchase service

Many companies have to provide **post-purchase service**, notably repairs, to fulfil the terms of their warranties. Other firms offer post-purchase services such as maintenance and repairs not only to satisfy their customers but also to augment their revenues. Companies that offer products such as automobiles and mechanical equipment, such as elevators or heating and ventilation systems, rely on their service contracts for a substantial portion of their sales and profits. With more complex products and increasingly demanding and vocal consumers, post-purchase service has become essential. A frequent consumer complaint is that manufacturers and retailers do not provide adequate repair service for the products they sell.

Many responsive companies have established toll-free telephone numbers that connect the customer directly with a customer-service representative. Many actually invite customers to complain, acting on the principle that if the customer doesn't complain, the company won't know there is a problem and can't take steps to correct it. This post-purchase service is also required for troubleshooting and assembly assistance for many products and services such as audio systems or Internet installation. Many companies post their toll-free customer-service numbers on the doors of their stores and feature them in their advertising. While it may not always be pleasant to listen to customer complaints, the alternative of customers taking their business elsewhere is much worse in the long run.

Post-purchase service has the potential to be either a differential advantage or a disadvantage for an organization. Therefore, it is an issue that managers must monitor on a regular basis.

◄ BACKSPACE

1. In marketing, what is bundling?
2. What are three reasons why management would consider changing the packaging of its product?
3. What is the purpose of a warranty?

Summary

Effective product management involves developing and then monitoring the various features of a product — its brand, package, labelling, design, quality, warranty, and post-purchase service. A consumer's purchase decision may take into account not just the basic good or service but also the brand and perhaps one or more of the other need- or want-satisfying product features. Each of these features has the potential of enhancing value from the customer's perspective.

A brand is a means of identifying and differentiating the products of an organization. Branding aids sellers in managing their promotional and pricing activities. The dual responsibilities of brand ownership are to promote the brand and to maintain a consistent level of quality. Selecting a good brand name — and there are relatively few really good ones — is difficult. Once a brand becomes well known, the owner may have to protect it from becoming a generic term.

Manufacturers must decide whether to brand their products and/or sell under an intermediary's brand. Intermediaries must decide whether to carry producers' brands alone or to establish their own brands as well. In addition, intermediaries must decide whether to carry generic products. Both producers and intermediaries must set policies regarding the branding of groups of products and branding for market saturation.

A growing number of companies are recognizing that the brands they own are, or can be, among their most valuable assets. They are building brand equity — the added value that brand recognition brings to a product. It's difficult to build brand equity but, if it can be done, it can be the basis for developing brand loyalty and relationships. As well, it can enhance product-mix expansion opportunities. Products with abundant brand equity also lend themselves to trademark licensing, a marketing arrangement that is growing in popularity.

Packaging is becoming increasingly important as sellers recognize the problems — as well as the marketing opportunities — associated with it. Companies can choose among strategies such as family packaging, multiple packaging, and changing the package. Labelling, a related activity, provides information about the product and the seller. Many consumer criticisms of marketing target packaging and labelling. As a result, several laws regulate these activities.

Companies are now recognizing the marketing value of both product design and quality. Good design can improve the marketability of a product; it may be the only feature that differentiates a product. Projecting the appropriate quality image and then delivering the level of quality desired by customers are essential to marketing success. In many cases, firms need to enhance product quality to eliminate a differential disadvantage; in others, firms seek to build quality as a way of gaining a differential advantage.

Warranties and post-purchase service require considerable management attention these days because of consumer complaints and government regulations. Product liability is an issue of great consequence to companies because of the financial risk associated with consumers' claims of injuries caused by the firms' products.

Many companies provide post-purchase service, mainly repairs, to fulfil the terms of their warranties and/or to augment their revenues. To promote customer satisfaction, a number of firms are improving their methods of inviting and responding to consumer complaints. A strong reputation for product quality, as well as for comprehensive post-purchase service and warranties, enhances the perceived value of the product to the consumer and contributes to brand equity and loyalty.

Key Terms and Concepts

brand 252
brand awareness 254
brand characteristics 254
brand equity 254
brand extensions 256
brand label 270
brand loyalty 254
brand mark 253
brand name 253
brand personality 254
brand recognition 254
brand relationship 254
branding 252
bundling 267
descriptive label 270
eco-labelling 270
express warranty 273
family packaging 269
family-brand strategy 265
generic name 261

grade label 270
image 252
implied warranty 273
intangible asset 255
label 270
multiple-brand strategy 265
multiple packaging 269
packaging 266
post-purchase service 274
private labels 253
producer's brand 253
product colour 272
product design 272
product quality 273
reputation 252
reuse packaging 269
service guarantees 274
statutory labelling requirements 271
trademark 253
warranty 273

Questions and Problems

1. Answer the following question to determine Heinz Ketchup's brand personality: If Heinz Ketchup was a person, what sort of person would it be? List five personality traits.

2. Evaluate each of the following brand names in light of the characteristics of a good brand, indicating the strong and weak points of each name.
   a. Xerox (office copiers).
   b. Club Monaco (retailer).
   c. Holiday Inns (hotels).
   d. Moschino (clothing)
   e. Red Lobster (restaurant).
   f. Ecco (footwear)

3. When does a company or product name become a brand? What distinction do you make between the concepts of "name" and "brand"? Does the term "brand" imply that the product or company has achieved a certain status?

4. Suggest some brands that are on the verge of becoming generic. What course of action should a company take to protect the separate identity of its brands?

5. Name some private-label products and determine which brand names compete with them. Which product do you prefer and why? (**Example**: President's Choice Decadent chocolate chip cookies versus Chips Ahoy!)

6. A manufacturer of a well-known brand of ski boots acquired a division of a company that marketed a well-known brand of skis. What brand strategy should the new organization adopt? Should all products (skis and boots) now carry the boot brand? Should they carry the ski brand? Would some other alternative be better?

7. Why do some firms sell an identical product under more than one of their own brands?

8. What changes would you recommend in the typical packaging of these products?
   a. Soft drinks.
   b. Hairspray.
   c. Adventure vacation.
   d. Toothpaste.

9. Give examples of products for which the careful use of the colour of the product has increased sales. Can you give examples to show that poor use of colour may hurt a company's marketing program?

10. How would the warranty policies set by a manufacturer of skis differ from those adopted by an automobile manufacturer?

Hands-On Marketing

1. Go to **www.aircanada.ca** and examine the company's use of its Web site to build its brand.

2. Interview five students who are not taking this course or five friends and ask them to tell you about their favourite brands. Note what kinds of products and services they are most likely to associate with a "brand." Ask them for reasons why these are their favourite brands. Try to determine what these brands mean to them and what roles the brands play in their lives.

Back to the Top

Consider the importance of the Birks blue box as discussed in the chapter opener. Why do you think the blue box became so important to Birks? What role did it play in reinforcing the Birks brand? Is it a package? Or, is it more than a package? Why do you suppose Birks management is considering changing to a different colour?

Want to get better grades, tips on how to study more effectively, and up-to-date information on happenings in the world of marketing? Then, visit the Online Learning Centre for practice tests, Study Smart software, and much more! **www.mcgrawhill.ca/college/sommers**

Interested in finding out what marketing looks like in the real world? *Marketing Magazine* is just a click away on your Online Learning Centre!

Case 3-1

Gap Inc.

Gap Girl Lost

Sarah was walking along Robson Street in Vancouver when she noticed a huge billboard with the slogan "For Every Generation." On it was a smiling Kris Kristofferson, sporting casual clothes. That had to be a Gap ad, thought Sarah. She found it interesting that Gap's new ad campaign reminded her of the old Gap 10 years ago. That was when Gap had first moved into Canada and Sarah, recently out of journalism school, had started shopping there regularly. At the time, she had just landed a job as a media specialist for a Vancouver-based, not-for-profit organization and, as a young professional, Gap's clothes suited her perfectly. Sarah had always valued her simple lifestyle and worked in a place where everyone dressed casually. Gap's clothes were perfect for work, for days off, and even for going out. She could always find the perfect outfit, no matter the occasion.

Until a few years ago, Sarah would shop at Gap regularly. She trusted the quality of the clothes and liked the styles. It was trendy, but not too trendy, and even though she was a tall woman, Sarah knew she could always find pants that were long enough. She bought everything from Gap, including socks, candles, and even Gap's own scented body spray. Sarah was always satisfied with her purchases. She knew that the clothes she bought were classic and wouldn't go out of style after six months. Sarah was practical, and these considerations were very important to her. She wanted to know that when she spent her hard-earned dollars, the clothes would last her a while. She was sure she would never grow tired of Gap jeans and khakis. In fact, Sarah still owned a pair of Gap khakis she had bought eight years before. They were her most comfy pair of pants. She would never part with them.

Then, about three years ago, Gap started to change. The new ads showed young, thin models wearing funkier clothes. Sarah's younger sister Jen and Jen's body-pierced friends even started shopping at Gap. Sarah and Jen could not have been more different, and Sarah couldn't imagine shopping at the same store as her sister. She just couldn't relate to Gap anymore. Sure, it still sold khakis, but somehow it didn't feel like the same store. Eventually, Sarah found other stores that suited her style better and she stopped going to Gap altogether. Now, as she walked by a Gap store in downtown Vancouver, she was tempted to go in and check out its new arrivals. It seemed like the old Gap again. But when she looked at her watch, Sarah realized that she was already late meeting her friends at Starbucks.

Questions

1. What factors contributed to Sarah's falling-out with her favourite store, Gap?

2. How can Gap win back customers like Sarah? Can it revive its brand image as a back-to-basics clothing store?

Source: Marina Strauss, "Gap tired brand in new old clothing," *The Globe and Mail,* August 16, 2002, p. B9.

Case 3-2

Procter & Gamble

Dryel: Do-It-Yourself Dry-Cleaning

About 80 percent of new products fail, according to some reports, but that doesn't stop companies like Procter & Gamble from developing new products and bringing them onto the market as quickly as they can. In order to be more competitive, the company that is known for brands such as Pampers, Crest, and Tide decided in 1999 not only to launch new products, but also to create entire new categories with the hope that they would catch on. Some of P&G's products have been hugely popular. Take, for instance, the Swiffer, an electrostatic mop with a disposable cloth intended for dusting dry surfaces. The Swiffer has become a household name, but other products haven't fared so well. Dryel, a home dry-cleaning kit launched in 1999, has been scrutinized by many since coming onto the market.

As a possible substitute for dry-cleaning, Dryel presents a threat to traditional dry-cleaners. For $16.99, consumers can purchase the Dryel kit that allows them to clean up to 16 "dry-clean only" items in their dryer. Each kit contains an instruction pamphlet; a bottle of stain remover; four absorbent pads; four pre-moistened, dryer-activated cloths; and a reusable Dryel bag. The user first checks the garments for spots and applies the Dryel stain remover to the affected areas, using the absorbent pads. Then one to four garments are placed in the Dryel bag with a single pre-moistened cloth. The bag is put into the home clothes dryer at medium to high heat for 30 minutes. After hanging the garment, wrinkles disappear and the garment is ready to be worn, just as if it had been picked up from the dry-cleaner. Or is it?

Dryel was supposed to revolutionize the way people handled their "dry-clean only" clothes. Instead, the product has received mixed reviews. CBC's *Marketplace* engaged the services of Edith Strasser, a professor of fabric in the fashion management department of George Brown College, to evaluate the product. Professor Strasser's conclusion was that Dryel partially removed some stains, but for the most part, although the garments looked and felt fresher, stains still remained after the Dryel procedure. She concluded, "I guess for stains as deep as that you're better off to go to a professional dry-cleaner, so this is not a replacement for dry-cleaning. It is OK to freshen things a bit, but for real dry-cleaning and any stains, it has to go to the dry-cleaners."

In addition to Professor Strasser's assessment of the product as not being a real substitute for dry-cleaning, many professional dry-cleaners accused Procter & Gamble of misleading advertising. The International Fabricare Institute in the United States even filed a complaint with the Federal Trade Commission, alleging that P&G had made false and deceptive claims in advising consumers to disregard "dry-clean only" label instructions. Amid these negative responses to its new product, Procter & Gamble was forced to rethink its marketing strategy for Dryel.

Questions

1. Did Dryel deliver on its promise to effectively clean "dry-clean only" clothes? Does Dryel create value for the customer?

2. Discuss the psychology of dry-cleaning. How do consumers know when something is clean?

3. Keeping Dryel in mind, why do you think up to 80 percent of new products fail?

Video source: CBC *Marketplace*, "Putting Dryel to the Test," November 2, 1999.

Case 3-3

Daniel and Jane Dine Out in Montréal

Daniel Stein smiled to himself as he slipped on his sports jacket. The 37-year-old marketing executive was having a great weekend in Montréal, a city he often visits on business. On this particular business trip, however, Jane had been able to take time off work to join him. As this didn't happen very often, Daniel suggested that they have dinner at Chez Antoine, an upscale French restaurant in the heart of Old Montréal. He knew the restaurant was very pricey but this was a special weekend for the couple. Both Jane and Daniel had hectic careers and lately they hadn't been able to spend much time together.

Although he had several favourite restaurants in Montréal, Daniel had chosen this one for its charming atmosphere and wonderful French cuisine. He was certain Jane would love it too. He had raved to her about Chez Antoine many times and had promised they would go there when she was able to join him in Montréal. They left the hotel on this windy, cold Friday evening in January, jumped into a taxi, and headed toward Chez Antoine, expecting to have a wonderful evening.

Arriving at the restaurant at 8 p.m., they noticed that the restaurant was very busy. Daniel gave his name to the hostess, expecting their reservation to be honoured right away. Instead, the hostess smiled apologetically and explained that a table would be available soon. Daniel and Jane grew more and more impatient as time went by. They considered leaving for another restaurant nearby, but they really had their hearts set on this one. A few minutes later, a couple walked in and gave their names to the hostess. She seated them right away. At this point, Daniel was about to object, but as the hostess returned from seating the other couple, she smiled at the Steins and said, "Your table is ready now. Please come this way." Almost half an hour after they had arrived, Daniel and Jane were finally seated and they couldn't wait to order. By now, they were famished. They ordered their favourite drinks, which the server brought right away.

After examining the menu, the couple waited for the server to return and take their order. Even by the time they had finished their drinks, though, the server was still frantically going from table to table, zipping by the Steins' table a few times without even looking at them. Daniel tried to make eye contact to suggest that they were ready to order but it was to no avail. Finally, he muttered in frustration, "This is unbelievable; I'm going to complain." Jane felt sorry for the server, who clearly had too many tables to handle. She felt that the manager was the one responsible for having only two servers working on a Friday evening, so it wasn't the server's fault. Daniel agreed, and refrained from complaining. Finally, 20 minutes later, the server came to their table and described the chef's special. Daniel ordered lamb, medium rare, and Jane ordered a seafood crepe in a cream sauce, a dish for which the restaurant was famous. The couple was eager to eat. They had had a light lunch earlier that day, and that was eight hours ago!

While they waited, they admired the quaint decor. Chez Antoine reminded them of a restaurant they had been to in Paris, bringing back memories of their first trip together to Europe. The couple reminisced about the wonderful time they had had and before they knew it, their meals had arrived. The server sprinkled fresh ground pepper on their dishes, asked politely if she could get them anything else, and left. Everything looked wonderful. The presentation was very nice and the food smelled terrific.

Jane tasted her crepe and marvelled at how delicious it was. Daniel, however, was not as pleased. His lamb was overcooked — even burned in places — dry, and tough. When Jane asked him what he thought of his dinner, he answered that it wasn't at all like the lamb he had eaten here before. Jane was disappointed for him. She told him he should complain to the server. Daniel agreed. When the server came back to ask whether they were enjoying their meals, Jane nodded and smiled. The server then looked at Daniel and asked, "And how's your lamb, sir?" Daniel thought for a moment, hesitated, and finally said that it was fine. The server was satisfied with this reply and turned to leave. Daniel stopped her and ordered a second bottle of wine.

Jane was confused. Why hadn't Daniel said anything? Daniel, on the other hand, had decided against complaining when he realized that he might have to wait another 30 minutes if he ordered more lamb. He knew Jane was enjoying her meal and did not want to make her wait longer than she already had. He realized that if the server took the lamb back to the kitchen, they would either have to eat their meals separately or Jane's would become cold. He didn't want the hassle, and besides, he felt uncomfortable about complaining. So he said nothing. The couple finished eating and realized that the second bottle of wine had not arrived. When the server came to take their plates, they reminded her about the wine. She turned red and apologized profusely. The couple told her that they no longer wanted it; instead, they ordered dessert.

When they were finished, the bill arrived and Daniel glanced at it briefly. It seemed very expensive for what they had ordered. Then he noticed that they had been charged for the second bottle of wine. Daniel was becoming frustrated again. Things were just not going well that evening.

He mentioned the extra wine on the bill to the server, who again turned red, apologized, and quickly left to prepare another bill. Jane could not believe how poor the service was. She was equally frustrated. When it was time to leave a tip, Jane told Daniel that he should leave a small one. Daniel felt uncomfortable doing that and even made excuses for the server! Jane felt annoyed at her husband but she didn't want to argue with him, especially not in the middle of this busy, upscale restaurant. The couple left, feeling disappointed by their dining experience at Chez Antoine.

****

Talin Vartanian has heard of scenarios like this one many times. "Citizen Talin," as she is called, keeps a close watch over the rights of consumers, and she is baffled by customers who won't complain about poor service in restaurants. Restaurateurs insist that when they ask customers, "How is everything this evening?" they want to hear the truth. But often, customers simply won't tell the truth. Either they are too timid, too embarrassed, or, as in the case of the Steins, they don't want to spoil the mood of the evening.

Vartanian is adamant that customers should complain when something goes wrong, instead of just putting up with the poor service, leaving a tip, and never returning to the restaurant. A customer who calmly and politely explains the problem to the server is much better off. And so is the owner of the restaurant, who may not be aware of the problem, which means it will happen again and again. This leads to silent defections — customers leave quietly, never to return. The customers are unhappy and what's worse for the restaurateur is that future revenue is lost. Disgruntled customers will not give the restaurant repeat business nor will they recommend it to anyone. Worse, they may tell all their friends and families about the unpleasant experience, and the restaurant loses more potential customers. The moral of Citizen Talin's story? Complain politely when service is poor and both the customer and the restaurant benefit.

Questions

1. Which parts of the Stein's experience were unacceptable? How could the hostess and server have handled these situations differently?

2. If you were Jane or Daniel Stein, how would you have handled the situation? What would this have accomplished, according to Talin Vartanian?

3. Which parts of the Steins' dining experience were good? If no part of the experience was horrible, why did the couple leave the restaurant feeling disappointed?

4. How do you think the Steins felt toward the hostess, the server, the restaurant, the food, the decor — the whole experience?

Video source: CBC *Marketplace*, "Restaurant Service," February 27, 2002.

PART 4

Marketing Communications

Informing, persuading, and reminding current and potential customers

Having just examined strategies for developing products and services, we now turn our attention to how they are to be promoted to customers and prospective customers — the task of marketing communications.

Chapter 10 presents an overview of integrated marketing communications, including the various types of marketing communications, how marketing communications work, and the management issues involved in developing marketing communications programs. Chapter 11 looks at advertising, probably the most obvious and public form of marketing communications. The selling process, sales promotion, public relations, and publicity are the subjects of Chapter 12.

CHAPTER 10

Marketing Communications Programs

This chapter will help you to understand how marketing communications decisions are made by describing what marketing communications is and how it fits into a firm's total marketing program. After studying this chapter, you should have an understanding of:

- The role of marketing communications.
- Different methods used in marketing communications.
- The concept of integrated marketing communications.
- How the process of communicating relates to effective marketing communications.
- The concept and design of the marketing communications mix.
- Considerations in developing a marketing communications program.
- Alternative marketing communications budgeting methods.
- Regulation of marketing communications.

Curious Vanilla

The theme of the campaign says it all: "Reward your curiosity." And what is there to be so curious about?

How about all of the new brands and flavours of pop being introduced by soft drink manufacturers? And why spend almost $20 million for a single campaign? Because soft drink sales are starting to bubble up after going flat a couple of years ago, thanks to all of the new juices, energy and health drinks, teas, and bottled waters that poured into the marketplace. Another reason may be that, with its Vanilla Coke, Coca-Cola was very careful to try to "get it right" before introducing a new flavour. Vanilla is only the second flavoured version, after cherry, to be offered by the company.

In tests, consumers saw vanilla as new and innovative. In developing the flavour, Coca-Cola wanted to provide "a new and different drinking experience, a smooth cola that would be unexpected," according to a company spokesperson, because younger consumers "are looking for variety, and we wanted to make a big statement that there is no other flavour like Vanilla Coke."

The supporting Vanilla Coke campaign, launched in the summer of 2002, aimed to prompt consumers — particularly younger consumers, who buy soda more often — to try the product by encouraging them to think of it as significantly different from all of the others. And how did Coca-Cola go about doing this? By piquing consumer interest through different forms of media, each with a consistent message.

The campaign, which included television, radio, the Internet, outdoor advertising, and product sampling, was focused on generating awareness and curiosity about the product and then persuading consumers to try it. The campaign's creative director noted that, while Coke itself is "so incredibly well known…the vanilla version is only partially known. That results in immediate curiosity and a need to find out about it." The whole idea behind the advertising was to show how people are very intrigued and curious about how Vanilla Coke might taste.

In commercials that were run on networks watched by younger consumers, a 20-something guy becomes the victim of his own curiosity. After peeking through a hole in a fence, the "victim" is grabbed in a headlock or yanked into a seedy hotel room — oh, no! But have no fear: The young peeper is rewarded for his youthful curiosity by experiencing a "nice Vanilla Coke soft drink." Each TV ad featured an imposing, dapper, *Sopranos*-like character with a looming "enforcer" sidekick. Our host explains that our unwitting victim will find "the delicate hint of vanilla alluring; the taste, smooth," before our boy finds himself banished back to the street with a Vanilla Coke in hand. Spots ended with the tag line "Reward your curiosity." In radio ads, actors were curious about whether "that mysterious-looking plant was poison ivy" and whether "Personals really worked." Ads ended "Admit it — you're curious." Internet components (**www.vanillacoke.com** and **www.vanilla.coke.com**) picked up on the momentum of the already-produced ads by promoting a contest to "make your own commercial" and win a $10,000 prize.

And once you've piqued all this curiosity — what next? You start giving the product away — more than 10 million, 591-ml bottles at the peak of advertising. This was done in 33 cities, with the locations provided on Web sites. The bottles were featured in outdoor ads — billboards, telephone kiosk posters, and transit signs that also contained the "Reward your curiosity" tag line. Co-ordinated newspaper ads also advertised special pricing on six-packs at retailers such as Kmart, ensuring that stores had an ample supply on hand. In-store (or point-of-purchase) displays featured the new product alongside Coca-Cola Classic and Cherry Coke.

The campaign resulted in strong initial sales of the product — in Canada, by July 2002, Vanilla Coke was the third best-selling soft drink in Canada, after Classic Coke and Pepsi. But, of course, products such as this make up only a small component of the soft drink market. Cherry Coke has only 0.7 percent of the market, but then again, that's good for an estimated $500 million in annual sales! Another good reason to spend almost $20 million to launch the product.[1]

The Role of Marketing Communications in Marketing

One of the main functions of marketing communications is to differentiate the offerings of a company from those of its competitors. The Vanilla Coke campaign works hard to convince potential consumers that the new flavour is really different from what competitors have to offer. In the absence of effective differentiation, consumers are likely to conclude that there are no differences and make their purchase decisions based largely on brand image or price. Therefore, differences are emphasized not only in the Vanilla Coke case but also when President's Choice bottled water and Banff Ice vodka focus on being made from iceberg and glacial water, or Becel margarine focuses on being the best margarine for heart health because it "takes your health to heart." Attempts are made to direct attention to those traits that distinguish the product from others competing in the market.

Becel shows how it can make a difference.

A firm also hopes that marketing communications will create a strong consumer relationship with the firm or its brand to affect consumer responses to price increases and decreases (demand elasticity), so that when prices go up, demand will decrease very little and when prices go down, demand will increase quite a bit. Management wants marketing communications to create an image and to send certain messages that will give the consumer a number of non-price reasons to acquire and use the product being advertised. In fact, one of the main roles of marketing communications is to create non-price value — to communicate sufficient value for the company and its products and services to take the customer's mind off price to a certain extent. It provides many other reasons to buy, over and above an attractive price.

Then there are products and services that would appear to actually be the same across providers — here you provide a little "personality" to the product or company through your communications efforts. Although available nationally, in Québec, people may say, "Call me on my Fido" — referring to a cellphone from Fido Microcell Solutions of Montréal (**www.fido.ca**), a personal communications services provider. The canine term has come to be used generically in this marketplace, as when people use terms such as Kleenex or Band-Aid. The marketing communications program has successfully branded a product and a service that have been fraught with price competition and have now come to be perceived as a commodity.

Fido Microcell Solutions

Communications in the context of marketing

marketing communications
All of the elements of an organization's marketing (usually advertising, publicity, public relations, personal sales, and sales promotion) that serve to inform existing and potential customers.

Marketing communications serves three essential roles: It informs, persuades, and reminds prospective customers about a company and its products. The relative importance of these roles varies according to the circumstances faced by a firm.

Communicating to inform   The most attractive product or brand will be a failure if no one knows it is available! Because distribution channels are often long, a product may pass through many hands between its producer and consumers. Therefore, a producer must inform wholesalers as well as end-consumers or business users. Wholesalers, in turn, must inform retailers, and retailers must inform consumers. As the number of prospective customers grows and the geographic dimensions of a market expand, the problems and cost of informing target consumers increase. Simply making available a good or useful product is not enough. A program of communication must be designed to reach different groups — and to reach them effectively through word and imagery. The use of imagery and visuals transfers a great deal of information rapidly and often remains after the words have been forgotten.

You can't rely on the idea that, once a product is packaged and on the store shelf, all has been done. A communications plan must be designed and implemented that will cause consumers to understand the product, recognize its features, demand it, and keep coming back for more. Consumers see hundreds of marketing communications each day and the average shopper spends slightly more than 20 minutes buying groceries, covering less than a quarter of the supermarket in the process and looking at a given product for just 2.5 seconds.

Panasonic

When Panasonic (**www.panasonic.ca**) wanted to launch the new line of Power Activator (PA) batteries aimed at the battery-eating electronics of today's youth markets, it knew it had to be "cool" about it, but without looking as if it was trying too hard. The solution was to employ "guerrilla" tactics aimed at building grass-roots awareness in the target market's own environment and culture. First, the product's logo was circulated without product identification through underground channels — posters were used in and around dance clubs, showing blown-out electronics and just the PA logo. Then the logo was emblazoned on T-shirts, hats, and stickers that were distributed at more than 30 events in major Canadian cities. Club DJs were also enlisted to assist by wearing the PA T-shirts at their clubs. Eventually,

MuchMusic

this merchandising was replaced with similar gear, but this time revealing the product itself in addition to the logo. The campaign was then tied in with MuchMusic and a MuchDance CD release. Also, a contest mini-site was connected to the MuchMusic Web site (**www.muchmusic.com**), with prizes of Panasonic electronics and, of course, PA batteries.[2]

Who knew what so-called "energy" or nutritional bars were a couple of years ago? Were they like granola bars or candy bars? But, thanks to marketers, we now understand what they are and where they fit as a food product. When Kellogg decided to introduce a Canadian-exclusive bar version of its new Vector Cereal, the Vector Energy Bar, this was a problem that the company faced. The solution was an integrated marketing campaign to educate consumers and support the proposed positioning of the product. It was positioned as a nutritional snack that tastes good against the saturated energy bar market, and as a nutritional bar against the snack bar category. Available in single servings and in 4- and 15-bar boxes in Cranberry Apple and Berry Burst flavours, the product was targeting active, health-conscious Canadians in their 20s and 30s. While available in supermarkets, the bars were made available where energy bars as well as the target group could be found — at the gym. A heavy sampling campaign was implemented in-store as well as at athletic events. The campaign's messages were also delivered through the use of Canadian athlete spokespersons and TV spots during the Salt Lake City Olympics.[3]

Campbell Soup Company

Communicating to persuade   Another purpose of marketing communications is persuasion. The intense competition among different industries, as well as among different firms in the same industry, puts tremendous pressure on the communications programs of marketers. Campbell (**www.campbellsoup.com**) has been selling soup for more than 120 years and has annual soup sales of close to $2 billion. Studies show that 96 percent of Canadian households have canned soup in their kitchen cupboards. Yet the firm spends more than $60 million each year advertising soup, since there is still room to "win more stomachs for Campbell's." To increase its share of the fast-growing, home-prepared soup market, Campbell continues to innovate to persuade non-Campbell users to switch brands. It does this by launching new varieties of canned, freeze-dried, and fresh-frozen soups. Other strategies have included ready-to-serve varieties, snacking soups, and Campbell's Supper Bakes sauces. All of these new products have to be advertised to non-users to make them aware of their features and benefits and how they meet existing consumer needs better than the soup brands now being used. Of course, they also have to be advertised to current users to persuade them to stay with the Campbell brand and to try new offerings.[4]

Persuading consumers to buy a company's offering also includes the packaging appearance and style — whether it's sitting on the shelf or making an impression in advertising, packaging says something. All communication uses "visual vocabulary"— more than 40 percent of communication is visual. And what is more visual than packaging? Further, 80 percent of this visual communication is driven by colour and shape — words tell and pictures sell! Text most often is forgotten, so marketers must rely on images, colours, and shapes to elicit a positive emotional response, while remaining true to brand character. Colour, for example, can make a package something it isn't: Black and dark colours impart visual weight, while light colours make packages appear to be less heavy. Dark colours can make them look compact, while light ones can make them look larger.[5]

Persuasion is also about positioning the product in consumers' minds. "Being a guy just got better"

Using persuasion to position for guys can be expensive.

IT'S GOOD TO BE A GUY.

according to Corby Distilleries' new multi-million dollar campaign for C.C.& G. — which apparently is just for guys! Targeting men in their 20s and 30s, it was "especially made for guys who like the taste of rye and aren't satisfied with vodka or rum coolers," according to the company. The ready-to-drink blend of Canadian Club and ginger ale is intended as a response to market research indicating that young men are looking for a refreshing alternative to beer.[6]

Music not only soothes but also keeps consumers from tuning out an advertiser's message, and sometimes a little help is needed persuading consumers to listen to or watch a message. According to a recent woman's magazine survey, nearly 47 percent of women 45 to 54 cited music as a key element in holding their attention during television commercials. Also, 43 percent of women 18 to 34 gave music as a top reason for why they watch commercials.[7] This doesn't mean spending a fortune for the rights to a rock and roll classic; simply matching the music to the product or market is all that's necessary. But sometimes a classic might be just what is needed. Popular musicians often license their music to be used with or without lyrics — Madonna's "Ray of Light" was used for the launch campaign for Windows XP, while Moby's "Porcelain" was used for Toyota's "You Belong Outside" campaign promoting its SUV products.

Communicating to remind Because of competitive clutter, consumers must be reminded about the availability of a product or brand and its potential to satisfy. In addition, they need to be reminded on occasion of broader messages that are related to the image of companies and not-for-profit organizations. Advertisers bombard the marketplace with thousands of messages every day in the hope of attracting new consumers and reinforcing their relationships with existing customers. Even an established firm must constantly remind people about its brand to retain a place in their minds. It is unlikely that a day goes by, for example, in which you don't see some form of marketing communications (an ad, in-store display, counter sign, billboard, or imprinted T-shirt) for Coca-Cola. Similarly, while we all grew up with Wrigley gums — Juicy Fruit, Doublemint — the company still spends tens of millions of dollars each year on "reminder" advertising.

Older brands often need to remind you that they're still out there and to keep their image current. Campbell, in addition to attempting to persuade non-users to switch soup brands, makes sure that it reminds users of the benefits of their brand loyalty. The makers of Kahlua liqueur, in order to keep up with trends in alcoholic beverages, have begun running vibrant ads with recipes to reflect the popularity of fruit coolers — such as the Kahlua Skrew, containing Kahlua, vodka, and orange juice.

Marketing Communications Methods

Marketing communications takes five basic forms: personal selling, advertising, sales promotion, public relations, and publicity. Each has distinct features that determine the role that it can play in a communications program.

- **Personal selling**, or just plain "selling" or "sales," is the direct presentation of a product or service to a prospective customer by a representative of the organization that is marketing it. This is the field to which we are referring when we talk about someone going into "sales" after graduation. It covers many different kinds of sales positions these days, from retail salespeople to pharmaceutical sales reps to telemarketers. Personal selling takes place face to face, over the telephone, or by means of an Internet "chat," and it may be directed to an intermediary or a final consumer. We list it first because, across all businesses, more money is spent on personal selling than on any other form of marketing communications.

- **Advertising** is non-personal mass communication that the sponsor has paid for and in which the sponsor is clearly identified. The most familiar forms of ads are found in the broadcast (TV and radio) and print (newspapers and magazines) media. However, there are many other advertising alternatives, from spots on heavily visited Internet pages, to direct mail, billboards, and the Yellow Pages. Product placement in movies and television shows is another, more subtle way of getting a brand in front of the consumer.

- **Sales promotion** is demand-stimulating activity designed to supplement advertising and facilitate personal selling. It is paid for by the sponsor and frequently involves a temporary incentive to encourage a purchase. Many sales promotions are directed at consumers, including the coupons that arrive in the mail and the contest that allows you to win tickets to a Barenaked Ladies concert. Many sales promotions, however, are designed to encourage a company's sales force or other members of its distribution channel to sell its products more aggressively. This latter category is called *trade promotion*. Included in sales promotion is a wide spectrum of activities, such as contests, trade shows, in-store displays, rebates, samples, premiums, discounts, and coupons.

MARKETING AT WORK 10-1: STRATEGY

I'll Have a Medium Double-Double and the Old Guy in the Pink Hat

Nine-year-old Jarod sits in front of the television, transfixed. As his favourite YTV show, *The Zone*, begins, he's hoping to win the coveted, cool, action figures featured in his favourite cartoon, "Dragon Ball Z." The show's hosts announce that the figures can be won, courtesy of Irwin Toy, through the YTV Web site. The Irwin Toy logo flashes on-screen periodically throughout the program, so nobody can forget who's footing the bill for the prizes.

Diesel, L'Oréal, and Wal-Mart all worked with an emerging Canadian musical act to reach their collective demographic. By associating itself with boy band i.d. (short for "identically different"), L'Oréal thought the opportunity stood out (or up) for its Radical Gel and Out of Bed Putty, as all five members of the group had radically spiky hair. This lent itself to a product placement in the group's new video released to support the launch of the Special FX hair product line. Wal-Mart hosted a summer-long tour for i.d. by closing down its parking lots for weekend concerts. Why? To publicize new locations and build the music reputation within its stores.

Remember the "True Stories" ads from Tim Hortons, particularly the one about Shorty Jenkins? He's the crusty old codger in the pink cowboy hat who goes from town to town making curling ice. Of course, he always goes to the nearest Tim's between putting down ice layers. Well, he made his movie debut in 2002 in *Men with Brooms*. Tim Hortons was asked to supply cups for the movie, and because Shorty's so well known by the curling set, he was swept up in the deal. Eagle-eyed viewers will notice Shorty just before the climatic curling scene, spraying the ice in his classic lasso style.

Welcome to the fast-increasing trend of meshing programming content with brand advertising. It's quickly going mainstream and has become a "must do" for the dozens of new digital channels struggling to stay afloat in Canada. It's an effective tool in a cluttered marketing environment, with the prime advantage being that the advertising message can

become an integral part of the editorial content, ensuring that people aren't looking away or flipping through channels. Whether it's a character in your favourite network sitcom drinking a particular brand of pop or the crew of a Discovery Channel adventure show using a particular brand of climbing gear, kayak, or SUV, these product placements shouldn't be underestimated. They can be valuable endorsements and a valuable component of a thoroughly integrated communications plan.

SOURCE: Rakshande Italia,"Ads That Are a Part of the Show," *Marketing Magazine*, February 25, 2002, p. 22; Mark Etting, "Tim's at the Movies," *Marketing Magazine*, April 1, 2002, p. 23; Marlene Milczarek, "Baby Boy Band Embraces Sponsors," *Marketing Magazine*, August 13, 2001, p. 3.

Unable to advertise easily, du Maurier uses other approaches.

● **Public relations** encompasses a wide variety of communications efforts to contribute to generally favourable attitudes and opinions toward an organization and its products. Unlike most advertising and personal selling, it does not include a specific sales message. The targets may be customers, shareholders, a government agency, or a special-interest group. Public relations can take many forms, including newsletters, annual reports, lobbying, and sponsorship of charitable or civic events. The Labatt hot-air balloon is a familiar example of a public relations device. Many large companies, such as the Royal Bank of Canada and Air Canada, gain national attention through their sponsorship of organizations and events such as symphony orchestras and the Special Olympics.

● **Publicity** is a special form of public relations that involves creating and placing a news story, editorial, or announcement about an organization or its products or services. Like advertising, it involves a non-personal message that reaches a mass audience through the media. But several things distinguish publicity from advertising: It is not paid for, the organization that is the subject of the publicity has little control over it, and it appears as news and therefore may have greater credibility or "legitimacy" than advertising. Organizations seek good publicity and frequently provide the material for it in the form of news releases, photographs, and press conferences. Publicity is not always positive — as in cases when a firm has lower than expected sales or earnings or it lays off a large number of employees.

◀━ BACKSPACE

1. Name the three essential roles that marketing communications plays.
2. What are the five basic forms of marketing communications?
3. What are the essential differences between advertising and public relations?

Integrated Marketing Communications

integrated marketing communications (IMC)

A strategic business process used to plan, develop, execute, and evaluate co-ordinated communication with an organization's customers and the general public.

While marketers have a variety of communications tools at their disposal, making effective use of them means that a company's personal selling, advertising, and other communications activities should form a co-ordinated program within its total marketing plan. However, in many firms, these activities are not well co-ordinated, with potentially damaging consequences. For example, advertising directors and sales force managers sometimes come into conflict over resources, or the sales force may not be adequately informed about the details of a sales promotion effort. This wouldn't happen if the elements comprising the marketing communications program were part of an **integrated marketing communications (IMC)** effort. IMC is a strategic business process used to plan, develop, execute, and evaluate co-ordinated communication with an organization's customers and the general public.[8]

IMC begins with a strategic planning effort designed to co-ordinate marketing communications with product planning, pricing, and distribution, the other marketing mix elements. The communications program is influenced, for example, by how distinctive a product is and whether its planned price is above or below that of the competition. A manufacturer or intermediary must also consider its promotional links with other firms in the distribution channel. For example, DaimlerChrysler and Ford recognize that their success is closely tied to the performance of their dealers. Therefore, in addition to advertising their automobiles directly to consumers, these firms have developed dealer certification processes to train dealers' sales and service personnel in how to provide the best experience possible for the customer. Chrysler's Five Star program involves ongoing monitoring of dealerships for employee training, customer satisfaction surveys, customer follow-up, and service standards. Ford's Blue Oval Certified program operates similarly, using a thumbprint in Ford's trademark blue colour to indicate certification status. According to one employee, the logo is "A symbol to show customers we've done everything in our power to make sure that their stay at the dealership was the best it could be."[9] Such programs also offer cash incentives to dealers with high customer-satisfaction scores. IMC efforts such as these often incorporate what is referred to as an **internal marketing component** — that is, marketing messages that inform, persuade, and remind employees — educating and helping employees to do their jobs well, thereby enhancing their employment experience and providing better product quality and customer service.

An audience perspective

An IMC approach adopts the position that a customer or prospect is exposed to many bits and pieces of information about a company or brand. Certainly, some of these bits are designed and presented by marketers but others, possibly the majority, come from other sources. These sources can include personal experience, the opinion of others, and comparisons made by competitors in their advertising. Based on all of this information, individuals make evaluations and form judgements. With so little control over what information consumers can use, a marketer's efforts must be highly co-ordinated and complementary to have a useful impact. That means anticipating the opportunities when the target audience will be exposed to information about the company or brand, and effectively communicating the appropriate message in those "windows of opportunity." Usually, this involves using several different communications methods and requires a high degree of co-ordination.

IMC elements

The use of the IMC approach to marketing communications is reflected in how managers think about the information needs of the message recipients. Organizations that have adopted an IMC philosophy tend to share several characteristics:

- An awareness of the target groups' information sources, as well as their media habits and preferences.

- An understanding of what such groups know and believe that relates to the desired response.

- The use of a mix of communications tools, each with specific objectives but all linked to a common overall goal.

- A concerted effort in which personal selling, advertising, sales promotion, public relations, and publicity are co-ordinated in order to communicate a consistent and continuous flow of information adapted to the audience's needs.

- A long-term perspective that focuses on continuing co-ordination and integration to contribute to the building of brand equity.

Implementing IMC

In developing integrated communications, a company co-ordinates its advertising, personal selling, sales promotion, public relations, and publicity to accomplish specific objectives. For example, a few years ago, IBM's communications efforts had become highly fragmented. The company was using more than 80 advertising agencies around the world, and its ads were sending mixed messages. To take care of the problem and co-ordinate efforts:

● The 80 agencies were replaced by 1.

● All packaging, brochures, and trade show booths were standardized to present a unified image.

● Sports sponsorships were consolidated into a few big events, such as the Olympics, to better showcase IBM technology.

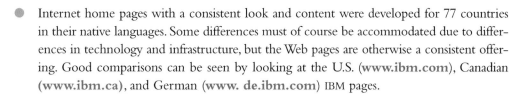

● Internet home pages with a consistent look and content were developed for 77 countries in their native languages. Some differences must of course be accommodated due to differences in technology and infrastructure, but the Web pages are otherwise a consistent offering. Good comparisons can be seen by looking at the U.S. (**www.ibm.com**), Canadian (**www.ibm.ca**), and German (**www. de.ibm.com**) IBM pages.

IBM (United States, Canada, Germany)

Communications at IBM is now built around the theme and content of being a technology innovator that is accessible and responsive.[10]

An IMC program may incorporate several different communications campaigns, with some even running concurrently. Depending on objectives and available funds, a firm may undertake simultaneous local, regional, national, and international programs. To increase its accessibility and responsiveness in the Canadian marketplace, IBM took e-business on the road in 2002. The "IBM e-Business Breakaway Tour" had company executives discussing business solutions and showcasing products and services across the country to businesses of all sizes. According to IBM Canada's vice-president of marketing and communications, it was "a great opportunity to get closer to companies within Canada, with a specific message on how to integrate technology for its business advantage."[11] Moreover, a firm may have one campaign aimed at consumers and another at wholesalers and retailers. We have discussed how, with so many products available, companies must go beyond designing an attractive product to actually communicating with and attracting the attention of the marketplace. This includes those in the supply chains that make decisions regarding carrying a product and reordering.

Coca-Cola

Coca-Cola (**www.cocacola.com**) is probably the best example of a truly global product — around the world, "It's the real thing." The company uses this phrase, which it owns, as a part of its global message — at least as close to it as can be literally and culturally communicated and translated. The "Coke" part of "Vanilla Coke" is extremely important in the international roll-out of this new flavour. Another global Coke campaign is the "Enjoy" branding campaign. Such efforts usually have a minimum of text communication, emphasizing visual and brand images. These global programs are designed to be easily tailored to specific markets. Coca-Cola also acts nationally, regionally, and locally to bolster individual markets. Coke has always initiated a variety of programs unique to Canada, such as the Coke Card promotion, but also uses programs with regional "flavouring," such as the hockey-themed campaign featuring a young girl singing the Canadian anthem. And to show that it's still "the real thing" in Atlantic Canada, the company produced an advertisement that showcased a series of well-known and familiar sites throughout the Atlantic provinces, in which Atlantic Canadians were shown enjoying the product.[12]

Evaluating IMC

The final step in IMC is evaluation. A program can be evaluated in a number of ways. One approach is to examine how it is implemented. For example, if the communications program of a large manufacturer of consumer goods is being carried out in a manner consistent with the notion of IMC, we would expect to find:

- An advertising program consisting of a series of related, well-timed, carefully placed ads that reinforce personal selling and sales promotional efforts.

- A personal selling effort that is co-ordinated with the advertising program. The firm's sales force would be fully informed about the advertising portion of the campaign — the theme, media used, and the schedule for appearance of the ads. The salespeople would be able to explain and demonstrate the product benefits emphasized in the ads and would be prepared to transmit the promotional message and supporting material to intermediaries so that they could take part in the campaign.

- Sales promotional devices such as point-of-purchase display materials that are co-ordinated with other aspects of the program. Incentives for intermediaries would be clearly communicated and understood. Retailers would be briefed about consumer promotions and adequate inventories would be in place.

- Public relations efforts scheduled to coincide with the other mix components and emphasizing the same theme.

- Publicity activities that "make" news for the advertiser.

More rigorous evaluation examines the results of the program. The outcome of each component is compared with the objectives set for it to determine if the effort was successful. Below are some typical objectives and some common measures associated with each of them.[13]

- *Awareness of a company or brand:* Competitive brand position studies; focus groups with distributors at trade shows; Web site "hits."

- *Interest in a product or brand:* Number of brochures or other company publications distributed; attendance at company-sponsored seminars; Web site traffic — number of pages viewed, time spent at the site, requests for company and product information.

- *Action:* Usage of and results from support tools provided to distributors and retailers; responses to direct mail; customer enquiries or store visits; sales.

To be meaningful, most of these measures need to be taken both before and after the communications effort, with the difference between the two measures indicating its effect. For example, Gap did not experience a meaningful increase in store traffic and sales during and after some recent TV campaigns. One in particular, featuring young people in khakis swing dancing, was disappointing because it was lauded by industry observers as an outstanding commercial. As a result, the retailer de-emphasized the TV component of its communications strategy, shifting more funds to in-store promotion, print advertising, and online advertising.[14] After an appropriate period of time, these new tools will also be evaluated. Sometimes, a campaign can be spectacularly successful in that it generates a great deal of publicity beyond the ads paid for by the company.

Barriers to IMC

Despite its attractiveness, an IMC approach is not universally supported. In some organizations, the communications functions are in different departments. The sales force may be in a unit separate from where advertising decisions are made. The result is a lack of internal communication and co-ordination. In other firms, there is a belief that communications activities are so imprecise that efforts to carefully design objectives and co-ordinate efforts would be unproductive. In still other firms, there is a history of relying on particular forms of communications and a resistance to consider alternatives.

Fully utilizing an IMC approach would probably require a firm to make several changes. One involves restructuring internal communications to ensure that all relevant parties involved in communications work together. Some firms have approached this by creating a marketing communications manager who oversees the planning and co-ordination of all promotional and communications efforts. A second change involves conducting research to gather the necessary information about the target audience. Firms utilize extensive databases for this purpose, but these are costly to create and expensive to maintain. Finally, and most importantly, senior management must support the effort to integrate marketing communications efforts. Strong leadership is essential to break down barriers and help create co-operative situations.

Next, we will examine how basic communication, the core of all marketing communications, actually works. We will then move on to key managerial issues in the marketing communications program.

The Communication Process

communication

Verbal or non-verbal transmission of information, through a medium or media, between a sender and a receiver.

Communication is the verbal or non-verbal transmission of information between someone wanting to express an idea and someone else expected or expecting to understand that idea. Because the components of marketing communications are examples of communication between two or more parties, much can be learned about structuring effective marketing messages by examining the communication process.

Fundamentally, communication requires only four elements: a message, a source of the message, a communication channel, and a receiver. In practice, however, important additional components come into play:

- The information that the sending source wants to share must first be encoded into a transmittable form. **Encoding** is the conversion of an idea into words, pictures, symbols in an advertisement, or some other form, such as a product display in a supermarket, a coupon, or a "hot button" on a Web site.

- Once the encoded message has been transmitted through some communication channel, the symbols must be **decoded** — perceived, or given meaning, by the receiver. The perceived message may be what the sender intended or something else, depending on the receiver's knowledge and experience.

- If the message has been transmitted successfully, there is some change in the receiver's knowledge, beliefs, or feelings. As a result of this change, the receiver formulates a **response**. The response could be non-verbal (a positive reaction, as indicated by a smile while watching an ad), verbal (suggesting to a friend that she try an advertised product), or behavioural (purchasing the advertised product).

response

The reaction (non-verbal, verbal, or behavioural) of an information receiver that serves as feedback to the sender of a communication.

- The response serves as **feedback**, telling the sender whether the message was received and how it was perceived by the recipient. Through feedback, the sender can learn why a communication failed and how to improve future communication.

- All stages of the process can be affected by **noise** — any external event or factor that interferes with successful communication, such as a competitive ad. Noise occurs when a television viewer sees ads for both Speedy and Midas within a short time period or when your system crashes while filling your shopping cart at a retail Web site.

Figure 10-1 illustrates these components of a communication process and relates them to marketing communications activities.

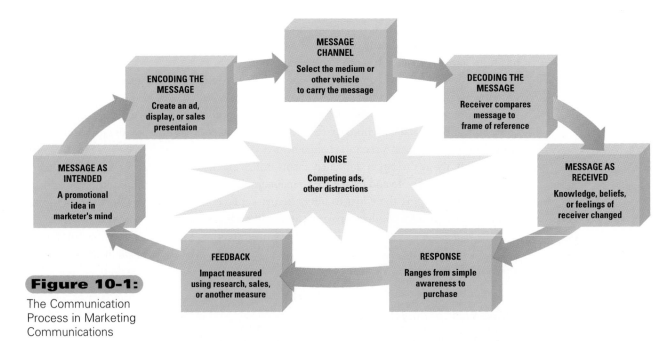

Figure 10-1:

The Communication Process in Marketing Communications

What does the communication process tell us about producing effective marketing communications programs? First, the act of encoding reminds us that messages can take many forms. Messages can be physical (a sample, a premium) or symbolic (verbal, visual), and there are many options within each of these categories. For example, a verbal message can be factual, humorous, or even threatening.

Second, the number of channels or methods of transmitting a message are limited only by the imagination and creativity of the sender. Most marketing communications messages are transmitted by familiar channels, such as the voice of a salesperson, the airwaves of radio, the mail, the side of a bus, or the lead-in to a feature film in a movie theatre. Each channel has its own characteristics in terms of audience reach, flexibility, permanence, credibility, and cost. In selecting a channel, a marketer must have clearly defined objectives and a familiarity with the features of the many alternatives.

Third, how the message is decoded or interpreted depends on its form (encoding and transmission) and the capability and interest of the recipient. In designing and sending messages, marketers must be sensitive to the audience. What is the vocabulary and level of verbal sophistication of audience members? What other messages have they received? What experiences have they had? What will get and hold their attention?

Finally, every component of the marketing communications program should have a measurable objective that can be determined from the response and feedback provided by the recipients. Feedback may be collected in many forms — changes in sales, recall of advertising messages, more favourable attitudes, increased awareness of a brand or an organization — depending on the objective of the marketing communications message. For some promotional activities, the objective may be modest; for example, an increase in the audience's awareness of a brand or stimulating trial of a new product. For others, such as a direct-mail solicitation, the objective would be a particular level of sales. Without objectives, the effectiveness of a message cannot be evaluated.

1. What is the purpose of IMC?
2. What are some of the barriers to IMC?
3. Define *communication*.

MARKETING AT WORK   10-2: STRATEGY

And, in This Corner...

If you saw a big flashy dude in tights and shades enter your favourite sports bar, what would go through your mind? Probably that you've had way too much to drink and you need assistance getting to a cab, right now! However, it's probably just one of the newest characters from the world of wrestling — The Molson EXterminator — performing a tag-team promotion for Molson and World Wrestling Federation Entertainment Canada to hype an upcoming WrestleMania event. In a 2002 promotion called "Belt Your Bartender," the EXterminator visited Toronto bars, challenging barkeeps to novel, but not-too-strenuous matches: thumb-wrestling (for opposable opponents), pose-downs (flex those pecs!), or trash-talking (the sport's favourite sideshow). The promotion was supported by in-house bar promotions and Molson radio spots. Yet another example of the

breadth of marketing communications and promotional tools used within the brewing industry to support brands.

The wrestling promotion was timed perfectly for Molson Export, following on the heels of the successful "Had Your EX Today?" advertising campaign, as well as being a perfect tie-in with the brand name. It was a "tongue-in-cheek way to tie into WrestleMania," according to Molson Export Marketing Manager Todd Lewin. Frequent prizes were given away by the fictitious wrestling star — even to unsuspecting bartender participants, who received a specially designed wrestling belt.

SOURCE: Sharon Younger, "Promomania: Guy Brands Leap into the Ring with WWF," *Strategy*, February 11, 2002, p. 3.

Determining the Marketing Communications Mix

marketing communications mix

The combination of personal selling, advertising, sales promotion, publicity, and public relations that is intended to help an organization achieve its marketing objectives.

A **marketing communications mix** is an organization's combination of personal selling, advertising, sales promotion, public relations, and publicity. An effective mix is a critical part of virtually all marketing communications strategies. Product differentiation, market segmentation, trading up and trading down, and branding all require effective communications with target audiences. Designing an effective marketing communications mix requires a number of strategic decisions, as we will now see.

Factors influencing the marketing communications mix

Five factors should be taken into account when determining the marketing communications mix: (1) the target market; (2) the objective of the communications effort; (3) the nature of the product or service being promoted; (4) the stage in the life cycle of the product or service; and (5) the amount of money available for marketing communications.

Target market   As in most areas of marketing, decisions on the marketing communications mix will be greatly influenced by the target market. At least four variables affect the choice of an approach to communicating with a particular market segment:

awareness

Stage 1 of buying readiness: The customer gains information about the product and the brand name.

- **Readiness to buy:** A target segment may be in any one of six stages of buying readiness. These stages — awareness, knowledge, liking, preference, conviction, and purchase — are called the *hierarchy of effects*, because they represent stages that a buyer goes through in moving toward a purchase, and each defines a possible goal or effect of marketing communications.

    At the **awareness** stage, the marketer's task is to let buyers know that the product or brand exists. Here the objective is to build familiarity with the product and the brand name. Recall the unconventional "shock" ads that Benetton (**www.benetton.com**) used to attract attention. A controversial series of print ads depicted various forms of human suffering, including a dying AIDS victim, refugees jumping overboard from a ship, and a pool of blood from a war casualty.

Benetton

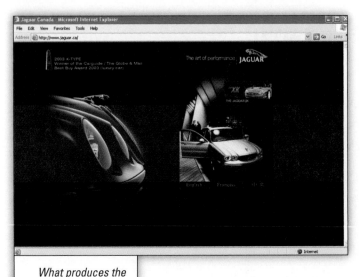

What produces the conviction in this ad?

knowledge
Stage 2 of buying readiness: A customers learns about a product's features and how it can meet a need.

liking
Stage 3 of buying readiness: The knowledgeable customer moves from being indifferent about the brand to having positive feelings about it.

preference
Stage 4 of buying readiness: The customer distinguishes among brands and prefers yours.

CDNOW

conviction
Stage 5 of buying readiness: The customer makes an actual decision or commitment to purchase.

purchase
Stage 6, the last stage of buying readiness: The customer overcomes any inhibitors that might delay or postpone purchase and buys the product.

Knowledge goes beyond awareness to learning about a product's features: The provider has to tell or show you what it is and what it can do for you. For example, what exactly can the new generation of cellphones do to make my life easier? What exactly is a personal VCR?

Liking refers to how the market feels about the product or brand. Marketing communications can be used to move a knowledgeable audience from being indifferent to actually liking a brand. A common technique is to associate the item with an attractive symbol or person. Buick, usually the choice of older consumers, as part of an integrated effort to lower the average age of its consumers, has redesigned some products and engaged a celebrity spokesperson, as well as using a little humour in its advertising. The result? Ads featuring Tiger Woods have attracted new, younger buyers, never before seen in Buick showrooms. Buick has also staked its territory as the official vehicle for the Professional Golf Association tour and the title sponsor of its four major events. By doing this, the company has tried to balance its popularity with younger and older age segments.[15]

Creating **preference** involves distinguishing among brands so that the market prefers yours. It is not uncommon for consumers to like several brands of the same product, but the customer can't make a decision until one brand is preferred over the alternatives. The Internet has recently provided one of the best venues for this type of marketing, allowing manufacturers the opportunity to present side-by-side comparisons of their products and those of the nearest competitors, often down to the smallest detail. This has become particularly popular with automotive and high-technology products such as personal computers. Ads that make direct comparisons with the competition are intended to create a preference.

Conviction entails the actual decision or commitment to purchase. The marketing communications objective here is to increase the strength of the buyer's need. Trying a product and experiencing the benefits that come from using it are very effective in strengthening the conviction to own it. Consider how video game, WebTV, and CD systems are set up ready to use in stores and how sites such as CDNOW (**www.cdnow.com**) provide sampling on the Internet.

Purchase can be delayed or postponed indefinitely, even for customers who are convinced that they should buy a product. The inhibitor might be a situational factor, such as not having enough money at the moment or a natural resistance to change. Action may be triggered through a marketing communications price discount or offering additional incentives. Postponement or cancellation can also be a challenge for Internet retailers, as e-shoppers will often abandon their cybercarts containing merchandise before submitting their orders. E-tailers try to encourage follow-up of this purchase intent by holding these items in the customers' cart until the customers remove the products themselves. Customers are also reminded on each return to the site that there are items in their shopping carts.

- *Geographic scope of the market:* Personal selling may be adequate in a small local market, but as the market broadens geographically, greater emphasis must be placed on advertising, using a variety of media. The exception would be a firm that sells to concentrated pockets of customers scattered around the country. For example, the market for certain plastics is heaviest in Ontario and Québec, because these plastics are used by component suppliers to the auto industry. In this case, emphasis on personal selling may be appropriate, because spending on advertising that is widely distributed would be wasteful.

Staples/Business Depot

- *Type of customer:* Marketing communications strategy depends in part on the level of the distribution channel that the organization hopes to influence. Final consumers and resellers sometimes buy the same product, but they require different marketing communications. This is common among computer products that are targeted toward business and personal applications. To illustrate, Staples/Business Depot (**www.staples.ca**) serves both consumer and business markets. Aside from other differences utilized, the company designs TV advertisements that communicate to both audiences.

- *Concentration of the market:* The total number of prospective buyers is another consideration. The fewer potential buyers there are, the more effective personal selling is, compared with advertising. For example, in Canada, there are only a handful of manufacturers of household vacuum cleaners. Clearly, for a firm selling a component part for vacuum cleaners, personal selling would be the best way to reach this market.

Nature of the product   Several product attributes influence marketing communications strategy. The most important are:

- *Unit value:* A product with a low unit value is usually relatively uncomplicated, involves little risk for the buyer, and must appeal to a mass market to survive. As a result, advertising would be the primary marketing communications tool. In contrast, high-unit-value products often are complex and expensive. These features suggest the need for personal selling. BMW dealers are being encouraged to have salespeople get out of the showroom and call on prospects. By increasing the personal selling effort through techniques such as delivering cars to potential customers for test-drives, BMW hopes to stimulate North American sales. Such a component to the program would be consistent with the service ideology of such a high-end product offering.

- *Degree of customization:* If a product must be adapted to the individual customer's needs, personal selling and service (or sometimes a technology-based equivalent) are necessary, so you would expect to find an emphasis on personal selling for something like home remodelling or an expensive suit. However, the benefits of most standardized products can be effectively communicated in advertising. The increasing number of firms making use of advanced production techniques and information management has made it possible to customize some products for large markets without a great deal of personal service, by relying on data warehousing and electronic communication.

- *Pre-purchase and post-purchase service:* Products that must be demonstrated, for which there are trade-ins, or that require frequent servicing to keep them in good working order lend themselves to personal selling, sometimes combined with Internet-based demonstrations, video cassettes, and displays of product performance. Typical examples are riding lawnmowers, powerboats, and personal computers. For example, Bombardier would want to show its Ski-Doo (**www.ski-doo.com**) and Sea-Doo (**www.sea-doo.com**) machines in action.

Bombardier

Stage of product life cycle   Marketing communications strategies are influenced by a product's life-cycle stage. When a new product is introduced, prospective consumers must be informed about its existence and its benefits, and wholesalers and retailers must be convinced to carry it. Both advertising (to consumers) and personal selling (to channel members) are therefore critical in a product's introductory stage. At introduction, a new product also may be something of a novelty, offering excellent opportunities for publicity. Later, if a product becomes successful, competition intensifies and more emphasis is placed on persuasive advertising. Table 10-1 shows how marketing communications strategies change as a product moves through its life cycle.

Funds available   Regardless of what may be the most desirable marketing communications mix, the amount of money available for marketing communications is the ultimate determinant of the mix. A business with ample funds can make more effective use of advertising than can a firm with limited financial resources. Small or regionally based companies are likely to rely on personal selling, dealer displays, or joint manufacturer-retailer promotions. For example, the Vancouver Grizzlies partner with corporate sponsors such as Air Canada, TELUS Mobility, and IBM Canada to produce premiums such as magnetic game schedules, megaphones, and mouse pads, which add value for basketball fans and keep them coming back to the Grizzlies games.[16]

Lack of money may limit the options a firm has for its marketing communications effort. For example, television advertising can carry a particular message to far more people and at a lower cost per person than can most other media. Yet a firm may have to rely on less expensive media, such as Yellow Pages advertising, because it lacks the funds to take advantage of television's broad coverage.

TABLE 10-1   Communications Strategies for Different Product Life-Cycle Stages

Market Situation	Promotional Strategy
Introduction Stage	
Customers are not aware of the product's features, nor do they understand how it will benefit them.	Inform and educate potential customers that the product exists, how it might be used, and what want-satisfying benefits it provides. In this stage, a seller must stimulate primary demand — the demand for a type of product — as contrasted with selective demand — the demand for a particular brand. For example, producers had to sell consumers on the value of compact discs in general before it was feasible to promote a particular brand. Normally, heavy emphasis must be placed on personal selling. Exhibits at trade shows are also used extensively in the communications mix. A trade show gives a new product broad exposure to many intermediaries. Manufacturers also rely heavily on personal selling to attract intermediaries to handle a new product.
Growth Stage	
Customers are aware of product's benefits. The product is selling well, and intermediaries want to handle it.	Stimulate selective (brand) demand as competition grows. Increase emphasis on persuasive advertising. Intermediaries share more of the total communications effort.
Maturity Stage	
Competition intensifies and sales level off.	Advertising is used more to remind and persuade rather than only to provide information. Intense competition forces sellers to devote larger sums to advertising and thus contributes to the declining profits experienced in this stage.
Decline Stage	
Sales and profits are declining. New and better products are coming into the market.	All communications efforts are cut back substantially. The focus becomes reminding remaining customers.

Choosing a push or a pull strategy

push strategy
A communications program aimed primarily at wholesalers and retailers.

pull strategy
A communications program aimed primarily at end-users.

True Value
Home Hardware

As we have seen, producers aim their marketing communications mix at both intermediaries and end-users. A communications program aimed primarily at wholesalers and retailers is called a **push strategy**, and a program directed primarily at end-users is called a **pull strategy**. It is not unusual for firms to use both types of strategies for the same brand. Figure 10-2 contrasts these two strategies.

When using a push strategy, a channel member directs its message primarily to the firms that are the next link forward in the distribution channel. The product is "pushed" through the channel. Take the case of a hardware manufacturer such as Stanley tools, which sells its products to household consumers through wholesalers and retailers such as True Value (**www.truevalue.com**) and Home Hardware (**www.homehardwaredealers.com**). The producer promotes heavily to wholesalers, which then also use a push strategy to retailers. In turn, the retailers promote to consumers. A push strategy usually involves a lot of personal selling and sales promotion, including contests for salespeople and displays at trade shows. Also, awards and prizes are promoted, based on the volume of product sold through individual outlets. Attractive display cases to showcase products may also serve as an incentive if space is available, as in large hardware stores and other warehouse-sized outlets. Discounting may also be used to encourage carrying a new product or buying larger quantities. This marketing communications strategy is appropriate for many manufacturers of business products, as well as for various consumer goods.

With a pull strategy, marketing communications messages are directed at end-users — usually the public. The intention is to motivate end-consumers to ask retailers for the product. The retailers, in turn, will request the product from wholesalers, and wholesalers will order it from the producer. In effect, marketing communications to consumers is designed to "pull" the product through the channel. This strategy relies on heavy advertising and various forms of consumer-directed sales promotions, such as coupons, samples in consumers' mailboxes, or in-store demonstrations. To promote its new Olay collection of cosmetics, Procter & Gamble (**www.pg.com**) mailed more than 1.5 million tiny lipstick samples in a first-ever campaign of this type. The cosmetics, aimed at women 25 and older, were sent to let consumers actually try the product and see the benefits.[17] Sunny Delight (**www.sunnydelight.com**) sent out small bottles of juice to consumers — using the same unique bottle shape as the large bottles, packaged in cardboard refrigerators with doors that open to reveal the product and coupons for future purchases. These are obviously expensive to produce and distribute, but they get the product into the consumer's hands — or, well, consumer's mouths in these examples.

Procter & Gamble
Sunny Delight

Figure 10-2:

Push and Pull
Strategies of
Marketing
Communications

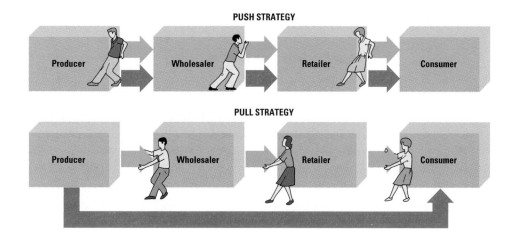

The Marketing Communications Budget

Establishing **marketing communications budgets** is extremely challenging, because management generally lacks reliable standards for determining how much to spend altogether on advertising or personal selling and determining how much of the total budget to allocate to each element of the marketing communications mix. A firm may have the alternative of adding seven salespeople or increasing its trade show budget by $400,000 per year, but it cannot determine precisely the increase in sales or profits it could expect from either expenditure. As a result, rather than one generally accepted approach to setting budgets, there are four common marketing communications budgeting methods: percentage of sales, all available funds, following the competition, and budgeting by task or objective. These methods are frequently discussed in connection with the advertising budget, but they may also be applied to any communications activity to determine the total marketing communications budget.

Percentage of sales

The marketing communications budget may be related in some way to company income, as a percentage of either past or anticipated sales. A common approach for determining the sales base is to compute an average of the previous year's actual sales and expected sales for the coming year. Some businesses prefer to budget a fixed amount of money per unit of past or expected future sales. Manufacturers of products with a high unit value and a low rate of turnover (automobiles or appliances, for example) frequently use the per-unit approach to setting budgets.

Because the percentage-of-sales method is simple to calculate, it is probably the most widely used budgeting method. Moreover, it sets the cost of marketing communications in relation to sales income, making it a variable rather than a fixed expense.

Two things must be noted about basing marketing communications expenditures on past sales. First, management is effectively making marketing communications a result of sales when, in fact, it is a cause of sales. Second, a percentage-of-past-sales method reduces marketing communications expenditures when sales are declining — just when advertising and other forms of communications usually are most needed.

All available funds

A new company or a firm introducing a new product or service frequently ploughs all available funds into its marketing communications program. The objective is to build sales and market share as rapidly as possible during those early, critical months and years. We have seen many Internet start-ups spending all of their funds in an effort to create awareness and Web site traffic — a few successfully, many not so successfully. After a time, management generally finds it necessary to invest in other things, such as new equipment or expanded production or distribution capacity, so the method of setting the marketing communications budget is changed.

Follow the competition

A weak method of determining the marketing communications budget, but one that is used occasionally, is to match the marketing communications expenditures of competitors or to spend in proportion to market share. Sometimes, only one competitor is followed. In other cases, if management has access to industry average expenditures on marketing communications through a trade association, these become company benchmarks.

This approach has at least two problems. First, the firm's competitors may be just as much in the dark regarding how to set a marketing communications budget. Second, a company's goals may be quite different from those of its competitors because of differences in the marketing strategies being followed.

Task or objective

The best approach for establishing the marketing communications budget is to determine the tasks or objectives that the communications program must accomplish and then decide what they will cost. The task method forces management to define realistically the goals of its marketing communications program. Sometimes, it may be defined as straightforwardly as wanting to increase revenue by 10 percent or unit sales by 5 percent, or increasing the price while maintaining a particular level of sales.

Sometimes this is called the *build-up method* because of the way it is constructed. For example, a company may decide to enter a new geographic market. Management determines this venture will require 10 additional salespeople. The compensation and expenses of these people will cost a total of $520,000 per year. Salary for an additional sales supervisor and expenses for an extra office and administrative needs will cost $70,000, so in the personal-selling component of the marketing communications mix, an extra $590,000 per year must be budgeted. Similar estimates can be made for the anticipated costs of advertising, sales promotion, and other communications tools. The budget is developed by adding up the costs of the individual marketing communications tasks needed to reach the goal of entering a new territory.

For the 2002 budget year, British Columbia Hydro decided to alter the goals of its communications plan and its budget accordingly. Instead of focusing on warm-and-fuzzy images and messages to promote the brand in the newly deregulated industry, management decided on a more task-oriented approach. To deal with the tight labour market situation in the province, it was decided that $1 million needed to be directed toward employee recruitment. Another $2 million would be split roughly evenly between public relations activities and advertising dealing with tenders, water flow levels, and community-impact activities. The decision that $3 million was required to achieve the goals of the plan meant that the company would actually spend $2 million less than in the previous year.[18]

Regulation of Marketing Communications Activities

Because the primary objective of marketing communications is to sell something by communicating with a market, marketing communications activities attract attention. Consequently, abuses by individual firms are easily and quickly noted by the public. This situation in turn soon leads to (1) public demand for correction of the abuses, (2) assurances that they will not be repeated, and (3) general restraints on marketing communications activities. To answer public demand, laws and regulations have been enacted by the federal government and by most provincial governments. In addition, many private business organizations have established voluntary codes of advertising standards to guide their own marketing communications activities. The advertising industry itself, through the Advertising Advisory Board and its Advertising Standards Councils, does a considerable amount of self-regulation.

The federal role

Broadcasting Act
Established the CRTC and provided for sweeping powers of advertising regulation.

A number of federal government departments administer legislation aimed at controlling various aspects of marketing communications, particularly advertising. The **Broadcasting Act** established the Canadian Radio-television and Telecommunications Commission (CRTC) and provided for sweeping powers of advertising regulation. The CRTC may make regulations concerning the character of broadcast advertising and the amount of time that may be devoted to it. While the potential for substantial control exists, the CRTC does not in reality approve each radio and television commercial — it has delegated authority in certain fields to other federal departments, such as Health Canada and Industry Canada.

MARKETING AT WORK 10-3: ETHICS

Wyeth-Ayerst Looks for the Better Way

Although they have been on the Canadian market since 1961 as consumer products, birth control pills and those who manufacture them have always been content to remain shy, discrete, and demure. Now, however, they are set to take centre stage — in more ways than one. For the first time in Canadian history, Wyeth-Ayerst Canada Inc., the pharmaceutical company that makes the Alesse birth control pill, is promoting its sometimes controversial product on national television with ads geared specifically to young people.

Pharmaceutical companies may advertise their drugs as long as they provide viewers with only the name, quantity, and price of their products. The rationale is that this is the bare minimum required for manufacturers to promote their products in a pharmacy. Manufacturers are also free to produce informational TV shots that make no mention of any specific product, but rather discuss the disease or condition that a product treats. The strategy is to motivate consumers to seek more information from their doctors, who will be able to list all available treatments, including (hopefully) the advertiser's.

Wyeth-Ayerst Canada Inc. has not developed commercials that name the drug and talk about what it does. The company developed two commercials, one talking about birth control options, the other providing a "lesson learned" feature and staying within Health Canada's guidelines of name, price, and quantity. Two 15-second TV spots advertise the Alesse brand (there is also a 60-second cinema ad) and one 30-second informational TV spot discusses the importance of birth control in general. With a 10-week run on Canada's MuchMusic network, the commercials are destined to hit its target market of "with-it" young women. In fact, all of the commercials feature such women talking about men and relationships. Each woman discusses "a lesson," such as a lesson in relationship break-ups: "Don't lend him anything you ever expect to get back" and a lesson in guys: "Never play hard to get. Be hard to get."

While the 15-second commercials identify the brand name and show a package of Alesse pills, the 30-second infomercial reveals neither. It does however wind up with a woman saying, "Talk to your doctor about your birth control options," to which another woman adds, "Less could make sense for you." Although the line refers to the pill's low-dose formula, it also sounds coincidentally like "Alesse could make sense for you." Come to think of it, all those "a lessons" sound coincidentally like "Alesse," too.

Wyeth-Ayerst's integrated advertising strategy — along with the TV and cinema commercials, posters will appear throughout city transit systems — is a classic device. Sending similar messages about a product through multiple media channels so that the consumer associates one with another and then combines them all into a unique, more complex message is nothing new. What is new is Wyeth-Ayerst's take on the integrated advertising approach. The information commercial and the branded commercial are not run at the same time. The firm has spaced these commercials according to Advertising Standards Canada (ASC) guidelines. After all, the similarity in the casting, copy, and overall look and feel of the ads ensures there will be overlap between the various Alesse "lessons." The fact that the ads are set to run during the same time period makes the overlap even more pronounced. The deciding factor will be: How much of an overlap will be too much?

If, for example, Wyeth-Ayerst placed the two kinds of ads in the same media time and space, where a consumer who saw one and then the other was likely to make a connection between birth control and Alesse, Health Canada would be forced to make a fuss. Or would it? Health Canada doesn't pre-screen prescription drug ads. That role is performed by the ASC, the ad industry's self-regulating organization. And the ASC has given the Alesse campaign a thumbs-up.

For years now, prescription drug makers have been pushing to loosen tight advertising regulations. They argue that consumers are being bombarded by brand-name drug ads from U.S. media and the Internet, anyway. If they can't compete on the same tough turf, how will Canadian manufacturers survive? Maybe Wyeth-Ayerst is giving more "Alessons" than it originally planned.

SOURCE: Adapted, in part, from Patrick Allossery, "Health Canada Challenge," *Financial Post,* May 15, 2000, p. C5; John Heinzl, "A lesson in drug advertising," *The Globe and Mail,* May 5, 2000, p. M1; and Shawna Cohen, "The Pill Is Controversial Once Again," *Marketing Magazine Online,* May 15, 2000.

Health Canada deals with advertising in the fields of drugs, cosmetics, and devices (officialese for birth control products), and it has sweeping powers to limit, control, rewrite, or ban certain communications for the products under its authority. The department deals with general types of prohibition aimed at preventing the treatment, processing, packaging, labelling, advertising, and selling of foods, drugs, and devices in such a manner as to mislead or deceive, or even to be likely to create an erroneous impression concerning the nature of the products. It also prohibits the advertising of whole classes of drugs and diseases or conditions for which a cure may not be advertised under any circumstances. This prohibition stands even if a professionally accepted cure exists. The logic for the prohibition of advertising, in spite of the existence of a cure, is that Health Canada does not want members of the general public to engage in self-diagnosis of a condition that can be treated.

Health Canada has been delegated, by the CRTC, absolute control over radio and television advertisements for the products under its jurisdiction. All such advertisements must be submitted to it at least 15 days prior to airing, and no radio or television station can air an ad without its having been approved by the department and, therefore, by the CRTC.

In contrast to the delegated review powers that Health Canada has over advertisements using the broadcast media, its position in relation to the print media is weak. Its formal control is over alleged Food and Drugs Act violations, which must be prosecuted in court. Given the lack of jurisprudence in this area, the department is loath to go to court in case it loses and thus sets a precedent, or in case its regulations (many of which have not been tested in court) are found to be illegal. What the department does is advise advertisers of its opinion of advertisements that are prepared for the print media. This opinion is not a ruling, and ads submitted, as well as those that are not, are still subject to the regulations for which the department has responsibility. This does not mean that the department does not monitor the print media: Newspapers and magazines are sampled and advertisements are examined.

What is actually on the product package is also a part of the marketing communications package — and is subject to regulation. Aside from legalities about the labelling of contents, size, etc., there are also regulations about what else you can say about your product. In recent years, the health dimension of a product has become a very popular marketing focus for many foods, from Becel margarine to Sun-Rype Fruit & Veggie bars to So Good soya beverages.

Legislation that became effective in January 2001 made Canada the first country to require cigarette manufacturers selling their products in this country to carry warnings accompanied by grotesque images depicting the potential damage that may result from using the product. One of the warnings (there are 16 different ones, in total) has to take up the top half of the front and back of each package. These messages are significantly more graphic than those required by the 1995 Supreme Court ruling.

Industry Canada has substantial responsibility in the area of regulating marketing communications. The Acts administered include (1) the Precious Metals Marking Act (definitions of sterling and carat weight), (2) the Trademarks Act, (3) the Consumer Packaging and Labelling Act, and (4) of greatest significance, the Competition Act. In the **Competition Act**, a number of sections pertain directly to the regulation of the following types of advertising and marketing communications activities:

- Manufacturers or wholesalers who offer marketing communications allowances to retailers must offer such allowances on proportionate terms to all competing purchasers.

- Misleading advertising in general is prohibited.

- "Bait and switch" advertising is not allowed.[19]

- The making of any false or misleading statement in relation to warranties is banned.

- When a retailer promotes a product at two different prices or when two prices appear on a product at the point of sale, the retailer must sell the product at the lower of the prices.

Competition Act

The major federal legislation in Canada that governs the marketing and advertising activities of companies and organizations operating in Canada.

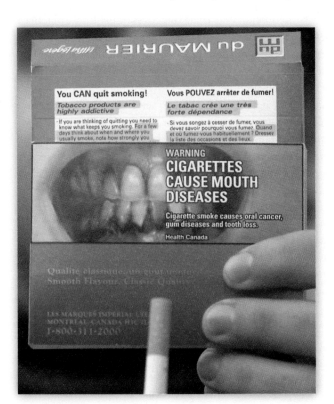

- An advertiser who promotes a product at a "sale" price must have sufficient quantities of the product on hand to satisfy reasonable market demand.

- Selling a "sale" item at a price higher than the advertised "sale" price is prohibited.

- Advertisers who promote contests must disclose the number and value of the prizes and the geographical areas in which prizes are to be distributed, and the prizes must be distributed on the basis of skill or random selection.

The provisions of the Competition Act relating to misleading advertising do not apply to publishers and broadcasters who actually distribute the advertising in question to the general public, provided that these publishers have accepted the contents of the advertising in good faith. In essence, this means that a newspaper cannot be prosecuted for misleading advertising if it accepted the advertising on the assumption that its contents were not misleading.

The provincial role

In each of the provinces, a considerable variety of legislation exists that is aimed at controlling various marketing communications practices. For instance, in Ontario, various degrees of control are exercised by the Liquor Control Board of Ontario, the Ontario Superintendent of Insurance, the Ontario Human Rights Commission, the Ontario Securities Commission, the Ontario Crime Control Commission, the Ontario Racing Commission, various ministries of the Ontario government responsible for financial, commercial, consumer, and transportation functions and services, and more. Most of the provinces have similar sets of legislation, regulatory bodies, and provincial departments. Each of the provinces, for example, regulates various aspects of the promotion of alcoholic beverages.[20] While much of the federal regulation must in the end result in argument and prosecution in a courtroom, the provincial machinery would appear to be much more flexible and potentially regulatory in nature, and if pursued, may have a more substantial effect on undesirable practices.

The powers of provincial governments in relation to the regulation of misleading advertising have been increased considerably in recent years. A number of provinces have legislation in place dealing with unfair and unconscionable trade practices. The trade practices legislation of British Columbia, Alberta, and Ontario, for example, contain "shopping lists" of practices that are illegal in those provinces. In reality, these pieces of legislation write into law practices that have been considered illegal by federal prosecutors for a number of years.

Relating to advertising, these Acts prohibit such practices as advertising a product as new when it is in fact used; advertising that fails to state a material fact, thereby deceiving the consumer; and advertising that gives greater prominence to low down payments or monthly payments rather than to the actual price of the product. The Alberta Fair Trading Act also contains a provision for corrective advertising. This provision means that a court, on convicting an advertiser for misleading advertising, can order that advertiser to devote some or all of its advertising for a certain period to informing customers that the advertiser had been advertising falsely in the past and to correcting the misleading information that had been communicated in the offending advertisements.

The Province of Québec has a section in its Consumer Protection Act that regulates advertising directed at children. This section forbids the use of exaggeration, endorsements, cartoon characters, and statements that urge children to buy. Québec's Charter of the French Language also contains a number of sections that govern the use of French and English in advertising in that province.

Regulation by private organizations

Several types of private organizations also exert considerable control over the marketing communications practices of businesses. Magazines, newspapers, and radio and television stations regularly refuse to accept advertisements that they feel are false, misleading, or generally in bad taste, and in so doing they are being "reasonable" in the ordinary course of doing business. Some trade associations have established codes of ethics that include points pertaining to sales force and advertising activities, and regularly censor advertising appearing in their trade or professional journals. Better Business Bureaus located in major cities across the country are working to control some very difficult situations. Advertising Standards Canada administers the Canadian Code of Advertising Standards; a number of other advertising codes, including the Broadcast Code for Advertising to Children (on behalf of the Canadian Association of Broadcasters); and a code regulating the advertising of over-the-counter drugs, which was developed in co-operation with drug firms and Health Canada.

◄ BACKSPACE

1. Five factors must be considered when determining the marketing communications mix. What are they?
2. What are the six stages of buying readiness?
3. What is the difference between a push strategy and a pull strategy?

Summary

Marketing communications, the fourth component of a company's total marketing mix, is essential in modern marketing. The three primary methods of marketing communications are personal selling, advertising, and sales promotion. Other forms include public relations and publicity.

The purposes of marketing communications are to inform, persuade, and remind customers. That means being able to make a product, service, or organization attractive to potential customers at any given price. It also means that marketing communications aims to increase the attractiveness of a product or service by providing the customer with evidence that it is different from the competition, thereby offering a number of non-price reasons for buying.

Marketing communications must be integrated into a firm's strategic planning, because effective execution requires that all elements of the marketing mix — product, price, distribution, and marketing communications — be co-ordinated. An IMC approach helps to assure necessary co-ordination.

Fundamentally, the marketing communications process consists of a source sending a message through a channel to a receiver. Communications success depends on how well the message is encoded, how easily and clearly it can be decoded, and whether any noise interferes with its transmission. Feedback, the response created by a message, is a measure of how effective a communication has been.

When deciding on the communications mix (the combination of advertising, personal selling, and other marketing communications tools), management should consider (1) the nature of the market, including the type of customer, the prospect's readiness to buy, and the geographic scope of the market; (2) the objective of the communications effort; (3) the nature of the product or service, including unit value, the degree of customization required, and the amount of pre-purchase and post-purchase service; (4) the stage of the life cycle of the product or service; and (5) the funds available for all forms of marketing communications.

A basic decision is how much marketing communications effort should be focused on intermediaries and how much should be directed to end-users. The options are a push strategy, which involves concentrating marketing communications efforts on the next link forward in the distribution channel, and a pull strategy, in which marketing communications is focused primarily on the final buyer.

Because the effects of communications are unpredictable, it is difficult to set a dollar figure for the total marketing communications budget. The most common method is to set the budget as a percentage of past or anticipated sales. A better approach is to establish the communications objectives and then estimate how much it will cost to achieve them.

As a result of criticism and concern regarding the use of advertising and marketing communications techniques, the federal government has enacted legislation that regulates marketing communications. The main federal laws are the Competition Act and the Broadcasting Act. Industry Canada and the Canadian Radio-television and Telecommunications Commission are charged with administering the legislation in this area. Marketing communications practices are also regulated at the provincial level through trade practices legislation and voluntary codes of businesses and trade associations, and by the advertising industry itself.

Key Terms and Concepts

advertising 287
awareness 295
Broadcasting Act 301
communication 293
Competition Act 303
conviction 296
decoding 293
encoding 293
feedback 293
inform 285
integrated marketing communications (IMC) 289
internal marketing component 290
knowledge 296
liking 296
marketing communications 285

marketing communications budgets 300
marketing communications mix 295
noise 293
personal selling 287
persuade 285
preference 296
public relations 289
publicity 289
pull strategy 299
purchase 296
push strategy 299
remind 285
response 293
sales promotion 288

Questions and Problems

1. Describe and explain the components of the marketing communications process in the following situations:
   a. A college student trying to convince her parents to buy her a used car.
   b. A salesperson trying to sell a car to a college student.

2. Explain how the nature of the market affects the marketing communications mix for the following products:
   a. Auto insurance.
   b. Golf balls.
   c. Plywood.
   d. Aircraft maintenance.
   e. Compact discs.
   f. Computers used as servers.

3. Describe how classifying consumer goods as convenience, shopping, or specialty goods helps determine the best marketing communications mix (refer to Chapter 7 for information on the classification of goods).

4. Explain whether personal selling is likely to be the main ingredient in the marketing communications mix for each of the following products:
   a. Chequing accounts.
   b. Home swimming pools.

   c. Liquid laundry detergent.
   d. A large order of fries at McDonald's.

5. Explain whether retailer trade promotion efforts should be stressed in the marketing communications mix for the following:
   a. Levi jeans.
   b. Sunkist oranges.
   c. Canada Saving Bonds.
   d. VISA card.

6. Identify the central idea — the core or basic theme — in three current marketing communications campaigns.

7. Assume that you are marketing a liquid that removes creosote (and the danger of fire) from chimneys used for wood-burning stoves. Briefly describe the roles you would assign to advertising, personal selling, sales promotion, and publicity in your marketing communications campaign.

8. Do you think we need additional legislation to regulate advertising? To regulate personal selling? If so, explain what you would recommend.

Hands-On Marketing

1. An advertisement should have a particular objective that would be apparent to a careful observer. For each of the following marketing communications objectives, find an example of a print ad:
   a. Primarily designed to inform.
   b. Primarily designed to persuade.
   c. Primarily designed to remind.

2. An IMC program or campaign is a co-ordinated series of marketing communications efforts built around a single theme and designed to reach a predetermined goal. It often includes advertising, sales promotion, personal selling, public relations, and publicity. For an important event at your school (such as homecoming, recruiting new students, fund raising), describe the marketing communications tools used in the campaign and evaluate their appropriateness based on the criteria in the chapter for designing a marketing communications mix.

Back to the Top

Think about the program used by Coca-Cola to launch its Vanilla Coke brand extension. It made use of many of the components of an integrated marketing communications program. Identify those components and think about how useful each could be to pique interest and communicate the uniqueness of a vanilla flavour of a soft drink. Which component could do the best overall job? Would there be any reason to use any of the other components to reinforce the objectives that Coca-Cola has for the new brand and its positioning in the market?

Want to get better grades, tips on how to study more effectively, and up-to-date information on happenings in the world of marketing? Then, visit the Online Learning Centre for practice tests, Study Smart software, and much more! **www.mcgrawhill.ca/college/sommers**

Interested in finding out what marketing looks like in the real world? *Marketing Magazine* is just a click away on your Online Learning Centre!

CHAPTER 11

Management of Advertising

This chapter examines the major non-personal, mass-communications promotional tool — advertising. After studying this chapter, you should have an understanding of:

- The nature, purpose, and scope of advertising and what it means to the individual firm.
- The characteristics of the major types of advertising.
- How advertising campaigns are developed and advertising media are selected.

Wrap It Up to Go!

What's that up front in traffic? What's written on that VW Beetle that just changed lanes — does it say something about panty lines? And what was written on that SUV yesterday? It was a Jeep Cherokee, but the slogan covering the entire side of the vehicle didn't seem to be too complimentary — something about not having enough horsepower. What's going on?

Forget about advertising on transit buses, on the company car, or delivery truck. Who notices that anymore, with all of the other clutter, advertising, and messages we see whenever we go outside? Billboards, bus shelters, subway stations — it's all been done. The way to go? Autowrapping! It's just like it sounds — the entire vehicle is actually "'wrapped" in advertising — and even better, the car belongs to someone else.

Autowraps is the first company to truly identify and use the automobile as an advertising medium. The unique characteristics of the automobile and its place in our culture make it a natural for advertising to a mobile, fragmented, and distracted consumer population. Characteristics such as mobility, flexibility, and interactivity, as well as sampling and distribution possibilities, give the wrapped vehicle a unique and distinct advantage over the usual outdoor media.[1]

Advertisers can hit specific demographics with a little calculation and ingenuity and really attract attention.

You're thinking: "Ads on vehicles? That's not new." But there's a difference — not just the impact of seeing it on the street, but consider who's driving the vehicle. Vehicle owners who register with the company and qualify for the program are compensated for driving their own cars — sometimes as much as they have to shell out for their monthly car payments.

So, how does it work? Well, car owners provide detailed demographic information about themselves and their lifestyles, as well as driving and parking habits. To determine a little more detail, a test is conducted: A global positioning system (GPS) is installed and locations, time, speed, and usual routes are tracked. This bundle of information is then used to "sell" this driver (and the vehicle) to an advertiser — actually, it's more like renting. The advertising is then designed to totally cover the vehicle, using high-quality vinyl adhesive. The driver must keep the advertising on the vehicle for the length of the advertising agreement.

Think about it — it makes good sense. If the driver matches a marketer's demographic, so should the people he or she knows and the places and the activities they all take part in — the ad would always be in the middle of the action, travelling and spending time where potential customers are. In large metro areas, it is estimated that in just one hour each day, about 2,500 impressions result from autowrapping — whether the vehicle is travelling in traffic or just parked at a meter.[2]

advertising

All activities involved in presenting to a group a non-personal, sponsor-identified message regarding a product or organization.

Advertising is the main mass-communications tool available to marketers. As the terminology suggests, mass communications uses the same message for everyone in an audience. The mass communicator trades off the advantage of personal selling (the opportunity to tailor a message to each prospective customer) for the advantage of reaching many people at a lower cost per person. However, as the emergence of interactive television advertising, the Autowraps innovation, and the use of the Internet illustrate, mass communications is becoming less mass and more closely targeted. Advertisers are constantly seeking ways to present their messages to more clearly defined audiences.

Nature and Scope of Advertising

All advertisements have four features: a verbal and/or visual message; a sponsor who is identified; message delivery through at least one medium; and payment by the sponsor to the media carrying the message.

Advertising, then, consists of all of the activities involved in presenting to an audience a non-personal, sponsor-identified, paid-for message about a product or organization. One of the most interesting changes taking place in advertising is the increasing ability of marketers to reach specific audiences with tailor-made messages. As a result, we will see advertising in the future becoming less non-personal in nature, as specialty channels, publications, and other media innovate and flourish. Viewers will be able to program individual entertainment preferences, database marketing will continue to be refined and based on actual individual consumption behaviour, and technological advances will push the trend, just as GPS tracking made it possible for Autowraps to locate its moving medium and target messages.

Types of advertising

Advertising can be classified according to (1) the target audience, either consumers or businesses; (2) what is being advertised, a product or service versus an organization or company; and (3) the objective sought, the stimulation of primary or selective demand. To fully appreciate the scope of advertising, it is essential to understand these three classifications.

consumer advertising

Advertisements directed to consumers.

Consumer and business-to-business advertising   An ad is generally directed at either consumers (consumer advertising) or businesses (business-to-business advertising). Most retailers by definition sell only to end-consumers, so they are not faced with the choice of whether to target a consumer or a business audience. There are exceptions — such as Staples/Business Depot — that target both. The publishers of *National Post* and similar newspapers and magazines must decide what portion of their advertising budgets will be used to attract advertisers (called *trade advertising*) and what portion will go toward gaining subscribers and selling magazines and newspapers.

business-to-business advertising

Advertisements directed to businesses rather than consumers.

Product and institutional advertising   All advertising may be classified as product (or service) or institutional (or corporate). Here, we are using the term *product* to include both tangible products and services. **Product advertising** focuses on a particular product or brand, and is subdivided into direct-action and indirect-action advertising:

direct-action advertising

Product advertising that seeks a quick response.

- **Direct-action advertising** seeks a quick response — for instance, a magazine ad containing a coupon or a toll-free number urges the reader to redeem the coupon or call immediately for a free sample, or a supermarket ad in a local newspaper stresses this week's specials. Many advertisements today include the advertiser's Web site address, inviting the consumer to "Check us out" or "Window-shop on the Web."

Life Fitness wants communication — by telephone, by clicks, or at bricks.

- **Indirect-action advertising** is designed to stimulate demand for a company's products or services over a longer period of time. It is intended to inform or remind consumers that the product exists and to point out its benefits. Most television advertising is of this type. Often the purpose of this form of advertising is to build awareness and recognition of a brand.

- **Institutional or corporate advertising** presents information about the advertiser's business or tries to make a good impression. It is intended to create a positive image of the company and its brands in the eyes of customers, prospective customers, and the general public. Two forms of corporate advertising are:

- **Customer-service advertising** presents information about the advertiser's operations.

indirect-action advertising

Product advertising that is intended to inform or remind consumers about a product and its benefits.

institutional advertising

Advertising designed either to present information about the advertiser's business or to create a good impression to build goodwill toward the organization.

Indirect-action or institutional advertising? No matter which, a special place to visit.

Public service advertising by Ford for the CIBC Run for the Cure

customer-service advertising

Advertising that presents information about the advertiser's operations.

public service advertising

Advertising designed to improve the quality of life and indicate that the advertiser is a responsible member of the community.

Avis

primary-demand advertising

Advertising designed to stimulate demand for a generic product.

selective-demand advertising

Advertising intended to stimulate demand for specific brands.

pioneering advertising

Primary-demand advertising is done in the introductory stage of the product life cycle.

Advertisements describing the level of personal service available at Esso service stations are an example. Avis (**www.avis.com**) has long been known for its "We try harder" slogan, demonstrating in its ads how its staff goes the "extra mile" to provide superior service.

● **Public service advertising** (PSA) is designed to show that the advertiser is a responsible member of the community. Such ads may urge the audience to avoid drugs or to support a local anti-pollution campaign, or may show how the advertiser is making a contribution by supporting worthwhile projects and community activities.

Primary-demand and selective-demand advertising Primary-demand advertising is designed to stimulate demand for a generic category of a product such as Colombian coffee or garments made from cotton. This is in contrast to selective-demand advertising, intended to stimulate demand for individual brands such as Nabob coffee, British Columbia produce, Sunkist oranges, and clothing from Gap.

Primary-demand advertising is used in either of two situations. The first is when the product is in the introductory stage of its life cycle. This is called pioneering advertising. A firm may run an ad about its new product, explaining the product's benefits but not emphasizing the brand name. The objective of pioneering primary-demand advertising is to inform, not to persuade, the target market.

Creating selective demand for a commodity

differential competitive advantage

Any feature of an organization or brand perceived by customers to be desirable and different from that of the competition.

Dairy Farmers of Canada

comparative advertising

Selective-demand advertising in which the advertiser either directly (by naming a rival brand) or indirectly (through inference) points out how the advertised brand is better.

co-operative advertising

Advertising for which two or more firms share the cost.

vertical co-operative advertising

Advertising for which firms at different levels of the distribution channel share the cost.

advertising allowance

A payment or cash discount offered by a manufacturer to a retailer to encourage the retailer to advertise or prominently display the manufacturer's product.

The second use of primary-demand advertising occurs throughout the product life cycle. It is usually done by trade associations trying to stimulate demand for their industry's product. So, the Dairy Farmers of Canada's ads (**www.dairybureau.org**) urge us to drink more milk. They don't really care what brand of milk and dairy products we buy, just that we use more of them.

Selective-demand advertising essentially is competitive advertising — it pits one brand against another. This type of advertising typically is used when a product has gone beyond the introductory life-cycle stage. The product is reasonably well known and in competition for market share with several brands. The objective of selective-demand advertising is to increase the demand for a brand. To accomplish this goal, it emphasizes the particular benefits — the **differential competitive advantages** — of the brand being advertised.

Comparative advertising is an important kind of selective-demand advertising that is used for a wide variety of products. Here, the advertiser either directly — by naming a rival brand — or indirectly — through inference — points out differences between the brands. In some comparative advertising, the competitor's name is not mentioned but is obvious to the reader or viewer. In other cases, the competitor's product is named or even shown.

Co-operative advertising **Co-operative advertising** promotes products of two or more firms that share the cost of the advertising. There are two types — vertical and horizontal. **Vertical co-operative advertising** involves firms on different levels of distribution. For example, a manufacturer and a retailer share the cost of the retailer's advertising of that manufacturer's product. Cannondale, Honda, or Kawasaki, for example, would share with their dealers across the country the cost of advertising their bikes or all-terrain vehicles in local newspapers and sometimes on television. Frequently, the manufacturer pays for the preparation of the actual ad, leaving space for the retailer's name and location. Then the manufacturer and retailer share the media cost of placing the ad. Many retail ads in newspapers are co-operative ads.

Another type of vertical co-operative advertising uses an **advertising allowance**, or cash discount offered by a manufacturer to a retailer, to encourage the retailer to advertise or prominently display a product. This approach is often used in retail advertising of grocery products and other household items. Major retailers such as Loblaws, Canadian Tire, and Wal-Mart Canada have much of the cost of preparing their flyers covered by the advertising allowances provided by the manufacturers whose products are featured in the flyers. The difference between co-operative advertising and allowances is the amount of control exerted by the manufacturer over how the money is actually spent.

horizontal co-operative advertising

Advertising that involves firms on the same level of distribution sharing the cost.

Horizontal co-operative advertising is undertaken by firms on the same level of distribution — such as a group of retailers — that share the costs of advertising. For example, all stores in a suburban shopping centre may run a joint newspaper ad. The principal benefit is that by pooling their funds, the firms can achieve much greater exposure than if they advertised individually.

Cost of advertising

The significance of advertising is indicated by the amount of money spent on it. In 1998, expenditures on advertising in Canada totalled almost $9 billion. Table 11-1 shows the estimated total revenue by medium. For many years, daily newspapers have been the most widely used medium, but the percentage of total expenditures accounted for by newspapers has been declining steadily, from approximately 30 percent in the mid-1970s to 18 percent in 1998. In fact, the percentage of total advertising expenditures going to the traditional mass media — radio, television, newspapers, and magazines — has been declining steadily, as many advertisers have been switching at least part of their advertising budgets to established media such as direct mail, directories, and weekly newspapers, and to new media such as the Internet and CD-ROMs.

Internet Advertising Bureau of Canada

Another change in advertising expenditures includes that now expended on Internet advertising. According to an Internet Advertising Bureau of Canada (**www.iabcanada.com**) and PricewaterhouseCoopers' survey, Canadian English advertising virtually doubled in 2000, reaching $110 million, while French-language advertising more than doubled that same year to reach $14 million. This can be contrasted with estimates for the United States of well over $2 billion ($US). It's projected that by 2005, the Internet will attract 6 percent of total ad spending — doubling outdoor advertising spending and pretty much equalling the spending

TABLE 11-1	Net Canadian Advertising Revenues by Medium (in millions of Canadian dollars)				
Medium		**1999**	**%**	**2000**	**%**
Television	Total	$2,377	27	$2,456	26
	Network	$449	5	$444	5
	Selective	$1,609	18	$1,615	17
	Specialty	$304	3	$381	4
	Infomercial	$15	0	$17	0
Radio		$952	11	$1,014	11
Daily newspapers (excluding classified ads)		$1,630	18	$1,732	18
Weeklies/community newspapers		$788	9	$820	9
Trade publications		$283	3	$295	3
Consumer magazines		$389	4	$434	5
Outdoor and transit		$270	3	$293	3
Internet		$56	1	$110	1
Other		$2,214	25	$2,250	24
	Yellow Pages	$975	11	$1000	11
	Direct mail	$1,190	13	$1,200	13
	Other print	$49	1	$50	1
TOTAL ALL MEDIA		**$8,959**		**$9,404**	

*Less than 0.5 percent.

SOURCE: *2001, Media Digest.* Published by *Marketing Magazine* as compiled by TVB from Statistics Canada, CRIC, CAN, CCNA/Les Hebdos du Québec, Canada/LNA, CARD, Mediacom/CAN, Tele-Direct, Canada Post, IAB\Ernst & Young, and industry estimates.

on magazine print ads. The Internet is the best way to reach a majority of the people in urban areas, with urban women more likely to be online than urban men. Today, the Internet plays an integral role in the buying cycle, especially for women researching big-ticket items such as cars, electronics, and travel.[3]

Advertising expenditures   Some industries in Canada spend a lot more money than others on advertising. The retail industry spent over $950 million on advertising in 1998 — much more than the $750 million spent by automobile manufacturers. This pattern of spending has been relatively consistent in recent years. Retailers represent a very large proportion of this spending because there are so many of them and some are very large. Some of the advertisers who spend a large amount of money on advertising each year actually devote a very small percentage of their total sales to advertising. Data collected by Statistics Canada indicate that the largest percentage of sales spent on advertising is by companies that manufacture health and beauty aids, soaps, and cleaning products. In general, companies in the consumer-products field spend a higher percentage of sales on advertising than do manufacturers of industrial products. Major companies spend an average of about 2 percent of total sales on advertising, while companies that manufacture consumer products spend approximately 3 percent on average.

Advertising cost versus personal selling cost   While we do not have accurate totals for the costs of personal selling, we do know that they far surpass advertising expenditures. In manufacturing, only a few industries (such as drugs, toiletries, cleaning products, tobacco, and beverages) spend more on advertising than on personal selling. Advertising runs from 1 to 3 percent of net sales in many firms, whereas the expenses of recruiting and operating a sales force are typically 8 to 15 percent of sales.

At the wholesale level, advertising costs are very low. Personal selling expenses, however, may run 10 to 15 times as high. Even among retailers in total — and this includes those with self-service operations — the cost of personal selling is substantially higher than that of advertising.

◄ B A C K S P A C E

1. What are the four features of all advertisements?

2. _____ consists of all of the activities involved in presenting to an audience a non-personal, sponsor-identified, paid-for message about a product or organization.

3. What is the difference between direct-action advertising and indirect-action advertising?

Developing an Advertising Campaign

advertising campaign

The total advertising program for a product or brand that involves co-ordination, a central theme, and specific goals.

W.K. Buckley Limited

An **advertising campaign** consists of all of the tasks involved in transforming a theme into a co-ordinated advertising program to accomplish a specific goal for a product or brand. For example, you have probably seen the now-infamous advertising for Buckley's Mixture, the famous cough remedy from W.K. Buckley Limited (**www.buckleys.com**), which uses the tag line "It tastes awful. And it works." Of course it tastes awful, it's made from Canada balsam, menthol, camphor, and pine needle oil — it should taste awful! This campaign has been running successfully for many years and has now been extended to include recent additions to the Buckley's line. It relies on a blend of humour and trust in the grandfatherly figure of the company's president, Frank Buckley. The campaign theme has been very effective and has transferred successfully to international markets as the company has extended distribution. Most products are not this fortunate — but a taste this bad is truly a global thing.

MARKETING AT WORK 11-1: GLOBAL

I Am ... a Great Advertising Campaign

It's not just an advertisement anymore — it identified and articulated who we are as Canadians — at least, with the 19- to 25-year-old beer drinker. But, it has reached far beyond that. It is a television ad that served to integrate a marketing program (I AM.Canadian) originally started in 1994 — and create such synergy that people could be whipped into a frenzy, standing at attention and yelling, "I am Canadian" when it was performed live at hockey games or came on TV at the local sports bar. The momentum of the I AM campaign for Molson's flagship brand (Canadian) still persists — the brand seems to have become an extension of the Canadian identity. Within weeks, several thousand Canadian-pride testimonials were posted by visitors to the Web site (www.iam.ca) and the company was inundated with e-mails, telephone calls, and letters of praise.

It states the obvious — "I don't live in an igloo, or eat blubber, or own a dogsled" (those things are fine for some, but most of us have chosen other alternatives) and it explains that a toque is a hat. Joe (meant to be seen as the average Joe) goes on to emote about peacekeeping, diversity, and how Canadians can proudly bear the flag of their country on their backpacks wherever they travel (the message there being that Americans can't make the same claim) and explaining that Canada is the "first nation of hockey." As his voice and the background music reach a feverish pitch, Joe declares with beaming pride — "I am Canadian!"

And while it was shown only in Canada, it was meant to express what many Canadians feel is misunderstood (especially by those pesky Americans) about our country, as well as the things we are proud of. The "rant," as it is often called, rev-

olutionized beer advertising in this country. The "in your face" flag-waving struck a chord with many age groups, because it came at a time when Canadians were becoming more open about expressing their national pride. We can only hope it wasn't too bruising to Americans to realize that their neighbour to the north is "the best part of North America."

SOURCE: Jonathon Gatehouse, "With Glowing Hearts We See Thee Advertise," *National Post*, April 12, 2000, pp. A1, A2, and Molson Canadian site (www.iam.ca), July 19, 2002.

Building on this homespun "flavour" of advertising, the company has recently begun airing ads in which real company employees read humorous letters that the company has received about its products. The TV and radio spots are intended to communicate to viewers that the employees of the relatively small Canadian company are dedicated to both its product and its effectiveness, while increasing awareness of the newer products (such as Jack & Jill cough syrup for kids) and shifting the emphasis more toward the effectiveness of Buckley's products than just the reputation of its flavour.[4]

An advertising campaign is planned within the framework of the overall strategic marketing program and the marketing communications campaign. Before designing an advertising campaign, management must:

● Know who the target audience is.

● Establish the overall promotional goals.

● Set the total promotional budget.

● Determine the overall promotional theme.

With these tasks completed, the firm can begin formulating an advertising campaign. The steps in developing a campaign are: defining objectives; establishing a budget; creating a message; selecting media; and evaluating the campaign's effectiveness.

Defining objectives

The purpose of advertising is to sell something — product, service, idea, person, or place — either now or later. This goal is reached by setting specific objectives that can be expressed in individual ads that are incorporated into an advertising campaign. Recall again from the buying-decision process discussed in Chapter 3 that buyers go through a series of stages from unawareness to purchase. The immediate objective of an ad therefore may be to move target customers to the next stage in the hierarchy, from awareness to interest, for example. Note also that advertising seldom is the only communications tool used by a firm. Rather, it is typically one part of a strategy that may also include personal selling, sales promotion, a company Web site, and other tools. Therefore, the objective of advertising may be to "open doors" for the sales force.

Specific advertising objectives will be dictated by the firm's overall marketing strategy. Typical objectives are:

- **Support personal selling:** Acquaint prospects with the seller's company and products, easing the way for the sales force.

- **Improve dealer relations:** Wholesalers and retailers like to see a manufacturer support its products.

- **Introduce a new product:** As well as being made aware of new products, consumers need to be informed about line extensions that make use of familiar brand names.

- **Expand the use of a product category:** Attempt to lengthen the season for a product (as Lipton did for iced tea); increase the frequency of replacement (as Fram and Purolator did for oil filters); or increase the variety of product uses (as Arm & Hammer and Cow Brand did for baking soda). Sometimes, it's really the same use but for a different group. Repackaging a product can also alter the advertising message.

- **Counteract substitution:** Reinforce the decisions of existing customers and reduce the likelihood that they will switch to alternative brands.

Establishing a budget

Once a marketing communications budget has been established (as discussed in Chapter 10), it must be allocated among the various activities making up the overall program. In the case of a particular brand, a firm may wish to have several ads, as well as sales promotion and public relations activities, directed at different target audiences, all under way at the same time.

The great dot-com boom and bust of the late 1990s illustrates what can happen to communications budgets when some fundamentals are not handled well. Many start-ups at that time ran into great budgeting difficulties, since many were unknown and spent heavily to gain attention and build market share. For example, Vancouver-based Savingumoney.com was launched as a new firm with a new concept: Instead of sending out promotional coupons to consumers, consumers would be asked to surf to the company's Internet site to select and print coupons in which they were interested. The firm, being completely unknown, set a number of communications goals, starting with selection of the company name, Savingumoney.com, as one way of introducing the concept of an electronic coupon.

Next, awareness and interest had to be generated to attract companies to supply coupons and consumers to use the coupons. The conundrum was that attracting each required the presence of the other. The company had to promote and position itself effectively and this requires a little more consideration than creating banner ads on a couple of Web sites. The target for electronic coupons, however, didn't appear to be a very good match with the typical Web-savvy shopper. The new coupons, which were essentially the already familiar and widely distributed ones used for traditional everyday products, differed only in their mode of delivery. The clippers of such coupons were largely female and skewed to a mature age category (45 to 54) — hardly the typical Web shopper.

A $6 million campaign was designed to convey the essence of Savingumoney.com's positioning — "Coupons online for just about anything." The campaign was also aimed at cultivating an engaging brand image: friendly, helpful and just a little on the clever side. This budget was about a hundred times the original budget used when the site was quietly launched the previous year. Aside from some online advertising, the linchpin for the campaign was newspapers — this allowed a broad reach (very critical), flexibility, and fast turnaround times. A consistent newspaper presence was maintained through early 2000, while also utilizing outdoor and radio ads. Television was used in some U.S. markets where significant coupon offerings were available. Ads were designed to look like a coupon — with the depiction of a dotted line and scissors. Images included a completely bare room with an offer for "free burglar alarm installation." Another showed a seagull and the tag line "20% off dry-cleaning."[5]

We see here a set of objectives, tasks defined, and a $6 million budget drawn up and spent on the various media selected to carry out these tasks. Sorry that we can't report happy results, or any results — Savingumoney.com is no longer in business. While the budgeting process followed was reasonable, it was based on flawed assumptions, flawed research, or both. Perhaps the concept offered no consumer value, or the wrong target market was chosen, or the budget was too small, or the media plan was flawed, or the execution was faulty. Many dot-com firms suffered the same fate at the time with much larger budgets. Perhaps the budget was not the essential problem.

More often than not, the goal of advertising is not category awareness, but simply trying to get a larger piece of the market action. This was the case when Lexus Canada decided it was going to get a larger share of the burgeoning SUV market. In 1997, Lexus managed to sell 195 of the 649,393 light trucks sold in Canada — not a large number, but at over $80,000 each for the LX 470, this is not a big surprise. To introduce its new $46,000 RX 300, as well as the redesign of its entire vehicle line, the company is reported to have increased advertising spending from $2.9 million to $15 million. Such a steep increase was the result of deciding (1) not to use U.S. advertising and (2) to use television for only the second time in Canada. The company felt the Canadian market was unique and it was necessary to create separate appeals for the French- and Mandarin-speaking markets, since these represent important segments in Canada for prestige automobiles. Direct mail was also employed, using personalized letters customized for 20 different market segments.[6]

Many firms, particularly smaller ones, find the establishment of an advertising budget to be a very difficult exercise. This is because many businesspeople find it difficult to measure the payback from advertising and therefore don't feel that they are in a position to decide where to place their advertising dollars to get the greatest return. The result is that a lot of advertising money is wasted, and many companies probably pay much more than they should for effective advertising.

Creating a message

attention
Getting people to notice your message.

Whatever the objective of an advertising campaign, the individual ads must accomplish two things: get and hold the **attention** of the intended audience, and **influence** that audience in the desired way. Remember that the ultimate purpose of advertising is to sell something and that the ad itself is a sales message. The ad may be a fast-paced sales talk, as in a direct-action TV ad by a car dealership. It may be a very long-range, low-key message, as are many institutional ads. Whatever the method, the goal is to sell something sooner or later.

influence
The ability to cause a change in a person's beliefs, attitudes, or intentions.

Attention, getting people to notice your message, can be achieved in many ways (recall the discussion of perception in Chapter 3). The most common approach is to present material in an unexpected or surprising way or to use an unconventional technique to capture the attention of the audience. Thus, a print ad may be mostly white space or a television commercial might

Nike

show the product in an unusual setting or address a topic from a new perspective. American Express gets attention when it features well-known personalities in the advertising for its credit cards. Nike (**www.nike.com**) used intensive, adrenaline-pumping, high-impact ads that stopped in a sudden freeze-frame: Would the character in the ad make it to safety? Would the Nike shoes get the person away fast enough? Viewers who wanted to see how these cliffhangers ended had to go to a special Nike Web site set up just for this ad campaign. Here, alternative endings could be viewed and voted for by visitors.[7] Some advertising for social programs, such as anti-smoking campaigns and appeals against drinking and driving, uses dramatic emotional content to shock viewers and get their attention.

If the ad succeeds in getting the audience's attention, the advertiser has a few seconds to communicate a message intended to influence beliefs and/or behaviour. The message has two elements: the appeal and the execution. The **appeal** in an ad is the reason or justification for believing or behaving. It is the benefit that the individual will receive as a result of accepting the message.

Some advertisers mistakenly focus their appeal on product features or attributes. They either confuse attributes with benefits or assume that if they present the product's attributes, the audience will infer the correct benefits. Telling customers that a cereal contains fibre (an attribute) is much less meaningful than telling them that, because it contains fibre, consuming it reduces the possibility of colon cancer (the benefit). Common appeals or benefits and examples of product categories in which they are frequently used include:

- Health (food, non-prescription drugs).
- Social acceptance (cosmetics, health and beauty aids).
- Material success (automobiles, investments).
- Recognition (clothing, jewellery).

appeal

The reason, justification, or argument presented in an advertisement to cause a message receiver to be influenced.

Does the appeal of these ads capture your attention?

- Sensory pleasure (movies, candy).

- Saving time (prepared foods, convenience stores).

- Peace of mind (insurance, tires).

Execution means to combine in a convincing, compatible way the feature or device that gets attention with the appeal. An appeal can be executed in different ways. Consider the ways you could communicate the benefit of reliable performance in a home appliance — presenting operating statistics, obtaining the endorsement of a respected person or organization, collecting testimonials from satisfied owners, or describing the meticulous manufacturing process. Rather than doing any of these, Maytag opted for "the lonely repairman," an amusing and memorable execution that gets attention and conveys the benefit of reliability.

Creating an advertisement involves writing the copy, selecting the illustration (for visual media), preparing the visual or verbal layout, and reproducing the ad for the selected media. The **copy** in an ad is all of the written or spoken material in it; it's the words. Copy in a print ad includes the headline, coupons, advertiser's identification, and the main body of the message. In a broadcast ad, the copy is the script.

For visual ads, the **illustration** is a powerful feature. The main points to consider about illustrations are (1) whether they are totally appropriate to the product advertised and (2) despite the adage "A picture is worth a thousand words," whether the illustration represents the best use of the space. The **layout** is the physical arrangement of all of the elements in an advertisement. In print ads, it is the appearance of the page. For television, the layout is the set, as well as the positioning of actors and props. The layout of a radio ad is the sequence in which information is presented. A good layout can hold interest as well as attract attention. It should lead the audience through the entire ad in an orderly fashion.

The cost of creating an ad can vary from almost nothing for a local radio spot written by the staff at a radio station to as much as $500,000 or even more for a complex television commercial. In recent years, production costs for network TV ads have escalated dramatically. As a result, fewer commercials are being made, and they are kept on the air longer or are modified to create a number of variations.

Selecting media

advertising media
The communications vehicles (such as newspapers, radio, and television) that carry advertising.

In describing the steps in developing an advertising campaign, we discussed creating an advertising message before describing the selection of **advertising media** in which to place the ad. In reality, these decisions are made simultaneously. The appeal and the target audience determine both the message and the choice of media. The following discussion focuses on selecting appropriate media in which to place advertising.

Advertisers need to make decisions at each of three successive levels to determine which specific advertising medium to use:

1. Which type of medium will be used — newspaper, television, radio, magazine, or direct contact through mail or the Internet? What about the less prominent media of billboards, specialty items, and the Yellow Pages, or even the Autowrap?

2. Which category of the selected medium will be used? Television has network and cable and a host of different channels; magazines include general-interest (*Maclean's, Time*) and special-interest (*Chatelaine, Ski Canada, Wallpaper**) categories; and there are national as well as local newspapers. On the Internet, there are e-magazines, news sites, and a variety of retail and general-purpose portals from which to choose.

3. Which specific media vehicles will be used? An advertiser who decides first on radio and then on local stations must determine which stations to use in each city.

Levi Strauss Shifts into Low Gear

The Problem

Need new jeans? If you did, what brands you would look at? Diesel, Tommy, Parasuco, Ralph Lauren, Gap, Pepe, and some others probably come to mind for most of you reading this. But what about Levi's? Could you be convinced to check out what they have to offer? To the company's consternation, it has had increasing difficulty attracting young consumers to its products.

Levi Strauss & Company has done very well in Europe and in other global markets, but it lost touch with its North American market and is now determined to get it back. The jeans-maker has also faced increasingly intense competition from a number of new firms that just keep nibbling away at market share as well as profits. Despite strenuous efforts on its part, North American sales continued to fall between 1997 and 2002. The company decided to scratch its last advertising agency after continuing to experience declining sales during this time, despite a continually changing series of campaigns that climaxed with a commercial for low-rider jeans featuring singing belly buttons!

It then initiated a new and ambitious effort to turn around its North American market and profit position. One of its moves was to bring in new management. Robert Hanson, who was very successful running the European division, was repatriated to San Francisco headquarters to take over the job of running the Levi brand. Another move was to develop and implement, as a corporate priority, the marketing strategy of re-enforcing Levi Strauss as the market leader by winning back and increasing market share by producing new and innovative products. The challenge for the company is to transfer the success it's been experiencing in Europe over to North America. According to Robert Hanson, "What we're basically doing is what we did in Europe. We've got to have a product-innovation leadership position; nothing else matters."

After several years of not being on the "A" list of denim brands for young consumers, the company has embarked on an ambitious effort to turn around its struggling U.S. operations with new products and a new campaign.

Based on marketing research results, it was decided to have an immediate focus on low-rise styles for *both* men and women. There is growing evidence that males aged 13 to 17 years of age are spending more than ever for jeans and that those 18 to 24 are not only spending more but also are shopping more and more like their female counterparts. As Hanson says, women's low-rise jeans have been "a product to strut in" for some time, but for men, low-rise has been available only in high-priced designer versions. Focus group interviews with young men revealed that low-rise gives them "a bit of swagger." Hanson wants the brand to have the swagger as well as the jeans wearer.

For the low-rise jeans, the goal is to portray the product as having characteristics that have not been associated with the brand image of late — grittiness, urban chic, daring, rebelliousness. Some of those traits were trademarks of the brand during its heyday of the 1950s and 1960s.

Since the new North American strategy was very similar to the one successfully implemented in Europe, it is no surprise that the European creative director, Caroline Parent, took up a similar post for North America in another management move.

The Objective

Given new management and the new marketing strategy, the advertising communications objective was to promote the new Levi's low-rise jeans for both men and women by portraying the product as having "dangerously low" possibilities of wearing your pants below the point of parental approval. Another objective was to re-invent some of the same daredevil characteristics that had been promoted and associated with the Levi's brand during its heyday, but not used or promoted lately.

The Agency and the Budget

The agency of record over the 1997–2001 period of less-than-stellar performance was TBWA/Chiat/Day, a division of TBWA Worldwide. Under the new management team, a new agency was appointed — the New York office of Bartle Bogle Hegarty. BBH was awarded the estimated $60-million account because, according to Hanson, the agency "has demonstrated consistently an ability to get into the genetic code of new products...and produce the kinds of creative product-based advertising that can be successful." BBH also happens to be the British agency that handles the Levi's brand in Asia and Europe.

Creating the Message

With the theme of "'dangerously low" possibilities and using the desired brand characteristics of urban chic, daringness, grittiness, and rebelliousness, the agency set to work to develop and execute the specific appeals. The group creative director at BBH, Thomas Hayo, worked exclusively on the Levi's account. His creative approach is summed up nicely in his own words: "Jeans have always been a part of the youth culture and rebellion, a little bit anti-establishment, the guy from the wrong side of town. People are intrigued by the more seedy after-hours bar downtown; maybe they only go one time a year, but those are the stories you tell. That was what felt right for these jeans."

With regard to working with the Levi Strauss brand, the campaign director said, "When you're trying to change the perception of a brand, you have to know what the brand is all about, and it extends from TV and print down to the store: the displays, the signage, the hang tags."

The initial print ads show fit (i.e., skinny) young hotties of both genders in dark locales, wearing both the low-rise jeans and tough looks. The settings are far from chic: bus stops, underground garages, strip malls. Some ads also show the models standing next to vintage cars from the 60s and 70s, like the Ford Mustang and Chevy Malibu. In each instance, a beam of light bisects a young hottie at waist level, drawing attention to the skin bared by the low-slung pants. Printed on the beam are the words "Dangerously low. Levi's Low-Rise Jeans." The ads needed to be able to work in a number of different types of publications (such as music, lifestyle, entertainment, and fashion magazines) and media, including the company's Web site (**www.levi.com**).

"The low cut is a little bit more adventurous, especially for guys," Hayo says. "Exposing a little more skin is more risky," which is why the ads were shot "at places you normally wouldn't hang out or go to, in kind of dodgy areas." At the same time, he claims that the models were intended to be "people whose sexiness comes from inner strength and confidence," rather than solely from their looks." Yeah, right! This is intended to be part of an integrated campaign, including TV spots, theatre commercials, signs, and support materials for stores.

The Media Plan

Since the target market was younger men and women who would have an interest in low-rise jeans, the print ads were scheduled to run in a large number of fashion, entertainment, lifestyle, and music magazines. Included were *Allure, Blender, Cosmo Girl, Entertainment Weekly,* FHM, *The Fader, Glamour, Interview, Maxim, Rolling Stone, Seventeen, The Source, Stuff, Teen People,* and YM. Ads were to appear from August to December of 2002. Television commercials were also produced, as well as store signage and other retailer support materials.

SOURCE: Adapted in part from Stuart Elliot's *In Advertising,* "Levi's Shifts into a Lower Gear," July 9, 2002, *The New York Times On The Web* (NYTDirect@nytimes.com); and Ruth La Ferla, "Boys to Men: Fashion Pack Turns Younger," *The New York Times,* July 14, 2002, pp. 9-1, 9-6.

Here are some general factors that influence media choice:

- **Objectives of the ad:** The purpose of a particular ad and the goals of the entire campaign influence the choice of which media to use. If the campaign goal is to generate appointments for salespeople, the company may rely on direct mail or telephone contact. If an advertiser wants to produce quick action, newspaper or radio may be the medium to use.

- **Audience coverage:** The audience reached by the medium should match the geographic area in which the product is distributed. Furthermore, the selected medium should reach the desired types of prospects with a minimum of wasted coverage. Wasted coverage occurs when an ad reaches people who are not prospects for the product. Many media — even national and other large-market media — can be targeted at small, specialized market segments. *Maclean's* magazine publishes regional editions with different ads in its Atlantic, Ontario, and Western editions, with a French-language edition for Québec. As well, many U.S. magazines print "split-runs" to allow for some separate editorial content and advertising specifically for Canadian audiences. Does the use of the GPS in the Autowrap approach provide well-targeted coverage?

- **Requirements of the message:** The medium should fit the message. Food products, floor coverings, and apparel are best presented visually. If the advertiser can use a very brief message (the rule of thumb is six words or less), as is common with reminder advertising, billboards may be a suitable medium — provided, of course, that the preferred audience includes people who are likely to drive or walk by the billboards.

- **Time and location of the buying decision:** The medium should reach prospective customers when and where they are about to make their buying decisions. Research shows that radio scores the highest in immediacy of exposure: More than 50 percent of adults were last exposed to radio within one hour of making their largest purchase of the day. This factor highlights one of the strengths of place-based advertising such as in-store ads (on shopping carts and in the aisles of supermarkets) — reaching consumers at the actual time of purchase.

- **Media cost:** The cost of each medium should be considered in relation to the budget available to pay for it and its reach or circulation. For example, the cost of network television exceeds the available funds of many advertisers.

cost per thousand (CPM)

The media cost of gaining exposure to one thousand people with an ad.

The **cost per thousand (CPM)** people reached ("M" is the Roman numeral for a thousand) is a standard measure routinely provided to prospective advertisers by all media. It allows an advertiser to compare costs across media. The CPM is computed as follows:

$$\text{CPM} = \frac{(\text{ad cost} \times 1{,}000)}{\text{circulation}}$$

For example, let's assume that the advertising rate for a full-colour, one-page ad in *Holiday Getaways*, a magazine with an international circulation, is $42,000 and the circulation is 1,200,000. Therefore, the CPM for the magazine is:

$$\text{CPM} = \frac{(\$42{,}200 \times 1{,}000)}{1{,}200{,}000} = \$35$$

MARKETING AT WORK 11-2: TECHNOLOGY

The Way to Pay — Internet Pricing Models

The most common pricing scheme for online ads currently is the CPM, or cost per 1,000 impressions. It's what is provided on about 90 percent of online publishers' "rate cards." Recently, however, "hybrid" pricing models have been popping up, easing advertiser concerns about the effectiveness of online advertising. What follows is a brief overview of these newer alternatives. When would each option work best for an advertiser? Where are the risks, and where can value be found?

CPM: With cost-per-thousand models, the publisher sets a boundary for pricing, which typically runs, on average, about $26, according to the most recent research from the Internet Advertising Bureau of Canada.

CPA: Cost-per-action models mean that the advertiser pays only when someone actually registers or purchases something. Although rare, CPA clearly represents a low risk for advertisers. Site publishers take a commission on all sales generated, usually up to about 10 percent. The risk to publishers is that they don't know what visitors do once they've clicked to visit a site.

CPC: With the cost-per-click payment model, an advertiser pays only for the number of click-throughs that it derives from an ad, rather that paying a flat rate to run an ad on a site.

CPL: Using the cost-per-lead online advertising payment model, an advertiser pays an amount based solely on the number of qualifying leads.

Flat rate: Flat-rate pricing means that an advertiser/marketer basically rents space online and pays a lump sum for that piece of "real estate." The best example is sponsorship. The sponsorship runs in a content area that is a relevant fit with the ad message, locking out the competition from advertising in that space. The advertiser incurs the same cost, regardless of the traffic through the site.

SOURCE: Adapted from *The Internet Advertising Handbook,* Marketing Media Group, Rogers Media Inc., Toronto, 2002.

Of course, it's essential to estimate what proportion of all people reached are truly prospects for the advertiser's product. If an advertiser is interested only in females over 50 years of age, we might find that there are 650,000 *Holiday Getaways* readers in this category. Therefore, we would have to calculate a weighted CPM:

$$\text{Weighted CPM} = \frac{(\$42,000 \times 1,000)}{650,000} = \$64.62$$

BACKSPACE

1. What tasks must management complete before designing an advertising campaign?
2. What are the five steps in developing an ad campaign?
3. Name the different types of media used to advertise products and services.

- -

Beyond these general factors, management must evaluate the advertising characteristics of each medium it is considering. We have chosen the term *characteristics* instead of *advantages* and *disadvantages*, because a medium that works well for one product is not necessarily the best choice for another product. To illustrate, a characteristic of radio is that it makes its impressions through sound and imagination. The roar of a crowd, running water, the rumbling of thunder, or screeching tires can be used to create mental images quickly and easily. But radio will not do the job for products that benefit from colour photography. Let's examine the characteristics of the major media.

Newspapers   As an advertising medium, newspapers are flexible and timely. They account for the largest portion of total advertising dollars spent in Canada and can be used to cover a single city or a number of urban centres. With the use of computer technology and regional printing in the publishing industry, once-local newspapers may be printed in regional centres for distribution across the country. Both the daily *National Post* and *The Globe and Mail*, while headquartered in Toronto, are printed regionally and distributed nationally.

While newspapers are attractive to a national advertiser, they remain the principal advertising vehicle for local advertisers, particularly when they are used as the distribution vehicle for advertising flyers. Ads usually can be inserted on one day's notice and can be cancelled on a few days' notice. Newspapers can give an advertiser intense coverage of a local market because a very large percentage of consumers read newspapers. Also, because they're produced locally, the ads can be adapted to local audiences and to social and economic conditions. Circulation costs per prospect are low. On the other hand, the life of a newspaper advertisement is very short. High-quality colour printing has improved the visual impact of this medium, allowing for more appealing graphic representations.

Television   Television is probably the most versatile and the most rapidly changing of all media. It makes its appeal through both the eye and the ear — products can be demonstrated as well as explained. It offers considerable flexibility in the geographic market covered and the time of message presentation. By making part of its impression through the ear, television can take advantage of the personal, dramatic impact of the spoken word.

But television can be an extremely expensive medium. The message is not permanently recorded for the message receiver. The prospect who is not reached the first time is lost forever, as far as a particular message is concerned. Television does not lend itself to long advertising copy, nor does it present pictures as clearly as magazines do. As with direct mail and radio, television advertisers must create their own audiences.

Cable has also changed television as an advertising medium. Canada is still among the most heavily "cabled" nations in the world, with more than 90 percent of homes in many urban areas wired for cable. Having cable television often allows Canadians access to upward of a hundred channels, many of which are American. Some "local" channels also carry ethnic-language programming appealing to very specific markets. Many channels carry specialized programming, including sports, weather, movies, youth programs, country music, arts and entertainment, and popular music formats. This increased access to television channels has resulted in a dramatic change in the nature and effect of television as an advertising medium.

In households with cable, television is now a much more focused medium. The sheer variety of channels has led to a situation described as **fragmentation**: Not only are fewer viewers tuned to a given channel compared with the past, but viewers regularly "zap" their way through the range of channels available, often when a commercial appears. This proliferation of channels through cable, coupled with the use of VCRs and DVD players, remote-control devices, commercial-skip devices, video games, and the Internet, has meant that the audience likely to be exposed to a television commercial is reduced, thereby limiting the effectiveness of television in reaching a mass market. As a result, some advertisers have begun to use shorter, more attention-getting commercials, or have moved some of their advertising budgets away from television to other media.

In the cluttered world of television, advertisers are constantly looking for ways to reach targeted audiences and to make their advertising messages stand out. Some large advertisers are experimenting with interactive television, which many feel will become a major element of media advertising in the near future. Others are developing infomercials, which are

fragmentation
The break-up of the mass audience for television or other media into smaller audiences as the result of technological innovations, such as the proliferation of channels, channel-zapping, skip devices, use of VCRs and DVD players.

intended to stand out from other forms of advertising on television. Finally, some companies have moved their advertising from the mainstream television networks to specialty channels in order to increase the likelihood of reaching their targeted audiences. Advertising on such specialty cable channels as CBC Newsworld, The Weather Network, MétéoMédia, TSN, Outdoor Life Network, CMT, MuchMusic, MusiquePlus, YTV, Bravo, Showcase, and Vision TV reaches millions of viewers every day in Canada. The result is that television is fast becoming much more of a targeted medium and less of a mass medium to reach mass audiences.[8]

We can expect to see television become even more fragmented and more competitive in the future. With the growth of national direct-to-home satellite TV services, Star Choice and ExpressVu, Canadians who subscribe to these services can now have access to up to 300 channels from all over the world that satisfy a multitude of interests.[9] Cable companies have responded by launching a host of cable channels, including the Comedy Channel, Teletoon, the History Channel, Home and Gardening, CTV all-news, and a science fiction channel. The result may be a confusing array of television-based options that leads some advertisers to rethink their use of the medium.[10]

While specialty channels may offer some advertisers a prime group of viewers, they often deliver in total about 1-percent share point in key demographics. This can be compared to "generic" broadcasters, such as CTV, which has about a 12-percent share of the audience in Canada. These channels are, however, beginning to understand the challenges of attracting advertisers and developing a better understanding of programming that appreciates audience flow and narrower targeting. Strategies include "theme" events or "appointment television," personality programming such as Debbie Travis' *Painted House* on WTN, and, when all else fails — if it succeeds on A&E, borrow the concept![11]

 # MARKETING AT WORK   11-3: STRATEGY

U8TV Lofter's Boot Camp

Close to 2,000 people auditioned for a chance to become a 2002 U8TV Lofter and, after a nationwide search, the producers narrowed those hopefuls down to 24 finalists. What did they have in common? They were all Canadian, 19 to 34 years of age, and wanted to be famous. From these would come the eight "stars" for the second season of the 24/7 Internet-broadcast reality show. Choosing these eight Lofters was the job of the viewers, who decided which of the lucky finalists would live together in a downtown Toronto loft equipped with cameras broadcasting their every move. The roaming eyes of these cameras could be monitored day or night on the U8TV Web site, while a digest version was broadcast each evening on the Life Network. Also broadcast from the site was specialty viewing hosted by members of the show. Usually broadcast from inside the loft, these offerings included shows such as *Male Bag, SoGay TV,* and *Love Shack.*

U8TV's blend of edgy, live programs was a hit with certain groups and provided a wealth of opportunities to advertise products and services. Instead of the traditional TV spot — although with 375,000 viewers, mostly in the 18- to 34-year-old demographic (79 percent), an advertiser could effectively target a preferred audience — there were opportunities such as prod-

uct placement in the loft where almost all of the programming was filmed, program sponsorship, netmercials, contests, banners, and pop-ups. To encourage viewers to vote, prizes of Blackberry Rim pagers were offered, as well as trips for two to Europe with Contiki Holidays.

The Internet broadcasts were plugged by showing teasers and tidbits of programming on the condensed cable version. Online was uncensored and offered a continuation of what viewers saw on TV. For the right marketers/advertisers, it provided a very focused target group. The site received 30 million hits a month — with 157,000 unique visitors each month. A loyal audience, with 59 percent visiting the site several times a week or daily, and an average viewing time of 50 minutes.

U8TV illustrates how television channels and their shows are designed as advertising tools and how new Internet and cable technologies can provide highly specialized, narrowly focused advertising opportunities.

SOURCE: Adapted from Sandy Brown, "Technology, Cable Lead TV Ad Opportunities," *Strategy,* May 21, 2001, p. 10, and the U8TV home page, June 2, 2002.

Concern about television viewing also arises from increasing Internet usage. While many are using the Internet for more reasons, this concern arises over increasing usage by 12- to 17-year-olds. This age group spends considerable amounts of time on the Web for entertainment purposes. Since this is an important consumer group, and if group members are spending more time somewhere on the Internet, then they are not watching TV advertisers' carefully designed ads placed just for them! While Nielsen Media Research says that levels have remained the same since 1996 — at about 16 hours per week — other youth-oriented research groups (Youth Culture and Corus Entertainment) believe there is cause for concern. Some suggest multi-tasking is the answer, but if the teen target is using the computer while watching TV, is the advertising message getting through?[12]

Magazines   Magazines are an excellent medium when high-quality printing and colour are desired in an ad. Magazines can reach a national market at a relatively low cost per reader. Through special-interest or regional editions of general-interest magazines, an advertiser can reach a selected audience with a minimum of waste circulation. Magazines are usually read in a leisurely fashion, in contrast to the haste with which other print media are read. This feature is especially valuable to the advertiser with a lengthy or complicated message. Magazines have a relatively long life, anywhere from a week to a month, and a high pass-along readership.

With less flexible production schedules than newspapers, magazines require ads to be submitted several weeks before publication. In addition, because they are published weekly or monthly, it is more difficult to use topical messages. Magazines are often read at times or in places — on planes and in doctors' offices, for instance — far removed from where a buying impulse can be acted on.

Direct mail   Direct mail has probably become the most personal and selective of all of the media and, if properly used, can do much to develop strong consumer and customer relationships. Because direct mail reaches only the market that the advertiser wants to contact, there is little waste circulation. Articles or other editorial matter does not accompany direct mail unless the advertiser provides it. That is, most direct mail is pure advertising. As a result, a direct-mail ad creates its own circulation and attracts its own readers. The cost of direct mail per prospect reached is quite high, compared with that of other media, but other media reach many people who are not real prospects and thus have higher waste-circulation costs. A severe limitation of direct mail is the difficulty of getting and maintaining good mailing lists. Direct-mail advertising also suffers from the stigma of being classed as "junk mail."

The effectiveness of direct mail has been increased in recent years through the application of technology to the process of identifying prospects to whom advertising materials are to be mailed. Highly specialized mailing lists can be purchased from mailing-list brokers, but many firms are now able to produce their own highly targeted mailing and contact lists from their own databases. Buying lists can be expensive, but they do offer advertisers the ability to target precisely the groups in which they are interested. Many companies have developed their own mailing lists through an effective design of their internal information systems. By capturing sales data in an appropriate way, for example, a travel agency can produce a list of all of the clients who made business trips to Europe in the past year, or took vacations in the southern United States, or made more than 15 business trips. These individuals then represent target segments for special-interest mailings. Wastage is dramatically reduced, because the advertising reaches precisely those people who are most likely to be interested.

Technology, the Internet, and the development of databases have made many contributions to furthering direct-mail effectiveness. The refinement of database software, along with a better understanding of how to meaningfully combine demographic or customer data, has led many firms, both store and non-store retailers, to tailor it into a mix that works for their organizations. Customer relationship and loyalty programs allow retailers to maintain much information on regular customers. These programs also allow a company to maintain a link or "personalized" connection to the consumer — not unlike cookie programs used by Internet retailers. Maintaining information on past consumers (those who have responded by mailing in cards, calling toll-free numbers, or visiting the company's Web site) provides a valuable target list for information regarding new products, services, or other information changes. These databanks can also be generated from delivery information, or simply by asking for name and postal code information at the cash register, which can be keyed into the terminal at the time of sale. This information can be used to generate a mailing list for flyers and other promotional information.

Bank of Montreal
La Senza Girl

The Bank of Montreal's First Canadian Funds (**www.bankofmontreal.com**) developed an interactive program on a floppy disk to position its Intuition fund as the most appropriate education savings plan. In a few minutes, recipients could quickly calculate the funds required for their children's education and how they could get these funds. The target for this campaign was selected by vetting customer lists in the bank's database and selecting those who had indicated that they were parents. The program was a success, generating a response three-and-a-half times greater than was expected. Some retailers offer discount cards for purchases that enable them to maintain customer information. La Senza Girl's VIP card (**www.lasenzagirl.com**) — aimed at girls 8 to 14 — costs $20 and offers 10 percent off all purchases and $15 in coupons. To purchase the card, customers must supply their names and street and e-mail addresses.

Westminster International

Based in Richmond Hill, Ontario, Westminster International (**www.westminster.ca**) has extended its mailing-services company to combine the Internet with traditional direct marketing as a response mechanism, thereby bringing direct mail into the information age. The database-driven electronic business-reply service allows recipients of direct mail to interact with the sender via a personalized Web page. Every outbound response card has a unique URL printed on it, allowing a recipient who responds to enter a personalized Web page, be greeted by name in the chosen language, and view answers to previous questions or information selected specifically to reflect the recipient's interests.[13]

While direct mail is widely regarded as one of the most cost-effective of advertising media, it is also one that must be managed very carefully. The effectiveness of a direct-mail advertising program is very heavily dependent on the accuracy of the mailing list being used. Some users of direct mail spend too little time on ensuring the accuracy of the mailing list, with the result that many people on the list may not be at all interested in the product or service (sound familiar?), while some will receive two or three mailing pieces because their names appear on the list in a number of different forms. When this occurs, people develop a low opinion of the medium. In a study conducted for National Public Relations, 7 out of 10 respondents considered direct mail to be the least credible way for them to learn about a company's new product or service.

Radio   During the last decades of the twentieth century, radio made a real comeback. Today, local radio (as contrasted with national networks) is especially strong. The medium accounts for just over 10 percent of all advertising revenues in Canada, attracting almost $840 million in sales annually.

Radio's big advantage is its relatively low cost. It also has tremendous reach — the ability to get to almost everybody. At the same time, with special-interest, targeted programming,

Difficulty of evaluation   It is hard to measure the sales effectiveness of advertising. By the very nature of the marketing mix, all elements — including advertising — are so intertwined that it is nearly impossible to measure the effect of any individual element. Factors that contribute to the difficulty of measuring the sales impact of advertising are:

- *Ads have different objectives:* Although all advertising is ultimately intended to increase sales, individual ads may not be aimed at producing immediate results. Some ads simply announce new store hours or service policies. Other ads build goodwill or contribute to a company's image.

- *Ads can have an effect over time:* Even an ad designed to have immediate sales impact may produce results weeks or months after it appears. A consumer may be influenced by an ad but may not be able to act on it immediately. Or an ad may plant in the consumer's mind a seed that doesn't blossom into a sale for several weeks. It is very difficult to determine (with the exception of mail-order advertising) when a particular ad or campaign produced specific results.

- *Measurement problems:* Consumers usually can't say when or if a specific ad influenced their behaviour, let alone if it caused them to buy. At any rate, a consumer decision is rarely explained by a single factor.

Regardless of these problems, advertisers try to measure advertising effectiveness because they must — and some knowledge is better than none at all. An ad's effectiveness may be tested before it is presented to the target audience, while it is being presented, or after it has completed its run.

Methods used to measure effectiveness   Ad effectiveness can be measured directly or indirectly. **Direct tests**, which measure or predict the sales volume attributable to an ad or a campaign, can be used only with a few types of ads. Tabulating the number of redemptions of a reduced-price coupon incorporated in an ad will indicate its effectiveness. Coupons frequently are coded so that they can also be traced to the publications from which they came. Another direct test used to predict sales measures the number of enquiries received from an ad that offers additional information to prospects who call or write in.

Most other types of measures are **indirect tests** of effectiveness, or measures of something other than actual purchase behaviour. One of the most frequently used measures is **advertising recall**. Recall tests are based on the premise that an ad can have an effect only if it is perceived and remembered. Three common recall tests are:

- *Recognition:* Showing people an ad and asking if they have seen it before.

- *Aided recall:* Asking people if they can recall seeing any ads for a particular brand.

- *Unaided recall:* Asking people if they can remember seeing any ads within an identified product category.

For broadcast media, this kind of testing can be conducted using a telephone survey, calling people at home within a few hours after an ad is aired or after a campaign has been running for several weeks.

Television ads are often tested before they are presented to the general public in what are called **pre-tests**. Commercials in finished or nearly finished form (to save production costs) are presented to panels of consumers for their reactions. This is often done in theatre settings, with the test ad shown along with other ads in the context of a regular TV

direct tests
Measures of the sales volume produced by an ad or an entire advertising campaign.

indirect tests
Measures of advertising effects that use something other than sales volume.

advertising recall
A measure of advertising effectiveness based on the premise that an ad can have an effect only if it is perceived and remembered.

pre-test
An activity in which commercials in finished or nearly finished form are presented to panels of consumers in order to gauge their reactions.

program. After viewing the program and the ads, the viewers are quizzed about the commercial being tested.

A criticism of pre-tests is that the testing situation is unrealistic. The ads often are not in the final forms that the actual target audience would see, the research respondents have been invited to a theatre to participate, and the respondents are usually given an incentive for their involvement. The testers argue that since these factors exist across all commercials tested, they in effect "wash out" and the scores provide useful comparative information.

Refinements are constantly being made in advertising testing, and developments in areas such as laboratory test markets and computer simulations show promise. However, the complexity of decision-making, combined with the multitude of influences on the buyer, will continue to make measuring the effectiveness of advertising a difficult task.

Organizing for Advertising

A firm can manage its advertising in three ways:

- Develop an internal advertising department.
- Use an outside advertising agency.
- Use a combination of an internal department and an outside advertising agency.

Regardless of which alternative is selected, basically the same specialized skills are necessary to do the advertising job. Creative people are needed to prepare the copy, generate illustrative material, and design the layouts. Media experts are required to select the appropriate media, buy the time or space, and arrange for the scheduled appearance of the ads. Managerial skills also are essential to plan and administer the entire advertising program.

Internal departments

All of the advertising tasks, some of them, or just the overall direction can be performed by an internal department. A company whose advertising is a substantial part of its marketing mix will usually have its own advertising department. Large retailers, for example, have their own advertising departments and many do not use advertising agencies at all.

Advertising agencies

advertising agency
An independent company rendering specialized services in advertising in particular and in marketing in general.

Many companies, especially manufacturers of consumer products, use advertising agencies to carry out some or all of their advertising activities. An **advertising agency** is an independent company that provides specialized advertising services and may also offer more general marketing assistance, including public relations and media relations.

Advertising agencies plan and execute entire advertising and communications campaigns. They employ more advertising specialists than their clients do, because they spread the cost over many client accounts. A client company can benefit from an agency's experience gained from other products and clients. Many large agencies offer "full services," which include sales promotion and public relations, and they are frequently called on to assist in new-product development, package design, and selection of product names. In fact, some have become integrated agencies, offering services from strategic planning to market research and Web page design that previously were performed by other outside specialists or by the advertisers themselves.

Internal department and outside agency

Many firms have their own advertising department and also use an advertising agency. The internal advertising department acts as a liaison with the agency, giving the company greater control over this major expenditure. The advertising department approves the agency's plans and ads, is responsible for preparing and administering the advertising budget, and co-ordinates advertising with personal selling. It may also handle direct marketing, dealer displays, and other promotional activities if they are not handled by the agency.

⬅ **BACKSPACE**

1. Name some of the general factors affecting the choice of media for a company that wants to advertise.
2. Which medium is used most frequently by local advertisers?
3. What do advertising agencies do?

Summary

Advertising is the non-personal, mass-communications component of a company's marketing communications mix. Advertising can be directed to consumers or businesses and can focus on products or institutions. Direct-action product ads call for immediate action, while indirect-action product ads are intended to stimulate demand over a longer time period. Product ads are also classified as being primary-demand and selective-demand stimulating. Primary-demand ads are designed to introduce a new product, to stimulate demand for a generic product, or to sustain demand for an industry's products. Selective-demand ads, which include competitive and comparative advertising, are intended to increase the demand for a particular brand.

In vertical co-operative advertising, manufacturers and their retail dealers share the cost of advertising the manufacturers' product at the local level. Horizontal co-operative advertising involves joint sponsorship of ads by firms at the same level of distribution.

Advertising expenditures are large, but the average cost of advertising in a firm is typically 1 to 3 percent of net sales. This is considerably less than the average cost of personal selling. Other frequently used advertising media are radio, magazines, the Yellow Pages, and outdoor displays.

An advertising campaign should be part of a total marketing communications program. The steps in designing a campaign include defining specific objectives, establishing a budget, creating a message, selecting media, and evaluating the advertising effort. Objectives can range from creating awareness of a brand to generating sales. The advertising message — consisting of the appeal and the execution of the ad — is influenced by the target audience and the media used to deliver the message.

A major task in developing a campaign is to select the advertising media — the general type, the particular category, and the specific vehicle. The choice should be based on the characteristics of the medium, which determine how effectively it conveys the message and its ability to reach the target audience.

With increasing fragmentation of viewing audiences for various media, it is becoming increasingly challenging to develop cost-effective strategies to maximize advertisement viewership. More and more advertisers will turn to emerging forms of advertising such as the Internet and newly developed forms of direct marketing. While many of the evolutions in advertising media are each reaching smaller audiences, these are more similar groups of consumers, allowing advertisers to better target individual efforts.

A difficult task in advertising management is evaluating the effectiveness of the advertising effort — both the entire campaign and individual ads. Except for sales results tests, commonly used techniques measure only recall of an ad. To operate an advertising program, a firm may rely on its own advertising department, an advertising agency, or a combination of the two.

Key Terms and Concepts

advertising 310
advertising agency 334
advertising allowance 313
advertising campaign 315
advertising media 320
advertising recall 333
appeal 319
attention 318
business-to-business advertising 310
comparative advertising 313
consumer advertising 310
co-operative advertising 313
copy 320
cost per thousand (CPM) 323
customer-service advertising 312
differential competitive advantage 313
direct-action advertising 310

direct tests 333
execution 320
fragmentation 325
horizontal co-operative advertising 314
illustration 320
indirect-action advertising 311
indirect tests 333
influence 318
institutional (corporate) advertising 311
layout 320
pioneering advertising 312
pre-tests 333
primary-demand advertising 312
product advertising 310
public service advertising (PSA) 312
selective-demand advertising 312
vertical co-operative advertising 313

Questions and Problems

1. Businesses in different industries demonstrate quite different patterns in their advertising expenditures. Some are heavy advertisers on television, while others use no television at all. Some advertise heavily in daily newspapers, while others rely on magazines. Some firms, such as those in the consumer-products field, spend as much as 15 percent of sales on advertising, while others, including many industrial marketers, spend less than 1 percent. How do you account for such variations in advertising expenditures?

2. Which advertising medium would you recommend as the best one for each of these products?
   a. Park benches.
   b. Pantyhose.
   c. Tax-preparation service.
   d. A Web-based bookseller.
   e. Funeral services.
   f. Toys for young children.
   g. Plastic clothespins.
   h. Internet-based investment services.
   i. Pet grooming services

3. Many grocery product and chocolate bar manufacturers earmark a good portion of their advertising budgets for use in magazines. Is this a wise choice of media for these firms? Explain.

4. Why do department stores use newspapers more than local radio stations as an advertising medium?

5. Why is it worthwhile to pre-test advertisements before they appear in the media? How could a test market be used to pre-test an ad? (You may want to refresh your memory with a review of test marketing in Chapter 6.)

6. What procedures can a firm use to determine the level of sales that resulted from a direct-mail ad?

7. If a manufacturing firm hires an advertising agency, should it close its own advertising department? Should it consider any changes?

8. Scan a current issue of a major national home and garden magazine and note the sales-promotion tools that appear in advertisements in that magazine. Which one do you consider to be particularly effective?

9. Is sales promotion effective for selling expensive consumer products such as houses, automobiles, or cruise trips? Is your answer the same for expensive business products?

10. Explain how sales promotion might be used to offset weak personal selling in retail stores.

11. Can a well-implemented company Web site help to offset weak or inconsistent selling in a company's retail outlets?

Hands-On Marketing

1. Bring to class four print ads or describe four radio or television ads that illustrate at least four of the specific advertising objectives outlined early in the chapter. As an alternative, find and describe two ads for the same brand that appear to be directed at different objectives.

2. Choose a brand that you like and perform a search on the Internet to find the brand's Web page. Then, flip through a magazine that you know advertises this brand and compare the two advertisements. What is different? The same? Discuss some of the challenges associated with advertising on the Web.

Back to the Top

Have you seen any mobile billboards driving around your city or town? Think back to our chapter opener in which we talked about the use of private vehicles as advertising tools. Would you agree to have your car dressed up as an ad? Why? Would your parents use their car in such a way? Apart from the money, what would you get from the experience? What products or services would you and your car be most appropriate to advertise? How would this be of value to the advertiser?

Want to get better grades, tips on how to study more effectively, and up-to-date information on happenings in the world of marketing? Then, visit the Online Learning Centre for practice tests, Study Smart software, and much more! **www.mcgrawhill.ca/college/sommers**

Interested in finding out what marketing looks like in the real world? *Marketing Magazine* is just a click away on your Online Learning Centre!

CHAPTER 12

Selling, Sales Promotion, and Public Relations

This chapter examines the selling function within an organization — what is involved in what is classically referred to as "sales." We will explore how the role of salespeople is changing in light of the changing consumer and marketplace, as well as the technological environment in which most companies work. We will also examine the role of the sales function in contributing to the establishment of successful relationships with customers. Finally, we will explore two related functions that are important components of the broader marketing communications program of a firm: sales promotion and public relations. After studying this chapter, you should have an understanding of:

- The nature and advantages of the sales function in an organization.
- The variety and nature of sales positions.
- The new focus and changing patterns in professional selling.
- The sales process.
- Key issues in operating and evaluating sales force performance.
- The scope and management of sales promotions.
- The role of public relations and publicity in the marketing communications program.

Tools of the Trade

Sarah Muldowney is a pharmaceutical sales representative for one of Canada's largest manufacturers of prescription drugs. She graduated 10 years ago with degrees in chemistry and business from Carleton University, and joined the sales staff of PharmaNational shortly thereafter. She enjoys the flexibility of her job and the opportunity it provides her to be on the leading edge of scientific developments in the pharmaceutical industry. She is proud of her company, which has been among the leading firms internationally in the development and launching of advanced heart drugs in recent years.

Sarah's job does not involve the actual sale of PharmaNational's products. Her role is to encourage physicians to prescribe her company's products to their patients. She is responsible for a sales territory in eastern Ontario that extends from Brockville to the Québec border and includes Kingston and the complex of hospitals in that city, most of which are affiliated with the medical school at Queen's University. She visits physicians in their offices and clinics on a regular basis, advising them of drugs coming on the market and explaining to them the most recent advances in research on illnesses and

diseases in which they might be interested. She attends sales conferences a couple of times a year, usually in resort locations, at which she and her fellow sales reps learn of new products and selling techniques. Sarah is provided with a company car, as she has to travel from her home in Kingston. Her generous expense allowance allows her to entertain physicians at local restaurants two or three times a week.

Since joining PharmaNational, Sarah has seen a lot of changes in the tools that are available to support her selling efforts. She carries a laptop computer and links to PharmaNational's Web site every evening to download her e-mail and product information. She has been most impressed recently with the database that PharmaNational provides for her that contains detailed information about the doctors on whom she calls. The database is compiled partly from information relating to each physician that Sarah inputs: the medical school each graduated from, years in practice, activities enjoyed, and certain details of each physician's practice and family. The database also contains data provided by many of Canada's largest drugstore chains that lets Sarah know what drugs each physician is prescribing and in what volumes.

Sarah Muldowney is part of the sales function at PharmaNational. Hers is a different kind of sales job in that she doesn't actually "sell" products and services in the classic sense of that word. Nevertheless, she is in sales.

In this chapter, we will examine the sales function in Canadian companies, how it operates, and its role in the building of customer relationships. We will also look at two related marketing communications functions: sales promotion and public relations.

Nature of the Sales Function

sales function
The part of a company that is responsible for sales.

The goal of all marketing efforts within a company or other organization is to increase profitable sales by satisfying consumers over the long run. The activity of sales personnel represents by far the major communications method used to reach this goal. The number of people employed in advertising is a small fraction of the number employed in sales. In many companies, sales represents the largest single operating expense, often 8 to 15 percent of a company's total sales revenue. In contrast, advertising costs average 1 to 3 percent of revenue.

sales
The process of selling products and services to customers; usually involves sales personnel who interact with customers.

We are referring in this case to the **sales function** within the firm. Let's make sure that we are clear on what this means. The word **sales** is used very widely within marketing, most often in an accounting sense to refer to the total revenue of a company. We also refer to making a sale, and we are going to talk about sales promotion later in this chapter. We refer to what salespeople do within a company as **selling**, or occasionally *personal selling*. This is the process of representing the company and its products and services to prospective customers. It is the part of a company or organization that is most in contact with the customer. We meet salespeople every day when we deal with companies, often face to face in a retail setting or increasingly on the telephone and through the Internet.

selling
The communication of information to persuade a prospective customer to buy a product, service, or idea.

As we will see in this chapter, sales or selling is a varied function, including such different jobs as retail furniture salespeople, pharmaceutical sales reps, and sales engineers for a chemical company. You or some of your friends may go into sales when you graduate. You could be working for a wide variety of companies and organizations, and you may or may not be engaged in actually trying to sell something; that is, in trying to convince customers to buy. The salesperson who serves you at a clothing store may not actually offer you assistance or advice, and may simply ring up the sale, but it is still considered a sales job. Similarly, many sales personnel today are called **customer-service representatives** and work in call centres.

customer-service representatives
Employees who represent the company to customers, usually providing advice and service over the telephone from call centres.

In Chapter 10, we discussed five factors that influence an organization's marketing communications mix — the target market, the objective, the nature of the product or service being promoted, the life-cycle stage of the product or service, and the budget available for promotion. Of the five factors, the sales function is likely to be responsible for a large portion of the marketing communications load when:

- The market is concentrated geographically, in a few industries, or in a few large customers. In this scenario, it is easier to contact people and actually meet them.

- The value of the product is not readily apparent to prospective customers. In other words, there are a lot of hidden factors to point out to them.

- The product has a high unit value, is quite technical in nature, or requires demonstration. Such products need the personal input of a salesperson to explain them, and they also are sufficiently high-priced that money can be spent on employing salespeople.

- The product must be fitted to an individual customer's need, as in the case of securities or insurance. In such a situation, the salesperson is needed to interpret the customer's need and to devise the right solution.

- The sale involves a trade-in. A salesperson is needed in this case to make an assessment of the value of the trade-in and to apply the value to the price of the item being bought. This is most common in automobile sales.

Products like these usually require a salesperson to explain features.

- The product is in the introductory stage of its life cycle. Since the customer is not familiar with the product and its features, a salesperson is needed to explain it.

- The organization does not have enough money for an adequate advertising campaign. Since mass advertising is costly, many start-up firms have to rely on the efforts of salespeople (often the owners) until they reach a stage of their development when they can afford to advertise widely.

Advantages of selling

Selling involves the direct personal communication of information, in contrast to the impersonal communication of advertising, sales promotion, and other marketing communications tools. This means that the sales effort can be more flexible than these other tools. Salespeople can tailor their presentations to fit the needs and behaviour of individual customers. They can see their customers' reaction to a particular sales approach and make adjustments on the spot.

Also, selling usually can be focused on prospective customers, thus minimizing wasted effort. In contrast, advertising messages are usually directed at much larger audiences that contain many who are not realistic prospects.

Another advantage of selling is that its goal is to actually secure a sale. Other forms of promotion are designed to move a prospect closer to a sale. Advertising, for example, often has the less-ambitious goal of attracting attention, providing information, and arousing desire. Aside from retail and direct-response advertising, it is rarely the sole factor responsible for stimulating buying action or completing the sale or transaction.

On the other hand, a full-fledged sales effort is costly. Even though a well-organized selling function can minimize wasted effort, the cost of developing and operating a sales force is high. Another disadvantage is that a company may often find it difficult to attract and retain the quality of salespeople needed to do the job. A successful career in sales requires a certain personality; otherwise, the person most often does not enjoy the job — and customers often don't enjoy the interaction either! At the retail level, many firms have abandoned the use of sales staff and shifted to self-service for this very reason. More recently, many firms have adopted an e-commerce approach to dealing with customers, delegating the sales function to a Web site, call centre, or some combination of the two.

Scope of the sales function

Elements of selling can be found in almost every human interaction: When a recent marketing graduate tries to convince a human resources specialist at Imperial Oil to recruit her, we often suggest that she has to "sell" herself; when a junior manager tries to convince a senior executive to change the company's approach to advertising, we observe that he is trying to "sell" the idea up the line; when your friends try to convince you to attend a movie with them, they are trying to "sell" you on the idea.

There are two kinds of sales roles, as shown in Figure 12-1. One is where customers come to the salespeople. Called **inside selling**, it primarily involves retail selling. In this kind of selling, we also include the thousands of employees who work in call centres across the country and who take orders over the telephone. This, too, is retail selling because it involves sales to the end-consumer. By far, most salespeople in Canada fall into this first category.

Regardless of whether face-to-face or technology-based interaction occurs between the customer and the salesperson, there are two distinct categorizations of inside selling, the first of which may be termed **proactive selling**. This involves an overt attempt on the part of the salesperson to convince the customer to buy. In such a situation, the selling effort is usually initiated by the salesperson and a creative process is followed to interest the customer in buying. This is the kind of selling that is often associated with automobile, furniture, and higher-end clothing sales. In situations in which the salesperson has to tailor the sales initiative to address specific customer needs and characteristics, creative selling is at work. Advice and information is often conveyed as the salesperson attempts to convince the customer to buy the product or service.

In many other cases, however, customers already know what they want to buy, or the purchase is so uncomplicated that little or no input is needed from salespeople. This is the situation in much of retail today, particularly in self-service environments such as supermarkets. We label this kind of selling **reactive selling**, as the salesperson does not actively have to sell, but simply processes the sale once the customer has decided.

inside selling
The kind of selling in which customers come to the salespeople; primarily face-to-face retail selling, but also includes phone-in ordering.

proactive selling
A situation in which the selling effort is initiated by the salesperson, who actively tries to interest the customer in buying.

reactive selling
A situation in which the sales process is initiated by the customer and the salesperson simply processes the sale.

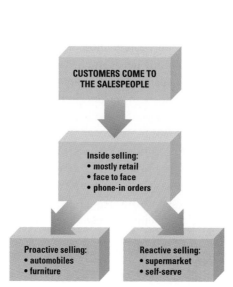
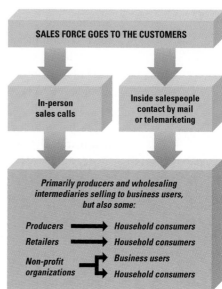

Figure 12-1:

Scope of the Sales Function

outside selling

The kind of personal selling in which salespeople go to the customers, making contact by mail, telephone, or face to face.

outside sales force

A group of sales reps engaged in field selling; that is, selling in person at a customer's place of business or home.

telemarketing

A form of non-store retailing in which a salesperson initiates contact with a prospect and closes the sale over the telephone.

Avon
Mary Kay
Dell
Gateway

In the other kind of selling situation, known as outside selling, salespeople go to the customer. Most sales forces operate outside the firm and usually represent producers or wholesaling intermediaries, selling to business customers and not to household consumers. Thus, we tend to associate the concept of an outside sales force with B2B marketing, as in the case of the pharmaceutical salesperson in our chapter opener or the sales reps for food manufacturing companies who sell to buyers at Loblaws and Sobeys. However, in our definition of an outside sales force we also include: (1) producers whose representatives sell directly to household as well as business customers, for example, insurance companies such as Great-West Life, and in-home sellers, such as those for Avon Products (www.avon.ca) or Mary Kay cosmetics (www.marykay.com); (2) representatives of retail organizations, such as those from home heating, home decorating, and renovations contractors, and also vacuum cleaner companies; and (3) representatives of non-profit organizations, for example, charity fund-raisers and workers for political candidates. Although this latter group is not typically thought to be in sales, their employees and volunteers who solicit donations are actually fulfilling a sales role.

A telephone-based sales function lies somewhere between inside and outside selling. It may also involve either proactive or reactive selling. The practice of telemarketing usually has salespeople engaged in proactive selling, because it involves outbound calling to prospective customers. Telephone sales representatives call customers and attempt to interest them in the purchase of a product or service. Such an approach to selling has become very popular in recent years, because it is based on the existence of large customer databases that are used to generate customer names. It has also succeeded in some situations in giving telemarketing a bad name, because the calls are usually unsolicited and are considered by many consumers to be intrusive or an invasion of their privacy.

Many call centres in Canada do not engage in telemarketing, but rather serve as order desks and customer-service centres. These centres receive toll-free inbound calls from customers who wish to order a product or service or to obtain information from customer-service representatives. These salespeople engage in reactive selling in that they respond to calls placed by customers.

With advances in telecommunication systems as integrated components of overall management information systems, the use of call centres and telemarketing representatives has grown exponentially in recent years. This practice became particularly popular with financial service providers and other companies with mass appeal. This sales approach works particularly well in combination with a significant Internet presence. Dell (www.dell.ca) and Gateway (www.gateway.com) computer companies have both become specialists in selling equipment and accessories through these channels.

Companies such as the Reader's Digest Association (Canada), Molson Breweries, and even chartered banks now use telemarketing. Reader's Digest has formed partnerships that have allowed it to develop inbound and outbound call centres offering collision coverage and fire insurance, as well as its traditional line of magazines, books, and videos. Molson has substantially reduced its personal sales force by hiring telephone reps to manage inventories and merchandising for smaller clients. Such telemarketing applications can cost as little as one-tenth that of a personal sales call and an efficient, experienced rep can often reach as many companies in a day as an employee in the field can in a week.[1]

Call-centre personnel take orders by telephone, but they are also in sales.

The new focus of selling

Consistent with the changes that have been taking place in marketing generally in recent years, the selling function within organizations is also being transformed by the shifting focus toward a longer-term emphasis on the building of relationships. Salespeople in companies are no longer being motivated merely to sell something, but rather are being given increasing responsibility to build relationships with customers. This is, of course, a natural extension of the sales role, as it is the salesperson who very often is the only point of personal contact between the company and the customer.

Customers of a company rarely meet a company's chief executive officer or the vice-president of marketing. The impressions they receive of a company are often based on their interaction with salespeople, whether retail sales staff or B2B sales representatives. To customers, the salesperson *is* the company, as impressions of the firm are based largely on interactions with sales personnel. All other employees are usually behind the scenes. Consequently, companies today seek to employ individuals in sales positions who are capable of developing relationships with customers, so that those customers will come back to do business with them (and the company) again. They want to hire salespeople who are outgoing, helpful, and friendly, people who can be trusted and on whom customers feel they can rely. They should be people with whom customers enjoy dealing.

Companies today, particularly in a B2B setting, want to employ sales reps who can become accepted as part of the customer's team. In an ideal relationship, the customer calls the sales rep with questions, to seek advice, and to request special services, and not simply to place an order. Many companies want to move beyond the status of "supplier" to become a trusted partner in the exchange relationship. In that regard, therefore, the sales rep becomes more than a salesperson and increasingly is viewed as a problem solver and solutions provider.

To play such a role, a sales rep has to be a special kind of person. In some industries, there is a high turnover rate in sales positions, because some people are very good at it and others are not. Successful salespeople are not only good at selling things, but also are good at gaining the confidence of customers and in building loyalty to them and their company. They have to be able to cope with rejection and with complaints from customers, because they are the first line of contact with customers.

Nature of sales jobs

The sales job of today is quite different from the stereotype of the past. The images of high pressure, false friendship, and fast talk are largely outdated. As more companies focus on hiring salespeople who can look beyond making the sale to the development of successful relationships with customers, the kind of people who are hired for sales jobs has changed.

The professional salesperson   A new type of sales rep has emerged: the **professional salesperson**. Today, these salespeople are managers of a market area: their territories or a customer category. They engage in a total selling job — serving their customers, building goodwill, selling their products, and training their customers' salespeople. Today's sales representatives act as a source of feedback on the market by relaying information back to the firm. They organize much of their own time and effort. They often take part in recruiting new salespeople, sales planning in their territories, and other managerial activities.

Sales and Marketing Management Magazine, in its surveys among sales executives and customers concerning the factors that are considered in selecting good sales employees, points to the following criteria:[2]

- *Accuracy:* Do the salespeople take care of details?

- *Availability:* Are the salespeople responsive to customers' requests?

Humpty Dumpty
IBM
Bombardier

● *Credibility:* Do customers view the salespeople as important resources?

● *Partnership:* Are the salespeople sought out for advice?

● *Trust:* Are customers confident that the salespeople will keep their word?

● *Discovery:* Do the salespeople offer ideas that improve customers' businesses?

Wide variety of sales jobs   The types of selling jobs and the activities involved in them cover a wide range. Consider the job of a Humpty Dumpty (**www.humpty dumpty.com**) driver-salesperson who calls routinely on a group of retail stores. That job is completely different from that of the IBM (**www.ibm.ca**) systems consultant who sells a computer system for managing hotel reservations to major hotel chains such as Fairmont or Four Seasons. Similarly, Sarah, the sales representative for PharmaNational in our chapter opener, has a job only remotely related to that of a Challenger 604 aircraft (**www.businessaircraft.bombardier.com**) sales engineer who leads the team that sells executive-type aircraft to large corporations around the world.

One way to classify sales jobs is on the basis of the creative selling skills required, from the simple to the complex. The classification that follows is updated and adapted from several classification schemes developed over time.[3]

driver-salesperson
A selling job in which the job is primarily to deliver the product; selling responsibilities, if any, are secondary to seeing that orders are filled correctly and on time.

1. **Driver-salesperson:** In this job, the salesperson primarily delivers the product, soft drinks or fuel oil, for example. Selling responsibilities are secondary, although most of these salespeople are encouraged to identify new business and are rewarded for finding opportunities to increase sales to existing accounts.

inside order taker
A selling job in which the primary function of the salesperson is to take orders in person or by telephone inside a store or other type of business.

2. **Inside order taker:** This is a position in which the salesperson takes orders at the seller's place of business; for example, a retail clerk standing behind the counter at a Bay store or a telephone representative of the Eddie Bauer catalogue retail operation. Most customers have already decided to buy. The salesperson's job is to serve them efficiently and courteously.

An effective inside order taker can adjust to a customer's reactions and build good customer relationships.

outside order taker

A selling job in which salespeople primarily go to customers in the field.

Para Paints

missionary salesperson

A selling job in which the salespeople are not expected to solicit orders but rather to influence decision-makers by building goodwill, performing promotional activities, and providing service to customers; called a *detail salesperson* in pharmaceuticals marketing.

Procter & Gamble
Merck
Eli Lilly

sales engineer

A selling job that often involves technically trained individuals selling sophisticated equipment; the emphasis is on the salesperson's ability to explain the product to the prospect and perhaps to adapt it to the customer's particular needs.

consultative salesperson

A selling job in which the person engages in the creative selling of goods and services.

xwave
Otis Elevator

3. **Outside order taker:** In this position, the salesperson goes to the customer in the field and accepts an order. An example is a sales representative for Para Paints (**www.para.com**) who calls on a building supplies store. Most of the sales made by outside order takers are repeat orders to established customers, and much of the salesperson's time is devoted to support activities such as assisting with promotion and helping train the account's salespeople. Outside salespeople are assigned targets, or goals, that require them to seek new customers and to introduce new products to existing customers.

4. **Missionary salesperson:** The job of a missionary salesperson is not to solicit orders but to build goodwill, perform promotional activities, and provide information and other services for the customers. These people may also be called *merchandisers* or *detail salespeople*. An example of this job is a missionary sales rep for Procter & Gamble (**www.pg.com**) who visits retailers regularly and may offer presentation suggestions, as well as assist in setting it up. They also help with special promotions. Also, there are "drug reps" like Sarah in our chapter opener who work for companies such as Merck (**www.merck.com**) or Eli Lilly (**www.lilly.com**), calling on doctors to introduce new products, provide information, and leave professional samples to be distributed to patients. This can be for both prescription and non-prescription products. Clearly, doctors don't buy these pharmaceutical products to resell, but they can potentially recommend or write prescriptions for these products.

5. **Sales engineer:** In this position, the major emphasis is on the salesperson's ability to explain the product to a prospective customer and also to tailor the product to the customer's particular needs. The products involved are typically complex, technically sophisticated items. A sales engineer usually provides technical support and works with another sales rep who regularly calls on a given account. Examples include producers of industrial equipment that develop manufacturing systems according to a client's requirements. Sales would be to new clients and also for replacement parts and replacement systems. As new developments occur, reps continue to sell existing clients on the increased benefits of the new technology. New clients and newly developed systems often require ongoing support while bugs are worked out, systems are fine-tuned to the particular processing requirements, and staff members learn to run and maintain the equipment. Also applicable here is the development and implementation of computer systems within organizations, or helping a company develop an Internet strategy and presence.

6. **Consultative salesperson:** This type of salesperson engages in the creative selling of goods and services. This category contains the most complex, difficult selling jobs, because customers can't see, touch, taste, or smell the product or service and often are not aware of their need for a seller's product. Consultative selling requires that a relationship of trust be established with the customer, because it often involves, for example, large-scale projects such as designing a system to fit the needs of a particular customer. For example, to make a sale, xwave (**www.xwave.com**) may design a flight arrivals and departures display system for an airport. Otis Elevator (**www.otis.com**) may develop a vertical lift system especially for a new office building. Such positions also involve technologically advanced products and computer systems.

Consultative selling does not have to involve highly technical outside selling. Some degree of consultation is also involved in certain retail situations where the customer is buying complex or tailored products that require the advice and opinion of a salesperson. For example, when most people are buying electronic equipment, computers, and certain items of clothing, they want to receive good advice from knowledgeable salespeople.

In summary, the above six types of sales jobs fall into three groups: **order taker** (categories 1, 2, and 3), **sales support personnel** (categories 4 and 5), and **order getter** (category 6). Order takers, unless they can find ways to provide added value for their customers, are the sales positions most threatened by Internet commerce.

The cost of personal selling   The cost of an outside sales call depends on the sales approach used. For firms selling commodities and emphasizing price, the cost can be from $100 or more per call. When the sales approach is to identify and design solutions for customers' problems, costs can range up to $200 or more per call. Add to this the fact that it can take from three to six calls to conclude a sale with a new customer and it becomes clear that personal selling is costly. Turnover can also be high, because certain personality traits are required to be successful in this profession. New salespeople require training and initially they are less productive — and perhaps less successful. High turnover among sales personnel sends a negative message to clients, suggesting that the company cannot keep good people. It is also disruptive to customer relationships, because good salespeople often develop such positive relationships with "their" customers that they take the customers with them when they leave a company to join another. In either case, sales may be lost.

The uniqueness of sales jobs   The features that differentiate sales jobs from other jobs are:

- The sales force is largely responsible for implementing a firm's marketing strategies in that they are the people who deal most directly with customers. Therefore, they have to be seen as spokespersons and ambassadors for the firm and guardians of its relationships and reputation.

- Salespeople represent their company to customers and to society in general. Many sales jobs require the salesperson to socialize with customers who frequently are upper-level managers in their companies. Opinions of the firm and its products are formed on the basis of impressions made by salespeople in their work and outside activities. The public ordinarily does not judge a company by its factory or office workers, but salespeople are on the front line and therefore have to be effective, personable, and easy to deal with.

- Sales personnel often operate with limited direct supervision. For success in selling, a sales rep must work hard physically and mentally, be creative and persistent, and show considerable initiative. This all requires a high degree of motivation.

- Salespeople have to have good people skills. They have to be empathetic and appear to be genuinely concerned with issues that customers have and committed to finding solutions. The best salespeople will go out of their way to solve customers' problems.

- Sales reps, particularly those who operate in a telemarketing context and other environments where they are "cold-calling" customers in an attempt to interest them in the firm's products and services, must have a high tolerance for rejection. Sales personnel in such roles may complete only one sale for every 50 or more calls made.

- Sales jobs often involve considerable travelling and time away from home, although many companies have reduced sales travel time by redesigning sales territories, routing sales trips better, and relying more on telephone and e-mail contact. Nevertheless, the other stresses of a sales job, coupled with long hours and travelling, require a mental toughness and physical stamina rarely demanded in other jobs. Personal selling is hard work!

BACKSPACE

1. _____ involves the direct personal communication of information, in contrast to the impersonal communication of sales promotion and other marketing communications tools.

2. Name the two kinds of sales roles.

3. What is a consultative salesperson?

Changing Patterns in Sales

Traditionally, selling was a face-to-face, one-on-one situation between a salesperson and a buyer, in both retail B2C sales and in B2B transactions. In recent years, however, some very different selling patterns have emerged. These new patterns reflect a growing expertise among consumers and business buyers, which in turn has fostered a growing professionalism in selling. They also reflect certain changes in the selling environment, including the always-important impact of technology. These changing approaches to selling are discussed below.

Team selling

team selling
Use of a number of sales personnel to represent a company, often calling on the same account; sometimes called a *selling centre*.

To match the expertise of the buying centre in business markets, a growing number of firms have adopted the organizational concept of a **selling centre**, or team selling. **Team selling** involves a group of people representing a sales department as well as other functional areas in a firm. This is also sometimes called a *sales team*.

Team selling is expensive and is used only when there is a potential for a high sales volume and profit. Procter & Gamble, for example, would have selling teams comprising salespeople and representatives from finance, distribution, and manufacturing assigned to cover a large retailer such as Wal-Mart. As an international retailer for most of P&G's products, the two firms work so closely together that Wal-Mart's scanner and inventory system is directly linked to P&G, allowing the company to perform inventory-control functions. The P&G sales team works closely with the retailer to develop, promote, and deliver products.

Most sales teams are ad hoc groups, assembled only to deal with a particular client or a large one-time opportunity. Except for the salesperson, the team members have other duties in the firm, which raises certain managerial issues. For example, who should direct the team: the most senior person, the person with the most experience with the situation at hand, or the salesperson who organized the team? What happens if a company decides it prefers working with a senior manager on the team or a technical expert who "speaks its language" rather than the salesperson? How should the team members be evaluated and compensated? Despite having to deal with these issues, the increasing complexity of sales has made team selling increasingly popular.

Systems selling

Xerox

The concept of **systems selling** means selling a total package of related goods and services — a system — to solve a customer's problem. The idea is that the system, the total package of goods and services, will satisfy the buyer's needs more effectively than selling individual products separately. Xerox (**www.xerox.ca**), for example, originally sold individual products, using a separate sales force for each major product line. Today, using a systems-selling approach, Xerox studies a customer's office information and operating problems, and then provides a total automated system of equipment and accompanying services to solve that customer's office problems.

Systems selling has several benefits, the most obvious being that it produces a larger initial sale, since a system rather than a product is being purchased. Second, it reduces compatibility problems, since all parts of the system come from the same supplier or they have been selected by the supplier to guarantee compatibility. Third, the supplier is usually retained to service the system because of the supplier's familiarity with it and its components. Finally, if the system performs effectively, the supplier is in an excellent position to sell upgrades as they are required. In some very technical situations, systems selling may involve a number of firms on the suppliers' side. This evolution into a "solutions" provider for the client fosters a reliance on the supplier as well as a stronger relationship between the two firms.

Global sales teams

Magna International

As companies expand their operations to various corners of the world, they expect their suppliers to do the same. Having products readily available and providing speedy service is essential to maintaining global customers, so many larger firms have established sales offices or distribution centres in some foreign locations to serve these customers. Now, to service their largest and most profitable customers, companies such as Bombardier, Magna International (**www.magna.ca**), and IBM form **global sales teams**. A global sales team is responsible for all of a client's requirements, for any of their locations, around the world.

Relationship Selling

Relationship selling means developing a mutually beneficial relationship with selected customers over time. Relationship selling can be a natural outcome from team selling or it can be developed by individual sales representatives in their continued dealings with customers. Relationship selling is based on the idea that instead of maximizing the number and size of individual transactions, the seller works to develop a deeper, longer-lasting relationship built on trust and mutual benefit. The salesperson must work with the client to determine what is in the best interest of the client, not the sales firm or the individual salesperson. This may mean taking the time and effort to understand the true needs and goals of the client's firm. The salesperson must place as much emphasis on the buyer-seller relationship as on the immediate sale during transactions and sales efforts. Sales representatives must receive the full support of the firm in these efforts in that their performance must be evaluated on relationship measures as well as sales performance.

Unfortunately, there is sometimes a lack of trust in the buyer-seller relationship, both in B2C and B2B selling. Too often, selling can become adversarial, with one side winning and the other side losing. Often the perception is that the sales representative's sole purpose is to increase the value of current sales without regard for future customer interactions. Prospective customers, therefore, are often wary of being sold something that they may not really need. When this does occur, it can be said that a relationship does not really exist, since the salesperson is more interested in selling than in meeting the customer's needs. In relationship selling, it must be accepted that *not* selling something may be the preferred solution if it leads to long-term customer satisfaction.

In the face of all of the hype about what technology can do, it's still people who form business relationships, understand customer needs, and fulfil them in a timely, cost-effective manner. Technology can speed up certain processes, but it's people like Grand & Toy's account managers, product specialists, space planners, and others who help customers determine what's best for their businesses, whether it's buying paper clips, figuring out the best value in a toner cartridge, or deciding on a new office layout. These employees have been trained to become trusted advisors who work together to provide customers with a single-source purchasing model for office and computer supplies, furniture, etc. This approach (and company culture) has developed for the company, which has been a leading supplier of office supplies for 119 years, trusting relationships with thousands of companies across the country.[4]

Subaru found a successful program that enabled one-on-one communication and relationship development with members of each of its target groups through an extreme version of the new car test-drive. As a bonus, this travelling program continues to generate publicity as it tours the country. In order to promote the Impreza WRX and attract current and potential customers into dealerships for a little "seat time," the company created the Subaru National Ride & Drive program, inviting visitors to auto shows and the company's Web site, along with customers referred by dealers, to attend the events in their cities. Activities included a classroom-style seminar, a "vehicle walk-around," and a course overview. Then participants were ready to climb aboard for a little of that "seat time." Participants did cornering sequences, a slalom course, torque cornering, and a stop box. Then professional drivers took participants on the ride of their lives in what was referred to as the "hot laps" portion of the event. Subsequent success continues with well-attended dealership tours of the company-sponsored rally team and cars. The company's rally participation and performance is also regularly documented on its Web site.[5]

Telemarketing and Internet selling

Telemarketing is the innovative use of telecommunications equipment and systems as part of the "going to the customer" category of personal selling. Under certain conditions, telemarketing is attractive to both buyers and sellers. Buyers placing routine reorders or new orders for standardized products by telephone use less of their time than with personal sales calls.

Many sellers find that telemarketing increases selling efficiency. With the high cost of keeping salespeople on the road, telemarketing reduces the time they spend on routine order-taking. Redirecting routine reorders to a telemarketing system or the Internet allows the field sales force to devote more time to creative selling, major account selling, and other more profitable selling activities. Some examples of selling activities that lend themselves nicely to such an approach are:

- Outbound telemarketing: This involves seeking leads to new accounts and identifying potentially good customers that sales reps can follow up with in-person calls.

Baxter International

- Processing orders for standardized products: In the case of Baxter International (**www.baxter.com**) and some of the customers for its hospital supplies, for example, the buyer's computer talks with Baxter's computer to place orders and determine shipping dates.

- Dealing with small-order customers, especially those with whom the seller would lose money if field sales calls were used: Routine orders may be placed over the telephone or through the supplier's Web site.

John Deere

- Improving relations with intermediaries: The John Deere farm equipment company (**www. deere.com**) "talks" via computers with its dealers about inventories, service, and financial management.

- Improving communications with intermediaries in foreign countries and competing better against manufacturers in those countries: In Europe, for example, the auto, chemical, steel, and shipbuilding industries have developed electronic communication systems involving manufacturers, suppliers, and even Customs and shipping agents.

Sales force automation

Equipping salespeople with laptop computers, wireless mobile phones, PDAs, fax machines, and pagers in order to give them access to databases, the Internet, e-mail, and other information and communication tools is called **sales force automation**. The concept is quite simple, since a wide range of software has been developed to help salespeople manage information about

Automation means he's never away from the office.

their accounts and prospects, generate proposals, submit reports, and manage their time and territories more efficiently. By arming sales representatives with the appropriate technology, a firm can increase a salesperson's productivity and efficiency. By reducing time spent on routine administrative tasks, more time is free for pursuing new clients, following up on existing clients, and strengthening relationships. Sales reps can, therefore, provide a higher level of service.

Automating a sales force can be expensive, depending on the level and degree of customization. For example, providing salespeople with pagers so they can keep in touch with customers would be a modest investment, compared to a system that permitted access to corporate databases.

Experiences with sales force automation have been mixed. As is often the case when new technology is implemented, many systems fail to meet expectations. However, a significant number of the problems that crop up seem to result from inadequate planning or implementation. Despite these difficulties, more and more sales forces are being automated.

The Sales Process

The sales process (see Figure 12-2) is a logical sequence of four steps that a salesperson takes in dealing with a prospective buyer. This process is designed to lead to some desired customer action and ends with a follow-up to ensure customer satisfaction. The desired action usually is to get the customer to buy a product or a service, but it may be to get the company on a preferred supplier list or to encourage a customer to engage in promotional activity for the supplier's brand.

prospecting
The stage in the personal-selling process that involves developing a list of potential customers.

Prospecting

The first step in the sales process is called **prospecting**. It consists of two activities — identifying prospects and then qualifying them, that is, determining whether they have the necessary willingness to buy, purchasing power, and authority.

Figure 12-2:
The Personal
Selling Process

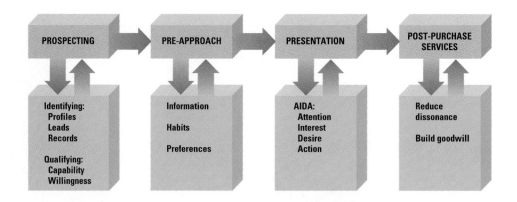

Identifying:
Profiles
Leads
Records

Qualifying:
Capability
Willingness

Information

Habits

Preferences

AIDA:
Attention
Interest
Desire
Action

Reduce
dissonance

Build goodwill

Identifying prospects The identification process is an application of market segmentation. By analyzing the firm's database of past and current customers, a sales representative determines the characteristics of the ideal prospect. Comparing this profile to a list of prospective customers produces a set of target prospects.

Many other sources can be used to build the list of prospects. The representative's sales manager may prepare a list, current customers may suggest new leads, trade association and industry directories can be a good source, and leads can come from people responding to the firm's marketing communications. These responses include customers mailing in coupons, calling a toll-free number given in an advertisement, or responding to a Web site.

A little thought often will suggest logical prospects. For example, The Brick furniture store (**www.thebrick.com**) can find prospects in lists of building permits issued. Toyota and Nissan auto dealers in Japan go door to door to seek prospects for new car sales. Insurance companies, real estate firms, and even local diaper services use such sources as marriage and birth announcements in newspapers.

The Brick

Qualifying the prospects After identifying prospective customers, a marketer should **qualify** them — that is, determine whether they have the necessary willingness, purchasing power, and authority to buy. To determine willingness to buy, a company can seek information about a prospect's relationship with its present suppliers. For example, a business firm or a household consumer may have had a long, satisfying relationship with The Co-operators insurance company for auto insurance. In this case, there would seem to be little chance that an Allstate (**www.allstate.ca**) salesperson could get that prospect's business, so the salesperson may be better advised to target other customers.

Allstate

Dun & Bradstreet

To determine a prospect's ability to pay, a marketer may refer to credit-rating services such as Dun & Bradstreet (**www.dnbcorp.com**). For household consumers or small businesses in an area, a seller may obtain credit information from a local credit bureau. Identifying the person who has the authority to buy for a business or a household can be difficult, as we saw in Chapter 5. In a business, the buying authority may rest with a committee or a senior manager at a distant location. Besides determining the buying authority, a seller also should identify the people who influence the buying decision. A purchasing agent may have buying authority, but the actual purchase may depend on the recommendation of office staff, factory engineers, or senior managers.

Pre-approach to individual prospects

Before calling on prospects, salespeople should learn as much as possible about them. This could mean finding out what products and services the prospects are now using and their reactions to them. In B2B selling, a salesperson or selling team should find out how buying decisions are made in the customer's organization. (Remember, in Chapter 5, we discussed the various roles played in the buying-decision process in business firms.) The right people can be targeted if the salesperson knows who the information gatekeeper is, who influences and/or makes the buying decision, and who actually makes the purchase.

Information about prospects also allows salespeople to tailor their presentations to individual buyers. That information extends to issues and problems that the prospective client is facing. By approaching the sales situation appearing to be well informed and having done their homework, sales reps are in a better position to propose solutions and to appear knowledgeable and helpful. Demonstrating such expertise and commitment often prompts a customer to observe that the sales rep "really understands my business."

Presenting the sales message

With the appropriate **pre-approach information**, a salesperson can design a **sales presentation** that will attract the prospect's attention. The salesperson then tries to hold the prospect's interest while building a desire for the product and, when the time is right, attempt to stimulate action by closing the sale. This approach, called **AIDA** (an acronym formed by the first letters of **a**ttention, **i**nterest, **d**esire, and **a**ction), is used by many organizations.

Attract attention — the approach   The first task in a sales presentation is to attract the prospect's attention and to generate interest. When the prospect is aware of a need and is seeking a solution, simply outlining the capabilities of the product may be enough. However, more creativity often is required.

For instance, if a customer referred the salesperson to the prospect, the right approach might be to start out by mentioning this common acquaintance. Or a salesperson might suggest the product benefits by making some startling statement. One sales training consultant often greets a prospect with the question, "If I can cut your selling costs in half and at the same time double your sales volume, are you interested?"

MARKETING AT WORK   12-1: ETHICS

"Roach-Bait Marketing" Gets Consumers to Spread the Word

That "tourist" asking to have her picture taken may be part of a covert marketing operation! Taking guerrilla marketing to a new level, Sony Ericsson Mobile Communications paid dozens of actors to pose as tourists at U.S. landmarks, such as the Empire State Building and Seattle's Space Needle, during the summer of 2002.

Without revealing their true purpose, the groups of two or three actors asked unsuspecting people to take their pictures, using the new T68I cellphone, which also serves as a digital camera. It's called "undercover" or "stealth marketing" — and in a world grown weary of ads, companies are increasingly using the method to push a range of products, from alcoholic drinks to personal-care items. The common goal: Fly under consumers' advertising radar and let them believe that they have had a spontaneous encounter with a user of a product — giving the item instant credibility. But critics say it's deceptive and unethical.

"It's the creep of ads into every nook and cranny of our lives and culture," according to the executive director of Commercial Alert, an anti-commercialism group based in Portland, Oregon. "It's the commercialization of human relationships."

Sony Ericsson defends the practice as a harmless way to engage consumers since no names are taken or junk mail sent out — the actors are just showing the product in a new and exciting way. It gets people talking about the product and passing the information to others — otherwise known as "viral marketing."

In another ruse, actresses perform scripted routines at trendy nightclubs — they answer their cellphones and then look at the caller's picture on its screen. In other situations, two "plants" sit at opposite ends of a bar competing in a video game on their cellphones.

Advocates of undercover marketing say it's an effective way to cut through the clutter of commercials, particularly when the target consumers are young people who have learned to tune out most forms of advertising. But, when they see another person using a product, it makes an impression.

Otherwise called "roach-bait marketing," the unsuspecting consumers are the "roaches," and they take the bait and spread it to family and friends!

SOURCE: Adapted from John Heinzl, "Beware Tourists With Talking Cameras," *The Globe and Mail*, August 1, 2002, pp. A1, A13.

Hold interest and arouse desire   After attracting the prospect's attention, the sales representative can hold it and stimulate further interest in the product with a sales talk. There is no common pattern here. Usually, however, a product demonstration is invaluable. Whatever pattern is followed in the talk, the salesperson must always show how the product will benefit the prospect. Increasingly, salespeople are using technology (often sales presentations on a laptop) to deliver a consistent sales message.

Many companies engaged in telemarketing or door-to-door selling often use a "canned" sales talk or a script — a memorized sales presentation designed to cover all points that management wants to have stated. Although many people feel that this is a poor practice, canned talks have time and again proved to be effective. Nevertheless, they are used less and less today in face-to-face sales situations, because companies believe that flexible presentations can be more personal and tailored for individual customers' needs.

Meet objectives and close the sale   After explaining the product and its benefits, a salesperson should try **closing the sale** — obtaining the customer's agreement to buy.

As part of the presentation, the salesperson may periodically venture a **trial close** to test the prospect's willingness to buy. By posing some "either/or" questions, a salesperson can bring the presentation to a positive result. For example, "Would you like the installation to begin next Monday or shall we book another time later in the week?"

The trial close is important because it gives the salesperson an indication of how close the prospect is to a decision or what objections the prospect has. If objections are stated, the salesperson then has an opportunity to handle them and clarify additional product or service benefits and to reinforce those that have already been presented.

Post-purchase service

An effective selling job does not end when the order is written up. The final stage of a selling process is a series of post-purchase activities that can build customer goodwill and lay the groundwork for future business. An alert salesperson will follow up sales to ensure that no problems occur in delivery, financing, installation, employee training, and other areas that are important to customer satisfaction. Many companies now have formalized customer contact after the sale to ensure that the product or service is meeting the customer's expectations. If it isn't, appropriate steps can be taken to restore that satisfaction by changing the product or offering needed information.

Post-purchase service reduces the anxiety that usually occurs after a person makes a buying decision. In this final stage of the selling process, a salesperson can minimize the customer's cognitive dissonance by (1) summarizing the product's benefits after the purchase, (2) repeating why the product is better than alternatives not chosen, and (3) emphasizing how satisfied the customer will be with the product.

Staffing and Operating a Sales Force

A majority of sales managers spend most of their time in staffing and operating a sales force. Since selling involves people dealing with people, it should come as no surprise that most of the activities we'll discuss in this section are, in fact, more closely related to human resources than they are to the traditional definition of marketing. We now turn our attention to these activities, as shown in Figure 12-3.

Figure 12-3:

Staffing and Operating a Sales Force

Recruitment and selection

Personnel selection is the most important management activity in any organization. This is true whether the organization is a business, an athletic team, or a university or college. Consequently, the key to success in managing a sales force is selecting the right people. Even when there are noticeable product advantages, if a sales force is distinctly inferior to that of a competitor, the competitor will win.

Sales force selection includes three tasks:

1. Determining the type of people wanted.

2. Recruiting an adequate number of applicants.

3. Selecting the most qualified persons from among the applicants.

Determining hiring specifications   The first step is to establish the proper hiring specifications, just as if the company was purchasing equipment or supplies. To establish these specifications, management must first know what the particular sales job entails. This calls for a detailed review of the marketing strategy to determine the salesperson's role. Then, a detailed job analysis and a written job description can be developed. This description will later be invaluable in training, compensation, and supervision decisions.

Determining the qualifications needed to fill the job is the most difficult part of the selection function. We still don't really know all of the characteristics that make a good salesperson, nor can we measure to what degree each characteristic should be present or to what extent an abundance of one can offset the lack of another. Some companies have analyzed the personal histories of its past sales representatives in an effort to determine the traits common to successful (and unsuccessful) performers.

Recruiting applicants   A planned system for recruiting a sufficient number of applicants is the next step in selection. A good recruiting system:

● Operates continuously, not only when sales force vacancies occur.

● Is systematic in reaching all appropriate sources of applicants.

● Provides a flow of more qualified applicants than immediately needed.

To identify recruits, large organizations often use placement services on university and college campuses or professional employment agencies or "head-hunters," some of which specialize in locating applicants for marketing and sales positions. Smaller firms that need fewer new salespeople may place employment ads in trade publications and daily newspapers. Many firms solicit recommendations from company employees, customers, or suppliers.

Matching applicants with specifications   Sales managers use a variety of techniques to determine which applicants possess the desired qualifications, including application forms, interviews, references, credit reports, psychological tests, aptitude tests, and physical examinations. Virtually all companies ask candidates to fill out application forms. In addition to providing basic screening information, the application form can indicate areas that should be explored in an interview.

No salesperson should be hired without at least one personal interview. It is usually desirable to have several interviews conducted by different people in different physical settings. Pooling the opinions of a number of people increases the likelihood of discovering any undesirable characteristics and reduces the effects of one interviewer's possible bias. An interview helps an employer to determine (1) the applicant's degree of interest in the job, (2) the match between the requirements of the job and the applicant's skills, and (3) the applicant's motivation to work hard.

The individuals involved in the selection process should be aware of the various provincial laws against discrimination to avoid inadvertent violations. Testing for intelligence, attributes, or personality, while legal, is somewhat controversial. Some companies avoid testing for fear that they will be accused of discrimination. However, employment tests are legitimate selection tools as long as they can be shown to predict job performance accurately.

Training a sales force

Both new and experienced salespeople need an effective **sales training program** to improve their selling skills, learn about new products, and improve their time- and territory-management practices. Recognizing that the recent college graduates it hires into its sales force are unlikely to have much experience with its appliances, Whirlpool devised an unusual training experiment.[6] Eight new hires spent two months living in a house together, using the products the company sells. Under the supervision of trainers, they cooked, cleaned, baked, and washed, using their company's products. At the end of the program, the trainees had the experience and confidence to go into the field and teach retail sales clerks how to demonstrate and sell Whirlpool appliances.

Motivating a sales force

Salespeople, especially outside sales forces, require a high degree of motivation. Consider how a sales job is different from most other jobs. Salespeople often work independently, without supervision and guidance from management. Outside salespeople work most of the time away from the support and comfort of home-office surroundings.

Consequently, management faces a challenge in **motivating salespeople**. One key is to determine what motivates a sales representative: Is it a need for status, control, accomplishment, or something else? People differ in what motivates them, and motivations change over time. A young person may be more motivated by monetary rewards alone, while older salespeople may be more interested in receiving recognition for building long-term relationships with important buyers. This means, of course, that a motivational program should reach the reps individually, as much as possible.

Sales executives can draw from a wide assortment of specific motivational tools.[7] Financial incentives — compensation plans, bonuses, fringe benefits — are frequently effective. Non-financial rewards — job enrichment; good, consistent feedback from management; recognition and honour awards (pins, trophies, or certificates) — may be appropriate. Sales meetings and sales contests are often considered to be enjoyable alternatives. Many firms provide cruises, resort trips, and other incentives as rewards for sales reps who meet or exceed various qualitative and quantitative sales goals.[8]

An important issue surrounding compensation relates to the type of behaviour that the firm wishes to reward. Many companies have motivated their sales personnel for many years by rewarding greater sales levels. This may involve simply paying salespeople a commission on all sales, or it may involve sales contests and bonuses for achieving certain sales targets. The common denominator here is that the salesperson is paid more for generating more sales.

As many companies have broadened their view of the role of sales personnel to include the development and maintenance of customer relationships, compensation systems have changed as a result. Many firms now motivate their salespeople to build solid customer relationships by including a component in the compensation program that encourages such behaviour.

Compensating a sales force

Financial rewards are still by far the most widely used tool for motivating salespeople. Consequently, designing and administering an effective **sales compensation plan** is a large part of a sales manager's job. Financial rewards may be direct monetary payments (salary, commission, bonuses) or indirect monetary compensation (paid vacations, pensions, insurance plans).

Establishing a compensation system calls for decisions concerning the level of compensation, as well as the method of compensation and the kind of behaviour for which the salesperson will be compensated and rewarded. The level refers to the total dollar income that a salesperson may earn over a period of time. The type of person required and the competitive rate of pay for similar positions influence the compensation level. The method is the system or plan by which the salesperson will reach the intended level. The behaviour to be encouraged refers to the comment above concerning whether the salesperson is to be rewarded only for making sales or whether there are other expectations.

Three widely used methods of compensating a sales force that are tied to sales are straight salary, straight commission, and a combination plan. A **salary** is a fixed payment for a period of time during which the salesperson is working. A salary-only plan (called a *straight salary*) provides security and stability of earnings for a salesperson. This plan gives management control over the selling efforts of the salesperson, and the sales representatives themselves are likely to cater to the customer's best interests. The main drawback of a straight salary is that it does not offer adequate incentive for salespeople to increase their sales volume. Also, a straight salary is a fixed cost, unrelated to sales volume or gross margin.

A **commission** is a payment tied to a specific unit of accomplishment; for example, a sales representative may be paid 5 percent of gross sales or 8 percent of gross margin. A commission-only plan (*straight commission*) tends to have just the opposite merits and limitations of a straight salary. A straight commission provides considerable incentive for salespeople, and it is a variable cost related directly to a representative's sales volume or gross margin. On the other hand, it is difficult to control straight-commission people, and it is especially difficult to get them to perform tasks for which no commission is paid. The straight-commission plan is most often used in retail selling situations and may have an unintended negative effect. The incentive behind such a system is to encourage salespeople to sell as much as possible. Many consumers do not like what they perceive to be the high-pressure approach that is often associated with commission-based selling.

There is no ideal method of compensation. Many firms combine some level of salary with a commission to create an incentive. Today, many companies are building into their compensation programs some component that rewards salespeople for achieving high levels of customer service, customer satisfaction, and customer relationships. To be able to reward salespeople for achieving these goals, a company must be able to measure outcomes, of course. This is a topic to which we will turn our attention later in this chapter.

Supervising a sales force

Sales force supervision is difficult because salespeople often work independently and where they cannot be observed. Yet supervision serves both as a means of continuing training and as a device to ensure that company policies are being carried out.

An issue that management must resolve is how closely to supervise. If too close, it can create a role conflict for the salesperson. One of the attractions of selling is the freedom it affords salespeople to develop creative solutions to customers' problems. Close supervision can stifle that sense of independence. Conversely, too little supervision can also cause problems: Salespeople who are not closely supervised may lack an understanding of the expectations of their supervisors and companies. They may not know, for example, how much time should be spent in servicing existing accounts and how much in developing new business.

The most effective supervisory method is personal observation in the field. Typically, at least half of a sales manager's time is spent travelling with or spending time on the sales floor with salespeople. Other supervisory tools are reports, e-mails, and sales meetings.

Evaluating Sales Performance

evaluating sales performance

The process of determining whether sales personnel have achieved objectives; important for compensation.

Managing a sales force includes **evaluating sales performance**. Sales managers must know what the salespeople are doing in order to reward them or to make constructive proposals for improvement. By establishing performance standards and studying salespeople's activities, management can develop new training programs for upgrading the sales force's efforts. And, of course, performance evaluation should be the basis for compensation decisions and other incentives and rewards.

Both quantitative and qualitative factors should be used as bases for performance evaluation. These are often referred to as "hard" and "soft" measures. The "hard" quantitative measures of sales performance generally have the advantage of being specific and objective and usually involve financial and other data that the firm collects automatically through its information system. The "soft" qualitative performance measures, although reflecting broader dimensions of desirable behaviour, are often limited by the subjective judgement of evaluators. For either type of appraisal, however, management faces the difficult task of measuring the desired outcomes and of setting standards against which a salesperson's performance may be measured.

Quantitative bases

Sales performance may be evaluated quantitatively in terms of inputs (efforts) and outputs (results). Together, inputs (such as number of sales calls per day or customer-service activity) and outputs (such as sales volume or gross margin over six months or longer) provide a measure of selling effectiveness. These have the advantage of being fairly easily measured, and with sophisticated information systems today, such measures can be tracked directly to each individual salesperson by the company's information system. It is precisely because such measures are easily obtained that many companies have continued to use them exclusively.

Useful quantitative input measures include:

- Call rate — number of calls per day or week.
- Number of formal proposals presented.
- Non-selling activities — promotion displays set up, training sessions held with distributors or dealers, client problem-solving sessions.

Some quantitative output measures that are useful as evaluation criteria are:

- Sales volume by product, customer group, and territory.
- Sales volume as a percentage of quota or territory potential.
- Gross margin by product line, customer group, and territory.
- Orders — number and average dollar amount.
- Closing rate — number of orders divided by number of calls.
- Accounts — percentage of existing accounts sold and number of new accounts opened.

An increasing number of firms, realizing the limitations of using an evaluation program that is tied only to quantitative measures, are incorporating measures of customer satisfaction or of service quality as a performance indicator. Satisfaction is measured a number of different ways, from detailed questionnaires that customers complete to counting the number of complaints received per customer. Assessing satisfaction reflects a recognition by companies that there is more to selling than making a sale and it also allows salespeople more scope in working with new and established customers.

Qualitative bases

Performance evaluation would be much easier if it could be based only on quantitative criteria, which would minimize the subjectivity and personal bias of the evaluators. However, many qualitative factors must be considered because they influence a salesperson's performance. The most important of these today relate to the objective of many firms to have sales representatives work at the development of customer relationships. While assessment of the quality of such relationships has been quite subjective in the past, today many progressive firms are beginning to quantify such previously qualitative variables. They have devised programs to actually measure the quality of customer relationships and are building such assessments into performance-evaluation programs. Some factors that have been considered to be qualitative but of considerable importance are:

- Knowledge of products, company policies, and competitors.

- Time management and preparation for sales calls.

- Customer relationships.

- Personal appearance.

A successful evaluation program appraises a salesperson's performance on as many different bases as possible. Otherwise, management may be misled. A high daily call rate may look good, but it tells us nothing about how many orders are being written up. A high closing rate (orders divided by calls) may be camouflaging a low average order size or a high sales volume on low-profit items. Historically, companies have tended to focus on short-term, historic, financial information relating mainly to sales and other variables measured within the company. Increasingly, companies are developing performance measures that are future-looking, non-financial, longer term, and collected from customers.

1. What is a selling centre?
2. _____ refers to selling a total package of related goods and services to solve a customer's problems.
3. What is the most widely used tool for motivating salespeople?

Sales Promotion

sales promotion
Activities, including contests for salespeople and consumers, trade shows, in-store displays, samples, premiums, and coupons, that are designed to supplement advertising and co-ordinate personal selling.

Sales promotion is one of the most loosely used terms in the marketing vocabulary. We define **sales promotion** here as tools and techniques used to stimulate demand in the short term, supplement advertising, and support the sales effort. Examples of sales-promotion devices are coupons, premiums, in-store displays and demonstrations, trade shows, samples, and contests.

Producers and intermediaries can both conduct sales promotions. The target for producers' sales promotions may be intermediaries, end-users — households or business users — or the producer's own sales force. Intermediaries direct sales promotions to their salespeople or prospects further down the distribution channel.

This eye-catching product ad could be a valuable addition to an in-store sales promotion.

Nature and scope of sales promotion

Sales promotion is distinct from advertising or selling, but these three forms of promotion are often used together in a co-ordinated fashion. For example, an in-store display (sales promotion) furnished by Michelin to dealers selling its tires may feature a slogan and illustrations (including, of course, the Michelin Man) from Michelin's current advertising campaign. This display, which helps retailers sell tires, also makes them more receptive to talking with Michelin salespeople. Or, as another example, prospective customers may be generated from people who enter a contest at the Canon copier exhibit at an office equipment trade show. These prospects might be sent some direct-mail advertising and then be contacted by a salesperson.

There are two categories of sales promotion: **trade promotions**, directed to the members of the distribution channel; and **consumer promotions**, aimed at consumers. Manufacturers as a group spend about twice as much on trade promotion as they do on advertising, and an amount about equal to their advertising on consumer promotions.

Since 1991, the number of coupons distributed in Canada has plummeted 75 percent. That year saw more than 22 billion coupons distributed, while by 2000, fewer than 6 billion were sent out, as retailers continued the trend away from in-ad couponing to other strategies, such as everyday low pricing and loyalty programs. There has also been a steady decline in redemption rates, from 5 percent in the 1970s to less than 1 percent today.

New formats continue to be tried and some success has been experienced with different targets. Free-standing inserts such as the Clip 'n' Save (essentially an all-coupon flyer inserted into newspapers) has been targeted toward female principal shoppers between 25 and 54 with a high incidence of children living at home. An advantage of this approach is that, as discussed earlier in this book, demographics and postal codes can be used to target the coupons where they will be most effective, reducing waste and costs.

New distribution methods and formats have also been explored, ranging from Web sites, wireless cellphones, and targeted e-mail distribution, to cash register tapes and parking meters that dispense coupons when you insert your parking fee.

Billed as Canada's first electronic-coupon magazine for packaged goods, save.ca (**www.save.ca**) guarantees clients a minimum of 250,000 visitors a month. Visitors click on the coupons they want, fill in their addresses, and indicate if they want to receive promotional offers, via e-mail, directly from the manufacturer. The coupons are then printed on high-gloss paper and mailed out the next business day. The challenge remains to keep visitors returning by continually offering new products and deals.[9]

As you walk past a local pizza shop, your Internet-enabled cellphone beeps, inviting you to save 25 percent on lunch. How can that be? Location-positioning technology can now deliver coupons at the point of purchase and, with an estimated 16.6 million Canadians estimated to be using these devices by 2003, there could be some potential there. L'Oréal Canada and Le Château are using their databases to send product information, discounts, and contest entries via permission-based e-mail. The savings, or chances to win, can triple when recipients

trade promotion
The type of sales promotion that is directed to members of a distribution channel.

consumer promotion
The type of sales promotion that is aimed at consumers.

save.ca

A coupon dispenser!

forward the message to three friends. Such viral campaigns can have surprising response rates — in one campaign, L'Oréal received 8,000 more contest entries than the total number of e-mails it sent out![10]

Toronto parking machines now do more than accept change — they dispense coupons as well as parking slips! Coupons from companies such as Pizza Pizza, Swiss Chalet, Foot Locker, and Petro-Canada to name a few. To ensure that motorists see the coupons before they place the parking slip in the car window, they are dispensed with the coupon facing up. They also are perforated, allowing motorists who park on business to redeem the coupon and still have the other half to claim as a business expense. These "pay and display" machines have the added bonus of providing municipalities with the opportunity of generating extra revenues from advertisers.[11]

Whether these new forms of couponing will result in an increase in their use (redemption) or increase their success in encouraging product trial remains to be seen, but for now they do offer unique promotion opportunities for firms as the technology that makes them possible becomes available and remains novel to consumers.

Several factors in the marketing environment contribute to the surging popularity of sales promotion:

- *Short-term results:* Sales promotions such as couponing and trade allowances produce quicker, more measurable sales results. They are generally intended to stimulate trial of a new product or to give sales a short-term boost. However, critics of this strategy argue that these immediate benefits come at the expense of building brand equity. They feel that an overemphasis on sales promotion may undermine a brand's future. While the intent (for the longer term) is to stimulate trial of a product, it is thought that as much as half of coupon redemption is from existing users.[12]

- *Competitive pressure:* If competitors are offering buyers price reductions, contests, or other incentives, a firm may feel forced to retaliate with its own sales promotions.

- *Buyers' expectations:* Once they are offered purchase incentives, consumers and distribution channel members get used to them and soon begin to expect them. Some companies seem to be offering continuous sales promotions, most of which offer customers reduced prices. In such cases, consumers often "catch on" and simply wait for the next promotion before buying.

- *Low levels of retail selling:* Many retailers use inadequately trained sales clerks or have switched to self-service. For these outlets, sales-promotion devices such as product displays and samples often are the only effective promotional tools available at the point of purchase.

- *Door openers:* When contact with salespeople is minimal, sales promotions often open the door to closer customer contact. When customers respond to a promotion, it provides a salesperson with an opportunity to make contact and to begin to establish a relationship.

MARKETING AT WORK 12-2: STRATEGY

Reaching the Unreachable

They've been called the unreachables, yet Generation Y is so attractive to marketers that it's being marketed to like no other in the history of capitalism. The children of the Boomers, now 9 to 25, have grown up with electronic media and technology, and that makes them harder to reach.

"The biggest difference with this generation is they're very media-savvy, very marketing smart. You can't try too hard, because that's the kiss of death," says managing director of DDB KidThink in Vancouver. And you can't use mainstream media alone. Many brands trying to reach youth through the old-school methods are not connecting with the key demographic they're going after. Advertising isn't enough.

Companies like Bell Mobility have asked Gen-Yers to help. Before the launch of Solo, a product aimed at teens, Bell consulted with an advisory panel of 16- to 24-year-olds. They are consulted on an ongoing basis, influencing everything from pricing to design, packaging, and how products are launched.

Today's youth are like chameleons — they move quickly in and out of trends. That's one of the reasons why smaller companies have had major success competing with the big guys for this market. What's hot today can turn cold before some of the bigger firms can manage to get to market with their versions. One example is Airwalk, a U.S.-based skateboard and snowboard clothing company that didn't even exist before the prominence of today's skate culture.

One firm taking the pulse of these trends is Masev Communications of Vancouver — an acronym for music, action sports and events. Masev's strategy is to involve its clients at the grass-roots level, such as sponsorship of a youth-oriented event, so it can connect with the target. Promotions are great ways of getting free things to the target group and word of mouth is very important to them, so public relations is an important way to reach them. The firm believes that "Companies need to create an experience youth will associate with that brand and support them," says the company president. "They know when you're supporting them and when you're not."

SOURCE: Adapted from Susan Heinrich, "To Reach the Unreachable Wallets of Generation Y," *Financial Post*, August 19, 2002, page FP12.

Management of sales promotion

Sales promotion should be included in a company's marketing communications plans, along with advertising and personal selling. This means setting sales-promotion objectives and strategies, determining a budget, selecting appropriate techniques, and evaluating the performance of sales-promotion activities.

One problem management faces is that many sales-promotion techniques are short-run, tactical actions. Coupons, premiums, and contests, for example, are designed to produce immediate (but short-lived) responses. As a result, they tend to be used as stopgap measures to reverse unexpected sales declines, rather than as integrated parts of a marketing program.

Determining objectives and strategies   Three broad objectives of sales promotion are:

- Stimulating business-user or household demand for a product.

- Improving the marketing performance of intermediaries and salespeople.

- Supplementing advertising and facilitating personal selling.

More specific objectives of sales promotion are much like those for advertising and personal selling. Examples are:

- *Gain trial for a new or improved product:* The companies that make Tetley tea or Neutrogena shampoo might send free samples through the mail.

- *Disrupt existing buying habits:* A coupon offering a large discount might cause a consumer to switch brands of a product that is viewed as generic, such as orange juice or motor oil.

- *Attract new customers:* Financial institutions have offered small appliances and other premiums to encourage consumers to open accounts.

- *Encourage greater use by existing customers:* Air Canada and most other airlines have frequent-flyer programs to encourage travellers to use their airlines more often. Other businesses have established similar loyalty programs, including the popular Air Miles program to which a number of major retailers belong.

- *Combat a competitor's promotional activity:* For example, one supermarket chain runs a lottery or game to attract shoppers, and a competitor retaliates by offering triple-value coupons.

- *Increase impulse buying:* End-of-aisle and island displays in supermarkets can increase sales of a product by as much as 50 percent.

- *Inspire greater retailer co-operation:* A sporting-goods manufacturer gets additional shelf space by setting up excellent point-of-purchase displays, training the retailers' salespeople, and providing tote bags to be given away with purchases.

The choice of sales-promotion tools derives directly from the objectives of the total marketing program. Consider the following situations and the different strategies available:

- A firm's objective is to increase sales, which calls for entering new geographic markets using a pull strategy. To encourage product trial and attract consumers away from familiar brands, possible sales-promotion tactics are coupons, cash rebates, free samples, and premiums.

- A firm's objective is to protect market share in the face of intense competition. This goal suggests a push strategy to improve retailer performance and goodwill. Training the retailers' sales forces, supplying effective point-of-purchase displays, and granting advertising allowances would be appropriate sales-promotion options.

Determining budgets   The sales-promotion budget should be established as a specific part of the budget for the total marketing communications mix. Including sales promotion in an advertising or public relations budget is not likely to foster the development of a separate sales-promotion strategy, and as a result, sales promotion may be overlooked or poorly integrated with the other components of marketing communications. Setting a separate budget for sales promotion forces a company to recognize and manage it.

Within the concept of developing an integrated marketing communications strategy, the amount budgeted for sales promotion should be determined by the task method. This forces management to consider specific objectives and the sales-promotion techniques that will be used to accomplish them.

Selecting the appropriate techniques   Common sales-promotion techniques are shown in Table 12-1, where they are divided into three categories based on the target audience:

- *Sales promotion directed at final consumers:* Many of the tools in Table 12-1 probably are quite familiar to you, but a brief discussion of some of them will give you a better sense of their significance.

  "Advertising specialties" is a miscellaneous category of small, usually inexpensive items imprinted with a company's name or logo that are given or sold by producers or intermediaries to customers and prospects. Examples are pens, calendars, key rings, paperweights, coffee cups, hats, and jackets.

- *Sales promotion directed at intermediaries:* Some of the tools just discussed may also be directed at intermediaries and their sales forces. In addition, trade associations in industries as diverse as shoes, travel, and furniture sponsor trade shows that are open only to wholesalers and retailers. Many producers also spend considerable time and money to train the sales forces of their wholesalers and retailers.

TABLE 12-1	Major Sales Promotional Tools, Grouped by Target Audience	
End-Users (Consumer or Business)	**Intermediaries and Their Sales Forces**	**Producers' Own Sales Force**
Coupons	Trade shows and exhibitions	Sales contests
Cash rebates	Point-of-purchase displays	Sales training manuals
Premiums (gifts)	Free goods	Sales meetings
Free samples	Advertising allowances	Packets with promotional materials
Contests and sweepstakes	Contests for salespeople	Demonstration model of product
Point-of-purchase displays	Training intermediaries' sales forces	
Product demonstrations	Product demonstrations	
Trade shows and exhibitions	Advertising specialties	
Advertising specialties		

- *Sales promotion directed at a producer's own sales force:* Again, there is an overlap between the tools directed at intermediaries and those designed for the producer's own sales force. Sales contests are probably the most significant of these tools, with many firms offering one type or another. The most common incentive is cash, used in over half of all contests. Other incentives include merchandise, plaques, jewellery, and travel. Visual sales aids (flip charts, slides) are prepared for salespeople, and brochures are developed to reinforce sales presentations.

A key step in sales-promotion management is deciding which devices will help the organization reach its promotional goals. Factors that influence the choice of promotional devices include:

- *Nature of the target audience:* Is the target group loyal to a competing brand? If so, a high-value coupon may be necessary to disrupt customers' purchase patterns. Is the product bought on impulse? If so, an eye-catching point-of-purchase display may be enough to generate sales.

- *The organization's marketing communications objectives:* Does a pull strategy or a push strategy best complement the rest of the marketing communications program?

- *Nature of the product:* Does the product lend itself to sampling, demonstration, or multiple-item purchases?

- *Cost of the device:* Sampling to a large market may be prohibitively expensive.

- *Current economic conditions:* Coupons, premiums, and rebates are good options during periods of recession or inflation, when consumers are particularly price-conscious.

Evaluating sales promotion Evaluating the effectiveness of sales promotions is much easier and the results are more accurate than is evaluation of the effectiveness of advertising. For example, responses to a premium offer or a coupon with a specified closing date can be counted and compared with a similar period when no premiums or coupons were offered. It is easier to measure sales promotion because:

- Most sales promotions have definite starting and ending points. Coupons must be redeemed by a certain date. Contest entries must be submitted before a particular deadline. Contests for the sales force include only the sales made during a specified period. This is quite different from advertising, where there can be significant residual effects and the results of one campaign may overlap with those of another.

● Most sales promotions are designed to drive sales directly. It is more difficult to measure a change in attitude or an increase in information about a product or brand than it is to count sales.

However, there are some pitfalls in measuring sales-promotion effects. First, not all sales promotions meet the conditions just mentioned. For instance, training given to a distributor's sales force may be valuable but may not produce immediate results. Second, current sales-promotion results may be inflated by sales "stolen" from the future. That is, a sales promotion may get buyers to act now, but they might have bought the product in the future anyway. An indication of this "cannibalizing" effect is a lower level of sales after the promotion ends, compared with the level before the sales promotion began. Third, any attempt at measurement must take into consideration external conditions, such as the behaviour of competitors and the state of the economy. A firm's market share may not increase following an expensive sales promotion, for example, but the promotion may have offset the potentially damaging impact of a competitor's promotional activity.

Public Relations

public relations
A broad communications effort designed to build or maintain a favourable image for an organization with its various publics.

Public relations is a management tool designed to build favourable attitudes toward an organization, its products, and its policies. It is an often-overlooked form of promotion, relegated far behind sales, advertising, and sales promotion. It is also often ignored until the company is facing a crisis or a problem that brings it into the public eye. In this sense, it is often viewed as a defensive tool. On the other hand, many companies today are realizing the role of public relations in supporting the reputation-building activities of the firm and in protecting its brand image.

In most companies, public relations is not the responsibility of the marketing department. If there is an organized effort, it is usually handled by a small public relations department that reports directly to the CEO. Only recently have many organizations come to appreciate the value of a solid public relations program. As the cost of marketing communications has gone up, firms are realizing that positive exposure through the media or as a result of community involvement can produce a high return on the investment of time and effort.

Nature and scope of public relations

Public relations activities typically are designed to build or maintain a favourable reputation and image for an organization and a favourable relationship with its various publics — customers, prospects, shareholders, employees, labour unions, the local community, and government.

Unlike advertising, public relations need not use the media to communicate its message. Good public relations can be achieved by supporting charitable projects (by supplying volunteer labour or other resources), participating in community service events, sponsoring athletic teams, funding the arts, producing an employee or customer newsletter, and disseminating information through exhibits, displays, and tours. Major companies often sponsor public events or special programs on television as part of their public relations efforts. Cultural organizations such as ballet companies and symphony orchestras would not survive without the support they receive from major corporations.

Publicity as a form of public relations

publicity
Media presentations about a product or organization that are not paid for and have the credibility of editorial material.

Publicity is any communication about an organization, its products, or policies through the media that is not paid for by the organization. Publicity usually takes the form of a news story appearing in a mass medium or an endorsement provided by an individual, either informally or in a speech or interview. This is good publicity.

There is also, of course, bad publicity — a negative story about a firm or its product appearing in the media. In a society that is increasingly sensitive about the environment and in which news media are quick to report mistakes, organizations tend to focus on this negative dimension of publicity. As a result, managers are so concerned with avoiding bad publicity that they overlook the potential of good publicity.

There are three approaches to gaining good publicity:

press release

News from a company sent to the media for publication.

1. *Prepare a story and circulate it to the media:* The intention of such a story, called a **press release**, is for the selected newspapers, television stations, or other media to report the information as news.

2. *Communicate personally with a group:* A press conference will draw media representatives if they feel the subject or speaker has news value. Company tours and speeches to civic or professional groups are other forms of individual-to-group communications.

3. *Engage in one-on-one personal communication, or lobbying:* Companies lobby legislators and other powerful people in an attempt to influence their opinions and, subsequently, their decisions.

Publicity can help to accomplish any communications objective. It can be used to announce new products, publicize new policies, recognize employees, describe research breakthroughs, or report financial performance — if the message, person, group, or event is viewed by the media as newsworthy. This is what distinguishes publicity from advertising: Publicity is not "forced" on the audience. This is also the source of its primary benefit. The credibility of publicity typically is much higher than that of advertising. If we tell you our product is great, you may well be sceptical, but if an independent, objective third party says on the evening news that our product is great, you are more likely to believe it.

Other benefits of publicity are:

- *Costs less than advertising or personal selling:* Publicity usually costs less because there are no media space or time costs for conveying the message and no salespeople to support.

- *Increased readership:* Many consumers are conditioned to ignore advertising or at least pay it little attention. Publicity is presented as editorial material or news, so it gets greater readership.

- *More information:* Because it is presented as editorial material, publicity can contain greater detail than the usual ad. More information and persuasive content can be included in the message.

- *Timeliness:* A company can put out a news release very quickly when some unexpected event occurs.

Of course, publicity also has limitations:

- *Loss of control over the message:* An organization has no guarantee that a press release will appear in the media. In fact, only a small proportion of all of the press releases a firm prepares are ever used. In addition, there is no way to control how much or what portion of a press release the media will print or broadcast.

- *Limited exposure:* The media typically uses publicity material to fill space when there is a lack of other news and will use it only once. If the target audience misses the message when it is presented, there is no second or third chance. There is no opportunity for repetition, as is the case in advertising.

- *Publicity is not free:* Even though there are no media time and space costs, there are expenses in staffing a public relations department and in preparing and disseminating press releases.

MARKETING AT WORK 12-3: ETHICS

A Crack in Their Reputation?

Hello, Bible Belt. That was the word after news came that Mediacom, a giant in billboard advertising, nixed a campaign for Parasuco Jeans, saying a shot of a woman's partially exposed bottom was too hot for bus shelters in the Greater Toronto Area. The ad already blanketed Montréal and New York.

Montréal-based Salvatore Parasuco and his jeans are hot all over: Milan, Hong Kong, Osaka. Nelly, the hip-hop star sings about them and, in the United States, youths are breaking into stores to get them. But when it came to Toronto bus shelters, the model was ordered, in effect, to hike up her drawers. Which is what happened, and a "sanitized" version was seen throughout Toronto the Good.

"You see a little butt cleavage," says Stephanie Gingras, who put together the campaign. "You don't see anything, and who doesn't see a little butt crack once in a while? What about all those construction workers and plumbers walking around? Nobody complains about them."

It seems that Mediacom was receiving calls about a number of shelter ads — particularly an ad for Diesel jeans that included a back view of a male with his jeans lowered slightly.

Two cities in the Greater Toronto Area, which will remain anonymous, ordered the Diesel ad to be pulled. But, look at the attention such a commotion generates! Who benefits?

Since 1963, the Canadian ad industry has policed itself through Advertising Standards Canada. That group is split into two: One section reviews ads in English Canada and a separate group previews ads in French Canada. Complaints about ads jumped 30 percent from 1998 to 1999, but this still amounts to only about 1,000 complaints a year. It doesn't take a lot of complaints to create a fracas — a handful of people can limit what the rest of us get to see.

Toronto can take some solace in the fact that there also was some concern in New York about the ads — they were pulled from buses travelling through predominantly Hasidic Jewish and Italian Catholic neighbourhoods. So, have no fear, there are those who are protecting us from jeans with low waistbands.

SOURCE: Adapted from Peter Kuitenbrouwer, "A Crack in Our Reputation," *National Post*, April 21, 2001, page H4.

Opportunities to promote and enhance a brand come in a variety of ways. West49, based in Burlington, Ontario, is riding the skateboard wave. From one store in 1996, there are now 49 in Canada and 3 in the United States. The company has its own 1,860-square-metre skate park in St. Catharines, allowing it direct and virtually unlimited opportunities to connect with its market. The West49 World Cup of Skateboarding is held there each year and is eastern North America's largest skateboarding event, with a cash purse of $70,000. The retailer also has its own skate team, consisting of professional boarder Pierre-Luc Gagnon and six amateurs, which tours locations, providing demonstrations and autographs.[13]

Absolut Vodka

Absolut Vodka sponsors a Web site that corresponds nicely with the brand's ongoing association with the art world. The site (**www.absolutdigitalart.com**) welcomes submissions from digital and non-digital artists who, if chosen, are featured online. The portal is often featured in universities and colleges that offer digital art courses, as well as at art events across Canada, exposing and building the brand with an important demographic. Absolut refers to these efforts not as sponsorships, but as partnerships, where art is the key driver, and includes associations with painters, sculptors, jewellery designers, and even architects.[14]

Evaluating public relations

Although few executives would argue that having a good image and staying in touch with an organization's publics are unimportant, evaluating public relations and publicity is difficult. In the past, evaluation usually involved a report of activities, rather than of results. Public relations departments maintained "scrapbooks" to show management how many stories were written and published, the number of employees who volunteered for civic projects, and similar information. These days, to justify expenditures, more organizations are requiring publicity departments to provide specific public relations objectives and show measurable results. Because it is impossible to relate public relations and publicity directly to sales, other measures must be used.

One is research to show, for example, increased awareness of a product or brand name, or changes in attitudes and beliefs about a firm.

More companies today are taking a scientific approach to the evaluation of public relations activities and opportunities. For example, before deciding to sponsor a particular group or event, or to associate with a particular business partner or spokesperson, some firms will conduct research to determine the "fit" between the firm and its brand on the one hand, and the event or organization or spokesperson on the other. If the fit (as perceived by the target audience) is not a good one, sponsorship money will be wasted and, more importantly, damage may be done to the firm and its brands.

BACKSPACE

1. Define *sales promotion*.

2. What are the three broad objectives of sales promotion?

3. _____ is a management tool designed to build favourable attitudes toward an organization.

Summary

Selling through a sales force is the main marketing communications tool used in North American business, whether measured by number of people employed, by total expenditures, or by expenses as a percentage of sales. The total field of selling comprises two broad categories. One covers selling activities when the customers come to the salespeople — primarily retail store or in-bound, telephone-based selling. The other includes all selling situations when the salespeople go to the customer — primarily outside sales forces.

The sales job has evolved — a new, professional salesperson has emerged. Sales jobs today range from order takers through support salespeople (missionary sellers, sales engineers) to order getters (creative sellers). Sales jobs differ from other jobs in several respects. Some changing patterns in personal selling have emerged in recent years — patterns such as team selling, systems selling, relationship selling, global team selling, Internet selling, and telemarketing.

The selling process consists of four steps, starting with prospecting for prospective buyers and then pre-approaching each prospect. The third step is the sales presentation, which includes attracting attention, arousing buyer interest and desire, handling objections, and then hopefully closing the sale. Finally, post-purchase activities involve follow-up services to ensure customer satisfaction and reduce dissonance regarding the purchase.

The sales management process involves planning, implementing, and evaluating sales force activities within the guidelines set by the company's strategic marketing planning. The tasks of staffing and operating a sales force present managerial challenges in several areas. The key to successful sales force management is to do a good job in selecting salespeople. Then, plans must be made to train new people. Management must set up programs to motivate, compensate, and supervise a sales force. The final stage in sales force management is to evaluate the performance of the individual salespeople.

Sales promotion consists of demand-stimulating devices designed to supplement advertising and facilitate personal selling. The amount of sales promotion has increased considerably in recent years, as management has sought measurable, short-term sales results.

Sales promotion should receive the same strategic attention that a company gives to advertising and personal selling, including setting objectives and establishing a budget. Sales promotion can be directed toward final consumers, intermediaries, or a company's own employees. To implement its strategic plans, management can choose from a variety of sales-promotion devices. Sales-promotion performance also should be evaluated.

Public relations is designed to favourably influence attitudes toward an organization, its products, and its policies. It is a frequently overlooked form of promotion. Publicity, a form of public relations, is any communication about an organization, its products, or policies through the media that is not paid for by the organization. Most often these two activities are handled in a department separate from the firm's marketing department. Nevertheless, the management process of planning, implementing, and evaluating should be applied to public relations and publicity performance in the same way that it is applied to advertising, sales promotion, and sales.

Today, firms are becoming increasingly creative in utilizing promotions, public relations, and publicity, as it would appear that some target groups are becoming desensitized to the barrage of traditional advertising they encounter daily.

Key Terms and Concepts

AIDA 353
closing the sale 354
commission 357
consultative salesperson 346
consumer promotion 360
customer-service representatives 340
driver-salesperson 345
evaluating sales performance 358
global sales team 349
inside order taker 345
inside selling 342
missionary salesperson 346
motivating salespeople 356
order getter 347
order taker 347
outbound calling 343
outside order taker 346
outside sales force 343
outside selling 343
post-purchase service 354
pre-approach information 353
press release 366
proactive selling 342
professional salesperson 344

prospecting 351
public relations 365
publicity 365
qualify 352
reactive selling 342
relationship selling 349
salary 357
sales 340
sales compensation plan 357
sales engineer 346
sales force automation 350
sales force selection 355
sales function 340
sales presentation 353
sales promotion 359
sales training program 356
sales support personnel 347
selling 340
selling centre 348
systems selling 348
team selling 348
telemarketing 343
trade promotion 360
trial close 354

Questions and Problems

1. The cost of a full-page, four-colour advertisement in one issue of a national magazine is higher than the cost of employing two salespeople for a full year. A sales manager is urging her company to eliminate a few of these ads and, instead, hire a few more salespeople. This executive believes that one good salesperson working for an entire year can sell more than one ad in one issue of a magazine. How would you respond?

2. If you were preparing a sales presentation for the following products and services, what information about a prospect would you seek as part of your preparation?
   a. Two-bedroom condominium.
   b. New automobile.
   c. Carpeting for a home redecorating project.
   d. Marketing research project for a local department store.
   e. Building cleaning service.

3. How would you go about recruiting sales applicants for each of the following firms? Explain your choice in each case.
   a. Delta Chelsea Hotel.
   b. IBM, for sales of mainframe (large) computers.
   c. Mount Pleasant Cemetery.

4. Compare the merits of straight-salary and straight-commission sales compensation. What are two types of sales jobs in which each plan might be desirable?

5. How might a firm determine whether a salesperson is developing relationships with customers?

6. Scan a current issue of a local or national newspaper and note the sales-promotion tools that appear in the advertisements. Which one do you consider to be particularly effective?

7. Explain how sales promotion might be used to offset weak personal selling in retail stores.

8. Can a well-implemented company Web site help to offset weak or inconsistent selling in a company's retail outlets?

9. Describe a recent public relations event in your community. How did it benefit the sponsor?

10. How does publicity differ from advertising?

Hands-On Marketing

1. Review your activities of the past few days and identify those in which:
   a. You did some personal selling.
   b. People tried to sell something to you.

   Select one situation in each category where you thought the selling was particularly effective, and explain why it was so.

2. Visit a supermarket, drugstore, or hardware store and make a list of all of the sales-promotion tools that you observe. Describe how each one relates to the sales-promotion objectives described in the chapter. Which are particularly effective? Why?

Back to the Top

Put yourself in the shoes of Sarah Muldowney, the sales rep in our chapter opener. There, we provided some insight into Sarah's job, which consists mainly of calling on physicians in their offices and clinics, advising them of new products and research results, and trying to convince them to prescribe PharmaNational's products. Your instructor may have shown you the clip from the CBC video that accompanies this textbook. This video suggests that some of the data that Sarah has in the PharmaNational database may not be appropriate as a sales tool. Think about the ethics of retail drugstore chains providing this information to pharmaceutical companies. How would you, as Sarah, handle such issues if they were raised by physicians?

Want to get better grades, tips on how to study more effectively, and up-to-date information on happenings in the world of marketing? Then, visit the Online Learning Centre for practice tests, Study Smart software, and much more! **www.mcgrawhill.ca/college/sommers**

Interested in finding out what marketing looks like in the real world? *Marketing Magazine* is just a click away on your Online Learning Centre!

Case 4-1

Adidas
Basketball Buzz

Roberto has been playing basketball since he was very young. Every day after school, a couple of his buddies would come over to shoot some hoops. Roberto was never the top player, but he was always pretty good. When he was old enough to join the school's basketball team, he signed up right away. His passion for basketball extended beyond the court: His room was plastered with Detroit Pistons posters, and as soon as an NBA game came on, Roberto was glued to the television.

For his twelfth birthday, Roberto's father bought him tickets to see Atlanta play the Pistons in Detroit. Roberto can still remember the excitement he felt as his father drove over the Ambassador Bridge from Windsor into Detroit. That night, as he cheered from the stands, he dreamed of one day playing in the NBA, a dream no doubt shared by many boys his age.

Now 16, Roberto takes basketball very seriously. He doesn't mind that his basketball coach is very demanding. After all, his team's chances of making it to the finals this year are great — especially with Sam on the team. The team's 1.95-m captain has been the top scorer this season. Whenever they play, a large crowd comes to watch the games. It has been rumoured that NBA scouts have been in the stands to watch Sam. Why, just the other day, a stranger approached Sam after the game and pulled him aside. Later, when asked about it, Sam dodged the question.

Yesterday at practice, Roberto noticed that Sam was wearing a new pair of Adidas shoes of a type that he hadn't seen before. During the practice, a couple of team members commented, "Cool shoes. Where'd you get them?" Sam mumbled the name of a sports store in the local mall. After practice, Roberto headed for the mall to see if he could find the shoes. As he walked into the store, he spotted them right away, but when he looked at the price tag, he saw that they weren't cheap. He wondered how he could convince his parents to buy him a pair.

What Roberto doesn't know is that the stranger in the audience was in fact a "product seeder" sent by Adidas to scout out the best player, or trendsetter, on his team to give him their latest shoes. The idea behind "buzz marketing," as it is called, is that friends and peers will notice the trendsetter's shoes and start talking about them. As word spreads and more kids buy the shoes, the benefits to the company are numerous, including the fact that brand awareness is heightened by the buzz. And the best thing about buzz marketing is that people don't know they are being advertised to. If Roberto found out how Sam got his shoes, would they have the same appeal for him?

Questions

1. Can buzz marketing be considered a marketing activity?

2. Why does Roberto want to get the same shoes as Sam? What value does he perceive in those shoes?

3. What do you think would be Roberto's reaction if he was to find out that what he thought was an NBA scout was in fact an Adidas rep, whose purpose was to get people talking about the shoes?

4. Can buzz marketing be called advertising if people don't know they are being advertised to?

Video source: CBC *Marketplace*, "Buzz Marketing," March 27, 2002.

Case 4-2

Altoids

The "Curiously Strong" Mint

"Did you see *Friends* last night?" was the last thing Andrew heard before he blocked out the conversation. Every coffee break was the same — who was dating whom on *Friends.* Mindless drivel as far as Andrew was concerned. Besides, who had time to watch television? Between his job, his friends, working out, and hiking, the young Royal Bank employee didn't know how anyone had time to eat, let alone watch sitcoms.

That evening, waiting for the bus to go home, Andrew was thinking about the hectic week ahead when he noticed a new ad on his bus as it pulled in. "We Double Dare You! Altoids, The Curiously Strong Mint" read the ad. "Cool," thought Andrew. "Haven't heard of those mints before. I wonder how they taste?" Later, after working at home for a while, Andrew decided it was time to get out of his apartment. He called his friend Laura and suggested they meet for coffee at the Second Cup around the corner.

Andrew got there first and found a table. He waited and waited for Laura to show up and kept looking at his watch impatiently. After 20 minutes, he decided to find a payphone and call her. Andrew was surprised to find a telephone booth just around the corner, but was even more surprised to see another ad for Altoids at the side of the booth. This one was even funnier than the one on the bus. It had a picture of a muscleman flexing and the tag line "Nice Altoids." Andrew was still laughing when he finally reached Laura. "I'm just going out the door — see you soon!" she said.

Bright and early the next day, as Andrew made his way to the bus stop, he noticed two men putting up a new poster ad. Could it be? Yes, it was! There on the shelter was another Altoids' ad. Like the others, this one was really quirky: "Pow, right in the kisser. Altoids, the curiously strong mint," it read. Andrew chuckled to himself as he got on the bus.

For the next month, Andrew kept noticing the ads wherever he went. They were on payphone booths, buses, and shelters, in his favourite music store's newsletter, on the subway — everywhere he looked. He didn't mind all the ads, though. In fact, every time he saw one, he smiled. One night on his way to a party, Andrew dropped into the local Mac's to pick up some chips, when a small tin container in the candy section caught his attention. There they were: Altoids! Andrew decided to buy them. After all, the ads were quirky and he was curious about the product. On his way out of the convenience store, Andrew popped one into his mouth. "Wow!" he said out loud. "These are strong!" Andrew couldn't help but feel good about the discovery he had just made.

Questions:

1. Why does Altoids use non-traditional media for its ads?

2. What do you think were the company's goals in designing this ad campaign?

Case 4-3

Rethink

Not Your Average Ad Agency

Does creativity fall victim to the politics and hierarchical structures often found in larger ad agencies? Chris Staples of Rethink, a small Vancouver ad agency, certainly thinks so. And that's the reason he and his two partners, Ian Grais and Tom Shepansky, left their former employer, Palmer Jarvis DDB, one of Canada's largest and most successful ad agencies — that is, of course, if you measure success based on revenues. Staples would prefer to measure success based on the effect that ads have on people.

After working more than 10 years for the conventional ad agency, the creative trio broke away to form their own company, Rethink, in October 1999. The small agency immediately began drawing media attention and clients, including large companies such as A&W and A&P/Dominion. And while it may seem surprising that such a small ad agency has managed to lure clients away from larger firms, it would appear that some of these clients are looking for new ideas and more exciting advertising.

The reason is that advertising is everywhere. Consumers are bombarded by hundreds of ads every day and people are getting bored with the same old advertising. Companies such as Labatt North America have grown tired of the traditional ad agency structure and approach and have dropped their lead agencies. Many favour smaller ad agencies because of their refreshing new approach to advertising, which includes more time spent on thinking and creating and less time on planning and strategy.

There is nothing traditional about Rethink. The founders have no business plan and don't believe in market research. Instead, they have a one-word philosophy: "Rethink." Believing that large agencies are trying to be everything to everybody, like big department stores, Rethink wants instead to be fabulous at just a few things, spending all of its creative energy thinking up unique ads. So in this sense, Rethink is not a full-service agency like the larger firms. Rather, it has carved out a niche for itself that appeals to companies that are bored with their current advertising and are looking for something bold and daring.

So far, Rethink has not needed to do much to attract new clients. Mostly, the partners have just had to pick up the telephone and propose an idea. The creative trio has a great reputation in the industry, having won a Cannes Lion award. Many clients have come knocking at their door, but Rethink won't take on just anybody — it's very picky about the companies it chooses. There must be chemistry, a passion for the product, and, above all, creative carte blanche. Staples, Grais, and Shepansky want the freedom to create, to be different, to stand out from the rest. They won't tolerate a lot of interference from clients. And rather than having a traditional agency-client relationship, Rethink prefers to think of itself as a part of the client's business.

As masters of self-promotion, the founders have been able to draw a lot of attention to their young company. Rethink's approach has been described as dynamic, refreshing, and unorthodox — and it works. Only four months after opening, the small ad agency had already picked up some large clients and $15 million in new business. The agency has also won numerous awards for its ads.

Rethink is more than just the name of the company; it is a brand that the founders intend to build. As Staples explains, many traditional ad agencies are named after "dead white guys." He means, of course, their founders, who are no longer alive. Staples wants Rethink to be a brand rather than a person's name, so that the brand will outlive its partners and take on an identity of its own. And they are building their brand by creating products that will carry the Rethink name. Their first such venture was beer.

After months of developing their product in co-operation with Tree Breweries, a British Columbia microbrewery, the agency launched its own Rethink beer in 2000. The beer even came in a cool, new package rather than in the traditional cardboard box. The idea behind Rethink beer was that the new product would provide free advertising for the agency. Despite many obstacles and delays in bringing Rethink beer to the market, it served its purpose. The buzz around the beer turned out to be great promotion for the small ad agency. The beer was also meant to show prospective clients that Rethink can do more than just advertise — it can think up products.

Rethink is not a small agency by necessity; it's small by choice, at the founders' insistence. Otherwise, it will risk losing its identity, its creativity, and its focus. Staples calls Rethink an ideas company, positioning itself as an agency that puts creativity first. It claims that it is not in it for the money. To prove this, Rethink tells its clients that if they are not satisfied, Rethink does not get paid all of its fees. The agency's goal is to earn its fees in performance. It gets involved with clients, rather than just treating them as clients. In fact, many small firms complain that when they go to the larger ad agencies, their accounts are often given to "B" teams. They know they are not a priority for the bigger ad agencies that have much larger clients. Smaller ad agencies like Rethink are therefore more appealing to these companies.

Is Rethink changing the face of advertising? Or is it simply carving out a niche that appeals to a certain type of client? Certainly, the partners' in-your-face attitude and their criticism of the larger agencies have elicited negative responses from the advertising industry. But their attitude and their philosophy is also the reason that major clients have signed on with them. Rethink brings refreshing ideas and clever advertising to clients — and these clients need to stick out in an increasingly competitive market. Rethink has succeeded in standing out and in making many of its clients stand out with outlandish ads.

Questions

1. How has Rethink positioned itself in the competitive advertising industry?

2. What are the advantages for an ad agency to stay small?

3. Are smaller ad agencies more creative than their larger counterparts?

4. Does Rethink's advertising style fit with every prospective client? Why or why not?

Source: Unknown, "The Princes of Pitch," *CBC's Venture,* July 24, 2001; Eve Lazarus, "True Believers," *Marketing Online,* November 26, 2001; Unknown, "Agency Report: Scouting Canada's Agencies 2000 — Part Three," *Marketing Online,* December 4, 2000; Mark Etting, "Mark Etting's Street Talk: Private-Label Chris," *Marketing Online,* November 8, 1999; Mark Etting, "Mark Etting's Street Talk: Re-thinking Rethink," *Marketing Online,* October 25, 1999; Eve Lazarus, "Rethinking ropes in $15M in business," *Marketing Online,* January 17, 2000; and Eve Lazarus, "The Young Turks," *Marketing Online,* February 15, 2001.

Video source: CBC *Venture,* "Rethinking the Advertising Game," January 9, 2001.

PART 5

Distribution

Systems for distributing products and services from producer to user, including channels and logistics

We are in the process of developing a marketing program to reach the firm's target markets and achieve the goals established in strategic marketing planning. So far, we have considered the product and communications functions in that marketing mix. Now, we turn our attention to the distribution system — the means for getting products and services to the market.

The system for getting products and services to customers is very complex. Consumers see and interact with one part of this system on a regular basis — the retailing system, which is presented in Chapter 13. In Chapter 14, we deal with more behind-the-scenes aspects of distribution, addressing the questions of how products and services get to the retailers and the various systems and processes that exist to ensure they do.

CHAPTER 13

Retailing

You have abundant experience with retailing — as a consumer. And perhaps you also have worked in retailing. This chapter builds on that experience and provides insights about retail markets, different types of retailers, and key strategies and trends in retailing. After studying this chapter, you should have an understanding of:

- The nature of retailing
- What a retailer is.
- Types of retailers.
- Retail marketing strategies.
- Forms of non-store retailing.
- Retailing on the Internet
- Trends in retailing.

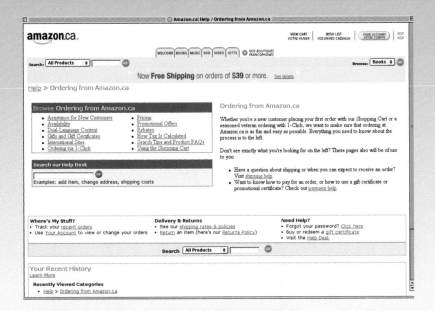

Read Any Good Books Lately?

When was the last time you bought a book? Other than this or another textbook, that is — textbooks don't count. You know — a novel, a biography, a how-to book, or for that matter, what about a CD or DVD? Better yet, how did you buy it? Was it over the Internet? When was the last time you browsed a bookstore? Book retailing has changed a lot over the last couple of years and it's been a pretty rough time to be a bookseller in Canada. Book retailing is one of the first product categories to successfully make the transition to cyber-retailing, increasing competition and making things quite difficult for small independent booksellers.

One of the largest book distributors has gone under and Indigo has had to come to the rescue of mega-bookseller Chapters. And now Amazon, which was already a leading online bookseller in this country, has opened a Canadian site — **www.amazon.ca** — meaning faster delivery and cheaper shipping charges. Nevertheless, online book sales account for only about 10 percent of overall book sales.

Not everyone is happy about this new arrival, and the salt in the wound is the free advertising for the Amazon site courtesy of Canada Post vehicles — a Crown corporation! It has partnered as exclusive delivery agent for Amazon in Canada, and this was a bonus of the deal. But, is this a bad thing? At least now the company is required by industry rules to purchase from Canadian distributors and publishers.

Does it make sense, though, to order a book from some other part of Canada, or even from the United States, when it is probably down the street at your local bookseller? Apparently it does, as many Canadians are ordering online instead of going to the bookstore. And they may be swayed to point their shopping carts in the direction of Amazon because its prices are routinely cheaper than Canadian-based Chapters/Indigo.

Do you buy online or do you prefer a trip to the bookstore? Why? What is it you're looking for — just the book, the lowest price, or a shopping and/or social experience? Is it something you see as an errand or an event with friends? What is the value for you as a consumer? People see value in different parts of the shopping experience — and now there are more options. The issue that remains for marketers is to try to determine the long-term effect of this trend on book and music retailing.[1]

Nature and Importance of Retailing

For every far-reaching retail superstar like Wal-Mart, Chapters/Indigo, Loblaws, or maybe Amazon, there are thousands of small retailers serving consumers, some in very limited and simple ways, some in very expansive and sophisticated ways. Despite their differences, all of these firms have one thing in common: They are the first contact that consumers have with the supply chain that began with producers located all over the world.

Retailing and retailers

Safeway
Sobeys
Shell
Petro-Canada

First, let's be clear about what is and what is not a retailer. If Safeway (**www.safeway.com**) or Sobeys (**www.sobeys.ca**) sells some floor wax to a gift shop operator to polish the shop floor, is this a retail sale? When a Shell (**www.shell.com**) or Petro-Canada (**www.petro-canada.ca**) service station advertises that tires are being sold at the wholesale price, is this retailing? Can a wholesaler or manufacturer engage in retailing? When a service such as hairstyling or auto repair is sold to an end-consumer, is this retailing? Obviously we need to define some terms, particularly *retailing* and *retailer*, to avoid misunderstandings later.

Retailing (or retail trade) consists of the sale, and all activities directly related to the sale, of goods and services to end-consumers for personal, non-business use. While most retailing occurs through retail stores, it may be done by any institution, whether down the street or in cyberspace. A manufacturer selling brushes or cosmetics door to door is engaged in retailing and so is Amazon on the Internet or a farmer selling vegetables at a roadside stand. Any firm — manufacturer, wholesaler, or retailer — that sells something to end-consumers for their own non-business use is making a retail sale.

retailing
The sale, and all activities directly related to the sale, of goods and services to end-consumers for personal, non-business use; same as *retail trade*.

And what we say about products applies equally to services. While one of the characteristics of services relates to the inseparability of the service from the individual or company that provides it, the marketing of services is often delegated to retailers. For example, travel agents are really retailers who sell to end-consumers the services offered by airlines, hotels, railroads, and car rental companies. Banks and other financial services companies retail Canada Savings Bonds on behalf of the Government of Canada. Ticketmaster (**www.ticketmaster.ca**) retails theatre and concert tickets.

Ticketmaster Canada

Characteristics of retailing

retailer
A firm engaged primarily in retailing.

All **retailers** — whether they are down-the-street, bricks-and-mortar stores or the Internet Web sites of Chapters/Indigo or Amazon — serve as purchasing agents for their customers and as sales specialists for their suppliers. To carry out these roles, retailers perform many activities, including anticipating customers' needs and wants, developing assortments of products, acquiring market information, and financing.

It is relatively easy to become a retailer. No large investment in production equipment is required, merchandise can often be purchased on credit, and store space can be leased with no down payment. Some retailers don't actually need to do this much: Retailers that sell over the Internet need only a virtual storefront — many Internet service providers will even assist their subscribers to set up shop. If not retailing a downloadable product such as software or information, there is still a requirement to have some sort of warehousing — but even this can be outsourced, eliminating the need for capital investment or expertise. This ease of entry results in fierce competition among retailers and better value for consumers.

To get into retailing is easy, but to be forced out is just as easy. To survive in retailing, a company must do at least a satisfactory job in its primary role — catering to consumers — as well as in its secondary role — serving its suppliers, producers, and wholesalers. This dual responsibility is both the justification for retailing and the key to retail success.

Retail Trends

Since retailing is dynamic, even volatile, it isn't easy to see where it is heading in the future, but certain trends can be seen:

Entertainment — On-site entertainment has become very popular with large and small retailers alike. Otherwise known as "retail-tainment," it includes whatever stimulates the senses or emotions, making shoppers want to stay, tell others, and/or come back again. The comfy couches at Chapters and the listening posts at HMV were just the beginning. Embattled jeans maker Levi Strauss has opened a flagship store that is a unique mix of music, technology, and art. The store features a hot tub, where consumers can soak their jeans — while still wearing them — and then dry them in a waist-high glass booth. Computers identify customers by fingerprint, while other high-tech devices measure consumers to ensure a perfect fit.

Service and convenience — Since consumers have less time and more things to do these days, they are spending less time shopping, going to fewer stores, and spending less time in each. Retailers are responding with extended hours, drive-through windows, delivery — offering what they know customers want. Loblaws' new retailing strategy is to be "the supplier of consumers' everyday household needs." This is reflected in a broader range of housewares and kitchen goods, larger stores, and a push into children's clothing. It offers a wide range of services in many of its stores, including pharmacies, photo labs, financial services, travel agencies, nurseries, and cigar shops. The store has increased its natural food offerings and has also introduced a line of organic products.

Specialty and "big box" — As we become more educated consumers, it seems we demand either specialties or specials. A generalist approach may no longer be effective in today's competitive environment — specialize or offer low prices! Shoppers Drug Mart, in order to contend with increasing competition from stores such as Costco, Wal-Mart, and Zellers, will open 20 to 25 big-box, stand-alone drugstores in 2002 and 2003. Sears is developing specialty stores to compete with rivals such as Home Outfitters (owned by the Bay) and to cash in on the expanding home decor market.

Managing customers — Customer retention and loyalty are key to success and a potential source of sustainable competitive advantage in today's environment. We continue to see the introduction, improvement, and reorganization of loyalty or customer-appreciation programs and other attempts at customer-relationship development. Technology has made possible the organization of databases that contain client information and purchase history. While this software is often referred to as customer-relationship management (CRM), it is only the beginning of what is required to organize the firm around developing relationships, or bonds, with customers.

Multi-channel retailing — More and more retailers are utilizing more than one channel to distribute their goods. The biggest change is the number of "traditional" retailers who have chosen to utilize the Web to retail their products. Often most successful are those companies that have already successfully established efficient distribution systems through catalogue retail experience such as L.L. Bean, Lands' End, and Sears. We are also seeing retailers gaining additional penetration by allowing other retailers to sell their products, such as Sears offering selected Roots merchandise, as well as Lands' End merchandise beginning in 2003.

SOURCE: Adapted from Lisa D'Innocenzo, "HMV Engages Customers with In-Store Displays," *Strategy*, March 12, 2001, page B12; Sarah Smith, "Checking Out the New Loblaw," *Marketing Magazine*, April 29, 2002, pp. 10, 11; "Sears Mulls Martha Stewart Stores," *Marketing Magazine*, June 17, 2002, page 3.

Size of the retail market

Statistics Canada reported in 2001 that there were about 242,852 retail stores in Canada in 2000, and the total sales volume of retail trade for 2001 was almost $290 billion (see Figure 13-1). In spite of growth in total population and consumer incomes over the past 30 years, the total number of retail stores has not increased consistently. In fact, the volatility of the retail business is reflected in the fact that the total number of retail stores in Canada actually dropped from 227,200 to 174,121 between 1988 and 1994, only to rise again and then drop dramatically in 1997 to 155,665. The numbers have increased since then. Incorporated into this trend is the recent spate of retail mergers in North America, impacting retail outlets in both Canada and the United States.

Retail trade accounts for 12 percent of all establishments, trailing far behind the services industry, which accounts for 35 percent. Canadian retailers have benefited from the buoyancy of consumer spending in recent years. For 2000, an analysis of sales-to-population ratios shows that consumers in Newfoundland spent 7.5 percent more than during the previous year, the highest growth rate in per-capita spending among the provinces and territories. Alberta's retailers were the biggest winners in 2000, posting absolute sales growth of 8.1 percent, almost 2.0 percentage points over the national average.[2]

Costs and profits of retailers

Information regarding the costs of retailing is very limited. By gleaning data from several sources, however, we can make some rough generalizations.

Total costs and profits As closely as can be estimated, the total average operating expense for all retailers combined is about 25 to 27 percent of retail sales. The expense ratios of retailers vary from one type of store to another. Table 13-1 shows average gross margins as a percentage of total operating revenue for different kinds of stores. These margins range from 17.1 percent for motor vehicle dealers to about 44 percent for shoe and clothing stores and for automotive parts and accessories businesses. The overall gross margin is 26.9 percent of total operating revenue. Table 13-1 also shows average profit (before depreciation and income taxes) for each type of store. These figures range from a very low 0.83 percent of sales for supermarkets and grocery stores to 9.42 for shoe stores.

Figure 13-1:

Total Retail Trade in Canada, Selected Years *Sales volume has increased tremendously, and the number of stores has grown as well.*

SOURCE: Statistics Canada, *Market Research Handbook,* 2001, cat. no. 63-224-XPB.

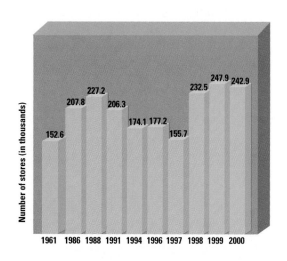

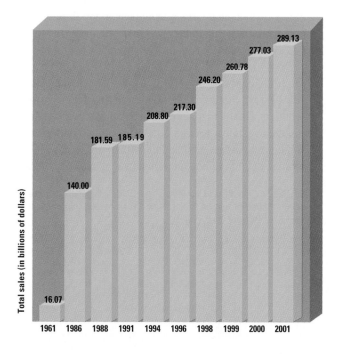

| TABLE 13-1 | Gross Margin and Net Profit as Percentage of Total Operating Revenue for Selected Types of Retailers | |

Gross margin (net sales minus cost of goods sold) is the amount needed to cover a company's operating expenses and still leave a profit. How do you account for the differences in operating expenses among various types of retailers?

Line of Business	Gross Margin (%)	Operating Profit (%) (taxes and depreciation not included)
Supermarkets and other grocery stores	20.75	0.83
All other food stores	36.74	6.17
Drug and patent medicine stores	28.57	4.29
Shoe stores	44.39	9.42
Men's clothing stores	43.74	5.98
Women's clothing stores	44.60	5.81
Household furniture and appliances	35.30	2.15
Motor vehicle and rv	17.11	5.05
Gasoline service stations	20.33	6.71
Automotive parts and accessories	43.95	6.39
TOTAL RETAIL TRADE (including all other categories)	26.86	4.52

SOURCE: Statistics Canada, *Wholesaling and Retailing in Canada*, 1998, cat. no. 63-236-XPB, p. 60.

Retail scale — store size

Most retail establishments are very small, with 15 to 20 percent of all retailers having annual sales of $100,000 or less. However, despite their numbers, such stores account for a very small percentage of total retail sales.

Loblaw
Bay/Zellers

At the same time, there is a high degree of concentration in retailing. This becomes increasingly the case as large retailers merge and departments stores decline in number. A small number of companies account for a substantial share of total retail trade. These companies, such as Loblaws (**www.loblaws.ca**) and the Hudson's Bay Company (the Bay and its sister store Zellers can both be found at **www.hbc.com**), own many individual stores and account for the considerable degree of concentration in the industry. For example, the companies highlighted in Table 13-2 and a small number in other selected categories, while numbering fewer than 40, probably account for close to half of all retail sales in Canada.

Stores of different sizes present different management challenges and opportunities. Buying, promotion, personnel relations, and expense control are influenced significantly by whether a store's sales volume is large or small. Store size brings with it certain advantages — see Table 13-3. Relatively large stores have a number of competitive advantages over small stores, but small retailers can and do still succeed:

contractual vertical market system

An arrangement in which independent firms (producers, wholesalers, and retailers) operate under a contract specifying how they will try to improve their distribution efficiency and effectiveness.

- Some are able to become part of a **contractual vertical marketing system** (VMS), in which independently owned firms join together under a contract specifying how they will operate (this is discussed in more detail later). These entities — called retailer co-operatives, voluntary chains, or franchise systems — give individual members certain advantages of large stores, such as specialized management, buying power, and a well-known store name.

- Many consumers seek benefits that small stores can often provide better than can large stores. A major one is accessibility and shopping convenience. Small outlets located near residential areas offer just that — and it is a valuable benefit.

TABLE 13-2 Canada's Largest Retailers

Company	Revenue ($000)	Profit ($000)
Department/Clothing/Specialty Stores		
Hudson's Bay Co.	7,457,636	72,750
Costco Wholesale Canada	7,044,959	N/A*
Sears Canada	6,726,400	94,100
Katz Group	6,000,000	N/A
Canadian Tire Corp.	5,374,759	176,653
Zellers	4,693,027	N/A
Shoppers Drug Mart	3,634,567	22,913
Jean Coutu (PJC)	2,924,844	105,941
Future Shop	1,985,177	32,376
RONA	1,834,544	24,633
Food Distribution		
Loblaw Companies	21,536,000	563,000
Sobeys Inc.	11,370,500	42,000
Westfair Foods	5,962,828	176,070
Canada Safeway	5,338,300	N/A
Metro Inc.	4,868,900	122,800
Hotels/Restaurants		
McDonald's Restaurants of Canada	2,240,151	N/A
Cara Operations	1,129,528	102,678
Intrawest Corp.	922,810	60,587
Fairmont Hotels & Resorts	598,400	69,600
A&W Food Services of Canada	388,000	N/A

*Not available.

SOURCE: Canada's Largest Retailers, "The Top 1000," *Report on Business Magazine*, July 2002, reprinted with permission of *The Globe and Mail*.

- Other consumers want high levels of personal service. A small store's highly motivated owner-manager and well-supervised staff may easily surpass a large store on this important patronage dimension. Small retailers have a better opportunity to develop strong functional and emotional relationships, particularly the latter, than do large ones. Frequently, the emotional component of a relationship can compensate for occasional functional lapses, and keep consumers returning.

Physical facilities

physical facilities
The location, design and layout of a retail store's site.

Some firms engage in non-store retailing — by selling through catalogues, the Internet, or door to door — but many more firms rely on retail stores. Firms that operate retail stores must consider three aspects of **physical facilities**:

1. *Location:* There are three keys to success in retailing: location, location, and location! Although overstated, this axiom does suggest the importance that retailers attach to location. A store's site should be the first decision made about facilities. Considerations such as surrounding population, traffic, and cost determine where a store should be located.

TABLE 13-3 Competitive Positions of Large and Small Retail Stores	
Selected Bases for Evaluation	**Who Has the Advantage?**
Division of labour and specialization of management	Large-scale retailers — their biggest advantage.
Flexibility of operations — merchandise selection, services offered, store design, reflection of owner's personality	Small retailers — their biggest advantage.
Buying power	Large retailers buy in bigger quantities and thus get lower costs.
Access to desirable merchandise	Large retailers promise suppliers access to large numbers of customers, whereas a single small retailer may be viewed as insignificant.
Development and promotion of retailer's own brand	Large retailers.
Efficient use of advertising, especially in citywide media	Large retailers' markets match better with media circulation.
Ability to provide top-quality personal service	Small retailers, if owners pay personal attention to customers and also to selecting and supervising sales staff.
Opportunity to experiment with new products and selling methods	Large retailers can better afford the risks.
Financial strength	Large retailers have resources to gain some of the advantages noted above (such as private brands and experimentation).
Public image	Small retailers enjoy public support and sympathy. However, this same public often votes with its wallet by shopping at big stores.

For Internet retailers as well as other non-store retailers, location also matters, as they require warehousing and call centres. But instead of wanting to be located in highly populated areas, these retailers focus more on outlying areas, where property and labour costs are usually lower. This must, of course, also be balanced with an optimal location that provides for timely and low-cost shipping provisions.

2. *Design:* This factor refers to a store's appearance, both exterior and interior. This is important for attracting and retaining customers, as well as setting the image or tone for the location. For the non-store retailer, design is of little importance, except to ensure that the working environment is not a source of dissatisfaction for employees. It is important to provide a pleasant working environment for employees, but not to the degree that it is important for traditional retailers to design environments with customer appeal.

3. *Layout:* The amount of space allocated to various product lines, specific locations of products, and a floor plan of display tables and racks make up the store's layout. The layout should be convenient for customers, while showcasing merchandise in the most prudent manner. For non-store retailers, the location's layout, like its design, is not to enhance the consumer's shopping experience but rather to facilitate the efficient, safe processing of customer orders.

As might be expected, retail store locations tend to follow the population. Consequently, the bulk of retail sales takes place in urban, rather than rural, areas. And suburban shopping areas continue to be popular, while many downtown areas have been weakened over the past 20 years or so. However, some counter-trends can be seen in new city-centre condominium and retailing development. In many Canadian cities, professional couples and retired empty-nesters are reinhabiting city cores. For example, the 2001 census indicated that 16,000 people had moved into central Vancouver since 1996 — a remarkable figure for a somewhat small city centre.[3]

The "new urbanism," as this trend is called, is about more than building places to live in the middle of the city. It's a reaction to more than a century of sprawling suburbanism. It's the idea that inner cities can be great places to live if they are planned right. That space for "living" must be incorporated into the development of the city, such as retail, entertainment, and green space. At the same time, it's also about planning for density: How else could you fit an extra 16,000 people with everything they own into downtown Vancouver?

Shopping centres are the predominant type of retail location in most suburban areas. A **shopping centre** consists of a planned grouping of retail stores that lease space in a structure that is typically owned by a single organization and can accommodate multiple tenants. For many, shopping is part entertainment, and this helps to explain the continuing popularity and investment in shopping centres in North America. With the increasing use of catalogue and online shopping, many shopping mall owners have been trying to create more reasons to visit the local mall — by increasing the number of services offered and the entertainment options available, from movie theatres to piano bars and amusement parks. Some newer developments have seen the inclusion of condominium developments with large retail components.[4]

shopping centre

A planned grouping of retail stores in a multi-unit structure, with the physical structure usually owned by a single organization.

MARKETING AT WORK 13-1: GLOBAL

IKEA: Is That Swedish for Meatballs?

On his way to the cash registers, he stops abruptly — something has gone horribly wrong! Mike Baker, manager of Canada's newest, largest, and most shrewdly engineered IKEA outlet groans, "The music isn't right." Two years in the making, at a cost of $75 million, the 30,658-square-metre Etobicoke store is opening today and someone has messed up the darned music list.

"The tunes are supposed to be upbeat in this area," he says, as a melancholy country song drifts overhead. "The point is to give people a lift, make them feel like opening their wallets. This is a hurtin' song." There's at least one other bug: The store is so big, it has its own radio station, which will transmit a stream of IKEA messages — once it's actually working.

Customers will file past 9,500 products, ranging from particle-board shelves to leather sofas and stainless steel-clad appliances. The music, from 300 speakers, changes as customers move between areas of the store: Moroccan kasbah-sounding in the carpet area, happy tunes in the children's area, and, in the cash lanes, acoustic guitar solos — better to calm the customers as they reach for their wallets.

"You shop with more than your eyes," explains Hilde Abbleloos, Etobicoke's project manager. "If I could have introduced smells to the store, I would have. Cookies baking in the kitchen area, that sort of thing."

The company studies all of its markets with anthropological zeal — it knows most Canadian couples argue when buying furniture, so the staff is trained in conflict resolution. Also, Vancouverites are obsessed with storage space, so displays are set up accordingly. Québec residents demand a superior selection of cookware. Torontonians are in a work-at-home phase, so the emphasis is on home offices at this location. Room settings have been painstakingly designed to reflect local tastes, such as an emphasis on lofts. Gone are the cardboard display electronics and TV sets — real ones are used for authenticity. One long-standing tradition remains — the room settings contain books written in Swedish.

Oh, there's one other tradition: The store has received a 27,215-kilogram shipment of IKEA's famous meatballs to serve up in the gleaming 350-seat restaurant. No, they weren't shipped from Sweden — these are Canadian-made.

SOURCE: Adapted from Brian Hutchinson, "IKEA: That's Swedish for BIG," *Financial Post*, October 17, 2001, p. FP1.

Traditional shopping centres can be classified by size and market served:

- **Convenience centre:** Usually consists of 5 to 10 outlets, such as a dry-cleaner, branch bank, convenience grocery store, and video rental store.

- **Neighbourhood centre:** Has 10 to 25 tenants, including a large supermarket and perhaps a drugstore.

- **Community centre:** Includes 25 to 50 stores and features a discount house or junior department store. It may also include a supermarket. Given its composition of stores, a community centre draws shoppers from a larger area than does a neighbourhood centre.

- **Regional centre:** Anchored by one or more department stores and supermarkets and complemented by as many as 200 smaller retail outlets, a regional centre is typically enclosed in a climate-controlled mall.

BACKSPACE

1. Define *retailing*.
2. What is multi-channel retailing?
3. What are the three aspects of physical facilities that retailers must consider?

Forms of Retailing

Different forms of retail ownership confer different strategic and operating advantages and disadvantages on owners and managers of retailing establishments. The major forms of ownership in retailing are independent, corporate chain, and the vertical marketing system. Within the VMS category are several types of organizations: wholesaler-sponsored voluntary chains, retailer-owned co-operatives, and franchise systems.

Independent stores

independent retailer
A company with a single retail store that is not affiliated with any type of contractual VMS.

The most numerous of all retailers, an **independent retailer** is a company with a single retail store that is not affiliated with any type of contractual vertical marketing system. Most retailers are independents, and most independents are quite small. Of course, an independent department store or supermarket can have $10 million or more in annual sales, so it may have more economic power than small chains consisting of only a few stores. Still, independents usually have the characteristics of small retailers that were presented in Table 13-3.

Independents are typically viewed as having higher prices than chain stores. On the other hand, they are usually more accessible than any other retail form and, of great importance, they have the best opportunity of developing strong relationships with consumers, both functional and emotional. As for the question of prices, because of differences in merchandise and services, it is difficult to compare directly the prices of chains and independents. For instance, chains often have their own private brands that are not sold by independents. Also, the two types of retailers frequently provide customers with different levels — and perhaps quality — of services. Many customers are willing to pay extra for services that are valuable to them, such as credit, delivery, alterations, installation, a liberal returns policy, and friendly, knowledgeable personal service.[5]

Corporate chain stores

corporate chain

An organization of two or more centrally owned and managed stores that generally handle the same lines of products.

A **corporate chain**, sometimes called a *chain store system*, consists of two or more centrally owned and managed stores that generally handle the same lines of products. Three factors differentiate a chain from an independent store and a contractual VMS:

1. Technically, two or more units constitute a chain. Today, however, many small-scale merchants have opened two or three units in shopping centres and in newly populated areas. These retailers ordinarily do not think of themselves as chains. Having four or more units is a good definitional basis for discussing chain stores.

2. Central ownership distinguishes corporate chains from contractual vertical marketing systems.

3. Because of their centralized management, individual units in a chain typically have little autonomy. Strategic decisions are made at headquarters, and there is considerable standardization of operating policies for all of the units in a chain.

Corporate chains continue to play a major role in retail trade in Canada, as shown in Table 13-4. The predominance of chains varies considerably, however, depending on the type of business. Organizations with four or more stores did about 35 percent of all retail business in Canada in 1998, the last date for which statistics are available.

The importance of chains varies considerably from one type of business to another. Chains account for 70 percent or more of total sales in the general merchandise, variety store, family clothing, and shoes categories. Among grocery stores, hardware stores, and pharmacies, however, chains account for 30 percent of sales or less. There are still a large number of independent food retailers in small towns and neighbourhoods throughout Canada.

Competitive strengths and weaknesses   Chain store organizations are large-scale retailing institutions and are subject to the general advantages and limitations of all large retailers.

Lower selling prices   Chain stores have traditionally been credited with selling at lower prices than do independents. But the claim of lower prices needs careful scrutiny, because it can be misleading. It was probably more justified in the past than it is today: Many independents have pooled their buying power so that, in many instances, they can buy products at the same price as the chains can. However, it is almost certainly true that chains have a cost advantage over independents.

It is very difficult to compare the prices of chains with those of independents. The merchandise is often not exactly comparable, because many chains sell items under their own brands — for example, it's difficult to compare the prices of Del Monte peaches with a Loblaws or Safeway brand of peaches. It is even more difficult to compare an item of apparel from Zellers with one from a "designer" store. The quality and durability of the fabric, the garment's construction, and other factors are almost impossible for the average person to knowledgeably compare. At least with peaches, the proof is in the eating! Also, it is not accurate to compare the price of a product sold in a cash-and-carry, no-customer-service store with the price of an identically branded product in a full-service store. The value of services should be included in the comparison.

TABLE 13-4	Chain Store Share of Total Retail Sales Volume (1979–1998)						
	1979	**1986**	**1989**	**1994**	**1996**	**1997**	**1998**
Percentage of total annual retail sales	41.5	41.5	39.3	37.3	37.5	38.4	35.6

SOURCE: Statistics Canada, "*Marketing Research Handbook,*" cat. no. 63-224-XPB, various years.

MARKETING AT WORK 13-2: RELATIONSHIPS

Redefining the Specialty Shop and CRM

When you think of a specialty department store, you probably don't expect 1,860 square metres and 1,000 employees. This $40-million, four-floor mega-boutique has a piano bar, vodka bar, sushi bar, art gallery, copper and enamel workshop, karaoke competitions, 49-seat cinema, nursery, and beauty salon.

Les Boutiques San Francisco hopes the ghosts of the former landmark Eatons store will not spook customers from its newest and largest store, Les Ailes de la Mode, recently opened in Montréal. It's what the company calls the largest specialty store of its kind in Canada. Communications Director Diane Jubinville explains, "We're trying to reinvent what shopping can be. Our promise is to constantly surprise people. We want them to spend more time with us, and enjoy being at Les Ailes."

Les Ailes — which focuses exclusively on fashion, beauty, and decor — is only eight years old, but it has not only established itself as a top retailer in Québec, but also as a credit card and loyalty program company and even as a publisher. The brand has built its name around customer relationships: Each piece fits into its home-grown CRM strategy to become a part of its customers' lifestyles. It's little things, little extras, such as free coat-checking,

baby-feeding rooms, highly trained staff (and more of them on the floor), and a place for people to go to read the newspaper.

The Les Ailes MasterCard has been targeted at an under-served segment of the "gold" market: women. The card has a rewards program that incorporates monthly coupons via an electronic gift card. Card members also receive the retailer's magazine. The Web site allows customers to check and exchange points, pay bills, and make hair appointments. With 105,000 people in the program, the biggest challenge is recruiting more men. Although the primary target is women, at least 30 percent of in-store customers are men.

"We're investing in our relationships, but it doesn't *have* to come with technology," says the vice-president of marketing. "We have invested in chip technology and the Internet, but at the same time, we bought a piano to boost the store brand experience."

SOURCE: Adapted from "San Francisco Chain Opens Huge Montreal Store," *Financial Post*, August 7, 2002, p. FP2; Lisa D'Innocenzo, "How Can Retailers Create a Distinctive and Profitable Store Environment?" *Strategy*, May 20, 2002, p. 2; Bernadette Johnson, "Quebec Success Story Proves CRM Strategy Can Work Even for Smaller Businesses," *Strategy*, May 20, 2002, p. D9.

Multi-store feature of chains Chain stores do not have all of their eggs in one basket (or in one store). Even large-scale independent department stores or supermarkets cannot match this advantage of the chains. A multi-unit operation has automatically spread its risks among many units. Losses in one store can be offset by profits in other units. Multi-store organizations can experiment quite easily, trying a new store layout or a new type of merchandise in one store without committing the entire firm.

A chain can make more effective use of advertising than can even a giant, single-unit independent store. A grocery chain may have 15 medium-sized stores blanketing a city. An independent competitor may have one huge supermarket doing three to four times the business of any single unit of the chain. Yet the chain can use the metropolitan daily newspaper as an advertising medium, with much less waste in circulation, than the independent can. Many chains can also make effective use of national advertising media.

On the negative side Standardization, the hallmark of a chain store system and a major factor in its success, is a mixed blessing. Standardization, while it can reduce marketing and operating costs, can also mean inflexibility. Often a chain cannot adjust rapidly to a local market situation. Chains are well aware of this weakness and have consequently given local store managers greater freedom to act in various situations. Also, with improved information systems, chains can better tailor their merchandising efforts to local markets. Implementing a relationship strategy is much more difficult in a chain operation than in an independent store or, sometimes, in a vertical marketing system.

Contractual vertical marketing systems

In a contractual vertical marketing system, independently owned firms join together under a contract specifying how they will operate. Three types of contractual VMSs are common:

Retailer co-operatives and voluntary chains   These both exist to increase the competitiveness of members and to provide members with management and administrative systems and assistance. The difference lies in how they are organized. A retailer co-operative is formed by a group of small retailers that agree to establish and operate a wholesale warehouse. In contrast, a voluntary chain is sponsored by a wholesaler that enters into individual supply contracts with interested retailers.

Historically, these two forms of contractual VMSs have been organized for defensive reasons — to enable independent retailers to compete effectively with larger chains. These forms of VMSs are able to do this by creating volume-buying power for members. Assistance is also provided with regard to store layout, training programs, promotion, accounting, and inventory-control systems. While retailer co-operatives are declining, there is still strong representation in groceries and hardware, such as True Value Hardware. Voluntary chains have been common in the grocery field, but are also found in hardware and auto supply operations.

Franchise systems   Franchising involves a continuing relationship in which a parent company provides the right to use a trademark and management assistance in return for payments from the owner of the individual business unit. The parent company is called a *franchiser*, and the owners of the individual business units are called *franchisees*. The combination of these individuals is called the *franchise system*. This type of contractual VMS has grown rapidly. According to the International Franchise Association (**www.franchise.org**), roughly 600,000 units are affiliated with about 2,500 different franchise systems.[6]

There are two kinds of franchising:

International Franchise Association

● ***Product and trade name franchising:*** Historically, the dominant type of franchising, product and trade name, is most prevalent in the automobile (Ford, Honda) and petroleum (Esso, Petro-Canada) industries. It is a distribution agreement in which a franchiser authorizes a franchisee-dealer to sell a product line, using the parent company's trade name for promotional purposes. The franchisee agrees to buy from the franchiser-supplier and also to abide by specified policies. The focus in product and trade name franchising is on what is sold.

Some product and trade name franchisees are very closely monitored by their franchisers.

- ***Business-format franchising:*** Much of franchising's growth and publicity over the past two decades has been associated with business-format franchising (including names such as KFC, Tim Hortons, Midas, and H&R Block, as can be seen in Table 13-5). This kind of franchising covers an entire format for operating a business. A firm with a successful retail business sells the right to operate the same business in different geographic areas. Quite simply, the franchisee expects to receive from the parent company a proven business format; in return, the franchiser receives payments from the individual business owner, as well as conformance to policies and standards. The focus here is on how the business is run — and the business must be run according to the format provided.

  What the franchiser provides to franchisees in this format is management assistance, especially marketing expertise. There is also a great deal of proven brand equity in the brand name of the organization, so the franchisee has a head start at further developing a functional relationship with customers, as well as being able to focus on the emotional relationship.

TABLE 13-5	Numerous Products Reach Consumer Markets through Business-Format Franchises	
Product/Service Category	**Sample Franchises**	
Fast food	McDonald's, Tim Hortons, Harvey's, Druxy's, Pizza Hut, Treats, A.L. Van Houtte	
Auto rental	National, Avis, Thrifty, Budget, Hertz	
Auto repair	Ziebart, Midas, Speedy, Thruway Muffler, Jiffy Lube, Mister Transmission	
Personal care/services	Regis, H&R Block, Money Concepts, Nautilus Fitness, Body Shop	
Home decor/services	Color Your World, Bathtub Doctor, Molly Maid, Weed Man, Servicemaster, College Pro Painters	
Printing/photography	Kwik-Kopy, Japan Camera, U Frame It, Kinko's	
Clothing	Sportchek, Benetton, Cotton Ginny, Mark's Work Warehouse, Rodier	
Computers and video	Compucentres, Computerland, Jumbo Video, Radio Shack	
Health and personal care	Nutri/System, Shoppers Drug Mart, Optical Factory, Tridont Health Centre	
Convenience stores	7-Eleven, Mike's, Mac's, Becker's, Green Gables, Red & White	

Retail Marketing Strategies

Whatever its form of ownership, a retailer must develop marketing-mix strategies to succeed in its chosen target markets. In retailing, the marketing mix emphasizes product assortment, price, location, promotion, and customer services.

Let's look at retail strategies by examining the major types of retail stores, paying particular attention to three elements of their marketing mixes (see Table 13-6):

1. Breadth and depth of product assortment.

2. Price level.

3. Number of customer services.

department store
A large-scale retailing institution that has a very broad and deep product assortment, prefers not to compete on the basis of price, and offers a wide array of customer services.

Department stores

Still a mainstay of retailing in Canada is the **department store**, a large-scale retailing institution that has a very broad and deep product assortment, tries not to compete on the basis of

TABLE 13-6 Retail Store Types and Key Marketing Strategies

Type of Store	Breadth and Depth of Assortment	Price Level	Number of Customer Services
Department store	Very broad, deep	Avoids price competition	Wide array
Discount house	Broad, shallow	Emphasizes low prices	Relatively few
Limited-line store	Narrow, deep	Traditional types avoid price competition; newer kinds emphasize low prices	Vary by type
Specialty store	Very narrow, deep	Avoids price competition	At least standard and extensive in some
Off-price retailer	Narrow, deep	Emphasizes low prices	Few
Category-killer store	Narrow, very deep	Emphasizes low prices	Few to moderate
Supermarket	Broad, deep	Some emphasize low prices; others avoid price disadvantages	Few
Convenience store	Narrow, shallow	High prices	Few
Warehouse club	Very broad, very shallow	Emphasizes very low prices	Few (open only to members)
Hypermarket	Very broad, deep	Emphasizes low prices	Some

price, and provides a wide array of customer services. Familiar department store names that can be found across the country include Sears and the Bay.

Traditional department stores offer a greater variety of merchandise and services than any other type of retail store. They feature both "soft goods " (such as apparel, sheets, towels, and bedding) and "hard goods" (including furniture, appliances, and consumer electronics). Department stores also attract — and satisfy — consumers by offering many customer services. The combination of distinctive, appealing merchandise and numerous customer services is designed to allow the stores to maintain the manufacturers' suggested retail prices. That is, department stores strive to charge full, or non-discounted, prices.

Department stores face mounting problems, however. Largely due to their prime locations and customer services, their operating expenses are considerably higher than those of most other kinds of retail business. Many manufacturers' brands that used to be available exclusively through department stores are now widely distributed and often carry discounted prices in other outlets. And the quality of personal service, especially knowledgeable sales help, has deteriorated in some department stores.

Intense horizontal competition is also hurting. Other types of retailers aim at consumers who have long supported department stores. Specialty stores, off-price retailers, and even some discount houses (all of which will be discussed later) have been particularly aggressive in trying to lure shoppers away from department stores. To varying degrees, retail chains such as Wal-Mart and Zellers compete directly against the conventional department stores.

Seeking to gain a competitive advantage in a market increasingly dominated by the

Retailers such as Winners specialize in offering the lowest prices.

Sears

large discounters and category-killer stores (discussed later in this chapter), the more conventional department stores have had to adopt new ways of doing business. For example, Sears (**www.sears.ca**), Canada's leading department store chain, is striving to establish its trademark as a statement of quality and value. Other strategies being used include redesigning stores, dropping or moving entire product lines, launching new ad campaigns, and stepping up sales and promotions. Sears is trying to increase strength in products such as apparel and home furnishings. The store has focused on building the brands of its own private-label apparel and has developed the Whole Home brand of furnishings and accessories for the entire home. In some markets, it has opened furniture stores under this name.

Discount houses

discount retailing

A retailing approach that uses price as a major selling point by combining comparatively low prices and reduced costs of doing business.

Discount retailing uses price as a major selling point by combining comparatively low prices and reduced costs of doing business. Several institutions, including off-price retailers and warehouse clubs, rely on discount retailing as their main marketing strategy.

Not surprisingly, the prime example of discount retailing is the **discount house**, a large-scale retailing institution that has a broad, shallow product assortment, emphasizes low prices, and offers relatively few customer services. A discount house normally carries a broad assortment of soft goods (particularly apparel) and grocery items, and may carry well-known brands of hard goods (including appliances and home furnishings). It also advertises extensively. Zellers and Wal-Mart are leading discount-house chains in Canada. Some observers believe that Amazon is a fledgling discount retailer. Do you think it fits into this category?

discount house

A large-scale retailing institution that has a broad and shallow product assortment, emphasizes low prices, and offers relatively few customer services.

The success of discount houses can be attributed to two factors. First, other types of retailers traditionally had large mark-ups on appliances and other merchandise, thereby providing discount houses with the opportunity to set smaller margins and charge lower prices. Second, consumers were receptive to a low-price, limited-service format. Discount houses have had a major impact on retailing, prompting many retailers to lower their prices.

Wal-Mart

Wal-Mart (**www.walmart.com**) has experienced tremendous success in Canada since it acquired the Woolco chain in 1994. That success has been built on the image of lowest prices, a position that has been promoted extensively by the chain. It also maintains state-of-the-art distribution technology, which builds on strong supplier relationships, behind-the-scenes ordering, and inventory management systems. Wal-Mart also prides itself on an up-front emphasis on customer service.[7]

Zellers has felt the strong competitive impact of Wal-Mart. In response, Zellers has developed Best Value locations, opened in many former Kmart locations, amended its low-price strategy, and complemented it with broader assortments. This has included the addition of the private label, Truly. The Truly line, consistent with the company's positioning as being truly Canadian was selected by the U.S. trade magazine *Private Label* as being one of the top five brands of its type. Zellers has changed its practice of featuring a large number of weekly specials in favour of an everyday low-pricing policy similar to Wal-Mart. It has also expanded its loyalty program to include purchases made at sister retailer the Bay and now offers Air Mile rewards.[8]

The Retail Council of Canada expects that the face of retailing will change in this country in the next 10 years, as it predicts that discount chains, particularly from European and Asian countries, will move into the marketplace. Retailers such as Target (United States), H&M (Sweden), and Carrefour (France) have already begun sizing up the Canadian retail environment.[9]

Limited-line stores

limited-line store

A type of retailing institution that has a narrow but deep product assortment; its customer services tend to vary from store to store.

Much of the action in retailing in recent years has been in **limited-line stores**. This type of institution has a narrow but deep product assortment and customer services that vary from store to store. Traditionally, limited-line stores strived for full or non-discounted prices. Currently, however, new types of limited-line retailers have grown by emphasizing low prices.

Breadth of assortment varies somewhat across limited-line stores. A store may choose to concentrate on:

- Several related product lines (shoes, sportswear, and accessories).

- A single product line (shoes).

- Part of one product line (athletic footwear).

We classify limited-line stores by primary product line — furniture store, hardware store, clothing store. Some retailers such as grocery stores and drugstores, which used to be limited-line stores, now carry much broader assortments.

specialty store
A type of retail institution that concentrates on a specialized product line or even part of a specialized product line.

Specialty stores   Specialty stores have very narrow and deep product assortments, often concentrating on a specialized product line (baked goods) or even part of a specialized product line (cookies). Examples of specialty stores are bake shops, furriers, athletic footwear stores, meat markets, and dress shops. (Specialty stores may carry any category of consumer goods, not just specialty goods.)

Most specialty retailers strive to maintain manufacturers' suggested prices and provide at least standard customer services. Some, such as the Running Room, emphasize extensive customer services and particularly knowledgeable and friendly sales help. Their success depends on the ability to attract and serve well the customers whose two primary concerns are deep assortments and extensive, top-quality services. They excel at functional and emotional relationship-building. In general, they are successful because they have clear strategies with a narrow focus, rather than the broad approach of department stores.[10]

Some specialty retailers are broadening their reach with what has been termed *lifestyle retailing*. These retailers realize that their store "is the brand" and they leverage their brands by selling a lifestyle concept that goes far beyond just clothing. The cachet of their labels has allowed once very limited-line retailers such as Club Monaco, Roots, La Senza, La Vie en Rose, Le Château (Châteauworks), and Northern Getaway to label products as varied as fragrances, household goods, furniture, massage oil, and feather-applied edible powder![11]

Specialty retailers such as Le Château continue to push the boundaries of their product lines.

off-price retailing
A strategy of selling well-known brands below the manufacturer's recommended retail price.

factory outlet
A special type of off-price retail institution that is owned by a manufacturer and usually sells only that manufacturer's clearance items, regular merchandise, and perhaps even otherwise unavailable items.

category-killer store
A type of retail institution that has a narrow but very deep assortment, emphasizes low prices, and offers few-to-moderate customer services; it is designed to "destroy" all competition in a specific product category.

IKEA
Toys "Я" Us
HMV

supermarket retailing
A retailing method that features several related product lines, a high degree of self-service, largely centralized checkout, and competitive prices.

supermarket
A type of retailing institution that has a moderately broad and moderately deep product assortment, spanning groceries and some non-food lines, that offers relatively few customer services and ordinarily emphasizes price in either an offensive or defensive way.

Off-price retailers   Positioning themselves below discount houses, with lower prices on selected product lines, **off-price retailers** are most in evidence in the areas of clothing and consumer electronics. They offer a narrow, deep product assortment; emphasize low prices; and offer few customer services. Store names such as Labels and Winners are now well known to consumers in many cities in Canada. A number of chains of off-price retailers now operate in various regions of the country.

Some off-price retailers buy manufacturers' excess output, inventory remaining at the end of a fashion season, or irregular merchandise at lower-than-normal wholesale costs. In turn, their retail prices are much lower than those for regular, in-season merchandise sold in other stores. Customers are attracted by the low prices and fairly current fashions.

Factory outlets   A special type of off-price retailer, **factory outlets** are often owned by manufacturers and usually sell a single manufacturer's clearance items, regular merchandise, and perhaps even otherwise unavailable items. Canadian retailers such as Danier Leather, Club Monaco, Parasuco, and Roots all operate factory outlets. As well, many other famous brands offer off-price locations in Canada, including Esprit, Guess, Liz Claiborne, and Mexx. Some large fashion retailers, such as Harry Rosen and Holt Renfrew, also operate discount outlets.

Category-killer stores   Featuring a narrow but very deep assortment, emphasizing low prices, and offering few-to-moderate customer services, **category-killer stores** are so-named because they are designed to destroy all competition in a specific product category. Highly successful category killers include IKEA (**www.ikea.ca**) with a broad assortment of assemble-it-yourself furniture, Future Shop in consumer electronics, and Toys "Я" Us (**www.toysrus.com**). Other product areas where category killers tend to operate include office supplies, sporting goods, housewares, and records, tapes, and compact discs.

This form of retail institution concentrates on a single product line or several closely related lines. The distinguishing feature of a category killer is a combination of many different sizes, models, styles, and colours of the product, coupled with low prices. For example, IKEA stocks literally thousands of furniture and home furnishing items. Music retailers such as the major stores of HMV (**www.hmv.ca**) carry such an assortment that consumers need to make only one stop to ensure that they can find particular compact discs.

The category killer's marketing goal is to dominate in such a way that the consumer believes this is the first store to visit and that the value will be better there. Although the major category killers tend to be found in large metropolitan markets, it is in fact easier for a major retailer to dominate a category in a smaller market, where the competition is not likely to be as fierce and where competitors tend to be smaller, local independents. However, most kinds of merchandise as well as many geographic areas will not generate the large sales levels that permit low prices through high-volume buying power. Existing category killers are not without problems — they face a major challenge in maintaining inventories that are large enough to satisfy customer demand but not so large as to result in excess inventories, requiring significant markdowns.

Supermarkets

As a method, **supermarket retailing** features several related product lines, a high degree of self-service, largely centralized checkout, and competitive prices. The supermarket approach to retailing is used to sell various kinds of merchandise, including building materials, office products, and — of course — groceries.

The term *supermarket* usually refers to an institution in the grocery-retailing field. In this context, a **supermarket** is a retailing institution that has a moderately broad, moderately deep product assortment, spanning groceries and some non-food lines, and offers relatively few customer services. Most supermarkets emphasize price. Some use price offensively by featuring low prices in order to attract customers. Other supermarkets use price more defensively by

IKEA has become an icon for low-priced, colourful home furnishings.

relying on leader pricing to avoid a price disadvantage. Since supermarkets typically have very thin gross margins, they need high levels of inventory turnover to achieve satisfactory returns on invested capital. In recent decades, supermarkets have added various non-food lines to provide customers with one-stop shopping convenience and to improve overall gross margins.

Today, stores using the supermarket method of retailing are dominant in grocery retailing. However, different names are used to distinguish these institutions by size and assortment:

- A superstore is a larger version of the supermarket. It offers more grocery and non-food items than a conventional supermarket does. Many supermarket chains are emphasizing superstores in their new construction.

- Combination stores are usually even larger than superstores. They, too, offer more groceries and non-foods than does a supermarket, but also offer most product lines found in a large drugstore.

For many years the supermarket has been under attack from numerous competitors. For example, a grocery shopper can choose among not only many brands of supermarkets (Loblaws, Safeway, A&P, and Sobeys) but also various types of institutions (warehouse clubs, gourmet shops, meat and fish markets, and convenience stores). Supermarkets have reacted to competitive pressures primarily in one of two ways: Some cut costs and stressed low prices by offering more private brands and generic products and few customer services. Others expanded their store size and assortments by adding more non-food lines (especially products found in drugstores), groceries attuned to a particular market area (foods that appeal to a specific ethnic group, for example), and various service departments (including video rentals, restaurants, delicatessens, financial institutions, and pharmacies).

The trend toward eating out more has cut into the profits of supermarkets. As well, the days of "made from scratch" are a thing of the past. Consumers today are looking for a 20/20 solution — that is, 20 minutes to get the shopping done and then just as quickly to prepare most meals. Supermarkets have responded by expanding home-meal replacement (HMR) offerings. An HMR is any frozen or fresh meal prepared in-store for immediate consumption at home. Some supermarkets provide cafe areas where many of the products can be consumed on-site.

From bagged salads to frozen lasagna, the trend has reshaped supermarkets across the country. It has become a battle to recapture food dollars that time-strapped Canadians have been shelling out to restaurants and fast-food outlets. In southern Ontario, Fortino's has added a sushi bar, along with a wine shop and a cigar counter. And Pete (otherwise known as the Fresh Prince of Papaya) of Pete's Frootiques in Bedford, Nova Scotia, has a power-juice bar and a professional piano player positioned over the grapes.[12]

Convenience stores

convenience store
A type of retailing institution that concentrates on convenience-oriented groceries and non-foods, has higher prices than found at most grocery stores, and offers few customer services.

To satisfy the increasing consumer demand for convenience, particularly in suburban areas, the convenience store emerged several decades ago. This retailing institution concentrates on convenience groceries and non-foods, has higher prices than most other grocery stores, and offers few customer services. Gasoline, fast foods, and selected services (such as car washes and automated banking machines) can also be found at many convenience stores.

The name *convenience store* reflects its main appeal and explains how the somewhat higher prices are justified. Convenience stores are typically located near residential areas and are open extended hours; some never close. Hence, the reputation for being convenient! Examples of convenience store chains are 7-Eleven (originally open from 7 a.m. to 11 p.m. but now always open in most locations), Mac's, Mike's, and Beckers. Couche-Tard, based in Laval, Québec, which operates these last three convenience chains and is the largest convenience store operator in Canada, has recognized the same trends as the supermarkets. The company has adapted by targeting the meal-replacement market, hoping to allow the stores to expand their customer base and lessen their reliance on tobacco sales. Aside from increasing fresh and frozen meal offerings, these stores have also added branded products such as Subway, Taco Bell, and Timothy's coffee. Through these diversified offerings and store renovations, the chains have increased their appeal beyond the typical 18- to 34-year-old market and are attracting more women and 35-plus customers.[13]

Convenience stores compete to some extent with both supermarkets and fast-food restaurants. Furthermore, gasoline companies have modified many service stations by phasing out auto repairs and supplies and adding a convenience store section. This has evolved as the convenience store has — Chevron advertises the fresh-baked Bread Garden products it carries in its convenience stores, while Couche-Tard plans to steal market share away from Tim Hortons and Dunkin' Donuts with its freshly brewed coffee and fresh sandwiches, doughnuts, and muffins.[14]

Warehouse clubs

warehouse club
A combined retailing and wholesaling institution that has a very broad but very shallow product assortment; offers very low prices but few customer services, and is open only to members (same as *wholesale club*).

Another institution that has mushroomed is the warehouse club, sometimes called a *wholesale club*. A combined retailing and wholesaling institution, it has very broad but very shallow product assortments, extremely low prices, and few customer services, and is open only to members. Costco (**www.costco.com**) is the major warehouse club chain in Canada.

A warehouse club, or big-box store, carries about the same breadth of assortment as a large discount house but in much less depth. For each item, the club stocks only one or two brands and a limited number of sizes and models. Many products are sold in larger, bulk sizes. It is housed in a warehouse-type building, with tall metal racks that display merchandise at ground level and store it at higher levels. Customers pay cash (credit cards are generally not accepted) and handle their own merchandise — even bulky, heavy items.

Market research suggests that the big-box trend will continue in Canada for some time, as more new theme retailers from the United States, such as Home Depot, continue to expand across the country. With 83 outlets already in operation, Home Depot has plans for another

Costco

37 mega-stores across Canada. The company is also planning to build up to 150 more locations based on smaller-store concepts.[15] This will last as long as, among other things, the demand for commercial real estate remains high, at which time growth will taper off. As with other retailing institutions, modifications and refinements can be anticipated as new demand slows and competition intensifies.

1. What are the three major forms of ownership in retailing?
2. Name the different types of retail stores.
3. What is the difference between discount houses and category killers?

Non-Store Retailing

non-store retailing

Retailing activities resulting in transactions that occur away from a retail store.

A large majority — over 80 percent — of retail transactions are carried out in stores. However, a growing volume of sales are taking place away from stores. Retailing activities resulting in transactions that occur away from a retail store are termed **non-store retailing**. In this section, we review the four types of "traditional" non-store retailing: direct selling, telemarketing, direct marketing, and automatic vending. Then, in the next section, we will discuss the most turbulent form of non-store retailing today — electronic transactions, or Internet retailing, or e-commerce, or e-tailing, or cybercommerce — whatever term you would prefer to use.

Direct selling

direct selling

A form of non-store retailing in which personal contact between a salesperson and a consumer occurs away from a retail store.

Statistics Canada defines **direct selling** as the retail marketing of consumer goods to household consumers by other than a regular retail store outlet. This represents a major growth area in Canadian retailing, as consumers increasingly turn to non-store retailers for the purchase of many products. In Canada, sales by direct selling total about $3.5 billion, a figure that does not include sales by foreign mail-order retailers, direct sales made to Canadians by the mail-order divisions of department stores (such as the Sears catalogue), or direct sales through vending machines or by wholesalers. We can expect the impact of non-store retailers to increase in the future, as consumers demand the convenience of shopping at locations and times that are convenient for them.

Amway
Electrolux

An increasing number of companies are turning to the direct-selling route to reach consumers in their own homes. Among the many well-known direct-selling companies are Avon, Mary Kay, Tupperware, Amway (**www.amway.com**), Electrolux (**www.electrolux.com**), and The Pampered Chef. Many diverse products are sold through the direct-selling route, most of which require some form of testing or demonstration (cosmetics, water purifiers, vacuum cleaners). Essentially, the direct-selling approach involves a salesperson contacting potential customers outside of a conventional retail store environment.

door-to-door selling

A kind of direct selling in which the personal contact between a salesperson and an individual prospect occurs at the prospective customer's residence or business.

The two major kinds of direct selling are door to door and party plan. Sometimes **door-to-door selling** simply involves "cold canvassing," without any advance selection of prospects. The use of door-to-door techniques has declined considerably as both adult partners increasingly work outside the home. More often, there is an initial contact in a store, by telephone, or by a mailed-in coupon.

party-plan selling

A type of direct selling in which a host or hostess invites some friends to a party at which a salesperson makes a sales presentation.

With **party-plan selling**, a host or hostess invites some friends to a party. These guests understand that a salesperson — for a cosmetic or a housewares company, for example — will make a sales presentation. The sales rep has a larger prospective market and more favourable selling conditions than if these people were approached individually, door to door, and the guests get

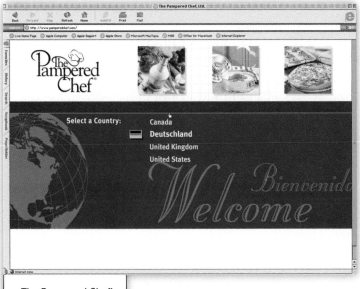

The Pampered Chef's Web site is designed to support and recruit "kitchen consultants."

to shop in a friendly, social atmosphere. The Pampered Chef (**www.pamperedchef.com**) "parties" involve food preparation using the company's products, with gifts of the firm's merchandise for the person who hosts the gathering and the food preparation. Tupperware (**www.tupperware.ca**), the best known of the party-plan retailers, continues after 54 years to market its extensive range of plastic houseware products primarily through in-home parties, involving 374,000 dealers in more than 100 countries. The company claims that 72 percent of U.S. women have attended its parties, with 34 percent having attended more than six. However, because of the changing nature of the North American market, Tupperware is now also marketed through catalogues, office parties, shopping mall kiosks, television infomercials, and the Internet.[16] Party-plan selling continues to expand as more companies see the advantage of selling in this relaxed social environment. For example, Fantasia hosts about 10,000 parties across Canada each year, demonstrating its lingerie and erotic products.[17]

Telemarketing

The Pampered Chef
Tupperware

Sometimes called telephone selling, **telemarketing** refers to a salesperson initiating contact with a shopper and also closing a sale over the telephone. As with door-to-door selling, telemarketing may mean cold canvassing from the telephone directory or it may rely on prospects who have requested information from the company or whose demographics match those of the firm's target market. This information may be obtained by purchasing client lists from other organizations.

The telemarketing business has really developed only within the past 10 years, as marketers found it increasingly difficult to reach consumers through conventional means. Also, the development of computerized mailing or calling lists and auto-dialling technology have meant that literally hundreds of calls can be made during a day by a single telemarketer. Many products that can be bought without being seen are sold over the telephone. Examples include home cleaning and pest-control services, magazine subscriptions, credit card and other financial services, telephone and energy services, and athletic club memberships. Not-for-profit organizations thrive, if not depend, on direct-marketing channels such as mail and telemarketing because they are efficient and accountable.[18]

Creative marketers have found some unlikely products to flog via the telephone. How about coming home at the end of a long day at school or work to find Leeza Gibbons, former host of *Entertainment Tonight*, on your answering machine. The friendly voice mail begins with Gibbons acknowledging that even though you don't know each other personally, she wants to tell you all about a radio station she thought you might enjoy listening to — giving you the reasons in detail. By the time the lengthy pre-recorded message ends, you're thinking: Why would I switch the dial based on the paid ramblings of a tabloid-TV quasi-celebrity?[19]

This form of selling is not without its concerns. Few sales representative last very long in this job — encountering hostile responses on the other end of the phone, receiving more rejections than closed sales, and often working under high-pressure conditions, it's not uncommon for these centres to be referred to as "boiler rooms." Annual turnover rates often average 100 percent. Telemarketing's reputation has also been damaged by the unethical sales practices of some firms. These firms tell consumers that they are conducting marketing research and "are not selling anything." Such unethical procedures hurt other telemarketing companies as well as legitimate research firms that conduct telephone surveys. Such practices are known as "sugging" — selling under the guise of research.

It is anticipated that some of the negative outcomes of telemarketing will be reduced as privacy regulations are enacted and fine-tuned at both the national and provincial levels in the next couple of years. The federal privacy regulations that went into effect in January 2001 are just the beginning, as the provinces have until 2004 to draft their own equivalent legislation. These changes are of concern to marketers in Canada, as they are unsure of how exactly they will be affected in the coming years. It is clear, however, that their practices will be restricted.[20]

The Canadian Marketing Association has called on the Canadian Radio-television and Telecommunications Commission to establish a national "do not call" service to reduce consumer annoyance with telemarketers. It is proposed that a fully bilingual, mandatory service would register customers who do not want to be reached by telemarketers. A proposed $5 per three-year registration fee would be charged to consumers, and companies would pay an annual fee ranging from $500 to $10,000.[21]

The approaches used by some telemarketing companies, coupled with a desire on the part of many consumers not to be bothered at home, has led to a consumer backlash against telemarketing in some areas. Aside from the high-pressure tactics used by some of these firms, it has also become a popular vehicle for outright fraud, particularly targeting seniors. Oddly enough, much of the fraud in Canada targets seniors in the United States, with the typical victim being a 70-year-old churchgoer and a resident of California, Texas, or Pennsylvania, according to the RCMP. The most common scams are fake lotteries and low-interest credit cards, and bogus fraud investigations with con artists posing as police officers or lawyers asking for money to "shut down" fraud rings. The "fraud capital" of Canada is Montréal, with 40 to 50 boiler rooms on average taking in about $1 million per week.[22]

Despite this problem, telemarketing sales have been increasing for several reasons. Certain consumers appreciate the convenience of making a purchase by telephone. Also, the introduction of outgoing WATS lines has made telemarketing to consumers in distant locations more cost-effective. Finally, computer systems today can automatically dial a telephone number or, going a step further, play a taped message and then, to complete the sale, record information that the consumer provides. Such systems reduce the normally high labour costs associated with telemarketing.

These advances in technology, despite their obvious contribution to the efficiency of the process, contribute further to the negative feeling that many consumers have toward being sold products and services in such an intrusive manner. The truly effective telemarketing programs are being run by companies that have adopted an approach to telemarketing that involves doing a better job of targeting those customers who are most likely to be interested in the product or service being offered, and conveying their sales message to the consumer in a polite, caring manner without pressuring the listener.

Direct marketing

direct marketing
A form of non-store retailing that uses non-personal media to contact consumers who, in turn, purchase products without visiting a retail store.

There is no consensus on the exact nature of direct marketing; in a sense, it comprises all types of non-store retailing other than the three already discussed. We define **direct marketing** as the use of non-personal media to contact consumers who, in turn, purchase products without visiting a retail store. (Be sure to distinguish among the terms *direct marketing, direct selling*, and *direct distribution*.)

To contact consumers, direct marketers use one or more of the following media: radio, TV, newspapers, magazines, catalogues, and direct mail. Consumers typically place orders by telephone or mail. Direct marketing is big business. Everywhere we go today, we are exposed to direct-marketing efforts. We see advertisements for recordings and exercise aids on television from direct-marketing retailers, and we are encouraged to call a toll-free number, with our VISA or MasterCard number handy, of course. We receive "bill stuffers" with our monthly

direct mail

An advertising medium in which the advertiser contacts prospective customers by sending some form of advertisement through the mail.

catalogue retailing

One form of direct marketing, in which companies mail catalogues to consumers or make them available at retail stores, and consumers make their purchases from the catalogues.

Tilley Endurables
Canadian Tire

television shopping

A form of direct marketing in which TV channels show consumer electronics, jewellery, and other products for sale at relatively low prices.

The Shopping Channel

Internet shopping

Use of the Internet to offer products for sale, providing information that can assist in sales being made elsewhere, but also offering an alternative way to purchase products.

gasoline bills, retail store invoices, and credit card statements. We order clothing and other items from mail-order catalogues, by either mailing back an order form or more likely calling a toll-free number. A large volume of direct-marketing effort is rarely seen by end-consumers because it is directed at the business-to-business market, where direct marketers have relied on catalogues and mailing pieces for many years.

Given its broad definition, there are many forms of direct marketing. The major types are as follows:

- *Direct mail:* Music and book clubs, magazine clearing houses, and credit card companies make wide use of direct mail. Store retailers, such as Holt Renfrew, also use this approach — mailing out postcards to remind customers of their semi-annual sales or new product arrivals.

- *Catalogue retailing:* In catalogue retailing, companies mail catalogues to consumers and to businesses or make them available at retail stores. Examples of the latter include Tilley Endurables (www.tilley.com) and Canadian Tire (www.canadiantire.ca). Catalogue retailers appear well suited to operating on the Internet, as they have the systems and distribution experience required for such an undertaking. In fact, according to one research firm, two catalogue retailers (Lands' End and L.L. Bean) quickly earned the top ratings in online apparel retailing.[23]

- *Television shopping:* There are basically two approaches to providing television shopping. We have mentioned one above, in which individual products are advertised and the consumer places an order by calling a toll-free number and providing a credit card number. The second involves the use of a dedicated television channel such as The Shopping Channel (www.TheShoppingChannel.com), which provides continuous advertisements for a variety of products such as housewares, jewellery, and other items that can be sold without the need for demonstration or trial.

- *Internet shopping:* Stated simply, Internet shopping is the use of the Internet to offer products for sale. While this may be considered the newest form of direct marketing, its impact and nature is so broad, and still unknown, that it is considered separately later in this chapter. It is a form of marketing that almost every type of retailer has exploited — whether simply to advertise and provide information regarding products and services, or to actually provide an alternative way to purchase products.

Direct marketing has been a major growth area in retailing. Its advantages relate particularly to its ability to direct the marketing effort to those consumers who are most likely to respond positively. Also, it offers products and services in a way that is most convenient for the consumer. A company that uses catalogues and direct mail to reach its target customers maximizes the effectiveness of its marketing programs by having the most accurate and complete mailing list possible. In fact, the success of most direct-marketing programs lies to a very great extent in the preparation and maintenance of an accurate mailing list.

Technology has kept pace with (or even led) developments in the direct-marketing field, as companies are now developing sophisticated computer databases of customers and prospective customers. These databases contain not only mailing addresses, but also other data on the characteristics of consumers and their households, and a history of purchases that these consumers have made. Companies such as VISA and American Express make very effective use of such databases for direct mailings to cardholders in their monthly statements. The types of advertisements that are sent to certain customers are determined to an extent by an analysis of their purchasing history using the credit card.[24]

Like other types of non-store retailing, direct marketing provides consumers with shopping convenience. Direct marketers often benefit from relatively low operating expenses because they do not have the overhead of retail stores. There are drawbacks to direct marketing, however. Consumers must place orders without seeing or trying on the actual merchandise (although they may see a picture of it). To offset this limitation, direct marketers must offer liberal return policies. Furthermore, catalogues (and, to some extent, direct-mail pieces) are costly and must be prepared long before they are issued. Price changes and new products can be announced only through supplementary catalogues or brochures. The biggest drawback is that some consumers react negatively to receiving unsolicited mailing pieces at their homes, spam in their e-mail, and telemarketing solicitations.

Automatic vending

The sale of products through a machine, with no personal contact between buyer and seller, is called **automatic vending** (or *automated merchandising*). Most products sold by automatic vending are convenience-oriented or are purchased on impulse. They are usually well-known brands with a high rate of turnover. For years, the bulk of automatic vending sales has come from three main product categories: coffee, soft drinks, and confectionery items.

Vending machines can expand a firm's market by reaching customers where and when it is not feasible for stores to do so. Thus, they are found virtually everywhere, particularly in schools, workplaces, and public facilities. Automatic vending has to overcome major challenges, however: Operating costs are high because of the need to continually replenish inventories, and the machines require occasional maintenance and repairs.

Technology can allow these machines to be monitored from a distance, thereby reducing the number of out-of-stock and out-of-order machines and increasing revenue. Coca-Cola is testing a machine with two-way communication ability that would allow long-distance price changes based on supply and demand considerations. These technological advances, however, are costly.[25]

While sales through vending machines have been somewhat volatile in recent years, there is reason to believe that we can expect to see more products sold through this form of non-store retailing in the future. The reason for this optimism relates to changes in vending machine technology and the continual flow of new products for these machines. As well, they can be set up to accept credit and debit cards. New product offerings include movie soundtracks (sold in theatre lobbies), freshly squeezed orange juice, prepaid calling cards, reheatable dinners, office supplies, and even live bait for fishing. In Japan, machines dispense everything from life insurance, to adult movies, to custom-made business cards.

You can get just about anything from a vending machine!

automatic vending
A form of non-store retailing in which the products are sold through a machine, with no personal contact between the buyer and seller; same as *automated merchandising*.

Online Retailing

When a firm uses a Web site to offer products and services for sale, and individuals or organizations use their computers to make purchases from this company, these parties are engaging in electronic transactions. It is these transactions that are the basis of **online**, or Internet, **retailing**, which has been discussed throughout this book. The majority of these transactions take place between businesses. In this chapter, we focus on sales by firms to end-consumers.

Online retailing is being carried out by an almost countless number of firms — many of them new companies, but many existing retailers have also been attracted to the Internet.

MARKETING AT WORK   13-3: TECHNOLOGY

No More Free Lunch

Not long ago, Leah Taylor visited egreetings.com, her favourite e-card site, only to find something had changed — a "Paid Members Only" section occupied most of the site.

The site, owned by American Greetings Corp., welcomes visitors with a pop-up window, letting them know they can still browse all cards and send a selection of "everyday" cards free, from love notes to jokes. But most of the site is reserved for subscribers who pay $11.95 per year to send the more popular online cards, as well as create paper cards, set up reminders for themselves, and compile a personal address book.

"I grew up thinking the Internet was free," says 23-year-old Leah, "but now I have to pay for my service provider and phone bill." Additional charges, she says, are intolerable.

Leah's experience isn't unusual. While the Internet remains a rich repository of freebies, visitors are increasingly being asked to pay for what, in the past, cost them nothing. Leah's reaction is a hint at the limits of the paid Internet — companies are unlikely to get away with slapping a fee on all of their con-

tent. Instead, most sites will still need to draw traffic with free content in order to tempt visitors with paid material.

Web experts say more and more companies will attempt such a mix, as they struggle with the new mantra of profitability in the wake of a ruthless Internet shakeout. Jupiter Media Metrix Inc. predicts revenue from paid online content will balloon (in U.S. dollars) to $5.8 billion in 2006 from an estimated $1.4 billion in 2002.

Now, many companies feel that they have no choice but to charge for some content, and they hope consumers will eventually go along. Advertising — Web sites' main support — has withered as legions of online marketers have gone under. Analysts predict the Internet will eventually mimic the cable-TV business: Consumers will be able to sign up for subscription plans with pricing levels similar to cable's basic and premium tiers, perhaps with additional content or services equivalent to pay-per-view shows.

SOURCE: Adapted from Mylene Mangalindan, "No More Free Lunch," *The Wall Street Journal*, April 15, 2002, p. R6.

New retailers that have chosen the Web include Chapters.Indigo.ca and Buy.com, while familiar retailers such as Sears and Lands' End have also found their way onto the Internet. Traditional retailers either operate on their own or in alliance with an Internet firm.[26] Some sites feature broad assortments, such as those of general merchandiser Wal-Mart. However, most e-tailers concentrate on limited product lines or categories that are obvious from their names, which usually are also the Internet locations where they can be found — garden.com, 1-800-flowers.com, or furniture.com, to name a few of the more obvious.

Whatever their differences, firms engaged in online retailing are likely to share a common attribute: They are struggling to be profitable. For those that are both "bricks and clicks" (multi-channel approach) in their structure, this doesn't mean that the company is unprofitable, but sometimes the cyber-component is not profitable. There are substantial expenses in establishing an online operation, many of which do not diminish once the site is set up — marketing costs continue to be high, as these still-early stages of Internet commerce require that firms continually remind consumers that they are actually there to serve customers' needs. Without a physical presence of some sort, it is difficult to remain in consumers' minds. While organizations are still struggling to turn a profit on the Internet, many have discovered that the secret may lie in controlling costs and developing a streamlined logistics system that efficiently fills and distributes orders, while minimizing inventories held.

The Boston Consulting Group (BCG) reports that the typical pure-play e-tailers spend $82 in U.S. dollars to land each *new* customer, while the bricks-with-clicks spend $12. As more pure-plays fall by the wayside, established stores are ploughing forward. Only e-tailers who carve out a niche or strike a partnership to get purchasing deals are going to make it in the face of competition from giants such as Sears Canada and Future Shop, according to BCG.[27]

While Canadians are active online, they aren't buying as much as Americans do. Only 28 percent of Canadians with Internet access have bought anything on the Web, compared with 54 percent of Americans. Despite glowing predictions of mass success, some Canadians remain wary about security issues involved in divulging their credit card numbers online.

A recent study by Léger Marketing found that while security was still a concern to Canadians, about 15 percent of respondents said they didn't buy online because in-store shopping was easier and more fun.[28]

Despite this, it is anticipated that online retail sales in Canada will grow tenfold in the next couple of years — to $24 billion by 2006, according to Forrester Research, Inc. That will represent about 8 percent of retail transactions in the country. However, in this same time, the Internet will come to influence another $59 billion in offline purchases, as consumers use the Web to research products before buying. Therefore, it should be appreciated that the Internet will become one of the most important places to interact with customers in the future.[29]

Turning browsers into buyers is one of the challenges of Internet retailing — beyond those consumers with safety issues. Online shopping-cart abandonment rates can be quite high — from 60 to 90 percent in some cases. Often, the buying process is long and unwieldy, with user-unfriendly navigation through what can seem like a maze. Ways to help convince browsers to take the plunge include providing complete product information and description, with clear graphics illustrating product features; reducing the number of steps in the buying process; and prominently displaying security features and guarantees.[30]

Aggressive efforts to attract shoppers and retain customers, through extensive advertising, low prices, and giveaways, are also clearly hampering profitability — at least in the short run. To this point, the substantial losses racked up by online enterprises have been accepted — even encouraged — by investors and industry analysts. The rationale was that all available funds should be used to gain a foothold in this growing market, subscribing to the principle of the first-mover advantage — that the pioneers in this new marketplace should do whatever they could to stake the biggest claim possible. Seemingly limitless financing was available to anyone with an idea for an Internet start-up. The values of Internet stocks were through the roof! But, what goes e-round eventually comes e-round. Attitudes changed as the new century began — as cash burn-rates for Web enterprises remained high and more "successful" sites were swallowed by black holes in cyberspace, the value of high-tech stocks dropped quickly and many predicted a shakeout in the e-tail arena. It was predicted that "clicks and bricks" firms stood the best chance of surviving, but that in the long run, as many as half of the e-tailers would disappear.

Survival of the fittest is predicted, because it is thought that those firms with unique products or services, strong brand names, and, of course, cash reserves will go on to survive. They will probably prosper, as they will be able to purchase flailing competitors for pennies on the dollar.[31]

Retail on the Internet is difficult to classify by country: By its very nature, marketers are not bound by geographical marketplaces. Firms may be based anywhere and have orders from anywhere, creating one truly global marketplace. Like most other trends in Canada, we usually adopt those behaviours that "catch on" in the United States. This makes sense because of proximity and many cultural similarities. There is a lag effect, however, with regard to retail shopping on the Internet: Canadians seem to welcome this opportunity, but there is delayed acceptance. It is not clear yet whether this is because we are a more conservative culture, simply leery of Internet commerce, or if it's just that the same momentum has not yet been established as in the United States, which has a population 10 times that of Canada. Either way, it would seem that we lag in these shopping patterns by about 18 months to two years. But, as e-commerce evolves, acceptance probably will as well.

Which product categories are consumers most likely to buy on the Internet? Well, this doesn't seem to vary much by geography. At the top of the list: books, music, and videos; computer hardware and software; travel; and apparel. What will they be most likely to buy on the Internet in the future? Given the speed of change in cyberspace, these categories soon may be surpassed by others — perhaps groceries, toys, health and beauty aids, auto supplies, or pet supplies.[32]

Retailing Management

Fundamental to managing a retailing firm is the planning of sound strategies. Central to strategic planning are the selection of target markets and product lines, and the development of customer relationships. Also, in the future, a factor called *retail positioning* will probably be even more critical.

Retail positioning

retail positioning
A retailer's strategies and actions designed to favourably distinguish itself from competitors in the minds (and hearts) of targeted groups of consumers.

Retailers are increasingly thinking about positioning as they develop marketing plans. Retail positioning refers to a retailer's strategies and actions designed to favourably distinguish itself from competitors in the minds (and hearts) of targeted groups of consumers. Such positioning centres on the three variables: product assortment, price, and customer services.

Let's briefly examine several positioning strategies.[33] When only price and service levels are considered, two strategies that have potential value are high price–high service and low price–low service. The former is difficult to implement because it requires skilled, motivated employees (especially salespeople); the latter necessitates careful management of operating expenses because gross margins are small.

When all three variables — product assortment, price, and customer services — are considered, two new options emerge. One is product differentiation, in which a retailer offers brands or styles different from those sold in competing stores. The second is service and personality augmentation, in which a retailer offers similar products but sets itself apart by providing special services and creating a distinctive personality or atmosphere for its stores.

A retailer's positioning strategy may include one or a combination of these options. Retail executives need to exhibit creativity and skill in selecting positioning strategies and implementing them.

Managing retail assortments: Keep an eye on fashion

Not all retail assortments are subject to seasonal or fashion cycles, but many are. A strategic approach to making retail product line decisions is based on how consumers view newness, styles, and fashions. Consumers seem to be constantly searching for "what's new" but not "too new" in products, styles, and colours. Often, consumers satisfy their hunger for newness through fashion, and retailers supply the fashions in various ways as part of their positioning strategy in relation to assortments.

style
A distinctive presentation or construction of any art, product, or activity.

Nature of style and fashion   A style is a distinctive manner of construction or presentation of any art, product, or endeavour. Thus, we have styles in automobiles (sedans, compacts, SUVs), in most clothing items (bathing suits can be one-piece, string bikini, or thong), in furniture (old Canadian pine, Mission, French Provincial), and in dance (waltz, break dancing, line dancing). Ethnic foods represent styles of food preparation.

fashion
A style that is popularly accepted by groups of people over a reasonably long period of time.

A fashion is any style that is popularly accepted and purchased by successive groups of people over a reasonably long period of time. Not every style becomes a fashion. To be considered a fashion, or to be deemed fashionable, a style must be accepted by many people. All of the styles listed in the preceding paragraph, except perhaps for break dancing, qualify as fashions. Fashion is rooted in sociological and psychological factors and furnishes us, as individuals, with the opportunity for self-expression.

fashion-adoption process
The process by which a style becomes popular in a market; similar to diffusion of an innovation.

Fashion-adoption process   The fashion-adoption process reflects the concepts of (1) large-group and small-group influences on consumer buying behaviour and (2) the diffusion of innovation. People usually try to imitate others at the same or the next higher status or socio-economic level by purchasing a product or using a service that is fashionable in the group they want to be like.

Thus, the fashion-adoption process is a series of buying waves that arise as a particular style is popularly accepted by one group, then another group, and then another, until it finally falls out of fashion. This movement, representing the introduction, rise, popular culmination, and decline of the market's acceptance of a style, is referred to as the *fashion cycle*.

There are three theories of fashion adoption (see Figure 13-2): the **trickle-down**, **trickle-across**, and **trickle-up theories**.

1. *Trickle-down:* A given fashion cycle flows downward through several status or socio-economic levels.

2. *Trickle-across:* The cycle moves horizontally and simultaneously within several status or socio-economic levels.

3. *Trickle-up:* A style first becomes popular at lower status or socio-economic levels and then flows upward to become popular among higher levels.

Traditionally, the trickle-down theory has been used to explain the fashion-adoption process. As an example, designers of women's apparel first introduced a style — through fashion houses or boutiques — to opinion leaders in the upper socio-economic groups. If they accepted the style, it quickly appeared in leading specialty clothing or fashion stores. Soon, the middle-income and then the lower-income markets wanted to emulate the leaders, and the style was mass-marketed in department and related stores. As its popularity waned, the style appeared in bargain-price stores and finally, no longer considered fashionable, appeared in second-time-around clothing shops.

Today, the trickle-across theory best explains the adoption process for most fashions. It's true that there is some flow downward and obviously there is an upward flow, but, by means of high-speed production, communication, and transportation, style information and products can be disseminated so rapidly that all social levels can be reached at about the same time. For example, within a few weeks of the beginning of the fall season, the same style of dress (but at different quality levels) appears (1) in small, exclusive dress shops appealing to the upper social class, (2) in large department stores appealing to the middle social class, and

Figure 13-2:

Fashion-Adoption Processes

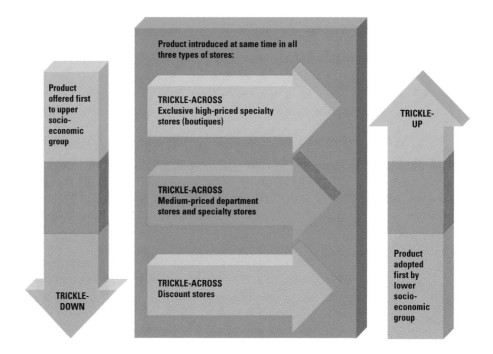

Fashionable mountain gear in mountain-inspired surroundings. Trickle across? Up? Down?

(3) in discount houses and low-price women's ready-to-wear chain stores, where the appeal is to the portion of the lower social class that has some disposable income.

Consider the popularity of mountain gear-inspired clothing for casual wear. Functional in design, these items were available at specialty stores for climbers and campers. Very durable and weather-resistant, such items were carefully constructed from special materials. They then became available in most sports stores, as people adopted them for various purposes. As they became a street fashion, clothing and department stores offered indoor and outdoor wear based on these styles. Although these durable fabrics have become cheaper with time, many lower-price outlets utilize common fabrics as this style becomes all about fashion and much less about function. Who by now doesn't have all-terrain sneakers, pants with pockets like pouches, and perhaps even zip-out leg bottoms or all-weather coats with a zillion zippers, drawstrings, and compartments? And how many members of the Mountain Equipment Co-op do you think are actually climbing mountains on the weekends?

Within each group, for example, clothing is purchased early in the season by the opinion leaders — the innovators. If a style is accepted, its sales curve rises as it becomes popular with the early adopters and then with the late adopters. Eventually, sales decline as the style loses popularity. This cycle is a horizontal movement, occurring virtually simultaneously within each of several socio-economic levels.

The trickle-up process also explains some product-adoption processes. Consider how styles of music such as jazz and rap became popular. Also look at acid-wash denim, T-shirts, Blacktop athletic footwear, boxer shorts peeking out over low-slung baggy pants, and even pasta in the 1990s. They all have one thing in common — they were popular first with lower socio-economic and inner-city groups. Only later did their popularity "trickle up" to higher-income markets.

Marketing considerations in fashion   When a retailer's product lines are subject to the fashion cycle, retail management and buyers must know what stage the cycle is in at all times. Managers must decide at what point to get into the cycle and when to get out, and remain consistent with the agreed positioning strategy. Accurate forecasting is critical to success in fashion merchandising but it is extremely difficult, because the forecaster must deal with complex sociological and psychological factors and their effects on target markets. Frequently, a retailer operates not only with large databases but also with intuition and inspiration, tempered by considerable experience.

Ordinarily, a retailer cannot participate successfully in all stages of the fashion cycle at the same time. Thus, a specialty apparel store — whose stocks are displayed in limited numbers without price tags — should get in at the start of a fashion trend. And a department store appealing to the middle-income market should plan to enter the cycle in time to mass-market the style as it is climbing to its peak of popularity. Fundamentally, retail executives must keep in mind the product's target market in deciding at which stage or stages of the life cycle its stores should offer fashionable apparel

Customer retention

customer-retention strategy
The measures that a company uses to retain current customers and have them make repeat purchases; includes getting to know customers in as much detail as possible in order to communicate effectively, and rewarding those who are loyal and continue to give the company their business.

In recent years, marketers in many businesses, especially in retailing, have begun to subscribe in increasing numbers to the philosophy that it makes considerably greater sense to retain the customers they have than to compete vigorously in order to attract new ones. This viewpoint acknowledges what should have been obvious to all marketers — that a company's most valuable assets are loyal customers. While not denying the importance of working to attract new customers, this approach to doing business places at least equal emphasis on keeping existing customers happy.

Two elements of a **customer-retention strategy** involve getting to know customers in as much detail as possible and rewarding those who are loyal and continue to give a company their business. The former implies the development and maintenance of a customer database and the latter often involves the establishment of a bonus program for frequent shoppers. Some of the most effective customer-retention programs combine these elements.

The best example of a customer-retention program (often called a *loyalty program*) in Canadian retailing is what was known as Club Z. In 2002, Zellers combined the Club Z customer data with the data of its sister retailer, the Bay, to form Hbc Rewards, creating what is probably the most comprehensive and far-reaching database in Canada. The purchases of its 8.5 million members are tracked at both retailers, and with these customers repeatedly redeeming their points for merchandise or flights, the Hudson's Bay Company has its finger on the pulse of about one-third of the adult Canadian population.[34]

wheel of retailing
The cyclical pattern of changes in retailing: A new type of store enters the market as a low-cost, low-price store and over time takes business away from unchanging competitors; eventually, the successful new retailer trades up, incurring higher costs and charging higher prices, making this retailer vulnerable to a new type of retailer.

Other retailers have had or have recently established similar programs to encourage shopper loyalty. High-end retailer Holt Renfrew has its Club Select and Canadian Tire has issued its well-known Canadian Tire money for many years, essentially giving customers discounts of up to 5 percent on purchases made in the store. Sears Canada relaunched its Sears Club, a frequent-shopper program that rewards users of the Sears credit card with savings of up to 4 percent on purchases. Even Tim Hortons found a way to reward faithful customers through its R-R-Roll Up the Rim to Win promotion.

Changing Retail Forms — the Wheel of Retailing

As consumers change, so do forms of retailing. Retail executives would like to anticipate changes in retailing before they occur. To some extent this is possible, as many of the evolutionary changes in retailing have followed a cyclical pattern called the **wheel of retailing**.[35] This theory states that a new type of retailer often enters the market as a low-cost, low-price store.

Other retailers, as well as financial firms, often do not take the new type of retailer seriously. However, consumers respond favourably to the low prices and shop at the new institution. Over time, this store takes business away from other retailers that initially ignored it and retained their old strategies.

Eventually, according to the wheel of retailing, the successful new institution trades up in order to attract a broader market, achieve higher margins, and/or gain more status. Trading up entails improving the quality of products sold and adding customer services. Sooner or later, high costs and, ultimately, high prices (at least as perceived by its target markets) make the institution vulnerable to new types of retailing as the wheel revolves. The next innovator enters as a low-cost, low-price form of retailing, and the evolutionary process continues.

There are many examples of the wheel of retailing. To mention a few, chain stores grew at the expense of independents during the 1920s, particularly in the grocery field. In the 1950s, discount houses placed tremendous pressure on department stores, which had become staid, stagnant institutions. The 1980s saw the expansion of warehouse clubs and off-price retailers, which have forced many institutions — supermarkets, specialty stores, and department stores — to modify their marketing strategies.

◄— BACKSPACE

1. What are the four types of "traditional" non-store retailing?
2. What is the difference between direct marketing and direct sales?
3. In retailing, to what does "bricks and clicks" refer?

Summary

Retailing is the sale of goods and services to ultimate consumers for personal, non-business use. Any institution (such as a manufacturer) may engage in retailing, but a firm engaged primarily in retailing is called a *retailer*.

Retailers serve as purchasing agents for consumers. They perform many specific activities, such as anticipating customers' needs and wants, developing product assortments, and providing financing.

Most retail firms are very small. However, small retailers can survive — and even prosper — if they remain flexible and pay careful attention to personally serving customers' needs.

Retailers need to carefully select markets and plan marketing mixes. Besides product, price, promotion, and customer services, executives also must make strategic decisions regarding physical facilities. Specific decisions concern location, design, and layout of the store. Downtown shopping areas have suffered, while suburban shopping centres have grown in number and importance.

Retailers can be classified in two ways: (1) by form of ownership, including corporate chain, independent store, and various kinds of contractual vertical marketing systems, such as franchising; and (2) by key marketing strategies. Retailer types are distinguished according to product assortment, price levels, and customer-service levels: department store, discount house, catalogue showroom, limited-line store (including specialty, off-price, and category-killer stores), supermarket, convenience store, and warehouse club. Mature institutions such as department stores, discount houses, and supermarkets face strong challenges from new competitors, particularly from different types of limited-line stores.

Although the large majority of retail sales are made in stores, an increasing percentage now occur away from stores. Four major forms of non-store retailing are direct selling, telemarketing, automatic vending, and direct marketing. Perhaps the greatest change in non-store retailing will be from the Internet, as more and more retailers set up shop on the Internet and as marketers refine their skills to attract shoppers to this new retail medium.

To remain competitive, retailers should consider positioning — how to favourably distinguish their stores from competitors' stores in the minds of consumers. Customer retention is also very important: A company's most valuable assets are loyal customers.

Various trends present opportunities or pose threats for retailers. Institutional changes in retailing can frequently be explained by a theory called the *wheel of retailing*. To succeed, retailers need to identify significant trends and ensure that they develop marketing strategies to satisfy consumers.

Key Terms and Concepts

automatic vending 400
catalogue retailing 399
category-killer store 393
contractual vertical marketing system 381
convenience store 395
corporate chain 386
customer-retention strategy 406
department store 389
direct mail 399
direct marketing 398
direct selling 396
discount house 391
discount retailing 391
limited-line store 391
door-to-door selling 396
factory outlet 393
fashion 403
fashion-adoption process 403
franchising 388
independent retailer 385
Internet shopping 399
limited-line store 391

non-store retailing 396
off-price retailer 393
online retailing 400
party-plan selling 396
physical facilities 382
retailer 378
retailing (retail trade) 378
retail positioning 403
shopping centre 384
specialty store 392
style 403
supermarket 393
supermarket retailing 393
telemarketing 397
television shopping 399
trickle-across theory 404
trickle-down theory 404
trickle-up theory 404
warehouse club (wholesale club) 395
wheel of retailing 406

Questions and Problems

1. Explain the terms *retailing, retail sale,* and *retailer* in light of the following situations:
   a. Avon cosmetics salesperson selling in offices.
   b. Farmer selling produce door to door.
   c. Farmer selling produce at a roadside stand.
   d. Sporting-goods store selling uniforms to a semi-professional baseball team.
   e. Chapters/Indigo selling books and music through its Web site.

2. How do you explain the wide differences in operating expenses among the various types of retailers shown in Table 13-1?

3. What recommendations do you have for reducing retailing costs?

4. Reconcile the following statements, using facts and statistics where appropriate:
   a. "Retailing is typically small-scale business."
   b. "There is a high degree of concentration in retailing today; the giants control the field."

5. Of the criteria given in this chapter for evaluating the competitive positions of large-scale and small-scale retailers, which ones show small stores to be in a stronger position than large-scale retailers? Do your findings conflict with the fact that most retail firms are quite small?

6. What course of action might a small retailer take to improve its competitive position?

7. What could a department store do to strengthen its competitive position?

8. "The supermarket, with its operating expense ratio of 20 percent, is the most efficient institution in retailing today." Do you agree with this statement? In what ways might supermarkets further reduce their expenses?

9. "Door-to-door selling is the most efficient form of retailing because it eliminates wholesalers and retail stores." Discuss.

10. Which of the retailing trends discussed in the last section of the chapter do you think represents the greatest opportunity for retailers? The greatest threat?

Hands-On Marketing

1. Arrange an interview with a representative of a small retailer. Discuss with this person the general positions of small and large retailers, as covered in this chapter. With which if any of these points does the small retailer's representative disagree, and why? Also ask what courses of action the company takes to achieve or maintain a viable competitive position. Interview a representative of another small retailer, ask the same questions, and compare the answers you received from both.

2. Go to a local independent bookstore that sells new or used books and think about the services offered by the bookstore and its competitive advantages in relation to online booksellers. Then, go to **www.amazon.ca** and examine the services offered to its customers. What are Amazon's competitive advantages relative to the small independent bookstore?

Back to the Top

Think about the books you have bought recently. What kind of books were they? Where did you buy them? Why did you buy where you did? Was there some reason why you chose to buy online or in a conventional bookstore? Think back to our chapter opener and discuss the competitive position of various online book retailers and conventional bookstores that have existed in Canadian towns and cities for generations. What customer segments is each targeting? On what occasions and in what circumstances will customers buy online versus buying from a bookstore?

Want to get better grades, tips on how to study more effectively, and up-to-date information on happenings in the world of marketing? Then, visit the Online Learning Centre for practice tests, Study Smart software, and much more! **www.mcgrawhill.ca/college/sommers**

Interested in finding out what marketing looks like in the real world? *Marketing Magazine* is just a click away on your Online Learning Centre!

CHAPTER 14

Supply Systems

This chapter will provide you with insight into how wholesale markets, wholesaling institutions, and physical-distribution activities relate to marketing and how manufacturers and other producers work with wholesalers and retailers to reach their markets. After studying this chapter, you should have an understanding of:

- The nature of wholesaling and the role of wholesalers.
- The services rendered by merchant wholesalers, agent wholesalers, and manufacturers' sales facilities.
- What a distribution channel is and how it is designed.
- Criteria for selecting individual wholesalers and retailers.
- Channel arrangements to distribute to international markets.
- The nature of conflicts and control within distribution channels.
- Legal considerations in channel management.
- How physical distribution strengthens marketing programs and reduces marketing costs by using the five subsystems within the physical-distribution system.

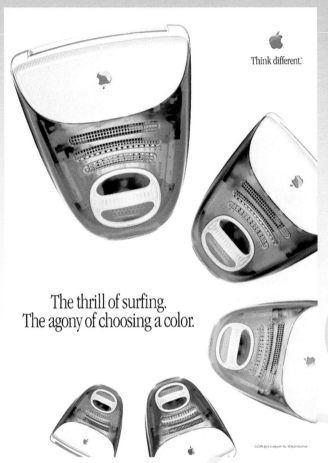

Think different.

The thrill of surfing.
The agony of choosing a color.

The Core of Customer Service

Apple Computer may appear to have come back from the near-dead: When it was introduced in 2000, the colourful iMac sold more than 1 million units in the first three months. Prior to this, the company's products were almost a specialty item, used primarily because of their desktop publishing and graphics capabilities. In 2002, the colours are gone, but the company continues to introduce innovative, eye-catching products.

Some believe the turnaround is a result of the loyalty of Mac fans, its technology, and superior capabilities. And,

of course, many attribute all of this to the sheer attention-getting value of the designs in a sea of beige and black boxes. But there is also something else, something that many consumers wouldn't realize: Apple focused hard on something that it hadn't before — it emphasized the distribution and reselling function within the organization. And this has enabled the revitalization of the brand.

Perpetual praise made for golden years in the 80s and early 90s, but Apple couldn't manufacture and keep product in stock. And Apple was accused of becoming arrogant with its distributors, resellers, and retailers — the very people on whom any manufacturer relies for its success. This contributed to the company's downward spiral. Now, however, in tandem with product innovation, the company has dedicated itself to channel structure and the needs of its channel members. It is also delivering its products through several different channels.

To negotiate more display space from retailers, the company has put in place greater support, ranging from employee training and technical product support to national television advertising. Intermediaries who wouldn't participate in this new effort were to be cut out — this new approach was meant to support channel members as well as the end-consumer.

The company also varied its supply system in different national markets. In Canada, sales to consumers and business markets are achieved primarily through a retail network and through its Internet-based sales channel, the Apple Store (**www.apple.ca**). In the United States, these channels are also used, as well as the Apple catalogue and the company-owned Apple Store at **www.apple.com**. Apple Canada believes the catalogue channel has not been successful because Canadian consumers need and desire more face-to-face service and aid in the buying process than do U.S. consumers. This has also resulted in the use of fewer mass merchandisers in the Canadian reseller network — Canadians are less comfortable making these purchases from such retailers and prefer resellers who specialize in the product category, because they can supply a higher level of training and support.[1]

Although you shop regularly at retail stores, you rarely see or hear of wholesalers. Also, beyond seeing company names on trucks and trains, you have little exposure to the way in which products actually are moved from the point of production to the point of final sale and consumption — through the channels of distribution. As a result, the role of wholesalers and physical-distribution activities are often a mystery. When was the last time, if ever, that you thought about how different Apple and Dell were in distributing their products? Apple uses a multi-channel approach, Dell uses direct delivery. But few companies operate as Dell does: Most use wholesalers — the essential connection in the movement of goods from producer to retailer.

Nature of Wholesaling

Wholesaling enables goods to be purchased for consumption. We already know that retailing involves sales to end-consumers for their personal use. Now we'll see that wholesaling has a different role in the marketing system.

Wholesaling and wholesalers

wholesaling
All activities directly related to the sale of goods and services to parties for resale, use in producing other goods and services, or operating an organization.

Wholesaling (or the wholesale trade) is the sale, and all activities directly related to the sale of goods and services to businesses and other organizations for (1) resale, (2) use in producing other goods or services, or (3) operating an organization. When a business sells shirts and blouses to a clothing store that intends to resell them to final consumers, this is wholesaling. When a mill sells flour to a large bakery for making bread and pastries, this is also a wholesale transaction. And when a firm sells uniforms to a business or another organization for its employees to wear in carrying out their duties, this is wholesaling as well.

Sales made by one producer to another are wholesale transactions, and the selling producer is engaged in wholesaling. Similarly, a discount house is involved in wholesaling when it sells software, laser printers, calculators, and office supplies to a business firm. Thus, wholesaling includes sales by any firm to any customer except an end-consumer who is buying for personal, non-business use. From this perspective, all sales are either wholesale or retail transactions — distinguished only by the purchaser's intended use of the good or service.

In this part of the chapter, we focus on firms engaged primarily in wholesaling — the wholesaling intermediaries.

The rationale for wholesaling

Most manufacturing firms are small and specialized. They don't have the capital to maintain a sales force to contact the many retailers or final users that are (or could be) their customers. Even for manufacturers with sufficient capital, some of their products or lines generate such a small volume of sales that it would not be cost-effective to establish a sales force to sell them.

At the other end of the distribution channel, most retailers and final users buy in small quantities and have only a limited knowledge of the market and sources of supply. Thus, there is often a gap between the seller (producer) and the buyer (retailer or final user).

A wholesaler can fill this gap by providing services of value to retailers and manufacturers. A wholesaler can pool the orders of many retailers and/or final users, thereby creating a market for a small producer. At the same time, a wholesaler selects various items from among many alternatives to form its product mix, thereby acting as a buying service for small retailers. Essentially, the activities of wholesalers create time, place, and/or possession or ownership value.

From a broad point of view, wholesaling brings to the total distribution system the economies of skill, scale, and transactions:

- Wholesaling *skills* are efficiently concentrated in a relatively few hands. This saves the duplication of effort that would occur if many producers had to perform wholesaling functions themselves.

- *Economies of scale* result from the specialization of wholesalers performing functions that might otherwise require several small departments run by producing firms. Wholesalers typically can perform wholesaling functions more efficiently than can most manufacturers.

- *Transaction economies* come into play when wholesalers are introduced between producers and their retailers and other customers. Let's assume that four manufacturers want to sell to six retailers. As shown in Figure 14-1, without a wholesaler, there are 24 transactions; with one wholesaler, the number of transactions is cut to 10. Four transactions occur when all of the producers sell to the wholesaler, and another six occur when the wholesaler sells to all of the retailers.

Wholesale market size

There are more than 54,000 wholesaling locations in Canada, which saw sales in excess of $394 billion in 2001. This represents a considerable increase from 1998, which saw wholesale sales of just over $333 billion.[2] As is the case in retailing, the sales generated by wholesaling establishments have increased dramatically in recent years. This has been especially the case for wholesalers of computers, packaged software, and other electronic machinery, suggesting that businesses are seeking further productivity gains by increasing their investment in new technologies. Part of this increase is accounted for by increases in prices that have occurred during the past 10 years or so, but even if sales were expressed in constant dollars, we would still see a substantial increase.

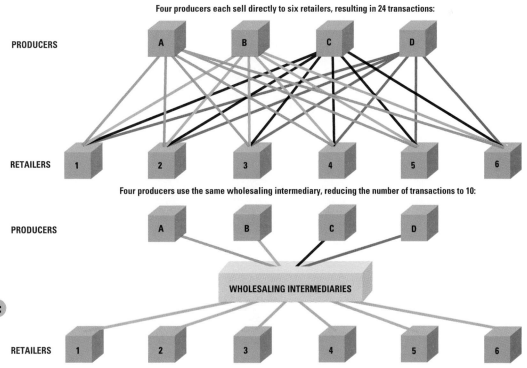

Figure 14-1:

The Economy of Transactions in Wholesaling

Profiling Wholesalers

Wholesalers are usually grouped into four major categories, as shown in Figure 14-2. These are: merchant wholesalers, manufacturers' sales facilities, agents and brokers, and primary-product agents. Later in this section, we will discuss these categories in more detail.

Wholesalers' customers

You might expect that total retail sales would be considerably higher than total wholesale trade, because the retail price of a given product is higher than the wholesale price. Also, many products sold at the retail price never pass through a wholesaler's establishment and so are excluded from total wholesale sales. But Figure 14-3, taken together with Table 14-1, belies this particular line of reasoning. In each year, the volume of wholesale trade is considerably higher than total retail sales and most wholesalers' sales are made to many customers other than retailers.

Operating expenses and profits of wholesalers

The average total operating expenses for wholesaling combined have been estimated at about 16.7 percent of wholesale sales. Profit margins for the wholesaling industry, at 34 percent, are approximately equivalent to profit margins for retailing. The most current figure on gross profit margins (before taxes) for the wholesale trade was approximately 5.4 percent, compared with profit margins for the retail trade of 5.05 percent.[3]

Figure 14-2:

Types of Wholesaling Institutions

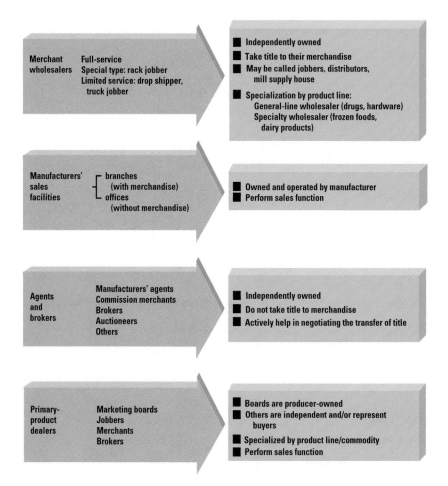

Merchant wholesalers
Full-service
Special type: rack jobber
Limited service: drop shipper, truck jobber

- Independently owned
- Take title to their merchandise
- May be called jobbers, distributors, mill supply house
- Specialization by product line:
  General-line wholesaler (drugs, hardware)
  Specialty wholesaler (frozen foods, dairy products)

Manufacturers' sales facilities
branches (with merchandise)
offices (without merchandise)

- Owned and operated by manufacturer
- Perform sales function

Agents and brokers
Manufacturers' agents
Commission merchants
Brokers
Auctioneers
Others

- Independently owned
- Do not take title to merchandise
- Actively help in negotiating the transfer of title

Primary-product dealers
Marketing boards
Jobbers
Merchants
Brokers

- Boards are producer-owned
- Others are independent and/or represent buyers
- Specialized by product line/commodity
- Perform sales function

Figure 14-3:

Wholesale Trade
Customers

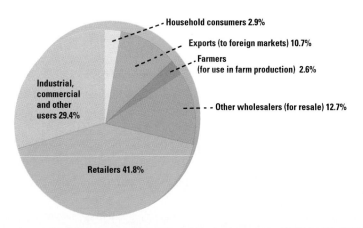

- Household consumers 2.9%
- Exports (to foreign markets) 10.7%
- Farmers (for use in farm production) 2.6%
- Other wholesalers (for resale) 12.7%

Industrial, commercial and other users 29.4%

Retailers 41.8%

TABLE 14-1	Total Wholesale and Retail Trade, Selected Years	
Year	Wholesale Trade ($millions)	Retail Trade ($millions)
1986	188,236	152,880
1990	255,081	192,555
1994	282,438	208,856
1998	333,236	246,675
1999	360,259	260,780
2000	384,567	277,033
2001	394,168	289,130

SOURCE: Statistics Canada, "Wholesale Trade — Historical Series, 1986–1996"; "Retail Trade — Historical Series, Canada, 1986–1996," *Wholesaling and Retailing in Canada*, 1996; and *Market Research Handbook, 2002*, cat. no. 63-224 xᴘʙ, pp. 163, 180. The explanation for this situation may be found in an analysis of the customers of wholesalers (see Figure 14–3).

Merchant Wholesalers

merchant wholesaler
An independently owned firm that primarily engages in wholesaling and ordinarily takes title to the products being distributed; same as *wholesaler*.

Merchant wholesalers take title to — buy in their own names — the products they handle, and account for the largest segment of wholesale trade, about 8 percent.

Full-service merchant wholesalers

An independent merchant wholesaler that performs a full range of wholesaling functions (from creating assortments to warehousing) is a **full-service wholesaler**. This wholesaler may handle consumer and/or business products that may be manufactured or grown or extracted, imported, exported, or made and sold domestically.

full-service wholesaler
An independent merchant wholesaler that normally performs a full range of wholesaling functions.

Full-service suppliers comprise the majority of merchant wholesalers. They have held their own in competitive struggles with other forms of indirect distribution, including manufacturers' sales facilities and agent wholesalers. While there has been an overall increase in full-service wholesalers' share of wholesale trade, there have been gains in some industries and losses in others.

Manufacturers in some industries have begun to distribute their products directly, eliminating some or all of the wholesalers in their channels. For example, Janes Family Foods (**www.janesfamilyfoods.com**), based in Concord, Ontario, a major frozen-foods manufacturer that produces more than 25 fish, chicken, cheese, and vegetable products, is now marketing directly to large restaurant chains, which follows its trend of selling directly to most major food retailers in Canada.[4]

Janes Family Foods

Full-service wholesalers survive and prosper by providing services needed by both their customers and producers; see Table 14-2 for a summary. Large wholesalers use their clout to obtain good prices from producers. They also apply the latest technology to develop computerized inventory systems for their customers. By helping customers keep their inventories lean, a full-service wholesaler can garner added loyalty.

TABLE 14-2	Full-Service Wholesalers' Typical Services to Customers and Producers
Service	**Description**
Buying	Act as purchasing agent for customers.
Creating assortments	Buy from many suppliers to develop an inventory matching needs of customers.
Subdividing	Buy in large quantities (such as a truckload) and then resell in smaller quantities (such as a dozen).
Selling	Provide a sales force for producers to reach small retailers and other businesses, at a lower cost than producers would incur by having their own sales forces.
Transportation	Make quick, frequent deliveries to customers, reducing customers' risks and investment in inventory.
Warehousing	Store products in facilities that are nearer customers' locations than are manufacturing plants.
Financing	Grant credit to customers, reducing their capital requirements. Aid producers by ordering and paying for products before purchase by customers.
Risk-taking	Reduce a producer's risk by taking title to products.
Market information	Supply information to customers about new products and producers' special offers and to producer-suppliers about customers' needs and competitors' activities.
Management	Assist customers, especially small retailers, in areas such as inventory control, allocation assistance of shelf space, and financial management.

Other merchant wholesalers

There are another two types of merchant wholesalers with distinctive operations:

truck jobber

A limited-function merchant wholesaler that carries a selected line of perishable and semi-perishable products and delivers them by truck to retail stores.

- Truck jobbers, also called *truck distributors*, carry a selected line of perishable products and deliver them by truck to retail stores. They are common in the food-products field. Each jobber carries a nationally advertised brand of fast-moving, perishable or semi-perishable goods, such as candies, dairy products, potato chips, and tobacco products. They furnish fresh products so frequently that retailers can buy perishable goods in small amounts to minimize the risk of loss. But truck jobbers are saddled with high operating costs, caused primarily by the small order size and inefficient use of their trucks (for example, during only parts of the day).

drop shipper

A limited-function merchant wholesaler that does not physically handle the product.

- Drop shippers, also known as *desk jobbers*, sell merchandise for delivery directly from the producer to the customer. They do not physically handle products. Drop shippers are common in coal, lumber, and building materials marketing, where typically sales are in large volumes and have high freight costs in relation to their unit value. An interesting number of new dot-com retailers have all of the appearances of drop shippers, except that they are in consumer products and do not have the volume of traditional drop shippers.

Agent Wholesalers

agent wholesaler

An independent firm that primarily engages in wholesaling and does not take title to the products being distributed, but does actively negotiate their sale or purchase on behalf of other firms.

As distinguished from merchant wholesalers, agent wholesalers (1) do not take title to products and (2) typically perform fewer services. Agent wholesalers receive a commission intended to cover their expenses and to provide a profit. Commission rates vary greatly, ranging from about 3 to 10 percent, depending mainly on the nature of the product and the services performed.

Agent wholesalers have lost market share to merchant wholesalers or direct distribution from producers. In the case of agricultural products and manufactured goods, agents are being replaced by merchant wholesalers or by direct sales to food-processing companies and grocery stores. As shown in Table 14–3, product characteristics and market conditions determine whether a distribution channel should favour an agent or merchant wholesaler.

On the basis of sales volume, the most significant types of agent wholesalers are manufacturers' agents, brokers, and commission merchants. These three types as well as several special types of agent wholesalers are described next.

TABLE 14-3	**Factors Suggesting Which Type of Wholesaling Intermediary Should Be Used in a Channel**	
	Favouring Agent	**Favouring Merchant**
Nature of product	Non-standard, perhaps made to order	Standard
Technicality of product	Simple	Complex
Product's gross margin	Small	Relatively large
Number of customers	Few	Many
Concentration of customers	Concentrated geographically and in a few industries	Dispersed geographically and in many industries
Frequency of ordering	Relatively infrequently	Frequently
Time between order and receipt of shipment	Customer satisfied with relatively long lead time	Customer requires/desires shorter lead time

SOURCE: Adapted from Donald M. Jackson and Michael F. d'Amico, "Products and Markets Served by Distributors and Agents," *Industrial Marketing Management*, February 1989, pp. 27–33.

Manufacturers' agents

manufacturers' agent

An independent agent wholesaler that sells part or all of a manufacturer's product mix in an assigned geographic territory.

An independent agent wholesaler that sells part or all of a manufacturer's product mix in an assigned geographic territory is a **manufacturers' agent**, or manufacturers' representative. Agents are not employees of the manufacturers; they are independent business firms. Still, they have little or no control over prices and terms of sale, which are established by the manufacturers they represent.

Manufacturers' reps have continuing, year-round relationships with the companies (often called *principals*) that they represent. Each agent usually serves several non-competing manufacturers of related products. A manufacturers' agent may specialize in toys and carry an assortment of non-competing lines in board games, dolls, learning materials, and outdoor play equipment.

When a manufacturer finds that it is not feasible to have its own sales force, a manufacturers' agent is often practical. An agent can be cost-effective because its major expenses (travel and lodging) are spread over a number of product lines. Also, producers pay agents a commission, which is a percentage of sales volume, so agents are paid only for what they actually sell — an average of 5.5 percent of sales.

An agent's main service to manufacturers is selling. Because a manufacturers' agent does not carry nearly as many lines as a full-service wholesaler, the agent can be expected to provide knowledgeable, aggressive selling — an important advantage. They are most helpful when:

● A small firm has a limited number of products and no sales force.

● A business wants to add a new and possibly unrelated line to its existing product mix, but the present sales force either is not experienced in the new line or cannot reach the new market.

● A firm wants to enter a new market that is not yet sufficiently developed to warrant the use of its own sales force.

broker

An independent agent wholesaler that brings buyers and sellers together and provides market information to either party.

primary-product agents

Intermediaries who trade in primary products as opposed to manufactured goods.

commission merchant

An independent agent wholesaler, used primarily in the marketing of agricultural products, that may physically handle the seller's products in central markets and has authority regarding prices and terms of sale.

auction company

An agent wholesaler that provides (1) auctioneers who do the selling and (2) physical facilities for displaying the sellers' products.

selling agent

A type of independent intermediary that essentially takes the place of a manufacturer's marketing department, marketing the manufacturer's entire output and often influencing the design and/or pricing of the products.

import-export agent

An agent wholesaler that arranges for distribution of goods in a foreign country.

There are limitations to what manufacturers' agents do. Agents do not carry an inventory of merchandise and typically are not equipped to furnish customers with extensive technical advice or repair service.

Brokers

Brokers ordinarily neither physically handle products being distributed nor work on a continuing basis with sellers or buyers. Instead, a broker is an independent agent wholesaler that brings buyers and sellers together and provides market information to either party. The broker furnishes information on many topics, including prices, products, and general market conditions. In recent years, manufacturers' agents and brokers have become more similar in relation to attributes and services.

Most brokers work for sellers, although some represent buyers. Brokers have no authority to set prices. They simply negotiate a sale and leave it up to the seller to accept or reject the buyer's offer. They are used in selling real estate and securities, but they are most prevalent in the food field. For example, a seafood broker handles the output from a salmon cannery, which operates only about three months each year. The canner employs a broker to find buyers among retail stores, wholesalers, and other outlets. Brokers provide limited services and, as a result, incur fairly low expenses, about 3 percent of sales. Likewise, they receive relatively small commissions — normally less than 5 percent.

Primary-product and other agent wholesalers

Two other types of agent wholesalers account for smaller shares of the wholesale trade but provide valuable services in the distribution of primary products such as agricultural commodities. These **primary-product agents** are:

● **Commission merchants**, common in the marketing of many agricultural products, set prices and terms of sale, sell the product, and perhaps physically handle it but do not take title.

● **Auction companies** help assembled buyers and sellers complete their transactions. They provide (1) auctioneers who do the selling and (2) physical facilities for displaying the sellers' products. Auction companies are extremely important in the wholesaling of used cars and certain agricultural products (such as tobacco, livestock, and fruit). They are now appearing on the Internet (see Marketing at Work 14-1, "Fresh as a Daisy: Reach and Speed in Cyberspace").

● **Selling agents** essentially substitute for a marketing department by marketing a manufacturer's entire output. Although selling agents transact only about 1 percent of wholesale trade, they play a key role in the distribution of textile products, coal, and, to a lesser extent, apparel, food, lumber, and metal products.

● **Import-export agents** bring together sellers and buyers in different countries. Export agents work in the country in which the product is made; import agents are based in the country where the product will be sold.

Channel Design: Putting Retailers, Wholesalers, and Producers Together

To this point, we have discussed retailing and retailers as well as wholesaling and wholesalers. We now turn to the perspective of producers of products and developers of services to examine how they access final customers and design a distribution channel or supply system.

MARKETING AT WORK 14-1: TECHNOLOGY

Fresh as a Daisy: Reach and Speed in Cyberspace

Does this make sense? A Brazilian orchid cultivator harvests highly delicate and perishable blossoms. They go to the airport and then halfway around the world to an auction house in Holland (where the majority of the world's flowers are assembled to be auctioned off). Our orchids are then bought by a Chilean wholesaler — so it's back to the airport and half way around the world to our Chilean wholesaler. Coincidentally, Chile is pretty darn close to Brazil! Doesn't this seem inefficient, costly, and not so great for our petally little product's well-being?

This is how 80 percent of the world's flower business is conducted, even though it means that up to 30 percent of the flowers rot, wilt, or die on the long and winding road to your local flower shop. Then, there is the way that the other 20 percent are sold — over the Internet. In auction houses such as Toronto-based e-Auction Global Trading Inc., perishable products such as flowers, fruit, and fish are getting a new lease on life. By streamlining industry processes in which "time to market" is key, losses are fewer, profits are higher, and products fresher!

The advantages are endless. A canning firm, for example, can reap the benefits of a Web site that auctions off raw tin as well as the equipment that processes it. And it doesn't matter if the firm in question is in Moncton or Mozambique — geography is no problem. For once, the company's presence is not required. Other advantages include less market fragmentation, fewer intermediaries, and less surplus inventory and spoilage. Sellers can sell more stuff, more quickly, while buyers get better selection and lower prices.

So why aren't more industries and firms doing it? Well, there are others, ranging from the Canadian grain-handling and transportation industry to NASDAQ, which has developed an electronic auction system for trading stocks. The truth is there are still some wrinkles to be ironed out — electronic auctions can sometimes be a little gangly and awkward. Major limitations are the absence of related services, ranging from insurance and foreign exchange to transportation and lines of credit. Growing pains aside, electronic auctions have made a difference and will continue to grow.

SOURCE: Adapted from Gaston Ceron, "NASDAQ Facing Off Against NYSE, Local Exchanges," *National Post*, January 10, 2002, p. IN2, and Tyler Hamilton, "Net Auctions Catch On," *The Globe and Mail*, April 27, 2000, p. T1.

What is a distribution channel?

A **distribution channel** consists of the set of wholesalers, facilitators, and retailers involved in moving and transferring the title to a product as it moves from producer to end-consumer or business user. A channel of distribution, such as that developed by Apple, always includes both the producer and the final customer for the product in its present form, as well as any retailers and wholesalers that are involved. In the case of services, the producer and the retailer are often one and the same.

The channel for a product extends only to the last person or organization that buys it without making any significant change to its form. When its form is altered and another product emerges, a new channel is started. When lumber is milled and then made into furniture, two separate channels are involved. The channel for the lumber might be lumber mill → broker → furniture manufacturer. The channel for the finished furniture might be furniture manufacturer → retail furniture store → consumer.

Besides the producer, wholesaler, retailer, and the final customer, other institutions facilitate the distribution process. Among these are banks, insurance companies, storage firms, voice- and data-transmission service providers, and transportation companies. However, because they do not take title to the products and are not actively involved in purchase or sales activities, these organizations are not formally included in the distribution channel.

◀ BACKSPACE

1. What is wholesaling?

2. What is the difference between merchant wholesalers, agent wholesalers, and brokers?

3. The _____ is the set of wholesalers, facilitators, and retailers involved in moving products from producer to the end-consumer or business user.

Designing distribution channels

Tupperware
Rubbermaid
Westin Hotels

Companies that appear to be similar often have very dissimilar channels of distribution. For example, Tupperware (**www.tupperware.ca**) sells its housewares primarily through a party-plan arrangement, in which customers buy products at Tupperware "parties" held in the homes of friends and neighbours. Rubbermaid (**www.rubbermaid.com**), on the other hand, sells its similar line of housewares through conventional department and variety stores. Some companies use multiple channels of distribution, as does Apple Computer. Hotels, such as Westin Hotels (**www.westin.com**), sell their products and services directly to walk-in customers, through travel agents, by mail, fax, telephone, through their Web sites, or even through Internet-based hotel room brokers.

Why do seemingly similar firms or the same firm wind up with such different channels? One reason is that there are numerous types of channels from which to choose. Also, a variety of factors related to the market, product, wholesalers and retailers, and the company itself influence the choice of channels actually used by a firm.

A company wants a distribution channel that not only meets customers' needs but also provides an edge on the competition. Some firms, such as Apple and Dell, gain a differential advantage with their distribution channels. Major corporations such as Caterpillar (**www.caterpillar.com**) in construction equipment and John Deere (**www.deere.com**) in farm equipment use dealers to provide many important services, ranging from advice about financing programs to rapid filling of orders for repair parts.

Caterpillar
John Deere

To design channels that satisfy customers and outdo the competition, an organized approach is required.[5] As shown in Figure 14-4, a sequence of four decisions is needed:

1. ***Specifying the role of distribution:*** A channel strategy should be designed within the context of the entire marketing mix. First, the firm's marketing objectives are reviewed. Next, the roles assigned to product, price, and promotion are specified. Each element may have a distinct role, or two elements may share an assignment. For example, a manufacturer of pressure gauges may use both traditional wholesalers and retailers and direct marketing via mail and Internet advertising to convince prospective customers that it is committed to servicing the product following the sale.

   In services marketing, the role of distribution is generally related to accessibility. Because the consumer is often involved during the process of service provision, as, for example, in legal services, the ability to access the service directly is crucial to its saleability. Determining the role of distribution in the marketing plan includes consideration of the human resources that will be applied to the delivery of the service. While more and more services are being delivered over the Internet — financial and travel information, and entertainment, for example — most cannot be delivered by e-mail or the post office, stored on a shelf and passed over a counter, or delivered through indirect systems. The producer must be able to meet face to face with the buyer.

   A company must decide whether distribution will be used defensively or offensively. Under a defensive approach, a firm will strive for distribution that is as good as, but not necessarily better than, other firms' distribution. With an offensive strategy, a firm uses distribution to gain an advantage over competitors. Canadian banks provide a good example of the use of offensive strategies — they are world leaders in moving rapidly to get the jump on their competitors with the use of telephone service options and secure online services.

The Internet is important in Westin Hotels' multi-channel distribution strategy.

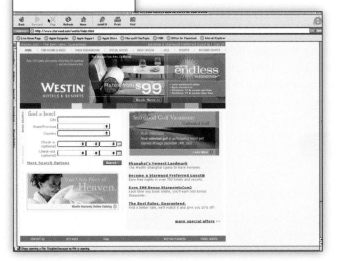

2. *Selecting the type of channel:* Once distribution's role in the overall marketing program has been agreed on, the most suitable type of channel for the company's tangible product or service must be determined. To illustrate the wide array of institutions available, as well as the difficulty of channel selection, consider a manufacturer of compact disc players. If the firm decides to use retailers to reach target markets, it must choose among many different types. At the retail level, the range of institutions includes specialty audio-video outlets, department stores, discount houses, mail-order firms, and Internet retail services. Sony, for example, utilizes all of these for their various lines of CD players. Another choice must be made if the firm decides to also use wholesalers to supply the retailers.

3. *Determining intensity of distribution:* The next decision relates to intensity of distribution, or the number of firms used at the wholesale and retail levels in a particular territory. The target market's buying behaviour and the product's nature have a direct bearing on this decision, as we will see later.

4. *Choosing specific channel members:* The last decision is selecting specific firms to distribute the product. For each type of institution, there are usually numerous companies from which to choose.

GetPlugged.com
Microsoft Network

Using our CD player example again, assume that the manufacturer prefers two types of retailers: department stores and specialty outlets. If the CD players will be sold in Toronto, the producer must decide which department stores and audio retail outlets — Sears, the Bay, Bay Bloor Radio, Toronto Music Super Store — will be asked to distribute its product line. Also, one or more audio Internet distributors — including, among others, GetPlugged.com (**www.getplugged.com**) and the Microsoft Network (**www.msn.com**) — may need to be considered. Similar decisions may be required for each territory in the firm's market.

When selecting specific firms to be part of a channel, a producer should assess factors related to the market, the product, its own company, and the nature of the wholesaler and retailer. Two additional factors are whether the intermediary sells to the market that the manufacturer wants to reach and whether the intermediary's product mix, pricing structure, promotion, and customer service are all compatible with the manufacturer's needs.

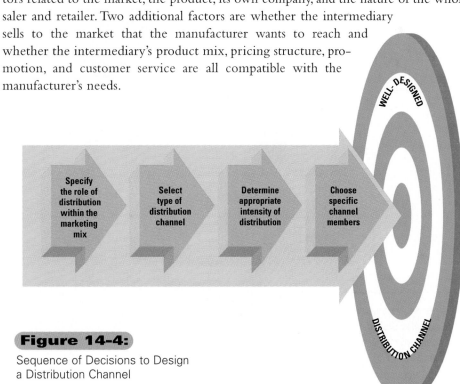

Figure 14-4:

Sequence of Decisions to Design
a Distribution Channel

Selecting the Type of Channel

direct distribution
A channel consisting only of producer and final customer, with no intermediaries providing assistance.

ServiceMaster
Schwan's

indirect distribution
A channel consisting of producer, final customer, and at least one level of intermediary.

Most goods-distribution channels include retailers and wholesalers, but some do not. A channel consisting only of producer and final customer, with no others providing assistance, is called **direct distribution**. ServiceMaster (**www.servicemaster.ca**) uses a direct approach to sell its cleaning and property maintenance services to both residential and commercial customers. Schwan's (**www.schwans.com**) sells a wide range of frozen food products from refrigerated trucks by door-to-door salespeople. Services are generally distributed directly because production and consumption usually occur simultaneously. Swiss Chalet restaurants, for example, produce the food they sell and distribute it directly to the consumer.

In contrast, a channel of producer, final customer, and at least one level of retailer or wholesaler represents **indirect distribution**. Air Canada and other airlines, while selling directly to consumers through offices and over the Internet, still rely on an indirect approach, through both travel agents and Internet-based travel services.

Major channels of distribution

The most common channels for consumer goods, business goods, and services are summarized in Figure 14-5. In viewing this figure, keep in mind that the producer and/or any one or more wholesalers and retailers can be located in Canada or any other national market.

Distributing expensive and complex pieces of equipment requires the building of strong relationships.

Figure 14-5:

Major Marketing
Channels for Different
Categories of Products

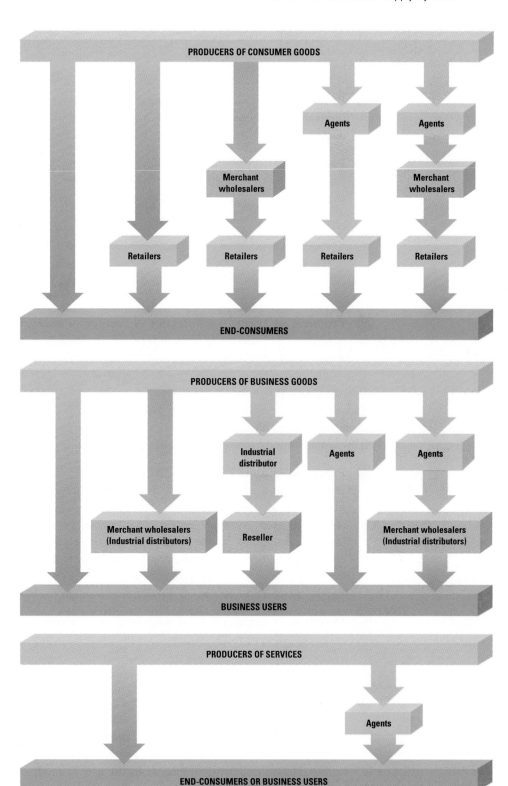

Distribution of consumer goods   Five channels are widely used in marketing tangible
products to ultimate consumers:

1. **Producer → consumer:** The shortest, simplest distribution channel for consumer
   goods is the direct one. The producer may sell from door to door, by mail, or on the
   Internet from Canada or another country, frequently the United States. For example,

Arcuri Jewellers
J. Crew

Arcuri Jewellers (**www.arcuri-jewellers.com**) offers complete catalogue jewellery sales direct to the consumer through its Canadian Web page, and J. Crew (**www.jcrew.com**) sells in Canada through its U.S. Web site.

2. **Producer → retailer → consumer:** Many large retailers buy directly from manufacturers and agricultural producers. Companies such as Loblaws and Wal-Mart maintain direct dealings with producers in a number of countries.

3. **Producer → wholesaler → retailer → consumer:** If there is a traditional channel for consumer goods, this is it. Small retailers and manufacturers by the thousands find this channel the only economically feasible choice. For imported goods, a foreign-based producer may use this channel as well.

4. **Producer → agent → retailer → consumer:** Instead of using wholesalers, many producers prefer to use agents to reach the retail market, especially large-scale retailers. For example, a manufacturer of a glass cleaner selected a food broker to reach the grocery store market, including large chains.

5. **Producer → agent → wholesaler → retailer → consumer:** To reach small retailers, producers often use agents, who in turn call on wholesalers that sell to large retail chains and/or small retail stores.

Distribution of business products   A variety of channels are available to reach organizations that incorporate the products into their manufacturing process or use them in their operations.[6] In the distribution of business products, the terms *industrial distributor* and *merchant wholesaler* are synonymous. The five common channels for business goods are:

Volkswagen

1. **Producer → user:** This direct channel accounts for a greater dollar volume of business products than does any other distribution structure. Manufacturers of large installations, such as airplanes, generators, and heating plants, usually sell directly to users. Companies also allow direct consumer purchases of items such as computers and other electronic items, although they do offer retail networks through other channels. Auto manufacturers have been trying to move consumers in this direction as well, as evidenced by Volkswagen (**www.vw.com**) in 2000 when it introduced limited-edition colours for the Beetle that could be purchased directly only through the Volkswagen Web site.

2. **Producer → industrial distributor → user:** Producers of operating supplies and small accessory equipment frequently use industrial distributors to reach their markets. Manufacturers of building materials and air-conditioning equipment are two examples of firms that make heavy use of industrial distributors.

3. **Producer → industrial distributor → industrial distributor → user:** This channel has been common for computer products and related high-technology items. The initial industrial distributor, usually a large firm, buys products from various manufacturers and then bundles them with related products for resale. These are often called *value-added resellers*. These firms then sell directly to the user as above or sell to smaller local firms, working closely with end-users to meet their needs for computer or communication system equipment and system design.

4. **Producer → agent → user:** Firms without their own sales departments find this a desirable channel. Also, a company that wants to introduce a new product or enter a new market may prefer to use agents rather than its own sales force. Producers in a growing number of industrial sectors are using Internet-based agents who create a virtual marketplace for them and buyers.

5. **Producer → agent → industrial distributor → user:** This channel is similar to the preceding one. It is used when, for some reason, it is not feasible to sell through agents directly to the business user. The unit sale may be too small for direct selling or decentralized inventory may be needed to supply users rapidly, in which case the storage services of an industrial distributor are required.

Distribution of services The intangible nature of services creates special distribution requirements. There are only two common channels for services:[7]

1. **Producer → consumer:** Because a service is intangible, the production process and/or sales activity often require personal contact between producer and consumer. Direct distribution is typical for many professional services, such as health care and legal advice, and personal services, such as haircutting and weight-loss counselling. Other services, including travel, insurance, and entertainment, also rely on direct distribution.

2. **Producer → agent → consumer:** While direct distribution often is necessary for a service to be performed, producer-consumer contact may not be required for distribution activities. Agents frequently assist a services producer with transfer of ownership (a sales task)

MARKETING AT WORK 14-2: TECHNOLOGY

Nygard Designs e-Supply Chains

Peter Nygard runs a $300-million company, with almost 3,000 employees in Winnipeg, Montréal, New York, Hong Kong, and Europe. Still others work in joint-venture manufacturing operations in Mexico and Asia and in more than 200 retail stores in Canada and the United States.

Quality manufacturing and clothing design are his hallmark and he's pretty sure his product is as good as it's gonna get! But, Nygard is looking for new directions to keep business booming. He believes the secret to his success has been and will continue to be streamlining the company's channels of distribution.

The firm has spent well over $30 million to automate the entire organization, allowing buyers to type in their orders and trigger a chain reaction of supply that begins with the fabric and component suppliers and ends with the billing department. As a bonus, customers are guaranteed delivery of the quantity in the time required. Most of his retailers are already connected, thanks to the firm's decision to cover the cost of the equipment and training for each retailer. Talk about adding service and value!

Ever-ambitious to increase the service aspect of his organization, Nygard is banking on the Internet to improve both the service and convenience aspects of doing business with his company. Buyers are able to see the garments at any time, with sample fabrics in their hands. The site is intended to be primarily for B2B — allowing retailers anywhere in the world to track down and order the exact model, colour, and size of an article they want — and it will be shipped within 24 hours.

End-consumers will also be served through this channel. According to Bianca, Nygard's daughter and appointed Web chief, customers will be able to enter personal information such as type of clothes preferred and lifestyle information, and the system will generate fashion suggestions. With that input, it is hoped Nygard can micro-market to them.

Although fashion is perhaps the hardest product to sell to consumers directly on the Internet, this obstacle has not fazed Nygard. Confident that no other clothing brand enjoys the same trust and loyalty that Nygard does, he is certain his cyber-time will come.

SOURCE: Adapted from Denise DeVeau, "Clear Challenge: Be Easy on the Eyes and Budget," *Computing Canada*, July 2002, p. 13; Martin Slofstra, "The Web and Fashion: Not Just a Pretty Face," *eBusiness Journal*, July 2001, p. 11; Serena French, "In the Company of Women," *National Post*, May 4, 2000, p. B1.

Ticketmaster

or related tasks. Many services, notably travel, lodging, advertising media, entertainment, and insurance, are sold through agents. For example, how often have you purchased tickets to a concert, sports event, or theatre production that were labelled Ticketmaster (**www.ticketmaster.ca**)? This firm is an agent that handles the logistics of selling admission to different venues. It doesn't know anything about organizing concert tours, directing plays, or running a circus or sports arena — its expertise is in ticket sales and distribution.

Multiple distribution channels

Many, perhaps most, producers are not content with only a single distribution channel. Instead, for reasons such as achieving broad market coverage, avoiding total dependence on a single arrangement, or entering a foreign market, they employ multiple distribution channels. Use of multiple channels, sometimes called *dual distribution*, occurs when:[8]

- The same product or service (for example, sporting goods or adventure tour packages) is being marketed to both consumer and business markets.[9]

- Unrelated products are being sold (margarine and paint; rubber products and plastics).

Multiple channels are also used to reach different segments within a single national market when:

- The size of the buyers varies greatly. An airline may sell directly to the travel departments of large corporations but use travel agents with physical outlets and Web-based solutions to reach small businesses and individual consumers.

- Geographic concentration differs across parts of the market. A manufacturer of industrial machinery may use its own sales force to sell directly to customers that are located close together, but may employ agents in sparsely populated markets.

Goodyear

A significant trend involves selling the same brand to a single market through channels that compete with each other. Nike shoes, Guess jeans, Levi's jeans, Maytag appliances, Sony electronics, Sherwin-Williams paints, and Goodyear tires (**www.goodyear.com**) are distributed through the manufacturers' own retail stores as well as through wholesalers, independent retailers, and large retail chains. Producers may open their own stores, thereby creating dual distribution, when they are not satisfied with the market coverage provided by existing retail outlets. They also may establish their own stores primarily as testing grounds for new products and marketing techniques.[9]

Although multiple distribution channels provide benefits to the producer, they can annoy existing channel members. Home Depot became so concerned with this increasing trend toward using the Internet as a cyber-intermediary that it wrote to many of its key suppliers in 1999, advising them that it would view any attempt to sell directly to consumers in a very negative way. It implicitly threatened suppliers — such as toolmaker Black & Decker — that it might drop their products from stores if they chose to sell directly through the Web.

Vertical marketing systems

vertical marketing system (VMS)
A tightly co-ordinated distribution channel designed to achieve operating efficiencies and marketing effectiveness.

In the past, distribution channels stressed the independence of individual channel members. Currently, the highly interdependent vertical marketing system has become perhaps the dominant form of distribution channel. A **vertical marketing system (VMS)** is a tightly co-ordinated distribution channel designed specifically to improve operating efficiency and marketing effectiveness. In a VMS, no marketing function is sacred to a particular level or firm in the channel. Instead, each function is performed at the most advantageous position in the channel. A vertical system obviously requires a great deal of trust among channel members and very strong relationships.

The high degree of co-ordination or control characterizing a VMS is formally achieved through one of three means: common ownership of successive levels of a channel, contracts between channel members, or the market power of one or more members. Loblaws, for example, is owned by George Weston Inc., which also owns a full range of bakery facilities, an ice cream production facility, and a soft drink bottling plant. Future plans involve the creation of a separate online grocery division.[10] As shown in Table 14-4, there are three distinct forms of vertical marketing systems: corporate, contractual, and administered.

TABLE 14-4 Types of Vertical Marketing Systems		
Type of System	**Control Maintained By**	**Examples**
Corporate	Ownership	Singer (sewing machines), Goodyear (tires), Radio Shack (electronics), Bata (shoes)
Contractual:		
Wholesaler-sponsored voluntary chain	Contract	IDA and Guardian Drugs, IGA stores
Retailer-owned co-operative	Stock ownership by retailers	Canadian Tire stores
Franchise systems:	Contract	
Manufacturer-sponsored retailers		Ford, Chrysler, and other auto dealers
Manufacturer-sponsored wholesalers		Coca-Cola and other soft-drink bottlers
Marketers of services		Wendy's, Speedy Muffler, Harvey's, Holiday Inn, Tilden car rentals
Administered	Economic power	Samsonite luggage, General Electric, Labatt

In a **corporate vertical marketing system**, a firm at one level of a channel owns the firms at the next level or owns the entire channel. Sherwin-Williams and Goodyear, for example, own retail outlets. Also, a growing number of apparel makers, such as Roots and Ralph Lauren, have opened retail stores to feature their brands of clothing. Some grocery chains own food-processing facilities, such as dairies, which supply their stores. In addition, some large retailers, including Sears, own all or part of the manufacturing facilities that supply their stores with many products.

In a **contractual vertical marketing system**, as discussed in Chapter 13, independent producers, wholesalers, and retailers operate under contracts specifying how they will try to improve the effectiveness and efficiency of their distribution. Three kinds of contractual systems have developed: wholesaler-sponsored voluntary chains (for example, IGA grocery stores), retailer-owned co-operatives (Canadian Tire), and franchise systems (Pizza Delight and Midas automotive maintenance and repairs).

An **administered vertical marketing system** co-ordinates distribution activities through the market and/or economic power of one channel member or the shared power of two channel members. This is illustrated by Corning in ovenware, Rolex in watches, and Kraft Foods in food products. Sometimes a producer's brand equity and market position are strong enough to gain the voluntary co-operation of retailers in matters such as inventory levels, advertising, and store display. However, retailers — especially giant ones such as Loblaws and the Bay — are more likely to dominate channel relationships now than in prior years.

corporate vertical marketing system

An arrangement under which a firm at one level of a distribution channel owns the firms at the next level or owns the entire channel.

administered vertical marketing system

A distribution system in which channel control is maintained through the economic power of one firm in the channel.

Factors affecting choice of channels

If a firm is customer-oriented, its channels are determined by consumer buying patterns and preferences: The nature of the target market should be the key factor in management's choice of channels. Other considerations are the product or service being marketed, the types of retailers and wholesalers available, and the company itself.

Well-run vertical marketing systems have benefited consumers, operators, and suppliers.

Market considerations A logical starting point is to consider the target market — its needs, structure, and buying behaviour:

- *Type of market:* Because end-consumers behave differently from business users, they are reached through different channels. Retailers, by definition, serve end-consumers, so they are not in the channels for business goods.

- *Number of potential customers:* A manufacturer with few potential customers (firms or industries) may use its own sales force to sell directly to ultimate consumers or business users. Canadair uses this approach in selling its jet aircraft. For a large number of customers, the manufacturer would probably use other firms. Tim Hortons relies on numerous franchisee outlets to reach the large number of consumers buying coffee. A firm using others does not need as large a sales force as a company selling directly to final consumers.

- *Geographic concentration of the market:* When most of a firm's prospective customers are concentrated in a few geographic areas, direct sale is practical. This is the situation in the textile and garment manufacturing industries. When customers are geographically dispersed, direct sale is likely to be impractical due to high travel costs. Sellers may establish sales branches in densely populated markets and use intermediaries in less concentrated markets.

- *Order size:* When either order size or total volume of business is large, direct distribution is economical. Thus, a food-products manufacturer would sell directly to large grocery chains. The same manufacturer, however, would use wholesalers to reach small grocery stores, whose orders are usually too small to justify direct sale.[11]

Product considerations While there are numerous product-related factors to consider, we will highlight three:

1. *Unit value:* The price attached to each unit of a product affects the amount of funds available for distribution. For example, a company can afford to use its own employee to sell a large aircraft engine part that costs more than $10,000. But it would not make sense for a company salesperson to call on a household or a business firm to sell a $2 ballpoint pen. Consequently, products with low unit value usually are distributed through indirect channels. There are exceptions, however. For instance, if order size is large because the customer buys many products at the same time from the company, then a direct channel may be economically feasible.

2. *Perishability:* Some goods, including many agricultural products, physically deteriorate fairly quickly. Other products, such as services, can be consumed only in the presence of the producer. Legal advice, for example, is only available directly from a law firm. As was discussed in Chapter 8, services are perishable due to their intangible nature. Perishable products require direct or very short channels.

3. *Technical nature:* A business product that is highly technical is often distributed directly to business users. The producer's sales force must provide considerable pre-purchase and post-purchase service; wholesalers normally cannot do this. Consumer products of a technical nature pose a real distribution challenge for manufacturers. Ordinarily, manufacturers cannot sell the goods directly to the consumer. However, with the development of the Internet, it is easier for products to be distributed directly from the manufacturer, with substantial amounts of technical support being provided on the Internet.

Channel member considerations   Here we begin to see that a company may not be able to arrange exactly the channels it desires:

- *Services provided:* Each producer should select firms that will provide those marketing services that the producer either is unable to provide or cannot economically perform. Foreign producers seeking to gain market share in Canada will utilize industrial distributors or importers.

- *Availability:* The potential channel members preferred by a producer may not be available. They may be carrying competitive products and may not want to add another line.

- *Producer's policies:* Sometimes manufacturers' choices of channels are limited because their marketing policies are not acceptable to certain types of firms. Some retailers or wholesalers, for example, are interested in carrying a line only if they receive assurance that no competing firms will carry the line in the same territory.

- *Channel position:* In some cases, a firm has achieved such a strong or even dominant position in the market that a manufacturer cannot afford not to distribute through them. For example, Staples/Business Depot and Chapters/Indigo occupy these types of positions.

Company considerations   Before choosing a distribution channel for a product, a company should consider its own situation:

- *Desire for channel control:* Some producers establish direct channels because they want to control their product's distribution, even though a direct channel may be more costly than an indirect channel. By controlling the channel, producers can achieve more aggressive promotion and can better control both the freshness of merchandise stocks and their products' and services' retail prices. Dell Computer became extremely successful with direct distribution systems via the Internet and mail order.

- *Services provided by seller:* Some producers make decisions about their channels based on the distribution functions desired and occasionally demanded. Numerous retail chains will not stock a product unless it is pre-sold through heavy advertising by the producer.

- *Ability of management:* The marketing experience and managerial capabilities of a producer influence decisions about which channel to use. Many companies lacking marketing know-how turn the distribution job over to others.

- *Financial resources:* A business with adequate finances can establish its own sales force, grant credit to its customers, and/or warehouse its own products. A financially weak firm uses other firms to provide these services.

In a few cases, virtually all factors point to a particular length and type of channel. In most cases, however, the factors send mixed signals. Several factors may point to the desirability of direct channels, others to the use of wholesalers and/or retailers. Or the company may find that the channel it wants is unavailable. If a company with an unproven product that has low profit potential cannot place its product with wholesalers, it may have no other option but to try to distribute the product directly to its target market.

Distribution to Foreign Markets

exporting
The activities by which a firm sells its product in another country, either directly to foreign importers or through import-export intermediaries.

export merchant
An intermediary operating in a manufacturer's country that buys goods and exports them.

export agent
An intermediary that operates either in a manufacturer's country or in the destination country, negotiating the sale of a product in another country; may provide additional services such as arranging for international financing, shipping, and insurance on behalf of the manufacturer.

company sales branch
A sales facility that carries a stock of the product being sold.

In deciding to market in a foreign country, management must select an appropriate channel and organizational relationship in the same manner that it does for Canadian markets. There is a range of channels for distributing in foreign markets (see Table 14-5), representing successively greater levels of market involvement. While the basic considerations for distribution to foreign markets are the same as those for the Canadian market, the details of these markets are different. They exist in a different context, and differences range from economic, governmental, legal, and social systems to the specific trade practices of wholesalers and retailers and the channels that are available.

Exporting

The simplest way of distributing goods to foreign markets is by **exporting**, either directly to foreign importers or through import–export intermediaries. In international markets, just as in domestic markets, there are both merchant and agent wholesalers.

An **export merchant** operates in the manufacturer's country, buying goods and exporting them. Very little risk or investment is involved. Also, minimal time and effort are required on the part of the exporting producer. However, the exporter has little or no control over merchant wholesalers.

An **export agent** may be located in either the manufacturer's country or in the destination country. The agent negotiates the sale of the product and may provide additional services, such as arranging for international financing, shipping, and insurance on behalf of the manufacturer. Greater risk is involved, since the manufacturer retains title to the goods. These types of organizations generally are not aggressive marketers, nor do they generate a large sales volume.

To counteract some of these deficiencies, management can export through its own **company sales branches** in foreign markets. Operating a sales branch enables a company to (1) promote its products more aggressively, (2) develop its foreign markets more effectively, and (3) control its sales effort more completely.

Because it is the easiest way to distribute to international markets, exporting is popular with small firms.

TABLE 14-5	The Range of Channels and Structures for Distributing in International Markets		
Exporting directly or through import-export intermediaries	Company sales branches	Licensing foreign producers	Contract manufacturing by foreign producers
Low involvement abroad ◄————————————————————————► High involvement abroad			

MARKETING AT WORK　　14-3: GLOBAL

Canadian Company Shows 'em What's Sexy

Where do you think a Canadian lingerie manufacturer would go to find new markets? Maybe Brazil, home of the "dental floss" bikini? Perhaps France, the destination for romance? Try the Muslim nations of the Middle East!

That's one of the places Montréal-based La Senza decided to offer its line of intimate apparel. The first country to (very discreetly) reap the lacy benefits was the ultra-conservative kingdom of Saudi Arabia. In public, Saudi women are required to wear hijabs to cover their faces and abayas to cover their bodies, but what goes on underneath the veil is up to the woman *and* her husband. Lately, lingerie has become a highly liberating, titillating, and popular form of expression in that country — there are now 34 La Senza stores successfully operating there.

Although the stores are modelled after the 194 La Senza lingerie stores located across Canada, there are a few regional differences. One, there are no fitting rooms. Another — which partially explains the first — is that all sales clerks are male.

La Senza's Saudi success has caused the company to branch out into other Gulf States. A licensing agreement with a

United Arab Emirate-based trading company has seen the opening of La Senza boutiques in the United Arab Emirates, Bahrain, Kuwait, Oman, and Qatar.

Interestingly, the radically different Arab culture is probably one of the biggest reasons for La Senza's success. The differences were of such an obvious magnitude that the company was forced to study the market very carefully with regard to its structure and consumer behaviour in relation to lingerie. It was also critical to learn the legal, political, social, and religious aspects of the country, as well as local business practices.

La Senza and La Senza Girl (clothing for girls 8 to 14) stores have also recently appeared in Malaysia, Morocco, and Poland. A La Senza lingerie store will also open in China in late 2002.

SOURCE: Adapted from Hollie Shaw, "La Senza to Expand to China: Licensing Agreement," *National Post*, June 13, 2002, p. FP6; "Lingerie Retailer La Senza Stretches Expansion Farther into Europe," *Canadian Press Newswire*, April 10, 2002; Zena Olijnyk, "La Senza Lingerie Heads East," *National Post*, April 25, 2000, pp. C1, C8.

---

contracting

A legal relationship that allows a firm to enter a foreign market indirectly, quickly establish a market presence, and experience a limited amount of risk.

licensing arrangement

A business arrangement whereby one firm sells to another firm (for a fee or royalty) the right to use the first company's brand, patents, or manufacturing processes.

Contracting　Contracting involves a legal relationship that allows a firm to enter a foreign market indirectly, quickly establish a market presence, and experience a limited amount of risk. One form of contracting is a licensing arrangement: granting to another producer — for a fee or royalty payment — the right to use one's production process, patents, trademarks, or other assets. For example, the Suntory brewery in Japan is licensed by Anheuser-Busch to produce Budweiser beer. La Senza of Montréal has licensed its successful lingerie brand for use in Saudi Arabia (see Marketing at Work 14-3 above).

Franchising has allowed Canadian service retailers, such as Pizza Pizza, Swiss Chalet, and Uniglobe Travel, to expand overseas. Franchising combines a proven operating formula with local knowledge and entrepreneurial initiative.

Pizza Hut franchises can be found worldwide.

In contract manufacturing, a marketer, such as the Bay, contracts with a foreign producer to supply products that are then marketed in the producer's country. For example, rather than importing certain tools and hardware for its planned stores in China, the Bay contracts with local manufacturers to supply certain items.

Contracting offers companies flexibility with minimal investment. It allows a producer to enter a market that might otherwise be closed to it because of exchange restrictions, import quotas, or prohibitive tariffs. At the same time, by licensing, producers may be creating future channel conflicts by building future competitors. A licensee may learn all it can from the producer and then proceed independently when the licensing agreement expires.

BACKSPACE

1. Describe the sequence of four decisions that need to be made when designing a channel.
2. When choosing channel members, what are some of the considerations companies should keep in mind?
3. _____ is the simplest way of distributing goods to foreign markets.

- -

Determining Intensity of Distribution

intensity of distribution
The number of intermediaries used by a producer at the retailing and wholesaling levels of distribution.

At this point in designing a channel, a firm knows what role has been assigned to distribution within the marketing mix, whether direct or indirect distribution is better, and which types of wholesalers and retailers will be used (assuming indirect distribution is appropriate). Next, the company must decide on the **intensity of distribution** — that is, how many firms will be used at the wholesale and retail levels in a particular territory.

There are many possible degrees of intensity. As shown in Figure 14-6, we consider the three major categories — intensive, selective and exclusive. Different degrees of intensity may be appropriate at successive levels of distribution. A manufacturer can often achieve intensive retail coverage with selective, rather than intensive, wholesale distribution. Or selective intensity at the retail level may be gained through exclusive intensity at the wholesale level. Of course, the wholesaling firm or firms will determine which retail outlets actually receive the product. Despite this lack of control, a producer should plan the levels of intensity needed at both the wholesale and retail levels.

Intensive distribution

intensive distribution
A strategy in which a producer sells its product in every available outlet where a consumer might reasonably look for it.

Under **intensive distribution**, a producer sells its product through every available outlet in a market where a consumer might reasonably look for it. Manufacturers of convenience goods use intensive distribution. Retailers often control whether a strategy of intensive distribution actually can be implemented. For example, a new manufacturer of toothpaste or a small producer of potato chips may want distribution in all supermarkets, but these retailers may limit their assortments to four best-selling brands.

Selective distribution

selective distribution
A strategy in which a producer sells its product through multiple, but not all, wholesalers and/or retailers in a market where a consumer might reasonably look for it.

In **selective distribution**, a producer sells through multiple, but not all possible, wholesalers and retailers in a market where a consumer might reasonably look for it. Selective distribution is appropriate for consumer shopping goods, such as various types of clothing and appliances, and for business accessory equipment, such as office equipment and handheld tools.

Figure 14-6:
The Intensity-of-Distribution Continuum

A company may shift to a selective distribution strategy after some experience with intensive distribution. The decision to change usually hinges on the high cost of intensive distribution or the unsatisfactory performance of current channel members. Some firms perennially order in small, unprofitable amounts; others may be poor credit risks. Eliminating marginal channel members may reduce the number of outlets but increase a company's sales volume. Companies have found that they were able to do a more thorough selling job with a smaller number of accounts.

A firm may move toward more selective distribution to enhance the image of its products, strengthen customer service, and/or improve quality control. The Italian firm Gucci concluded that its brand was on too many leather goods and fashion accessories and was carried by too many retailers. As part of a new marketing strategy, Gucci (**www.gucci.com**) slashed both its product line and the number of outlets carrying its goods.

Gucci

Exclusive distribution

exclusive distribution
A strategy in which a producer agrees to sell its product to only one wholesaling intermediary and/or retailer in a given market.

Under exclusive distribution, the supplier agrees to sell its product only to a single wholesaler and/or retailer in a given market. At the wholesale level, such an arrangement is normally called an *exclusive distributorship*; at the retail level, an *exclusive dealership*. A manufacturer may prohibit a firm that holds an exclusive distributorship or dealership from handling a directly competing product line.

Producers often adopt an exclusive distribution strategy when it is essential that the retailer carry a large inventory. Exclusive dealerships are frequently used in marketing consumer specialty products such as expensive suits. This strategy is also desirable when the dealer or distributor must furnish installation and repair service. For this reason, manufacturers of farm machinery and large construction equipment grant exclusive distributorships.

Exclusive distribution helps a manufacturer control the last level of supply before the final customer. A retailer or wholesaler with exclusive rights is usually willing to promote the product aggressively. Why? Interested customers will have to purchase the product from this firm because no other outlets in the area carry the same brand. However, a producer suffers if its exclusive retailers in various markets do not serve customers well. Essentially a manufacturer has "all of its eggs in one basket."

An exclusive dealer or distributor has the opportunity to reap all of the benefits of the producer's marketing activities in a particular area. On the other hand, a wholesaler or retailer may become too dependent on the manufacturer. If the manufacturer fails, the firm also fails (at least for that product). Another risk is that once sales volume has been built up in a market, the producer may add other dealers or, worse yet, drop all dealers and establish its own sales force.

Conflict and Control in Channels

Distribution occasionally is characterized by goals shared by suppliers and customers and by co-operative actions. But conflicts as well as struggles for control are more typical, whether the channel is a domestic or international one. To manage distribution channels effectively requires an understanding of both conflict and control, including techniques to (1) decrease conflict, or at least its negative effects, and (2) increase a firm's control within a channel.

channel conflict
A situation in which one channel member perceives another channel member to be acting in a way that prevents the first member from achieving its distribution objectives.

Channel conflict exists when one channel member perceives another channel member to be acting in a way that prevents the first member from achieving its distribution objectives. Firms in one channel often compete vigorously with firms in other channels; this represents horizontal conflict. Even within the same channel, firms might argue about operating practices and try to gain control over other members' actions; this illustrates vertical conflict.

Horizontal conflict

horizontal conflict
A form of channel conflict occurring between firms on the same level of distribution, between intermediaries of the same type, or between different types of intermediaries.

Horizontal conflict occurs among firms on the same level of distribution. The cellphone field provides an excellent example. Cellphones and services can be purchased at a multitude of places — office supply outlets, department stores, warehouse clubs, consumer electronics retailers, and telecommunications providers such as TELUS and Bell Canada, with their own stores, toll-free lines, and Web sites.

Horizontal conflict may occur between:

● Firms of the same type: Maryvale Home Hardware versus Fred's Friendly Hardware, for example.

● Different types of firms on the same level: Maryvale Home Hardware versus St. Clair Paint and Wallpaper versus Wal-Mart.

The main source of horizontal conflict is scrambled merchandising, in which competitors diversify by adding product lines not traditionally carried by their type of business. Supermarkets, for instance, expanded beyond groceries by adding health and beauty aids, small appliances, recordings, and various services such as snack bars. Retailers that originally sold these product lines became irritated both at supermarkets for diversifying and at producers for using multiple distribution channels.

Vertical conflict

vertical conflict
A form of channel conflict occurring between firms at different levels of the same channel, typically producer versus wholesaler or producer versus retailer.

Perhaps the most severe conflicts in distribution involve firms at different levels of the same channel. Vertical conflict typically occurs between producer and wholesaler or producer and retailer.

Producer versus wholesaler   Tensions occasionally arise between producers and wholesalers. A producer and wholesaler may disagree about aspects of their business relationship. For instance, John Deere has argued with distributors about whether they should sell farm equipment made by other companies or should restrict their efforts to the Deere brand.

Why do conflicts arise? Manufacturers and wholesalers have differing points of view. On the one hand, manufacturers think that wholesalers neither promote products aggressively nor provide sufficient storage services, and that wholesalers' services cost too much. On the other hand, wholesalers believe producers either expect too much or do not understand the wholesalers' primary obligation to customers.

Channel conflict typically stems from a manufacturer's attempts to bypass wholesalers and deal directly with retailers or consumers. The presence of the Internet makes this much easier to do. Direct sale occurs because (1) producers are dissatisfied with wholesalers' services or (2) market conditions call for direct sale. Ordinarily, battles about direct sale are fought in consumer goods channels. Such conflicts rarely arise in channels for business goods, because a tradition of direct sale to end-customers in business markets already exists.

To bypass wholesalers, a producer has two alternatives:

1. *Sell directly to consumers:* Producers may employ Internet, house-to-house, or mail-order catalogue selling. Producers may also establish their own distribution centres in different areas or even their own retail stores in major markets.

2. *Sell directly to retailers:* Under certain market and product conditions, selling directly to retailers is feasible and advisable. An ideal retail market for this option consists of retailers that buy large quantities of a limited line of products.

Direct distribution — a short channel — is advantageous when the product (1) is subject to physical or fashion perishability, (2) carries a high unit price, (3) is custom-made, or (4) requires installation and technical service. Direct distribution, however, places a financial and managerial burden on the producer. Not only must the manufacturer operate its own sales force and handle physical distribution of its products, but a direct-selling manufacturer also faces competition from its former wholesalers, who no doubt now sell competitive products.

Wholesalers too can improve their competitive position and thereby reduce channel conflict. Their options include:

- *Improve internal management* by modernizing operations, upgrading the calibre of their management, building new, low-operating-cost facilities.

- *Provide management assistance to retailers* by helping to meet certain retailers' needs and providing assistance with functions such as store layout, merchandise selection, promotion, and inventory control.

- *Form voluntary chains* (discussed in Chapter 13) by agreeing to furnish a group of retailers with management services and volume buying power. In turn, retailers promise to buy all, or almost all, of their merchandise from the wholesaler. IGA supermarkets are an example of this approach.

- *Develop private brands*, since a voluntary chain of retailers provides a built-in market for the wholesaler's brand.

slotting allowance
A fee that some retailers demand from manufacturers to place manufacturers' products on store shelves.

Producer versus retailer   Another struggle for channel control takes place between manufacturers and retailers. Conflict can arise over terms or conditions of the relationship between any two parties, or producers may compete with retailers by selling direct via the Internet, by catalogue, or through producer-owned stores. A number of apparel makers — including Ralph Lauren, Levi Strauss, and Liz Claiborne — have opened retail outlets. In doing so, they have annoyed department stores and specialty retailers that also carry their brands.

Producer and retailer may also disagree about terms of sale or conditions of the relationship between themselves. Large retail outlets continually demand lower prices as well as more service from suppliers. Some retailers demand a so-called slotting allowance to place a manufacturer's product on store shelves. This is most evident in the grocery products field. In some cases, companies with new products are required to pay a fee ranging from $100 to more than $1,000 per store for each version of the product, or payment may be in the form of free products. Of course, not all manufacturers are paying all of these fees, and some small producers cannot afford them. Manufacturers criticize slotting allowances, claiming they stifle the introduction of new products, particularly those developed by small companies. Retailers defend them as a way to recoup the costs of reviewing the flood of new products, stocking some of them, and removing failures.

Producers and retailers both have methods to gain more control. Manufacturers can:

- **Build strong consumer brand loyalty.** Creative and aggressive promotion is a key to creating such loyalty.

Well-known brands present their own faces, as well as being represented in other outlets.

- **Establish one or more forms of a vertical marketing system.**

- **Refuse to sell to unco-operative retailers.** This tactic has to be defensible from a legal standpoint.

  Effective marketing weapons are also available to retailers. They can:

- **Develop strong consumer relationships** with skilful advertising, strong store brands, and good service and customer handling.

- **Improve computerized information systems** to be able to determine what sells and how fast it sells and use such information in negotiating with suppliers.

- **Form a retailer co-operative** by having a group of retailers (usually fairly small ones) band together to establish and operate a wholesale warehouse and gain lower merchandise costs through volume buying power.[12]

Who controls channels?

channel control

The ability to influence the behaviour of other channel members.

Traditionally, manufacturers have been viewed as having **channel control** — making the decisions regarding types and number of outlets, participation of individual firms, and business practices to be followed by a channel. But this is a one-sided, outdated point of view. In many lines of trade, power has shifted to the big-box store brands and the category-killer retailers because of the volume of sales they control. Other strong retailers have gained much control because of the strong relationships they have developed with their customers.

Certainly the names Safeway, Loblaws, and Sears Canada mean more to consumers than the names of most brands sold in these stores. Large retailers are challenging producers for channel control, just as many manufacturers seized control from wholesalers years ago. Even small retailers can be influential in local markets, because their prestige may be greater than their suppliers' prestige.

A channel viewed as a partnership

Sometimes, members see a channel as a fragmented collection of independent, competing firms. The reality is that a channel is not something to "command and control," but rather it is a partnership aimed at satisfying end-users' needs.[13] Thus, co-ordination and relationship-building is needed throughout a distribution channel.

Legal Considerations in Channel Management

In various ways, organizations may try to exercise control over the distribution of their products as they move through the channel. Generally speaking, any attempts to control distribution may be subject to legal constraints. Four control methods that are frequently considered by suppliers (usually manufacturers) in attempting to exercise control are:

dealer selection

Under section 75 of the Competition Act, it is illegal for a manufacturer or supplier to refuse to supply a wholesaler or retailer unless the wholesaler or retailer is unwilling or unable to meet the usual trade terms of the supplier.

1. *Dealer selection:* In **dealer selection**, the manufacturer wants to select its customers and refuses to sell to some. Under section 75 of the Competition Act, it is illegal for a manufacturer or supplier to refuse to supply a wholesaler or retailer unless the wholesaler or retailer is unwilling or unable to meet the usual trade terms of the supplier. For example, selling the supplier's product as a loss leader or failing to provide adequate service or product support. Generally, it would be illegal to refuse to supply a product if the company carried a competitor's product or resisted a tying contract (see method 3).

exclusive dealing

The practice by which a manufacturer prohibits its dealers from carrying products of competing manufacturers.

tying contract

A contract under which a manufacturer sells a product to an intermediary only under the condition that this intermediary also buys another (possibly unwanted) product from the manufacturer.

exclusive territory

Under this arrangement, a manufacturer requires each intermediary to sell only to customers located within the intermediary's assigned territory.

2. *Exclusive dealing:* In exclusive dealing, the manufacturer wants to prevent dealers from carrying competitors' products. Exclusive dealing contracts are unlawful if the manufacturer's sales volume is a substantial part of the total volume in a market or if the volume done by the exclusive dealers is a significant percentage of the total business in an area.

3. *Tying contracts:* A tying contract exists when a manufacturer sells a product only under the condition that the buyer also buys another (possibly unwanted) product from the manufacturer. A dealer can be required to carry a manufacturer's full line as long as this does not impede competition in the market. The arrangement may be questionable, however, if a supplier forces a dealer or a distributor to take slow-moving, less attractive items in order to acquire the really desirable products.

4. *Exclusive (closed) territories:* Under an exclusive territory arrangement, the manufacturer requires the buyer to sell only to customers who are located within an assigned territory. However, closed sales territories can create area monopolies and restrict trade among competitors who carry the same brand. Exceptions are generally provided when a company is small or is a new entrant to the market, in order to facilitate market entry.

None of these arrangements is automatically illegal. The Competition Act deals with such practices in Part VII, in which certain dealings between manufacturers and intermediaries are deemed illegal if they restrict competition.

Nature and Importance of Physical Distribution

physical distribution

Activities involved in the flow of products as they move physically from producer to consumer or industrial user; used synonymously with *logistics*.

After a company establishes its channels of distribution, it must arrange for the physical distribution of its products through these channels. Physical distribution, a term that we use synonymously with *logistics*, consists of all of the activities concerned with moving the right amount of the right products to the right place at the right time. In its full scope, physical distribution for manufacturers includes the flow of raw materials from their sources of supply to the production line and the movement of finished goods from the end of the production line to the final users' locations. Wholesalers and retailers manage the flow of goods onto their shelves, as well as from their shelves to customers' homes, stores, or other places of business.

The activities making up physical distribution are inventory location and warehousing, materials handling, inventory control, order processing, and transportation. A decision regarding any one of these activities affects all of the others. Location of a warehouse influences the selection of transportation methods and carriers; the choice of a carrier influences the optimum size of shipments.

Systems approach to physical distribution

We have occasionally alluded to marketing as a total system of business action, rather than a fragmented series of operations, but physical-distribution activities are still too often unco-ordinated. Managerial responsibility for it is delegated to various units that often have conflicting, perhaps opposite, goals. The production department, for instance, is interested primarily in long production runs to reduce unit-manufacturing costs, even though the result may be high inventory costs. In contrast, the finance department wants a minimum of funds to be tied up in inventories. At the same time, the sales department wants to have a wide assortment of products available at locations near customers.

Unco-ordinated conditions like these make it impossible to achieve a flow of products that satisfies the firm's goals. To alleviate this problem, firms are establishing separate departments responsible for all logistics activities and taking a total cost approach. The total cost concept is integral to effective supply chain management. A company should determine the set of activities that produces the best relationship between costs and profit for the entire physical-distribution system. This approach is superior to focusing strictly on the separate costs of individual distribution activities.

Strategic use of physical distribution

The strategic use of physical distribution may enable a company to strengthen its competitive position by providing more customer satisfaction and/or by reducing operating costs. The management of physical distribution can also affect a firm's marketing mix, particularly distribution channels. The opportunities that can result from the strategic use of physical distribution are described below.

Improve customer service   A well-run logistics system can improve the service that a firm provides its customers, and the level of customer service directly affects demand. This is true especially in marketing undifferentiated products (such as chemicals and most building materials), when effective service may be a company's only differential advantage. To ensure reliable customer service, management should set standards of performance for each subsystem of physical distribution. These standards should be quantitatively measurable. Some examples:

- Electronics manufacturer: Make delivery within seven days after receiving an order, with no more than 20 percent of the shipment by air.

- Sporting-goods wholesaler: Fill 98 percent of orders accurately without increasing the size of the order-filling staff.

- Industrial distributor: Maintain inventory levels that enable fulfilment of at least 85 percent of orders received from inventory on hand, but maintain a stock turn of 30 days.

Reduce distribution costs   Many avenues to cost reductions may be opened by effective physical-distribution management. For example, eliminating unneeded warehouses will lower costs. Inventories — and their attendant carrying costs and capital investment — may be reduced by consolidating stock at fewer locations.

Create time and location value   Storage is essential to correct imbalances in the timing of production and consumption. An imbalance can occur when there is year-round consumption but only seasonal production, as in the case of agricultural products. In other instances, warehousing helps adjust year-round production to seasonal consumption. Transportation adds value to products by creating location value. A fine suit hanging on a manufacturer's rack in Montréal has less value than an identical suit displayed in a retailer's store in Vancouver. Transporting the suit adds value to it.

Stabilize prices   Careful management of warehousing and transportation can help stabilize prices for an individual firm or for an entire industry. If a market is temporarily glutted with a product, sellers can store it until supply and demand conditions are better balanced.

Influence channel decisions   Decisions regarding inventory management have a direct bearing on a producer's selection of channels. Logistical considerations may become paramount, for example, when a company decides to decentralize its inventory. In this case, management must determine (1) how many sites to establish and (2) whether to use wholesalers, the company's own warehouses, or public warehouses. One producer may select merchant wholesalers that perform storage and other warehousing services. Another may prefer to use a combination of (1) manufacturers' agents to provide aggressive selling and (2) public warehouses to distribute the products ordered.

Control shipping costs Managers with shipping responsibilities need to ensure that their companies enjoy the fastest routes and the lowest rates for whatever mode of transportation they use. The pricing of transportation services is one of the most complicated parts of North American business. The rate, or tariff, schedule is the carrier's price list. Typically, it is complex; to give one example, shipping rates vary for many different types of goods, depending on many factors, including not only the distance to the destination but also the bulk and weight of the products. Therefore, being able to interpret a tariff schedule properly is a money-saving skill for a manager with shipping responsibilities.

Tasks in physical-distribution management

Regardless of whether a firm is part of a logistics alliance or handles this function by itself, effective physical-distribution management is built around five interrelated activities: order processing, inventory control, inventory location and warehousing, materials handling, and transportation.

Order processing The starting point in a physical-distribution system is order processing — a set of procedures for receiving, handling, and filling orders promptly and accurately. This activity should include provisions for billing, granting credit, preparing invoices, and collecting past-due accounts.

There have been various computer-based advances in order processing, notably electronic data interchange (EDI). Under EDI, orders, invoices, and other business information are transmitted by computer network. EDI speeds up the process, reduces paperwork, and allows invoices, payments, and order information to pass instantaneously between manufacturers, suppliers, and retailers. IBM expects all order processing from suppliers to be done electronically; General Motors and Ford demand the same of all of their suppliers.

Inventory control Inventory control, maintaining control over the size and composition of inventories, which represent a sizeable investment for most companies, is essential to any physical-distribution system. The goal of inventory control is to fill customers' orders promptly, completely, and accurately, while minimizing both the investment and fluctuations in inventories.

- *Customer-service requirements:* Inventory size is determined by balancing costs and desired levels of customer service. That is, what percentage of orders does the company expect to fill promptly from inventory on hand? Out-of-stock conditions result in lost sales, loss of goodwill, even loss of customers. Generally speaking, about 80 percent more inventory is required to fill 95 percent of the orders than to fill only 80 percent.

- *Economic order quantity:* Management must establish the optimal quantity for reorder when it is time to replenish inventory stocks. The economic order quantity (EOQ) is the volume at which the sum of inventory carrying costs and order-processing costs are at a minimum. Typically, as order size increases, (1) inventory carrying cost goes up (because the average inventory is larger) and (2) order-processing cost declines (because there are fewer orders).

In Figure 14-7, EOQ represents the order quantity with the lowest total cost. Actually, the order quantity that a firm considers best (or optimal) often is larger than the EOQ. That's because management must try to balance the sometimes-conflicting goals of low inventory costs and responsive customer service. For various reasons, such as gaining a differential advantage, a firm may place a higher priority on customer service than on inventory costs. To completely fill orders in a timely manner may well call for a larger order quantity than the EOQ — for example, quantity X in Figure 14-7.

physical-distribution management
The development and operation of efficient flow systems for products.

order processing
The subsystem of physical-distribution management that consists of the set of procedures for receiving, handling, and filling orders.

electronic data interchange (EDI)
Computer-to-computer transmission of orders, invoices, or other business information.

inventory control
The subsystem of physical-distribution management that involves maintaining control over the size and composition of inventories in order to fill customers' orders promptly, completely, and accurately while minimizing both the investment and fluctuations in inventories.

economic order quantity (EOQ)
The optimal quantity for reorder when replenishing inventory stocks, as indicated by the volume at which the inventory carrying cost plus the order-processing cost are at a minimum.

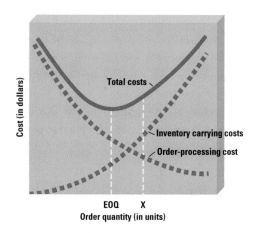

Figure 14-7:

Economic Order Quantity

just-in-time (JIT) inventory control

An inventory-control system that involves buying parts and supplies in small quantities just in time for use in production and then producing in quantities just in time for sale.

market response system

A form of inventory control in which a purchase by a final customer activates a process to produce and deliver a replacement item to inventory.

warehousing

A broad range of physical-distribution activities that include assembling, doing any necessary repacking, storing products, and then preparing them for reshipping.

private warehouse

A warehouse that is owned and operated by the firm whose products are being stored and handled at the facility

Just-in-time: A popular form of inventory control, purchasing, and production scheduling is the **just-in-time (JIT)** concept. The idea of JIT is that you buy in small quantities that arrive just in time for production and then produce in quantities just in time for sale. In Canada and the United States, the JIT philosophy was first adopted in the auto industry, but the concept has been adopted by leading firms in other industries, such as IBM, Xerox, Apple, Black & Decker, and General Electric. For some firms, the results have been quite positive. Xerox eliminated 4,700 suppliers in one year, and Black & Decker cut more than 50 percent of its suppliers in two years.[14] A producer that relies on JIT tends to use fewer suppliers, because they must be close to the producer's facilities and also because there must be strong partnerships with suppliers, which is not feasible with large numbers of suppliers.

An updated version of JIT, labelled JIT II, stresses closer working relationships between manufacturers and suppliers. Under JIT II, a company provides a supplier with sales forecasts and other useful information, some of which may be confidential. In turn, a supplier may place one of its employees at the customer's plant to handle all or part of the purchasing function.[15] This obviously can't be done unless there is a substantial relationship between the two firms, with high levels of trust. Such an arrangement has developed between The Foxboro Company, Dell Computer, and Software House International. Foxboro's purchasing unit has established a strategy for buying personal computers and peripherals that allow the company to cut buying costs, improve process efficiencies, and satisfy internal and external customer requirements.[16]

Market response systems: The focus of JIT inventory control tends to be on production and the relationship between the producer and its suppliers. A parallel trend involves producers or distributors of finished goods and their customers. We refer to this counterpart of JIT as a **market response system**, sometimes called a *quick response system*. The central idea is that a purchase by a final customer, one who intends to consume the product, should activate a process to produce and deliver a replacement item to inventory. In this way, a product is pulled through a channel on the basis of demand rather than being pushed through on the basis of short-term price reductions or other inducements that often result in excessive inventory costs.

The intent of a market response system is similar to that of JIT — to have the right volume of goods to satisfy consumers and to replenish exhausted stocks rapidly. By resulting in better inventory control, a market response system can both reduce stock carrying and operating costs.

Inventory location and warehousing Management must make critical decisions about the size, location, and transporting of inventories. These areas are interrelated in often quite complex ways. The number and location of inventory sites, for example, influence the inventory size and transportation method. One important consideration in managing inventories is **warehousing**, which embraces a range of functions, such as assembling, doing any necessary repacking, storing products, and then preparing them for reshipping.

Types of warehouses: Any producer, wholesaler, or retailer has the option of operating its own **private warehouse** or using the services of a public warehouse. A private warehouse is more likely to be an advantage if (1) a company moves a large volume of products through a warehouse, (2) there is very little, if any, seasonal fluctuation in this flow, and (3) the goods have special handling or storage requirements.

public warehouse
Operated by an independent firm that provides storage and handling facilities.

A **public warehouse** offers storage and handling facilities to individuals or companies. Public warehousing costs are a variable expense. Customers pay only for the space they use, and only when they use it. Public warehouses can also provide office and product display spaces, and accept and fill orders for sellers.

distribution centre
A concept in warehousing that develops under one roof an efficient, fully integrated system for the flow of products, taking orders, filling them, and delivering them to customers.

- **Distribution centres** are planned around markets rather than transportation requirements. The idea is to develop under one roof an efficient, fully integrated system for the flow of products — taking orders, filling them, and preparing them for delivery to customers. IKEA, the Scandinavian furniture retailer, expanded very slowly in Canada and the United States because the company wanted to find locations and facilities that effectively met the needs of its distribution centres. Nintendo of America (**www.nintendo.com**) has a 35,303-square-metre distribution centre that receives products in large sealed containers shipped from Japan and fills orders with a 99.996 percent accuracy rate.

Nintendo of America

materials handling
The subsystem of physical-distribution management that involves selecting and operating the equipment and warehouse building used in physically handling products.

Materials handling   Selecting the proper equipment to physically handle products, including the warehouse building itself, is the **materials-handling** subsystem of physical-distribution management. Equipment that is well matched to the task can minimize losses from breakage, spoilage, and theft. Efficient equipment can reduce handling costs as well as the time required for handling.

Modern warehouses are often huge, one-storey structures located in outlying areas, where land is less expensive and loading platforms are easily accessed by trucks and trains. Conveyor belts, forklift trucks, and other mechanized equipment are used to move merchandise. In some warehouses, the order fillers are even outfitted with in-line skates!

Online grocers use different methods to deliver goods. Toronto area-based Grocery Gateway takes orders for all major brand goods and uses its more than 140 trucks to deliver from its 26,012-square-metre warehouse with three climate-controlled areas (freezer, refrigerator, room temperature), but has JIT arrangements with supermarkets for fresh produce. In the United States, San Francisco-based Webvan Group, now defunct, invested $35 million to set up a distribution network in the San Francisco Bay area, including 120 delivery vans and 170 drivers. Processing some 2,000 orders a day, the company set up a "hub and spokes" delivery system of delivery routes; the system was too expensive, given the sales volume generated.[17]

containerization
A cargo-handling system in which shipments of products are enclosed in large metal or wooden containers that are then transported unopened from the time they leave the customer's facilities until they reach their destination.

- **Containerization** is a cargo-handling system that has become standard practice in physical distribution. Shipments of products are enclosed in large metal or wooden containers. The containers are then transported unopened from the time they leave the customer's facilities (such as a manufacturer's plant) until they reach their destination (such as a wholesaler's warehouse). Containerization minimizes physical handling, thereby reducing damage, lessening the risk of theft, and allowing for more efficient transportation.

transportation
The function of shipping products to customers.

Transportation   A major function of the physical-distribution system in many companies is **transportation** — shipping products to customers. Management must decide on both the **mode of transportation** and the particular carriers.

mode of transportation
The manner in which the movement of goods is carried out; leading modes of transportation are railroads, trucks, ships, and airplanes.

- ***Major modes:*** Railways, trucks, ships, and airplanes are the leading modes of transportation. In Table 14-6, these four methods are compared on the basis of criteria likely to be used by physical-distribution managers in selecting a mode of transportation.

TABLE 14-6 Comparison of Transportation Methods

Selection Criteria	Transportation Method			
	Rail	Water	Highway	Air
Speed (door-to-door time)	Medium	Slowest	Fast	Fastest
Cost of transportation	Medium	Lowest	High	Highest
Reliability in meeting delivery schedules	Medium	Poor	Good	Good
Variety of products carried	Widest	Widest	Medium	Somewhat limited
Number of geographic locations served	Very many	Limited	Unlimited	Many
Most suitable products	Long hauls of carload quantities of bulky products, when freight costs are high in relation to product's value	Bulky, low-value non-perishables	Short hauls of high-value goods	High-value perishables, where speed of delivery is all-important

intermodal transportation
When a mode of transportation is so configured that it can be used to move freight by another mode or modes in order to save on loading and unloading costs, as well as time taken in transit.

piggyback service
Transporting loaded truck trailers on railroad flatcars.

fishyback service
Transporting loaded trailers on barges or ships.

freight forwarder
A specialized transportation agency that consolidates less-than-carload or less-than-truckload shipments into carload or truckload quantities and provides door-to-door shipping service.

● *Intermodal transportation:* When two or more modes of transportation are used to move freight, this is called **intermodal transportation**. The intent of intermodal transportation is to take advantage of multiple forms of transportation.

One type of intermodal transportation involves trucks and railways: Called **piggyback service**, it involves carrying truck trailers on railroad flatcars. This type of intermodal transportation provides (1) more flexibility than railroads alone can offer, (2) lower freight costs than trucks alone, and (3) less handling of goods. **Fishyback service** transports loaded trailers on barges or ships. The trailers may be carried piggyback-fashion by railroad to the dock, where they are transferred to the ship. Then, at the other end of the water trip, the trailers are loaded back onto trains for completion of the haul.

● *Freight forwarders:* A specialized marketing institution serving firms that ship in less-than-carload quantities is called a **freight forwarder**. Its main function is to consolidate less-than-carload or less-than-truckload shipments from several shippers into carload and truckload quantities. The freight forwarder picks up the merchandise at the shipper's place of business and arranges for delivery at the buyer's door. A small shipper benefits from the speed and minimum handling associated with large shipments. A freight forwarder also provides the small shipper with traffic-management services, such as selecting the best transportation methods and routes.

● *Package-delivery firms:* Companies that deliver small shipments of packages and high-priority mail, such as United Parcel Service (UPS), Federal Express (FedEx), and Loomis, compete directly with Canada Post. These commercial package-delivery giants attempt to position themselves more favourably than their competition by trying to surpass each other in relation to delivery times, technology that allows customers to prepare and track their shipments, and — of course — low prices.[18]

In many respects, these companies offer the same services as freight forwarders. However, whereas the typical freight forwarder does not have its own transportation equipment, package-delivery firms do. Companies such as UPS and FedEx essentially are integrated as cargo airlines and trucking companies. Furthermore, package-delivery firms, in effect, use intermodal transportation. Consider FedEx, for example: A package is picked up by truck, shipped intercity or overseas by plane, and delivered locally by truck.

The Changing Face of Distribution

Largely as a result of advancing technology and the changing balance of power within distribution channels, we are witnessing a change in the nature of distribution and in the means by which products and services reach the end-consumer.

Shopping from home is expected to be a growth area in retailing in the future, as systems become more sophisticated and as catalogue companies and other direct retailers become even better at serving their customers. We will see much more use of the Internet and a host of personal wireless appliances that can be used to connect with retailers, as well as others, from anywhere.

Distribution involves the movement of more than just the physical product. Many costs are involved in the administrative function of distribution. The Internet has had an impact on various marketing functions. While very few products can physically be distributed through this medium (some entertainment exceptions excluded, of course, plus downloadable products) most firms have found ways to aid distribution through the Internet if only for its promotional value. There are real costs, however, to be saved through this medium. Transaction costs have three parts, which individually or together can be quite prohibitive. These are:

- *Search costs:* Finding what you need takes time, resources, and out-of-pocket costs. Determining whether to trust a supplier adds more costs.

- *Contracting costs:* Every exchange requires a separate price negotiation and contract. Such processes can be expensive to arrange and formalize.

- *Co-ordination costs:* These are the costs of co-ordinating resources and processes.

More and more of these searching and acquisition activities are taking place in cyberspace markets, with examples of savings in the online market appearing daily as manufacturers in all industries post their requirements on the Web. Ford and General Motors have developed parts-supply marketplaces for their requirements, while three of the top five computer manufacturers have announced plans to join with nine suppliers to create a similar marketplace for that industry.[19]

BACKSPACE

1. In distribution, what is the difference between horizontal conflict and vertical conflict?
2. What are four methods used by suppliers when they want to exercise control?
3. What is meant by *physical distribution*?

Summary

Wholesaling consists of the sale, and all activities directly related to the sale, of goods and services for resale, use in producing other goods or services, or operating an organization. Firms engaged primarily in wholesaling, called *wholesaling intermediaries*, provide economies of skill, scale, and transaction to other firms involved in distribution.

Three categories of wholesaling intermediaries are merchant wholesalers, agent wholesaling intermediaries, and manufacturers' sales facilities. The first two are independent firms; a manufacturer owns the third. Merchant wholesalers offer the widest range of services and thus incur the highest operating expenses. The main types of agent wholesalers are manufacturers' agents and brokers. Because they perform more limited services, agent wholesalers' expenses tend to be lower than those of merchant wholesalers.

A distribution channel includes producer, final customer, and the wholesalers and retailers that participate in the process. Designing a channel of distribution for a product occurs through a sequence of four decisions: (1) delineating the role of distribution within the marketing mix; (2) selecting the proper type of distribution channel; (3) determining the appropriate intensity of distribution; and (4) choosing specific channel members. Because of deficiencies in conventional channels, vertical marketing systems — corporate, contractual, and administered — have grown into major forces.

Numerous factors need to be considered prior to selecting a distribution channel for a product. The primary consideration is the nature of the target market; other considerations relate to the product, the wholesalers and retailers, and the company itself.

Distribution intensity refers to the number of intermediaries used at the wholesale and retail levels in a particular territory. It ranges from intensive to selective to exclusive.

Devising distribution channels for international markets requires an examination of the same considerations that are necessary for distribution in Canadian markets.

Firms distributing goods and services sometimes clash. There are two types of conflict: horizontal (between firms at the same level of distribution) and vertical (between firms at different levels of the same channel). Vertical conflict typically pits producer against wholesaler or retailer. Manufacturers' attempts to bypass intermediaries are a prime cause of vertical conflict. All parties may be served best by viewing channels as a system requiring co-ordination of distribution activities.

Physical distribution is the flow of products from supply sources to the firm and then from the firm to its customers. The total cost concept should be applied to physical distribution but with a balance between customer service and total cost.

The operation of a physical-distribution system requires management's attention and decision-making in five areas: (1) inventory location and warehousing, (2) materials handling, (3) inventory control, (4) order processing, and (5) transportation. These should not be treated as individual activities but as interrelated components within a physical-distribution system.

Key Terms and Concepts

Questions and Problems

1. Which of the following institutions are intermediaries? Explain.
   a. Avon salesperson.
   b. Electrical wholesaler.
   c. Real estate broker.
   d. Railroad.
   e. Auctioneer.
   f. Advertising agency.
   g. Grocery store.
   h. Stockbroker.
   i. Bank.
   j. Radio station.

2. "The great majority of business sales are made directly from producer to business user." Explain the reason for this, first in relation to the nature of the market and then in relation to the product.

3. Is a policy of intensive distribution consistent with consumer buying habits for convenience goods? For shopping goods? Is intensive distribution normally used in the marketing of any type of business goods?

4. From a producer's viewpoint, what are the competitive advantages of exclusive distribution?

5. What are the drawbacks to exclusive distribution from a retailer's point of view? To what extent are these alleviated if the retailer controls the channel for the particular brand?

6. What role is the Internet playing in changing distribution networks? Provide examples to illustrate the changes that are occurring.

7. Which of the following are wholesaling transactions?
   a. Colour Tile sells wallpaper to an apartment building contractor and also to the contractor's family for its home.
   b. General Electric sells motors to Whirlpool for its washing machines.
   c. A fish "farmer" sells fish to a local restaurant.
   d. A family orders carpet from a friend, who is a home decorating consultant, at 50 percent off the suggested retail price. The carpet is delivered directly to the home.
   e. Weber Supply sells nails to Home Hardware.
   f. A local bakery delivers goods to Sobeys.

8. Which type of wholesaling intermediary, if any, is most likely to be used by each of the following firms? Explain your choice in each instance.
   a. A small manufacturer of a liquid glass cleaner to be sold through supermarkets.
   b. A small canner in Nova Scotia that packs a high-quality, unbranded fruit product.
   c. A small-tools manufacturing firm that has its own sales force selling to the business market and now wants to add backyard barbecue equipment to its product mix.
   d. A Québec textile mill producing unbranded towels, sheets, pillowcases, and blankets.
   e. A virtual bookstore that has no existing physical infrastructure other than its call centre for receiving orders.
   f. A software e-tailer that features only downloadable products.

9. Looking to the future, which types of intermediaries do you think will increase in importance and which ones will decline? What continuing impact, if any, will Internet technology have on the role of intermediaries in distribution? Explain.

10. Name some products for which you think the cost of physical distribution constitutes at least one-half of the total price of the goods at the wholesale level. Can you suggest ways of decreasing the physical-distribution cost of these products?

Hands-On Marketing

1. A manufacturer of precision lenses used in medical and hospital equipment wants to ship a 5-kg box of these lenses from your town to a laboratory in Stockholm, Sweden. The lab wants delivery in five days or less. The manufacturer wants to use a package-delivery service but is undecided as to which shipper to choose. Compile and compare the types of services provided and prices charged by Federal Express, United Parcel Service, and one other package-delivery firm.

2. Arrange an interview with either the owner or a top-level manager of a small manufacturing firm. Inquire about (a) what distribution channel(s) the company uses for its primary product, (b) what factors were the greatest influences in choosing the channel(s), and (c) whether the company would prefer some other channel(s).

Back to the Top

Why is distribution so important to Apple Computer and to other manufacturers of technology products? Think about the chapter opener and the efforts that Apple has made to have its products conveniently available for Canadian con-sumers. Think also about the completely different distribution strategies used by Dell and Gateway computer companies. Why do both approaches seem to work?

Want to get better grades, tips on how to study more effectively, and up-to-date information on happenings in the world of marketing? Then, visit the Online Learning Centre for practice tests, Study Smart software, and much more! **www.mcgrawhill.ca/college/sommers**

Interested in finding out what marketing looks like in the real world? *Marketing Magazine* is just a click away on your Online Learning Centre!

Case 5-1

Clodhoppers

Sugar High

Chris and Larry were sitting in their Winnipeg office discussing the successful company they had built. The two high school friends had been in business together for six years and wondered what they would do next. They already supplied major retailers, but now they were wondering where else they could sell their product. They wanted to increase their sales volume and felt that the only way they could do it was to build relationships with more retailers. They had grown a lot, but they were still looking to increase their revenue and thought that their distribution would play a key role.

In 1995, Chris Emery and Larry Finnson were just two guys from Winnipeg tossing around a business idea. They had a delicious product: Chris's grandmother's vanilla fudge-graham wafer-chopped cashew clusters, which they called Clodhoppers. They knew the candy would sell, but they had a lot of decisions to make and a lot of questions remained unanswered. Where would they get start-up capital? Where would they produce their Clodhoppers candy? How would they package it? Who would sell it for them?

Within a year, their company, Krave's Candy Co., was up and running. Chris and Larry had a 65-square-metre warehouse in which they produced some 25 kilograms of candy per hour. But if their candy was going to compete with large successful candy companies like Hershey, Nestlé, and Cadbury, Chris and Larry were going to have to convince large retailers like Wal-Mart, Zellers, and Shoppers Drug Mart to sell their product.

The first thing the two Winnipegers did to become more competitive was to change the packaging of their Clodhoppers. Chris and Larry went from a fancy black-and-gold box to a box with a picture of their faces and the slogan "highly addictive." They even introduced a 225-gram metallic bag and a snack-size bag. They also added chocolate fudge and a peanut butter Clodhoppers. Their aim was to move away from being a seasonal specialty item to become a snack that consumers would eat regularly. Now that they had changed the positioning of their product, they wanted to get it out there. First, they had to find the right retailers.

They decided their snack-size package would be perfect for convenience stores. Mac's and Circle K seemed perfect. But what about the bigger bag and the small box? Chris and Larry had their sights set on Wal-Mart — a deal with the huge retailer would raise awareness of their brand and get the volume of sales they needed to make money and pay off their large initial investment. As luck would have it, Chris and Larry met the president and CEO of Wal-Mart's U.S. operation at a trade show in Toronto. They were invited to Wal-Mart's Arkansas headquarters to strike a deal. That was their big break: Clodhoppers now sells in all 2,765 Wal-Marts. In addition, they also supply their delicious candy to Shopper's Drug Mart, Safeway, Zellers, and Loblaws. Even Dairy Queen makes a Clodhoppers Blizzard from the chocolate fudge version of the candy.

In 2002, the business was very successful: They expected to make $6 million — not bad for a company that started with sales of $57,000. Chris and Larry have a great product and good relationships with major retailers. Distribution has played an important part in their success. No matter how delicious their candy, Chris and Larry could not have grown without large retailers to sell their product.

Pertinent Web Sites

www.kraves.com
www.clodhoppers.tv/kraveskit.pdf

Questions

1. What would have happened to the company if Chris and Larry had been unable to find nationwide retailers?

2. What should they look for when they search for new distributors/retailers?

Video source: CBC *Venture*, "Sugar High," December 7, 1999.

Case 5-2

Salvation Army Thrift Stores

It's Chic to Be Cheap!

The Salvation Army's goal is to help the needy, but that doesn't stop those who aren't needy from shopping at its Thrift Stores! People of all ages and socio-economic levels now shop there and at other used-clothing stores. It's become chic to be cheap and the trend has spread quickly. As Canadians become more value-conscious, they refuse to pay exorbitant prices for clothing they can find elsewhere at much lower prices. But this doesn't mean that they will settle for low quality. Consumers want to pay less but still expect a certain level of quality — there's a new generation of Canadians that's demanding more bang for its bucks. So far, they've managed to find quite a lot of bang at the Salvation Army Thrift Stores.

The popularity of used-clothing stores has been driven by more than just cheap prices. In recent years, retro styles and vintage clothing have become trendy, bringing new prestige to bargain hunting and used clothing — or, as it is often referred to today, pre-owned, previously loved, gently used, or second-time-around items. It is not uncommon to hear someone bragging about how little he paid for a really cool pair of pants or how she can't believe how lucky she was to have found such a funky shirt. The best part about used-clothing stores: You don't have to worry about showing up at a party and finding someone else wearing the same shirt!

The Salvation Army has become too popular, causing it to lose its status as a tax-exempt registered charity and it is now considered a profit-making business. The Thrift Stores attract so many Canadians that they actually present a threat to other retailers such as Le Château, whose clothing tends to be retro and funky. But why would you pay $80 for hip-huggers when you can get the real thing at a Thrift Store? This may explain why the Salvation Army is now one of the fastest-growing retailers in Canada!

Salvation Army Thrift Stores were once viewed as being drab, and didn't really try to compete with other retailers. Donations of clothing and other items were revitalized and presented as attractively as possible, with the hope that these items would meet the needs of the less-advantaged who would buy the clothes at low prices. But as Canadians flock to these stores in record numbers, the whole feel of the store has changed. Now, one finds teenagers and young adults sorting through racks in search of a good find — as they say, one person's junk is another's treasure. And a low price increases the value of the treasure, making it more difficult for traditional clothing retailers to sell retro clothes at steep prices.

Pertinent Web Site

www.salvationarmy.ca

Questions

1. Do Le Château and the Salvation Army appeal to the same target market? Why or why not?

2. What factors (social, psychological, etc.) other than price influence a consumer's decision to buy at the Salvation Army Thrift Stores and other types of second-hand clothing stores?

Source: This case was prepared by Natalie Slawinski, with content from the original case written by Peter A. Dunne and published in the ninth edition of this textbook.

Case 5-3

CBC

Grocery Gateway

Redefining "Bricks and Clicks"

Grocery Gateway Inc. has been successful in a market that has seen so many others fail. As an online grocer, Grocery Gateway has certainly faced an uphill battle but has managed so far to overcome many obstacles. The biggest challenge has been working out the logistics of its business: how to get an Internet order off the shelves of its warehouse, into bags, then into a truck, then into a building, and finally into the customer's kitchen without breaking anything, without making a mistake with the order, without the ice cream melting, without the milk going sour.... Essentially, this is a logistical nightmare — if any one of those things goes wrong, you've got an unhappy customer who won't order from you again. In this business, you must be quick, efficient, accurate, and consistent.

Why has Grocery Gateway succeeded when so many other e-commerce merchants have failed? Why is the company thriving in an environment where, despite predictions of an e-revolution, dot-coms have fared poorly? Many thought that e-commerce would take off and revolutionize the way business is done. Instead, the outcome has been disappointing. Many dot-coms invested huge sums in start-up capital, only to achieve less-than-satisfactory returns. Quite a few have gone bankrupt. With these poor odds, investors have become more impatient. In this bleak environment, Grocery Gateway has done well, thanks largely to its philosophy that the only way to measure progress is whether a service or product simplifies people's lives. If it can't use technology to make people's lives simpler, the company knows it won't be in business long. That's why it prides itself on its simple, user-friendly Web site, where customers go down the aisles, view items, and create personal shopping lists. The site even has a "Meal Planner" that allows customers to purchase all of the ingredients for a recipe at the click of a mouse. Service is personalized to cater to shoppers' individual needs. Costs are totalled as items are added to the virtual shopping cart. It really is shopping made easy!

Many Canadians have hectic lives and certainly value this kind of service. Grocery Gateway's value proposition is that the service saves time, something many people are short of these days. The company does not compete on the basis of price, even though its prices are similar to those of supermarkets. At present, Grocery Gateway serves the Greater Toronto Area. It does not want to repeat the mistake made by some U.S. online grocers who expanded too quickly and went broke or had to merge. Before they even consider expanding to other parts of Canada, Grocery Gateway wants to prove to investors that providing groceries online is lucrative. To do this, the company has had to be very efficient and had achieved near-capacity in its warehouse within months of its opening.

Grocery Gateway's management team members understand the business they're in, the business of logistics. They know that the groceries they sell must be good, but that's a given. What will make or break them is the logistics of getting the groceries to the customer quickly and with no mistakes. To help, the company has warehouse-management software that groups the orders and puts them through to various radio-frequency-tracked order pickers. Then, route-management software allocates the orders to different trucks and decides which trucks go where. Only with this level of sophisticated technology is Grocery Gateway able to get a handle on its complicated logistics. Its highly automated warehousing, picking, and distribution system has made the online grocer a feasible business.

So far, Grocery Gateway has managed to get delivery time down to 90 minutes or less. About 95 per cent of orders are satisfactory. But that's not good enough, says CEO Bill Di Nardo. In the online grocery business, they need to get the orders right 99.9 percent of the time. And still, that's not enough to satisfy customers. Employees delivering the groceries have to be helpful, friendly, and courteous, in addition to being fast and efficient. They must take their shoes off at customers' doors and even load the pantry shelves when customers can't do it themselves. Every part of the experience must be great to keep customers shopping online. Grocery Gateway knows that it can be successful only if it builds a loyal customer base. As the company wins over whole neighbourhoods, it will be easier for it to deliver groceries faster and more efficiently. And with its fleet of more than 140 trucks, delivery time has continued to fall.

Grocery Gateway believes it has the key to e-commerce success: Di Nardo feels that e-businesses have failed largely because they have not understood the value proposition. Logistics is key to the success of online retailers. Grocery Gateway isn't the only grocer offering online service — Canadian grocery chains have been dabbling in online selling, but they have done this mostly to gauge the threat of newcomers like Grocery Gateway. These traditional supermarkets' businesses remain in the realm of bricks and mortar. They cannot compete with Grocery Gateway, a company that has remained focused on its core competencies. And as its CEO explains, if the company can handle the complicated logistics of low-margin groceries, it can certainly handle books, CDs, etc. In fact, Grocery Gateway is now delivering wine, beer, books, videos, hardware, and toys, and it will continue to expand its product offering.

Grocery Gateway is not only Toronto's leading online grocer but it has also become the largest consumer-direct online company in Canada. The company has succeeded in making online grocery shopping a pleasant experience that simplifies customers' lives. The online grocer may never capture a huge market share or put traditional supermarkets out of business, but as long as it understands its customers and continues to deliver on its value proposition of fast, accurate delivery, it will thrive in the $59-billion grocery industry. Not only is Grocery Gateway reinventing the grocery business, but its success may even pave the way for other e-businesses.

Pertinent Web Sites

www.grocerygateway.com
www.grogate.com

Questions

1. What challenges do online grocery stores face?

2. Why has e-commerce failed to live up to expectations?

3. What does Grocery Gateway offer that traditional grocery stores can't?

4. How has Grocery Gateway positioned itself relative to the competition operating in traditional stores? Illustrate this through the use of a positioning map.

Source: Rajiv Sekhri, "Grocery Gateway unscathed as online grocers succumb," *The Industry Standard*, August 23, 2001.

Video source: CBC *Venture*, "Grocery.com," October 3, 2000.

PART 6

Pricing

The determination of the price for a product or service and its connection to the creation of value

By turning our attention to price in Chapter 15, we complete our tour of the traditional marketing mix. Having already addressed product, communications, and distribution, we turn now to pricing, where we face two tasks. First, we must understand the role of price as seen by the customer and appreciate its role as a tool to communicate value. Then, we must turn our attention to the task of setting price and implementing pricing strategies.

CHAPTER 15

Price and Value

In this chapter, we address the importance of price in the marketing of products and services — what price is, how it functions as a marketing tool, and how it is set. After studying this chapter, you should have an understanding of:

- How consumers think about price and the messages price can communicate.
- What makes up the price we pay for goods and services.
- The concept of value and how it relates to price.
- Pricing objectives and goals.
- Factors influencing how a price is set.
- The types of costs incurred in producing and marketing a product.
- Approaches to pricing and the role of break-even analysis.

The Price of Friendship

It's the last week of August and Air Canada has just announced a seat sale covering travel during the next three months. Great timing! You have been planning to spend a long weekend this fall visiting your friend Pat, who's returning to McGill for her second-year commerce course. The Air Canada ad in the Halifax *Chronicle-Herald* indicates a price of $159 each way, from Halifax to Montréal and return. Although you haven't flown a lot, this strikes you as a pretty good price.

The Air Canada Web site offers a number of possible flights between Halifax and Montréal. You select a flight leaving at 5 p.m. on November 7, which would allow you to attend your accounting class at 1 p.m. You would return on a flight leaving at 6:20 p.m. on November 12, getting you back to Halifax in time to get ready for your favourite course, marketing, at 9 a.m. on the 13th. The fare is, indeed, $318, but you are surprised at the additional taxes, surcharges, security charge, and airport improvement fee, which when added to the basic fare, bring the total for your ticket to $467.39. The ticket is non-refundable. The Web site says you have to book before September 1, so you decide to check other airlines.

Air Canada's regional airline Tango has flights available on those days, leaving Halifax at 6:40 p.m. on November 7, returning at 7:55 p.m. on the 12th. The total fare on Tango is $323.64. CanJet's Web site offers a special Web fare of $84 each way, but the taxes and other charges bring the total to $294.89. In addition, you'd have to leave Halifax at 1:20 p.m. on November 7 (missing your accounting class) and leave Montréal at 2:35 on the 12th, cutting short your visit with Pat. A new entrant into Canadian skies, Jetsgo, offers a total return fare to Montréal of $398.39, but you would have to travel to Montréal and back via Toronto. While you could leave Halifax at 3:45 p.m. on the 7th, you would have to leave Montréal at 9:30 a.m. on the 12th, not getting back to Halifax until 2:55 p.m.

You are confused. Which airline should you use? Maybe Pat can come back to Halifax to see you. Maybe you can convince your parents to send you to Montréal on their frequent-flyer points.

This chapter may help to make sense of the often-confusing world of pricing. The quandaries involved in selecting an airline to visit a friend are not at all untypical, and the confusing array of airline prices found is equally common. So, what *does* it cost to fly to Montréal from Halifax? The answer, of course, is that there is no single price. What an airline charges and what a customer is prepared to pay depend on many factors. How badly do you want to see Pat? How important are the arrival and departure times? What is your impression of each of the airlines involved? Had you decided on the Air Canada seat-sale option, you may have found yourself seated next to a businessperson on the return flight who is going to Halifax for a business meeting and then back to Montréal. She is paying a fare of $1,249.66. What additional value is she getting for that price? We will address questions such as these in this chapter.

Deciding How Much to Charge

The issue of how much a company or organization should charge for its products and services involves many factors. As the chapter opener shows, the value that consumers perceive in a product or service is always a factor influencing the price that can be charged. And costs are always present and must be paid. As a result of technological advances and increased competition, lower costs generally will lead to lower prices. There are, of course, many other factors that must be taken into consideration, including the target segment for the product or service, the image and market positioning desired, and the prices being charged by competitors. These factors must be taken into account when a company introduces a new product or service or considers changing the price of an existing one. Pricing is about much more than how much a firm can get from the consumer — it should be all about delivering value for money. Price is the most important and universally accepted indicator of value — price is used by consumers as a tool to reflect value.

In this chapter, we will discuss methods used by companies and other organizations to determine prices. Before being concerned with actual price setting, however, managers — and you — should understand the meaning and importance of price.

The Meaning of Price

price
The amount of money and/or other resources needed to acquire some combination of a product and its accompanying services.

Some pricing difficulties occur because of confusion about the meaning of **price**, even though the concept is easy to define in familiar terms. Simply, price is the amount of money and/or other resources that are needed to acquire a product.

Generally, we tend to think of price in strictly monetary terms: A sweater costs $100, a movie ticket costs $10. But how much does a trip to a doctor's office cost? Because of our health-care system, very few of us have any idea what a visit to a doctor costs because we don't pay for it, at least not directly. It may be useful to think of price as what it costs us to acquire something, whether that something is a tangible product or service. But, price is only part of what it costs the customer.

What it costs to acquire that sweater is more than $100. It involves shopping time and effort and it may involve other non-monetary considerations, such as having to find a parking space, or arranging public transit, or having to visit several stores to find the size and other features you need. Viewing price as a monetary factor oversimplifies the buying process. When customers decide whether they are satisfied with a sweater or with a meal at a restaurant, they implicitly think about the value received. As a result, we often hear customers say, "I'll never go back there. It's just not worth the _____." They may fill the blank with "money," but it's just as likely that they'll include words like "time," "hassle," or "aggravation."

value of a product/service
The ratio of perceived benefits of a product/service to perceived costs, including price and other incurred costs.

Therefore, we need to consider the **value of a product** or service when we talk about price. A marketer who is interested in creating customer satisfaction will focus on creating value for the customer. There are many ways to create or add value, only one of which is to reduce price. But, because our economy utilizes money as the medium of exchange, we tend to state prices in monetary terms. As you read this chapter, however, it may be useful to think of the effect that price has in communicating value to customers.

Price is the most important way that marketers have of communicating value. It is an indicator to consumers of what a product or service is "worth." On seeing the price, the consumer must decide whether the product or service is worth it. A great deal of psychology is at work, as the consumer often makes an immediate and subconscious decision whether or not to buy. Some, on hearing a price, will respond with comments like "I'd never pay that kind of money for that," or "There's no way that's worth it." But, there are also circumstances in which customers are prepared to pay much higher prices for what would appear to be very similar if not identical products and services.

Price, therefore, must be set in the context of what the customer is seen to be getting in return. It also must be viewed in light of what else the customer is expected to commit to its purchase. Customers will generally expect to pay less if they have to take the table home from IKEA and assemble it themselves. They will similarly expect to pay more for a table from another retailer that is fully assembled and delivered. Customers are generally prepared to pay more for products and services that are made available conveniently and with high levels of support services. Despite the opinion of many managers that customers are always looking for lower prices, many are often heard to comment that they would be prepared to pay *higher* prices "If the company would only _____."

Practical problems also arise when we try to state simply the price of a product or service. In our chapter opener, Air Canada announced that its seat-sale price to Montréal was $318, but the total price is $467.39. Most customers would not stop to think that, for the total price, they are also getting dependable air traffic control services, buying enhanced airport security, contributing to the general revenues of federal and provincial governments through the sales tax, and helping to pay for the recent renovations and improvements at the Halifax International Airport. So, you are buying more than a trip to Montréal. The trip is simply the core product.

This example indicates that the definition of price depends on determining exactly what is being purchased. A seller usually is pricing a combination of (1) the specific core product or service that is the object of the transaction, (2) several supplementary services (such as a warranty), and (3) in a very real sense, the need- or want-satisfying benefits provided by the

Price Is What You Pay for What You Get

Here are prices under various names:

- Tuition → Education.
- Interest → Use of money.
- Rent → Use of living quarters or a piece of equipment for a period of time.
- Fare → Taxi ride or airline flight.
- Fee → Services of an accountant or lawyer.
- Retainer → Lawyer's or consultant's services over a period of time.
- Toll → Long-distance phone call or travel on some highways.
- Salary → Services of an executive or other white-collar employee.
- Wage → Services of a blue-collar employee.
- Commission → Salesperson's services.
- Dues → Membership in a union or a club.

And in socially undesirable situations, there are prices called blackmail, ransom, or bribery.

SOURCE: Suggested in part by John T. Mentzer and David J. Schwartz, *Marketing Today*, 4th ed. (San Diego: Harcourt Brace Jovanovich, 1985), p. 599.

product. Sometimes it is difficult to define even the price of the core product or service itself. On one model of automobile, a stated price may include radio, power steering, and power brakes. For another model of the same brand, these three items may be priced separately. So, to know the real price of a product, you need to look at the identifiable components that make up that product.

The price paid, therefore, will depend on various factors: the amount of planning that has gone into the purchase, how badly the customer needs the product, and how much the customer is prepared to put into the purchase — how much it is valued. If a businessperson absolutely has to attend a meeting in Halifax on short notice, she may indeed be prepared to pay a higher price. In other circumstances, business travel is booked ahead of time, even though uncertainty exists at the time about whether the trip will need to be taken. For this reason, Scandinavian airline SAS is able to charge business travellers higher fares, even though they no longer receive upgraded in-flight service. The curtain separating business and economy travellers has disappeared on SAS, but business travellers can change tickets once they're booked and travel on more flexible terms than holiday travellers can.[1]

If you absolutely have to have your favourite group's new CD right away, you'll pay more for the instant gratification, even though you could have obtained it more cheaply on the Internet. It's not that much different than deciding to send your film away for processing or zipping out to the mall for one-hour processing. It all depends on how the customer defines the value associated with the purchase.

MARKETING AT WORK 15-1: STRATEGY

What Do You Give the Customer Who Has Everything?

"Let me tell you about the very rich," said F. Scott Fitzgerald. "They are different from you and me."

When it comes to the well-heeled, brand loyalty and purchasing intentions are usually motivated more by recognition, exclusivity, and excellent customer service than by the low interest rates or gifts-with-purchases that start the pulse racing for us ordinary folk. While young international travellers may be interested in airline points for their next vacation, affluent, more seasoned executives want ease of processing at airports and perks that cater to their comfort and convenience. Hence, there

are two types of airport lounges for those with first-class tickets: lounges for Silver members — the occasional first-class travellers — and lounges for the jet-set Gold members, which are equipped like luxury hotels with mini-gyms, showers, and spas.

As with all demographics, though, it's a mistake to believe that the motivation of every upper-income consumer is the same. The best approach for a marketer is to use personal information to create personalized incentives.

One example of matching incentives to the target demographic is that used by BMW Canada. The company doesn't do a lot of promotions, but has had huge success with one idea that fits well with the performance demands of its typical patron. It combines a compelling offer with brand and loyalty-building, according to Tony Chapman, president of Toronto-based Capital C Communications, who believes the best incentives for the moneyed set provide recipients with a sense of prestige and exclusivity.

"When you buy a BMW 5-Series car, you get a day in the BMW Driver Training Program. It's a nice tie-in to the brand — performance car, performance driving — and it probably costs a lot less than the $2,500 rebates Chrysler is giving away," says Chapman. "It allows the customer to get a benefit, an incentive that's not financial. They take part in a day of training and get to appreciate and understand their vehicle much better."

SOURCE: Adapted from Patti Summerfield, "What Do You Give the Customer Who Has Everything?" *Strategy*, October 22, 2002, p. B13.

It may be useful to view price in the context of an equation. If customers feel that what they have obtained for what they paid is somewhat in balance, there will be satisfaction with the price. The consumer will feel that what was obtained was "worth it." If there is an imbalance, however, the customer will either be delighted at having obtained a real deal or bitterly disappointed at having paid too much. When customers conclude that something isn't worth it, the price is not necessarily being questioned. What is being questioned is the value that is being offered for the price charged. Therefore, marketers should pay more attention to making the value proposition as attractive as possible, rather than concentrating always on bringing prices down.

Importance of Price

Price is significant to an individual firm and in the minds of consumers. It is a very obvious component of a marketing program that determines whether a firm's offer is acceptable to the customer. Price epitomizes and makes tangible the notion of value that lies at the heart of the exchange process. Let's consider just how important price is for both customers and companies.

In the consumer's mind

price sensitivity
Extent to which the market or a certain segment of it will respond to price changes or is focused on price when buying.

At the retail level, a small segment of customers is interested primarily in low prices — they have a high level of price sensitivity. Another segment may be indifferent about price in making purchases. The majority of consumers are somewhat sensitive about price but are also concerned with other factors such as brand image, the nature of the shopping situation, store location, convenience, quality, and, ultimately, value. Consumers who utilize the Internet to comparison-shop and research prices are often much more price-sensitive about some goods because they can compare prices very easily — others are not as price-sensitive. Consumers' relative interest in price also can vary across demographic groups. Consumers with large families, single parents, and those on low incomes and/or fixed incomes are likely to be much more price-sensitive. But even customers in these situations will, on occasion, be prepared to pay more to get what they consider to be better value. Further, even those with generous resources at their disposal may still seek value for their money, cautiously assessing benefits and features versus price before purchasing.

Economic conditions may dictate for some consumers that they focus mainly on low prices, but in today's increasingly hectic environment, other costs beyond the price, as previously discussed, are figuring into the calculation of these costs. We could think of this as cost-sensitivity, using *cost* in the broadest sense of that term. And, as already stated, there will always be those who are not looking primarily for the lowest price. In the purchase of many routine products and services, the greatest cost to some consumers is the time required in an already hectic schedule and the mental effort involved. Time and psychological effort may be more expensive than money, so these consumers will pay extra for convenience, expediency, or just to get exactly what they want.

quality
The characteristics of a product or service in relation to the expectations of the customer.

Another consideration is that some consumers' perceptions of product and service quality vary directly with price. Typically, the higher the price, the better the quality is perceived to be. Have you ever questioned product quality — when you're looking at ads for DVD players or stereo equipment, for example — when the price shown was unexpectedly low? Or, at the other extreme, have you ever selected a restaurant for a special dinner because you heard it was fairly expensive, assuming this meant it would be very nice? Consumers' perceptions of quality are, of course, influenced by other factors, such as store reputation, product colour or texture, advertising, or the nature of the service and sales encounter. Many consumers are prepared to pay more for good service.

Price is so central to the decision process and to perception of value that many consumers live by rules of thumb, many of them learned from their parents. How many of us have been berated by our parents when a low-priced item of clothing falls apart at the first washing? The rule of thumb invoked on this occasion may be "You get what you pay for" — meaning had you paid more, you would have received better quality.

More and more customers, in both B2C and B2B markets, are demanding better value in the goods and services they purchase. Value is the ratio of perceived benefits to perceived costs, including price and other incurred costs. Time associated with shopping for the product, time spent on the Internet browsing to gather information to determine exactly what you want, gasoline used travelling in search of your purchase, and time (and perhaps aggravation) assembling the product are examples of these other incurred costs.

When we say a product has value, we don't necessarily mean it is inexpensive. Rather, good value indicates that a particular product has the kinds and amounts of potential benefits — such as product quality, image, and purchase convenience — that consumers expect from that product at a particular price level.

Many businesses are responding to consumers' calls for more value by devising new products and services. The intent is to improve value (or more correctly, **value for money**) — essentially, the ratio of benefits to price. And benefits, real or otherwise, have to be perceived. This can be thought of in the following way:

$$\text{value for money} = \frac{\text{perceived benefits}}{\text{price}}$$

Improving value can be accomplished by maintaining essential elements, adding new elements or features, dropping other elements to cut costs, lowering prices, or more effectively communicating benefits that already exist. In other words, by increasing what is in the numerator of our ratio.

Some major retailers, such as Zellers and Wal-Mart, have essentially adopted a low-price strategy, offering their customers good value for money. Other businesses are striving for better value with existing products. Fast-food firms such as Wendy's, Burger King, and McDonald's, have reduced prices on basic items by taking a "combination meals" approach, which bundles several items for a lower price than if the items were purchased separately. The inclusion of small toys representing popular movie characters and animated figures has also been seen by many consumers as adding value to these restaurants' offerings, owing to the popularity of these toys among children (and some adults). These restaurants believe the toys are strong premiums that provide extra value to existing customers and that they are not the primary reason customers come to their stores.[2]

In the individual firm

The price of a product or service is an important determinant of the market demand for it. Price affects a firm's competitive position and its market share. But, more than anything, price has a considerable bearing on a company's revenues and net profits. Through prices, money comes into an organization.

Some businesses use higher prices to convey an image of superior quality, but this would make sense only to consumers who consider quality to be important. Differentiated product features, a favourite brand, high quality, convenience, or some combination of these and other factors may be more important to consumers than price.

As we saw in Chapter 9, one object of branding is to decrease the effect of price on the demand for a product. Some brands have been so successful in creating a solid, high-value image that they rarely if ever have to reduce their prices. Heinz Ketchup is the "gold standard" in the ketchup category, and customer loyalty to the brand is so strong that the product is rarely discounted — consumers are prepared to pay regular price all of the time. The same is true with many fashion brands, such as Chanel, whose famous No. 5 fragrance is almost never discounted.

value for money
Customer's perception of what is received for the price paid.

Price plays a very important role in positioning the firm and its brands. Many companies will use the price of their products and services to send a message to customers that they are prestige or discount brands. Thus, some hairstylists will cut your hair for $8, while a haircut at a fashionable salon could cost you $30 or more. You can eat lunch for $5.99 at a downtown diner, but lunch at a trendy cafe could set you back $50. A black Stanfield's T-shirt costs $15, but a black Hugo Boss T-shirt could cost $60 or more. What contributes to the price difference? Certainly, the cost of the materials used and the skills of the service provider will contribute to the difference, but some cynical observers will comment, "You're paying for the name." So, what's wrong with that? Many people are obviously prepared to pay more to wear Hugo Boss (**www.hugoboss.com**) or Issey Miyake (**www.isseymiyake.com**), or to be seen carrying a Prada bag (**www.prada.com**). This is an obvious part of a company's positioning strategy. For example, while both are well-recognized brand names, Prada's leather goods are not positioned in the same market space as Roots' leather goods; Wal-Mart is not considered to be a direct competitor of Harry Rosen.

Hugo Boss
Issey Miyake
Prada

The price that a company charges must also be part of a co-ordinated strategy, one that fits with other elements of the marketing mix. Price is only one of the elements of the mix, and it has to be consistent with the messages being sent by the other elements. Thus, it is difficult to charge higher prices when product quality is questionable or inconsistent, or when advertising messages suggest that prices are competitive, or when service is poor or the method of distribution is inconvenient. The price charged must reflect the value being offered and must be acceptable to consumers, considering the other elements of the marketing mix being offered — particularly quality, service and convenience.

value strategy
An overall strategy of a company to offer value to its customers; price is part of this strategy.

Price is, therefore, an important component of a firm's **value strategy**. The company must decide what it intends to mean to customers in terms of the value being offered, and how it will deliver that value. Ideally, a firm needs to achieve a position where customers believe its prices are reasonable and fair. To deliver on a high-price strategy, a company has to be seen to be delivering value in many ways to justify its higher prices. When a company stresses low prices, customers do not expect value to be added in other areas.

Pricing Objectives

pricing objective
The goals that management tries to reach with its pricing structure and strategies.

Every marketing activity — including pricing — should be directed toward a goal, so management should decide on its **pricing objective** as part of its overall value strategy before determining the actual price. Yet, as logical as this may sound, few firms consciously establish, or explicitly state, a pricing objective.[3]

To be useful, the pricing objective that management selects must be compatible with the overall goals set by the company and the goals for its marketing program. Let's assume that an established company's goal is to increase return on investment from its present level of 15 percent to 20 percent within three years. It follows that the pricing goal during this period must be to achieve some stated percentage return on investment. It would not be logical, in this case, to adopt the pricing goal of maintaining the company's market share or of stabilizing prices. We will discuss the following pricing objectives:

- **Profit-oriented:**
  - To achieve a target return.
  - To maximize profit.

- **Market-oriented:**
  - To achieve a certain image or market position
  - To increase sales volume.
  - To maintain or increase market share.

- **Status quo-oriented:**
  - To stabilize prices.
  - To meet competition.

Profit-oriented goals

Profit goals may be set for the short or long run. A company may select one of two profit-oriented goals for its pricing policy.

target return

A pricing goal that involves setting prices to achieve a certain percentage return on investment or on net sales.

mark-up

The dollar amount that is added to the acquisition cost of a product to determine the selling price.

Achieve a target return   A firm may price its product to achieve a **target return** — a specified percentage return on its sales or on its investment. Many established retailers and wholesalers use a target return on sales as a pricing objective for short periods, such as a year or a fashion season. They add an amount to the cost of the product, called a **mark-up**, to cover anticipated operating expenses and provide a desired profit for the period. A chain of men's clothing stores may have a target profit of 7 percent of sales, and price its products accordingly. Safeway or Loblaws, for example, may price to earn a net profit of 1.5 percent on a store's overall sales. Achieving a target return on investment is measured in relation to a firm's net worth (the firm's assets minus its liabilities). The leading firm in an established industry often selects this pricing goal.

This approach is not necessarily useful nor even easily used in fast-changing, high-technology industries. Cost and price structures, as well as competitive forces, change so rapidly these days that this method reduces effective forecasting — if forecasting can even be considered to be accurate in some of these industries. As well, advances of technology can be so rapid that prices must be able to be quickly adapted to impending advancements.

profit maximization

The pricing objective of making as much money as possible.

Maximize profits   The pricing objective of making as much money as possible — using a "what the market will bear" approach — is followed by some firms, particularly in industries in which there is relatively little competition. The trouble with this goal is that, to some people, **profit maximization** has an ugly connotation, suggesting profiteering, high prices, and monopoly. Sometimes, this description appears to be too close to the mark, if a firm attempting to maximize its revenues in this way is the only provider of a product or service. Alternatively, a firm may be trying to get what it can before other providers enter the market, or a fad or trend passes, or the next technology arrives that lessens the market value of the current product.

In both economic theory and business practice, and for most of us budgeting our own time, there is nothing wrong with profit maximization. Theoretically, if profits become high in an industry because supply is short in relation to demand, new competitors will enter the market. This will increase supply and eventually reduce profits to normal levels. In a marketplace where there is real competition, it is difficult to find many situations where profiteering has existed over an extended period of time. Substitute products are available, purchases can be postponed, and competition can increase to keep prices at a reasonable level.

Market-oriented goals

In some companies, management's pricing policy is focused on driving sales volume or on market positioning. The pricing goal may be to increase sales volume, to increase the firm's market share, or to achieve a certain image.

Increase sales volume   The pricing goal of **increasing sales volume** is typically adopted to achieve rapid growth or to discourage potential competitors from entering a market. The goal is usually stated as a percentage increase in sales volume over some period, perhaps one year or three years. Management may seek higher sales volume by discounting or by some other aggressive pricing strategy, perhaps even incurring a loss in the short run. Thus, clothing stores run end-of-season sales and auto dealers offer rebates and below-market financing rates on new cars to stimulate sales. Many vacation destinations, such as golf courses and resorts, reduce prices during off-seasons to increase sales volume.

market share targets

When a company sets a certain share of the market as its objective when setting prices.

Maintain or increase market share   In some companies, both large and small, the pricing objective is to achieve certain **market share targets**. Why is market share protected or pursued so vigorously? In growing fields such as computers, information technology, and communications, companies want a large market share in order to gain leverage with vendors and to aid in driving down production costs and other costs that are sensitive to economies of scale.

Most other industries today are not growing much, if at all, and, if they have not yet rationalized their operations, have excess production and operations capacity. Since the size of the market "pie" isn't growing in most cases, businesses that need added volume have to grab a bigger "slice of the pie" — that is, greater market share. The North American auto and airline industries illustrate this situation.

Achieve market position   As we observed briefly above, some firms use price strategically to present a particular image of their companies or brands, or to achieve a certain market position. In such cases, price plays a very important role in sending messages to customers about the position of the company against its competitors. Thus, some companies will want to be seen as the low-price leader that will not be undersold, while another will stake out a position in the market as the value leader — you will pay higher prices but it will be worth it.

Status quo goals

stabilizing prices
A pricing goal designed to achieve steady, non-volatile prices in an industry.

Two closely related goals — **stabilizing prices** and **meeting competition** — are the least aggressive of all pricing goals. They are intended simply to maintain the firm's current situation — the status quo. With either of these goals, a firm seeks to avoid price competition.

Price stabilization often is the goal in B2B markets in which the product is highly standardized (such as lumber products or bulk chemicals) and in which one large firm historically has acted as a leader in setting prices. Smaller firms in these industries tend to "follow the

MARKETING AT WORK   15-2: TECHNOLOGY

Netting a Net Profit

If someone asked you why you shop on the Internet, you would probably say, like most Net shoppers, that obtaining lower prices was a major reason. According to a recent study by Ernst & Young, 75 percent of customers cited low price as an important factor in their decision to buy online.

But don't take that answer to the bank. We don't always behave in a way that is consistent with what we say we'll do, and nowhere is this truer than with pricing. One of the worst ways to find out about customers' price sensitivity is to ask them directly about price. Invariably, they will tell you they are more price-sensitive than they really are. New pricing research has developed a number of more indirect methods that can provide truer measures of sensitivity.

Research by McKinsey & Company of the "clickstream" behaviour of 50,000 active online Internet users indicates that, contrary to popular belief, the Internet does not negatively affect pricing in most industries. Analysis indicates that neither consumers nor businesses are *overly* aggressive online price shoppers.

Consider the following:

- 89 percent of online book buyers purchase from the first site they visit, as do 84 percent of toy, 81 percent of music, and 76 percent of electronics buyers online.

- Most consumers stick with the brand they trust, or use the Internet because it's convenient, not because it's cheap.

- 29 percent of users can be categorized as "simplifiers," looking more for convenience than price.

- 36 percent use the Internet primarily to connect with family and friends, and generally default to their offline preferences if they do buy online.

- Only 8 percent of users are "bargainers" who aggressively search for the best deals online.

The lowest-price dot-com competitors seldom dominate the market. In fact, during the late 1990s, when online retailing first experienced exponential growth, e-tailers such as Amazon and Barnes & Noble increased prices by 8 percent and 7 percent, respectively, while discounter Books-a-Million lowered prices by 30 percent — even with the proliferation of price-comparison software (shopping bots), Amazon and B&N increased their market shares considerably.

SOURCE: Adapted from Paul Hunt, "Pricing to Make a Net Profit," *Marketing Magazine*, January 29, 2001, p. 29.

leader" when setting their prices. What is the reason for such pricing behaviour? A price cut by any one firm is likely to be matched by all other firms in order to remain competitive; therefore, no individual firm gains, but all may suffer smaller profits. Conversely, a price boost is unlikely to be matched, but the price-changing firm faces a differential disadvantage because other elements of a standardized product, such as gasoline, are perceived to be fairly similar.

Even in industries in which there are no price leaders, countless firms deliberately price their products to meet the prevailing market price. This pricing policy gives management an easy means of avoiding difficult pricing decisions. Many stores have adopted a price-matching policy, such as Future Shop (**www.futureshop.ca**) and Staples/Business Depot (**www.staples.ca**). This allows the onus to be placed on the consumer to present a lower price to be matched or beaten by a fixed percentage, while allowing the retailer to advertise having the lowest prices available.

Firms that adopt status quo pricing goals to avoid price competition are not necessarily passive in their marketing. Quite the contrary! Typically, these companies compete aggressively, using other marketing-mix elements — product, distribution, customer service, and especially promotion. This approach is called **non-price competition**, and its objective is to provide the customer with reasons other than price for buying the firm's products or services. It is never desirable to depend on differentiation based only on price, as this will simply escalate price-matching and reduce profits all around. Some consumers will pay extra for better service, greater convenience, or other attributes that they believe offer incremental value. Non-price competition is discussed in more detail in the "Price Competition" section of this chapter.

Future Shop
Staples/Business Depot

non-price competition

A strategy in which a firm tries to compete based on some factor other than price; for example, promotion, product differentiation, or variety of services.

◀ BACKSPACE

1. What are some of the factors, other than cost, that a company must take into consideration when it sets the price for its product or service?

2. Value for money can be thought of as an equation. What does it equal?

3. Name three pricing objectives that a company can choose, depending on its overall goals and strategy.

Factors Influencing Price Determination

base price

The price of one unit of the product at its point of production or resale; same as *list price*.

Knowing the objective of its pricing, a company then can move to the heart of price management: determining the base price of a product. **Base price**, or **list price**, refers to the price of one unit of the product or service at its point of production, resale, or delivery. This price does not reflect discounts or special allowances, delivery or freight charges, or any other modifications. In the chapter opener, Air Canada's list price was $318 for the return trip to Montréal.

Estimating demand

In pricing, a company must estimate the total demand for the product or service. This is easier to do for an established product than for a new one. The steps in estimating demand are (1) determine whether there is a price that the market expects and (2) estimate what the sales volume might be at different prices.

The **expected price** of a product is the price at which customers consciously or unconsciously value it — what they think the product is worth. Expected price usually is expressed as a range of prices rather than as a specific amount. Thus, the expected price might be "between $250 and $300" or "not over $20." The expected price will vary by circumstances and across individuals. One customer may expect not to pay more than $15 for a haircut, while another may expect to pay $40 or more in a certain salon. The expected price also depends on the image of the company or brand, and on the situations in which customers

expected price

The price at which customers consciously or unconsciously value a product; what they think the product is worth.

find themselves. You will expect to pay more for a round of golf at 9 a.m. on a Saturday in July than you will at twilight in mid-November.

A producer must also consider an intermediary's reaction to price. Intermediaries are more likely to promote a product if they approve of its price. Sometimes they don't approve. For example, in the mid-1990s, Wal-Mart did not approve when Rubbermaid attempted to raise its prices on housewares. Rubbermaid was faced with a substantial cost increase for resin, a major ingredient in its houseware products. But since Wal-Mart was such an important (i.e., large-volume) reseller, Rubbermaid settled for a smaller increase (which meant smaller profit margins) than it had originally considered. Accepting this still resulted in a greater increase in profits than if the huge reseller had decided not to carry the Rubbermaid line any more.

It's possible to set a price too low. If the price is much lower than the market expects, sales may be lost. For example, it probably would be a mistake for MAC Cosmetics (**www.maccos-metics.com**), a trendy cosmetics maker, to put a $1.49 price tag on its lipstick or for L'Oréal (**www.lorealparis.ca**) to price its hair-colouring products at $5.99, well below its competitors' prices. This would not be consistent with the image of the company that built its reputation on the slogan "Because you're worth it." In all likelihood, customers would be suspicious about product quality, or their self-concept would not let them buy such low-priced products.

Although many consumers know that a high price does not necessarily mean high quality, most believe that a low price is an indication of lower quality. The prices just discussed would be significantly lower than expected from these brands and would signal inconsistency with the traditional products and images of those cosmetics companies. After all, the well-known slogan "Because you're worth it" doesn't mean much if the hair colour is only $4.99. And most consumers know that a "Rolex" priced at $15 in a sidewalk vendor's jewellery tray is not likely to be the real thing.

After raising a product's price, some organizations have experienced a considerable increase in sales. This situation is called **inverse demand** — the higher the price, the greater the unit sales. Inverse demand usually exists only within a given price range and only at lower price levels. Suppose a leading-edge electronics company such as Sony increased the prices of its line of DVD players. Would you wonder if perhaps this was the brand everyone was buying, or that the marketplace must recognize these as superior to other players? Perhaps you'd believe that it

MAC Cosmetics
L'Oréal

inverse demand
A price-volume relationship: The higher the price, the greater the unit sales.

You're prepared to pay more for these products, because you're worth it.

means they're in short supply and you should get one while you can. However, at some point, inverse demand ends and the usual pattern — declining demand as prices rise — becomes evident.

It is extremely helpful to estimate what the sales volume will be at several different prices. By doing this, the seller is in effect determining the demand curve for the product. Moreover, the seller is gauging price elasticity of demand, which refers to the responsiveness of quantity purchased to price changes. Estimates of sales at different prices also are useful in determining break-even points (we'll discuss this topic later).

price elasticity of demand

The responsiveness of quantity purchased to price changes.

Competitive reactions

Competition greatly influences base price. A new product is distinctive only until the inevitable arrival of competition. The threat of potential competition is greatest when the field is easy to enter and profit prospects are encouraging. This may provide a good opportunity for a firm to exercise its competitive intelligence skills. Competition can come from these sources:

- *Directly similar products:* Nike versus Adidas or Reebok running shoes.
- *Available substitutes*: Air freight versus truck shipping or rail freight.
- *Unrelated products seeking the same consumer dollar:* A Palm handheld PDA versus a portable CD player, bicycle, or a trip to Montréal for the weekend.

In the case of directly similar products, a competitor may adjust its prices. In turn, other firms have to decide what price adjustments, if any, are necessary to retain their customers.

Other marketing-mix elements

A product's base price is influenced greatly by the other components of the marketing mix, such as the product itself, distribution, promotion, and service.

Do I buy this Palm handheld or go to see Pat for the weekend?

Product We have already observed that a product's price is affected by whether it is a new item or an established one. Over the course of the life of a product — its life cycle — price changes are necessary to keep the product competitive. The end-use of the product must also be considered. For instance, there is little price competition among manufacturers of packaging materials or producers of industrial gases, so their price structure is stable. These business products are only an incidental part of the final article, so customers will buy the least expensive product consistent with the required quality. The price of a product is also influenced by whether (1) the product may be leased as well as purchased outright, (2) the product may be returned to the seller, and (3) a trade-in is involved.

Distribution The channels and types of intermediaries selected will influence a producer's pricing. A firm selling both through wholesalers and directly to retailers often sets a different factory price for these two classes of customers. The price to wholesalers is lower because they perform services that the producer would have to perform otherwise — such as providing storage, granting credit to retailers, and selling to small retailers.

Also, in some cases, a more direct distribution channel may allow a firm to charge higher prices, because customers are generally prepared to pay more for convenience and speedy delivery. Insurance companies that sell direct, as opposed to using agents, illustrate how cost savings can be passed to customers because of a major change in a distribution channel.

Promotion   The extent to which the product is promoted by the producer or intermediaries and the methods used are added considerations in pricing. If major promotional responsibility is placed on retailers, they ordinarily will be charged a lower price for a product than if the producer advertises it heavily. Even when a producer promotes heavily, it may want its retailers to use local advertising to tie in with national advertising. Such a decision must be reflected in the producer's price to these retailers. The promotional message must also be consistent with the pricing strategy of the company, so that customers know what to expect. Promotion is also important in establishing the market position of the brand, which is reinforced by its price.

Service   The price being charged must be consistent with the level of service being offered to the customer and may reflect that level of service. Thus, customers expect to pay less to pump their own gas or to shop at supermarkets where they bag and carry out their own groceries. Most customers expect to pay less on the Internet because they are performing many of the functions that companies normally provide. Price also reflects the quality of service. We expect a "better" and more stylish haircut from a trendy downtown salon where we pay more, probably because we expect the stylist to have more experience or skill.

Cost-Based Pricing

cost-based pricing
A company uses its costs as the basis for setting its prices and does not take the customer or market into account.

Many companies today still attempt to establish their prices based on total cost plus a desired profit.

Let's discuss **cost-based pricing**, which means setting the price of a product or service mainly on the basis of the total cost of producing that product or service, plus some desired profit. Suppose that Regency Builders, a housing contractor, figures that the labour and materials required to build and sell 10 condominiums will cost $750,000, and other expenses (office rent, depreciation on equipment, management salaries, and so on) will be $150,000. The contractor wants to earn a profit of 10 percent on the total cost of $900,000. Cost plus desired profit is $990,000, so each of the 10 condos is priced at $99,000.

While it is an easily applied method, cost-based pricing has limitations. One is that it does not recognize various types of costs or the fact that these costs are affected differently by changes in level of output. What if the company is unable to sell all of the units and the price has to be reduced to sell the remaining ones? This changes the entire pricing structure.

A second and more important limitation of this pricing approach is that market demand is ignored (which might explain why we have unsold condos). That is, cost-based pricing assumes that all of the output will be produced and sold. If fewer units were produced, each would have to sell for a higher price to cover all costs and show a profit. But if the condominium market is becoming depressed or the location of the units is not that desirable, output must be cut, as it is not wise to raise the unit price. Another limitation of this method is that it doesn't recognize that total unit-cost changes as output expands or contracts. However, a more sophisticated approach to cost-based pricing can take such changes into consideration.

One approach to cost-based pricing is to set prices based, at least, on variable costs only, not total costs. This is **variable-cost pricing**. Assume that a firm cannot obtain a price to cover its total costs because of, for example, extreme short-term competitive conditions — an Air Canada seat sale on the domestic and international routes brought about because of a downturn in demand and an oversupply of competitive seat sales. If the firm can sell the product or service for any price in excess of its variable costs, the excess contributes to the payment of fixed costs. The firm can continue with this kind of pricing only if it has other sources of revenue to cover its total costs.

Pricing by intermediaries

At first glance, cost-based pricing appears to be widely used by retailing and wholesaling intermediaries. A retailer, for example, pays a certain amount to buy products and have them delivered to the store. Then the retailer adds an amount, a mark-up, to the acquisition cost. This mark-up is estimated to be sufficient to cover the store's expenses and provide a reasonable profit. Thus, a building materials outlet may buy a power drill for $30, including freight, and price the item at $50. The $50 price reflects a mark-up of 40 percent based on the selling price, or 66.7 percent based on the merchandise cost. Of course, in setting prices, intermediaries also should take into account the price expectations of their customers.

Various types of retailers require different percentage mark-ups because of the nature of the products handled and the services offered. A self-service supermarket has lower costs and thus can have a lower average mark-up than a full-service delicatessen. Figure 15-1 shows examples of mark-up pricing by intermediaries.

Is cost-based pricing really used by intermediaries? For the following reasons, it's safe to say that cost-based pricing is not widely used:

- Most retail prices are really only offers. If customers accept the offer, the price is fine. If they reject it, the price usually will be changed quickly, or the product may even be withdrawn from the market. Prices are always on trial.

- Many retailers don't use the same mark-up on all of the products they carry. A supermarket will have a mark-up of 6 to 8 percent on sugar and soap products, 15 to 18 percent on canned fruit and vegetables, and 25 to 30 percent on fresh meats and produce. These different mark-ups for distinctive products reflect competitive considerations and other aspects of market demand.

- The intermediary usually doesn't actually set a base price but only adds a percentage to the price already set by the producer. The producer's price is set to allow each intermediary to add a reasonable mark-up and still sell at a competitive retail price. The producer sets the key price with an eye on the final market.

Since a firm should be market-oriented and cater to consumers' wants, why are we considering cost-based pricing? Simply, cost-based pricing must be understood because it is referred to often in business. Further, it is used by many firms in the B2B market.

The traditional perspective has been that costs should be a determinant of prices, but not the only one. Costs are a floor under a firm's prices — particularly variable costs, as we pointed out earlier. If goods are priced under the cost floor for a long time, the firm will be forced out of business. But when it is used by itself, cost-based pricing is a weak and unrealistic method, because it ignores competition and market demand.

Figure 15-1:

Examples of Mark-Up Pricing by Retailers and Wholesalers

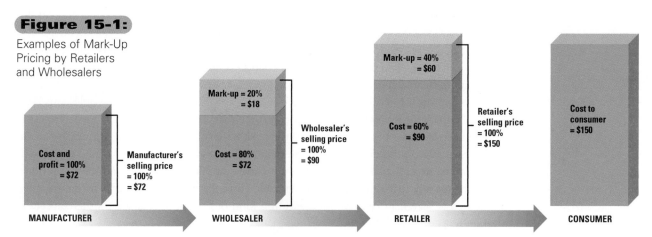

Break-Even Analysis

break-even point
The level of output at which revenues equal costs, assuming a certain selling price.

One way to consider both market demand and costs in price determination is to use **break-even analysis** to calculate break-even points. A **break-even point** is that quantity of output at which total revenue equals total costs, assuming a certain selling price. There is a different break-even point for each different selling price. Sales exceeding the break-even point result in a profit on each additional unit. The higher sales are above the break-even point, the higher will be the total and unit profits. Sales below the break-even point result in a loss to the seller.

Determining the break-even point

The method of determining a break-even point is illustrated in Table 15-1 and Figure 15-2. In our example, the Futon Factory's fixed costs are $25,000 and variable costs are assumed to be constant at $30 per unit.

The total cost of producing one unit is $25,300 — the Futon Factory obviously needs more volume to absorb its fixed costs! For 400 units, the total cost is $37,000 ($30 multiplied by 400, plus $25,000). In Figure 15-2, the selling price is $80 a unit, and variable costs of $30 per unit are incurred in producing each unit. Consequently, any revenue over $30 contributes to covering fixed costs (sometimes called *overhead*). When the price is $80, that contribution would be $50 per unit. At a price of $80, the break-even point is 500 units, because a $50 per-unit contribution will just cover the overhead of $25,000.

Stated another way, variable costs for 500 units are $15,000 and fixed costs are $25,000, for a total cost of $40,000. This amount equals the revenue from 500 units sold at $80 each. So, at an $80 selling price, the break-even volume is 500 units. Figure 15-2 shows a break-even point for an $80 price, but it is highly desirable to calculate break-even points for several different selling prices.

The break-even point can be found with this formula:

$$\text{break-even point in units} = \frac{\text{total fixed costs}}{\text{unit contribution to overhead}}$$

Because unit contribution to overhead equals selling price less the average variable cost, the working formula becomes:

$$\text{break-even point in units} = \frac{\text{total fixed costs}}{\text{selling price} - \text{average variable cost}}$$

TABLE 15-1 Futon Factory: Computation of Break-Even Point

At each of several prices, we wish to find out how many units must be sold to cover all costs. At a unit price of $100, the sale of each unit contributes $70 to cover overhead expenses. The Futon Factory must sell about 357 units to cover its $25,000 in fixed costs.

(1) Unit price	(2) Unit variable costs	(3) Contribution to overhead (1) − (2)	(4) Overhead (total fixed costs)	(5) Break-even point (rounded) (4) ÷ (3)
$60	$30	$30	$25,000	833 units
80	30	50	$25,000	500 units
100	30	70	$25,000	357 units
150	30	120	$25,000	208 units

Figure 15-2:

Break-Even Chart
for Futon Factory

*Here the break-even point
is reached when the
company sells 500 units.
Fixed costs, regardless of
quantity produced and
sold, are $25,000. The
variable cost per unit is
$30. If this company sells
500 units, total costs are
$40,000 (variable cost of
500 × $30, or $15,000, plus
fixed costs of $25,000). At
a selling price of $80, the
sale of 500 units will yield
$40,000 revenue, and
costs and revenue will
equal each other.
At the same price, the
sale of each
unit above 500
will yield a profit.*

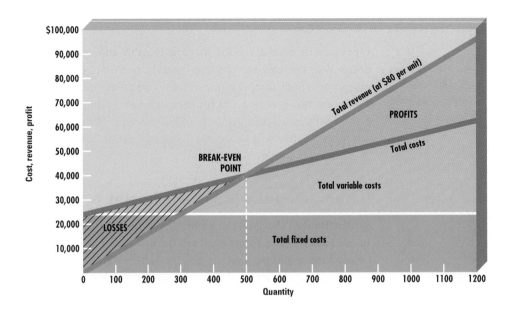

Evaluation of break-even analysis

Two basic assumptions underlie break-even analysis: Total fixed costs are constant and variable costs remain constant per unit of output. Actually, fixed costs may change, although not rapidly, and average variable costs normally fluctuate. Therefore, break-even analysis cannot be used conclusively in most companies, but it does provide some guidance.

Another drawback of break-even analysis is that it cannot tell marketers whether they can actually sell the break-even amount. Table 15-1, for example, shows what revenue will be at the different prices if the given number of units can be sold at these prices. The number the market will buy at a given price, however, could be below the break-even point. If that happens, the firm will not break even — it will show a loss.

Despite these limitations, management should not dismiss break-even analysis as a pricing tool. Even in its simplest form, break-even analysis is helpful because, in the short run, many firms experience reasonably stable cost-and-demand structures.[4] The break-even exercise tells marketers what they will have to sell at each price to cover costs. It assumes that the marketer's cost estimates are accurate, but does not give any indication whether the prices selected are reasonable in light of competitive activity or customer expectations. Nevertheless, it is a valuable exercise to force a company to focus on whether selling the break-even volume of units is a reasonable target.

Market-Based Pricing

Cost-based pricing is one extreme among pricing methods. At the other extreme are methods in which a firm's prices are set in relation to the market price. The seller's price may be set right at the market price to meet the competition, or it may be set above or below the market price.

Pricing to meet competition

Pricing to meet competition is simple to carry out. A firm ascertains what the market price is and, after allowing for customary mark-ups for intermediaries, arrives at its own selling price. To illustrate, let's take the high end of athletic shoes and a manufacturer like Nike. Nike's market research indicates that the Air Metal Max IV cross-trainer should be priced around $160 on the store shelf. Let's suppose that retailers want about a 40 percent average mark-up, based on their selling price. Consequently, after allowing $64 for the retailer's mark-up, Nike's price is $96. This manufacturer then has to decide whether $96 is enough to cover the associated costs and provide the desired level of profit. Sometimes, a producer faces a real squeeze if costs are rising but the market price is holding firm.

One situation in which management might price a product right at the market level is when competition is keen and the firm's product is not differentiated significantly from competing products: Product differentiation is absent, buyers and sellers are well informed, and the seller has no discernible control over the selling price. Most producers of agricultural products and small firms marketing well-known, standardized products use this pricing method. This describes the market condition known as **commoditization**, in which non-differentiated products are treated as commodities by customers.

commoditization
A situation in which consumers perceive little or no difference among the products of various companies and therefore focus on price as a differentiator.

Pricing below competition

A variation of market-based pricing is to set a price below the level charged by a firm's main competitors. **Pricing below competition** is done by discount retailers, such as Zellers and Wal-Mart, that compete against major department stores. They stress low mark-up, high volume, and fewer customer services (including fewer salespeople). They price some heavily advertised, well-known brands below the suggested list price that is normally charged by full-service retailers. Even full-service retailers may price below the competitive level by eliminating specific services. Some gas stations offer a discount to customers who pay with cash instead of a credit card. Canadian Tire gasoline stations distribute bonus coupons for its Canadian Tire money that provide consumers with four or five times the "cash" if they pay by cash or debit card.

The risk in pricing below competition is that consumers begin to view the product as an undifferentiated commodity, such as coal and bulk salt, with all of the focus on price differences. If that happens, and some would say it already has in fields such as personal computers, then consumers choose the brand with the lowest price. In turn, competing firms are likely to wind up in a price war that diminishes or eliminates profits. One important problem faced by firms that consistently adopt a low-price strategy is that they have great difficulty ever raising their prices if they decide to adopt a different positioning strategy in the future.

Godiva

Pricing above competition

Producers or retailers sometimes set their prices above the prevailing market level. Usually, **pricing above competition** works only when the product is distinctive or when the seller is staking out a prestige market position. Most communities have an elite clothing boutique and a prestigious jewellery store in which price tags are noticeably above the level set by other stores with seemingly similar products. However, a gas station that has a strong advantage based on a superior location (perhaps the only such station for many kilometres on the Trans-Canada Highway) may also be able to use above-market pricing.

Above-market pricing often is used by manufacturers of prestige brands of high-cost products, such as automobiles (Porsche, Mercedes), clothing (Prada, Dolce & Gabbana), leather products (Gucci, Fendi), and watches (TAG Heuer, Rolex). Above-market pricing is sometimes found even among relatively low-cost products — chocolates, for example. Godiva (**www.godiva.com**), a brand of imported Belgian chocolates, follows this practice in Canada and the United States. Recently, even simple

A higher price sets this product apart from other drinks.

SoBe
Jones Soda

daily-use products have become premium-priced niche products. Mature, and highly competitive, product categories can provide some examples: Crest has gone beyond toothpaste and toothbrushes to offer "dental gum," a tooth-cleaning chewing gum, for about $2 a package, and so-called "energy" drinks such as SoBe Sports System (**www.sobebev.com**) and Jones Whoop Ass (**www.jonessoda.com**), also about $2 a pop, have stirred up both the soda and juice categories. Providing convenience and portability has also allowed producers to set premium prices — Listerine PocketPaks, 24 small, quick-dissolve, mouthwash wafers, retail for about the same price as the 1.5 litre bottle of Listerine.[5]

BACKSPACE

1. What are the factors that influence price determination?
2. Competition can come from similar products, available substitutes, or _____.
3. What is the break-even point?

Price Competition

In developing a marketing program, a firm decides on the positioning of its offerings and then manages the elements of its marketing mix to achieve and maintain the position — or reposition, if necessary. Some firms decide to compete primarily, but not exclusively, on the basis of price. Others use such non-price approaches as concentrating on quality of product or service and/or distribution, advertising, and promotion, but always with a compatible pricing policy.

A firm engages in **price competition** by:

price competition
A strategy in which a firm regularly offers prices that are as low as possible, usually accompanied by a minimum of services.

1. Regularly offering products priced as low as possible and accompanied by a minimum of services. Zellers, Wal-Mart, and other discount houses and off-price retailers compete in this way.

2. Instigating changes in price that change the consumer's perception of product value without relying on other marketing factors. Supermarkets that rely on heavily discounted weekly specials to attract customers are an example of this practice. The "Bay Days" promotion regularly scheduled by the Bay department store is another such example.

3. Reacting to competitors' price changes with price changes of its own; for example, dropping prices to remain price-competitive.

Many companies today attempt to avoid price competition by striving to maintain prices and by attempting to protect or improve their market positions by emphasizing other aspects of their marketing programs. This does not mean that price setting is not an important component of the marketing mix. If the price of a product or service appears unreasonable in the marketplace, few consumers will buy it, regardless of how catchy the advertising jingle or how excellent the service reputation. In non-price competition, the seller is interested in creating value for the customer by offering something that will cause the customer not to focus on obtaining a lower price. When marketers are successful in adding such value, either through service or attractive features, the customer is often prepared to pay more.

In non-price competition, a manufacturer, retailer, or service provider will attempt to maintain or increase demand for its product by focusing on product differentiation, promotional activities, distribution, superior service, or some other technique. Some factor is chosen to distinguish this provider from others in the marketplace. This factor represents incremental value to the consumer beyond simply the cash price of the product or service, often proving to be a more enduring factor in consumer loyalty than is price. Price competition generally leads to customers switching brands in search of lower prices.

There are different ways to compete on a non-price basis, other than through the development of individual customer relationships previously discussed in this textbook. One similar way is through achieving mind share — clicking with customers on an emotional, non-price-related basis. Retailers such as Gap, Old Navy, and Williams-Sonoma have achieved this. Forget about selling merchandise, sell the brand! Loblaws has done a good job of catering to and anticipating consumer needs, delivering a comprehensive array of products and services that forge a true brand connection. On the fashion front, few retailers have created a platform for their brand as strongly as Roots has achieved. It has all of the hallmarks of a true brand: Not only has it spun its retail roots from shoes, bags, and clothes to Roots Home and Roots Camp, it has also been able to ink licensing deals for various other products.[6]

Finding ways to deliver value unrelated to price is another method. It seems Canadian consumers have thumbed their noses at environmental concerns and embraced convenience as their mantra — offered by a wide variety of single-use, disposable products in the marketplace. Today, we have personal care wipes for face, toes, and virtually all regions in between, as well as household wipes for basically every cleaning need. Even a stodgy brand like Old Spice is getting in on the action with Cool Contact, Old Spice-scented deodorant body wipes targeted to college-aged men.[7]

Value pricing

Earlier in this chapter, we discussed how more consumers are seeking better value in their purchases. In response, many companies in diverse industries are using what's called **value pricing**. This form of price competition aims to improve a product's perceived value — the ratio of its benefits to its price and related costs. Using value pricing:

- A firm may offer products with lower prices but the same, or perhaps added, benefits. Through bundling products or services, consumers may receive the benefit of reduced prices per item.

- At the same time, a firm may seek ways to reduce expenses so that profits do not suffer. If a company can manage to maintain costs or decrease them through increased efficiency, then there is a reduced need to increase prices as often and profit levels can be maintained.

Department stores have dropped like flies in the last decade, but really have only themselves to blame. Shoppers, battered by a nasty recession in the early 1990s, demanded bargains, but department stores didn't deliver. The ultimate challenge came when Wal-Mart achieved a strong foothold in Canada by purchasing insolvent Woolco in the mid-1990s. Canadians found religion in price and now retailers must focus on achieving the optimum blend of quality and price that maximizes the value delivered to their target markets. The Bay has heeded the warning and renewed its commitment to value pricing in 2002 with a strategy to compete against Sears that will see the retailer boost its share of value-priced house brands through what it calls "The Bay Value Program" — a promotional push on 120 items sold at an everyday low price. This program, which will grow to about 300 items in its first year, is more a reaction to the developing global trend of lower apparel prices than a response to a lacklustre economy. The spirit of the program is captured in the retailer's new tag line, "the Bay — more than you came for."[8]

It might be helpful to think of value pricing as a compromise or blend of price and non-price factors. Many things shape consumers' perception of value. Also, there is some variation among consumers as to what represents value. As discussed earlier, additional effort and cost must often be invested to enhance the offering, and yet there is an emphasis on reducing the final cash price to the customer. But, as also discussed, there are other components of total price beyond the cash that is exchanged between buyer and seller. A business can influence this by offering several value components at a number of levels — not just product features.

Many times, if marketers can add value in some way, this will allow them to maintain price. If a competitive price gives the consumer greater flexibility and reduces risk or commitment, then this has provided more value to the consumer while not costing the seller a great deal.

Relationship pricing

Differentiated marketing is critical to attracting more loyal, longer-term customers. Companies have made advances in this area by discovering ways to reward their best customers for giving the companies their business. Many are developing value propositions for customers that correspond to their consumption patterns and value to the firm. In short, marketers are pricing in a way that encourages relationship-building, or at least customer retention.

relationship pricing
Related to the concept of value pricing, in which benefits are shared with customers to ensure that they receive better value and therefore remain loyal.

Relationship pricing is one of the elements of a broader customer–relationship strategy. You will recall that relationship marketing is about developing long-term, ongoing relationships with customers, the benefits of which include customer loyalty and reduced costs of doing business. In relationship pricing, some of these benefits are shared with customers to ensure that they receive better value and have another incentive to remain loyal. In other words, the firm gives a better price to its more valuable customers. In relationship pricing, customers are given a price incentive to encourage them to do all or most of their business with one supplier. For example, if you maintain a chequing account, savings account, mortgage account, and retirement fund with one bank, you will very likely be offered reduced interest rates on any borrowing or invited to join a plan that provides no-cost transactions. The bank is attempting to establish a relationship with you as a customer by offering you a preferred rate and is therefore encouraging you to do all of your business with it.[9] Insurance companies may offer a percentage discount based on the number of policies carried with the company.

Relationship pricing can be thought of as pricing based on bundling products or services over the longer term — sort of like a bulk purchase, but over time. It is pricing based on the long-term potential of the relationship determined on a discretionary one-to-one basis within a range of possible discount levels. Initially, relationship pricing is based on the perceived potential of future business to encourage a consumer to select this provider. Future exchanges may enhance the perception of a special relationship and express to customers their value to the firm, or combat the risk of defection. Beyond special pricing considerations, this approach might involve some free services or products and extra or discretionary services.

Market-Entry Pricing Strategies

In preparing to enter the market with a new product or service, management must decide whether to adopt a market-skimming or a market-penetration pricing strategy.

market-skimming pricing
A pricing strategy in which the initial price is set high in the target market's range of expected prices.

Market-skimming pricing

Setting a relatively high initial price for a new product is referred to as market-skimming pricing. Ordinarily, the price is set high in relation to the target market's range of expected prices. That is, the price is set at the highest possible level that the most interested consumers will pay for the new product. This strategy assists in the recovery of research, development, and introductory costs as quickly as possible before decreasing the price to attract the next price-sensitive level of customers.

Intel

Intel (**www.intel.com**) has long utilized this strategy in the pricing of its computer processor chips. Possessing a very strong dominant market position, the company is able to command the highest price possible, given the benefits it provides over competing products when it introduces the newest generation of its product. The price is relatively stable at this level until the company introduces the next generation or sales begin to decline as competitors begin to catch up with new-product introductions.

Market-skimming pricing has several purposes. Since it should provide healthy profit margins, it is intended primarily to recover research, development, and other introductory costs as quickly as possible. Further, lofty prices can be used to connote high quality and/or cutting-edge innovation and technology. Moreover, market-skimming pricing is likely to curtail demand to levels that do not outstrip the firm's production capacities. Finally, it provides the firm with flexibility, because it is much easier to lower an initial price that meets with consumer resistance than it is to raise an initial price that has proven to be too low to cover costs.

Market-skimming pricing is suitable under the following conditions:

- The new product has distinctive features strongly desired by consumers.

- Demand is fairly inelastic — most likely the case in the early stages of a product's life cycle. Under this condition, lower prices are unlikely to produce greater total revenues.

- The new product is protected from competition through one or more market-entry barriers, such as a patent.

Market-penetration pricing

market-penetration pricing
A pricing strategy in which a low initial price is set to reach the mass market immediately.

In market-penetration pricing, a relatively low initial price is established for a new product or service. The price is low in relation to the target market's range of expected prices. The primary aim of this strategy is to penetrate the mass market immediately and, in so doing, generate substantial sales volume and a large market share. At the same time, it is intended to discourage other firms from introducing competing products.

Market-penetration pricing makes the most sense under the following conditions:

- A large mass market exists for the product.

- Demand is highly elastic, typically in the later stages of the life cycle for a product category.

- Substantial reductions in unit costs can be achieved through large-scale operations. In other words, economies of scale are possible.

- Fierce competition already exists in the market for this product or can be expected to materialize soon after the product is introduced.

When computer firms introduced clones that imitated IBM or Apple models a number of years ago, they were relying on market-penetration pricing by undercutting the prices of the large, well-known producers. Now, a number of years later, pricing approaches have changed again. In an attempt to optimize price points, some manufacturers, such as IKEA and Compaq Computer Corp., follow a pricing philosophy called "design to price." They figure out the price point consumers are willing to pay for a particular item, then they build the best product they can to meet that price point and achieve their profit objectives. In the case of Compaq, it determined that under $2,000 was a key price for personal computers. It designs its computers accordingly, cutting back on some options and specifications to meet that price point and capture that share of the market. Other PC manufacturers partner with software producers in order to equip their products with pre-installed, in-demand programs as part of the purchase price.[10]

Discounts and Allowances

Discounts and allowances result in a deduction from the base (or list) price. The deduction may be in the form of a reduced price or some other concession, such as free merchandise or advertising allowances. Discounts and allowances are commonplace in business dealings.

MARKETING AT WORK 15-3: TECHNOLOGY

Raising the Bar on Price Codes

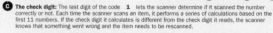

How bar codes work

The bar code, or UPC (Universal Product Code) can be found on most retail products. Manufacturers in Canada and the U.S. use a 12-digit number, those in other parts of the world use a 14-digit system. Canadian retailers are being asked to modify their equipment to be able to read the longer codes. The UPC symbol printed on a package has two parts; a machine-readable bar code and a human-readable UPC number.

In Canada, UPCs originate with the Electronic Commerce Council of Canada which issues each manufacturer a six-digit manufacturer identification number.

A **Manufacturer identification number:** The first six digits of the UPC number – **064420.**

B **Item number:** The next five digits – **00081** – are the item number. The manufacturer is responsible for assigning item numbers to products, making sure the same code is not used on more than one product and retiring codes as products are removed from the product line.

C **The check digit:** The last digit of the code **1** lets the scanner determine if it scanned the number correctly or not. Each time the scanner scans an item, it performs a series of calculations based on the first 11 numbers. If the check digit it calculates is different from the check digit it reads, the scanner knows that something went wrong and the item needs to be rescanned.

How the check digit is calculated: Using the code 06442000081 example shown above, add together the value of all of the digits in odd positions (0 + 4 + 2 + 0 + 0 +1 = 7). Multiply that number by 3. (7 * 3 = 21). Add together the value of all of the digits in even positions (6 + 4 + 0 + 0 + 8 = 18). Add this sum to the value in step 2. (21 + 18= 39). Take the number in Step 4. To create the check digit, determine the number that, when added to the number in step 4, is a multiple of 10. (39 + 1 = 40). The check digit is therefore 1.

SOURCE: WWW.HOWTHINGSWORK.COM   DOUGLAS COULL / THE GLOBE AND MAIL

The universal product code (UPC), or bar code, can be found on pretty much everything we buy. We all know that somehow it contains the price — but how exactly does it work?

In Canada and the United States, manufacturers use a 12-digit number, while elsewhere a 13-digit code is used. It is recommended that by January 1, 2005, all manufacturers will convert to a 14-digit code in an effort to bring universal standards to databases for retailers. Large retailers such as Shoppers Drug Mart and the Hudson's Bay Company are making preparations, but it's expensive and may be a problem for some smaller retailers.

The UPC symbol printed on a package has two parts: a machine-readable bar code and a human-readable UPC number. In Canada, UPCs originate with the Electronic Council of Canada, which issues each manufacturer a six-digit manufacturer identification number. The first six digits of any bar code are the manufacturer's identification number — 0-64420, for example.

Next comes the item number — the next five numbers — say, 00081. The manufacturer is responsible for assigning these item numbers to products, making sure that the same code isn't used on different products and retiring codes as products are removed from the product line.

Lastly, there is the check digit — the last digit of the code (we'll make it 1 for our example) — that allows the scanner to determine if it scanned the product correctly. Each time the scanner scans an item, it performs a series of calculations based on the first 11 numbers. If the check digit it calculates is different from the check digit it reads, the scanner knows something went wrong and the item must be rescanned.

Using the code 0-64420-00081-1 example from above, add together the value of all of the first 11 digits that are in odd positions (the result should be seven) and multiply that number by three (that's 21). Add together the value of all of the first 11 digits in even positions (the total is 18). Add this sum to the odd-digit count: 21 + 18 = 39. Take this total (39) and, to ensure that the check digit is correct, determine the number that, when added to the first 11 digits, produces a multiple of 10 (39 + 1 = 40). Our check digit of 1 is therefore correct!

SOURCE: Adapted from Marina Strauss, "Big Chains Set for a Globalized 14-Digit Bar Code," *The Globe and Mail*, August 19, 2002, p. B3.

Quantity discounts

quantity discount
A reduction of the list price when large quantities are purchased; offered to encourage buyers to purchase in large quantities.

non-cumulative quantity discount
A quantity discount based on the size of an individual order of products.

Quantity discounts are deductions from the list price that are intended to encourage customers to buy in larger volumes or to buy most of what they need from the firm offering the discount. Such discounts are generally based on the size of the purchase, either in dollars or in units.

A **non-cumulative quantity discount** is based on the size of an individual order of one or more products. A pro shop may sell golf balls at $2 each or at three for $5. A manufacturer or wholesaler may set up a quantity discount schedule such as the following, used by a manufacturer of industrial adhesives:

Boxes purchased in single order	Percent discount from list price
1–5	None
6–12	2.0
13–25	3.5
Over 25	5.0

Non-cumulative quantity discounts are intended to encourage large orders. Many expenses, such as billing, order filling, and salaries of salespeople, are about the same whether the seller receives an order totalling $10 or one totalling $500. Consequently, selling expense as a percentage of sales decreases as orders grow in size. With a non-cumulative discount, a seller shares such savings with a purchaser of large quantities.

cumulative quantity discount

A quantity discount based on the total volume purchased over a specified period of time.

A cumulative quantity discount is based on the total volume purchased over a specified period. This type of discount is advantageous to a seller because it ties customers more closely to that firm. The more total business a buyer gives a seller, the greater the discount. Airlines' frequent-flyer and hotels' frequent-guest programs are a form of cumulative discount. Cumulative discounts also are common in selling perishable products. These discounts encourage customers to buy fresh supplies frequently, so that merchandise will not become stale.

Trade discounts

Trade discounts, sometimes called *functional discounts*, are reductions from the list price offered to buyers in payment for marketing functions that the buyers perform, such as storing, promoting, and selling the product. A manufacturer may quote a retail price of $400 with trade discounts of 40 percent and 10 percent. The retailer pays the wholesaler $240 ($400 less 40 percent) and the wholesaler pays the manufacturer $216 ($240 less 10 percent). The wholesaler is given the 40 and 10 percent discounts. The wholesaler is expected to keep the 10 percent to cover costs of the wholesaling functions and pass on the 40 percent discount to retailers.

Cash discounts

A cash discount is a deduction granted to buyers for paying their bills within a specified time period. The discount is computed on the net amount due after first deducting trade and quantity discounts from the base price. Every cash discount includes three elements, as indicated in Figure 15-3:

- The percentage discount.
- The time period during which the discount may be taken.
- The time when the bill becomes overdue.

Let's say that a buyer owes $360 after other discounts have been granted and is offered terms of 2/10, n/30 on an invoice dated November 8. This means that the buyer may deduct a discount of 2 percent ($7.20) if the bill is paid within 10 days of the invoice date — by November 18. Otherwise the entire (net) bill of $360 must be paid in 30 days — by December 8.

Figure 15-3:

Parts of a Cash Discount

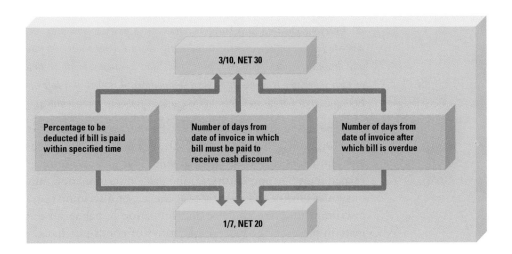

Most buyers are eager to pay bills in time to earn cash discounts. The discount in a 2/10, n/30 situation may not seem like very much, but this 2 percent is earned just for paying 20 days in advance of the date on which the entire bill is due. If buyers fail to take the cash discount in a 2/10, n/30 situation, they are, in effect, borrowing money at a 36-percent annual rate of interest.

Other discounts and allowances

seasonal discount
A discount for placing an order during the seller's slow season.

A manufacturer of goods such as air conditioners or snowmobiles purchased on a seasonal basis may consider granting a **seasonal discount**. This discount of, for example, 5, 10, or 20 percent is given to a customer who places an order during the slack season. Off-season orders enable manufacturers to better use their production facilities and/or avoid inventory carrying costs. Many services firms also offer seasonal discounts. For example, Club Med, other vacation resorts, and cruise lines lower their prices during the off-season.

forward dating
A combination of a seasonal discount and a cash discount under which a buyer places an order and receives shipment during the off-season, but does not have to pay the bill until after the season has started and some sales revenue has been generated.

Forward dating is a variation on both seasonal and cash discounts. A manufacturer of fishing tackle might seek and fill orders from wholesalers and retailers during the winter months, but the bills would be dated April 1, with terms of 2/10, n/30 offered as of that date. Orders filled in December and January help to maintain production during the slack season for more efficient operation. The forward-dated bills allow the wholesale or retail buyers to pay their bills after the season has started and they can generate some sales revenue from the products delivered earlier.

promotional allowance
A price reduction granted by the seller as payment for promotional services rendered by the buyer.

A **promotional allowance** is a price reduction granted by a seller as payment for promotional services performed by buyers. To illustrate, a producer of builders' hardware gives a certain quantity of free goods to dealers who prominently display its line. Or a clothing manufacturer pays one-half the cost of a retailer's ad featuring its product.

Regulation of Pricing

The discounts and allowances discussed in this section may result in different prices for different customers. When price differentials exist, there is price discrimination. In certain situations, price discrimination is prohibited by the Competition Act. This is one of the most important federal laws affecting a company's marketing program. Below are some excerpts from the Act (in italics) and their implications for common pricing strategies.

Price discrimination

Competition Act section 50 (1):

(a) Everyone engaged in a business who ... is a party or privy to, or assists in, any sale that discriminates to his knowledge, directly or indirectly, against competitors of a purchaser of articles from him in that any discount, rebate, allowance, price concession or other advantage that, at the time the articles are sold to such purchaser, is available to such competitors in respect of a sale of articles of like quality and quantity ... is guilty of an indictable offence and is liable to imprisonment of two years.

The following conditions must be met in order for a conviction to be registered for price discrimination: (1) a discount, rebate, allowance, price concession, or other advantage must be granted to one customer and not to another; (2) the two customers concerned must be competitors; (3) the price discrimination must occur in relation to articles of similar quality and quantity; (4) the act of discrimination must be part of a practice of discrimination. Not all price discrimination is, per se, an offence. It is lawful to discriminate in price on the basis of quantities of goods purchased.

Predatory pricing

Competition Act section 50 (1):

(c) Everyone engaged in a business who engages in a policy of selling products at prices unreasonably low, having the effect or tendency of substantially lessening competition or eliminating a competitor, or designed to have such effect, is guilty of an indictable offence and is liable to imprisonment for two years.

It must be shown that prices are unreasonably low and that such prices have the effect of reducing competition. The word *products* in the Competition Act includes articles and services.

Granting promotional allowances as an offence

Competition Act section 51 (1):

In this section, "allowance" means any discount, rebate, price concession or other advantage that is or purports to be offered or granted for advertising or display purposes and is collateral to a sale or sales of products but is not applied directly to the selling price.

The Act requires that promotional allowances be granted proportionately to all competing customers. An allowance is offered on proportionate terms only if, according to section 51 (3):

(a) The allowance offered to a purchaser is in approximately the same proportion to the value of sales to him as the allowance offered to each competing purchaser is to the total value of sales to such competing purchaser.
(b) In any case where advertising or other expenditures or services are exacted in return, the cost thereof required to be incurred by a purchaser is in approximately the same proportion to the value of sales to him as the cost of such advertising or other expenditures or services required to be incurred by each competing purchaser is the total value of sales to such competing purchaser, and;
(c) In any case where services are exacted in return therefore, the requirements thereof have regard to the kinds of services that competing purchasers at the same time or different levels of distribution are ordinarily able to perform or cause to be performed.

These provisions apply to the sale of both articles and services. Discrimination in the granting of promotional allowances is a per se offence, not requiring proof of the existence of either a practice of discrimination or a lessening of competition. A company that wishes to discriminate among its customers may do so through the legal practice of granting quantity discounts.

Resale price maintenance

Some manufacturers want control over the prices at which retailers resell the manufacturers' products. This is most often done in Canada by following a policy of providing manufacturers' suggested list prices, where the price is just a guide for retailers. It is a list price on which discounts may be computed. For others, the suggested price is "informally" enforced. Enforcement of a suggested price, termed *resale price maintenance*, has been illegal in Canada since 1951. In this country, attempts on the part of the manufacturers to control or to influence upward the prices at which retailers sell their products have been considered akin to price fixing.

The Competition Act prohibits a manufacturer or supplier from requiring or inducing a retailer to sell a product at a particular price or not below a particular price. On occasion, a supplier may attempt to control retail prices through the use of a "suggested retail price." The use of suggested retail prices is permitted only if the supplier makes it clear to the retailer that the product may be sold at a price below the suggested price and that the retailer will not in any way be discriminated against if the product is sold at a lower price.

Other legislation: Loss-leader pricing

loss-leader pricing
Involves temporarily reducing the prices of well-known items; the price cuts are made with the idea that these "specials" (loss leaders) will attract customers to the store.

Many firms, primarily retailers, temporarily cut prices on a few items to attract customers. This price and promotional strategy is called **loss-leader pricing** and the items for which prices are reduced below the retailer's cost are called *loss leaders*.

Loss leaders should be well-known, heavily advertised articles that are purchased frequently. The idea is that customers will come to the store to buy the advertised loss-leader items and then stay to buy other regularly priced merchandise. The net result, the firm hopes, will be increased total sales volume and net profit.

Three provinces — British Columbia, Alberta, and Manitoba — have legislation dealing with loss-leader selling. The approach has been to prohibit a reseller from selling an item below invoice cost, including freight plus a stated mark-up, which is usually 5 percent at retail.

These laws have some glaring weaknesses. In the first place, the provinces do not establish provisions or agencies for enforcement. It is the responsibility and burden of the injured party to seek satisfaction from the offender in a civil suit. Another limitation is that it is difficult or even impossible to determine the cost of doing business for each individual product. The third weakness is that the laws seem to disregard the fundamental idea that the purpose of a business is to make a profit on the total operation, not necessarily on each sale of each product.

Geographic Pricing Strategies

In pricing, a marketer must consider the costs of shipping physical products to the buyer. These costs grow in importance as freight becomes a larger part of total variable costs. Pricing policies may be established under which the buyer pays all of the freight expense, the seller pays the entire cost, or the seller and buyer share this expense. The strategy chosen can influence the geographic limits of a firm's market, the locations of its production facilities, the sources of its raw materials, and its competitive strength in various geographic markets.

Free on board (f.o.b.) point-of-production pricing

f.o.b. factory pricing
A geographic pricing strategy whereby the buyer pays all freight charges from the selling facility location to the destination.

In one widely used geographic pricing strategy, the seller quotes the selling price at the factory or at some other point of production or origin. In this situation, the buyer pays the entire cost of transportation. This is usually referred to as **f.o.b. factory pricing**. Of the four strategies discussed in this section, this is the only one in which the seller does not pay any of the transport costs. The seller pays only the cost of loading the shipment aboard the carrier — hence the term f.o.b., or free on board.

Under an f.o.b. factory pricing strategy, the seller nets the same amount on each sale of similar quantities. The delivered price to the buyer varies according to the freight charge. However, this pricing strategy has serious economic and marketing implications. In effect, f.o.b. factory pricing tends to establish a geographic monopoly for a given seller, because transportation costs prevent distant competitors from entering the market. The seller, in turn, is increasingly priced out of more distant markets.

uniform delivered pricing
A geographic pricing strategy whereby the same delivered price is quoted to all buyers, regardless of their location; same as *postage-stamp pricing*.

Uniform delivered pricing

Under the **uniform delivered pricing** strategy, the same delivered price is quoted to all buyers, regardless of their locations. This strategy is sometimes referred to as "postage-stamp pricing" because of its similarity to the pricing of first-class mail service. The net revenue to the seller varies, depending on the shipping cost involved in each sale.

A uniform delivered price is typically used where transportation costs are a small part of the seller's total costs. This strategy is also used by many retailers who feel that "free" delivery is an additional service that strengthens their market position.

Under a uniform delivered price system, buyers located near the seller's factory pay for some of the costs of shipping to more distant locations. Critics of f.o.b. factory pricing are usually in favour of a uniform delivered price. They feel that the transportation expense should not be charged to individual customers any more than is any other single marketing or production expense.

Zone-delivered pricing

zone-delivered pricing
A geographic pricing strategy whereby the same delivered price is charged at any location within each geographic zone.

Under a zone-delivered pricing strategy, a seller would divide the Canadian market into a limited number of broad geographic zones. Then, a uniform delivered price is set within each zone. Zone-delivered pricing is similar to the system used in pricing parcel post services and long-distance telephone service. A firm that quotes a price and then says "slightly higher west of the Lakehead" is using a two-zone pricing system. The transportation charge built into the delivered price is an average of the charges at all points within a zone area.

Freight-absorption pricing

freight-absorption pricing
A geographic pricing strategy whereby the seller pays for (absorbs) some of the freight charges in order to penetrate more distant markets.

A freight-absorption pricing strategy may be adopted to offset some of the competitive disadvantages of f.o.b. factory pricing. With an f.o.b. factory price, a firm is at a price disadvantage when it tries to sell to buyers located in markets closer to competitors' plants. To penetrate more deeply into such markets, a seller may be willing to absorb some of the transportation costs. Thus, seller A will quote to the customer a delivered price equal to (1) A's factory price plus (2) the freight costs that would be charged by the competitive seller located closest to that customer.

A seller can continue to expand the geographic limits of its market as long as its net revenue after freight absorption is larger than its marginal cost for the units sold. Freight absorption is particularly useful to a firm with excess capacity, whose fixed costs per unit of product are high and whose variable costs are low. In these cases, management must constantly seek ways to cover fixed costs, and freight absorption is one answer.

Special Pricing Strategies

To set initial prices and evaluate existing prices, a firm needs to consider a number of distinctive strategies. It's likely that at least one, but probably not all, will apply to a particular pricing situation.

One-price and flexible-price strategies

one-price strategy
A strategy under which a seller charges the same price to all customers of the same type who buy the same quantity of goods.

flexible-price strategy
A pricing strategy under which a company sells similar quantities of merchandise to similar buyers at different prices; same as variable-price strategy.

Rather early in its pricing deliberations, management should decide whether to adopt a one-price strategy or a flexible-price strategy. Under a one-price strategy, a seller charges the same price to all similar customers who buy similar quantities of a product. Under a flexible-price strategy (also called a variable-price strategy), similar customers may each pay a different price when buying similar quantities of a product.

In Canada, a one-price strategy has been adopted more often than flexible pricing. Most retailers, for example, follow a one-price policy — except in cases in which trade-ins are involved, and then flexible pricing abounds. A one-price policy builds customer confidence in a seller, whether at the manufacturing, wholesaling, or retailing level. Weak bargainers need not feel that they are at a competitive disadvantage.

When a flexible-pricing policy is followed, the price often is set as a result of buyer-seller bargaining. In automobile retailing — with or without a trade-in — price negotiating (bargaining) is quite common, even though window-sticker prices may suggest a one-price policy. Variable pricing may be used to meet a competitor's price.

Psychological pricing

Considerations for final pricing decisions may often involve more than just calculations about covering costs and how much you can get the customer to pay: Thought is also given to how the price of an item or service can be used to communicate information to the consumer — to let the price tell the consumer (or let consumers think) something about the product. Price is used to communicate price level, of course, but the use of certain numbers influence the consumer's perception of that level and therefore the value received. Price also is used to connote quality, value, and up-to-date and cutting-edge innovation. While a high price does not mean high quality, it can be taken as an indication in many consumers' minds.

Psychological pricing means setting a price to have a special appeal to a particular segment of consumers. Loss-leader pricing (as discussed earlier) is intended to attract customers by selling some products at a very low price, perhaps at a loss, to get people into the store. This is often used for weekly supermarket sales. Or there is **bait pricing**, baiting consumers with a low-priced feature item but then pointing out its weaker details in order to sell a more expensive version. This approach also can work in the other direction — by raising prices above competitive levels, sometimes to such a degree that it is referred to as **prestige pricing**. Swiss watchmaker TAG Heuer is one such example — the company's average watch price went from $250 to almost $1,000. The company's sales also increased — sevenfold![11]

Price lining involves selecting a limited number of prices at which a business will sell related products. It is used extensively by clothing retailers. A sporting-goods store, for instance, may sell several styles of running shoes at $99.95 a pair, another group at $119.95, and a third at $149.95. For the consumer, the main benefit of price lining is that it simplifies buying decisions. For the retailer, price lining helps in planning purchases. The buyer for the sporting-goods store can go to market looking for shoes that can be retailed at one of its three prices.

Odd pricing, another psychological strategy, is commonly used in retailing. Odd pricing sets prices at uneven (or odd) amounts, such as 49 cents or $19.95, rather than at even amounts. Autos often are priced at $19,995 rather than $20,000, and houses sell for $189,500 instead of $190,000. Odd pricing is often avoided in prestige stores and on higher-priced luxury items. A man's suit at Holt Renfrew, for example, may be priced at $1,000, but not $999.95. The Hyundai Tiburon is advertised at $13,999 while the Infiniti I30 is advertised for $41,000.

The rationale for odd pricing is that it suggests lower prices and, as a result, yields greater sales than even pricing. According to this reasoning, a price of 98 cents will bring in more revenue than a $1 price for the same product. Research indicates that odd pricing can be an effective strategy for a firm that emphasizes low prices.[12]

Everyday low pricing (EDLP) is "the hottest retailing price trend," according to one analyst.[13] While it may be trendy, it certainly is not new. Basically, it involves consistently low prices and few if any temporary price reductions. Both Wal-Mart and Zellers have been extremely successful with this type of pricing, as have warehouse stores such as Costco and Staples/Business Depot. Some of these stores support this pricing policy with a guaranteed price-matching or

psychological pricing
Setting a price to have a special appeal to a particular segment of customers.

bait pricing
Attracting consumers with a low-priced feature item and then pointing out its weaknesses in order to sell a more expensive version.

prestige pricing
Raising prices above competitive levels.

price lining
Involves selecting a limited number of prices at which a business will sell related products.

odd pricing
A form of psychological pricing that consists of setting prices at odd amounts ($4.99 rather than $5.00, for example) in the belief that these seemingly low prices will result in larger sales volume.

everyday low pricing (EDLP)
A pricing strategy that involves consistently low prices and few if any temporary price reductions.

price-beating policy. This feels like "insurance" to consumers and may reassure them that this particular store must offer the lowest prices in order make this claim.

Many firms do not engage in EDLP but rather in **high-low pricing**, which involves charging relatively low prices for some products and higher prices for others. This strategy combines frequent price reductions and aggressive promotion to convey an image of very low prices. Many supermarkets and some department stores and chain drugstores rely on this approach.

BACKSPACE

1. What is non-price competition?
2. What is the difference between market-skimming and market-penetration pricing strategies?
3. Pricing very low to get people into a store or raising prices above the competition to make the product seem more prestigious are both examples of _____ pricing.

Summary

In our economy, price influences the allocation of resources. In individual companies, price is a significant factor in achieving marketing success, and in many purchase situations, price can be of great importance to consumers. However, it is difficult to define price. A rather general definition is: Price is the amount of money and/or other resources needed to acquire a product.

Before setting a product's base price, management should identify its pricing goal. Major pricing objectives are to (1) earn a target return on investment or on net sales, (2) maximize profits, (3) increase sales, (4) hold or gain a target market share, (5) stabilize prices, and (6) meet competition's prices.

Besides the firm's pricing objective, other key factors that influence price setting are (1) demand for the product, (2) competitive reactions, (3) strategies planned for other marketing-mix elements, and (4) cost of the product. The concept of elasticity refers to the effect that unit-price changes have on the number of units sold and on total revenue.

Two major methods used to determine the base price are cost-based pricing and setting the price in relation only to the market. For cost-based pricing to be effective, a seller must consider several types of costs and their reactions to changes in the quantity produced. The main weakness in cost-based pricing is that it completely ignores market demand. To partially offset this weakness, a company may use break-even analysis as a tool in price setting.

For many products, management will often set the price at the level of competition. Because markets are constantly changing and evolving, this still requires that pricing policies and strategies be assessed frequently. Pricing at prevailing market levels makes sense for firms selling well-known, standardized products and sometimes for individual firms in a market shared by a small number of producers or sellers.

After deciding on pricing goals and setting the base price, marketers must establish pricing strategies that are compatible with the rest of the marketing mix. Although price competition was widespread in the 1990s, most firms prefer non-price competition. Price competition establishes price as the primary, perhaps the sole, basis for attracting and retaining customers. A growing number of businesses are adopting value pricing to improve the ratio of benefits to price and, in turn, win customers from competitors.

When a firm is launching a new product, it must choose a market-skimming or a market-penetration pricing strategy. Market skimming uses a relatively high initial price, market penetration a low one. It is also important to consider that the lowest price is not always the most important variable to a consumer at all times or for all products.

Strategies also must be devised for discounts and allowances — deductions from the list price. Management has the option of offering quantity discounts, trade discounts, cash discounts, and/or other types of deductions. Transportation costs must be considered in pricing. A producer can require the buyer to pay all or none of the freight costs, or the two parties can share the freight costs.

Management also should decide whether to charge the same price to all similar buyers of identical quantities of a product (a one-price strategy) or to set different prices (a flexible-price strategy). Many organizations, especially retailers, use at least some of the following special strategies: price lining — selecting a limited number of prices at which to sell related products; odd pricing — setting prices at uneven (or odd) amounts; and loss-leader pricing — temporarily cutting prices on a few items to attract customers to a store.

Market opportunities and/or competitive forces may motivate companies to initiate price changes or, in other situations, to react to other firms' price changes. A series of successive price cuts by competing firms creates a price war, which can harm the profits of all participating companies.

Key Terms and Concepts

bait pricing 480
base price (list price) 462
break-even analysis 467
break-even point 467
cash discount 475
commoditization 469
cost-based pricing 465
cumulative quantity discount 475
everyday low pricing (EDLP) 480
expected price 462
f.o.b. factory pricing 478
flexible-price (variable-price) strategy 479
forward dating 476
freight-absorption pricing 479
high-low pricing 481
increasing sales volume 460
inverse demand 463
loss-leader pricing 478
market share targets 460
market-penetration pricing 473
market-skimming pricing 472
mark-up 460
meeting competition 461
non-cumulative quantity discount 474
non-price competition 462
odd pricing 480
one-price strategy 479

prestige pricing 480
price 454
price competition 470
price elasticity of demand 464
price lining 480
price sensitivity 457
pricing above competition 469
pricing below competition 469
pricing objective 459
pricing to meet competition 468
profit maximization 460
promotional allowance 476
psychological pricing 480
quality 457
quantity discount 474
relationship pricing 472
seasonal discount 476
stabilizing prices 461
target return 460
trade (functional) discount 475
uniform delivered pricing 478
value for money 458
value of a product/service 454
value pricing 471
value strategy 459
variable-cost pricing 465
zone-delivered pricing 479

Questions and Problems

1. Explain how a firm's pricing objective may influence the promotional program for a product. Which of the six pricing goals involves the largest, most aggressive promotional campaign?

2. What marketing conditions might logically lead a company to set "meeting competition" as a pricing objective?

3. Name at least three products for which you think an inverse demand exists. For each product, within which price range does this inverse demand exist?

4. Why is the status quo goal of meeting the competition considered to be the least aggressive of all of the pricing goals?

5. A small manufacturer sold ballpoint pens to retailers at $8.40 per dozen. The manufacturing cost was 50 cents for each pen. Expenses, including all selling and administrative costs except advertising, were $19,200. How many dozens of pens must the manufacturer sell to cover these expenses and pay for an advertising campaign costing $6,000?

6. For each of the following products, should the seller adopt a market-skimming or a market-penetration pricing strategy? Support your decision in each instance.
   a. High-fashion dresses styled and manufactured by Yves Saint Laurent.
   b. An exterior house paint that wears twice as long as any competitive brand.
   c. A cigarette that is totally free of tar and nicotine.
   d. A tablet that converts a litre of water into a litre of automotive fuel.

7. A manufacturer of appliances quotes a list price of $800 per unit for a certain model of refrigerator and grants trade discounts of 35, 20, and 5 percent. What is the manufacturer's selling price? Who might get these various discounts?

8. The Craig Charles Company (CCC) sells to all of its customers at the same published price. One of its sales managers hears that Jamaican Enterprises is offering to sell to one of CCC's customers, Mountain Sports, at a lower price. CCC then cuts its price for Mountain

Sports but maintains the original price for all other customers. Is CCC's price cut for Mountain Sports a violation of the Competition Act?

9. An eastern firm wants to compete in western markets, where it is at a significant disadvantage because of freight costs. What pricing alternatives can it adopt to overcome the freight cost differential?

10. Under what conditions is a company likely to use a flexible-price strategy? Can you name firms that use this strategy other than when a trade-in is involved?

Hands-On Marketing

1. Visit a local discount store such as Wal-Mart or Zellers. Note the prices of three products, including a child's toy, a piece of electronic equipment such as a CD player, and a small appliance. Check these prices at other outlets that sell on the basis of high-low pricing, such as Sears or the Bay. Determine whether there is a difference in price. Are the products selling at high or low prices in the non-discount outlets?

2. Karina's Pizza produces two products, 12-inch pizzas and 16-inch pizzas, with the following characteristics:

	12-Inch Pizza	16-Inch Pizza
Selling price	$500,000 ($5/unit)	$900,000 ($6/unit)
Variable cost	$300,000	$300,000
Expected sales (units)	100,000	150,000

The total fixed costs for the company are $700,000.

a. What is the anticipated level of profits for the expected sales volumes?

b. Assuming that the product mix in units would be the same as above at the break-even point, compute the break-even point in terms of number of units of each of the products.

c. If the product sales mix was to change to four 12-inch pizzas for each 16-inch pizza, what would be the new break-even volume for each of the products? Comment on the number of units required to break even for this sales mix, compared with the original sales mix.

Note: Question 2 was prepared by Assistant Professor Judith A. Cumby, Faculty of Business Administration, Memorial University of Newfoundland, as a basis for class discussion and is not intended to reflect either an effective or an ineffective handling of a management problem.

Back to the Top

Have you ever been confused by airline prices? Have you heard other people complain about the cost of air travel or express amazement at the fact that some people travel at one-quarter of the fare paid by others? The chapter opener is intended to make you think about what contributes to price in this industry and in others. What contributes to the price being charged to a particular customer to fly on a particular routing at a particular time? Why is this so difficult for consumers to understand?

Want to get better grades, tips on how to study more effectively, and up-to-date information on happenings in the world of marketing? Then, visit the Online Learning Centre for practice tests, Study Smart software, and much more! **www.mcgrawhill.ca/college/sommers**

Interested in finding out what marketing looks like in the real world? *Marketing Magazine* is just a click away on your Online Learning Centre!

Case 6-1

Hudson's Bay Company
Sale Day at the Bay

Bob Jones was walking through the men's wear department of the downtown Bay department store, taking a shortcut to the restaurant where he was meeting Denise for lunch. As he neared the door, Bob noticed a rack of men's cotton slacks, above which was displayed a large sign announcing "Special! 50% off." Although Bob had not intended to buy slacks that day, he was attracted by the sign and stopped to look at the goods.

As Bob examined the slacks on the rack, he noticed that the brand was Ruff Hewn and that the original price was $80. He thought, "I could use a pair of slacks and this is a really good price." He had a couple of Ruff Hewn cotton shirts hanging in his closet, and he was pretty sure that the sweater Denise had given him for his birthday was Ruff Hewn as well. He picked out a dark-green pair, size-32 waist, and tried them on. They fitted perfectly, so he decided to buy them.

"Will that be on your Bay account, sir?" asked the sales clerk. Bob replied that he would be paying cash and took a $50 bill from his wallet. The clerk then asked, "Do you have your Bay Day card?" Bob indicated that he wasn't familiar with the Bay Day card. The clerk explained that he should have been handed one as he entered the store and that, since this was a Bay Day, he was entitled to scratch a certain part of the card to reveal the discount that he would receive on his purchase. As Bob didn't have a card, she reached under her counter and gave him one. Bob scratched the latex portion of the card and saw the words "30% off."

Bob was certain that he wouldn't receive an extra 30 percent off pants that were already reduced by 50 percent. He wasn't disappointed, though, because he thought that, at 50 percent off, the pants were already a good bargain. He showed the card to the sales clerk and commented, "Too bad I can't use this, because the pants are already 50 percent off." The clerk smiled at him and said, "Oh no, you get an additional 30 percent off the sale price. Let's see, that's another $12, so the price of the slacks will be $28." Bob was delighted. He really hadn't expected to get the pants for such a low price — he'd thought that he was getting a good deal at $40. He paid the $28, plus tax, thanked the sales clerk, and rushed off to apologize to Denise for being late.

Questions

1. What was the price of the pants that Bob bought?

2. What factors influenced his decision to buy?

3. What would Bob have done if he'd seen a rack of pants at the Bay with a sign reading "Cotton slacks $28" or one that said "Cotton slacks $80"?

Case 6-2

A Question of Ethics?
A Great Deal on Heating Oil

The Maxwell Oil Company had been marketing home heating oil to homeowners in the Westville area for more than 50 years. The company operated an annual payment/purchase plan, offering customers a package that, for $99 per year, gave them regular maintenance, service, and insurance on their furnaces, and the fuel at 34 cents per litre.

During the past year or so, the company had noticed it was receiving a number of telephone calls from customers who were calling to cancel their annual plan because a local competitor was offering them home heating oil at 30 cents per litre. At first, the company apologized and said there was nothing it could do about this. But, after the company began losing many customers, Maxwell's management decided that they had to do something about this. They called a meeting and decided that the only thing they could do to keep their customers was to match the competitor's price on oil. To ensure that profits didn't drop too much, management agreed that only those customers who called to complain would get the new price on oil. If the other customers didn't complain about the price, there was no need to reduce it for them — or so they thought! Now, when customers called to complain about the price of oil, Maxwell agreed to match the deal, thereby giving only those customers who contacted the company a reduction of 4 cents per litre from the current contract price.

Once it became generally known in certain Westville neighbourhoods that Maxwell was prepared to match the competitor's price, even more customers called in to complain. The company began to regret its decision. But the worst was yet to come. Soon, Maxwell began getting a number of calls from very angry customers who were upset at the fact that some of their neighbours, who apparently had signed up for the same contract, had been receiving their fuel at 4 cents less per litre — simply because they had called and asked for it. Those who were still paying the higher price were not happy and threatened to leave. They told Maxwell that it was unfair to charge different prices to different customers. Some had been Maxwell customers for 30 years or more and felt "hurt" at being treated this way. Maxwell's management team immediately regretted its decision and felt it never should have offered the lower price in the first place. But as one manager pointed out, they still would have lost customers. What was Maxwell to do now?

Questions

1. What obligation, if any, did Maxwell have to offer the same price reduction to all customers who were currently under contract for the annual plan?

2. What options did the company have when it first realized that the competition was offering fuel at 4 cents less per litre? Should it have let some of its customers go or tried to keep as many as possible?

3. Is an ethical issue involved when prices are lowered for some customers and not for others?

Case 6-3

Paying the Price for a Healthy Pet

Penny's not a picky eater. She'll eat just about anything you put in front of her. In fact, the three-year-old pug will eat whatever she finds — even things she's not supposed to eat. Ted Rowen, her owner, wants what's best for his pet and he'll do whatever is necessary to keep Penny healthy.

Recently, Ted noticed that Penny was starting to gain weight and she seemed to wheeze more than usual when he took her for walks. He knew that pugs were prone to putting on weight and that they could become obese quickly if their diet went unchecked. Worried, he began taking her on three walks a day instead of two. He decided he would wait a couple of weeks to see if Penny's weight returned to normal. In the meantime, Ted consulted a few friends who were dog owners to see if they had any suggestions. His friend Bob suggested that Ted should change to a diet-formula dog food, while his other friend Larry told him that the no-name brand he'd been feeding Penny was not good quality, especially for an expensive pure-bred.

The next time Ted went grocery shopping, he went to the pet food aisle to choose a new brand. He'd always bought no-name because he was convinced it was no different from the brand-name dog foods: He'd read the list of ingredients and they were essentially the same. The only difference, as far as Ted was concerned, was the price. Ted looked for diet dog food. The no-name diet food cost $7.99 for an 8-kg bag, while the next cheapest brand, President's Choice, cost $10.99. After that, the other brand names were much pricier. Purina sold for $14.99 for an 8-kg bag. Why should he pay more for the same thing, he thought? He decided he should at least try another brand to see if it would make a difference. He thought for a moment. Maybe the more-expensive brand really was better somehow. He examined the Purina package carefully. The package boasted that Purina had extra nutrients to meet all of the nutritional needs of an adult dog, while helping the dog to lose weight. It seemed that the extra nutrients were the reason for the higher cost. Satisfied, Ted picked up the Purina package and went to the checkout.

After a couple of weeks on the Purina diet, Penny's weight had not changed, so Ted decided it was time to take her to the vet. Dr. Smith examined and weighed Penny. She was 2.5 kg over the normal, healthy weight for a pug. The vet decided that the problem was her diet, which he said was too high in fat and not high enough in protein. He explained that, if Penny continued to gain weight and became obese, she would develop other health problems and have a shorter life span. Ted became very worried. He even felt a little guilty. Ted asked the vet how to get more protein into his pet's diet. Dr. Smith recommended a specially formulated premium diet dog food that he sold in his office. It cost $25 for a bag that was just under 8 kg.

Ted couldn't believe the price. It seemed like a lot to pay, especially when he considered how much more it would cost him per year. He did a quick calculation in his head. He usually bought about one 8-kg bag of no-name a month. At this rate, he would be spending almost $300 per year instead of the usual $96. Fresh out of teacher's college, Ted had just started a new job teaching history at a local high school. He had accumulated quite a lot of debt as a student and now had to pay it off. And with his car payments and rent, money was a little tight.

But he couldn't think about all that right now. The important thing was Penny's health. He would pay whatever he needed to. The vet, sensing Ted's hesitation, explained that the more-expensive dog food was so rich in protein and other nutrients that Ted would need to give the dog portions that were only half the size he usually fed Penny. If he took that into account, then the premium dog food was not that much more expensive. Ted did another calculation in his head and figured he would be spending about $150 per year. Satisfied, Ted bought a bag of premium dog food and decided he would try it for a couple of weeks to see if there was any improvement.

Ted felt better about his dog's health as he left the vet's office. He was sure the more-expensive dog food would do the trick. He put Penny on the diet right away. After one week, he weighed his dog and saw that she had put on another kilogram. Frustrated, Ted decided to get another vet's opinion. He took Penny to see Dr. Eva Martin. After Ted explained to her the events of the past few weeks, Dr. Martin nodded and said there was no doubt in her mind that the premium dog food had more nutritional value. The problem was that once Penny had consumed the required protein, the remaining protein was converted into fat. Dr. Martin thought that Ted should continue to buy the regular diet food from the supermarket because it had a sufficient amount of proteins and nutrients, but that he should reduce the portions by one-third. She also told Ted to look for dog food with the CVMA label on the package. That meant the dog food was approved by the Canadian Veterinary Medical Association and that it met the pet's nutritional requirements.

Ted went back to the grocery store and looked for the CVMA label. He saw that both the no-name brand and the President's Choice had the CVMA certification, while the Purina brand was certified by the Pet Food Association of Canada. Again, Ted hesitated. He knew that he could buy the less-expensive, no-name brand because it had the proper certification, but he couldn't help thinking about what his friend Larry had said about no-name being a lower-quality dog food. Even though the vet had told him it was fine, Ted felt bad feeding it to his pet. He decided to buy President's Choice because it seemed like a better dog food but was not as pricey as the Purina brand.

Penny didn't seem to mind yet another change in her dog food. She happily ate whatever Ted gave her. After a week, it was time to put Penny back on the scale: She had lost a half-kilogram! Ted was thrilled. He thought about all of the vet bills he could have saved had he just bought the President's Choice in the first place. Oh well, he thought. As long as Penny was healthy, he didn't care.

Questions

1. Why did Ted choose the no-name dog food in the first place?

2. What were the factors involved in his decision to purchase President's Choice?

3. Why did he decide to spend so much more on the premium dog food on his first visit to the vet?

4. How would you decide which dog food to buy if Penny was your dog? What considerations would be the most important to you?

Video source: CBC *Marketplace*, "Premium Pet Food," October 31, 2000.

PART 7

Tying Marketing Together

An overview of the company's marketing function; reviewing the role of marketing in society, and considering where marketing is heading in the future

Up to this point, we have dealt separately with how a firm selects its target markets and then develops and manages the elements of its marketing strategy for those markets. In the first part of Chapter 16, we bring those separate areas together, as we present an overview of the role of marketing within an organization, proposing a very holistic view of what marketing entails. We reinforce our view that marketing starts with the customer. This is followed by a discussion of marketing implementation and evaluation. Then, we review the current position of marketing in our society, examine how various organizations have responded to the changing face of marketing, and consider where marketing is headed in the future.

CHAPTER 16

Marketing: A State of Mind

In this chapter, we discuss an holistic (all-inclusive) view of marketing in an attempt to communicate how the marketing function is evolving in progressive firms, whether they are retail, service, or not-for-profit organizations. Strategic management of the marketing function is becoming increasingly important in today's global marketplace. The planning, careful implementation, and systematic evaluation of marketing programs are critical to this end. Management must periodically assess the appropriateness of its goals and its performance in reaching them.

This final chapter also addresses a number of criticisms of marketing, as well as ethical issues and current responses to these. Finally, we will peer into a crystal ball and consider some of the prospects for the future of marketing. After studying this chapter, you should have an understanding of:

- The holistic view of marketing.
- The role of implementation in the strategic management process.
- A broadened perspective for evaluating marketing performance.
- Criticisms of marketing and the responses of various stakeholders.
- Ethical issues in today's marketing environment.
- Trends influencing future marketing activity.

Who Are Our Best Customers?

Joanne Henson is a junior consultant with a large international consulting company that she joined just two months ago, after 10 years of working in financial services with one of Canada's chartered banks. She has just returned from her first business trip to Europe, which involved meeting with a number of the company's clients in France, Germany, Sweden, and the United Kingdom. On the flight home, she is thinking about the lessons she has learned about how different companies approach their customers and how they practise marketing.

One of her first meetings was with a telecommunications company that is perplexed by a continually high customer "churn," or turnover rate, in its cellphone business. While the company seemed to realize that it is essentially in a commodity business — one that is dominated by severe price competition — it seemed to be at a loss to decide how to differentiate itself from its competitors and to create a higher level of customer retention.

Joanne recalled a meeting with senior marketing managers of a supermarket chain who indicated that this company is focused on building customer loyalty.

When one of Joanne's colleagues asked how they define "loyalty," the managers indicated that they use a sophisticated model to identify the most loyal customers. The model is based on the shopping patterns of customers and takes into consideration how recently customers have shopped there, how often they shop, and how much they spend. The company's frequent-shopper program is geared toward rewarding with discounts and special offers those customers who shop most often and spend the most money.

Joanne was impressed by what she perceived to be an enlightened approach to marketing that was fairly common across the companies whose representatives she had met. There seemed to be a general acceptance of the fact that loyal customers are more valuable than those who flit from company to company. Most firms seemed to be focused on treating their best customers really well. When she asked them how they identified their best customers, most replied that they have extensive databases that allow them to pinpoint those who spend the most with them or even those that are most profitable. Joanne couldn't get out of her mind, however, the response that a Swedish senior marketing manager of IKEA had given. "That's simple," he said. "Our best customers are those who like us the most."

Throughout this book, we have tried to present a new and different view of marketing, one that is focused on the customer and on the building of relationships with customers. It suggests that marketing is as much about how you view business and its dealings with customers as it is about a set of tools that are used to market a company and its products and brands. We have suggested that the term *marketing* is legitimately defined as virtually any aspect of an organization that has the potential to affect long-term customer satisfaction. This is a different view than has been practised by many companies and organizations in the past, and many are just now coming around to accepting it.

Marketing: The Holistic View

holistic view of marketing

The view that virtually everything a company does has an impact on customer satisfaction and is, therefore, part of marketing.

We have proposed what we call an **holistic view of marketing**. This means that we need a "big picture" perspective of all of the things that should be included in marketing. We suggested earlier that marketing now extends well beyond the areas that have traditionally been considered the responsibility of the marketing department. In the past, these have generally been referred to as the four elements of the marketing mix — the product, communications, distribution, and price. While we have suggested the broadest possible definitions of these areas of responsibility and we have devoted several chapters of this book to explaining how each of these contributes, we have also encouraged you to think about lots of other things that have the potential to make customers satisfied or dissatisfied. Forward-thinking firms adopt a sense-and-respond marketing mindset that integrates customer demand management, internal and external resource allocation, and network collaboration.[1]

Therefore, we suggest that marketing is essentially how the firm views its dealings with customers. If the prevailing view is one of how to sell them more products and services, we suggest that this firm has a sales emphasis, rather than a modern marketing emphasis. What's interesting is that this company may feel it is customer-focused, and indeed it is! It is focused on figuring out how to sell more to its customers, but that's not marketing — at least not how we view it.

customer-centric

Focused on customers and on achieving customer satisfaction; the customer is at the centre of management thinking.

Today, it has become fashionable for companies and other organizations to portray themselves as customer-focused or **customer-centric**. The implication is that such firms are concentrating on their customers and doing things that will be considered attractive by those customers. While more and more companies are moving toward this customer-centric positioning, others are only part-way along the road. To be truly customer-centric means that a company not only must understand its customers intimately, but also must appreciate that many different things that are under the control of the company have the potential to contribute to the satisfaction of those customers, not only the things that have been considered to be part of the marketing department's responsibility.

It may be useful to think about the factors that we discussed in Chapter 1 that contribute to customer satisfaction. We suggested then that it's not enough to have great products at attractive prices and to advertise and distribute them effectively. It is also important to think about the many ways that a company can, on the one hand, make a customer feel important and valued or, on the other hand, angry and frustrated. We have suggested throughout this book that there is an important emotional side to what a company offers its customer — its value proposition — and that the emotional is at least as important as the so-called functional side of the offer in driving customer satisfaction. Thus, having great products and great prices is not enough if the customer is constantly frustrated in trying to deal with the company or encounters rude and unhelpful employees.

The most effective companies today understand that a wide array of things has the potential to create customer satisfaction and dissatisfaction, and they also realize that it is critically important that customers enjoy dealing with them. This is what lies behind the comment made by the Swedish IKEA manager in our chapter opener. IKEA is a company that works very hard at creating the right atmosphere for customers (see Marketing at Work 13-1, "Is That Swedish for Meatballs?" in Chapter 13). It is also a company that *does* have great products at attractive prices, but it knows that this is not enough.

Extending the view

This relationship-based view of marketing has been extended even further by more progressive companies to apply to others who have the potential to affect the company's ability to serve and interact positively with its customers. Thus, we see companies establishing **supplier-relationship programs** to ensure that the firm has more of a partnership relationship with its suppliers. Because suppliers provide the products and services that allow a company to operate effectively and often supply items that are sold to customers, a company must realize that it cannot operate efficiently unless suppliers are efficient and helpful as well. So, successful companies today are surrounding themselves with suppliers they can trust and depend on; in short, they are building supplier relationships based on the notion of partnership. This closed, full-loop approach to supplier relationships is enhanced through the use of technology, such as that available through SAP (**www.sap.com**), which supports supply strategy, sourcing, purchase execution, contract management, and relationship management.[2]

The concept of supply-chain management also requires a company to realize that a customer's satisfaction with its products and services is very much influenced by the channel through which those products and services are distributed. In many cases, those channel members are not under the direct control of the company whose products and services are being distributed. This is obviously the case with many consumer products, where the responsibility to get the products and services to customers is delegated to wholesalers and retailers. To ensure the highest level of co-operation from channel members, many companies have established **channel-relationship programs** to ensure that channel relationships are as positive as possible.

We observed in Chapter 8 that delivering superior service and generally interacting successfully with customers involves the employees of a firm. They must understand the potential they have to create satisfied customers and how important they are in building customer relationships. More and more companies are acknowledging the importance of having satisfied employees who will be more likely to treat customers well, and have established **employee-relationship programs** that are the joint responsibility of the human resources and marketing departments.

Siebel, a company that develops customer-relationship-management software, has developed a product for helping firms to organize themselves around managing relationships with their own employees. Internal testing in its 34 offices around the globe reportedly resulted in increased productivity of employees in all offices. It improved organizational flexibility, improved employee training, enhanced the ability to respond to changing market conditions, and reduced human resource processing costs.[3]

The firm and the brand

Our holistic view of marketing must be extended even beyond relationships with obvious channel members to address the fact that how the firm is managed and its role in the broader community are also important. The extent to which employees buy into this view of marketing and feel themselves to be an important part of how its customers feel toward the firm will depend to a very large extent on how they are treated and whether they enjoy working for the firm. Therefore, we should include a discussion of the **corporate culture** in our definition of marketing. Happy employees generally create happy customers. It is easy for customers to know when an employee is unhappy working for a firm, because it is often reflected in the employee's attitude and behaviour toward customers.

supplier-relationship program
A program intended to develop solid relationships with suppliers, knowing that they contribute to the company's ability to satisfy its customers.

SAP

channel-relationship program
A program intended to develop positive relationships with distribution channel members, such as wholesalers and retailers.

employee-relationship program
A program intended to "market" the company to its employees, to get employees on-side in terms of an emphasis on treating customers well.

corporate culture
The atmosphere that prevails within a company, which contributes to employees' satisfaction and influences how they treat customers.

The atmosphere within a firm and its culture — whether it is a pleasant place to work — is a function of the leadership of the firm and how the firm treats its people. That leadership rests with the CEO or general manager. It is not uncommon today in more progressive companies to hear the observation that the CEO is the main marketing executive of the company, or that the "CEO owns the customer."

Finally, we should look outside the doors of the firm and beyond its obvious marketing activities to examine its role within the broader community. How a company conducts itself in its dealings with customers, suppliers, its employees, and other groups, and how it demonstrates its role as a member of the community in which it operates will influence its reputation in that community. Its reputation is an important element in how the company is viewed by prospective customers and employees. If that reputation is a positive one, customers and others are more likely to want to deal with the company. Managing that reputation is of critical importance and again is the responsibility of senior executives.

Therefore, in the broadest possible definition, we could argue that how a company behaves as a member of a community — the charities it supports, the events it sponsors, and the other businesses with which it associates — is also part of its marketing program, because this can have an important impact on whether customers will want to deal with the company.

In Figure 16-1, we summarize the many facets of the new view of marketing, one that is focused on creating high levels of customer satisfaction that lead to customer retention and solid relationships. We suggest in this illustration that a firm's ability to create an environment leading to such results rests with the leadership of the company as provided by the senior management team, led by the CEO or equivalent. With the right kind of enlightened leadership, a culture will be created within the firm that will be conducive to employee satisfaction and to the employees treating customers well.

When customers experience excellent service and excellent treatment at the hands of the employees of a firm, they will be satisfied and will tend to return to do business again, leading to higher levels of customer retention. Once customers establish a pattern of repeat business, there is an opportunity for a customer relationship to be established. If a company enjoys high levels of positive relationships with large numbers of customers, that enhances the value of the company to its owners. Thus, we have a fairly direct link between the leadership provided by a CEO and the value that is created for the shareholders.

It is important to point out that the service provided by employees of the firm is only one component of the factors that drive customer satisfaction. At the same time, the four components of the conventional marketing mix — product, promotion, distribution, and price — are at work and must succeed in creating the right value for customers Also, decisions that the company's management team makes in portraying the company to the general public and the community are also important in influencing the image and reputation of the company and its brands, and in turn how they are viewed by customers. The important message here is that marketing is much more than getting the four elements of the marketing mix right.

Figure 16-1:

Leadership Leads to Shareholder Value

Beyond Borders and Business

It is important to note that the principles we have been discussing in this book and the view of marketing that we have described in the preceding sections of this chapter are equally applicable in international markets and in non-business settings. Understanding the principles is important.

Today, many companies are exposed to international marketplaces and international competitors. In fact, it is difficult to think of an organization that does not interact with an international factor that has the potential to influence its success. Because consumers have so many options today as a result of technology, firms and other organizations often find that their competitors are no longer down the street, in the next town or even in Canada. Customers have the option, through the Internet and other channels, to buy products and services from companies that don't even operate in Canada. In that sense, a very large percentage of firms operate in a global marketplace, possibly without even realizing it.

At the same time, many firms have chosen to compete directly in foreign markets, exporting their products and services to other countries. Whenever these organizations venture into other markets, they are exposed to different customs and customer values and different ways of doing business. All of the concepts that we examined in Chapter 3 pertaining to customer behaviour also apply in other countries, but may not be at all similar to the situation in Canada. It is important, therefore, that companies get to know the marketplaces in which they plan to compete, because these are almost certainly different in some respects from the Canadian marketplace. Even marketing in the United States, a country that is right next door and one that many Canadians know quite well, presents numerous challenges as a result of marketplace and customer differences.

One of the best organizations at creating value for its stakeholders

Having said that, the principles of marketing that we have been discussing in this book apply as well in international marketing as they do at home. The goal of the marketer is still to create high levels of customer satisfaction, leading to repeat business, positive word of mouth, and eventually to relationships with customers. It is almost certainly true, however, that the route to achieving this satisfaction may be different in other countries.

The same may be said about not-for-profit organizations. These entities do not operate in a classic business context, but rather offer their "customers" intangible services as diverse as police protection, symphony performances, food bank assistance, and religion. Thus, the definition of not-for-profit organizations is very broad and includes governments at all levels, charities such as the Canadian Cancer Society, cultural groups such as Symphony Nova Scotia and the Stratford Festival, religious bodies such as the Salvation Army, public transit organizations such as the la Société de transport de Montréal and the Toronto Transit Commission, and educational institutions such as your college or university.

"It's a lot like directing a play," according to Antoni Cimolino, general manager of the Stratford Festival. "Although we are not trying to drive shareholder value, we are trying to drive value for our artists, our audience members, and the corporations that support us." Government funding for such organizations has dropped substantially in recent years, but Stratford recently made a record $4.2 million and increased visitors by 17 percent over previous seasons.[4]

Again, while the objectives and motivations of such organizations are not exactly the same as those of Shoppers Drug Mart or

General Motors Canada, the principles of marketing still apply. It is important that not-for-profit organizations also strive for customer satisfaction, even though they may refer to their customers as members, taxpayers, donors, patrons, or passengers. In many cases, they don't want people to buy things from them as much as they want their donations, patronage, or simply support. To achieve that, not-for-profit organizations have to present an attractive value proposition, just as a retailer or a bank does. It has to appreciate the fact that it is operating in a competitive marketplace, where it is competing for the attention of its target audience in the same way that Mark's Work Warehouse competes with Eddie Bauer.

One of the problems associated with not-for-profit organizations is that their leaders or executive members often are reluctant to practise marketing because the term is associated in their minds with commercial applications. They may respond that they can't be seen to be competing in the same way that Loblaws or Wal-Mart competes. However, the fact is that such organizations *do* compete. They compete for donations, for the time of volunteers, for public service announcements on radio, and for the hearts and minds of supporters. To be successful, there must be a realization that what they offer their target audience must be seen to be attractive.

MARKETING AT WORK   16-1: STRATEGY

Relationships and Customer Service — College-Style

Do marketing strategies such as customer service, acquisition, and retention have a place in the business of higher education? Some would say no. While recognizing the traditional roles of education, that of generating knowledge and intellectual pursuits, marketers also see the value that such an approach has had south of the border.

A good example of a marketing plan geared toward student-relationship development is Aims Community College in Colorado, which, after experiencing declining enrolments, developed an enrolment-management strategy geared toward recruiting and retaining students.

The plan involves about 75 people, no less than 22 percent of the college's staff, and is a top priority for the entire institution. Aim's integrated approach does not stop at advertising — its recruitment tactics include such efforts as:

- A "gentle introduction to college" that allows graduating high school students to take a semester of classes tuition-free (everyone likes free samples!).

- One-hour information sessions, campus tours every Tuesday, and many campus events to lure potential students onto the campus.

- An enquirer follow-up program that is triggered whenever someone expresses interest in attending Aims. This includes calling registered students one week before classes start to ensure that they are still planning to attend.

- The Aims Web site (www.aims.edu) refers to convenient locations, a caring and friendly atmosphere, and how students can walk from their cars to the classroom in less than two minutes.

- Scheduling of many course offerings after 5:30 p.m. in order to allow full-time workers to take courses.

What has been the result of these efforts? Enrolment has increased by 20 percent or more. And those telephone calls? Those alone have increased retention by about 5 percent.

Will we see a major shift in the marketing of higher education in Canada in the near future? Believe it or not, it has already begun. The British Columbia Institute of Technology offers the chance to win a Palm Pilot by registering online, while the Certified Management Accountants of British Columbia (who refer to students as customers) use an integrated plan that includes print advertising, personalized direct mail, information sessions, a free transcript review offer, and telephone and e-mail follow-up.

SOURCE: Adapted from Maureen Rutherford, "Customer Service, College-Style," *Marketing Magazine*, April 2, 2001, p. 18.

Implementation in Marketing Management

There should be a close relationship among planning, implementation, and evaluation. Without strategic planning, as discussed in Chapter 2, a company's operational activities — its implementation tactics — can go off in any direction, like an unguided missile. Good planning cannot overcome poor implementation, but effective implementation often can overcome poor planning.

Okay, you're standing in a line-up outside the theatre, deciding which film to see. Will it be the multi-million-dollar blockbuster with the star-studded cast or that low-budget, home-grown Canadian flick about curling? Chances are, you'll go for the flashy one — it seems a safer bet! Rarely do Canadian movies receive much recognition: Small budgets are partly responsible, but also distributors often don't use the right type of marketing.

One Canadian movie that appeared to break that mould is *Men with Brooms*, a romantic comedy about a group of curlers, starring Paul Gross and Leslie Neilson. More than $1 million was spent to promote the film, a pittance by Hollywood standards but a lot for a Canadian film. It was enough to get people talking about the movie and generate the highest-recorded opening weekend for a Canadian film. In the early planning stages, promotional deals were struck with Roots, Chapters/Indigo, and the CIBC, and four different TV spots were aired during the 2002 Winter Olympics on CBC. In addition to a movie-theatre trailer, the marketing plan included a cross-country press junket with the film's stars, which generated substantial media interest. A 15-track soundtrack was released and an e-mail campaign was launched through the Canadian Curling Association.[5]

Marketing implementation comprises three activities:

1. *Organizing the marketing effort:* Once a company has developed its strategic marketing plan, an early activity is to organize the people who will implement it. The relationship between marketing and the other functional divisions of the firm must be defined. Then, within the marketing department, management must design an organization that will implement both strategies and tactics.

2. *Staffing the organization:* For plans to produce an intended result, an organization needs skilled, dedicated people to carry them out well, so selection of the right people is very important. Organizations are beginning to rediscover the importance of the people who make up the firm.

   A sales manager's success depends greatly on the people whom the manager selects. The success of relationship-marketing programs rests substantially on the sales force as the key implementers of strategies and tactics.

3. *Directing the execution of marketing plans:* In this third phase of implementation, revenues are generated. To do so, management needs to direct the work of the people who have been selected and organized as the company's marketing team. Success in this phase depends on four important aspects of managing employees — delegation, co-ordination, motivation, and communication.

Organizing for implementation

Organizational structures are receiving increasing attention in companies around the world as management recognizes that yesterday's structures may hinder operations in today's dynamic environment. Satisfying customers profitably requires talking to them — and listening carefully to what they have to say. Teamwork across functional areas of a business, including marketing, human resources, finance, and manufacturing, is also essential. Traditional organizational structures isolate different functions, however, and have many managerial layers between customers and decision-makers. Recognizing this, larger organizations in particular have made significant organizational changes in recent years to ensure that marketing works closely with other parts of the business that have the potential to affect customer satisfaction.

In a very real sense, traditional vertical structures are being replaced by horizontal organizations.[6] Several specific trends are noteworthy:

- **Fewer organizational levels:** The intent is to facilitate communication among the executives who develop the strategic plans, the employees who have continuing contact with the market, and the firm's customers.

- **Employee empowerment:** Granting more authority to middle-level executives in decentralized locations can stimulate innovation and generate faster responses to market shifts. Empowering customer-contact personnel can boost both customer satisfaction and repeat business. With that in mind, the Ritz-Carlton hotel chain allows any employee who hears that a customer has a problem to spend up to $2,000 trying to rectify that problem.[7]

- **Cross-functional teams:** By having personnel from various departments work on a project, not only are barriers among functions broken down, but the best combination of expertise and experience can be focused on the assignment. Empowering cross-functional teams is a recommended approach for developing new products, particularly in high-technology industries.[8]

- **Sharing of information:** Assisted by the use of information systems and accessible databases, more and more companies are sharing customer information across the various departments, so that all employees can have a view of the customer and be informed about account history and other pertinent information when it is needed.

◄ BACKSPACE

1. What is an holistic view of marketing?
2. What role does corporate culture play in customer satisfaction?
3. What does *employee empowerment* mean?

Evaluating Marketing Performance

Soon after a firm's plans have been put into operation, the process of evaluation should begin. Without evaluation, management cannot tell whether a plan is working and what factors are contributing to its success or failure. Evaluation logically follows planning and implementation. A circular relationship exists, as illustrated in Figure 16-2. Plans are made and put into action, the results of those actions are evaluated, and new plans are prepared on the basis of this evaluation.

Previously we discussed evaluation as it relates to individual parts of a marketing program — the product-planning process, the performance of the sales force, and the effectiveness of the advertising program, for instance. Now let's look at evaluation of the total marketing effort.

The marketing audit: A total evaluation program

marketing audit
A comprehensive review and evaluation of the marketing function in an organization.

A marketing audit is an essential element in a total evaluation program. An audit implies a review and evaluation of some activity. Thus, a **marketing audit** is a comprehensive review and evaluation of the marketing function in an organization — its philosophy, environment, goals, strategies, organizational structure, human and financial resources, and performance.

It's true that a marketing audit involves evaluation. But it is much more than that. In advocating the value of marketing audits in the banking industry, one writer stressed, "Simply stated, a strategic marketing plan should be written only after completion of an intensive, objective, marketing audit."[9]

A complete marketing audit is an extensive and difficult project. That's why it is conducted infrequently — perhaps every two or three years. However, a company should not delay a marketing audit until a major crisis arises.

The rewards of a marketing audit can be great. Management can identify problem areas in marketing and, by reviewing its strategies, the firm is likely to keep abreast of its changing marketing environment. Successes can also be analyzed so that the company can capitalize on its strong points. The audit can spot lack of co-ordination in the marketing program, outdated strategies, or unrealistic goals. Furthermore, an audit should anticipate future situations. According to one marketing specialist, it is intended for "prognosis as well as diagnosis…. It is the practice of preventive as well as curative marketing medicine."[10]

Misdirected marketing effort

Figure 16-2:

The Circular Relationship among Management Tasks

One of the benefits of evaluation is that it helps to correct **misdirected** (or misplaced) **marketing effort**.

80-20 principle

A situation in which a large proportion of a company's marketing units (products, territories, customers) accounts for a small share of the company's volume or profit, and vice versa.

The 80-20 principle In most firms, a large proportion of the total orders, customers, territories, or products accounts for only a small share of total sales or profit. Conversely, a small proportion produces a large share of sales or profit. This relationship has been characterized as the 80-20 principle — 80 percent of the orders, customers, territories, or products contribute only 20 percent of sales or profit. On the other hand, 20 percent of these selling units account for 80 percent of the volume or profit. We use the 80–20 figure simply to highlight the misplacement of marketing effort. In reality, of course, the percentage split varies from one situation to another.

iceberg principle

A concept related to performance evaluation, stating that the summary data (tip of the iceberg) regarding an activity may hide significant variations among segments of this activity.

Reasons for misdirected marketing effort Frequently, marketing managers cannot uncover their misdirected effort because they lack sufficient information. The **iceberg principle** is an analogy that illustrates this situation. Only a small part of an iceberg is visible above the surface of the water, and the large submerged portion is the dangerous part. The figures representing total sales or total costs on an operating statement are like the visible part of an iceberg. The detailed figures representing sales, costs, and other performance measures for each territory or product correspond to the dangerous submerged segment.

Total sales or cost figures are too general to be useful in evaluation; in fact, they often are misleading. A company may show satisfactory overall sales and profit figures, but when these totals are subdivided by territory or products, serious weaknesses often are discovered. A manufacturer of audio equipment showed an overall annual increase of 12 percent in sales and 9 percent in net profit on one product line one year. But management wasn't satisfied with this "tip of the iceberg." When it analyzed the figures more closely, it found that the sales change within territories ranged from an increase of 19 percent to a decrease of 3 percent. In some territories, profit increased as much as 14 percent, and in others it was down 20 percent.

A more basic cause of misplaced marketing effort is that executives must make decisions based on inadequate knowledge of the exact nature of marketing costs. In other words, management often lacks knowledge of (a) the disproportionate spread of marketing effort, (b) reliable standards for determining what should be spent on marketing, and (c) what results should be expected from these expenditures. This is illustrated in the chapter opener, when we consider how some companies define their best customers or measure the value of a customer to the company. When the focus is on revenue alone, the company is missing essential information related to how much a customer costs the company. Most firms do not yet have sufficiently sophisticated cost accounting systems to allow them to determine what it costs to serve a customer.

Evaluating marketing

Before we can begin to appraise marketing, we have to agree on a basis for evaluating performance — what the objective of marketing should be. In our discussion of the marketing concept, we said that an organization's objective is to determine consumers' needs or wants and satisfy them. Thus, from the point of view of the individual organization, if the firm's target market is satisfied and the organization's objectives are being met, the marketing effort can be judged to be successful.

However, this standard makes no distinction between organizations whose behaviour is detrimental to society and whose activities are socially acceptable. Firms that pollute the environment or stimulate demand for harmful products or services would qualify as good marketers right along with firms that behave responsibly. Therefore, we should take a broader, societal view that incorporates the best interests of others as well as the desires of a particular target market and the objectives of the marketer to satisfy that market. Marketing must balance the needs and wants of consumers, the objectives of the organization, and the welfare of society.

Marketing cannot, and certainly does not, exist in a vacuum. Practically speaking, consideration must be given to the cost-effectiveness of marketing efforts. In other words, how much does marketing contribute to the revenue of the firm or to the coffers of the owners — the shareholders? Corporate performance is evaluated as a means of measuring the performance of management and the decisions they have made. Various means are used, but one method is through measurement of shareholder value. Have the operations of the firm over a particular period increased the value of the organization for its shareholders? Unfortunately, these are often taken as short-term measurements when many marketing efforts take some time to yield results.

The principal objective of management is the creation of shareholder value. By this measure, the firm is assessed according to easily measured financial indicators. However, marketing results can sometimes be less easily measured. Marketing is about developing customer relationships. Organizations must recognize that relationships are required to establish long-term shareholder value through accumulative effects that provide future streams of value. Such intangibles are difficult to measure in the short term, yet customer relationships must be assessed for the long-term health of the firm.

Relationships, like marketing, require an understanding of what the customer wants, how to provide it, and where the firm is strong and where it is weak. Measures include customer value, service quality, and customer satisfaction. To develop a sustainable stream of shareholder value a wider group of stakeholders should be considered, aside from shareholders. These include employees, suppliers, and customers.

Real shareholder value is created by guaranteeing the long-term viability and growth of the company. Value creation, therefore, is intimately tied to customer loyalty. Loyal customers deliver a stream of revenues as long as they are satisfied. Satisfaction drives customer relationships. Relationships are aided and influenced through well-planned and integrated marketing efforts.[11]

Evidence of the interrelationship of these three criteria is all around us. If a product does not meet the needs of consumers or if a firm is unable to provide the level of service that customers want, the consumer will not buy that product or service. The business world is littered with companies that have gone out of business because they were unable to satisfy their customers. Likewise, if a firm behaves in a fashion that is viewed by consumers or the public to be detrimental to society, government will probably intervene, as it does in regulating the advertising of alcohol, tobacco, and other products judged to be potentially damaging to the health and safety of consumers. Finally, companies regularly change advertising and promotional campaigns as their organizational objectives change.

MARKETING AT WORK 16-2: RELATIONSHIPS

Accountants: 1, Marketers: 0

Here's a sobering thought. The accounting profession may understand more about branding than some marketers — at least as far as a brand's actual value is concerned. In other words, how it is performing.

Sure, marketers understand all about how to influence people to buy brands and get employees all excited about their brands, but when it come to understanding and communicating the actual financial value of brands, that's another story.

The accounting profession realizes that modern companies attribute a significant component of their value to intangibles — patents, licences, contracts, brands, etc. More importantly, these assets are far too complex and nuanced to continue to be lumped under the catch-all label of "goodwill." As a result, we are seeing a series of international accounting standards, indicating the desire to bring certainty to the valuation and understanding of intangible assets.

The UK accounting profession started the ball rolling with *Financial Reporting Standard 10*. Americans jumped on the bandwagon with their *Financial Accounting Standard 142*. Here in Canada, accountants have dutifully brought in similar standards, found in *Generally Accepted Accounting Practices 3062*.

These accounting standards all currently have two serious problems. First, they apply only to brands acquired from another company, not in-house brands. But, more importantly, the issue of how to go about actually valuing the brands remains unresolved.

It all stems from understanding net present value as it applies to a brand. For example, someone offers to sell you a magic goose. To determine its value today, you need to estimate risk — how many eggs it would lay, the profit from those eggs, expected life of the goose, other ways you could invest your money, and whether golden eggs might someday go out of style.

The challenge is getting the accountants to agree on how to measure the various risks. But that doesn't mean companies should avoid doing internal valuations of brands, relationship equity, customer growth and retention, and similar intangibles. In fact, that very exercise will provide a whole new toolbox of decision-making instruments that, in the long run, will enable the firm to tweak bottom-line performance.

SOURCE: Adapted from Mark Szabo, "Accountants 1, Marketers 0," *Strategy*, July 1, 2002, p. 13

Criticisms of Marketing

Criticisms of marketing focus on actions (or inaction) that relate to the balance between organizational objectives and the needs of customers and/or the well-being of society. These issues can be categorized as follows:

- **Exploitation:** Marketers are sometimes accused of taking unfair advantage of a consumer or of a situation. Examples of exploitation are price gouging during a shortage and misleading consumers with false or incomplete information. These behaviours are clearly in conflict with marketing's goal of long-term customer satisfaction.

- **Pervasiveness:** Marketing is everywhere. Or, more correctly, what many people associate with marketing is everywhere. For many people, marketing is advertising and other outward evidence of marketing in action. Some people are becoming tired of the fact that, everywhere they turn, they encounter advertising, flyers, contests, and other tools of marketing.

- **Inefficiency:** Some critics feel that marketing uses more resources than necessary. Accusations include ineffective promotional activity, unnecessary distribution functions, and excessive numbers of brands in many product categories. Inefficiency results in higher costs to organizations, higher prices to consumers, and a waste of society's resources.

- **Demand stimulation:** A number of marketers have been accused of encouraging consumers or businesses to purchase products that are harmful in some way to the individual or the organization. For example, debate has raged throughout the Western world for the past 25 years or more concerning the marketing of cigarettes. The issue tends to revolve around the fact that tobacco is a legal product, although there are regulations in Canada that prohibit the sale of tobacco products to teens and children. Although the marketing of such products may meet the needs of some consumers and satisfy the objectives of the organizations that produce and sell them, the marketing of tobacco products is controversial because society generally agrees that the product is detrimental to people's health.

- **Inappropriate values:** Related to the concept of unwholesome demand is that of the promotion of inappropriate values. The use of sexual imagery has often been criticized in advertising as well as the association of alcohol consumption and tobacco products with images of the "good life." This refers to images of "successful" or "popular" individuals that infer to viewers that the product has a role in delivering such desirable attributes.

- **Illegal behaviour:** Laws are passed to protect individuals, organizations, and society in general. Marketers are expected to abide by these laws, even when violating a law might benefit consumers or an organization. Price collusion, for instance, is detrimental to competitors of the colluding firms. Therefore, since the behaviour is unfair to others in society, it is unacceptable.

- **Poor service:** Some of the most vocal criticisms of marketing in recent years have been reserved for the way service is delivered to customers when they come into contact with marketing organizations, particularly at the retail level.

  Service has many dimensions — it is a form of product that comprises activities, benefits, satisfactions, and outcomes. The quality of delivery of each of these greatly impacts the quality of the product received. There is no doubt that some companies and organizations have made great strides and have developed well-deserved reputations for providing superior service; others have not.

  Customers' expectations with regard to how they want to be treated have risen, and many organizations have simply not met the challenge. The result is considerable consumer dissatisfaction with service. The problem is that many firms and employees do not realize this. The physical service or product provided, the attitude projected, and the efforts of these individuals all combine to represent the quality of service that a consumer receives.

- **Reliance on technology:** The use of database marketing and direct-mail systems has led many firms to believe that an effective and appropriate marketing program simply pops out of a computer tailored to the organization's needs. This is not the case. Efforts at relationship marketing have been jeopardized by this blind allegiance to technology. It has led to the use of meaningless information to design meaningless marketing programs and waste company resources. This has contributed to the image of direct-mail programs as "junk mail" without sensitivity to the consumer's needs.

- **Short-term goals:** Within the firm, marketing decisions may be determined ultimately outside of the marketing department. Short-term sales and budget projections may shape what resources are available for marketing efforts. This may be at the cost of the long-term equity of the brand and of the provision of superior service to customers. Some managers feel marketing efforts are extraneous and that whatever funds are left over can be used for marketing. In response to a drop in sales, some managers will "compensate" with a drop in marketing expenditure: If sales have already dropped, can less marketing and promotion effort improve the situation?

Understanding the criticisms

To evaluate criticisms against marketing, we must understand what actually is being criticized. Is the object of the complaint ultimately the economic system? An entire industry? A particular firm? If the criticism applies to a firm, is the marketing department or some other department the culprit?

The free-enterprise system encourages competition, and government regulatory bodies for many years have judged competition by the number of competitors in an industry. Thus, when we complain about the number of toothpaste or cereal brands on the market, we're really criticizing the system. In a particular firm, a faulty product may result from production mistakes, not from marketing problems. Clearly, a failure in manufacturing does not make consumers' complaints less valid. The point is that marketing is not to blame for such business mistakes, although it may be left to the marketing or customer-service department to handle the fallout.

This possible confusion raises a very important question that has been implicit in several sections of this book: What exactly is "marketing"? Or, more correctly, what are the boundaries around the marketing function in an organization? We observed in Chapter 1 that the single most important objective of marketing is customer satisfaction. But a customer may become dissatisfied with a company for a variety of reasons, many of which have nothing to do directly with what historically would be considered the responsibility of the marketing function in a company.

If the marketing department in an organization has the responsibility for customer satisfaction, then it is essential for it to work closely with other departments in the organization. Also, this points out the need for other components of the firm to be marketing-oriented — they must have an appreciation of the fact that their functions have as much potential to influence long-term customer satisfaction and dissatisfaction as do the things that traditionally are considered to be the responsibility of marketing.

We also need to consider the sources of criticism directed at marketing. Some critics are well intentioned and well informed. They point out real weaknesses or errors needing correction, such as deceptive packaging, misleading advertising, and irresponsible pricing. But some critics are simply ill informed. They do not understand the functions associated with distribution or are not aware of the cost of producing and selling a product. As a result, although their criticisms may have popular appeal, these criticisms cannot withstand careful scrutiny. There are other critics whose views do not reflect the sentiments of society but, to serve their own interests, they vociferously criticize behaviour they find objectionable. Some of the protests against the use of advertising in political campaigns is an example. We must examine criticism carefully to separate the legitimate from the erroneous and self-serving.

Responses to Marketing Issues

Efforts to address the issues that arise from marketing activities have come from consumers, the government, and business organizations. In the following sections, we discuss some of these **responses to marketing issues**.

Consumer responses

consumerism
Protests by consumers against perceived injustices in marketing, and the efforts to remedy these injustices.

One response to marketing misdeeds, both actual and alleged, has come from consumer activists. The term **consumerism** was popularized just over 30 years ago when, in response to increasing consumer protests against a variety of business practices, Canada became the first country in the world to establish a government department at the federal level to be responsible for the rights of consumers (Industry Canada, Office of Consumer Affairs: **www.strategis.ic.gc.ca**; click on "Consumer Information"). The emphasis has been on protecting consumers from harmful products and from false and misleading advertising.

Industry Canada, Office of Consumer Affairs

Government responses

Interest in consumer issues is not likely to disappear. The main reason for this forecast is that today it is politically popular to support various consumer, social, and environmental causes. All of the provinces have legislation and consumer protection programs in place.

A significant number of these laws were designed to protect the consumer's right to safety — especially in situations when consumers cannot judge for themselves the risk involved in the purchase and use of particular products. Legislation such as the Food and Drugs Act regulates and controls the manufacture, distribution, and sale of food, drugs, and cosmetic products. The Hazardous Products Act establishes standards for the manufacture of consumer products designed for household, garden, personal, or recreational usages, or for use by children.

One controversial area of product safety legislation is the paternalistic type of law that is intended to protect consumers — whether or not they want that protection. Thus, it is mandatory to equip automobiles with seat belts and it is illegal to operate an automobile unless the seat belts are fastened. In many cities, bicycle riders are required to wear helmets. In effect, somebody else is forcing a consumer to accept what the other person feels is in the consumer's best interests — truly a new and broadening approach to consumer legislation.

Another series of laws and government programs support the consumer's right to be informed. These measures help in such areas as reducing confusion and deception in packaging and labelling, identifying the ingredients and nutritional content of food products, advising consumers of the length of life of certain packaged food products, providing instructions and assistance related to the care of various textile products, and determining the true rate of interest in financial transactions.

Business responses

An increasing number of businesses are making substantive responses to consumer problems. Here are a few examples:

- *Better communications with and information for consumers:* Toll-free telephone numbers now appear on many manufacturers' packages or in their advertising. Increasingly, advertisers are including their Web site addresses in advertisements and are encouraging consumers to contact them via e-mail. Manufacturers' instruction manuals on the use and care of their products are more detailed and easier to read. Often, package labels are more informative than they were in the past. Many companies also have installed call-centre operations that are staffed around the clock, allowing consumers to call with questions or problems using the company's toll-free number. The vast majority of larger companies now have Web sites that contain much more information than was available to the public in the past and in a much more accessible form.

- *Product improvements:* More marketers are making a concerted effort to incorporate feedback from consumers in the designs of their products. As a result of consumer input or complaints, many companies have made improvements in their products. For example, detergent manufacturers have produced concentrated products that are more environmentally safe and scent-free products that contain no perfumes that might irritate people with allergies.

- *Service quality measurement:* Many companies have realized that it is becoming increasingly difficult to gain a competitive advantage through product design and that the key to success is to offer the customer the best possible service. Realizing also that they need feedback so that they know how well they are doing, many have developed and introduced programs that allow them to measure consumers' perceptions of the level of service they are receiving.

- *More carefully prepared advertising:* Many advertisers are extremely cautious in approving ads prepared by their advertising agencies, in sharp contrast to past practices. Advertisers also are involving their legal departments in the approval process.

- *Customer-service departments:* A growing number of companies have established departments to handle consumer enquiries and complaints. In addition to dealing with complaints, customer-service departments also gauge consumer tastes, act as sounding boards for new ideas, and often gain consumer feedback on new products.

Some trade associations see themselves as defenders of their respective industries or professions. In that capacity, they try to moderate government anti-business legislation by lobbying and head off criticism with arguments to justify almost any behaviour. More enlightened associations have recognized the necessity for responsible corporate behaviour. Such associations reflect those marketers that have been responsive to changes in the social fabric and marketplace that make up Canada. Although they still engage in lobbying, these groups actively respond to consumer problems by setting industry ethics standards, conducting consumer education, and promoting research among association members.

← **BACKSPACE**

1. A/an _____ is a comprehensive review of the marketing functions in an organization

2. What is the 80-20 principle?

3. What is shareholder value? What does it measure?

Ethics and Marketing

ethics
The rules and standards of moral behaviour that are generally accepted by a society.

Ethics are standards of conduct. To act in an ethical fashion is to conform to an accepted standard of moral behaviour. Undoubtedly, virtually everyone prefers to act ethically. It is easy to be ethical when no hardship is involved — when a person is winning and life is going well. The test comes when things are not going so well — when pressures build up. These pressures arise in all walks of life, and marketing is no exception.

Marketing executives face the challenge of balancing the best interests of consumers, their organizations, and society into a workable guide for their daily activities. In any situation, they must be able to distinguish what is ethical from what is unethical and act accordingly, regardless of the possible consequences. However, there are many circumstances in which determining ethical behaviour is far from straightforward.[12]

Setting ethical guidelines

Many organizations have formal codes of ethics that identify specific acts (bribery, accepting gifts) as unethical and describe the standards by which employees are expected to live their business lives. A large percentage of major corporations have ethics codes, as do many smaller businesses. These guidelines lessen the chance that an employee will knowingly or unknowingly violate a company's standards. In addition, ethics codes strengthen a company's hand in dealing with customers or prospective customers who encourage unethical behaviour. For young or inexperienced managers, these codes can be valuable guides, helping them to resist pressure to compromise personal ethics in order to move up in the firm.

However, every decision cannot be taken out of the hands of the manager. Furthermore, determining what is right and what is wrong can be extremely difficult. When faced with an ethical problem, honest answers to the following questions help to indicate which route a manager could follow:

● Would I do this to a friend?

● Would I be willing to have this done to me?

● Would I be embarrassed if this action was publicized nationally?

Socially responsible behaviour

social responsibility
The commitment on the part of a company to improving the well-being of society.

Avon Canada

Canadian Marketing Association

Ethical behaviour goes beyond avoiding wrongdoing. Ethical marketers recognize that the position they hold in society carries with it certain obligations. This **social responsibility** involves improving the well-being of society. Besides obeying the law and meeting the normal and reasonable expectations of the public, socially responsible organizations and individuals lead the way in setting standards of business and community performance. Some companies encourage their employees to join volunteer groups and will pay the fees for staff to join service clubs that are involved in community projects. Many companies donate money raised from the sale of certain items to charitable organizations. Since 1993, Avon Canada (**www.avon.ca**) has raised more than $8 million for breast cancer research, prevention, and education through the sale of its Avon Flame Crusade products. In 2001 alone, the Avon Flame Teddy Bear raised more than $1.5 million, the most raised in a single year. CIBC and Ford are major sponsors of the "Run For The Cure" and promote breast cancer research, education, diagnosis, and treatment year-round on their Web sites. Such companies wisely choose social causes that may best identify with core or expanding target groups of consumers.[13]

Protecting the customer's right to privacy

One of the most troublesome issues facing marketers relates to behaviour that threatens the customer's right to privacy. This is especially important today, because more and more companies are collecting information on customers from a number of sources and storing the data on databases to be used for marketing purposes. Some consumers object to businesses having the information in the first place and to their use of it to sell them things. The point is that the technology is available to permit the integration of databases, making it possible to obtain information about the characteristics of consumers and their households and to match that information with data about purchases, credit card usage, and other consumption behaviour.

Nowhere is the issue of privacy more pertinent than in the area of telemarketing. As the use of the telephone has increased to contact people in their homes for the purpose of marketing products and services, so too has the public outcry against such a practice. Many members of the public object to being telephoned at home, so they have installed answering machines or a call-management service provided by a telephone company that will allow them to screen calls or have paid extra for unlisted telephone numbers. The issue has now also found its way onto the Internet, as many consumers object to the amount of unsolicited advertising that appears each day in their e-mail inboxes.

The direct-marketing industry has taken steps to police itself with regard to offering protection to consumers against invasion of privacy. The industry association, the Canadian Marketing Association (**www.the-cma.org**), has adopted a code of standards that regulates its members, who account for about 80 percent of all direct marketers in Canada.

As discussed previously, regulation of the Internet has begun. This started with privacy legislation Bill C-6 (2001), which changed the nature of how *all* companies are allowed to handle client information. By 2004, companies will have

Many companies support worthy social causes.

ADOPTION NOTICE.

Very cute, cuddly individual,
Loves being around people.
Looking to be adopted by
someone special to help find
a cure for breast cancer.

This fall, 500,000 teddy bears will be up for adoption.
The adoption fee is only $5.00. All profits go to breast cancer research.
You can get one from an Avon Sales Dealer.

PLEASE CARE. ADOPT A BEAR.

Contact your Avon Sales Dealer, or call 1-800-265-2866

AVON
www.avon.ca

to be able to secure, dispose of, and disseminate this information in a controlled manner. The foundation for this legislation rests on the Canadian Standards Association's Moral Code and provides for three levels of consent regarding personal information collected by Web site operators who may attempt to use the information for purposes other than that for which it was collected. It is hoped that such practices, if enforced by law, will reduce consumers' fears about conducting transactions online.[14]

Advertising and social responsibility

Benetton

The issue of the social responsibility of marketing is also often related to the advertising that businesses present to their target consumers. For example, Benetton (**www.benetton.com**), the international Italian-owned clothing manufacturer and retailer, has in recent years employed rather controversial approaches in its advertising. Some consumers in many countries have been shocked by the content of Benetton ads.

Advertising is also criticized for the way in which certain groups in society are presented or for the effect that it may have on them. There has been considerable objection, for example, to the portrayal of ultra-thin young models in fashion advertising for such brands as Calvin Klein and Club Monaco. Critics suggest that such advertising promotes the view that thinness is glamorous and may contribute to eating disorders.[15] Similar public discussion surrounds such issues as whether manufacturers of prescription drugs should be allowed to advertise them to prospective consumers. The United States and New Zealand are the only countries that permit direct-to-consumer advertising of pharmaceuticals, but you'd be excused for thinking Canada has few laws restricting it.

The legislation overseeing advertising of prescription drugs in Canada dates from 1953 and stipulates that pharmaceutical ads may provide information about a disease or can show the name of the product, but they cannot do both at the same time. A new area of pharmaceutical advertising emerged recently when viewers started seeing, for instance, a man celebrating a "good morning" after using Viagra the night before or women discussing contraception over a product shot of Alesse.

This ad presents the brand but can tell you nothing about the condition it treats.

When Alesse (Wyeth-Ayerst Canada Inc.) was released, it was promoted through a series of spots on MuchMusic. Such ads are prohibited from giving in the same commercial both the product name and the condition or disease it is intended to treat. Two different commercials, called "reminder ads" or "help-seeking ads," were run within a few moments of each other that, together, provided both pieces of information. Some felt that this was a violation of existing legislation.[16]

Much advertising that appears in the mass media is controversial for a number of reasons. What is often interesting to observe is that the most violent criticism and the most strident demands for removal of the offending advertising often come from people who are clearly not in the advertiser's intended target market segment.

What Lies Ahead for Marketing?

Let's now consider what lies ahead for marketing. It can be seen that the scope of marketing has been broadening recently to include everything that has the potential to affect the consumer. It is possible to infer that this trend will continue as consumers themselves change, as the technology that reaches into our homes becomes more pervasive, and as competition in the marketplace continues to intensify.

In the future, in order to be more effective and efficient, and to increase levels of customer satisfaction, what do marketers need to know and what do they need to do?

Changes in the marketing environment

Many trends bear watching. We discussed numerous aspects of the external environment in Chapter 2. In this section, we focus on the implications for marketing of four areas: demographic changes, shifts in consumer values and attitudes, the impact of technology, and the growth of information.

Consumer demographics Changes in demographics — the population's age distribution, income, education, ethnic composition, and household structure — all affect marketers' activities. For example, the population is getting older, and senior citizens are the fastest-growing age group. This shift creates expanded marketing opportunities in such areas as travel, tourism, health, and medical care. Another demographic change is the greater ethnic diversity in Canada's cities, resulting primarily from increases in the level of immigration from Asia and other areas. These groups are large enough to attract the attention of marketers, but they present interesting challenges.[17]

What do demographic changes tell us? They indicate that some markets will practically disappear and new ones will emerge. Marketers must remain abreast of these developments and adjust their strategies accordingly.

Values and attitudes Values — the widely held beliefs in a society — change slowly, as do consumers' attitudes. When they do change, however, the impact on existing institutions and the opportunities for innovative marketers can be great. Value shifts often accompany demographic changes. As the Canadian population ages and changes in other ways, we can expect some adjustments in values. For example, we are seeing:

- *Broadened perspectives:* Some forecasters see a shift away from a self-orientation to an "other-orientation." For example, volunteerism is on the upswing. Indications are that people may be disturbed by the materialism of the 1990s, a period in which self-gratification governed many choices. Today, many consumers seem to be motivated by quality of life, rather than by the accumulation of assets.

- *Increased scepticism:* Education is at its highest level ever. Consumers have more confidence in their ability to make judgements and are less willing to accept unsubstantiated claims. Authority is subject to challenge. Consumers demand information and are willing to question traditions. The concerns of Canadians with regard to cuts in social programs, including health care and education, are causing considerable scepticism about the leadership of elected officials. Some people are becoming quite jaded and tired of the pace of life and materialism that seem to dominate society.

● *Balanced lifestyles:* From a society that focused on work to produce a richer lifestyle, we are moving to a society that wants to balance work and leisure to enjoy a lifestyle. This will mean increasing concern with wellness in the form of nutrition and exercise; the allocation of more time to home, family, and leisure; and a desire to become involved in activities viewed as worthwhile and fulfilling. Younger Canadians in particular do not appear to be driven to succeed nearly as much as their parents were.

● *Greater self-confidence:* In part because of their higher levels of education but also in part because of their greater knowledge of the world around them, consumers today have more self-confidence and are more decisive. They understand how the marketplace works and are not at all reluctant to take their business elsewhere if they are not satisfied. As a result, many companies are, as in the example of the cellphone company in our chapter opener, experiencing high levels of customer churn.

● *Demands for good service:* The success of businesses such as Four Seasons Hotels, FedEx, and Kinko's makes it clear that consumers reward good service. It is also apparent that many firms recognize this opportunity. Recognizing the need to offer good service is often easier than finding and training employees to provide it. A major challenge for organizations in the future will be to design and implement systems that provide consumers with high-calibre service. There is increasing evidence that the offering of superior customer service represents a strategic competitive advantage for successful companies.[18]

What do these changes mean for marketing? We are likely to see increasing emphasis on quality over quantity in consumption and a more careful evaluation of the value of product features that seem to add more to style than to substance. One area in which values are evident is a heightened interest in the future quality of life. International concern over the dissipation of the atmosphere's ozone layer, the disappearance of rainforests, increases in acid rain, and the greenhouse effect is obvious. Other environmental issues of interest to consumers are waste disposal and landfills, air and water pollution, and biodegradability.

Technology   There can be little doubt that marketing has been revolutionized in recent years because of the impact of technology. The development of advanced technology has been so rapid that it has created both opportunities and problems that have serious implications for how marketing is carried out in just about every organization. The developments in technology are so vast that we can provide only a brief overview here, but we will touch on a number of key areas where marketing has been affected.

● *Internet marketing:* One opportunity that is obvious from the advances in technology in recent years is use of the Internet to market products and services to prospective customers around the world. Virtually every major company and many smaller ones have created Web sites, and many of these are designed to sell things.

● *Fragmentation and customization of the electronic media:* Technology is revolutionizing the media to which consumers are exposed. Not only are there many more television stations, but there are numerous ways for consumers to access entertainment and educational programming. The result is a mind-boggling array of alternatives, most of them delivered through electronic media and on the Internet.

● *Impact on service delivery:* Technology has had a very definite impact on the delivery of customer service. On the one hand, some argue that the introduction of such technology as automated banking machines, interactive voice-response telephone systems, and call-management software has created an impenetrable barrier between some companies and their customers. This suggests that, at a time when companies are generally interested in establishing close relationships with customers, there is a very real danger that technology will get in the way of a company being able to do so. On the other hand, this is a very good example of the "two-edged sword" nature of technology. At the same time that technology seems to be getting in the way of service delivery, there are many examples of how technology actually facilitates service delivery.

● *Customer monitoring:* Technology has made it possible for companies to get to know their customers far better than has ever been the case in the past. Supermarket scanners and other forms of technology essentially observe the purchase patterns and behaviour of customers and maintain a running record of what has been purchased, where, and when. The result is the comprehensive databases that we will discuss in the next section.

Growth of customer information   Marketers have the ability to pinpoint trends and individual customers as never before. Using scanner data that produces detailed purchase behaviour on a store-by-store basis, Statistics Canada gathers data that provide demographic information down to the city block and, using a variety of other sources such as warranty registration cards, contest entries, and rebate requests, firms can build detailed customer and prospective customer profiles. With this information, they are able to design products and assortments tailored specifically to a customer's needs.

market fragmentation

The identification of smaller and smaller market segments.

Knowing more about the market has led to market fragmentation and to niche marketing — the identification of smaller and smaller market segments. There was a time when a packaged-goods manufacturer could develop a quality product, advertise it nationally using the national media, stock retailers' shelves, and have a reasonable chance of success. But the situation has changed — marketers can no longer expect large numbers of consumers to compromise their needs and wants and buy standardized products. Rather, they must tailor goods and services to meet the needs of small market segments. The strategy of niche marketing significantly complicates the marketer's job. One version of a product is replaced by several. Different ads must be produced and new media must be found to reach different consumers. Retailers must choose among many product variations, not all of which can be stocked. The added variety complicates inventory management, distribution, and personal selling.

There are no indications that the trend toward niche marketing will end. In fact, with more sophisticated electronic data collection methods being developed and the diversity of the population increasing, all indications point to even greater fragmentation in the future. The reaching of smaller and smaller market segments is facilitated largely through advances in technology that make it possible to design a unique marketing program to address the needs of individual customers.

Strategic Marketing Response

One common response to change is simply to react as it occurs. However, realizing that change is always occurring, marketers should initiate strategic proactive efforts to improve performance. Seven are described in this section.

1. Instilling a market-driven orientation   Describing the marketing concept in this book and implementing it in an organization are two different things. The concept — combining a customer orientation with co-ordinated marketing and the organization's goals —

certainly has intuitive appeal, yet many organizations seem unable to practise it consistently. Despite the fact that marketing has been taught in college and university business schools for more than 50 years, effective implementation of marketing is the exception rather than the rule. What does practising a marketing orientation require?

- The marketing concept involves a philosophy of business that focuses on the customer's needs. However, when faced with the choice of putting the customer first or meeting their own needs, some employees often find it difficult to give the customer priority. Instilling this orientation requires top-management commitment. Lip service is not sufficient. Employees must see management putting the customer first.

- There must be a reward system within the company that encourages a customer orientation. Employees must be empowered to make decisions that recognize the importance of customers and be publicly rewarded for those decisions. Managing the employees in a customer-centric organization will increasingly be seen as a partnership between marketing and human resources.

- Organizations must stay in close contact with the market. This means having detailed, accurate market knowledge. Consumers are becoming less and less willing to compromise to satisfy their desires. Marketers must develop more marketing programs for smaller markets. In consumer marketing, this means conducting research on a continuous basis. In business-to-business marketing, it may mean creating new structures. Progressive research firms have helped their clients by developing research programs to measure the quality of service being delivered and to examine the state of customer relationships with service companies.

- Consumers must be offered the best value possible. Many companies have realized that offering discounts and "specials" does little to build long-term customer loyalty and have instead turned to other ways to create value for their customers. The concept of adding value is of such importance that we will return to it later in this chapter.

- Listen to the customer. Successful companies no longer assume that they know what their customers want. Consequently, many are doing more marketing research than they have in the past. They have also learned that they can do nothing to improve the service to customers unless they know when customers are having problems or concerns.

- All exchange partners, not just customers, must be satisfied. The exchange partners of an organization include its customers, suppliers, intermediaries, owners, regulators, and anyone else with whom it interacts. If suppliers, for example, feel their exchanges with an organization are unsatisfactory, they will not do everything in their power to ensure that the needs of end-customers will be met. The same is true of employees. Essential to satisfying the final customers are strong, positive relationships among all of the parties who contribute to bringing a product or service to market.

2. Competing more effectively   Today, most businesses (and not-for-profit organizations, as well) are facing greater and more effective competition than ever before. The array of choices available to consumers today is much more vast than it has ever been. As we observed earlier, competition is coming from all sides, locally, nationally, and internationally. Such a marketing environment changes how a company must compete. It is no longer sufficient (if it ever was!) to merely put products into the marketplace and hope that customers will find them attractive. We have stressed a strategic approach to marketing in this book because it is more important today than ever before for a company to have a strategy in order to compete. This means that it must understand the marketplace, the customer, and the competition better than ever before. It also means that business has to be much more creative in how it practises marketing, so that the company will stand out from the competition and give the customer a reason to deal with it.

MARKETING AT WORK 16-3: STRATEGY

Head-On Marketing Strategy

Affichage Astral *Media*

Four flannel-clad hunters sit around a table in a cabin; laughter and congratulatory backslapping erupt. Above them on the wall is the subject of their latest exploit — a moose head. But, it's not your average hunting trophy, as a shattered car windshield hangs around the moose's neck.

"Peu importe ce qui arrive..." ("Whatever happens...") is flashed on-screen.

This TV spot helped revitalize the image of Lebeau Vitres d'autos almost overnight — with a little help from that giant moose head. With a diminishing market share, the parent company, Montréal-based Belron Canada, set about developing an innovative marketing plan intended to serve as the foundation for marketing in the coming years.

The Goal: After more than 50 years in business, brand recognition was not the problem — personality was, though. Clear positioning was required. The approach led to the new "Whatever happens" slogan, intended to convey the peace of mind that comes from knowing Lebeau can fix your windshield quickly and inexpensively.

The Strategy: Find a way to build Lebeau's image that was accessible across the province and cost-effective. Without a unique selling proposition and with a limited budget, the company had to let the population of drivers know it was different — not necessarily better, just different. Humour and exaggeration would work — in Québec, advertising can be a little more risqué, as "The population doesn't mind laughing at itself," according to Julie Dubé, strategic director of the project.

The Execution: The hunter spot had two runs in 2001 — in the spring and then again in fall. But what really took Montréal by storm was the 1,975-kilogram, 10-metre-wide moose head mounted on a billboard. The billboard travelled to a new location once, receiving a great deal of media coverage. The truck that shipped the billboard was even followed by commuters wondering where it was going.

Spring 2002 saw a switch to radio — continuing with the successful slogan. The spots explained the different kinds of windshield cracks such as the "bullseye" and the "cloverleaf."

The Results: Results were immediate and measurable. During the first TV run in the spring, sales jumped 10 percent. When the campaign ran in the fall, sales went up 17 percent, compared to the year before.

SOURCE: Adapted from Geoff Dennis, "Meeting the Challenge Head On," *Strategy*, July 1, 2002, p. 23.

3. Adopting a global orientation   To be successful in the future, marketers must adopt a global orientation toward markets, products, and marketing activity. In the past, most firms could be successful by focusing on the domestic market and outperforming local rivals, but that has changed: Now firms, both large and small, are going where the markets are the most attractive.

The cliché that we live in a "small world" is a reality for marketers. Virtually instantaneous communication has greatly increased global awareness. Economic, social, and political developments on one side of the world have an impact everywhere else. On the evening television news, we are as likely to hear about developments on the Japanese stock market as we are about activity on Bay Street.

Despite problems, the trend toward global marketing will accelerate. The lure of millions of consumers, combined with an improved understanding of the markets and marketing practices necessary to be successful, will increase the attractiveness of such opportunities. Internet technology has made every marketplace an international market. Consumers and businesses can now obtain information and place and receive orders from across the continent as easily as from across the province. Potential clients and competitors can be from anywhere around the world.

4. Understanding the concept of value and its relationship to customer needs

One of the most talked-about but least-understood concepts in marketing is value. We hear a great deal in marketing circles about adding value for customers. Presumably, this involves adding something over and above what the customer would normally get, in order to make the offering more attractive than that of a competitor. Often overlooked, however, is the fact that, in order to add value, marketers must have a very good understanding of what it is that customers value most. Few companies have invested sufficiently in research to be able to answer the question: What do customers value? The telecommunications company featured in our chapter opener is not unique. In businesses such as this, where the core product is essentially a commodity, relatively few companies have been successful in creating sufficient customer value over and above the core product or service to differentiate themselves. The result is lots of churn.

This issue of adding value is very closely related to the concept of customer needs, as discussed above and in Chapter 1. Customers value what allows them to better meet their needs. Thus, to add value for clients, marketers must be able to understand their needs.

5. Emphasizing quality and customer satisfaction

The emphasis on quality in products and services that is sweeping businesses today requires a rethinking of the role of marketing and even of what marketing means. In fact, there may be some justification in arguing that marketing and quality really refer to the same thing — efforts to produce satisfied customers. They both refer to intrinsic values in organizations that are customer-focused: an attitude, an orientation toward doing whatever is necessary to satisfy the customer. The job of a company's marketing program is not simply to increase sales or even to make sales. Marketing has one objective: to create customers, to create an environment that causes customers to appreciate the benefits of doing business with your firm. It is a strategic function of the organization — or, at least it should be! Things are changing in the Canadian marketing profession — a new rung has been added to the corporate ladder: the chief marketing officer (or CMO). While the form this position takes differs from firm to firm and, in fact, seems to still be changing within firms, what it demonstrates is experimentation with the marketing function, whereby responsibility for customer relationships and satisfaction become part of senior strategy-makers' job descriptions.[19]

Quality in many forms clearly is critical to customer satisfaction and therefore must have a high priority with management. The challenge for managers will be to identify or develop systems that can be successfully implemented and sustained within the existing business culture.

6. Designing environmentally sound strategies

Quality applies to more than making products that work better or longer. A broader issue is the general quality of everyday life and the way we treat the environment. In the past, commitments to single-issue efforts (for example, making a product biodegradable or eliminating chlorofluorocarbons) were enough to win consumer approval. In the future, however, environmental acceptance will be based on a product's entire life cycle, from design through disposal.

Firms will be forced to move away from looking for an exploitable or promotable feature to making environmental concerns an integral part of the business system. This will require a new way of thinking about consumption. One example is to make products so that the materials, components, and packages can be used longer and reused either in part or whole, a process called reconsumption.[20] Forms of reconsumption include:

● **_Reusing:_** Packaging material is often discarded long before it is unusable. Lego, the Danish toy manufacturer, delivers its products to retailers in large, durable boxes that are returned to Lego for reuse.

• ***Refilling:*** Rather than discarding a container when it is empty, if it is properly designed, it can be refilled. More than 30 million laser-printer cartridges are used and disposed of every year. Several companies have designed their cartridges so that they can be refilled.

SKF

• ***Repairing:*** With proper maintenance, products can be used longer. Thus, rather than waiting to act until after a product fails, SKF (**www.skf.se**), a Swedish bearing manufacturer, has developed a series of preventive support services and diagnostic techniques that its customers can use to greatly lengthen the life of its bearings.

• ***Restoring:*** Some products can be returned to their original condition by replacing some parts and reconditioning others. BMW and Mercedes-Benz are now restoring damaged auto parts that in the past were simply discarded.

The key to making reconsumption work is developing methods of manufacturing and marketing that make it profitable. This isn't easy. McDonald's invested nearly 60 percent of its research and development budget to attempting to develop a soluble plastic for packaging. Reconsumption also requires new ways of thinking. For years, manufacturers have focused on ways of assembling things efficiently. Now, the focus must switch to developing technologies for separating materials. For example, finding a method to remove the ink from newsprint economically will be crucial to its recycling.

7. Building relationships   One of the most important aspects of the current new way of looking at marketing is the emphasis that many companies now put on the development of relationships with customers. There is growing appreciation of the fact that it costs a company a great deal more to attract a new customer than it does to keep an existing customer happy. Therefore, we have seen a change in emphasis away from getting customers and toward keeping customers. In fact, some authors have suggested that in the future marketers must pay increasing attention to the "four Rs" of marketing: relationships, retention, referrals, and recovery.[21]

In this new way of thinking, marketers will stress building relationships with customers who will generate long-term profits for the company, developing strategies that will keep them satisfied so that they will stay with the company, and creating strategies that will deal with recovering from problems and mistakes when these occur. As the following box reflects, there is a considerable difference between this new way of looking at marketing and what has been practised in the past.

Old Marketing Model	New Marketing Model
• Focus on the product.	• Focus on process for serving customers.
• Define the target group.	• Feed and nourish the relationship.
• Set brand objectives.	• Extend respect and value to customers.
• Opportunity comes from analysis.	• Opportunity comes from synergy.
• Focus on brand benefit.	• Develop and refresh relevance.
• Create strategic advertising.	• Open the doors for dialogue.
• Operate against a brand plan.	• Improvise to sustain the relationship.
• Driven by a marketing group.	• A pervasive interdisciplinary attitude.

SOURCE: John Dalla Costa, "Towards a Model Relationship," *Marketing Magazine*, June 27, 1994, p. 12. Reprinted with permission.

One final issue that should be addressed concerns the type of relationship that a company should establish with its customers. There are some who believe that having a customer's name in a database and sending regular mailings to that customer constitutes a relationship. But a genuine relationship that will last a long time requires the company to demonstrate sincere interest in customers and in their well-being — not really different from those factors that contribute to relationships between people.[22]

← BACKSPACE

1. Many organizations have _____ that describe the standards by which employees are expected to live their business lives.
2. What is social responsibility?
3. Name the seven strategic proactive efforts to improve performance discussed in this chapter.

Summary

The marketing function should be based on a "big picture" perspective of what should be included in the marketing of the organization. This holistic, or strategic, view requires marketing planning to begin at a high level within the organization to ensure that all relevant functional areas are included in the planning process.

The management process in marketing is the planning, implementation, and evaluation of the marketing effort in an organization. Implementation is the stage in which an organization attempts to carry out its strategic planning. Strategic planning is virtually useless if it is not implemented effectively.

Implementation includes three activities — organizing, staffing, and operating. In organizing, the company first should co-ordinate all marketing activities into one department whose top executive reports directly to the CEO.

The evaluation stage in the management process involves measuring performance results against predetermined goals. Evaluation enables management to determine the effectiveness of its implementation and to plan corrective action when necessary. In today's rapidly changing environment, firms should periodically reassess their goals to determine if these remain feasible and relevant. A marketing audit is a key element of a total marketing evaluation program. Most companies are victims of at least some misdirected marketing effort. Too many companies do not know how much they should be spending on marketing activities, or what results they should get from these expenditures.

A firm's marketing performance should be appraised from a broad, societal perspective. Thus, evaluating an organization's marketing efforts must consider how well it satisfies the wants of its target customers, meets its own needs, and serves the best interests of society.

Marketing has been criticized for being exploitative, inefficient, and illegal, and for stimulating unwholesome demand. Many criticisms of marketing are valid. Fortunately, the offensive behaviour is confined to a small minority of all marketers.

Consumer responses to marketing problems have included protests, political activism, and the support of special-interest groups. Conditions that provide an impetus for widespread consumerism — sensitivity to social and environmental concerns, and the willingness to become actively involved — are present today. Governments at the federal, provincial, and local levels enforce consumer-protection legislation. Businesses have responded to criticism by improving communications, providing more and better information, upgrading products, and producing more sensitive advertising.

Many organizations have established codes of conduct to help employees behave ethically. However, it is not possible to have a rule for every situation. Managers can use a form of cost-benefit analysis to evaluate the ethics of alternatives. Another method of judging the ethics of a particular act is to ask three questions: Would I do this to a friend? Would I be willing to have this done to me? Would I be embarrassed if this action was publicized nationally? Besides being morally correct, ethical behaviour by organizations can restore public confidence, avoid government regulation, retain the power granted by society, and protect the image of the organization.

Prospects for the future of marketing are reflected in projected changes in consumer demographics, shifts in values, and the expansion of information. Marketers must react to these and other changes to remain competitive in the twenty-first century. Among the necessary adjustments are instilling a market-driven orientation, adopting a global orientation, gaining a better understanding of key concepts such as value, emphasizing quality and satisfaction, and retaining customers by building relationships.

Key Terms and Concepts

80-20 principle 497
channel-relationship program 491
consumerism 501
corporate culture 491
customer-centric 490
employee-relationship program 491
ethics 503
holistic view of marketing 490
iceberg principle 497

market fragmentation 508
marketing audit 496
marketing implementation 495
misdirected marketing effort 497
niche marketing 508
responses to marketing issues 501
social responsibility 504
supplier-relationship program 491

Questions and Problems

1. "Good implementation in an organization can overcome poor planning, but good planning cannot overcome poor implementation." Explain, using examples.

2. Give examples of how advertising and personal selling activities might be co-ordinated in a company's marketing department.

3. Can all of the criticisms of marketing be dismissed on the basis of critics being poorly informed or acting in their own interests?

4. How can a company's leadership affect customer satisfaction and retention?

5. What are the social and economic justifications for "paternalistic" laws such as seat-belt regulations and warnings on cigarette packages and alcoholic beverage containers?

6. Discuss some ethical implications of the fact that many companies today are able to obtain a considerable amount of data about consumers and what they buy, and other information that some consumers may wish to keep confidential. What are reasonable boundaries on the use of such information for marketing purposes?

7. Describe a firm whose behaviour toward its customers reflects, in your opinion, the adoption of a customer-focused strategy.

8. Choose two firms in the retail clothing industry that you think have opposite views of marketing. How does each practise marketing?

9. In the previous question, which firm would you say does not have an holistic view of marketing? What would it need to change in order to think beyond the traditional view of the marketing mix?

10. In question 8, choose the firm that has the most progressive view of marketing. How can this firm use the "four Rs of marketing" to improve customer loyalty and to build relationships with its customers? Use specific examples.

Hands-On Marketing

1. Interview a marketing executive to find out how the total marketing performance is evaluated in her or his company. As part of your report, include your appraisal of this company's evaluation program.

2. Ask the managers of three firms in the same industry:
   a. What foreseeable developments will have the greatest impact on marketing in their industry over the next five years?
   b. How they think the industry should respond to the developments.

Back to the Top

Think back to our chapter opener and Joanne Henson's experience in meeting some of her company's clients for the first time. Her work experience had been limited to financial services and she has now been exposed to some different thinking. What advice do you think she can provide to the companies who define loyalty as shopping behaviour and who seem to have difficulty differentiating themselves? Why do you suppose she was impressed by IKEA's definition of its best customers? What are the implications of this kind of thinking for how marketing is practised in that company?

Want to get better grades, tips on how to study more effectively, and up-to-date information on happenings in the world of marketing? Then, visit the Online Learning Centre for practice tests, Study Smart software, and much more! **www.mcgrawhill.ca/college/sommers**

Interested in finding out what marketing looks like in the real world? *Marketing Magazine* is just a click away on your Online Learning Centre!

Case 7-1

Canadian Blood Services
Lori Gives Blood

Lori's family had always given blood. She remembers how her whole family made an annual visit to a local high school gymnasium where the Red Cross was set up. There were always cookies and muffins and juice. She was 10 years old and a little nervous the first time she gave blood, but when she didn't feel any pain, her nervousness went away. She remembers asking her father why they were giving blood and he explained to her that sick people sometimes didn't have enough and needed it. He told her that her blood would be used to save lives. Lori was satisfied and didn't think about it any more.

A few years later, Lori's brother Brad was in a motorcycle accident. He was rushed to the hospital, where he was given a blood transfusion. Fortunately, Brad survived and Lori's father explained to her that without the blood transfusion, her brother would have died. The family's visits to the Red Cross Blood Donor Clinic were now much more meaningful, until the day they discovered that Brad had hepatitis C. The doctor explained that Brad had contracted the disease when he received the blood transfusion; there was no other possible explanation. Lori and her family were shocked. How could this have happened? They had always trusted the Red Cross. It was supposed to be safe. What later became known as the "tainted blood scandal" was to change Brad's life forever.

Lori never gave blood to the Red Cross again. She felt that she and her family had been betrayed, along with thousands of other Canadians. Some time later, the Canadian Blood Services (CBS) took over management of the blood supply for Canadians. This newly formed not-for-profit organization had an enormous challenge ahead of it. How was it going to rebuild the trust of Canadians that the Red Cross had lost? CBS needed to make it clear to Canadians that it was handling the blood differently and that it was committed to safety. The organization needed to find a way to connect with its target market — Canadians who were willing to give blood.

Canadian Blood Services therefore launched a huge ad campaign designed to appeal to the emotions of Canadians. Ads featuring real people who needed blood transfusions appeared on television and in movie theatres, with the tag line "Blood. It's in you to give." These dramatic ads struck a chord with Lori, whose social conscience pushed her to give blood once again. She hesitated at first, fearing that the blood could be mishandled as it had been by the Red Cross. But eventually, she was convinced that the new organization took safety very seriously. She went back to giving blood once a year, as she always had when she was growing up. She felt that her small contribution could save a life. It made her feel good to give blood.

Questions

1. What challenges did CBS face when it took over from the Red Cross?

2. How did marketing help the organization to achieve its goals?

3. Lori gives blood to CBS, but what does she get in return? Is it an exchange?

Case 7-2

Mystery Shoppers

John has worked part-time at Roots for almost a year. While he usually enjoys his job, he wasn't enjoying himself on this particular Tuesday evening. The 21-year-old student was unable to concentrate. All he had on his mind was his biology mid-term at 9 a.m. the next day. He'd tried to switch shifts, but none of his co-workers were able to work for him that night. So, he was stuck with his shift and completely stressed about it. He would have to stay up half the night studying if he wanted to pass that exam. He had just handed in two papers for other courses that day and was hoping to have the rest of the day and evening to study. But, here he was, exhausted from staying up the night before to write his papers and only four hours into an eight-hour shift. Besides that, he had to close the store that night, which meant at least an extra 20 minutes. At this rate, he wouldn't get home before 10 pm.

John was stressed. In the last month, he had contemplated quitting his job several times but needed the income to supplement his student loan. He was making only slightly more than minimum wage, but this did allow a little spending money. And, with his employee discount, John could afford some nice clothing.

That night, John had brought his biology book to work. He knew Tuesdays were slow and that he'd be able to put in a bit of time studying. Besides, Mike was working with him and told him that he'd take care of customers while John studied.

No sooner had John opened his book than a woman walked into the store. She looked around, seeming to go through every single rack, picked out some items, and walked up to Mike to ask him questions. John was focused on the chapter he was reading and didn't hear the conversation. After what seemed like 10 minutes, the woman approached John and started asking him detailed questions about the clothing, the material it was made of, the available sizes, the washing instructions. Mike walked over to the counter, looking helpless. The woman had clearly not been satisfied with his answers and now she was waiting for John to be more helpful. She explained to him that they didn't have her size. John apologized and, while he knew he could have phoned another store and had them send over the right size, he didn't want to make Mike look incompetent. He simply shrugged his shoulders. The woman put the clothes down on the counter and left the store.

Mike turned to John and said, "She seemed awfully curious. Do you think she was one of those mystery shoppers?" John looked puzzled: "A what?" Mike explained what he had seen on television the night before. CBC's *Marketplace* had shown a segment on mystery shoppers, people hired by stores to examine service quality, among other things. Mystery shoppers look like ordinary customers, so employees don't know they're secretly being evaluated. John shook his head. "No, man, you're just paranoid" but as he said it, he wasn't convinced. Maybe the company had hired someone to check up on them.

Questions

1. If the woman was indeed a mystery shopper, was it fair to evaluate John when he was having a bad day?

2. Is it ethical to spy on your staff? How would you feel if you worked in a clothing store and knew that management hired mystery shoppers?

3. Do managers have other options for evaluating staff and making sure they are delivering high-quality service to customers?

Video source: CBC *Marketplace*, "Mystery Shoppers," January 9, 2001.

Case 7-3

Jack Garrett's View of Marketing

Jack Garrett sat back in his chair and sighed. From his office window, he could see the Toronto skyline. He loved the view from his office, but he wasn't so sure about his job anymore. He almost regretted taking this new job as marketing director at Urban Clothiers, a national clothing chain with corporate headquarters in Toronto. He had been with the company only two months, but already he was feeling as though he'd made a bad move. At the time, it seemed like an exciting career change, not to mention a huge promotion. Only six years out of a commerce program at a well-known east-coast university, Jack was quite young to have the position, especially with such a successful company.

Prior to taking the job, he worked for ThinkTank Consultants, a small marketing consulting firm in Montréal. There, he put in many long hours and his work had paid off. He had landed some major contracts, which made him very appealing to potential employers when he began looking for a new job. Jack remembered how he had sat down with the president of Urban Clothiers, Larry Macintosh, during a second interview. Larry had told Jack how the company needed new blood and that he was hoping Jack could bring in some new ideas. Jack had left the meeting elated. This was exactly what he was looking for!

Jack smiled as he thought back to that meeting. Suddenly, there was a knock on the door. Larry walked in. "Hi, Jack. I was just thinking about the meeting we had yesterday and I think you're right. We really need to focus on customer loyalty. I was thinking that we need to give more to our customers." For a moment, Jack felt relieved. Maybe Larry was finally coming around to his way of thinking. Then Larry suggested a loyalty program, using a card. Jack frowned. No, Larry just didn't get it. Jack felt, more than ever, that he should have stayed with his old firm. The pay wasn't as good, but at least management thought the way he did about marketing. Building customer loyalty was far more complex than Larry thought. It could not be done just by using a so-called loyalty program. The company had to go beyond that. It had to create value by finding out what the customers wanted. But there was no point in arguing with Larry: Jack felt that there was no way to make him understand.

Jack went home that night frustrated. When he lived in Montréal, he had gone to a talk by Elliott Ettenberg, a top-level marketing executive. Ettenberg was something of a business radical, but many were starting to listen to his gloomy predictions about the future of marketing. He spoke about future demographic and societal trends that would shake up the world of marketing as we've known it for the past 30 years. The "four Ps of marketing" — product, price, promotion, and place — will be pushed aside by the "four Rs of marketing" — relationships, relevancy, retrenchment (going directly to the consumer), and reward, explained Ettenberg to an attentive crowd. According to the native Montréaler, we are moving into the Next Economy.

Recently, Jack had picked up a copy of Ettenberg's book *The Next Economy*, in which he argues that a collapse in consumer spending is looming that will turn into a long and deep recession lasting 20 years or more. Ettenberg explains that as Baby Boomers near retirement, the results will be dramatic. Jack had read how this generation represents the single largest age group in North America, and as they begin to retire, Boomers will start to spend much less. Once the best shoppers, Baby Boomers will now be putting their wallets away. What's worse, the generation that follows — Generation X — is half the size of the Boomers and much tighter with its money. Ettenberg argues that this recession will last until Generation Y — those who are now between the ages of 8 and 25 — reaches middle age and starts spending. Jack couldn't put the book down. If Ettenberg's predictions were right, he thought, then mass marketing would no longer be effective.

What does this mean for the marketer? A lot, according to Ettenberg. As Boomers become more careful with their money, they will become more selective about what they buy — they'll be harder to please. Ultimately, the marketer will need to spend more time and money gaining a deeper insight into what customers want. Marketers will no longer be able to simply group people into demographic categories. They'll *really* need to know who their customers are. Understanding the psychographic characteristics of a customer will be necessary to delve more deeply into what the customer wants. Knowing what customers really want will mean researching their values, beliefs, habits, and lifestyles.

Jack had to agree with Ettenberg. When he was working at ThinkTank, he and his co-workers often discussed how companies could better understand their customers. As a consultant, Jack had worked with many companies and had been able to convince most with his way of thinking. But with Larry, there was no hope. Jack wouldn't be able to implement these ideas at Urban Clothiers.

The company simply didn't understand its customers. Sure, Urban Clothiers was successful, but if it was going to grow, it was going to have to gain a competitive advantage in the highly competitive world of retail clothing. Jack knew that mass marketing would no longer be effective. The customer of the future would be more sophisticated and more demanding and would no longer accept being grouped with the masses. Why? Because technology enables customers to become more knowledgeable about products and services. These customers increasingly know what they want and demand respect. And if they don't get it, they'll go elsewhere. In his book, Ettenberg argues that as demand drops and customers become pickier, firms will need to compete on the basis of their ability to please customers and build relationships with them. Jack thought Ettenberg was dead-on. The problem remained how to convince Larry.

Jack knew that Larry didn't want to hear about the gloomy future Ettenberg was predicting. Larry's thinking was: Everything's great — why change it? Jack could hear his boss saying, "We're making money and our shareholders are happy. Everything's fine." But Jack knew that this thinking was outdated. It used to be (and still is, for many firms) that company goals revolved around increasing shareholder value. The more money firms made for their shareholders, the better. But in the future, Ettenberg argues, business priorities will need to shift from satisfying shareholders to delighting customers. Until now, firms have been obsessed with the short term, but this will have to change, the author explains. Building relationships with customers is a long-term strategy that is often overlooked by short-sighted executives. Jack knew this only too well. After all, he himself seemed to be working for a short-sighted executive.

Jack decided to give it one last try. Armed with Ettenberg's advice from *The Next Economy*, Jack explained to Larry that the company needed to prepare for the gloomy future. He explained how Ettenberg urges firms to concentrate their efforts on building customer loyalty and forming genuine relationships with the top two-fifths of their customers. That means ranking customers according to the number of dollars they spend with the company each year and focusing the company's marketing efforts on those who fall into the top two-fifths. In the Next Economy, profits will be more important than market share and traditional measures of success will have to change. Higher margins and share of wallet will be the new measures of success. Larry nodded as Jack spoke, but he kept looking at his watch. He was obviously distracted. Finally, he cut Jack off, patted him on the shoulder and said, "Sounds interesting. We'll talk about this again sometime." Jack knew that "sometime" meant never. He would start looking for a job with a more progressive company as soon as he could.

Questions

1. What do Ettenberg's predictions mean for the marketing departments of large companies? How must they change in the future to remain competitive?

2. What is Larry's view of marketing? How does it differ from Jack's? Why does this frustrate Jack?

3. Why will the four Rs of marketing be more important than the four Ps in the Next Economy?

4. How does Ettenberg propose that businesses should build relationships with their customers?

Source: J. Burton Eller, "The Next Economy," *Textile Rental Magazine*, June 2002; Unknown, "Business's New Customer," *McGraw-Hill Ryerson: Press Releases*, January 28, 2002; Susan Reda, "Sophisticated new tools help retailers evaluate the payoff from advertising and marketing," *Stores Online*, May 1998; Lesley Daw, "Ettenberg leaves Bozell to set up shop," *Marketing Online*, May 3, 1999; Gordon Pitts, "New Style advocated for 'Next Economy': Marketer advises targeting best customers," *The Globe and Mail*, February 22, 2002, p. B11.

Video source: CBC *Venture*, "Boomer Doom," May 26, 2002.

Glossary

80-20 principle: A situation in which a large proportion of a company's marketing units (products, territories, customers) accounts for a small share of the company's volume or profit, and vice versa.

accessory equipment: In the business market, capital goods used in the operation of a firm.

activities, interests, and opinions: The bases of an individual's lifestyle; these characterize how people lead their lives.

activity indicator of buying power: A market factor that is related to income generation and expenditures; sometimes, a combined indicator of purchasing power and the number of business users.

actual self-concept: The way you really see yourself, as distinguished from *ideal self-concept*.

administered vertical marketing system: A distribution system in which channel control is maintained through the economic power of one firm in the channel.

advertising: All activities involved in presenting to a group a non-personal, sponsor-identified message regarding a product or organization.

advertising agency: An independent company rendering specialized services in advertising in particular and in marketing in general.

advertising allowance: A payment or cash discount offered by a manufacturer to a retailer to encourage the retailer to advertise or prominently display the manufacturer's product.

advertising campaign: The total advertising program for a product or brand that involves co-ordination, a central theme, and specific goals.

advertising media: The communications vehicles (such as newspapers, radio, and television) that carry advertising.

advertising recall: A measure of advertising effectiveness based on the premise that an ad can have an effect only if it is perceived and remembered.

agent wholesaler: An independent firm that primarily engages in wholesaling and does not take title to the products being distributed, but does actively negotiate their sale or purchase on behalf of other firms.

agribusiness: The business side of farming; usually involves large, highly mechanized farming operations.

annual marketing plan: A written document that details the planned marketing activities for a business unit or product for a given year.

appeal: The reason, justification, or argument presented in an advertisement to cause a message receiver to be influenced.

attention: Getting people to notice your message.

attitude: A learned predisposition to respond to an object or class of objects in a consistently favourable or unfavourable way.

auction company: An agent wholesaler that provides (1) auctioneers who do the selling and (2) physical facilities for displaying the sellers' products.

automatic vending: A form of non-store retailing in which the products are sold through a machine, with no personal contact between the buyer and seller; same as *automated merchandising*.

awareness: Stage 1 of buying readiness: The customer gains information about the product and the brand name.

B2B marketing: The marketing of goods and services to business users, rather than to end-consumers.

bait pricing: Attracting consumers with a low-priced feature item and then pointing out its weaknesses in order to sell a more expensive version.

base price: The price of one unit of the product at its point of production or resale; same as list price.

behavioural segmentation: Market segmentation based on consumers' product-related behaviour; typically, the benefits consumers desire from a product and the rate at which they use the product.

benchmark: The process of comparing a company with its competitors and others in related industries.

Boston Consulting Group (BCG) matrix: A strategic planning model that classifies strategic business units or major products according to market shares and growth rates.

brand: A name, term, symbol, special design, or some combination of these elements that is intended to identify the products of one seller or a group of sellers.

brand awareness: The first stage in building an association between customers and a brand; they become aware of it.

brand characteristics: The stage of the development of a brand relationship in which customers are able to associate certain characteristics with the brand.

brand equity: The value a brand adds to a product.

brand extensions: New products or services that are launched by a company under an existing brand name.

brand label: The application of the brand name alone to a product or package.

brand loyalty: The situation in which a customer buys a certain brand on a regular basis because of its performance and appeal.

brand mark: The part of a brand that appears in the form of a symbol, picture, design, or distinctive colour or type of lettering.

brand name: The part of a brand that can be vocalized: words, letters, and/or numbers.

brand personality: The acquisition by a brand of certain characteristics normally associated with people; reflects the people who are most likely to buy the brand.

brand recognition: The stage in a brand's association with customers where it is recognized and many customers are familiar with it.

brand relationship: The ultimate stage of association between customers and a brand: They have an emotional attachment to it.

branding: The process of a company or product name acquiring a certain meaning over time; it comes to stand for something in the minds of customers.

breadth of product mix: The number of product lines offered for sale by a firm.

break-even point: The level of output at which revenues equal costs, assuming a certain selling price.

Broadcasting Act: Established the CRTC and provided for sweeping powers of advertising regulation.

broker: An independent agent wholesaler that brings buyers and sellers together and provides market information to either party.

bundling: The process of grouping together a number of services that are sold as a single unit.

business analysis: The stage of new-product development in which a surviving idea is expanded into a business proposal and management identifies product features; estimates market demand, competition, and profitability; establishes a development program; and assigns responsibility for further study.

business product: A product that is intended for purchase and use in producing other products or in rendering services in a business.

business (B2B) market: The market consisting of business users.

business user: An organization that buys goods or services to resell, use in its own business, or make other products.

business-to-business advertising: Advertisements directed to businesses rather than consumers.

buy classes: Three typical buying situations in the business market: new-task buy, straight rebuy, and modified rebuy.

buyers: The people in a buying centre who select the suppliers, arrange the terms of sale, and process the actual purchase orders.

buying centre: All of the people in an organization who participate in the buying-decision process.

buying-decision process: The series of logical stages through which a prospective purchaser goes when faced with a buying problem. The stages differ for consumers and organizations.

buying motive: The reason why a person buys a specific product.

cash cows: Strategic business units that are characterized by high market shares and do business in mature industries (those with low growth rates).

catalogue retailing: One form of direct marketing, in which companies mail catalogues to consumers or make them available at retail stores, and consumers make their purchases from the catalogues.

category-killer store: A type of retail institution that has a narrow but very deep assortment, emphasizes low prices, and offers few-to-moderate customer services; it is designed to "destroy" all competition in a specific product category.

Census Metropolitan Area (CMA): One of the major population centres of Canada, as defined by Statistics Canada; generally contains population centres of 100,000 or more.

channel conflict: A situation in which one channel member perceives another channel member to be acting in a way that prevents the first member from achieving its distribution objectives.

channel control: The ability to influence the behaviour of other channel members.

channel-relationship program: A program intended to develop positive relationships with distribution channel members, such as wholesalers and retailers.

cognitive dissonance: Anxiety created by the fact that in most purchases the alternative selected has some negative features and the alternatives not selected have some positive features.

commercial information environment: All marketing organizations and individuals that directly or indirectly communicate with consumers.

commercial services: The services marketed by business or professional firms with profit-making motives, as compared with the services offered by public and not-for-profit organizations.

commission merchant: An independent agent wholesaler, used primarily in the marketing of agricultural products, that may physically handle the seller's products in central markets and has authority regarding prices and terms of sale.

commoditization: A situation in which consumers perceive little or no difference among the products of various companies and therefore focus on price as a differentiator.

communication: Verbal or non-verbal transmission of information, through a medium or media, between a sender and a receiver.

company sales branch: A sales facility that carries a stock of the product being sold.

comparative advertising: Selective-demand advertising in which the advertiser either directly (by naming a rival brand) or indirectly (through inference) points out how the advertised brand is better.

Competition Act: The major federal legislation in Canada that governs the marketing and advertising activities of companies and organizations operating in Canada.

competitive bidding: The characteristic form of government procurement, in which a government agency advertises both offline and online for bids, using a format that states the specifications of the intended purchase. The agency must accept the lowest bid that meets these specifications.

consultative salesperson: A selling job in which the person engages in the creative selling of goods and services.

consumer: An individual or organizational unit that uses or consumes a product or service.

consumer advertising: Advertisements directed to consumers.

consumer product: A product that is intended for purchase and use by household consumers for non-business purposes.

consumer promotion: The type of sales promotion that is aimed at consumers.

consumerism: Protests by consumers against perceived injustices in marketing, and the efforts to remedy these injustices.

containerization: A cargo-handling system in which shipments of products are enclosed in large metal or wooden containers that are then transported unopened from the time they leave the customer's facilities until they reach their destination.

contracting: A legal relationship that allows a firm to enter a foreign market indirectly, quickly establish a market presence, and experience a limited amount of risk.

contractual vertical market system: An arrangement in which independent firms (producers, wholesalers, and retailers) operate under a contract specifying how they will try to improve their distribution efficiency and effectiveness.

convenience goods: A class of consumer products of which the consumer has prior knowledge and purchases with minimum time and effort.

convenience sample: A sample that is selected in a non-random way, so that every member of the universe does not have an equal chance of being included.

convenience store: A type of retailing institution that concentrates on convenience-oriented groceries and non-foods, has higher prices than found at most grocery stores, and offers few customer services.

conviction: Stage 5 of buying readiness: The customer makes an actual decision or commitment to purchase.

co-operative advertising: Advertising for which two or more firms share the cost.

core services: Services that are the main purpose or object of a transaction.

corporate chain: An organization of two or more centrally owned and managed stores that generally handle the same lines of products.

corporate culture: The atmosphere that prevails within a company, which contributes to employees' satisfaction and influences how they treat customers.

corporate vertical marketing system: An arrangement under which a firm at one level of a distribution channel owns the firms at the next level or owns the entire channel.

cost-based pricing: A company uses its costs as the basis for setting its prices and does not take the customer or market into account.

cost per thousand (CPM): The media cost of gaining exposure to one thousand people with an ad.

culture: A complex of symbols and artifacts created by a given society and handed down from generation to generation as determinants and regulators of human behaviour.

cumulative quantity discount: A quantity discount based on the total volume purchased over a specified period of time.

customer: An individual or organization that makes a purchase decision.

customer-centric: Focused on customers and on achieving customer satisfaction; the customer is at the centre of management thinking.

customer expectations: What customers expect to occur when they enter a service encounter, or what they would like to happen, based in part on their personal experiences.

customer-interest stage: A company realizes that satisfying its customers is critical to its success; generally involves trying to know customers better.

customer loyalty: A state achieved when a customer not only deals regularly with a company, but also feels an emotional attachment to it and recommends it to others.

customer relationship: Close association between company and customers, characterized by strong feelings of loyalty, trust, and commitment; the ultimate connection, based not only on quality of products and service, but also on how the company makes its customers feel.

customer-relationship management: A strategic orientation of a company toward the development of positive, long-term relationships with customers.

customer-relationship stage: A company actively tries to cultivate long-term relationships with its customers, based not only on great products, price, and service, but also on establishing an emotional connection.

customer retention: The behavioural connection between regular customers and a company; characterized by repeat buying behaviour, but not yet a relationship because it may be lacking an emotional component.

customer-retention strategy: The measures that a company uses to retain current customers and have them make repeat purchases; includes getting to know customers in as much detail as possible in order to communicate effectively, and rewarding those who are loyal and continue to give the company their business.

customer satisfaction: The degree to which a customer's experience with a product or organization meets or exceeds his or her expectations.

customer service: That part of the company's value proposition that addresses how the company interacts with its customers, as compared with the core service or services that it offers.

customer-service advertising: Advertising that presents information about the advertiser's operations.

customer-service representatives: Employees who represent the company to customers, usually providing advice and service over the telephone from call centres.

customer-service stage: A company at this stage places emphasis on providing excellent service to its customers, usually through improved systems and employee-customer interaction.

customer value: The value that a customer or customers bring to a company or organization; made up of short-term sales, long-term repeat business, positive influence, and referrals.

data analysis: The process of extracting relevant information from data collected through research; usually associated with the application of statistical tools.

database: A set of related data that is organized, stored, and updated on a computer.

data mining: Method used to identify patterns and meaningful relationships in masses of data that might be unrecognizable to researchers.

data warehouse: A collection of data from a variety of internal and external sources, compiled by a firm for use in conducting transactions.

dealer selection: Under section 75 of the Competition Act, it is illegal for a manufacturer or supplier to refuse to supply a wholesaler or retailer unless the wholesaler or retailer is unwilling or unable to meet the usual trade terms of the supplier.

deciders: The people in a buying centre who make the actual buying decision regarding a product and/or supplier.

decision-maker: The individual in a household or organization who has the responsibility of deciding what to buy.

decline stage: The fourth, and final, part of a product life cycle, during which the sales of a generic product category drop and most competitors abandon the market.

demography: The statistical study of human population and its distribution.

department store: A large-scale retailing institution that has a very broad and deep product assortment, prefers not to compete on the basis of price, and offers a wide array of customer services.

depth of product line: The assortment within a product line.

derived demand: A situation in which the demand for one product is dependent on the demand for another product.

differential advantage/differential competitive advantage: Any feature of an organization or brand perceived by customers to be desirable and different from that of the competition.

direct-action advertising: Product advertising that seeks a quick response.

direct distribution: A channel consisting only of producer and final customer, with no intermediaries providing assistance.

direct mail: An advertising medium in which the advertiser contacts prospective customers by sending some form of advertisement through the mail.

direct marketing: A form of non-store retailing that uses non-personal media to contact consumers who, in turn, purchase products without visiting a retail store.

direct selling: A form of non-store retailing in which personal contact between a salesperson and a consumer occurs away from a retail store.

direct tests: Measures of the sales volume produced by an ad or an entire advertising campaign.

discount house: A large-scale retailing institution that has a broad and shallow product assortment, emphasizes low prices, and offers relatively few customer services.

discount retailing: A retailing approach that uses price as a major selling point by combining comparatively low prices and reduced costs of doing business.

discretionary purchasing power: The amount of disposable income remaining after fixed expenses and essential household needs are covered.

distribution centre: A concept in warehousing that develops under one roof an efficient, fully integrated system for the flow of products, taking orders, filling them, and delivering them to customers.

distribution channel: The set of people and firms involved in the flow of ownership of a product as it moves from producer to ultimate consumer or business user.

diversification: A product-market growth strategy in which a company develops new products to sell to new markets.

dogs: Strategic business units that are characterized by low market shares and operate in industries with low growth rates.

door-to-door selling: A kind of direct selling in which the personal contact between a salesperson and an individual prospect occurs at the prospective customer's residence or business.

driver-salesperson: A selling job in which the job is primarily to deliver the product; selling responsibilities, if any, are secondary to seeing that orders are filled correctly and on time.

drivers of customer satisfaction: Factors that contribute to customer satisfaction.

drop shipper: A limited-function merchant wholesaler that does not physically handle the product.

early adopters: The second group (following innovators) to adopt something new. This group includes opinion leaders, is respected, and has much influence on its peers.

early majority: A more deliberate group of innovation adopters that adopts just before the "average" adopter.

eco-labelling: Seals of approval awarded by a government to encourage environmentally safe products.

economic order quantity (EOQ): The optimal quantity for reorder when replenishing inventory stocks, as indicated by the volume at which the inventory carrying cost plus the order-processing cost are at a minimum.

electronic data interchange (EDI): Computer-to-computer transmission of orders, invoices, or other business information.

emotional value: The value that an organization is able to create for its customers that addresses the feelings that the customer has toward the company or its brands.

employee-relationship program: A program intended to "market" the company to its employees, to get employees on-side in terms of an emphasis on treating customers well.

end-consumers: People who buy products for their personal, non-business use.

environmental scanning: Gathering information regarding a company's internal and external environment, analyzing it, and forecasting the impact of the conditions and trends that the analysis suggests.

ethics: The rules and standards of moral behaviour that are generally accepted by a society.

evaluating sales performance: The process of determining whether sales personnel have achieved objectives; important for compensation.

everyday low pricing (EDLP): A pricing strategy that involves consistently low prices and few if any temporary price reductions.

exchange: The voluntary act of providing a person or organization with something of value in order to acquire something else of value in return.

exclusive dealing: The practice by which a manufacturer prohibits its dealers from carrying products of competing manufacturers.

exclusive distribution: A strategy in which a producer agrees to sell its product to only one wholesaling intermediary and/or retailer in a given market.

exclusive territory: Under this arrangement, a manufacturer requires each intermediary to sell only to customers located within the intermediary's assigned territory.

expectations: What customers expect to encounter when dealing with a company or buying a product or service, based on past experience and desired outcomes.

expected price: The price at which customers consciously or unconsciously value a product; what they think the product is worth.

experimental method: A method of gathering primary data in which the researcher is able to observe the results of changing one variable in a situation while holding all others constant.

export agent: An intermediary that operates either in a manufacturer's country or in the destination country, negotiating the sale of a product in another country; may provide additional services such as arranging for international financing, shipping, and insurance on behalf of the manufacturer.

export merchant: An intermediary operating in a manufacturer's country that buys goods and exports them.

exporting: The activities by which a firm sells its product in another country, either directly to foreign importers or through import-export intermediaries.

express warranty: A statement in written or spoken words regarding restitution from seller to customer if the seller's product does not perform up to reasonable expectations.

external macro-environmental forces: Market forces that are generally beyond the control of companies: demographics, economic conditions, competition, social and cultural trends, technological developments, and political and legal forces.

external micro-environmental forces: Forces affecting a particular firm that can readily be influenced by the company: the sets of marketing relationships a firm has with its customers, its suppliers, and the wholesalers and retailers through which the company sells its products and services.

factory outlet: A special type of off-price retail institution that is owned by a manufacturer and usually sells only that manufacturer's clearance items, regular merchandise, and perhaps even otherwise unavailable items.

family: A group of two or more people related by blood, marriage, adoption, or common practice living together in a household.

family-brand strategy: A branding strategy in which a group of products is given a single brand.

family life cycle: The series of life stages that a family goes through, starting with young, single people and progressing through married stages with young and then older children, then ending with older married and single people.

family packaging: A strategy of using either highly similar packages for all products or packages with a common and clearly noticeable feature.

fashion: A style that is popularly accepted by groups of people over a reasonably long period of time.

fashion-adoption process: The process by which a style becomes popular in a market; similar to diffusion of an innovation.

fishyback service: Transporting loaded trailers on barges or ships.

flexible-price strategy: A pricing strategy under which a company sells similar quantities of merchandise to similar buyers at different prices; same as *variable-price strategy*.

f.o.b. factory pricing: A geographic pricing strategy whereby the buyer pays all freight charges from the selling facility location to the destination.

forward dating: A combination of a seasonal discount and a cash discount under which a buyer places an order and receives shipment during the off-season, but does not have to pay the bill until after the season has started and some sales revenue has been generated.

"four Rs" of marketing: Guideposts for the new way of thinking in marketing: customer retention, relationships, referrals, and recovery from negative experiences.

fragmentation: The break-up of the mass audience for television or other media into smaller audiences as the result of technological innovations, such as the proliferation of channels, channel-zapping, skip devices, use of VCRs and DVD players.

franchising: A type of contractual vertical marketing system that involves a continuing relationship in which a franchiser (the parent company) provides the right to use a trademark plus management assistance in opening and operating a business in return for financial considerations from a franchisee (the owner of the individual business unit).

freight-absorption pricing: A geographic pricing strategy whereby the seller pays for (absorbs) some of the freight charges in order to penetrate more distant markets.

freight forwarder: A specialized transportation agency that consolidates less-than-carload or less-than-truckload shipments into carload or truckload quantities and provides door-to-door shipping service.

full-service wholesaler: An independent merchant wholesaler that normally performs a full range of wholesaling functions.

functional value: The value that a company creates for its customers that is based on the quality of its products and the efficiency of its services.

gatekeepers: The people in a buying centre who control the flow of purchasing information within the organization and between the buying firm and potential vendors.

geographic segmentation: The process of segmenting a market into geographic regions and developing a different marketing strategy for each region.

"give and get": An illustration of the exchange process as both customer and company giving something and getting something in return.

government market: The segment of the business market that includes federal, provincial, and local government units buying for government institutions such as schools, offices, hospitals, and research facilities.

grade label: Identification of the quality (grade) of a product by means of a letter, number, or word.

growth stage: The second part of a product life cycle, during which the sales and profits of a generic product category rise and competitors enter the market; profits start to decline near the end of this part of the cycle.

heterogeneity (of a service): A characteristic of a service indicating that each unit is somewhat different from other units of the same service.

high-involvement level: A purchase decision that involves all six stages of the buying-decision process.

high-low pricing: A pricing strategy that involves charging relatively low prices for some products and higher prices for others.

holistic view of marketing: The view that virtually everything a company does has an impact on customer satisfaction and is, therefore, part of marketing.

horizontal business market: A situation in which a given product is usable in a wide variety of industries.

horizontal conflict: A form of channel conflict occurring between firms on the same level of distribution, between intermediaries of the same type, or between different types of intermediaries.

horizontal co-operative advertising: Advertising that involves firms on the same level of distribution sharing the cost.

household: A single person, a family, or any group of unrelated persons who occupy a housing unit.

iceberg principle: A concept related to performance evaluation, stating that the summary data (tip of the iceberg) regarding an activity may hide significant variations among segments of this activity.

ideal self-concept: The way you want to be seen or would like to see yourself, as distinguished from *actual self-concept.*

implied warranty: An intended but unstated assurance regarding restitution from seller to customer if the seller's product does not perform up to reasonable expectations.

import-export agent: An agent wholesaler that arranges for distribution of goods in a foreign country.

impulse buying: Low-involvement purchase made with little or no advance planning.

independent retailer: A company with a single retail store that is not affiliated with any type of contractual VMS.

indirect-action advertising: Product advertising that is intended to inform or remind consumers about a product and its benefits.

indirect distribution: A channel consisting of producer, final customer, and at least one level of intermediary.

indirect tests: Measures of advertising effects that use something other than sales volume

inelastic demand: A price-volume relationship in which a change of one unit on the price scale results in a change of less than one unit on the volume scale.

influence: The ability to cause a change in a person's beliefs, attitudes, or intentions.

influencers: The people in a buying centre who set the specifications and aspects of buying decisions because of their technical expertise, financial position, or political power in the organization.

informal investigation: The stage in a marketing research study at which information is gathered from people outside the company, such as distribution channel members, competitors, advertising agencies, and consumers.

innovation-adopter categories: Five categories, based on the point in time when individuals adopt a given innovation, comprising innovators, early adopters, early majority, late majority, and laggards.

innovator: The member of a reference group who is most likely to adopt something new (good, service) first.

inseparability: A characteristic of a service indicating that it cannot be separated from the creator/seller of the service.

inside order taker: A selling job in which the primary function of the salesperson is to take orders in person or by telephone inside a store or other type of business.

inside selling: The kind of selling in which customers come to the salespeople; primarily face-to-face retail selling, but also includes phone-in ordering.

installations: In the business market, long-lived, expensive, major industrial capital goods that directly affect the scale of operation of an industrial firm.

institutional advertising: Advertising designed either to present information about the advertiser's business or to create a good impression to build goodwill toward the organization.

intangibility: A characteristic of a service indicating that it has no physical attributes and, as a result, is impossible for customers to taste, feel, see, hear, or smell before buying.

integrated marketing communications (IMC): A strategic business process used to plan, develop, execute, and evaluate co-ordinated communication with an organization's customers and the general public.

intensity of distribution: The number of intermediaries used by a producer at the retailing and wholesaling levels of distribution.

intensive distribution: A strategy in which a producer sells its product in every available outlet where a consumer might reasonably look for it.

intermodal transportation: When a mode of transportation is so configured that it can be used to move freight by another mode or modes in order to save on loading and unloading costs, as well as time taken in transit.

internal marketing: The process of directing programs to staff members with the intention of encouraging them to deliver superior service to customers and generally to adopt a customer focus in all that they do.

internal non-marketing forces: The environment within a firm composed of working relationships between employees and departments.

Internet shopping: Use of the Internet to offer products for sale, providing information that can assist in sales being made elsewhere, but also offering an alternative way to purchase products.

interview guide: The equivalent of a questionnaire used in qualitative research; a list of questions or areas of enquiry designed to guide the depth interview or focus group.

introduction stage: The first part of a product life cycle, during which a generic product category is launched into the market in a full-scale marketing program.

inventory control: The subsystem of physical-distribution management that involves maintaining control over the size and composition of inventories in order to fill customers' orders promptly, completely, and accurately

while minimizing both the investment and fluctuations in inventories.

inverse demand: A price-volume relationship: The higher the price, the greater the unit sales.

just-in-time (JIT) inventory control: An inventory control system that involves buying parts and supplies in small quantities just in time for use in production and then producing in quantities just in time for sale.

knowledge: Stage 2 of buying readiness: A customer learns about a product's features and how it can meet a need.

label: The part of a product that carries written information about the product or the seller.

laggards: Tradition-bound people who are the last to adopt an innovation.

late majority: The sceptical group of innovation adopters who adopt a new idea late in the game.

learning: Changes in behaviour resulting from previous experiences.

licensing arrangement: A business arrangement whereby one firm sells to another firm (for a fee or royalty) the right to use the first company's brand, patents, or manufacturing processes.

lifestyle: A person's activities, interests, and opinions.

lifetime value of customers: The value to a company of a customer over the lifetime of that customer's association with the firm; more than direct purchases.

liking: Stage 3 of buying readiness: The knowledgeable customer moves from being indifferent about the brand to having positive feelings about it.

limited-line store: A type of retailing institution that has a narrow but deep product assortment; its customer services tend to vary from store to store.

line extension: One form of product-mix expansion in which a company adds a similar item to an existing product line with the same brand name.

loss-leader pricing: Involves temporarily reducing the prices of well-known items; the price cuts are made with the idea that these "specials" (loss leaders) will attract customers to the store.

low-involvement level: A purchase decision in which the consumer moves directly from need recognition to purchase, skipping the stages in between.

mail survey: Gathering data by means of a questionnaire mailed to respondents and, when completed, returned by mail.

mall intercept: A method of gathering data by conducting personal interviews in central locations, typically regional shopping centres.

manufactured parts and materials: Materials that become part of other finished products, distinguished from raw materials in that they have already been processed and bought by manufacturers for assembly into their final products. Some undergo further processing and may be referred to as *fabricating materials*.

manufacturer's agent: An independent agent wholesaler that sells part or all of a manufacturer's product mix in an assigned geographic territory.

market: People or organizations with needs or wants to satisfy, money to spend, and the willingness to spend it.

market aggregation: A strategy whereby an organization treats its total market as a unit — as one mass market in which the parts are considered to be alike in all major respects.

market development: A product-market growth strategy in which a company continues to sell its present products, but to a new market.

marketer: Any person or organization that desires to make exchanges.

market fragmentation: The identification of smaller and smaller market segments.

market penetration: A product-market growth strategy in which a company tries to sell more of its present products to its present markets.

market-penetration pricing: A pricing strategy in which a low initial price is set to reach the mass market immediately.

market response system: A form of inventory control in which a purchase by a final customer activates a process to produce and deliver a replacement item to inventory.

market segmentation: The process of dividing the total market for a product into several parts, each of which tends to be homogeneous in all significant aspects.

market share targets: When a company sets a certain share of the market as its objective when setting prices.

market-skimming pricing: A pricing strategy in which the initial price is set high in the target market's range of expected prices.

market tests: The stage of new-product development that involves tests with actual consumers.

marketing: A total system of business activities designed to plan, price, promote, and distribute need-satisfying products or services to target markets in order to achieve organizational objectives.

marketing audit: A comprehensive review and evaluation of the marketing function in an organization.

marketing communications: All of the elements of an organization's marketing (usually advertising, publicity, public relations, personal sales, and sales promotion) that serve to inform existing and potential customers.

marketing communications mix: The combination of personal selling, advertising, sales promotion, publicity, and public relations that is intended to help an organization achieve its marketing objectives.

marketing concept: A philosophy of doing business that emphasizes customer orientation and co-ordination of marketing activities in order to achieve the organization's performance objectives.

marketing information system (MkIS): An ongoing organized set of procedures and methods designed to generate, analyze, disseminate, store, and retrieve information for use in making marketing decisions.

marketing intermediaries: Firms that render services directly related to the purchase and/or sale of a product as it flows from producer to consumer.

marketing mix: A combination of the four elements — product, pricing structure, distribution system, and promotional activities — that comprise a company's marketing program. Many marketers now consider service and the "people" side of marketing to be a fifth component of the marketing mix, especially in the marketing of services.

marketing research: The process of specifying, assembling, and analyzing information used to identify and define marketing opportunities and problems; generate, refine, and evaluate marketing actions; monitor marketing performance; and improve the understanding of marketing as a process.

mark-up: The dollar amount that is added to the acquisition cost of a product to determine the selling price.

Maslow's hierarchy of needs: A needs structure consisting of five levels and organized according to the order in which people seek need gratification.

materials handling: The subsystem of physical-distribution management that involves selecting and operating the equipment and warehouse building used in physically handling products.

maturity stage: The third part of a product life cycle, during which sales of a generic product category continue to increase (but at a decreasing rate), profits decline largely due to price competition, and some firms leave the market.

merchant wholesaler: An independently owned firm that primarily engages in wholesaling and ordinarily takes title to the products being distributed; same as *wholesaler*.

missionary salesperson: A selling job in which the salespeople are not expected to solicit orders but rather to influence decision-makers by building goodwill, performing promotional activities, and providing service to customers; called a *detail salesperson* in pharmaceuticals marketing.

mission statement: Indicates the boundaries of an organization's activities.

mix extension: A way of expanding the product mix by adding a new product line to the company's current assortment.

mode of transportation: The manner in which the movement of goods is carried out; leading modes of transportation are railroads, trucks, ships, and airplanes.

modified rebuy: In the business market, a purchasing situation between a new-task rebuy and a straight rebuy in terms of time required, information needed, and alternatives considered.

motive: A need sufficiently stimulated that an individual is moved to seek satisfaction.

multiple-brand strategy: A strategy in which a firm has more than one brand of essentially the same product, aimed either at the same target market or at distinct target markets.

multiple buying influences: A situation in which a purchasing decision is influenced by more than one person in the buyer's organization.

multiple packaging: The practice of placing several units of the same product in one container.

multiple-segment strategy: A strategy that involves the selection of two or more groups of potential customers as target markets.

needs and wants: The focus of a customer-oriented company wanting to satisfy these in order to achieve customer satisfaction.

new-product strategy: A plan that defines the role new products are to play in helping the company achieve its corporate and marketing goals.

new-task buy: In the business market, a purchasing situation in which a company considers buying a given item for the first time.

niche marketing: A strategy in which goods and services are tailored to meet the needs of small market segments.

non-adopters: Consumers who never adopt an innovation.

non-business market: Includes such diverse institutions as churches, colleges and universities, museums, hospitals and other health institutions, political parties, labour unions, and charitable organizations.

non-cumulative quantity discount: A quantity discount based on the size of an individual order of products.

non-price competition: A strategy in which a firm tries to compete based on some factor other than price; for example, promotion, product differentiation, or variety of services.

non-store retailing: Retailing activities resulting in transactions that occur away from a retail store.

North American Industry Classification System (NAICS): System that allows business marketers to locate codes for present customers and obtain coded lists of similar firms, and provides a rapid, low-cost approach to identifying changes in the growth of various industry sectors.

objective: A desired outcome; same as *goal*.

observational method: Gathering data by observing personally or mechanically the actions of a person.

odd pricing: A form of psychological pricing that consists of setting prices at odd amounts ($4.99 rather than $5.00, for example) in the belief that these seemingly low prices will result in larger sales volume.

off-price retailing: A strategy of selling well-known brands below the manufacturer's recommended retail price.

one-price strategy: A strategy under which a seller charges the same price to all customers of the same type who buy the same quantity of goods.

operating supplies: The "convenience goods" of the business market: short-lived, low-priced items purchased with a minimum of time and effort.

opinion leader: The member of a reference group who is the information source and who influences the decision-making of others in the group.

order processing: The subsystem of physical-distribution management that consists of the set of procedures for receiving, handling, and filling orders.

outside order taker: A selling job in which salespeople primarily go to customers in the field.

outside sales force: A group of sales reps engaged in field selling; that is, selling in person at a customer's place of business or home.

outside selling: The kind of personal selling in which salespeople go to the customers, making contact by mail, telephone, or face to face.

packaging: For products, the activities in product planning that involve designing and producing the container or wrapper for a product; for services, bundling and promotion activities are involved.

party-plan selling: A type of direct selling in which a host or hostess invites some friends to a party at which a salesperson makes a sales presentation.

patronage motives: The reasons why a consumer chooses to shop at a certain place.

perception: Collecting and processing information from the environment in order to give meaning to the world around us.

perishability: A characteristic of a service indicating that it is highly perishable and cannot be stored.

personal disposable income: Personal income remaining after all personal taxes are paid.

personal interview: A face-to-face method of gathering data in a survey.

personality: An individual's pattern of traits that influences behavioural responses.

physical distribution: Activities involved in the flow of products as they move physically from producer to consumer or industrial user; used synonymously with *logistics*.

physical-distribution management: The development and operation of efficient flow systems for products.

physical facilities: The location, design and layout of a retail store's site.

piggyback service: Transporting loaded truck trailers on railroad flatcars.

pioneering advertising: Primary-demand advertising is done in the introductory stage of the product life cycle.

positioning: A company's strategies and actions related to favourably distinguishing itself and its products from those of competitors in the minds of selected groups of consumers.

post-purchase behaviour: Efforts by the consumer to reduce the anxiety often accompanying purchase decisions.

preference: Stage 4 of buying readiness: The customer distinguishes among brands and prefers yours.

press release: News from a company sent to the media for publication.

prestige pricing: Raising prices above competitive levels for the purpose of giving the impression of higher quality or of adding prestige value for the brand.

pre-test (of commercials): An activity in which commercials in finished or nearly finished form are presented to panels of consumers in order to gauge their reactions.

pre-testing (of questionnaires): The process of testing a questionnaire before it is used in a survey, to identify problems and areas of confusion.

price: The amount of money and/or other resources needed to acquire some combination of a product and its accompanying services.

price competition: A strategy in which a firm regularly offers prices that are as low as possible, usually accompanied by a minimum of services.

price elasticity of demand: The responsiveness of quantity purchased to price changes.

price lining: Involves selecting a limited number of prices at which a business will sell related products.

price sensitivity: Extent to which the market or a certain segment of it will respond to price changes or is focused on price when buying.

pricing objective: The goals that management tries to reach with its pricing structure and strategies.

primary data: Original data gathered specifically for the project at hand.

primary-demand advertising: Advertising designed to stimulate demand for a generic product.

primary-product agents: Intermediaries who trade in primary products as opposed to manufactured goods.

private warehouse: A warehouse that is owned and operated by the firm whose products are being stored and handled at the facility

proactive selling: A situation in which the selling effort is initiated by the salesperson, who actively tries to interest the customer in buying.

producer's brand: A brand that is owned by a manufacturer or other producer; same as *national brand*.

product: A product might be a tangible product, service, place, person, or idea; it has a set of tangible attributes, including packaging, colour, price, quality, and brand, plus the services and reputation of the seller.

product-adoption process: The stages that an individual goes through in deciding whether to accept a new product or innovation.

product development: A product-market growth strategy that calls for a company to develop new products to sell to its existing markets.

product diffusion: The process by which a new product or innovation is spread through a market or social system over time.

product-focus stage: The stage at which a company is focused mainly on producing high-quality products and services.

product-in-use situation: The stage in the interaction when the customer has bought the product and is using it; evaluation of the success of the purchase takes place.

product life cycle: The stages a product goes through from its introduction, to its growth and maturity, to its eventual decline and death (withdrawal from the market or deletion from the company's offerings).

product line: A broad group of products intended for essentially similar uses and possessing reasonably similar physical characteristics.

product–market growth matrix: A planning model that consists of four alternative growth strategies, based on whether an organization will be selling its present products or new products to its present markets or new markets.

product mix: All products offered for sale by a company.

product-mix contraction: The elimination of an entire line or simplification of the assortment within a line to weed out low-profit and unprofitable products.

product-mix expansion: Increasing the depth within a particular product line and/or the number of lines a firm offers to consumers.

product modification: Improvement of an established product as a less risky and more profitable alternative to developing a completely new product.

product or service differentiation: The strategy of setting a company or brand apart from its competition in the minds of its customers or prospective customers.

profit maximization: The pricing objective of making as much money as possible.

promotional allowance: A price reduction granted by the seller as payment for promotional services rendered by the buyer.

prospecting: The stage in the personal selling process that involves developing a list of potential customers.

psychographics: A concept in consumer behaviour that describes consumers in terms of a combination of psychological and sociological influences.

psychological pricing: Setting a price to have a special appeal to a particular segment of customers.

public relations: A broad communications effort designed to build or maintain a favourable image for an organization with its various publics.

public service advertising: Advertising designed to improve the quality of life and indicate that the advertiser is a responsible member of the community.

public warehouse: Operated by an independent firm that provides storage and handling facilities.

publicity: Media presentations about a product or organization that are not paid for and have the credibility of editorial material.

pull strategy: A communications program aimed primarily at end-users.

purchase: Stage 6, the last stage of buying readiness: The customer overcomes any inhibitors that might delay or postpone purchase and buys the product.

purchaser: The person in the household or organization who actually makes the purchase of a product or service.

push strategy: A communications program aimed primarily at wholesalers and retailers.

qualitative research: A form of marketing research usually employed for exploratory purposes that examines consumers' deeply held views, opinions, and feelings; includes focus group interviews and one-on-one depth interviews.

quality: The characteristics of a product or service in relation to the expectations of the customer.

quantitative research: A form of marketing research that is intended to obtain statistical information about a sample of consumers or members of the public; usually relies on surveys to collect the data.

quantity discount: A reduction of the list price when large quantities are purchased; offered to encourage buyers to purchase in large quantities.

question marks: Strategic business units characterized by low market shares but high industry growth rates.

questionnaire: A data-gathering form used to collect information in a personal, telephone, or mail survey.

random sample: A sample that is selected in such a way that every unit in the defined universe has a known probability of being selected.

raw materials: Business goods that have not been processed in any way and that will become part of another product.

reactive selling: A situation in which the sales process is initiated by the customer and the salesperson simply processes the sale.

reciprocity: The policy of "I'll buy from you if you'll buy from me."

reference group: A group of people who influence a person's attitudes, values, and behaviour.

referral: The process of recommending a company or brand to others; positive word of mouth.

relationship-insensitive forces: Forces that do not afford a firm a particular advantage or the opportunity to develop particularly strong bonds or connections with its customers.

relationship pricing: Related to the concept of value pricing, in which benefits are shared with customers to ensure that they receive better value and therefore remain loyal.

relationship segmentation: The process of segmenting a market on the basis of the types of relationships that customers want to have with a company or brand.

relationship-sensitive forces: Forces that can be managed to varying degrees and therefore are part of a firm's marketing system.

repositioning: The process of moving a company, store, or brand to a new position in the minds of target customers, usually by changing its image.

research hypothesis: A tentative supposition that, if proven, would suggest a possible solution to a problem.

research objectives: The purpose of conducting the research; questions the marketer and researcher want to have addressed and areas that they want to have explored.

reseller market: Wholesaling and retailing intermediaries that buy products for resale to other business users or to consumers; a segment of the business market.

response: The reaction (non-verbal, verbal, or behavioural) of an information receiver that serves as feedback to the sender of a communication.

retail positioning: A retailer's strategies and actions designed to favourably distinguish itself from competitors in the minds (and hearts) of targeted groups of consumers.

retail scanner: The electronic device at retail checkouts that reads the bar code on each item.

retailer: A firm engaged primarily in retailing.

retailing: The sale, and all activities directly related to the sale, of goods and services to end-consumers for personal, non-business use; same as *retail trade*.

sales: The process of selling products and services to customers; usually involves sales personnel who interact with customers.

sales engineer: A selling job that often involves technically trained individuals selling sophisticated equipment; the emphasis is on the salesperson's ability to explain the product to the prospect and perhaps to adapt it to the customer's particular needs.

sales function: The part of a company that is responsible for sales.

sales-orientation stage: The stage in the evolution of marketing management in which the emphasis is on selling whatever the organization produces.

sales promotion: Activities, including contests for salespeople and consumers, trade shows, in-store displays, samples, premiums, and coupons, that are designed to supplement advertising and co-ordinate personal selling.

seasonal discount: A discount for placing an order during the seller's slow season.

secondary data: Information already gathered by somebody else for some other purpose.

segments: Parts of markets.

selective attention: The process that limits our perceptions so that, of all of the marketing stimuli to which our senses are exposed, only those able to capture and hold our attention have the potential of being perceived.

selective-demand advertising: Advertising intended to stimulate demand for specific brands.

selective distortion: The process of mentally altering information that is inconsistent with one's beliefs or attitudes.

selective distribution: A strategy in which a producer sells its product through multiple, but not all, wholesalers and/or retailers in a market where a consumer might reasonably look for it.

selective retention: The process of retaining in memory some portion of what is perceived.

self-concept: A person's self-image.

selling: The communication of information to persuade a prospective customer to buy a product, service, or idea.

selling agent: A type of independent intermediary that essentially takes the place of a manufacturer's marketing department, marketing the manufacturer's entire output and often influencing the design and/or pricing of the products.

service encounter: In services marketing, a customer's interaction with any service employee or with any tangible element, such as a service's physical surroundings.

service failure: The failure of a service to meet customer expectations or standards, resulting in disappointment, frustration, or similar emotions.

service guarantees: Guarantees that companies offer to their customers that attest to the quality of their service.

service quality: The value that consumers perceive they are receiving from their purchase of services; generally very difficult to measure.

service recovery: The process of correcting the situation when a customer is dissatisfied with service provided. A company may attempt to recover from a poor service experience by apologizing or by offering the customer a price reduction or other form of compensation.

services: Identifiable, intangible activities that are sometimes the main object of a transaction and at other times support the sale of tangible products or other services.

services market: The market for service activities, including all transportation carriers and public utilities; communications firms, financial, insurance, legal, and real estate firms; and organizations that produce and sell services such as rental housing, recreation and entertainment, repairs, health care, personal care, and business services.

services value proposition: The value proposition of a services company, which must include elements of the service provided to customers and the emotional value created.

share of wallet: The share of a customer's total spending in a product or service category that is given to a particular company or brand.

shopping centre: A planned grouping of retail stores in a multi-unit structure, with the physical structure usually owned by a single organization.

shopping goods: A class of consumer products purchased after the buyer has spent some time and effort comparing price, quality, colour, and/or other attributes of alternative products.

simulated test market: A variation of test marketing in which consumers are shown advertising for a product and then are allowed to "shop" in a test facility in order to measure their reactions to the advertising, the product, or both.

single-segment concentration strategy: The selection of one homogeneous segment from within a total market to be the target market.

single-source data: Data that allow marketers to trace to individual households any connection between exposure to television advertising and product purchases.

situation analysis: The stage in strategic company planning that involves gathering and studying information important to the strategies and tactics of an organization.

situational influences: Temporary forces, associated with the immediate purchase environment, that affect behaviour.

slotting allowance: A fee that some retailers demand from manufacturers to place manufacturers' products on store shelves.

social information environment: Family, friends, and acquaintances who directly or indirectly provide information about products.

social responsibility: The commitment on the part of a company to improving the well-being of society.

specialty goods: A class of consumer products with perceived unique characteristics; consumers are willing to expend special effort to buy them.

specialty store: A type of retail institution that concentrates on a specialized product line or even part of a specialized product line.

stabilizing prices: A pricing goal designed to achieve steady, non-volatile prices in an industry.

stages in the product-adoption process: The six stages a prospective user goes through in deciding whether to purchase something new, including awareness, interest, evaluation, trial, adoption, and confirmation.

stars: Strategic business units characterized by high market shares and high industry growth rates.

statutory labelling requirements: Federal and provincial laws regulating packaging and labelling.

stimulus–response theory: The theory that learning occurs as a person responds to some stimulus and is rewarded with need satisfaction for a correct response or penalized for an incorrect one.

straight rebuy: In the business market, a routine purchase with minimal information needs.

strategic business unit (SBU): A separate division for a major product or market in a multi-product or multi-business organization.

strategic company planning: The level of planning that consists of defining the organization's mission, analyzing the situation the company is facing, setting organizational objectives, and selecting strategies to achieve the organization's objectives.

strategic marketing planning: The level of planning that consists of conducting a situation analysis, determining marketing objectives, identifying target markets and measuring the market, deciding on positioning and differential advantage, and designing a marketing mix.

strategy: Broad, basic plan of action by which an organization intends to achieve its objectives.

style: A distinctive presentation or construction of any art, product, or activity.

subculture: Groups that exhibit characteristic behaviour patterns sufficient to distinguish them from other groups within the same culture.

supermarket: A type of retailing institution that has a moderately broad and moderately deep product assortment, spanning groceries and some non-food lines, that offers relatively few customer services and ordinarily emphasizes price in either an offensive or defensive way.

supermarket retailing: A retailing method that features several related product lines, a high degree of self-service, largely centralized checkout, and competitive prices.

supplementary services: Services that support or facilitate the sale of a tangible good or another service.

supplier-relationship program: A program intended to develop solid relationships with suppliers, knowing that they contribute to the company's ability to satisfy its customers.

supply partnership: A partnership that occurs when a buyer and seller with mutual trust and interests adopt certain policies, procedures, and co-ordinated relationships to lower production and supply costs and increase consumer product value.

survey: A method of gathering data by interviewing a limited number of people (a sample) in person or by telephone or mail.

SWOT assessment: Identifying and evaluating an organization's most significant **s**trengths, **w**eaknesses, **o**pportunities, and **t**hreats.

syndicated data: Research information that is purchased from a research supplier on a shared-cost basis by a number of clients.

tactic: An operational means by which a strategy is implemented or activated.

target market segment: A group of customers (people or firms) to whom a company specifically aims its marketing efforts.

target return: A pricing goal that involves setting prices to achieve a certain percentage return on investment or on net sales.

team selling: Use of a number of sales personnel to represent a company, often calling on the same account; sometimes called a *selling centre*.

telemarketing: A form of non-store retailing in which a salesperson initiates contact with a prospect and closes the sale over the telephone.

telephone survey: A method of gathering data in a survey by interviewing people over the telephone.

television shopping: A form of direct marketing in which TV channels show consumer electronics, jewellery, and other products for sale at relatively low prices.

test marketing: A marketing research technique in which, before committing to a major marketing effort, a firm markets its product in a limited geographic area, measures the sales, and then, from this sample, projects (a) the company's sales over a larger area and/or (b) consumer response to a strategy.

trademark: A brand that is legally protected.

trade promotion: The type of sales promotion that is directed to members of a distribution channel.

trading down: A product-line strategy in which a company adds a lower-priced item to its line of prestige goods in order to reach a market that cannot afford the higher-priced items.

trading up: A product-line strategy in which a company adds a higher-priced, prestige product to its line in order to increase sales of the existing lower-priced products in that line and attract a higher-income market.

transportation: The function of shipping products to customers.

truck jobber: A limited-function merchant wholesaler that carries a selected line of perishable and semi-perishable products and delivers them by truck to retail stores.

tying contract: A contract under which a manufacturer sells a product to an intermediary only under the condition that this intermediary also buys another (possibly unwanted) product from the manufacturer.

uniform delivered pricing: A geographic pricing strategy whereby the same delivered price is quoted to all buyers, regardless of their location; same as *postage-stamp pricing*.

unsought goods: A type of consumer product that consists of new products of which the consumer is not yet aware or products that the consumer does not yet want.

usage rate: The rate at which people use or consume a product.

users: The people in a buying centre who actually use a particular product.

value: The quantitative measure of the worth of a product to attract other products in exchange.

value chain: The relationships by which the roles of suppliers, producers, distributors, and end-users contribute to the final product.

value for money: Customer's perception of what is received for the price paid.

value of a product/service (to consumer): The ratio of perceived benefits of a product/service to perceived costs, including price and other incurred costs.

value proposition: The sum total of what the company offers the customer; much more than product and price.

value strategy: An overall strategy of a company to offer value to its customers; price is part of this strategy.

values (as distinct from *value*): The principles that individuals hold to be important and by which they lead their lives.

vertical business market: A situation in which a given product is usable by virtually all of the firms in only one or two industries.

vertical conflict: A form of channel conflict occurring between firms at different levels of the same channel, typically producer versus wholesaler or producer versus retailer.

vertical co-operative advertising: Advertising for which firms at different levels of the distribution channel share the cost.

vertical marketing system (VMS): A tightly co-ordinated distribution channel designed to achieve operating efficiencies and marketing effectiveness.

warehouse club: A combined retailing and wholesaling institution that has a very broad but very shallow product assortment; offers very low prices but few customer services, and is open only to members (same as *wholesale club*).

warehousing: A broad range of physical-distribution activities that include assembling, doing any necessary repacking, storing products, and then preparing them for reshipping.

warranty: An assurance given to buyers that they will be compensated in case the product does not perform up to reasonable expectations.

wheel of retailing: The cyclical pattern of changes in retailing: A new type of store enters the market as a low-cost, low-price store and over time takes business away from unchanging competitors; eventually, the successful new retailer trades up, incurring higher costs and charging higher prices, making this retailer vulnerable to a new type of retailer.

wholesaling: All activities directly related to the sale of goods and services to parties for resale, use in producing other goods and services, or operating an organization.

word of mouth: The process of customers discussing companies and brands with which they have come in contact; may be either positive or negative.

zone-delivered pricing: A geographic pricing strategy whereby the same delivered price is charged at any location within each geographic zone.

Notes and References

Chapter 1

1. James G. Barnes, Peter A. Dunne, and William J. Glynn, "Self-Service and Technology: Unanticipated and Unintended Effects on Customer Relationships," in Teresa A. Swartz and Dawn Iacobucci, eds., *Handbook of Services Marketing and Management* (Thousand Oaks, CA.: Sage Publications, 2000), pp. 89–101.
2. Lara Mills, "What A Rush," *Marketing Magazine*, March 11, 2002, pp. 7, 8.
3. James L. Heskett, Thomas O. Jones, Gary W. Loveman, W. Earl Sasser Jr., and Leonard A. Schlesinger, "Putting the Service–Profit Chain to Work," *Harvard Business Review*, March–April 1994, pp. 164–174.

Chapter 2

1. Paul Brent, "Chrysler to Target Cars: Carmaker Reduces Reliance on Trucks, Vans and SUVs," *Financial Post*, July 26, 2002, p. FP3.
2. For a detailed review of the demographics of the Baby Boomers and how demographics influence buying behaviour, see David K. Foot with Daniel Stoffman, *Boom, Bust & Echo 2000: Profiting from the Demographic Shift in the New Millennium* (Toronto: Macfarlane Walter & Ross, 1998).
3. Data obtained from Statistics Canada Web site, www.statcan.ca, 2000.
4. Data obtained from Statistics Canada Web site, www.statcan.ca, June 2002.
5. Milton Parissis and Michael Helfinger, "Ethnic Shoppers Share Certain Values," *Marketing Magazine*, January 11, 1993, p. 16.
6. Ontario Transportation Capital Corporation, "Ontario Transportation Minister Registers for a Highway 407 Transponder," Press Release, Canada NewsWire, May 30, 1997.
7. Peter A. Dunne and James G. Barnes, "Internal Marketing: A Relationships, Value-Creation View," published in *Internal Marketing: Directions for Management*, by Barbara R. Lewis and Richard J. Varey (London: Routledge, 2000).
8. *Pulse of the Middle Market—1990* (New York: BDO Seidman, 1990), pp. 12–13.
9. Paul Feriss, "Mitsubishi Prepares for Early Entry," *Marketing Magazine*, February 25, 2002, p. 3.
10. Sarah Smith, "Tango Aimed at Price-Conscious Fliers," *Marketing Magazine*, October 22, 2001, p, 3.
11. Jamie Butters, "GM Will Phase Out Oldsmobile Brand," Auto.com Web site, December 13, 2000.
12. PricewaterhouseCoopers Global Web site: http://www.pwcglobal.com/nl/eng/iaa/igoransoff.html

Chapter 3

1. R. Craig Endicott, "Advertising Fact Book," *Advertising Age*, January 6, 1992, p. S-11.
2. Clyde Kluckholn, *Culture and Behaviour* (New York: Free Press, 1962), p. 26.
3. Jo Marney, "Counting Ethnic Canadians In," *Marketing Magazine*, June 4, 2001, p. 24.
4. "The Marketing Report on Multicultural Marketing," *Marketing Magazine*, September 14, 1998, pp. 15–25.
5. Jo Marney, "Counting Ethnic Canadians In," *Marketing Magazine*, June 4, 2001, p, 24.
6. Tony Pigott and Michael Sullivan, "Including Visible Minorities," *Marketing Magazine*, June 4, 2001, p. 24.
7. For statistical information regarding languages spoken in Canada, see the Statistics Canada Web site at www.statcan.ca. The information reported is based on the most recent 1996 Canadian census data.
8. For more information see, Dwight Thomas, "Culture and Consumption Behavior in English and French Canada," in Bent Stidsen, ed., *Marketing in the 70s and Beyond* (Edmonton: Marketing Division, 1975), pp. 255–261. Also, Francois Vary, "Quebec Consumer Has Unique Buying Habits," *Marketing Magazine*, March 23, 1992, p. 28, and Louise Gagnon, "Eaton's Quebec Ads Target Hip Shoppers," *Marketing Magazine*, June 16, 1997, and "Price Cuts Escalate Beer Battle," *Marketing Magazine*, June 30, 1997.
9. *CIA World Fact Book:* www.cia.gov/publications/fact book, June 03, 2002.
10. Astrid Van Den Broek, "Speaking the Same Language," *Marketing Magazine*, June 21, 1999, p. 13.
11. Julie Look, "Understanding Tween Culture," *Marketing Magazine*, August 2, 1999, p. 16.
12. Anita Lahey, "Bauer Gets A Boost at World Cup of Hockey," *Marketing Magazine*, September 2, 1996, p. 2; Daniel Greeno, Montrose Sommers, and Jerome Kernan, "Personality and Implicit Behaviour Patterns," *Journal of Marketing Research*, February 1973, vol. 10, pp. 63–69.
13. See Elihu Katz and Paul Lazarsfeld, *Personal Influence* (New York: Free Press, 1955), especially p. 325.
14. Sara Curtis, "Radio Show Targets Children 8 to 12," *Marketing Magazine*, October 7, 1996, p. 3.
15. Mikala Folb, "Totally Girl," *Marketing Magazine*, January 4/11, 1999, pp. 10, 12.
16. A. H. Maslow, *Motivation and Personality* (New York: Harper & Row, 1954), pp. 80–106.
17. Steven Reiss and Susan M. Havercamp, "Toward a Comprehensive Assessment of Fundamental Motivation: Factor Structure of the Reiss Profile," *Psychological Assessment*, June 1998, pp. 97–106.

18. Other schools of thought on learning, principally the cognitive approach and gestalt learning, are discussed in books on consumer behaviour. See David Louden and Albert J. Della Bitta, *Consumer Behavior*, 3rd ed. (New York: McGraw-Hill, 1988).

19. Daniel Greeno, Montrose Sommers, and Jerome Kernan, "Personality and Implicit Behaviour Patterns," *Journal of Marketing Research*, February 1973, vol. 10, pp. 63–69.

20. Andrew Poon and Dawn Walton, "Tables Turning on Fast Food," *The Globe and Mail*, July 5, 1997, pp. B1, B3.

Chapter 4

1. Barb Grant, "An Exciting New Hybrid," *Marketing Magazine*, June 10, 2002, p. 19; Wendy Cuthbert, "The Hardest We've Ever Hit," *Strategy*, July 1, 2002, p. 21, "Molson Gives Beer Drinkers Something They Can Use," *Strategy*, April 8, 2002, p. B4; "Urban Campaign Lures New York Singletons," *Strategy*, May 6, 2002, p. 6.

2. Chris Daniels, "Xbox's Inner Workings," *Marketing Magazine*, November 19, 2001, pp. 8–9.

3. Jennifer Lewington, "Canada Facing Age Crunch," *The Globe and Mail*, July 17, 2002, p. 1; Jane Armstrong, "Newest Territory Boasts Highest Birthrate," *The Globe & Mail*, p. A6.

4. Margaret Wente, "Census Allows a Peek at Our Future," *The Globe and Mail*, July 17, 2002, pp. A1, A8)

5. For Canadian statistics including current and projected population figures, visit the Statistics Canada Web site at www.statcan.ca.

6. "Kellogg, YTV Get in the Box," *Marketing Magazine*, January 1/8, 2001, p. 1.

7. Lucy Saddleton, "Youth May Help Car Makers Weather Downturn," *Strategy*, October 22, 2001, p. 2.

8. Duncan Hood & Chris Maddever, "They're Not Like You and Me," *Strategy*, May 6, 2002, p. B13; Lisa D'Innocenzo, "Marketers Ramp up Activity in Canadian Skateboard Scene," *Strategy*, June 3, 2002, p. 1.

9. Lisa D'Innocenzo, "Ear to the Ground: Students Wary of Campus Marketing," *Strategy*, November 19, 2001, p. 19.

10. Jennifer Lewington, "Universities Give Recruitment Old College Try," *The Globe and Mail*, July 4, 1997, p. A1.

11. David Eggleston, "CHIP Sells Seniors on Reverse-Mortgage Idea," *Strategy*, January 31, 2000, p. D3.

12. Bernadette Johnson, "Mature Market Fast Becoming Prime Target for Online Marketers," *Strategy*, April 22, 2002, p. D1.

13. For Canadian statistics, visit the Statistics Canada Web site at www.statcan.ca.

14. For a view of the family life cycle that reflects the growing number of single adults, with or without dependent children, see Patrick E. Murphy and William A. Staples, "A Modernized Family Life Cycle," *Journal of Consumer Research*, June 1979,

pp. 12–22. Also *New Trends in the Family: Demographic Facts and Features* (Ottawa: Statistics Canada, 1999), cat. no. 91-535E.

15. Greg Goldin, "When Brand is Grand," *World Business*, November/December 1996, pp. 19–23. Also Anita Lahey, "The Total Brand Experience," *Marketing Magazine*, March 27, 2000, pp. 13–14.

16. Lisa D'Innocenzo, "Nike Wants Women," *Strategy*, March 26, 2001, p. 5; www.nikegoddess.com, July 30, 2002.

17. Allanna Sullivan, "Mobil Bets Drivers Pick Cappuccino Over Low Prices," *The Wall Street Journal*, January 30, 1995, p. B1. For information regarding Mobil Speedpass, consult the company's Web site at www.exxon.mobil.com.

18. Chris Daniels, "Esso Locations to Offer Full Tim's Menu," *Marketing Magazine*, April 1, 2002, p. 4.

19. Sarah Smith, "Heinz Kickers Target Adult Taste Buds," *Marketing Magazine*, June 3, 2002, p. 3; www.heinz.com, July 30, 2002; "Say Something Ketchuppy: Heinz Gives Ketchup Connoisseurs a Chance to Talk Back," *Business Wire*, July 10, 2002; "Color It Gone: Heinz EZ Squirt Mystery Color Disappearing From Grocery Shelves," *Business Wire*, June 26, 2002.

20. Marina Strauss, "Holt's renews focus on rich with designer-brand goods," *The Globe and Mail*, September 13, 2002, p. B12.

21. Mark Maremont, "They're All Screaming for Häagen-Dazs," *Business Week*, October 14, 1991, p. 121.

22. "Theodore Fires Up Gatorade Spot," *Marketing Magazine*, May 13, 2002, p. 2; www.gatorade.com, August 3, 2002.

23. Norma Ramage, "Dell Connects With Critical Mass," *Marketing Magazine*, June 10, 2002, p. 3; www.dell.ca, August 3, 2002.

24. www.drmartens.com, August 4, 2002.

25. Sharon Younger, "Strap on Some Star Power," *Strategy*, June 4, 2002, p. B2.

26. Simon Ashdown, "Fashion Retailers Reach Out to Plus-Size Teens," *Strategy*, October 8, 2001, p. 7.

27. Patti Summerfield, "Big Brewers Miss Out in Growing Demo," *Strategy*, May 6, 2002, p. 1; Wendy Cuthbert, "The Hardest We've Ever Hit," *Strategy*, July 1, 2002, p. 21.

28. Geoff Dennis, "Image Isn't Everything in Canada's Local Beer Wars," *Strategy*, June 17, 2002, p. 1.

29. Sally Donnelly, "Business Classy," *Time*, July 1, 2002, p. 38.

30. Allan J. Magrath, "Niche Marketing: Finding a Safe, Warm Cave," *Sales and Marketing Management in Canada*, May 1987, p. 40; Robert E. Linneman and John L. Stanton Jr., "Mining For Niches," *Business Horizons*, May/June 1992, pp. 43–51.

31. Alex Taylor III, "Porsche Slices Up Its Buyers," *Fortune*, January 16, 1995, p. 24.

32. James Pollack, "PharmaPlus Pushes New Health Store Formats," *Marketing Magazine*, September 23, 1996, p. 4.

33. Fawzia Sheikh, "Zellers Unveils Plan to Fight Wal-Mart," *Marketing Magazine*, June 18, 1998, p. 2.

34. Chris Powell, "On A Roll," *Marketing Magazine*, July 1, 2002, pp 10–11.

Chapter 5

1. Statistics Canada, *Market Research Handbook*, catalogue 63-224 (Ottawa, 2001).

2. 1996 Annual Report, Safeway.

3. Statistics Canada, *Market Research Handbook*, catalogue 63-224 (Ottawa, 2001).

4. Diane Trommer, *Electronic News*, vol. 46, no. 24, June 12, 2000, p.38.

5. *Direct Marketing*, vol. 64, no. 6, October 2001, p. 20.

6. Earl D. Honeycutt, Theresa B. Flaherty, and Ken Benassi, "Marketing Industrial Products on the Internet," *Industrial Marketing Management*, January 1998, pp. 63–72.

7. Sang-Lin Han, David Wilson, and Shirlish P. Dant, "Buyer-Seller Relationships Today," *Industrial Marketing Management*, November 1993, pp. 331–338.

8. "Xerox Multinational Supplier Quality Survey," *Purchasing*, January 1995, p. 112.

9. Background on relationship-building is described in F. Robert Dwyer, Paul H. Schurr, and Sejo Oh, "Developing Buyer-Seller Relationships," *Journal of Marketing*, April 1987, pp. 11–27. See also Patricia Doney and Joseph Cannon, "An Examination of the Nature of Trust in Buyer-Seller Relationships," *Journal of Marketing*, April 1997, pp. 31–51.

10. An interesting description of value imaging, the psychological influences on business buying behaviour, can be found in Paul Sherlock, "The Irrationality of 'Rational' Business Buying Decisions," *Marketing Management*, Spring 1992, pp. 8–15.

11. Robert D. McWilliams, Earl Naumann, and Stan Scott, "Determining Buying Center Size," *Industrial Marketing Management*, February 1992, pp. 43–49.

12. Ken Yamada, "Apple to Unveil Mail Order Catalog and Sell Directly to Big Companies," *The Wall Street Journal*, September 17, 1992, p. B7.

13. For examples of benefit segmentation as used in the business market, see Mark L. Bennion Jr., "Segmentation and Positioning in a Basic Industry," *Industrial Marketing Management*, February 1987, pp. 9–18. Also Cornelius A. de Kluyver and David B. Whitlark, "Benefit Segmentation for Industrial Products," *Industrial Marketing Management*, November 1986, pp. 273–286.

14. For an excellent discussion on industrial market segmentation, see Richard E. Plank, "A Critical Review of Industrial Market Segmentation," *Industrial Marketing Management*, May 1985, pp. 75–91. Also, detailed coverage of the topic is contained in

Thomas V. Bonoma and Benson P. Shapiro, *Segmenting the Industrial Market* (Lexington, MA: Lexington Books, 1983).

Chapter 6

1. Sharon Younger, "Online Surveys More Hype Than Action," *Strategy*, January 28, 2002, p. 25.

2. Justin Martin, "Ignore Your Customer," *Fortune*, May 1, 1995, pp. 121–126; Astrid Van Den Broek, "Are You Sure They Want It?" *Strategy*, July 15, 2002, p. 29.

3. Colin Tener, "A Practical Approach to Internet Privacy," *Strategy*, January 29, 2001, p. D11.

4. Robert Everett-Green, "The Great Canadian Hunt for Home-Grown Movies," *The Globe and Mail*, June 13, 1996, p. A13.

5. Ivor Thompson, "Why Response Rates Matter," *Marketing Magazine*, May 27, 2002, p.18.

6. Ivor Thompson, "Why Response Rates Matter," *Marketing Magazine*, May 27, 2002, p.18.

7. Brad Edmondson, "The Wild Bunch: Online Surveys and Focus Groups Might Solve the Toughest Problems in Market Research," *American Demographics*, June 1997, pp. 10–15.

8. *The Internet Advertising Handbook*, Marketing Media Group, Rogers Media, Inc., Toronto, 2002.

9. Scott Gardiner, "A Truly Awesome Database," *Marketing Magazine*, April 29, 2002, p. MD2.

10. For a more detailed discussion of scanner panels and single-source data, see James G. Barnes, *Research for Marketing Decision Making* (Toronto: McGraw-Hill Ryerson, 1991), pp. 137–140.

11. Lara Mills, "Playing hard to get," *Marketing Magazine Online*, April 24, 2000: www.marketingmag.ca; "Privacy Commission Arms Orgs With Free Assessment Tool," *Strategy*, September 10, 2001, p. D3; Lesley Young, "Provincial Privacy Regs On The Way," *Marketing Magazine*, August 27, 2001, p. 3.

Chapter 7

1. Adapted from: Geoff Dennis, "Condom Site Turns Strategy Writer into Sex Expert," *Strategy*, April 22, 2002, p. 4.

2. For a different classification scheme that provides strategic guidelines for management by relating products and prices, along with a bibliography on product classification, see Patrick E. Murphy and Ben M. Enis, "Classifying Products Strategically," *Journal of Marketing*, July 1986, pp. 24–42. Also see Ernest F. Cooke, "The Relationship between a Product Classification System and Marketing Strategy," *Journal of Midwest Marketing*, Spring 1987, pp. 230–240.

3. Brian Dunn, "Taking on Tropicana," *Marketing Magazine*, November 2, 1998, p. 16.

4. Gary MacIntosh, "Just Ask Mom," *Marketing Magazine*, July 17, 2000, p. 8.

5. Marina Strauss, "Canada Rated 6th in Quality of Its Manufactured Goods," *The Globe and Mail*, February 10, 1994, p. B6.

6. Jan Field, "Ice With Edge," *Marketing Magazine*, February 7, 2000, p. 17.

7. Kathy Tyrer, "Selling Hockey in the Land of La La and Disney," *Marketing Magazine*, November 8, 1993, p. 5.

8. Sony Web site: www.sonystyle.com, July 14, 2002.

9. John Burghardt, "Old Product, New Use, Good Campaign," *Strategy*, November 5, 2001, p. 15.

10. Glenn Collins, "The Cola War Is Expected to Heat Up," *The New York Times*, January 25, 1997, pp. 37, 39.

11. James Pollack, "Ikea Puts Focus on Office Furniture," *Marketing Magazine*, November 4, 1996, p. 4.

12. Susan Caminiti, "Will Old Navy Fill the Gap," *Fortune*, March 18, 1996, p. 59.

13. "Makeovers for Aging Brands," Astrid Van Den Broek, *Marketing Magazine*, August 7, 2000, p. 14.

14. Thomas Pigeon, "The Message Is in the Bottle," *Marketing Magazine*, October 8, 2001, pp 22–23.

15. Jo Marney, "Too Much of a Good Thing," *Marketing Magazine*, January 24, 1999, p. 21.

16. "Kraft Buzzing About Honey Cereal," *Marketing Magazine*, August 2, 1999, p. 1.

17. Jo Marney, "What's in Your Face Counts," *Marketing Magazine*, September 11, 2000, p. 24.

18. David Menzies, "The Museum of Mortal Marketing Mistakes," *Marketing Magazine*, April 23, 2001, pp. 9–11.

19. David Menzies, "The Museum of Mortal Marketing Mistakes," *Marketing Magazine*, April 23, 2001, pp. 9–11.

20. Eugene Carlson, "Some Forms of Identification Can't Be Handily Faked," *The Wall Street Journal*, September 14, 1993, p. B2.

21. Honda Motor Company home page: www.honda.com, April 2000.

22. Andrew Stodart, "The Road More Traveled," *Marketing Magazine* Online, July 19/26, 1999: www.marketingmag.ca.

23. The benefits cited are from a study reported in Robert G. Cooper and Elko J. Kleinschmidt, "New Product Processes at Leading *Industrial Firms*," Industrial Management, May 1991, pp. 137–147. For an approach to improve the management of multiple new-product development projects, see Steven C. Wheelwright and Kim B. Clark, "Creating Project Plans to Focus Product Development Stages," *Harvard Business Review*, March-April 1992, p. 70–82.

24. For a report on the criteria used in making "go – no-go" decisions in the product- development process, see Ilkka A. Ronkainen, "Criteria Changes Across Product Development Stages," *Industrial Marketing Management*, August 1985, pp. 171–178.

25. "Study: Launching New Products Is Worth the Risk," *Marketing News*, January 20, 1992, p. 2.

26. For more on the first two stages, see Linda Rochford, "Generating and Screening New Product Ideas," *Industrial Marketing Management*, November 1991, pp. 287–296.

27. For the foundations of diffusion theory of innovation, see Everett M. Rogers, *Diffusion of Innovations*, 3rd ed. (New York: Free Press, 1983).

28. "Kodak Video Tape Feature Differentiation," Kodak home page: www.kodak.com, April 2000.

29. William C. Symonds, "Would You Spend $1.50 for a Razor Blade?" *Business Week*, April 27, 1998, p. 46; Mark Maremont, "Gillette Finally Reveals the Future, and It Has Three Blades," *The Wall Street Journal*, April 14, 1998, pp. A1, A10; www.mach3.com, July 10, 2002.

30. Dean Takahashi, "Intel to Unveil Speedier Chips on Monday," *The Wall Street Journal*, October 22, 1999, p. B6; Andy Reinhardt, "Intel Is Taking No Prisoners," *Business Week*, July 12, 1999, p. 38; www.mach3.com, July 10, 2002.

31. Kevin Coughlin, "Are CD's Days Numbered? Two New Technologies Join the Battle for the World's Ear," *St. Louis Post-Dispatch*, September 5, 1999, p. E1; Robert A. Starrett, "Burning Down the House: Home Recorders are Here," *E-Media Professional*, May 1999, p. 50.

32. Lucy Saddleton, "Anti-Aging Products Are Multiplying Like Tribbles," *Strategy*, March 11, 2002, p. 2.

33. For more on this subject, see Steven P. Schnaars, "When Entering Growth Markets, Are Pioneers Better Than Poachers?" *Business Horizons*, March-April 1986, pp. 27–36.

34. Reiji Yoshida, "Sega Plays Survival Game with Dreamcast," *Japan Times Weekly*, International Edition, December 14–20, 1998, p. 13; Chris Daniels, "Xbox's Inner Workings" *Marketing Magazine*, November 19, 2001, pp. 8–9.

35. Lesley Daw, "How to Market A Milestone," *Marketing Magazine*, March 10, 1997, pp. 10–11.

36. Mikala Folb, "Playskool Beats Bacteria," *Marketing Magazine*, March 17, 1997, p.3.

37. Hardy Green, "The Last Word in New Words," *Business Week*, August 30, 1999, p. 6; also the St. Martin's Press home page for scholastic publications: www.stmartins-scholarly.com, April 2000.

38. Bill Saporito, "How to Revive a Fading Firm," *Fortune*, March 22, 1993, p. 80.

Chapter 8

1. These statistics can be found on the Statistics Canada Web site at www.statcan.ca.

2. "The Flip Side of Flipping Hamburgers," *The Globe and Mail*, April 8, 1996, p. A6.

3. Leonard L. Berry and Terry Clark, "Four Ways to Make Services More Tangible," *Business*,

October/December 1986, p. 53. Also see Betsy D. Gelb, "How Marketers of Intangibles Can Raise the Odds for Consumer Satisfaction," *Journal of Service Marketing*, Summer 1987, pp. 11–17.

4. Lisa D'Innocenzo, "Celling to Youth," *Strategy*, April 8, 2002, p. 1.

5. "New Optimum Visa Debuts," p. 1, and "Amex Tees Up Tiger's Card," p. 2, *Marketing Magazine*, May 13, 2002.

6. Leonard A. Schlesinger and James L. Heskett, "The Service-Driven Service Company," *Harvard Business Review*, September-October 1991, pp. 71–81.

7. Patti Summerfield, "How Would You Market the New Digital Television Channels?" *Strategy*, January 14, 2002, p. 2.

8. Leonard L. Berry, "Improving America's Service," *Marketing Management*, 1992, vol. 1, no. 3, pp. 28–38. For each of the five fundamental mistakes, the author discusses several examples, the reasons for the mistakes, and suggests correcting the situation.

Chapter 9

1. Adapted from Alan Hustak, "Jewellery store's fabled blue box may be history," *National Post*, August 13, 2002, p. A8.

2. The 1993 study of personal computers was summarized in Kyle Pope, "Computers: They're No Commodity," *The Wall Street Journal*, October 15, 1993, p. B1.

3. George Stalk Jr. "What's in a Brand? It's the Experience," *The Globe and Mail*, May 23, 1997, p. B11.

4. Marina Strauss, "Gap a tired brand in new old clothing," *The Globe and Mail*, August 16, 2002, p. B9.

5. Howard Schlossberg, "Brand Value Can Be Worth More than Physical Assets," *Marketing News*, March 5, 1990, p. 6.

6. Peter Vamos, "Fairmont Hotels Put on Ad Blitz," *Strategy*, January 29, 2001, p. 6.

7. Elizabeth Nickson, "The American founders of Roots have been accused of branding the wilderness," *The Globe and Mail*, March 23, 2000.

8. For an in-depth discussion of the value of branding, see David Arnold, *The Handbook of Brand Management* (London: Pitman Publishing, 1992).

9. Ruth Shalit, "The Name Game," Salon online: www.salon.com, November 30, 2001.

10. Jamie Beckett, "Inventing a Product Name Is Part Science, Part Art," *The Globe and Mail*, October 27, 1992, p. B4.

11. Matthew Friedman, "Master of Your Domain: Overcrowding in the .com Domain Space Led to the Creation of New Domains That No One Uses," *Computing Canada*, May 10, 2002, p. 30.

12. Albert Leonardo, "Web Adds Seven New TLDs," *ComputerWorld Canada*, January 25, 2002, p. 27.

13. Jill Vardy, "Smut Peddlers Quick to Grab Domain Names to Redirect Traffic," *Financial Post*, March 8, 2002, p. FP7.

14. Kim Robertson, "Strategically Desirable Brand Name Characteristics," *The Journal of Product and Brand Management*, Summer 1992, pp. 62–72.

15. Dean Takahashi, "In Pursuit of Pokemon Pirates," *The Wall Street Journal*, November 8, 1999, pp. B1, B4.

16. Kanran Kashani, "A Future for Brands," *Financial Times, Mastering Management* (London: Pitman, 1997), pp. 171–174.

17. For an excellent discussion of the nature and benefits of this strategy, see Donald G. Norris, "Ingredient Branding: A Strategy Option with Multiple Beneficiaries," *The Journal of Consumer Marketing*, Summer 1992, pp. 19–31.

18. Russell Mitchell, "Intel Isn't Taking This Lying Down," *Business Week*, September 30, 1991, pp. 32–33.

19. "Air Canada and Second Cup Forge New Partnerships from the Grounds Up," Canada NewsWire press release, February 17, 1997.

20. For a look at the success of Loblaws' private-label business and at the developer of the program, Dave Nichol, see Mark Stevenson, "Global Gourmet," *Canadian Business*, July 1993, pp. 22–23; see also Anne Kingston, *The Edible Man: Dave Nichol, President's Choice and the Making of Popular Taste* (Toronto: Macfarlane Walter & Ross, 1994).

21. For a discussion of this topic, see Leonard L. Berry, Edwin F. Lefkowith, and Terry Clark, "In Services, What's in a Name?" *Harvard Business Review*, September/October 1988, pp. 38–40. Some of the examples were drawn from this source.

22. Lesley Young, Gatorade Targets Pint-Sized Jocks, *Marketing Online*, August 19, 2002: www.marketingmag.ca.

23. "PAC Weary of Further Government Meddling," *Canadian Packaging*, June 2001. p. 6; "Packaging Bill on Hold," Canadian Plastics, March 2002, pp. 9, 11.

24. Anheuser-Busch home page: www.anheuser-busch.com, August 20, 2002.

25. Information on this program can be obtained from Environment Canada's Web site: www.ns.ec.gc.ca.

26. "Labelling Cooperation Urged," *Marketing News*, May 9, 1994, p. 17.

27. For information related to this Act, the government has set up the Competition Bureau, which can answer any questions. You can write to Industry Canada, 50 Victoria Street, Hull, PQ, K1A 0C9 (1-800-248-5358). Industry Canada's Web site is www.ic.gc.ca. All federal government departments can be reached through www.canada.gc.ca.

28. For further information on any federal acts or regulations, access the Government of Canada Web page at www.canada.gc.ca.

29. "Will Gross Cigarette Labels Stop Smoking, *Toronto Star*, February 8, 2000, p. C4.

30. Frank Gibney and Belinda Luscombe, "The Redesigning of America," *Time*, March 20, 2000, p. 44; Lucy Saddleton, "Innovation Lures Customers to Cosmetic Counters," *Strategy*, June 3, 2002.

31. For a more detailed discussion of service guarantees, see Valarie A. Zeithaml and Mary Jo Bitner, *Services Marketing*, 3rd ed. (New York: McGraw-Hill Irwin, 2003, pp. 205–211).

Chapter 10

1. Stuart Elliot, "Curious Vanilla," *The New York Times*, online version: www.nytimes.com, July 2, 2002; Gordon Pitts, "Coke unit president prizes company's speedier strategy," *The Globe and Mail*, September 2, 2002, p B5.

2. "Guerrilla Tactics Get Panasonic Noticed," *Strategy*, March 27, 2000, p. BMP10.

3. " Kellogg Unveils Vector Bar," *Marketing*, November 26, 2001, p.1.

4. Emily Nelson, "Penney to Launch Free Teen Magazine," *The Wall Street Journal*, April 6, 1999, p. B2; "Campbell's Debuts Snacking Soup" *Marketing Magazine Online*, October 25, 2000: www.marketingmag.ca; www.Campbellkitchen.com, July 15, 2002.

5. Jo Marney, "What's in Your Face Counts," *Marketing*, September 11, 2000, p. 24.

6. "Corby's C.C.&G. Just For Guys," *Marketing*, April 1, 2002, p. 1.

7. "What's Hot: Tune In, Turn On Your Customers," *Strategy*, July 19, 1999, p. 5.

8. This is a condensed version of the definition offered by Don E. Shultz and Heidi F. Shultz, "Transitioning Marketing Communications into the Twenty-First Century," *Journal of Marketing Communications*, March 1998, pp. 9–26.

9. Ford Motor Company home page: www.ford.com, July 16, 2002.

10. This example is based on information in Bradley Johnson, "Abe Kohnstann: IBM," *Advertising Age*, June 26, 1995 and Sloane Lucas, "One on One," *Brandweek*, September 20, 1999, p. 16.

11. Sarah Smith, "IBM takes e-business on the road," *Marketing Magazine*, December 3, 2001, p. 3.

12. Adapted from Lara Mills, "Coke May Move Toward Localizing," *Marketing Magazine*, February 7, 2000, p. 3. Also, Lara Mills, "Coke Is Thinking and Acting Locally," *Marketing Magazine*, March 20, 2000, p. 3.

13. Russ Green, "Making Measuring Simple: Plan Marcomm, Evaluate Criteria," *Advertising Age's Business Marketing*, September 1999, p. 49.

14. Alice Z. Cuneo, "Bridging the Gap," *Advertising Age*, December 13, 1999, p. 22.

15. Dan Thompson, "Bigger, Fewer, Better," *Strategy*, March 11, 2002, p. 30.

16. Fawzia Sheikh, "Power Premiums, *Marketing Magazine*, August 18/25, 1997, p. S4.

17. "Tiny Lipsticks Sent Direct," *Marketing Magazine*, October 18, 1999, p. 17.

18. Eve Lazarus, "B.C. Hydro to Slash 2002 Ad Budget," *Marketing Magazine*, December 17, 2001, p. 3.

19. "Bait and switch" advertising is prohibited by the Competition Bureau of Industry Canada. The Bureau's role is to promote and maintain fair competition so that Canadians can benefit from lower prices, product choice, and quality services. For more information or to report unfair business practices, you can contact the Competition Bureau at 1-800-348-5358 or access its Internet site at www.cb-bc.gc.ca.

20. See "Marketer's Guide to Liquor Advertising Regulations," *Marketing Magazine*, August 21/28, 1997, pp. 14–16.

Chapter 11

1. Autowraps home page: www.autowraps.com, July 20, 2002.

2. Autowraps home page: www.autowraps.com, July 20, 2002.

3. *2000-2001 Media Digest*, p. 12. Published by *Marketing Magazine* as compiled by TVB from Statistics Canada, CRIC, CAN, CCNA/Les Hebdos du Quebec, Canada/LNA, CARD, Mediacom/CAN, Tele-Direct, Canada Post, IAB\Ernst & Young and industry estimates.

4. *The Internet Advertising Handbook*, Marketing Media Group, Rogers Media Inc., Toronto, 2002.

5. Lesley Young, "Buckley's Ads Highlight Employees," *Marketing*, November 19, 2001, p. 2.

6. David Eggleston, "summedia Turns Coupon Clippers into Coupon Clickers," *Strategy*, November 8, 1999, p. D10; also, David Todd, "Savingumoney.com Builds Awareness Offline," *Strategy*, February 28, 2000, p. NP7.

7. David Bosworth, "Lexus Revs Up Biggest DM Campaign," *Strategy*, January 28, 1998, p. DR2; also, Lara Mills, "Lexus Plans to Drive Up Utility Market," *Marketing Magazine*, February 23, 1998, p. 3.

8. "Write Your Own Ads, Say Advertisers," *Strategy*, March 13, 2000, p. 6.

9. Doug Sanders, "Advertisers Aim to Fragment TV Audience," *The Globe and Mail*, August 9, 1997, p. C3.

10. Harvey Enchin, "ExpressVu Launches Satellite TV Service," *The Globe and Mail*, September 11, 1997, p. B8.

11. Matthew Fraser, "Welcome to the Information Superhighway," *The Globe and Mail*, September 13, 1997, pp. D1, D2.

12. Janet Callaghan, "Specialties Adopting Smarter Strategies," *Strategy*, June 21, 1999, p. B14.

13. Carey Toane, "Teen Internet Use Survey Challenged," *Marketing Magazine*, June 5, 2000, p. 4; also, Bernadette Johnson, "Teen Study Raises Debate," *Strategy*, June 5, 2000, p. 3.
14. Bernadette Johnson, "Westminster Links Direct Mail Back to Internet," *Strategy*, July 19, 1999, p. D5.
15. Doug Checkeris, "Leaner, Meaner and Better?" *Marketing Magazine*, November 18, 1996, p. 11.
16. *The Internet Advertising Handbook*, Marketing Media Group, Rogers Media Group, Toronto, 2002.
17. Bernadette Johnson, "Internet Ad Revenues Soaring," *Strategy*, July 19, 1999, p. 6.
18. "Canadian E-tailers Lagging Behind U.S.," *Strategy*, March 13, 2000, p. 6.
19. Bernadette Johnson, "E-mail Comes into Its Own," *Strategy*, March 25, 2002, p. D8.

Chapter 12

1. John Burghardt, "Why Appreciate Your Customers When You Can Piss Them Off?" *Strategy*, July 29, 2002, p. 16; Bernadette Johnson, "Dion Steers Double-Digit Growth in New Business Lines," *Strategy*, January 28, 2002, p. D1.
2. Geoffrey Brewer et al., "1995 Best Sales Force Awards," *Sales & Marketing Management*, October 1995, pp. 52–63.
3. Robert N. McMurray, "The Mystique of Super-Salesmanship," *Harvard Business Review*, March-April 1961, pp. 113–122; Derek A. Newton, *Sales Force Performance and Turnover* (Cambridge, MA: Marketing Science Institute, 1973).
4. "Grand & Toy: Building Relationships," *Purchasing B2B*, January 2001, p. 19.
5. Roman Szostak, "Takin' It to the Streets: Subaru Rediscovers the Test-Drive," *Marketing Magazine*, January 10, 2002, p. 34.
6. Rekha Balu, "Whirlpool Gets Real with Customers," *Fast Company*, December 1999, pp. 74–76.
7. For a discussion of the importance of recognition in motivating a sales force, see Greg Cochrane, "Recognition Key to Sustaining Staff Passion," *Strategy*, August 18, 1997, pp. 16.
8. See Mark de Wolf, "What Really Motivates the Salesperson Today," *Strategy*, August 18, 1997, pp. 19, 22. Also, Ann Kerr, "Incentive Travel Buoyed by Economic Recovery," *The Globe and Mail*, September 17, 1996, p. C11.
9. Chris Powell, "Click and Save," *Marketing Magazine*, July 23, 2001, p. 8.
10. Chris Daniels, "E-mails With Edge," *Marketing Magazine*, February 18, 2002, p. 8
11. Pat Finelli and Rita Mcparland, "Just the Ticket," *Marketing Magazine*, March 11, 2002, p. 10.
12. Wayne Mouland, "How to Use Coupons to Get More Trial," *Marketing Magazine Online*, November 22, 1999: www.marketingmag.ca.

13. Lisa D'Innocenzo, "Marketers Ramp Up Activity in Canadian Skateboard Scene," *Strategy*, June 3, 2002, p. 1.
14. Lisa D'Innocenzo, "Absolut Considers TV Advertising as Competition Heats Up," *Strategy*, March 11, 2002, p. 1; Holly Wyatt, "Finding the Absolut Fit," *Strategy*, March 11, 2002, p. 32.

Chapter 13

1. Adapted from Mathew Ingram, "On Balance, Amazon.ca Is Likely a Good Thing," *The Globe and Mail*, June 26, 2002, p. B12; Hollie Shaw, "Amazon.com Takes Direct Aim at Indigo: Canadian Launch Today," *National Post*, June 25, 2002, pp. FP1, FP8.
2. Statistics Canada, *Market Research Handbook*, 2001, cat. no. 63-224-XPB.
3. Alison Appelbe, "Urban Chic," *BC Business Magazine*, June 2002, p. 40.
4. Liz Katynski, "Ka-ching, Ka-ching! On the Trail of Retail Development," *Manitoba Business*, November 2001, pp. 12, 14.
5. For an interesting insight into how a small family-owned kitchenware retailer in Calgary operates with an emphasis on personalized service, see Cathryn Motherwell, "Where the Business Is Cooking," *The Globe and Mail*, August 24, 1993, p. B28.
6. Dale D. Buss, "New Dynamics for a New Era," *Nation's Business*, June 1999, pp. 45–48.
7. "Advertising Age — 1995 Power 50 — Retail," *Advertising Age Online*, June 19, 1997; Angela Kryhul, "The Wal-Mart Decade," *Marketing Magazine Online*, December 20/27, 1999: www.marketingmag.ca.
8. David Eggleston, "Zellers Freshens Up Gen Z," *Strategy*, May 22, 2000, p. D3; Scott Gardiner, "A Truly Awesome Database," *Marketing Magazine*, April 29, 2002, p. 12.
9. Andy Georgiades, "Serious Overseas Competition Targets Canada," *Financial Post*, June 29, 2002, p. FP8; Garry Marr, "Target Eyes Canadian Retail Landscape," *Financial Post*, April 1, 2002, pp. FP1, FP4.
10. James Pollack, "Specialists Thrive on High-End Positioning," *Marketing News*, March 10, 1997, p. 3.
11. Sonja Rasula, "Beyond Clothes," *Marketing Magazine*, May 10, 1999, pp. 16–17.
12. Shawna Cohen, "One-Stop Shopping for Dinner," *Marketing Magazine*, February 1, 1999, pp. 10, 12; Jennifer Bain, "Raw Fish and Piano Bars," *The Globe and Mail*, January 29, 2000, p. R15.
13. Shawna Cohen, "One-Stop Shopping for Dinner," *Marketing Magazine*, February 1, 1999, pp. 10, 12.
14. Eve Lazarus, "Chevron Reimages Town Pantry Brand," *Marketing Magazine*, July 12, 1999, p. 2; Brian Dunn, "The King of Bread, Butts, and Beer," *Marketing Magazine*, October 25, 1999, p. 23.
15. Hollie Shaw, "Home Depot to Launch Urban Stores," *Financial Post*, June 15 2002, p. FP3.

16. Peter Verberg, "Party Time: Tupperware Has Been Keeping Food Fresh for Over 50 Years," *Canadian Business*, March 18 2002, p. 27.

17. Fantasia home page: www.kwic.com, August 20 2002.

18. "Challenging Times for Fundraisers," *Marketing Magazine*, April 29 2002, p. MD6.

19. Hailey Biback, "Crossing the Line," *Canadian Printer*, April/May 2002, p. 38.

20. Lesley Young, "Ontario's Privacy Folly," *Marketing Magazine*, March 11 2002, p. 26.

21. "CMA Seeks 'Do Not Call' Service," *Marketing Magazine*, December 10, 2001, p. 1.

22. "Some Facts on Telemarketing Fraud in Canada," Canadian Press Newswire, February 14, 2002.

23. Calmetta W. Coleman, "Retailers Strive for Shopping Synergy," *The Wall Street Journal*, December 20, 1999, pp. B1, B6; also "Lands' End, Bean Lead Pack," *Daily News Record*, November 3, 1999, p. 12.

24. Statistics Canada, *Vending Machine Operators*, 1997, cat. no. 63-213; Mary Gooderham, "Your Supermarket Knows Who You Are," *The Globe and Mail*, August 17, 1993, pp. A1, A4.

25. "Coke Tests Machine That Adjusts Prices," *St. Louis Post-Dispatch*, October 28, 1999.

26. For more on established retailers going online, see Greg Farrell, "Clicks-and-Mortar World Values Brands," *USA Today*, October 5, 1999, pp. 1B, 2B; Wendy Zellner and Stephanie Anderson Forest, "The Big Guys Go Online," *Business Week*, September 6, 1999, pp. 30–32.

27. Howard Solomon, "Pick a Niche, Study Warns E-tailers," *eBusiness Journal*, June 2001, p. 7; Timothy Hune, "Beyond Point and Click," *National Post Business*, May 2001, pp. 50–56.

28. Conway Daly, "Canadians Leery of Online Shopping," *Financial Post*, August 19, 2002, FP5.

29. Howard Solomon, "Customers in the crosshairs," *eBusiness Journal*, January 2002, p. 4.

30. Chris Daniels, "Turning Browsers into Buyers," *Digital Marketing*, March 2002, pp. 7–8.

31. Eric Reguly, "Dot-Coms Learning What Goes e-Round Comes e-Round," *The Globe and Mail*, May 2, 2000, p. B17.

32. Cristine Lourosa-Ricardo, "Picking the product," *The Wall Street Journal*, November 22, 1999, pp. R8, R10.

33. Positioning based on price and service is discussed in George H. Lucas Jr. and Larry G. Gresham, "How to Position for Retail Success," *Business*, April–June 1988, pp. 3–13. Positioning that combines all three variables is presented in Laurence H. Wortzel, "Retailing Strategies for Today's Mature Marketplace," *The Journal of Business Strategy*, Spring 1987, pp. 45–56.

34. Scott Gardiner, "A Truly Awesome Database," *Marketing Magazine*, April 29, 2002, p. 12.

35. Stephen Brown, "Variations on a Marketing Enigma: The Wheel of Retailing Theory," *The Journal of Marketing Management*, Summer 1996, pp. 63–66.

Chapter 14

1. Adapted from Barry Base, "Likeable But Pointless Doesn't Make the Grade," *Strategy*, July 15, 2002, p. 26; Apple Computer home page: http://www.apple.ca, August 10, 2002; David Akin, "Focus on Core Business to Apple's Success," *National Post*, April 22, 2000, p. D5.

2. Statistics Canada, CANSIM II Table 081-0002 and cat. no. 63-008-XIB, August 2002.

3. Data relevant to this discussion is contained in *Wholesaling and Retailing in Canada*, 1996 (Ottawa: Statistics Canada, 1999), cat. no. 63-236-XPB.

4. Lesley Daw, "Look! See Janes Build Frozen-Food Empire," *Marketing Magazine*, March 24, 1997, p. 3; Janes Family Foods home page: www.janesfamily foods.com, May 25, 2000.

5. An alternative approach that emphasizes market analysis is presented in Allan J. Magrath and Kenneth G. Hardy, "Six Steps to Distribution Network Design," *Business Horizons*, January-February 1991, pp. 48–52.

6. An excellent discussion of distribution channels for business goods and services is found in Michael D. Hutt and Thomas W. Speh, *Business Marketing and Management*, 4th ed. (Ft. Worth, TX: Dryden Press, 1992), pp. 359–392. For a review of emerging issues on business channels, see Al McGrath, "Managing Distribution Channels," *Business Quarterly*, Spring 1996, pp. 57–65.

7. For a discussion of this topic, see Donald H. Light, "A Guide for New Distribution Channel Strategies for Service Firms," *The Journal of Business Strategy*, Summer 1986, pp. 54–64.

8. Rowland T. Moriarty and Ursula Moran, "Managing Hybrid Marketing Systems," *Harvard Business Review*, November-December 1990, pp. 146–155.

9. For extensive discussion of this strategy, see John A. Quelch, "Why Not Exploit Dual Marketing?," *Business Horizons*, January-February 1987, pp. 52–60.

10. Zena Olijnk, "Loblaw Considers Creating Separate Online Division," *National Post*, May 5, 2000, pp. C1, C12.

11. For more on the idea that market considerations should determine a producer's channel structure, see Louis W. Stern and Frederick D. Sturdivant, "Customer-Driven Distribution Systems," *Harvard Business Review*, July-August 1987, pp. 34–41.

12. For further discussion of the strategies that either create or offset conflict between manufacturers and retailers, see Allan J. Magrath and Kenneth G. Hardy, "Avoiding the Pitfalls in Managing Distribution Channels," *Business Horizons*, September-October 1987, pp. 29–33.

13. Allan J. Magrath, "The Hidden Clout of Middlemen," *Journal of Business Strategy*, March/April 1990, pp. 38–41.

14. Ernest C. Raia, "Journey to World Class (JIT in USA)," *Purchasing*, September 24, 1987, p. 48;

15. Brian Milligan, "What's It Going to Take to Make It Work?," *Purchasing*, September 2, 1999, pp. 40–44.
16. Susan Avery, "Foxboro's Strategy for PCs and Peripherals Cuts Costs," *Purchasing*, May 20, 1999, p. 87.
17. John Peel, "Saturday Morning Syndrome," *The Economist*, February 26, 2000, p. survey 37.
18. "Out of the Box at ups," *Business Week*, January 10, 2000, p. 76; and Douglas A. Blackmon, "Overnight, Everything Changed for FedEx; Can It Reinvent Itself?" *The Wall Street Journal*, November 4, 1999, pp. A1, A16.
19. Don Tapscott, "Online Parts Exchange Heralds New Era," *Financial Post*, May 5, 2000, p. C7.

Chapter 15

1. Robert Pletzin, "SAS Pulls Back Curtain on Economy Class," *Financial Post*, March 21, 2002, p. FP12.
2. Sarah Smith, "Toy Versus Toy," *Marketing Magazine Online*, January 17, 2000: www.marketingmag.ca.
3. For a review of pricing strategies, see Nessim Hanna and H. Robert Dodge, *Pricing: Policies and Procedures* (London: McMillan Press, 1995).
4. Thomas L. Powers, "Break-Even Analysis with Semi-Fixed Costs," *Industrial Marketing Management*, February 1987, pp. 25–41.
5. Lisa D'Innocenzo, "When You Have No Time for Personal Hygiene…," *Strategy*, August 27, 2001, p. 9.
6. Mary Maddever, "Forget About Selling Merchandise, Sell the Store," *Strategy*, February 12, 2002, p. 16.
7. Patti Summerfield, "Wipeout! Convenience Checkmates Conservation for Canadian Consumers," *Strategy*, March 11, 2002, p. 6.
8. Steven Theobald, "Department Stores Fumbled but 'Quality Will Come Back into Vogue': Bay Chief Says," Canadian Press Newswire, April 25, 2002.
9. Discussions on relationship pricing are included in Tony Cram, *The Power of Relationship Marketing: Keeping Customers for Life* (London: Pitman Publishing, 1994). Also Leonard L. Berry, "Relationship Marketing," in Adrian Payne, Martin Christopher, Moira Clark, and Helen Peck, *Relationship Marketing for Competitive Advantage: Winning and Keeping Customers* (Oxford: Butterworth-Heinemann, 1996), pp. 65–74.
10. Paul Hunt, "Analysing the Psychology of Pricing," *Marketing Magazine*, February 25, 2002, p. 27.
11. "Buying Time," *Fortune*, September 8, 1997, p. 192.
12. Robert M. Schindler and Lori S. Warren, "Effects of Odd Pricing on Price Recall," Journal of Business, June 1989, pp. 165–177; Robert Blattberg and Kenneth Wisniewski, "How Retail Price Promotions Work: Empirical Results," *Marketing Working Paper No. 42* (Chicago: University of Chicago, 1987).
13. Gene Kaproski, "The Price Is Right," *Marketing Tools*, September 1995, p. 56.

Chapter 16

1. "It's Your Move," *Marketing Magazine*, June 24, 2002, p. 46.
2. "SAP Releases New Supply Management Tool," *Canadian Transportation Logistics*, February 2002, p. 15.
3. Andrew Allentuck, "CRM Finds a New Niche," *eBusiness Journal*, July 2002, p. 19.
4. "All the World's a Market, and All the Men and Women Potential Customers," *Financial Post*, May 15, 2000, pp. C1, C14.
5. Lucy Saddleton, "How Can the Struggling Canadian Film Industry Build Momentum?" *Strategy*, March 25, 2002, p. 2.
6. Seven elements of a horizontal organization are described in John A. Byrne, "The Horizontal Corporation," *Business Week*, December 20, 1993, pp. 76–81.
7. Evelyn Theiss, "Research Shows Good Service Is Getting Harder to Find," *St. Louis Post-Dispatch*, June 28, 1999, p. BP22.
8. Avan R. Jassawalla and Hemant C. Sashittal, "Building Collaborative Cross-Functional New Product Teams," *The Academy of Management Executive*, August 1999, p. 50; also Donald Gerwin, "Team Empowerment in New Product Development," *Business Horizons*, July-August 1999, p. 29.
9. Dale Terry, "Does Your Bank's Marketing Size Up?" *Bank Marketing*, January 1995, pp. 55–58.
10. Abe Schuchman, "The Marketing Audit: Its Nature, Purpose and Problems," in *Analyzing and Improving Marketing Performance: "Marketing Audits" in Theory and Practice* (New York: American Management Association, 1959), Management Report no. 32, p. 14. This article is the classic introduction to the marketing audit concept.
11. James G. Barnes, *Secrets of Customer Relationship Management: It's All About How you Make Them Feel*, Chapter 8 (New York: McGraw-Hill Companies, 2001).
12. For a very good overview of the ethical issues involved in marketing and advertising, see Jack Mahoney, "Buyer Beware: Are Marketing and Advertising Always Ethical?" *Financial Post*, December 14/16, 1996, pp. MM10–MM12; reprinted in *Financial Times Mastering Management* (London: Pitman Publishing, 1997), pp. 375–378.
13. Avon Canada home page: www.avon.ca, September 9, 2002.
14. Robert Colman, "Safe from Prying Eyes," *CMA Management*, August 2002, pp. 30–33.
15. Angela Kryhul, "Waif' Ads under Fire," *Marketing Magazine*, November 22, 1993, p. 2.
16. Chris Thatcher, "New Ads Walk a Fine Line," *Canadian Pharmaceutical Journal*, April 2002, p. 10.
17. For a detailed overview of changes in Canada's population, see David K. Foot and Daniel Stoffman, *Boom,*

Bust & Echo 2000: Profiting From the Demographic Shift in the New Millennium (Toronto: Macfarlane Walter & Ross, 1998).

18. Brian McGrory, "Happiness Is a Warm Hotel," *The Globe and Mail*, September 3, 1997, pp. D1, D2.

19. Lesley Young, "The Rise of the Chief Marketing Officer," *Marketing Magazine*, June 18, 2001, pp. 9,10; Lesley Young, "Strange Hybrids," *Marketing Magazine*, February 11, 2002, pp. 11, 12.

20. Sandra Vandermerwe and Michael Oliff, "Corporate Challenges for an Age of Reconsumption," *Columbia Journal of World Business*, Fall 1991, pp. 23–28.

21. James G. Barnes, "Close to the Customer: But Is It Really a Relationship," *Journal of Marketing Management*, 1994, vol. 10, pp. 561–570.

22. Daphne A. Sheaves and James G. Barnes, "The Fundamentals of Relationships," in Teresa A. Swartz, David E. Bowen, and Stephen W. Brown, eds., *Advances in Services Marketing and Management*, vol. 5 (Greenwich, CT: JAI Press, Inc., 1996); and James G. Barnes, "Closeness, Strength and Satisfaction: Examining the Nature of Relationships Between Providers of Financial Services and Their Retail Customers," *Psychology and Marketing* (Special Issue on Relationship Marketing), 1997.

Photo Credits

Chapter 1

Page 3, Donna Day/PhotoDisc/Getty Images; page 9, Courtesy Canadian Blood Services; page 10, CP/Nick Ut; page 11, Courtesy PBB Global Logistics; page 12, Courtesy of IAMS; page 14, Courtesy Sears Canada; page 18, ® ™ of The Pillsbury Company, a subsidiary of General Mills Inc. Used with permission; page 22, CP/Frank Gunn.

Chapter 2

Page 31, Courtesy of Mazda Canada; page 38, Advertising Agency: Zig, Toronto, Canada. Illustrator: Marcos Chin; page 43, CP/Quebec City Le Soleil; page 48, Courtesy Novartis; page 53; Courtesy Sony of Canada Ltd.; page 54, Courtesy of DaimlerChrysler Canada Inc.

Chapter 3

Page 61, © Alison Derry; page 68, Courtesy of Amazon.com Inc.; page 71, CP/Ryan Remiorz; page 73, Courtesy of Tropicana; page 75, Printed with the permission of the Tourette Syndrome Foundation of Canada, www.tourette.ca; page 79, CP/ Richard Buchan; page 86, Courtesy of Cara Operations.

Chapter 4

Page 97, Travelocity.com , www.travelocity.com; page 109, Courtesy of DaimlerChrysler Canada Inc.; page 111, Courtesy Glaxo Smith Kline; page 116, Hispanic Communications Inc. (Covveo Canadiense); page 119, Courtesy of P&G; page 122, Courtesy of Holt Renfrew; page 124, Dr.Martens AirWair USA LLC.

Chapter 5

Page 133, Courtesy www.mywebgrocer.com; page 135, Courtesy Terra; page 145, © Alison Derry; page 148, Courtesy Purchasing Management Association of Canada.

Chapter 6

Page 157, Mark Thomas/FoodPix/Getty Images; page 163, *National Post*; page 169, CP/Atsushi Tsukada; page 172, Yellow Dog Productions/Image Bank/Getty Images; page 179, Courtesy of CIBC.

Chapter 7

Page 193, Courtesy Hotspex Inc.; page 194, Sony Ericsson's P800 "Smart Phone"; page 199, Courtesy Panasonic Canada; page 206, 2003 Honda Insight Courtesy Honda Canada; page 207, Courtesy Crosskate; page 207, Annabelle Breakey/Freebord.

Chapter 8

Page 225, © Alison Derry; page 230, Photo courtesy of Peanuts © United Feature Syndicate, Inc. Metlife; page 231, PhotoDisc/Getty Images; page 234, CP/Ryan Remiorz; page 236, CP/Firdia Lisnawati Wor; page 238, CP/Jacques Boissinot.

Chapter 9

Page 251, Alison Derry; page 256, CP/*Toronto Star*/Keith Beaty; page 257, CP/Keith Srakocic; page 258, Courtesy Fairmont Hotel; page 264, Courtesy of Loblaw Co.; page 269, Courtesy Campbell Soup Company USA; page 271, Reprinted with permission from *The Globe & Mail*.

Chapter 10

Page 283, "Coca-Cola" trademarks appear courtesy of The Coca-Cola Company and Coca-Cola Ltd.; page 284, Used subject to agreement with Unilever Canada; page 286, Courtesy of Corby Distilleries; page 288, Justin L. Levine, Groove Music Canada; page 289, Courtesy of Harbourfront Centre; page 296, Trade-marks and copyrighted material used with the permission of Jaguar Canada; page 303, CP/Jacques Boissinot.

Chapter 11

Page 309, Courtesy of Autowraps; page 311, Ad courtesy of Life Fitness; page 311, Courtesy Newfoundland and Labrador Tourism; page 312, Courtesy Ford Motor Company; page 313, Courtesy of BC Hot House Foods Inc.; page 315, Richard J. Botto—Publisher, RAZOR Magazine; page 317, © 2000 Molson Canada; page 320, Courtesy MADD Canada; page 322, CP/Kevin Frayer.

Chapter 12

Page 339, Romilly Lockyer/Image Bank/Getty Images; page 341, PhotoDisc/Getty Images; page 343, Courtesy of Avon Canada Inc.; page 343, Eyewire/Getty Images; page 345, Courtesy of Canadian Tire; page 351, Eyewire/Getty Images; page 360, Photographer: Philip Rostvon, Instil Productions. Illustration: Rene Zamic/Reactor. Courtesy of Pepsi Co.; page 361, Dick Hemingway Photographs.

Chapter 13

Page 377, Courtesy of Amazon.com Inc.; page 381, Courtesy Les Ailes; page 384, Used with the permission of Inter IKEA Systems B.V.; page 388, © Alison Derry; page 388, © Alison Derry; page 390, © Alison Derry; page 392, Courtesy of Le Chateau. Dominic Colavecchio Photographie; page 393, Used with the permission of Inter IKEA Systems B.V.; page 397, The Pampered Chef, Ltd http://www.pamperedchef.com/; page 400, Courtesy Joe Boxer; page 405, Courtesy of Mountain Equipment Co-Op.

Chapter 14

Page 411, Courtesy of Apple; page 420, Courtesy of Starwood Hotels & Resorts Worldwide, Inc.; page 420, Photos courtesy of Deere and Company, Moline, Illinois, USA.; page 426, CP/Macleans/Peter Bregg; page 427, Courtesy of Canadian Tire; page 431, Courtesy La Senza International; page 431, CP/Sergei Karpukhin; page 435, © Alison Derry.

Chapter 15

Page 453, CP/ Adrian Wyld; page 456, © 2002 BMW Canada Inc. All Rights Reserved. The BMW trademark and logo are registered trademarks. Reproduced with the permission of BMW Canada Inc. for educational and non-commercial purposes only.; page 463, Courtesy of L'Oreal; page 464, Courtesy of Palm, Inc.; page 469, Courtesy of Jones Soda; page 474, Reprinted with permission from *The Globe & Mail*.

Chapter 16

Page 489, Used with the permission of Inter IKEA Systems B.V.; page 493, CP/*Toronto Star*/Boris Spremo; page 494, Courtesy of BCIT www.bcit.ca; page 504, Courtesy of Avon Canada Inc.; page 505, Taxi/Pfizer Canada; page 510, Courtesy of Lebeau Vitres D'Autos.

Subject Index